T0313239

The Routledge Handbook of Hospitality Studies

In recent years there has been a growing interest in the study of hospitality as a social phenomenon. This interest has tended to arrive from two communities. The first comprises hospitality academics interested in exploring the wider meanings of hospitality as a way of better understanding guest and host relations and its implications for commercial settings. The second comprises social scientists using hosts and guests as a metaphor for understanding the relationship between host communities and guests as people from outside the community – migrants, asylum seekers and illegal immigrants.

The Routledge Handbook of Hospitality Studies encourages both the study of hospitality as a human phenomenon and the study for hospitality as an industrial activity embracing the service of food, drink and accommodation. Developed from specifically commissioned original contributions from recognised authors in the field, it is the most up-to-date and definitive resource on the subject. The volume is divided into four parts: the first looks at ways of seeing hospitality from an array of social science disciplines; the second highlights the experiences of hospitality from different guest perspectives; the third explores the need to be hospitable through various time periods and social structures, and across the globe; while the final section deals with the notions of sustainability and hospitality. This handbook is interdisciplinary in coverage and is also international in scope through authorship and content. The 'state-of-the-art' orientation of the book is achieved through a critical view of current debates and controversies in the field as well as future research issues and trends. It is designed to be a benchmark for any future assessment of the field and its development.

This handbook offers the reader a comprehensive synthesis of this discipline, conveying the latest thinking, issues and research. It will be an invaluable resource for all those with an interest in hospitality, encouraging dialogue across disciplinary boundaries and areas of study.

Conrad Lashley holds the Professorship in Hospitality Studies in the Academy of International Hospitality Research at Stenden University of Applied Science, the Netherlands. He has held professorial appointments at several UK universities, and regularly makes keynote research presentations in Australia, New Zealand, the USA and Sweden as well as in Great Britain. He is the author or editor of eighteen books, and has published over a hundred papers in refereed research journals and sets of conference proceedings. He is currently co-editor of *Research in Hospitality Management* and Editor Emeritus of *Hospitality & Society*. He has worked extensively within the industry and generated commercial income from research and consultancy, as well as in-company management programmes. His research interests are principally concerned with understanding the meanings of hospitableness as a social phenomenon that has significance for commercial provision.

The Routledge Handbook of Hospitality Studies

Edited by Conrad Lashley

Routledge
Taylor & Francis Group

LONDON AND NEW YORK

First published 2017 by Routledge

2 Park Square, Milton Park, Abingdon, Oxon OX14 4RN

605 Third Avenue, New York, NY 10017

Routledge is an imprint of the Taylor & Francis Group, an informa business

First issued in paperback 2022

British Library Cataloguing in Publication Data
A catalogue record for this book is available from the British Library

Library of Congress Cataloging in Publication Data
A catalog record has been requested for this book

ISBN: 978-1-138-93112-1 (hbk)
ISBN: 978-1-03-233983-2 (pbk)
DOI: 10.4324/9781315679938

Typeset in Bembo
by Book Now Ltd, London

The Open Access version of chapter 4 was funded by Saxion University.

This book is edited in dedication to the memory of Sue: artist, mother, wife and friend; lost but never forgotten.

'In the cherry blossom's shade there's no such thing as a stranger'
(Kobayashi Issa, 1763–1828)

This quotation by the Japanese poet Kobayashi Issa has particular significance for this edited text on the study of hospitality. At face value it makes reference to the tree as a symbol of welcome, because the tree offers shelter or shade to all, without discrimination or exclusion. Indeed, many other cultures employ the tree as a metaphor for hospitality. The quotation also provides more evidence of the international and universal nature of hospitableness, because it was written in Japan two hundred years ago. Issa's comment is poignant because it was written during the time of the Japanese Sakoku, or 'closed country'. For just over two hundred years, between the 1630s and 1866, contact with the outside world was severely restricted by the Tokugawa shogunate. This was introduced in response to Spanish and Portuguese missionaries preaching and making converts to Christianity in Japan, thereby challenging traditional Japanese culture.

This incident symbolises an example of hosts restricting the offer of hospitality to guests, because guests have not behaved in a way that respects the host's culture. Ultimately, the study of hospitality has to be mindful of the underlying fear of strangers, and the potential hostility between guest and host. Pronouncements made about the need to welcome the stranger are moral instructions aimed at reducing hostility, and increasing harmony between those who receive and those who enter.

Conrad Lashley
Editor

Contents

Contents

Contents

Illustrations

Figures

Tables

Contributors

Isabel Baptista is a researcher at Portuguese Catholic University, Porto, Portugal.

David Bell is senior lecturer in critical human geography at the University of Leeds, United Kingdom, where he is also currently Head of School.

Martine Berenpas is a doctoral candidate in the Institute of Philosophy at Leiden University, the Netherlands.

Bastienne Bernasco is senior lecturer and researcher at Saxion University of Applied Sciences in Deventer, the Netherlands.

Bob Brotherton is a Visiting Professor in Hospitality Management at the NHTV University of Applied Sciences, Breda, the Netherlands.

Judi Brownell is a professor at the School of Hotel Administration, Cornell University, United States of America.

Leandro Benedini Brusadin is Professor Adjunto, Escola de Direito, Turismo e Museologia, Universidade Federal de Ouro Preto, Ouro Preto (MG), Brazil.

Elena Cavagnaro is Professor of Sustainability in Hospitality and Tourism, Stenden University of Applied Sciences, the Netherlands.

Prokopis Christou is the course leader of Hospitality & Tourism Management at the University of Central Lancashire-Cyprus.

Helena Catão Henriques Ferreira is Associate Professor and researcher in the Tourism Department of the Faculty of Tourism and Hospitality, University Federal Fluminense, Niterói, RJ, Brazil.

Aguinaldo César Fratucci is Associate Professor and researcher in the Tourism Department of the Faculty of Tourism and Hospitality, University Federal Fluminense, Niterói, RJ, Brazil.

Sjoerd Gehrels is UAS Professor Innovation in Hospitality at Stenden Hotel Management School, the Netherlands.

Szilvia Gyimóthy is Associate Professor and Head of Research at the Tourism Research Unit, Department of Culture & Global Studies, Aalborg University, Denmark.

Ko Koens is a senior lecturer at the Academy of Hotel and Facility Management, NHTVBreda University of Applied Sciences, the Netherlands.

Ricardo Lanzarini is Professor in the Tourism Management Course, Instituto Federal de Educação, Ciência e Tecnologia de São Paulo (IFSP), Brazil.

Conrad Lashley holds the Professorship in Hospitality Studies in the Academy of International Hospitality Research at Stenden University of Applied Science, the Netherlands.

Peter Lugosi, PhD, is a Reader at the Oxford School of Hospitality Management, Oxford Brookes University, United Kingdom.

Kim Meijer-van Wijk is a lecturer at the Hospitality Business School, Saxion University of Applied Sciences, Deventer, the Netherlands.

Barry O'Mahony is Dean of the Faculty of Business at the University of Wollongong in Dubai.

Shobana Nair Partington is the Acting Head of Department for the Department of Food and Tourism Management, Manchester Metropolitan University, United Kingdom.

Olga Araujo Perazzolo is a researcher at Universidade de Caxias do Sul (UCS), Brazil.

Siloe Pereira is a researcher at Universidade de Caxias do Sul (UCS), Brazil.

George Ritzer is Distinguished University Professor at the University of Maryland, United States of America.

Victoria N. Ruiter is a lecturer in the Tourism and Leisure School, Stenden University of Applied Sciences, the Netherlands.

Marcia Maria Cappellano dos Santos is a researcher at Universidade de Caxias do Sul (UCS), Brazil.

Leanne Schreurs is a researcher at Saxion University of Applied Sciences, Deventer, the Netherlands.

Ana Paula Garcia Spolon is a professor and researcher at Universidade Federal Fluminense, Brazil.

Judith Still is Professor of French and Critical Theory and Head of the School of Cultures, Languages and Area Studies at the University of Nottingham, United Kingdom.

Javed Suleri is a research projects coordinator in the Academy of International Hospitality Research, Stenden University of Applied Sciences, the Netherlands.

Elizabeth Telfer is formerly a member of Department of Sociology, University of Glasgow, Glasgow, United Kingdom.

Luiz Gonzaga Godoi Trigo is Professor in Leisure and Tourism, Escola de Artes, Ciências e Humanidades da Universidade de São Paulo (EACH-USP), São Paulo, Brazil.

John K. Walton was formerly a professor at the Universidad del País Vasco UPV/ EHU, Bilbao, Spain.

Desmond Wee is Professor of Tourism Sciences and Spatial Theories at the Karlshochschule International University, Germany.

Ruud Welten is a professor in the Faculty of Philosophy, Erasmus University Rotterdam, a philosophy lecturer at School of Humanities, University of Tilburg and lecturer in ethics and global citizenship at Saxion University of Applied Sciences, Deventer, the Netherlands.

Roy C. Wood is Professor in Hospitality and Gaming Management and Associate Dean (Curriculum and Teaching) in the Business Administration Faculty of the University of Macau, China.

1

Introduction

Research on hospitality: the story so far/ways of knowing hospitality

Conrad Lashley

> **Key themes**
>
> Studying the domains of hospitality
>
> The continuum of hospitality
>
> Hospitableness
>
> Themes

Hospitality is making your guests feel at home, even though you wish they were.

(Anon)

The study of hospitality has been stimulated by academics engaged in hospitality research and hospitality management education, and by academics from an array of social science fields interested in the study of relationships between guests and hosts. Although I have been primarily involved in hospitality management education, I recognised the need to explore social sciences insights into the study of host and guest relations. This interest resulted in a text co-edited with Alison Morrison, *In Search of Hospitality: Theoretical Perspectives and Debates* (Lashley and Morrison, 2000), followed by a second book, *Hospitality: A Social Lens* (Lashley et al., 2007). Around the same time, Jennie Germann Molz and Sarah Gibson edited *Mobilizing Hospitality: The Ethics of Social Relations in a Mobile World* (2007). The last-mentioned book emerged as the result of an interest in increasing global mobility from social science perspectives. Subsequently, researchers came together from both fields to launch the refereed research journal *Hospitality & Society*. This current edited volume is, therefore, the latest stage in the emerging academic field of 'hospitality studies'. It encourages both the study *of* hospitality as a human phenomenon and the study *for* hospitality as an industrial activity embracing the service of food, drink and accommodation in commercial and non-commercial settings.

DOI: 10.4324/9781315679938-1

Studying the domains of hospitality

Before going on to discuss the outline of this text, it is perhaps useful to go back over some of the ground that the study of hospitality encourages. Figure 1.1 reproduces a Venn diagram that was included in Lashley and Morrison's book (2000). While this might be accused of being somewhat simplistic and crude, it does suggest that studying hospitality as a commercial activity is just one domain, and that study of hospitality through the cultural/social domain and in the private/domestic domain can be interesting fields of academic enquiry in their own right, but can also better inform the development of managers destined to manage hospitality operations. Interestingly, the host–guest relationship has emerged as a metaphor for any setting where one person (guest) enters the space of another (host). Hospital services, banking and transport are examples of sectors where there is interest in hospitableness as a means of delivering customer experiences that enhance satisfaction and loyalty.

The *cultural/social domain* of hospitality activities suggests the need to study the social context in which particular hospitality activities take place. Current notions about hospitality are a relatively recent development (Lashley and Morrison, 2000; Germann Molz and Gibson, 2007; Lashley *et al.*, 2007). In pre-industrial societies, hospitality occupies a much more central position in the value-system (O'Gorman, 2007). Indeed in contemporary pre-industrial societies, hospitality and the duty to entertain both neighbours and strangers represent a fundamental moral imperative (Heal, 1990; Cole, 2007; Meehan, 2012; Melwani, 2009). Frequently, the requirement to provide hospitality, to act with generosity as a host and to protect visitors is

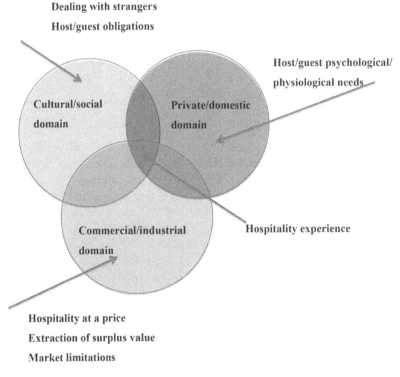

Figure 1.1   The domains of hospitality

more than a matter left to the preferences of individuals. Beliefs about hospitality, and obligations to others, are located in views and visions about the nature of society and the natural order of things. Thus any failure to act appropriately is treated with social condemnation. The centrality of hospitality activities has been noted in a wide range of studies of Homeric Greece, early Rome, medieval Provence, the Maori, Indian tribes of Canada, early modern England and in Mediterranean societies, for example. While modern industrial economies no longer have the same intensive moral obligations to be hospitable, and much hospitality experience takes place in commercial settings, the study of the cultural domain provides a valuable set of insights with which to critically evaluate and inform commercial provision. Part I of this book, entitled 'Disciplinary perspectives', includes chapters by authors that explore some of the more social and cultural dimensions to the study of hospitality.

The *private/domestic domain* helps with the consideration of some of the issues related to the meaning of hospitality, hosting and 'hospitableness'. Hospitality involves supplying food, drink and accommodation to people who are not members of the household. While much current research and published material focuses exclusively on the commercial market exchange between the recipient and supplier of hospitality, the domestic setting is revealing because the parties concerned are performing roles that extend beyond the narrow market relationships of a service interaction. The provision of food, drink and accommodation represents an act of friendship; it creates symbolic ties between people that establish bonds among those involved in sharing hospitality. In most pre-industrial societies, the receipt and kindly treatment of strangers was highly valued, though as Heal (1990) shows the motives were not always solely altruistic. Receiving strangers into the household helped to monitor the behaviour of outsiders. Visser (1991) links the relationship between the host and the guest through the common linguistic root of the two words. Both originate from a common Indo-European word that means 'stranger' and thereby 'enemy' (hospitality and hostile have a similar root), but the link to this single term 'refers not so much to the individual people, the guest and the host, as to the relationship between them' (Visser, 1991: 91). It is a relationship frequently based on mutual obligations and ultimately on reciprocity. The guest may become the host on another occasion. Importantly, however, most individuals have their first experiences of both consuming and supplying food, drink and accommodation in domestic settings. Indeed, few employees, or would-be entrepreneurs, enter the commercial sectors of hospitality as workers without having some experiences of hospitality in domestic settings.

One of the key issues relating to hospitality provision in the *commercial/industrial domain* relates to the authenticity of the hospitality provided. Are commercial hospitality products and services merely another service? Can commercial hospitality ever be genuinely hospitable? Are models of cultural and private hospitality of any value? Slattery (2002) argues that restaurant, bar and hotel services are essentially economic and involve a management activity. The study of hospitality from wider social science perspectives has, therefore, limited utility. In this view, the guest–host transaction is essential a monetary transaction.

Ritzer (2007) agrees by suggesting that there are powerful drivers in commercial hospitality organisations that will lead hospitality provision to become 'inhospitable'. Ritzer's comments on 'McDonaldisation' (2004) state that corporate drivers to increase efficiency, calculability, predictability and control lead ultimately to the creation of systems that act as a barrier to the frontline delivery of hospitableness. These McDonaldising processes inhibit performances that are hospitable, and at the same time they generate customer feelings of being undervalued as individuals. Standardising and systemising processes, therefore, are a fundamental aspect of the approach to managing hospitality services in bars, restaurants and hotels, and, in effect, remove the 'hospitableness' from the transaction. In Telfer's terms (2000), the commercial transaction provides an ulterior motive for offering hospitality and therefore prevents 'genuine' hospitality. Warde and Martens (2000) found that interviewees regarded eating out in restaurants as less than authentic. In contrast to the somewhat pessimistic views of Warde and Martens (2000) and Ritzer (2007), Telfer (2000) does suggest that it is not inevitable that commercial hospitality will invariably be a less than authentic version of hospitality in the home. She suggests that it is possible that those who have an interest in, and who value, hospitality will be drawn to work in the commercial hospitality sector. They may run their own hospitality businesses or choose to work in roles that enable them to be hospitable.

The problem is that many hospitality and tourism operators give priority to tangible aspects of the customer offer – the quality of the food, facilities and comfort of the room, the range and quality of the drinks on offer and so on – but fail to see that it is the quality of the employee performance which creates guests' emotional experiences that impact upon long-term customer satisfaction and loyalty. Herzberg's concept of motivation theory (1966) provides a useful metaphor. The physical aspects of the resort, the decor, physical facilities, the meals and drinks supplied are potentially '*dissatisfiers*'. If standards do not meet expectations, customers will be dissatisfied. However, exceeding their expectations in these tangible aspects will not produce satisfaction (Balmer and Baum, 1993). Customer satisfaction will be created by the quality of the emotions generated from their experiences. Staff performance, the qualities of hospitableness delivered, their fellow diners and the behaviour of line management are the key elements to producing customer satisfaction, through their emotional experiences as guests. Long-term customer loyalty and repeat custom to the venue are dependent on the emotions generated by these elements. Highly satisfied hospitality and tourism visitors are more likely to return or to recommend the establishment to family and friends.

Hospitality and hospitableness

This text embraces the study of hospitality from wider social science perspectives that enable an understanding of guest and host transactions that can inform much management practice and prerogatives. Traditional understandings of hospitality require hosts to be primarily concerned with ensuring guest well-being. Using some of these traditional models of hospitality offers the opportunity to convert strangers into friends. In a commercial context, this could be translated to converting customers into friends (Lashley and Morrison, 2000), thereby providing the basis for competitive advantage by building a loyal customer base. At root, operators can be trained to recognise and engage with the provision of hospitality experiences that rely heavily on the emotional dimensions of these experiences.

Combining the work of Heal (1984), Nouwen (1998), Telfer (2000) and O'Gorman (2007) it is possible to detect a number of motives for hosts offering hospitality to guests. Figure 1.2 provides a graphical representation of this array of motives. These can be mapped along a continuum showing the more calculative reasons for providing hospitality through to the most generous. In other words, where hospitality is offered with the hope of ensuing gain, to situations whereby hospitality is offered merely for the joy and pleasure of hosting.

Ulterior motives hospitality	Containing hospitality	Commercial hospitality	Reciprocal hospitality	Redistributive hospitality	Altruistic hospitality

Figure 1.2   A continuum of hospitality

Telfer (2000) identified the offering of food, drink and accommodation with some expectation of subsequent gain as 'ulterior motives hospitality'. It is assumed that the guest is able to benefit the host, and hospitality is offered as a means of gaining that benefit. Here, the business lunch or dinner for the boss, or the client, can be examples of hospitality being offered with the intention of creating a favourable impression that will ultimately benefit the host. Writing in the early 1500s, Niccolò Machiavelli advised, 'Keep your friends close, but your enemies closer'. In this sense 'containing hospitality' is motivated by a fear of the stranger, but one that advocates close monitoring by including the stranger in the household. Wagner's opera *Die Walküre* involves Hunding offering Seigmund hospitality even though Hunding knows Seigmund to be an enemy. This provides an insight into the obligation to offer hospitality to all, irrespective of who they are, but also suggests that the motive is to monitor and contain the enemy (Wagner, 1870).

On one level, 'Treat the customers as though they were guests in your own home' is attempting to tap into restaurant workers' hosting experience in domestic settings (Ashness and Lashley, 1995). Hopefully, the service worker will engage on an emotional level, as hosts serving their customers, as personal guests. Yet the provision of commercial hospitality involves a financial transaction whereby hospitality is offered to guests at a price, and would be withdrawn if the payment could not be made. Hence, 'commercial hospitality' can be said to represent a contradiction and cannot deliver true hospitableness (Ward and Martens, 2000; Ritzer, 2004, 2007). Telfer (2000), however, reminds us that this is a somewhat simplistic view because it may be that hospitable people are drawn to work in bars, hotels and restaurants, and offer hospitableness beyond, and in spite of, the commercial transaction and materialistic instructions from owners. Also, it may be that hospitable people are drawn to set up hospitality businesses in guesthouses, pubs and restaurants because it allows them to be both entrepreneurial and hospitable at the same time.

A number of writers suggest that hospitality involves reciprocity whereby hospitality is offered on the understanding that it will be reciprocated at some later date (O'Gorman, 2007). Hospitality practised by elite families in Augustinian Rome was founded on the principle of reciprocity as an early form of tourism. Affluent Romans developed networks of relationships with other families with whom they stayed as guests and then acted as hosts when their former hosts were intending to travel. Cole's work with the Ngadha tribe in Indonesia (2007) provides some fascinating insights into contemporary hospitality and tourism in a remote community today. The tribe practise reciprocal hospitality through tribe members hosting pig-roasting events for other tribe members. Thus, 'reciprocal hospitality' involves hospitality being offered within a context whereby hosts become guests and guests become hosts, at different times. Yet another form of hospitality takes place when redistributive hospitality is offered in settings where food and drink are provided with no immediate expectation of return, repayment or reciprocity. Those who have more share with those who have less, and the status of families and individuals is a reflection of what they give, not what they acquire. The study of the potlatch practised by North American Indians is an example of this redistributive effect. Clearly, the inclusion of the poor and needy in hospitality settings offered in the early Middle Ages noted by Heal (1990) also had a redistributive effect.

Finally, 'altruistic hospitality' involves the offer of hospitableness as an act of generosity and benevolence, and a willingness to give pleasure to others. Telfer (2000) describes this as 'genuine' hospitality, while Derrida (2002) calls it 'radical' hospitality. It provides an ideal type, or a pure form, of hospitality, devoid of personal gain for the host, apart from the emotional satisfaction arising from the practice of hospitableness. I prefer to label this as altruistic hospitality because it more clearly expresses the motive for offering hospitality as being about generosity. According to the work of Matthew Blain, altruistic hospitality is ultimately about generosity (Blain and Lashley, 2014). The research instrument developed by Blain is an attitude survey that appears to

> - The desire to please others
> - General friendliness and benevolence
> - Affection for people; concern for others and compassion
> - The desire to meet another's need
> - A desire to entertain
> - A need to help those in trouble
> - A desire to have company or to make friends
> - A desire for the pleasures of entertaining

Figure 1.3   The qualities of hospitableness

Source: Telfer (2000).

identify a consistent set of statements that identify individuals who are hospitable. Using a Likert scale, these statements are organised around three themes: desire to put guests before yourself, desire to make guests happy and desire to make guests feel special. The full set of questions and the questionnaire developed by Matthew Blain are featured in the last chapter of this book. The list of statements developed by Blain is consistent with the features of hospitableness listed in Figure 1.3 (Lashley and Morrison, 2000).

Themes

This edited book is organised around themes that have emerged as the result of the study of hospitality from social science perspectives. The chapters are organised under four themes. Part I 'Disciplinary perspectives' contains thirteen chapters that are written by authors who are mostly informed by social science views; Part II 'Experiencing hospitality' includes chapters exploring the experiences of being hosts and guest; Part III 'Hospitality through time and space' explores the worldwide human practices and obligations to be hospitable; and finally Part IV 'Sustainable hospitality' includes a number of chapters that look to the impact of hospitality in the future.

Part I 'Disciplinary perspectives' contains chapters that are written by authors who are mostly not hospitality management educators, though some are. Roy Wood, for example, was a long time academic at Strathclyde University in Edinburgh, though he is now working at the University of Macau in China. His chapter, 'Sociological perspectives on hospitality', makes the case that sociologists, and social scientists in general, have a significant contribution to make to the study of hospitality and hospitableness. David Bell's contribution, 'Geographies of hospitality', provides a geographers' perspective on the study, specifically sharing a concern for the role hospitality venues play in facilitating travel and venues for social intercourse. Kim Meijer-van Wijk's chapter, 'Levinas, hospitality and the feminine other', addresses the fundamental question of why and how people are hospitable towards each other by analysing the philosophy of Emmanuel Levinas. In 'The philosophy of hospitableness', Elizabeth Telfer provides a base for recognising there are different motives for offering hospitality. 'The hospitality trades: a social history' by John Walton sets the development of hospitality in a historical context through the increased travel generated by increased commercialisation to mass tourism in industrial/service economies. Bob Brotherton's chapter, 'Hospitality – a synthetic approach', argues for a clear definition of hospitality both conceptually and practically. Szilvia Gyimóthy's 'Dinner sharing: casual hospitality in the collaborative economy' explores the peer-to-peer marketplace covering social dining and the interconnecting of visitors with locals and eating in private dwellings. 'Religious perspectives on hospitality' by Conrad Lashley touches on both historical and philosophical issues to demonstrate hospitableness and the duty to be hospitable across different historical and geographical settings.

Marcia Santos, Olga Perazzolo, Siloe Pereira and Isabel Baptista provide an insight into the social psychological dimension between hosts and guest in their chapter, 'Hospitality and social ties: an interdisciplinary reflexive journey for a psychology of hospitality'. Judith Still explores the role of women in hospitality, particularly the character of Circe in Homer's *Odyssey* in 'Hospitalities: Circe writes back'. A key theme of Homer's work involves incidents with the strange Other, and Ruud Welten follows this up with the storyline in Moby Dick where Ishmael has to share a bed with a fellow sailor who is a cannibal. His chapter, 'On the hospitality of cannibals', explores the potential contradictions between the strangeness of the Other and the hospitality settings where the strangeness has to be set aside. The cross-cultural, historical and global reach of hospitality and the duty to host the stranger is further explored in Martine Berenpas's chapter, 'An Asian ethics of hospitality: hospitality in Confucian, Daoist and Buddhist philosophy'. Leanne Schreurs' work concerns the language used in hospitality exchanges. In 'Observing hospitality speech patterns' she explores the degree of formality and informality, as well the distance and intimacy of the encounter dependent on the nature of the interaction. The chapters in this section confirm the view that acts of hospitality and the engagement of hosts and guest are of considerable interest to social scientists. Academics from philosophy, history, geography, religious studies, social psychology and linguistics have contributed chapters to this section.

The second theme of the book highlights the experiences of hospitality from an array of perspectives including the immediate industrial context providing food, drink and accommodation, but also in a more metaphorical sense where hospitality and the host–guest interaction can be said to be in play where one person enters the space of another. Part II opens with a chapter by Barry O'Mahony which discusses the overlaps between hospitality and migration. 'Hospitality, migration and cultural assimilation' is a case study of Irish migration to Australia. It exposes some of the contradictions and inequalities that hosts display in relation to guests, best summed up as 'all welcome, but not them!' Judi Brownell also discusses unequal treatment, but with a focus on the treatment of women in the hospitality sector. 'Women experience hospitality as travelers and leaders' discusses a number of themes about the treatment of women both as employees and as customers. The hospitality industry has a high level of female employees, yet a much lower number in management positions. Hotel design and services are frequently male-oriented and frequently fail to recognise the needs of female guests. 'Hospitality employment', by Shobana Partington, deals with the some of the contradictory employment policies practised by the sector employers. Low wages, poor training and high staff turnover are not consistent with a service operation that relies on employee performance to create customer satisfaction and loyalty. Despite this situation, many come to work in the sector because of the fast moving and changing nature of the work.

Peter Lugosi's chapter, 'Consuming hospitality', suggests that consumers of hospitality are looking for different experiences depending on the occasionality of their visit. Their choices are then likely to shape their expectations of the service encounter, and signifiers of success. George Ritzer's chapter also deals with consumption of hospitality. 'Hospitality and prosumption' points to trends in both provision and customer expectations, for customers produce some, or all, of the service they consume. Self-check-in/check-out is just one obvious example of this tendency. Sjoerd Gehrels deals with the service of alcohol in hospitality settings. 'Liquid hospitality: wine as the metaphor' discusses the link between the experiences of serving and consuming wine with acts of hospitableness. The role of wine in the experiencing of hospitality and the impact of wine on the well-being of the consumer are issues pursued.

In 'Hospitality, territory and identity: reflections from community tourism in Aventureiro Village, Ilha Grande/RJ, Brazil' Helena Catão Henriques Ferreira and Aguinaldo Fratucci explore the impact of tourism on communities with limited experience of receiving tourists and the interaction with visitors with the community's cultural traditions of receiving guests. Visitors are attracted by the authenticity of the community, but their impact might ultimately distort or even destroy that which they come to see. The boundaries and inconsistencies of the duty to be hospitable are discussed via an analysis of the novel *Adventures of Huckleberry Finn* by Mark Twain in Bastienne Bernasco's chapter, 'Fluid hospitality in *Adventures of Huckleberry Finn*'. The relationship between Huck and Jim the runaway slave are at the heart of the plot and while they move through a variety of settings they are welcomed or rejected because of who they are rather than being subject to universal hospitableness.

Part III 'Hospitality through time and space' shares a cluster of chapters that report upon the concept of hospitality in different social, cultural and historical contexts. The global and temporal dimensions of hospitality set in an African context are the subject of Victoria Ruiter's chapter, 'Hunter and gatherer hospitality in Africa'. Hospitality through feasting enabled the collective community to benefit from individual gains. Moving across both time and space, 'The gift theory of Marcel Mauss and the potlatch ritual: a triad of hospitality', by Leandro Brusadin, highlights the hospitality practices of North American Indians prior to colonisation. Sharing the results of hunting with other tribe members was not just a duty, but also a signifier of social worth.

Anna Spolon reports upon the receiving of migrants into Brazil during the periods of mass colonisation when many of these migrants brought with them the disease of leprosy. 'Hospitality, sanitation services and immigration: leprosaria and hostels for immigrants in Brazil' suggests that leprosaria were hostels designed to both welcome migrants and protect the host population from the harmful effects of those arriving with diseases. This is an interesting case study of hospitableness that may have some insights for our contemporary context, where Europe is dealing with unprecedented levels of refugees from conflict zones, and hosts are complaining about being overwhelmed by 'migrant' guests. Interestingly, the terminology used to describe them is varied and communicates varying degrees of empathy with these would-be guests. Asylum seekers and refugee guests suggest more of a people in need perception, whereas migrants/immigrants imply economic motives for their need to leave their homeland. Javed Suleri, who originates from the Indian sub-continent, reports upon his personal experiences of being received into different countries and cultures, his experiences of moving around, in 'Experiencing hospitality and hospitableness in different cultures'. In some settings he was welcomed as a fellow human being and shown the best the good host could present. In other cases he was treated as 'one of them' and subjected to inhospitable behaviour. 'Transcending the limits of hospitality: the case of Mount Athos and the offering of philoxenia', by Prokopis Christou, introduces the notion of 'philoxenia' as the love of the guest and draws links to both ancient and contemporary religious cultures to demonstrate that this obligation has a geographical expression in various sites on Mount Athos in modern Greece. It provides an interesting insight into the role that hospitableness plays in helping to define the moral expression of a particular culture.

In 'Fifty shades of hospitality: exploring intimacies in Korean love motels' Desmond Wee and Ko Koens explore the use of love motels in South Korea. Love motels are a feature of many Far Eastern societies where domestic space is limited and frequently shared with parents and grandparents. Love motels describe commercial accommodation provision specifically available for couples to hire for intimacy and privacy. Rooms can be hired for one or two hours or overnight as with a traditional hotel. The authors report that these rooms are frequently decorated in a manner that reinforces their purpose, via extensive use of mirrors and so forth. Continuing the theme of hotel venues and sex, 'Hospitality between the sheets', by Ricardo Lanzarini and Luiz Trigo, discusses the role that hotels and other hospitality venues play in first engendering contact between potential sexual partners and subsequently providing private spaces for purposes of intimacy.

Part IV of this volume deals with the theme of sustainable hospitality. Elena Cavagnaro's chapter, 'Creating value for all: sustainable hospitality', deals with the general concerns of the sustainability of commercial hospitality provision. The issues of design and operational practice suggest that there is much that commercial operators can do to reduce wasteful practices. Conrad Lashley's chapter, 'Liberating wage slaves: towards sustainable employment practices', suggests that exploitative employment practices are counterproductive and ultimately more costly than more participative and inclusive approaches. The problem is that many management account-ability processes are narrowly focused on financial performance measures, and do not account for the cost of labour turnover, low training and poor employee satisfaction levels. In 'Hospitality studies: developing philosophical practitioners?' Lashley suggests that a less practitioner-driven curriculum would enable the development of future managers more able to cope with a fast changing environment because they appreciate the principles involved.

Conclusions

Although this book is not intended as a text that is principally concerned with demonstrating the global nature of hospitality, it is satisfying to note that it involves contributions from around the globe. Thirty-six authors from ten different countries spanning six continents have contributed chapters. If nothing else, this profile demonstrates the international interest in hospitality and hospitableness, further reinforcing Derrida's point that the means and rituals associated with the receiving of strangers into a community are a defining feature of all societies.

The hospitality studies agenda reflected in this text suggests that the study of hospitality is an academic field with a broad base and a long-term future. I currently hold a Professorship in Hospitality Studies and I firmly believe that other such appointments will emerge in the future. Time will tell, but in the interim this volume aims to contribute to the development of the study of hospitableness with both immediate commercial value and the long-term understanding of the relationships between hosts and guests.

References

Ashness, D. and Lashley, C. (1995) Empowering service workers at Harvester restaurants, *Personnel Review* 24, 8: 501–519.

Balmer, S. and Baum, T. (1993) Applying Herzberg's hygiene factors to the changing accommodation environment, *International Journal of Contemporary Hospitality Management* 5, 2: 32–35.

Blain, M. and Lashley, C. (2014) Hospitableness: the new service metaphor? Developing an instrument for measuring hosting, *Research in Hospitality Management* 4, 1/2: 1–8.

Cole, S. (2007) Hospitality and tourism in Ngadha: an ethnographic exploration. In Lashley, C., Lynch, P. and Morrison, A. (eds) *Hospitality: A Social Lens*, Amsterdam: Elsevier, pp. 61–71.

Derrida, J. (2002) *Acts of Religion*, London: Routledge.

Germann Molz, J. G. and Gibson, S. (eds) (2007) *Mobilizing Hospitality: The Ethics of Social Relations in a Mobile World*, Aldershot: Ashgate.

Heal, F. (1984) The idea of hospitality in early modern England, *Past and Present* 102, 1: 66–93.

Heal, F. (1990) *Hospitality in Early Modern England*, Oxford: Clarendon Press.

Herzberg, F. (1966) *Work and the Nature of Man*, New York: Staple Press.

Lashley, C. and Morrison, A. (eds) (2000) *In Search of Hospitality: Theoretical Perspectives and Debates*, Oxford: Butterworth-Heinemann.

Lashley, C., Lynch, P. and Morrison, A. (eds) (2007) *Hospitality: A Social Lens*, Amsterdam: Elsevier.

Meehan, S. (2012) Hospitality in Islam: the joy of honoring guests, *Understanding the Ethics of Islam*. Available at http://eislaminfo. blogspot.com/2012/12/hospitality-in-islam.html. Accessed 20 June 2016.

Melwani, L. (2009) Hindu hospitality: the gods amongst us, *Hinduism Today*, 27 September. Available at http://www.lassiwithlavina.com/features/faith/hindu-hospitality-the-gods-amongst-us/html. Accessed 20 June 2016.

Nouwen, H. (1998) *Reaching Out: A Special Edition of the Spiritual Classic including Beyond the Mirror*, London: Fount (an Imprint of HarperCollins).

O'Gorman, K. D. (2007) The hospitality phenomenon: philosophical enlightenment?, *International Journal of Culture, Tourism and Hospitality Research* 1: 189–202.

Ritzer, G. (2004) *The McDonaldization of Society*, rev. New Century edn, London: Sage.

Ritzer, G. (2007) Inhospitable hospitality? In Lashley, C., Morrison, A. and Lynch, P. (eds) *Hospitality: A Social Lens*, Amsterdam: Elsevier, pp. 129–140.

Slattery, P. (2002) Finding the hospitality industry, *Journal of Hospitality, Leisure Sport and Tourism* 1, 1: 19–28.

Telfer, E. (2000) The philosophy of hospitableness. In Lashley, C. and Morrison, A. (eds) *In Search of Hospitality: Theoretical Perspectives and Debates*, Oxford: Butterworth-Heinemann, pp. 255–275.

Visser, M. (1991) *The Rituals of Dinner: The Origin, Evolution, Eccentricities and Meaning of Table Manners*, Toronto: HarperCollins.

Wagner, R. (1870) *Die Walküre*, Libretto.

Warde, A. and Martens, L. (2000) *Eating Out: Social Differentiation, Consumption, and Pleasure*, Cambridge: Cambridge University Press.

Part I
Disciplinary perspectives

2

Sociological perspectives on hospitality

Roy C. Wood

Key themes

Hospitality and social theory

Strangerhood

Gifts, social exchange and hospitality

Conspicuous consumption

> What is more kindly than the feeling between host and guest?
>
> *(Aeschylus)*

In 1994, a conference was held at The Scottish Hotel School of the University of Strathclyde in Glasgow. Entitled 'Tourism – the State of the Art', it was a major event of its kind and led to the publication of selected papers in a large volume intended as a benchmark reference work (Seaton *et al.*, 1994). My contribution, beyond being a member of the book's editorial team, was a paper that offered what I still believe to be the first published synthesis of the then extant literature proposing a broadly sociological viewpoint on the topic of hospitality (Wood, 1994a). Of course, and by definition, there had been some previous explicit commentaries on hospitality from sociological perspectives. There were even one or two traceable, but unpublished, attempts at synthesis. I remember being particularly proud of my contribution at the time, but of course, with the benefit of more than twenty years of hindsight, it is easy now to see what could have been included that was not.

During the same decade, a number of people teaching and researching in the field of hospitality management began to reflect in private and in public on the nature and meanings of hospitality, the most prominent probably being Brotherton (1999; see also Brotherton, 2005). The term 'hospitality management' was, at that time, in the ascendency over previous descriptors such as 'hotel management' and 'catering management' for reasons that have been explored

DOI: 10.4324/9781315679938-3

in some detail elsewhere and need not detain us here (Wood, 2015a, 2015b). Brotherton and a small number of other hospitality academics sought to reflect on the nature of hospitality as a generalised social, economic and historical phenomenon rather than a narrow industrial one. In 2000, many of the first fruits of these contemplative processes were published in a landmark book, *In Search of Hospitality* (Lashley and Morrison, 2000), which benefited from having a broad mixture of contributions from scholars and researchers in subjects other than hospitality management (see also the earlier, US collection of papers, edited by Cummings *et al.*, 1998, which is undeservedly less well known).

In Search of Hospitality marked the beginning of a more thoroughly social scientific approach to the study of hospitality. Indeed, in the decade and a half since its publication, the field of 'hospitality studies' complementary to 'hospitality management' has been spawned. Relative to other subjects and disciplines, the number of hospitality management researchers around the globe is small and those who proclaim themselves to be in the hospitality studies field is even smaller. Yet now, in the second decade of the twenty-first century, in terms of contribution to theory and concept development, those in the latter area are beginning to make the running. In 2011, the editor of this volume and others established the academic journal *Hospitality & Society*. The current editor of the journal is Dr Paul Lynch who, in 2013, became the first Professor of Critical Hospitality and Tourism at Napier University Edinburgh, the title of his chair notice-ably devoid of the word 'management'. The 'hospitality studies' approach is not unproblematic. To begin with, it does not offer a monolithic or coherent perspective on hospitality but rather a number of varying and fragmented approaches, some of which appear to favour ignoring hospitality management as one form of hospitality in society altogether. Then again, as we shall see in this chapter, sociological perspectives on hospitality (where 'sociology' and 'sociological' are defined very broadly) are themselves fragmented and piecemeal. In undertaking to write this new and revised synthesis of the field, the intention is to try to forge a loose temporal and spatial framework to aid understanding of the sociological contribution to the study of hospital-ity, thereby maintaining a wholly justified social scientific imperative in the field.

Sociological beginnings

In UK higher education (and indeed elsewhere) in the 1970s, sociology was still a relatively young subject. Most courses required students to take a module or unit in classical sociological theory, which more often than not centred on the 'big three' founding fathers of the discipline – Karl Marx (1818–1883), Max Weber (1864–1920) and Émile Durkheim (1858–1917). Some syllabi also included Sigmund Freud (1856–1939) and, if you were lucky (or, perhaps, unlucky), you might also get to study the work of such luminaries as August Comte (1798–1857) and Herbert Spencer (1820–1903), who were often half-heartedly invoked as further evidence, if it were required, of sociology's historical claim to disciplinary legitimacy. *Tempora mutantur, nos et mutamur in illis.* In the second decade of the twenty-first century the definition of clas-sical sociological theory has expanded considerably. A casual glance through current textbook offerings reveals the work of numerous other individuals now embraced by the term, including Theodore Adorno (1903–1969), Karl Mannheim (1893–1947), Herbert Marcuse (1898–1979), George Herbert Mead (1863–1931), Robert K. Merton (1910–2003), Talcott Parsons (1902–1979), Georg Simmel (1859–1918) and Thorstein Veblen (1857–1929). Feminist sociologists have additionally made the case to include previously ignored female scholars as being among the 'founding mothers' of the discipline, examples including Harriet Martineau (1802–1876) and Charlotte Perkins Gilman (1860–1935) (see, for example, Goodwin and Scimecca, 2006).

Few of the founding fathers (or mothers) had very much to say *directly* on the subject of hospitality but their works influenced associates and have subsequently informed extrapolation and commentary by various 'disciplinary descendants'. Thus it is Durkheim we must partially thank for the work of his nephew Mauss (2000 [1922]). It is to Weber we turn in qualified gratitude for George Ritzer's more recent work on the McDonaldisation of hospitality. Georg Simmel and Thorstein Veblen spoke – usually, but not always, indirectly – to aspects of the phenomenon of hospitality but their work has not yet received the study or credit it deserves among proponents of the 'hospitality studies' approach noted earlier. One *contemporary* social theorist who *has* been latched onto by hospitality studies researchers is Jacques Derrida (1930–2004), to whom discussion will return in the chapter's conclusion.

On some of these there will be more later in this chapter, but the piecemeal interest of sociologists in hospitality suggests two ways in which accounts of the field may be approached. The first is essentially historiographic and descriptive, charting the contribution of individuals, movements and themes over time. The second approach is arguably more analytic, identifying and concentrating on themes from the outset and then seeking to impose some conceptual and theoretical order upon them. The latter approach was attempted by Wood (1994a) and will be deployed here, although what follows makes no pretence to be either comprehensive or exhaustive: sociologically speaking we are still very much at the starting line when it comes to understanding hospitality.

Hospitality as duty and protection

The giving of hospitality as a means of both protecting and controlling strangers has a long history, much of it rooted in religious values that acquired civic force in pre-industrial societies. Heal (1990), studying England between *c.*1400 and 1700, articulates a popular distinction in the sociological literature between hospitality as a social duty rooted in domesticity, and contemporary hospitality which is depicted as relatively free of such overtones. Visser, a sociologist and historian of food and eating, emphasises the domestic angle thus:

> The laws of hospitality deal firstly with strangers – how to manage their entry into our inner sanctum, how to protect them from our own automatic reaction, which is to fear and exclude the unknown, how to prevent them from attacking and desecrating what we hold dear, or from otherwise behaving in a strange and unpredictably dangerous manner. We remember that we too might one day need a stranger's help. So we behave in the prescribed civilized manner.
>
> *(1992: 93)*

Cultural historians such as Zeldin also see domesticity and control of the stranger as intertwined:

> Today in the rich countries, hospitality means, above all, entertaining friends or acquaintances in one's home; but once upon a time it meant opening one's house to total strangers, giving a meal to anyone who chose to come, allowing them to stay the night, indeed imploring them to stay, although one knew nothing about them. This kind of open hospitality has been admired and practiced in virtually every civilization that has existed, as though it fulfils a basic human need.
>
> *(1994: 437)*

Zeldin goes on to lament the decline of this 'domestic' hospitality, which he sees as beginning as early as in the sixteenth century, arguing that:

> As soon as the rich appointed almoners to do their charitable work for them, they lost direct touch with their visitors; as soon as distress was dealt with impersonally by officials, hospitality was never the same again ... Free hospitality was superseded by the hospitality industry.
>
> *(1994: 438)*

The juxtaposition between domestic and 'other' forms of hospitality becomes, in Zeldin's hands, a contrast between the purity of the former and its subsequent pollution as a result of industrialisation, whereby the provision of hospitality sheds many of its overtones of duty and instead becomes a collection of commercial propositions largely devoid of sentiment. There is a kind of vulgar Orwellianism at work here – domestic hospitality good, commercial hospitality bad (Brotherton and Wood, 2000, 2008). The distinction, in one form or another, can be found in earlier sociological commentaries. Indeed, Georg Simmel saw the position of the stranger as fundamentally ambivalent in the increasingly industrialised world of the nineteenth and early twentieth century – ambivalent because the stranger was simultaneously feared and desired and socially near yet far – occupying on the social battlefield, as it were, a no-man's land (Pickering, 2001; Frisby, 2002). In a contribution on 'hospitality' to a major social scientific encyclopaedia of the time, Mühlmann wrote:

> The germ of the decay of hospitality is inherent in the institution itself, in that it inevitably extends frontiers and the domain of peace and promotes trade; as a result there arise public legal principles, which go beyond the personal and the familiar and take the place of hospitality ... Primitive hospitality was addressed to the public enemy; in the modern world the distinction between friend and enemy in the political sense is irrelevant. The old hospitality was a social or religious obligation; that of modern times rests with the discretion of the individual.
>
> *(1932: 464)*

For Mühlmann, hospitality 'represents a kind of guarantee of reciprocity – one protects the stranger in order to be protected from him' (1932: 463). We shall examine the role of reciprocity in hospitality momentarily, but it is important here to note that, like Zeldin, Mühlmann appears to be reacting against a perceived debasement of the moral foundations to hospitality and its replacement with the impersonal provision of hospitality based on monetary exchange. Many of those social scientists who have focused on the stranger–hospitality relationship have evolved, then, a romantic view on that phenomenon. How reliable is such a perspective?

A fine romance

The history of ideas is replete with concepts that romanticise or over-romanticise social phenomena or sketch grand theories of a kind that intellectually fascinate but are of practical limitation (see Skinner, 1990, for essays offering a largely positive account of such theories). In considering the putative distinction between a (domestic, noble and moral) pre- and (commercial, ignoble and possibly amoral) post-industrial hospitality, it is necessary to bear in mind that, empirically, we are far short of the extensive evidence required to verify whether such differences bear scrutiny (though see Symons, 2013, for a plausible refutation of this dichotomy in the context of evidence pertaining to the rise of restaurants in post-revolutionary France). Indeed, it is not even clear that the contrast itself is constructed in a manner that encourages the comparison of like with like. It seems plausible that both domestic and commercial hospitality have been, and continue to be, extremely diverse in form.

A useful check on assuming too much here can be found in 'developmental' perspectives on human behaviour much loved by some social anthropologists, particularly those working in the field of food and foodways (e.g. Harris, 1986; see also Mennell *et al.*, 1992). For example, much has been made of the symbolic and religious origins of duties of hospitality, not least in the case of the Benedictine order (e.g. O'Gorman, 2006a). While the role of monasteries and similar religious houses in providing hospitality at times in history when few people travelled can be understood as the articulation of a particular philosophy, it is also the case that for those who did travel, places to stay were few and far between and religious houses often offered a greater range of facilities than inns and similar establishments (and for some of a stay at least, they were often free, for what were inns but commercial enterprises – see Clark, 1983).

Similarly, defining hospitality in terms of protecting strangers in order to protect ourselves is intellectually appealing but hardly sufficiently evidenced. Although it is a cliché, the scene played out in fiction, film and television where 'strangers' walk into a local inn with an animated clientele who suddenly become completely silent and sullen contains, like all clichés, a glimpse of truth. Strangers are not always welcome. Moreover, the historically invoked concept of the stranger encountered earlier in this discussion cannot be assumed to have retained its objective integrity in the modern world.

Stranger still

Much of the literature reviewed above makes little of Georg Simmel's (1971 [1908]) contribution to the concept of the stranger. This is perhaps not all that surprising. Despite the popularisation of Simmel's work in the last half-century, he still enjoys a less than central position in the sociological canon (Goodwin and Scimecca, 2006). Further, despite forensic analyses of the kind offered by Frisby (2002), his writing style, at least in translation, is often opaque, a factor that has contributed, in the case of the concept of the stranger, to some confusion as to his meaning. A useful short summary of some of these issues is given by McLemore (1970: 86), who observes that Simmel purposely uses the term 'stranger' in an idiosyncratic way, citing the following passage:

> The stranger will thus not be considered here in the usual sense of the term, as the wanderer who comes today and goes tomorrow, but rather as the man who comes today and stays tomorrow – the potential wanderer, so to speak, who, although he has gone no further, has not quite got over the freedom of coming and going.
>
> *(Simmel 1971 [1908]: 143)*

These and many of Simmel's other observations on the stranger have led, as McLemore (1970) shows, to a history of differing interpretations of his idea of the stranger, many of these being, in effect, misreadings of the original work. As McLemore notes:

> Simmel's (1908) view of the 'stranger' has given impetus and visibility to the sociological study of the newcomer but ... Simmel's ... principal interest clearly is not in the newcomer as such. His main interest is in a particular configuration of social attributes which

may characterize a group member who has come from somewhere else ... The focus of analysis here ... upon the newcomer who fails to become a fully participating member of the group.

(1970: 88–89)

The Simmelian concept of the stranger is much more in line with that branch of migratory studies with its origins in social anthropology that examines hospitality and other social phenomenon at a macro-social level. Yet there is nothing in Simmel's original essay that precludes the possibility of exploring his particular take on strangerhood in the context of more limited social scenarios, as in the cases examined thus far in this chapter. Indeed, one can make the case that, contemporarily, the work of Zygmunt Bauman to some degree does just this (Welten, 2015).

In his book *Thinking Sociologically*, Bauman (1990: 54) offers a complex and, on occasion, obscure interpretation of the concept of strangerhood. For all the fact that a specific and individual stranger is by definition someone unfamiliar, someone not known well, in order to label someone as a stranger we must know many things about strangers in general to be able to draw on contextual knowledge of their differences from 'non-strangers'. Bauman (1990: 61) comments on the range of possible responses to the ambiguous position of the stranger in society. At the macro-social, migratory level, one such response is of the 'send them back to where they come from' kind. Sometimes, separation occurs between migratory incomers and the rest of society as, for example (though Bauman does not employ this example), in the creation – deliberately or otherwise – of ghettos. This is a relatively rare occurrence, however, because, as Bauman (1990: 62–63) points out, most industrial societies encourage high density living and, in the contemporary world, people travel a great deal, if only within a comparatively delimited geography. The consequence of this for Bauman is that:

> The world we live in seems to be populated mostly by strangers; it looks like the world of *universal strangerhood*. We live among strangers, among whom we are strangers ourselves. In such a world, strangers cannot be confined or kept at bay. Strangers must be lived with.
>
> *(1990: 63)*

This argument is subsequently revisited in Bauman's later work on 'liquid modernity' (Bauman, 2000), a concept in part intended to counter many of the notions proposed by writers who claim we live in a postmodern world. The world of liquid modernity is one in which we, as individuals, are subjected to continual uncertainty, and where the breakdown of social networks permits greater fluidity in the range of social identities that can be adopted. It is a world of increasing individualism and atomised relationships. There is little that is fundamentally new in these ideas (see, e.g., Brittan, 1977) save for Bauman's identification of civility (a concept he borrows from fellow sociologist Richard Sennett) as the means by which society facilitates encounters by strangers. Civility consists of those activities which facilitate encounters between strangers, protect strangers from each other, but permit them to enjoy each other's company in public places without being prevailed upon to betray something of their inner self (think of the stereotype of English people who meet in a public space and whose conversation, if any, is focused on the weather). In other words, civility is a controlling or auto-controlling mechanism that in any encounter maintains the status of strangers *as* strangers.

Despite the fluidity of his writing, Bauman's arguments are, like Simmel's, not always easy to grasp. He appears to be suggesting that 'we are all strangers now' to the extent that controlling mechanisms, whether external or internalised, are required to ensure hospitable behaviour between strangers. In terms of physical space, such controls are articulated through rules of entitlement to admission enforced by (sometimes literally so) gatekeepers such as security guards and receptionists (Bauman, 1990: 65). In terms of what we might call mental space, codes of 'civility' serve as a means of control, even if some of the behaviours embraced by this civility seem less than the term demands – for example, Bauman (1990: 66–67) cites Erving Goffman's concept of 'civil inattention' (Goffman, 1963), whereby in a studied way we do not look at, or listen to, the strangers around us, most commonly evidenced in the avoidance of eye contact.

Hospitality as a gift: reciprocity and social exchange

The notion that we protect strangers in order to protect ourselves, as outlined in the previous section, resonates with another sociological tradition of research into hospitality which has its origins in the work of Marcel Mauss and his *Essai sur le donne* (in English: *The Gift*), first published in the early 1920s (some sources date it to 1922, others, for example Lechte, 1994, date it to 1923–24: the edition referred to here is that published in 2000). Mauss (2000) rejects simplistic and deterministic approaches to understanding social relationships based on economic exchange and instead argues for these relationships to be understood in terms of a complex interaction between economic and social factors, specifically, and in addition to, any prevailing practice of economic rationality, the interplay of shared values and trust. As Scott puts it:

> Mauss presented an account of the exchange of gifts in tribal societies, but he showed that these exchanges involved a norm of 'reciprocity' that was quite distinct from the economic logic of the market. Although many exchange theorists have attempted to build norms of obligation and reciprocity into their work, this has always been a problematic exercise. Economic theorists, the mainstream of exchange theory, and recent 'rational choice' theories have all been more at home with those forms of action that can be assumed to follow a purely rational 'economic' or 'market' orientation.
>
> *(1995: 75)*

Burgess (1982) adopts the view of the gift as metaphor in seeking to explain hospitality and hospitable behaviour and makes four important points. First, gifts have symbolic, communicative qualities, as well as material qualities such that gift-givers often seek to transfer, or at the very least convey, something of themselves to the recipient, for example respect, warmth and sincerity. In the practice of hospitality this manifests itself in the ways in which hosts, including the managers and proprietors of hospitality businesses, imprint their own personality and personal style on the delivery of hospitality (a phenomenon perhaps most remarked upon by writers who have experienced small-scale commercial hospitality focused on the home – see, for example, Goffman, 1959 on his experiences in Orkney; Stringer, 1981, on bed and breakfast providers; and Lynch, 2000, on the 'homestay' sector).

Second, gifts convey information about, and confer identity on, those who give. The nature and quality of a gift conveys data about the status and standing of the donor, while simultaneously revealing their perceptions of, and feelings towards, the recipient. It defines the general identity of both donor and recipient in terms of (often) abstract concepts of entitlement. In the context of hospitality, whether commercial or non-commercial, such abstraction manifests itself in the form of ambiguities that host and guest must manage. For example, in non-commercial home-based hospitality and in commercial hospitality centred on the host's domestic residence, most such ambiguities pertain to (often unarticulated) restrictions on the physical spaces within an edifice that guests are entitled to access. Stringer (1981) notes that in bed and breakfast establishments the ambivalence of the 'host' over the degree of access to certain parts of the building, or the availability of certain facilities, can create doubts about the extent to which guests are welcome. In other words, it creates doubt about their status. In more industrialised forms of commercial hospitality, for example the large hotel, the design and range of facilities is such that these ambiguities are reduced, guest and non-guest areas more clearly defined and the emphasis is thus on controlling the guest's interaction with the property (Wood, 1994b).

Third, and following Mauss, Burgess argues that gift exchange and hospitality share a pre-occupation with optimising the bonds of trust between givers and receivers. A long-standing source of recurring humour in the UK used to be the gifts given on birthdays and Christmas to male teenagers and young men by mature female relatives – typically in the form of bought handkerchiefs or ties, or in terms of something that has been produced by the donor, for example woollen mittens or scarves. Trust derived both from the reliability with which gifts of this nature appeared on these festive occasions and, more generally, from the fact that the recipient was not forgotten. Although such gifts might not be welcomed, they were evidence of at least some thought and commitment to a relationship in contrast to those gifts that took the form of a bank note stuffed into an envelope or a shopping voucher (usually a book token) of some kind which, while perhaps possessing greater utility, suggested the absence of thought and commitment and a desire for expedience on the part of the donor. The parallel in hospitality lies in the complex concept of guest or customer service and whether it is perceived by guests/customers as authentic and sincere. Scripted clichés of the 'have a nice day' kind pronounced by hospitality employees are both manufactured and insincere yet for large commercial hospitality organisations a need is felt for such standard procedures. Guests/customers buy into the concept that they are individuals with individual needs, desires and problems that should be addressed individually. Hospitality organisations, in contrast, treat guests/customers as if they were largely a homogeneous mass, and procedures for dealing with a breakdown in trust (for example training in how to handle 'difficult' – i.e. non-conforming guests/customers) are regarded as a necessary but peripheral evil.

Finally, Burgess (1982) suggests that gift exchange and hospitality are both oriented towards establishing an 'interaction order', whereby the character of exchanges is developed according to *implicit* rules understood by parties to the exchange. Extending Burgess' analysis, we can take this to mean that for 'effective' exchange, both parties must have some shared understanding of what is and what is not acceptable in terms of behaviour and action. Examples might include mutual respect of the public and private areas of hotels (Goffman, 1959), participation in the rituals of the hospitality organisation (Hayner, 1969 [1936]) and a minimum commitment to maintaining accepted standards of decorum (Wood, 1994b). This interaction order is fundamentally based on Mauss' central concept of reciprocity interpreted by Burgess in terms of the construction of a shared responsibility for the *positive* outcome of any exchange process between givers and receivers.

The 'gift' of hospitality

The interconnections between Maussian gift donation as presented by Burgess and others (see, e.g., Davis, 2000) and hospitality on the one hand, and the prelapsarian-like accounts of pre- and post-industrial hospitality considered earlier on the other, are not difficult to discern. As Christian (1979) observes, while, historically, private domestic hospitality may have been offered on the basis of protecting and circumscribing the behaviour of strangers without charge or monetary expectation, some form of reciprocity *was* expected, even if that reciprocity was limited to observing the rules of the interaction order. As suggested elsewhere (Brotherton and Wood, 2008), the notion of protecting the stranger via the rituals of hospitality is indivisible from at least the expectation of some 'return', even if that return is not equal. This is a point noted by Telfer who, in a discussion of the philosophy of 'hospitableness' and 'hospitality', argues that 'Being a good host is not even a necessary condition of being hospitable' (1996: 82) or, in other words, it is entirely possible to 'achieve' hospitality and hospitableness without being intrinsically motivated by reasons of altruism or duty, a fact to which the modern hospitality industry more than adequately testifies.

In short, the 'virtuous' and primarily domestic hospitality lauded by such writers as Zeldin (1994) – indeed all forms of hospitality – appear to be bound up with expectations as to reciprocity and trust. In respect of the latter, trust is invested both in the *institution* of hospitality (trust that it will be provided) and in the *mechanics* of various hospitality experiences which may be governed by one or both of explicit and implicit rules. Both types of rule may require negotiation but implicit rules must be navigated carefully as their purpose is not simply to establish mutual control in host–guest relationships, but to build a satisfactory 'interaction order', one of trust, by demonstrating that parties to a hospitality 'exchange' know and are practising such rules.

There is every reason to suppose that the principles of reciprocity and trust are just as important in post-industrial 'commercial' hospitality as they are in domestic hospitality, although their forms will vary not least because of the economic circumstances and legal frameworks in which the former operate. Both deploy, in Bauman's terms, mechanisms for regulating entitlements to admission. Thus, if Douglas (1975) is to be believed, the forms of hospitality provided in the home will structurally vary according to the status of the recipient. Hotels and restaurants reserve the right to determine who they will and will not serve. Public providers of hospitality may make more of physical controls to entitlement (security guards, receptionists, instructional artefacts – for example signs on doors stating 'Staff only', windows of time within which meals must be eaten and so on). Similarly, the concept of reciprocity as evident in Maussian analysis might well mutate – a hotel or restaurant will provide x, y and z not in the expectation that guests will return such favours if the hotelier or restaurateur turns up at their private residence, but in anticipation that the guest reciprocates by behaving in 'appropriate' ways (including paying their bill!).

There is much to be said for sociological approaches to understanding hospitality predicated on parallels with the gift. Advocates of materialist approaches to understanding hospitality (see, e.g., Slattery, 2002) emphasise contemporary commercial hospitality in terms of economic transactions, but it is self-evidently more than this because hospitality companies promise so much more, both implicitly and explicitly, than is implied by the exchange of monies. In business jargon, there are the elements of 'added value' which include behavioural and material components, the imperatives bearing on host and guest to act in certain ways, and the provision of 'touches and things' (Riley, 1984) which have no rational reason to be included in the basic economic exchange – for example the provision of in-room televisions, hot drink making facilities, trouser presses and the like.

Hospitality and conspicuous consumption

The literature on the treatment of strangers and the possibilities of hospitality as a form of gift both touch upon the role of status. The expectation of the quality of hospitality likely to be demonstrated in specific circumstances is status-related and the capacity for reciprocity is necessarily structured by status and the economic and social circumstances that underpin it. Status is at the heart of this discussion on Thorstein Veblen.

Nearly always regarded as a puzzling writer and rarely viewed as part of the intellectual mainstream, Thorstein Veblen published his *The Theory of the Leisure Class* in 1899 and introduced the world to the concept of 'conspicuous consumption'. Like Marx, Veblen (2007 [1899]) is concerned with what happens when capitalist economic systems begin to produce large-scale surpluses (indeed, there is an ongoing debate about how close Marx and Veblen are in their analysis of the economics of capitalist exploitation – see, for example, Ford and McColloch, 2012). The 'leisure class' are those who appropriate such surpluses (which are produced in the main by the working class) and use them to invest in property, which is the ultimate form of status and honour. As capitalism is normalised, 'property now becomes the most easily recognized evidence of a reputable degree of success as distinguished from heroic or signal achievement. It therefore becomes the conventional basis of esteem' (Veblen, 2007 [1899]: 24).

Of course, to demonstrate status, one must demonstrate one's possessions, or wealth, or at least display indicators of the same. This is achieved in two ways – for Veblen both inherently wasteful. First, the leisure class as its name suggests indulges a wide range of 'leisure activities' marking their 'exemption from "menial offices"' (Veblen, 2007 [1899]: 29). Leisure is: 'non-productive consumption of time. Time is consumed non-productively (1) from a sense of the unworthiness of productive work, and (2) as an evidence of pecuniary ability to afford a life of idleness' (Veblen, 2007 [1899]: 33). Second, status is communicated by members of the leisure class engaging in 'conspicuous consumption', which has quantitative and qualitative dimensions:

> The ... gentleman of leisure ... consumes of the staff of life beyond the minimum required for subsistence and physical efficiency, but his consumption also undergoes a specialisation as regards the quality of the goods consumed. He consumes freely and of the best, in food, drink, narcotics, shelter, services, ornaments, apparel, weapons and accoutrements, amusements, amulets, and idols or divinities.
>
> *(Veblen, 2007 [1899]: 52)*

The leisure class is itself subject to internal differentiation, there being a hierarchy of value such that: 'wealth acquired passively by transmission from ancestors or other antecedents presently becomes even more honorific than wealth acquired by the possessor's own effort' (Veblen, 2007 [1899]: 24).

Although the term 'conspicuous consumption' has passed into the English mainstream, Veblen's work very much remains a minority (even if a significant minority) interest in economics and sociology, and for that matter in marketing where the concept of conspicuous consumption might be thought to be of particular importance (see Mason, 1984). A careful reading of the original work reveals several avenues of inquiry relevant to hospitality but we will briefly consider only two of these here.

First, Veblen maintains that elite leisure practices 'trickle down' to the lower social classes who, desirous of sharing at least in part in the culture of esteem value, emulate their 'betters' as far as possible. This view has been criticised by numerous modern commentators (e.g. Rojek, 2000; Trigg, 2001). Rojek (2000: 7–8) argues that the once obvious division in society between rich and poor is less significant contemporaneously than that which exists between, on the one hand, the large corporations that produce goods and services, and, on the other, the consumers who buy these goods and services. The habits of aristocrats and/or corporate tycoons are less significant in influencing leisure than these products and services whose appeal is enhanced by celebrity endorsements. Rojek asserts that 'the celebrity elite has become a more important component of symbolic capital in the leisure market' (2000: 7) and goes on to argue that this elite is now the 'decisive influence on mass leisure choices, lifestyles, and values' (2000: 8). Relevant to this position, and articulated particularly well by Trigg (2001: 99ff.), is the notion that so-called 'trickle down' effects are often countered by 'trickle up' processes, whereby it is those at the bottom of the hierarchy who establish trends and fashions – a view that supports a picture of consumption as less dependent on social class than on 'lifestyles', which generally cross class boundaries. Drawing on comparisons with the work of French sociologist Pierre Bourdieu (especially his *Distinction*, 1984), Trigg (2001: 107) proposes a 'trickle-round' model of consumption influence where taste is transmitted between classes in a continuous circuit as opposed to in linear fashion (i.e. upper class to middle class to working class).

Second, Rojek (2000) among others suggests that far from flaunting their wealth, today's super-rich are more likely to go to great extremes to disguise its true size and value. This is an interesting and carefully expressed view if only because efforts to disguise the size/value of personal wealth do not, as an imperative, preclude conspicuous display of the possession of that wealth. The very celebrity that Rojek positions at the heart of modern consumption may be manifest in people from diverse social backgrounds and represent the full spectrum of taste from vulgar 'bling' to more evidently refined display, but there is rarely celebrity without wealth, and very obviously displayed wealth at that.

Evidence of conspicuous consumption has never been difficult to identify within certain domestic hospitality contexts – in the case of food production and service, for example, this would include the use of expensive and/or distinctive (e.g. organic) ingredients in food preparation through the possession of diverse apparatus of culinary production to the quality of tableware. In the hospitality industry, hotels and restaurants are arranged in various hierarchies that function to 'layer' entitlements to admission. The fluid use of celebrity is also found. For example, the upscale Mandarin Oriental Hotel Group enjoys the endorsement of a variety of global celebrities.[1] In the UK, a relatively superior 'budget' hotel group, Premier Inn, employs the much loved comedian and actor (Sir) Lenny Henry in its advertising.[2] Like the poor, conspicuous consumption are always with us. The arguable costs to society of supporting this edifice of indulgence are the topic to which attention now turns.

The new romantics?

Karl Marx and Max Weber had almost nothing to say directly on the subject of hospitality, but at least two more recent commentators on these founding fathers, respectively Harry Braverman and George Ritzer, have contributed interesting insights on the topic.

Harry Braverman's book *Labour and Monopoly Capital*, first published in 1974, has proven one of the most influential texts in the sociology of work and industry ever published. It extends Marx's theory of the exploitation of labour in the partial context of the emergence of oligopolistic corporations, focusing particularly on the concept of the labour process. Braverman rehearses Marx's argument that the labour process:

a   comprises three elements: purposeful human activity directed to work; the objects on which work is performed (natural or raw materials); and the instruments of work; and
b   is geared, under capitalism, to the creation of profit rather than satisfaction of human needs, thus generating a conflict of interests between labour and capital that can only be resolved by the agents of capital securing maximum control over the labour process.

For Braverman, it is the application of Taylor's scientific management to industry throughout the course of the twentieth century that has facilitated capitalist control of the labour process ensuring separation of the planning and execution of work with workers confined to the latter tasks, and thus, in essence, deskilled (though Braverman never uses the term), their labour economically cheapened (because the cost of labour to employers is reduced as workers are deprived of their skills and delimited to performing routinised processes), and also spiritually denuded.

From the point of view of this chapter, Braverman's most important contribution is to the understanding of labour processes in service work. At a time when sociologists of work were largely uninterested in service employment, Braverman ventured the following definition of services:

> what if the useful effects of labour are such that they cannot take shape in an object? Such labour must be offered directly to the consumer, since production and consumption are simultaneous ... the useful effects of labour themselves *become* the commodity. When the worker does not offer this labour directly to the user of its effects, but instead sells it to a capitalist, who re-sells it on the commodity market, then we have the capitalist form of production in the field of services.
>
> *(1974: 360; emphasis in original)*

Braverman's concept of service is deliberately narrow, the 'true' form of service labour being where the effects of labour themselves are the commodity for sale. This is because he goes on to argue that the concept of service labour is essentially artificial, most forms of service work being more typically akin to manufacturing work. The work of chefs and other restaurant workers, Braverman writes, is not unlike that of manufacturing employees because it takes form in a tangible product, thus: 'restaurant labour, which cooks, prepares, assembles, serves, cleans dishes and utensils etc., carries on tangible production just as much as labour employed in any other manufacturing process' (1974: 360). Similarly, Braverman asserts:

> Chambermaids are classed as service workers, but their labours are not always different, in principle, from those of many manufacturing workers, in that they take shape in a tangible result. When ... chambermaids ... make beds they do an assembly operation which is not different from many factory assembly operations ... the result is a tangible and vendible commodity.
>
> *(1974: 361)*

Braverman's comments are, of course, contentious, not least on service work. However, they do approximate to the findings of other strands of research into services that are regularly ignored by many mainstream scholars in the field of management studies, for example the well-evidenced ideas that (a) the extent of service work in modern societies has been greatly exaggerated (Miles, 2000; Jansson, 2009) and (b) many so-called service jobs depend for their existence on the continuing prevalence of extractive and manufacturing industries (see Greenfield, 2002; also Wood, 1997, for an extended account of Braverman in the hospitality context, and Thompson and Smith, 2010, to obtain a good sense of the general progress of the labour process debate).

However, for our purposes here, the interesting aspect of Braverman's work (and to some degree, by inference, Marx's original conceptualisation of exploitative capitalist relations) is the extent to which it embraces the romanticism of the most un-Marxist commentaries on the stranger reviewed earlier. In essence, Braverman implies a (largely unspecified) pre-capitalist form of hospitality that has been eradicated and replaced by commercial arrangements characterised by, if not the concrete mechanisation of work, then the spiritual mechanisation of work *processes* in the service arena. The strength of his argument lies in the effective denial of any real theoretical differences in the outcomes of service and non-service labour processes. The principal weakness of Braverman's position is that these outcomes are viewed as necessarily the outcome of capitalist relations of production, implying, *inter alia*, that pre-capitalist services were in some way fundamentally different in a roseate past – a point to which we shall return later in this discussion.

The work of George Ritzer on 'McDonaldisation', first outlined in his 1993 book *The McDonaldization of Society*, in many ways runs parallel to that of Braverman but from the perspective of the work of Max Weber rather than Karl Marx. Specifically, Weber's conceptions of rationality and bureaucracy are central to Ritzer's case. Bureaucratic organisations embrace and embody rational systems of administration, production and related processes, and these systems are predicated on efficiency, predictability, calculability and control (normally through technology). For Ritzer, McDonald's is the archetypal bureaucratic organisation of the modern age and the spread of the McDonaldisation process is in effect the spread of dehumanising conditions of work and, eventually, dehumanising products and services. It is a phenomenon that embraces 'notably homogeneous products, rigid technologies, standardized work routines, deskilling, homogenization of labour (and customer), the mass worker, and homogenization of consumption' (Ritzer, 1993: 1).

The Ritzer bandwagon has rolled on since 1993, having been joined by social scientists of almost every variety. It rolls more slowly today but remains a force in the 'hospitality studies' movement described in the opening paragraphs of this chapter. Critics of the McDonaldisation thesis – fairly few in number – have largely been ignored. The two main objections to Ritzer's thesis can be summarised fairly simply. First, even in 1993, there was very little that was new about the McDonaldisation thesis as Braverman's work amply demonstrates. Even before these two, however, Levitt (1972) outlined a theory of the 'industrialization of service', the content of which anticipates those parts of Braverman's and Ritzer's work addressed to that topic. Second, there has been a feeling in some quarters that Ritzer's conception of McDonaldisation is itself a reflection of the phenomenon itself in action: rationalised, over simplified and populist. Thus Gilling tore into the original book, commenting that 'is too simplistic and sloppy to have much educational value. It is not sociology and it would certainly not teach students how to reason' (1996: 24). Roberts postulated a more intriguing if perhaps mildly paranoid notion concerning what she calls the 'Ritzerization' of academic management texts, remarking: 'there is a formula present in Ritzer's book, which can be found in many academic texts. Such formulae are not primarily designed to create a highly effective tool for learning and developing the knowledge of readers, but, rather, to maximize the commercial success of the book' (2005: 58). Of course, Ritzer himself has moved on, most recently seeking to establish how McDonaldisation in the hospitality sector gives rise to 'inhospitality', once again a far from novel idea introduced and tackled with some originality as early as 1989 by Finkelstein, though giving rise to little debate at the time (see Finkelstein, 1989; Warde and Martens, 1999; Ritzer, 2015).

A very tentative sociological explanation for the success of Ritzer's work consists of two elements. The first of these is the relative lack of appeal of Marx and Marxism in modern American society, which, to a degree, is reflected in the practice of sociology in that country. Critiques of capitalism devoid of obvious Marxism (no matter how much such critiques are *indirectly* indebted to Marxist thinking) are perhaps more likely to command legitimacy than accounts predicated on the inevitability of the triumph of socialism and communism. The second element is related but more speculative. Since the collapse of the Soviet Union a few years before the publication of Ritzer's book, we have heard constant proclamations about the death of Marxism, communism, socialism and every other left-of-centre ideology, almost all of them misplaced. Ritzer's deployment and 'updating' of Weberian imperatives could be construed as Marx without the Marxism, for McDonaldisation lacks the ideological overtones of Marxism but still facilitates reasonably penetrating and attractive critiques of work and consumption without any of the baggage that that ideology carries in the US context.

Whatever the case, both Braverman and Ritzer present simplistic perspectives on hospitality that are at the very least implicitly indebted to (usually unspecified) notions of halcyon days gone by, and the former has been regularly singled out on this account by otherwise sympathetic critics (e.g. Rose, 1985). In short, both writers, though coming from vastly different traditions, frame their analyses in much the same way as those commentators on strangerhood we encountered earlier. Unfortunately, nostalgia is not what it used to be and nor is the spirit of romanticism. As forms of cultural criticism, the work of all these writers lacks completeness, and balance, based upon an analysis of the benefits as well as the disadvantages that might flow from the processes of industrialisation and commercialisation as they have acted upon hospitality. These processes have produced a reasonable, if somewhat artificial variety, as well as guaranteed product and service standards and thus predictable quality of hospitality experiences.

Conclusions

This chapter has sought to give a somewhat episodic flavour of selected sociological contributions to the understanding of hospitality, but at the start of these concluding remarks, it is entirely justified to give some brief account of, and explanation for, certain omissions.

At the beginning of the chapter it was noted how certain 'hospitality studies' researchers have invoked Derrida's foray into the analysis of hospitality as of some importance. Derrida's contribution to the sociological analysis of hospitality is undoubtedly somewhat less opaque than many of his other works, although, like that of other writers considered in this discussion, it rests for the most part on a very limited output (principally Derrida, 2000; see also O'Gorman, 2006b, 2007, for adequate accounts of Derrida's main ideas). The main thrust of Derrida's observations falls well within the 'strangerhood' theme considered earlier and, for this writer at least, adds nothing new to the discussion. Undoubtedly, for someone who has been described as one of the twentieth century's greatest philosophers and still, many years after his death, inspires an almost irrational if not messianic following among many scholars in the humanities and social sciences (and also a high degree of detestation from what is perhaps a significant minority therein), Derrida is a potentially useful ally for a developing area of scholarship that feels the need for a splash of 'mainstream' social scientific legitimacy but if that is what those committed to a 'hospitality studies' approach actually seek, then, as this chapter has shown, there are other possible areas to be explored. One such that has not been discussed at length here, precisely because it would merit a chapter on its own, is the sociology of food and eating. Much of the scholarship in this area is focused on food, eating and hospitality, and demonstrates theoretical pluralism (embracing several varieties of structuralism, the figurational sociology of writers such as Norbert Elias, 1978, and Stephen Mennell, 1985, and the neo-Marxism of Pierre Bourdieu, 1984) and a high degree of philosophical engagement (Finkelstein, 1989; Curtin and Heldke, 1992; Telfer, 1996). Similarly, for reasons of space, study of the increasingly rarefied phenomenon of social and economic exchange and its relevance for hospitality has been excluded (see Brotherton and Wood, 2008, for a somewhat elementary coverage of the topic).

Important though these omissions are their absence should not disguise the potential utility of those areas that *have* been covered in this chapter, not least in terms of two recurring themes. The most important of these, and the one begging for further sociological explication, is the romanticism that permeates a number of the perspectives considered. This in part appears attributable to a naive rendering of pre- and post-industrial history and its supposed impacts on the forms taken by hospitality. To develop understanding here, a more rigorous explanation of the effects of industrial capitalism (past, present and continuing) on the development of concepts of hospitality is required. A second theme that emerges, although much less obviously, is the role of hierarchy and status in hospitality – from the beneficence shown to strangers in pre-industrial society, through the creation and reinforcement of reciprocity in gift-oriented perspectives, to the trickle 'this way or that' of theories of conspicuous and other forms of consumption. Some sociologists have not been immune from (unintentionally?) reproducing assumptions of status and hierarchy in their study of hospitality as is at least evident in the sneering attitude often taken to so-called 'McJobs', those supposedly degraded forms of employment that characterise much service employment (see Wood, 2015a).

Hospitality in all its forms is a subject ripe for more meaningful intellectual exploration, and sociology and sociologists have a role to play in this, as indeed do those from other disciplines. To achieve progress will require a more systematic and comprehensive, less piecemeal, approach to theory than has hitherto been the case in the field, as well as extensive empirical investigations of the meanings of hospitality to different social groups in varying contexts. It is hoped that at least a little of the potential excitement of such an exercise has been conveyed in this chapter.

Notes

1 See www.mandarinoriental.com/celebrity-fans/. Accessed 2 October 2015.
2 See, for example, www.express.co.uk/finance/city/560526/Lenny-Henry-adverts-Premier-Inn-s-sales-soar. Accessed 2 October 2015.

References

Bauman, Z. (1990) *Thinking Sociologically*, Oxford: Blackwell.
Bauman, Z. (2000) *Liquid Modernity*, Cambridge: Polity.
Bourdieu, P. (1984 [1979]) *Distinction: A Social Critique of the Judgement of Taste*, London: Routledge.
Braverman, H. (1974) *Labour and Monopoly Capital*, New York: Monthly Review Press.
Brittan, A. (1977) *The Privatised World*, London: Routledge & Kegan Paul.
Brotherton, B. (1999) Towards a definitive view of the nature of hospitality and hospitality management, *International Journal of Contemporary Hospitality Management* 11, 4: 165–173.
Brotherton, B. (2005) The nature of hospitality: customer perceptions and implications, *Tourism and Hospitality Planning and Development* 2, 3: 139–153.
Brotherton, B. and Wood, R. C. (2000) Hospitality and hospitality management. In Lashley, C. and Morrison, A. (eds) *In Search of Hospitality*, Oxford: Butterworth-Heinemann.
Brotherton, B. and Wood, R. C. (2008) The nature and meanings of 'hospitality'. In Brotherton, B. and Wood, R. C. (eds) *The Sage Handbook of Hospitality Management*, New York: Sage, pp. 37–61.
Burgess, J. (1982) Perspectives on gift exchange and hospitable behaviour, *International Journal of Hospitality Management* 1, 1: 49–57.
Christian, V. A. (1979) The concept of hospitality: a position paper. Mimeograph, School of Hotel Administration, Cornell University, Ithaca, New York.
Clark, P. (1983) *The English Alehouse: A Social History, 1200–1830*, London: Longman.
Cummings, P. R., Kwansa, F. A. and Sussman, M. B. (eds) (1998) *The Role of the Hospitality Industry in the Lives of Individuals and Families*, New York: The Haworth Press.
Curtin, D. W. and Heldke, L. M. (eds) (1992) *Cooking, Eating, Thinking: Transformative Philosophies of Food*, Bloomington: Indiana University Press.
Davis, N. Z. (2000) *The Gift in Sixteenth Century France*, Oxford: Oxford University Press.
Derrida, J. (2000) *Of Hospitality – Anne Dufourmantelle Invites Jacques Derrida to Respond*, trans. R. Bowlby, Stanford, CA: Stanford University Press.
Douglas, M. (1975) Deciphering a Meal. In Douglas, M. (ed.), *Implicit Meanings*, London: Routledge & Kegan Paul.
Elias, N. (1978) *The Civilising Process*, vol. 1: *The History of Manners*, Oxford: Basil Blackwell.
Finkelstein, J. (1989) *Dining Out: A Sociology of Modern Manners*, Cambridge: Polity Press.
Ford, K. and McColloch, W. (2012) Thorstein Veblen: a Marxist starting point, *Journal of Economic Issues* 46, 3: 765–777.
Frisby, D. (2002) *Georg Simmel*, London: Routledge.

Gilling, A. (1996) Where there's Mc there's brass. *Times Higher Education Supplement*, 19 August: 24. Available at http://www.timeshighereducation.co.uk/books/where-theres-mc-theres-brass/162237. article. Accessed 26 March 2014.

Goffman, E. (1959) *The Presentation of Self in Everyday Life*, New York: Doubleday.

Goffman, E. (1963) *Behaviour in Public Places: Notes on the Social Organization of Gatherings*, New York: The Free Press.

Goodwin, G. A. and Scimecca, J. A. (2006) *Classical Sociological Theory: Rediscovering the Promise of Sociology*, Belmont, CA: Thomson Wadsworth.

Greenfield, H. I. (2002). A note on the goods/services dichotomy, *Service Industries Journal* 22, 4: 19–21.

Harris, M. (1986) *Good to Eat: Riddles of Food and Culture*, London: George Allen & Unwin.

Hayner, N. S. (1969 [1936]) *Hotel Life*, College Park, MD: McGrath (originally published by the University of North Carolina Press).

Heal, F. (1990) *Hospitality in Early Modern England*, Oxford: Clarendon Press.

Jansson, J. O. (2009) The myth of the service economy – an update, *Futures* 41: 182–189.

Lashley, C. and Morrison, A. (eds) (2000) *In Search of Hospitality*, Oxford: Butterworth-Heinemann.

Lechte, J. (1994) *Fifty Key Contemporary Thinkers: From Structuralism to Postmodernity*, London: Routledge.

Levitt, T. (1972) Production line approach to service, *Harvard Business Review*, Sept–Oct: 41–52.

Lynch, P. A. (2000) Host attitudes towards guests in the homestay sector, *International Journal of Tourism and Hospitality Research: The Surrey Quarterly Review* 1, 2: 119–144.

McLemore, S. D. (1970) Simmel's 'stranger': a critique of the concept, *Pacific Sociological Review* 13, 2: 86–94.

Mason, R. (1984) Conspicuous consumption: a literature review, *European Journal of Marketing* 18, 3: 26–39.

Mauss, M. (2000) *The Gift*, London: Routledge.

Mennell, S. (1985) *All Manners of Food: Eating and Taste in England and France from the Middle Ages to the Present*, Oxford: Basil Blackwell.

Mennell, S., Murcott, A. and van Otterloo, A. (1992) *The Sociology of Food: Eating, Diet and Culture*, London: Sage.

Miles, S. (2000) *Social Theory in the Real World*, London: Sage.

Mühlmann, W. E. (1932) Hospitality. In Seligman, E. R. A. (ed.) *Encyclopaedia of the Social Sciences*, vol. 7, New York: Macmillan, pp. 462–464.

O'Gorman, K. D. (2006a) The legacy of monastic hospitality: 1 The rule of Benedict and rise of western monastic hospitality, *Hospitality Review* 8, 3: 35–44.

O'Gorman, K. D. (2006b) Jacques Derrida's philosophy of hospitality, *Hospitality Review* 8, 4: 50–57.

O'Gorman, K. D. (2007) The hospitality phenomenon: philosophical enlightenment?, *International Journal of Culture, Tourism and Hospitality Research* 1, 3: 189–202.

Pickering, M. (2001) *Stereotyping: The Politics of Representation*, Basingstoke: Palgrave.

Riley, M. (1984) Hotels and group identity, *Tourism Management* 5, 2: 102–109.

Ritzer, G. (1993) *The McDonaldization of Society*, Thousand Oaks, CA: Pine Forge Press.

Ritzer, G. (2015) Hospitality and prosumption, *Research in Hospitality Management* 5, 1: 9–17.

Roberts, J. (2005) The Ritzerization of knowledge, *Critical Perspectives on International Business* 1, 1: 56–63.

Rojek, C. (2000) Leisure and the rich today: Veblen's thesis after a century, *Leisure Studies* 19: 1–15.

Rose, M. (1985) *Industrial Behaviour: Theoretical Development Since Taylor*, 2nd edn, Harmondsworth: Penguin.

Scott, J. (1995) *Sociological Theory: Contemporary Debates*, Aldershot: Edward Elgar.

Seaton, A. V., Jenkins, C. L., Wood, R. C., Dieke, P. U. C., Bennett, M. M., MacLellan, L. R. and Smith, R. (eds) (1994) *Tourism: the State of the Art*, Chichester: John Wiley.

Simmel, G. (1971 [1908]) The stranger. In Levine, D. N. (ed.) *Georg Simmel: On Individuality and Social Forms*, Chicago: Chicago University Press, pp. 143–149.

Skinner, Q. (ed.) (1990) *The Return of Grand Theory in the Human Sciences*, Cambridge: Canto Books.

Slattery, P. (2002) Finding the hospitality industry, *Journal of Hospitality, Leisure, Sport and Tourism Education* 1, 1: 19–28.

Stringer, P. F. (1981) Hosts and guests: the bed-and-breakfast phenomenon, *Annals of Tourism Research* 8, 3: 357–376.

Symons, M. (1994) Simmel's gastronomic sociology: an overlooked essay, *Food and Foodways* 5, 4: 333–351.

Symons, M. (2013) The rise of the restaurant and the fate of hospitality, *International Journal of Contemporary Hospitality Management* 25, 2: 247–263.

Telfer, E. (1996) *Food For Thought: Philosophy and Food*, London: Routledge.

Thompson, P. and Smith, C. (2010) *Working Life: Renewing Labour Process Analysis*, Basingstoke: Palgrave Macmillan.

Trigg, A. B. (2001) Veblen, Bourdieu and conspicuous consumption, *Journal of Economic Issues* 35, 1: 99–115.

Veblen, T. (2007 [1899]) *The Theory of the Leisure Class*, Oxford: Oxford University Press.

Visser, M. (1992) *The Rituals of Dinner*, London: Penguin Books.

Warde, A. and Martens, L. (1999) Eating out: reflections on the experience of consumers in England. In Germov, J. and Williams, L. (eds) *A Sociology of Food and Nutrition: The Social Appetite*, Oxford: Oxford University Press, pp. 116–134.

Welten, R. (2015) Hospitality and its ambivalences: on Zygmunt Bauman, *Hospitality and Society* 5, 1: 7–21.

Wood, R. C. (1994a) Some theoretical perspectives on hospitality. In Seaton, A. V. *et al.* (eds) *Tourism: The State of The Art*, Chichester: John Wiley, pp. 737–742.

Wood, R. C. (1994b) Hotel culture and social control, *Annals of Tourism Research* 21, 1, 65–80.

Wood, R. C. (1997) *Working in Hotels and Catering*, 2nd edn, London: International Thompson Business Press.

Wood, R. C. (2015a) *Hospitality Management: A Brief Introduction*, London: Sage.

Wood, R. C. (2015b) 'Folk' understandings of quality in UK higher hospitality education, *Quality Assurance in Education* 23, 4: 326–338.

Zeldin, T. (1994) How humans become hospitable to each other. In *An Intimate History of Humanity*, London: Minerva, pp. 426–464.

3

Geographies of hospitality

David Bell

> **Key themes**
>
> Spaces and scales of hospitality
>
> Hotels, or the comfort of strangers
>
> Hospitelity: spaces of care in medical tourism
>
> Eating together

I want to begin this chapter by considering three 'moments' of hospitality (Bell, 2007b). The first is the great annual migration of the festive holiday season, and the experiences of hosting and guesting that come with visiting friends and relatives, to use a tourism industry term. Families coming together in seasonal cheer or stress (or both), people finding ways to be together that are often partly ritualised, partly improvised: I think of my own recent experience of being first a guest in a familiar (in both senses of the word) place, gradually re-finding my sense of at-home-ness there, and, in turn, acting as a host when other guests arrive. I think of the importance placed on rituals of eating and drinking together, of being together and being togetherness. Of course, commercial hospitality spaces have important roles to play, too – the bars and hotels, restaurants and bed and breakfast places stage their own versions of togetherness at this time of year – but many of us make up togetherness in our own informal ways. I called this time of year 'the great annual migration' partly as a joke, but also to remember that so many of us are travelling to reconnect with family and friends; the traffic on the UK's motorways a couple of days either side of Christmas Day are a vivid display of the mass-ness of this movement, cars packed with people and gifts, all coalescing and congregating in venues – most often in homes – for a moment of hospitality, of welcomes (and gifts) given and received, of food and drink shared, of nights spent under familiar roofs. Michael Herzfeld comments that, 'hospitality seems to render the gift in spatial terms' (2012: 212), and this festive coming-together seems emblematic of this assertion.

My second 'moment' of hospitality is very particular to this time/date (late December 2015) and place (Yorkshire, England), and concerns a current major UK news story about flooding.

DOI: 10.4324/9781315679938-4

The drive back home was made both more urgent and more anxious by the developing story of floods around Leeds and York, and the coverage in the media reminds us of both the importance of home (and the devastation of being rendered homeless) and the ordinary (and extraordinary) acts of kindness that unfold when incidents like this take place. We see images of people helping out, mucking in, offering support, providing food and shelter. And we see the formal and informal work of repair – both infrastructural repair and 'social repair' (Hall and Smith, 2015; Thrift, 2005) as communities rally and respond. While such stories of community resilience risk becoming a cliché, another instance of localism and voluntarism evoking the 'human spirit', there is something in these moments of kindness that speaks of the 'good city' (Amin, 2006) and of hospitality as a practice of this 'goodness', this generosity. In one news item I half-heard yesterday, attention turned to the question of having to stay away from one's own home, not just for days, but potentially for months, maybe even years. People in flood-warned areas were urged to look for alternative accommodation should they need to evacuate their homes. Staying in hotels was discussed as some sort of emergency remedy, but as a very poor substitute for being at home (we will check back in to the hotel later in this chapter).

Of course, the experiences of those in flood hit areas being forced from their homes and losing their possessions – at least until the loss adjustors ship in – brings to mind one of the consistently biggest news stories of 2015, the plight of millions of displaced people crossing vast distances in the hope of a welcome, in what journalists and pundits here like to shorthand as 'the migrant crisis' and/or 'the refugee crisis'. This is my third and most ambivalent, troubled and troubling moment of hospitality. The scale of loss of life and untold misery for migrants and refugees often shown very provisional and contingent welcomes – or, perhaps, *unwelcomes* – reveals the politics of hospitality in its most global and most human form. As politicians in the European Union argue over quotas and policies (and while some swiftly erect fences and walls or pass new laws), large numbers of people continue to attempt perilous journeys, fleeing war zones and escaping persecution in the hope of a hospitable arrival elsewhere. The great philosopher of hospitality Jacques Derrida is of course well known for this work exploring this precise question, and his discussion of the tension between unconditional and conditional hospitality seems more prescient than ever (Derrida, 2001; Still, 2010).

The Archbishop of Canterbury, leader of the Church of England, used the theme of hospitality repeatedly in his New Year speech, urging the UK to show a true welcome to these new arrivals that have risked so much. We wait to see if 2016 can bring better news of the plight of all the people caught up in this catastrophe. Like my other two moments of hospitality, this situation is of course intensely geographical; it concerns the sites and scales of hospitality. Geographers have, in fact, been at the forefront of exploring (both empirically and theoretically) many different spaces of hospitality, and in the next section of this chapter I provide a brief, non-comprehensive overview of some of these lines of enquiry, before focusing on three particular instances of hospitable space: the hotel, the 'hospitel' and spaces of commensality. I round off the chapter with a reiteration of the main points.

Spaces and scales of hospitality

Here I want to offer a provisional, somewhat fragmentary, 'archive' of 'geographical'[1] work on hospitality, which has only quite recently become programmatic – in line with the so-called 'critical turn' in hospitality studies. My route through this archive is subjective, personal, reflecting my own route into hospitality studies as much as anything. So it begins with historical geography, which – like history – has long held an interest in the development and distribution of spaces of commercial hospitality, from inns to coffee houses, hotels to fast food joints (e.g. Schivelbusch, 1993). Of course, these spaces also created new ways of relating, from the coffee house as a place for political debate (Laurier and Philo, 2007) to the fast food outlet as a site for 'prosumption' (Ritzer, this volume). But as all good geographers know, space isn't simply the maker of behaviours, it is also made by them: space is produced by our actions in it, even as our actions are shaped by the spaces we inhabit. Geographical work on spaces of hospitality has been increasingly attuned to this two-way interaction, building increasingly sophisticated analysis of, among other things, sitting alone in a café or serving behind a bar. David Seamon's humanistic geography (1979) drew our attention to the former, in an account of a man who frequents the same café every day, and partakes in the same daily rituals – arrives at the same time, drinks the same drink, reads the same newspaper and sits in the same solitude.

Seamon's delightful description of the 'place ballet' – that part scripted, part improvised, largely unspoken dance we all do around each other as we go about our daily lives – seems to speak volumes about the informal and often fleeting moments of hospitality that take place and make place intersubjectively (a theme also explored by those with symbolic interactionism and/or ethnomethodological persuasions – see below). Of course, not all bars and cafés are the same, in terms of who goes there and what takes place. Cultural geographer Barbara Weightman (1980) deserves special mention here for her pioneering work on gay bars in the USA, especially for her close reading of both exteriors and interiors of such spaces when they were marginal, illegal and precarious. Her great discussion of gay bars as (paradoxically) private spaces echoes that well-known phrase from historian George Chauncey (1996) – 'privacy could only be had in public'. Weightman's work was an important contribution to a body of research on 'gay space' which should be seen as making insightful contributions to our understandings of the practices and meanings of commercial hospitality in relation to questions of identity and power – a strand of work that continues to develop important new insights (Lugosi, 2007).

With the onset of postmodernism in human geography, new perspectives on space and place emerged, and iconic among these in terms of hospitality was Fredric Jameson's at once bewitched, bothered and bewildered encounter with the atrium of the Bonaventure hotel in LA (1984) (of which, more later). While postmodernism did much to revivify the discipline, or at least wrong-foot it, subsequent 'returns' to hospitality – which have begun to combine into a more coherent research agenda – did not particularly follow Jameson's lead into the vertiginous sublime. Instead, parallel strands of work on eating and drinking places (and some on spaces of accommodation) provided detailed examinations of both commercial and informal/social hospitality as a socio-spatial practice. Here, a few way markers will suffice to point interested travellers to productive stepping-off points: work on geographies of drinking and socialising, such as bars, cafés and clubs (Malbon, 2002; Chatterton and Hollands, 2003; Laurier and Philo, 2006a, 2006b; Lugosi, 2007, 2008), on restaurants and other eating places (Crang, 1994; Bell and Valentine, 1997; Bell and Binnie, 2005), and on hotels and other rest-stops (see below). Importantly, this work included studies of the production of hospitality as well as its consumption, shedding light on employment practices and working conditions (e.g. Tufts, 2006). So, for at least a decade, we can trace a consolidating research agenda bringing together the 'critical' work in hospitality studies with what we might see as the post-postmodern concerns of 'critical' human geography.

Attentive readers will have noticed that this section is headed 'spaces and scales', and will perhaps be wondering when that second term will come into play. Spatial scale is an enduring if sometimes vexed concept in geography (Herod, 2010), loved and loathed in equal measure. I have always found it *useful*, at least practically, and have deployed it to organise my thoughts on, among other things, the geographies of food consumption, beginning at the scale of the body (Bell and Valentine, 1997). Judith Still makes a fleeting mention of the same scalar thinking, writing that 'the body is the first sphere of hospitality' (2010: 22), and there has emerged a rich seam of work looking at the bodily acts of hospitality, the tiny gestures and one-off encounters, the flickering moments of hosting, guesting and host-guesting (Laurier and Philo, 2006a, 2006b; Bell, 2007b). This work is often attentive to the micro-geographies, the 'cold shoulders and napkins handed' referred to in the title of a particularly good example of this genre (Laurier and Philo, 2006a). Drawing on the legacy of work in symbolic interactionism and/or ethnomethodology, it has provided valuable insights into both commercial hospitality spaces and informal, sometimes momentary, comings-together, welcomes extended, invitations accepted (or not). Its focus is on the business and busy-ness of everyday life, but it prefers to see this not as alienated or anomic but as full of nourishing interactions, even if these are almost unnoticed most of the time, and even when it turns attention towards the 'hazards' as well as the pleasures of sociability (on scales of hospitality, see also Candea and da Col, 2012). This research is also concerned to detail the work of conviviality – work carried out by all players, by consumers as well as those paid to provide service (Laurier and Philo, 2006a, 2006b; Bell, 2012).

Other studies have productively focused on a single site or venue, like Seamon's man in the café: exploring the experiences of working in a bar or restaurant (Crang, 1994; Lugosi, 2007) or being a customer in a coffee bar (Laurier *et al.*, 2001). Still, others have looked at the neighbourhood scale, investigating convivial spaces both formal and informal that together constitute the 'feel' of a place as people come together to produce and consume hospitality there (Latham, 2003; Koch and Latham, 2013). Pull back the focus further, and we see work looking at the city scale, both that which takes 'the city' as an archetype and that which explores particular cities and their configurations of hospitality and hospitableness (Thrift, 2005; Amin, 2006; Bell, 2007a; Broek Chavez and van der Rest, 2014; Hubbard and Wilkinson, 2015). Here, as with the following discussion, we begin to see a clear imprint of the turn towards continental philosophy in critical hospitality studies, and especially of Derrida's work on this topic, for example in his discussion of the 'city of refuge' (Derrida, 2001). Derrida's deconstructive approach to unpicking the hostility latent in hospitality, and to underscoring the power, even violence, playing across the threshold when host meets guest, has been especially important for understanding what he himself labelled the 'foreigner question', not least in the French context (with which he was particularly familiar; see Still, 2010).

Work tracing similar lines has here focused on 'French hospitality' and 'postcolonial hospitality', and has sought to shed critical light on the conditional and provisional extent of the welcome extended to the 'stranger' (Jelloun and Bray, 1999; Rosello, 2001; Gibson, 2003). Geographers including Clive Barnett (2005) and Mustafa Dikeç (2002) have written eloquently on this *problematique*, exploring ways of relating to 'otherness' and the often tense and fractured spaces of hospitality in the postcolonial context (Dikeç *et al.* 2009). National scale discussions of hospitality, therefore, return us to the issues of migration and movement, whether forced or voluntary. Who can move freely, and who is welcomed when they arrive? Of course, Derrida's critique is grounded at least in part in Kant's discussion of universal hospitality; unconditional and unquestioning, the absolute openness to welcome the other with no thought of reciprocity or obligation. At a global scale, then, we can similarly theorise (as well as empirically witnessing or experiencing) the politics of the welcome, the flows of people that cross the globe in ever-changing 'ethnoscapes' (Appadurai, 1990), pushed and pulled by forces of global geopolitics and economics. Of course, the 'ideal' of universal hospitality stands in stark contrast to the actually experienced relations of (in)hospitableness that are the outworking of these global processes.

Having provided a provisional route map of some of the lines of enquiry concerned with geographies of hospitality, in the remainder of this chapter I have chosen to focus on three different cases that bring to light somewhat different configurations of hospitable sites and scales (though there are connecting threads, as I hope will become clear).

Hotels, or the comfort of strangers

A hotel is for staying in. But it is a kind of staying that includes its opposite: leaving.

(Walsh, 2015: 69)

While arguably less extensively and intensively studied by geographers than spaces of eating and drinking (and less too than informal sites of hospitality), hotels provide interesting windows into the business, pleasure and fraught nature of hospitality. As Joanna Walsh notes, they invite a particular type of staying – temporary, always prefigured by leaving, by checking out. They also, she adds, provide an escape from ordinary life – though also an escape that is temporary: 'A hotel's secret is that it's only a seeming mini-break from the rights and wrongs of home. A hotel is an occasion for *unheimlich* longing' (Walsh, 2015: 14). In her short book *Hotel*, Walsh combines aphorisms, dreams, postcards and fictional encounters (with Sigmund Freud, Groucho Marx and others); the book is also a meditation of her collapsing marriage and an account of her job as a hotel review blogger. In its own way, it adds to the body of work 'decoding' hotel space – trying to understand the work of being in a hotel, as a guest or as a host. While Walsh asserts that 'I can't think in a hotel' (2015: 72), she in fact gives her readers a lot to think with, capturing something of that *unheimlich* experience of a temporary escape from home life. She breaks the hotel down into its constituent parts – rooms, corridors, pools, bars, restaurants and lobbies. Like Jameson, and, before him, Siegfried Krakauer and many others, she is drawn to the hotel lobby as a perplexing, paradoxical space: 'Nowhere is more lonely … I'm only one of many. It never feels right, that's the lobby problem' (Walsh, 2015: 74).

And so it is in the lobby that we will begin our brief encounter with hotel space. Before Jameson had diagnosed the Bonaventure Hotel's lobby as a postmodern 'mutation in built space itself' (1984: 80) – and we'll join him there presently – the hotel lobby had been figured as 'emblematic of certain aspects of *modernity*: broadly speaking, its routine yet kaleidoscopic, assembling and disassembling character' (Tallack, 2002: 141; my emphasis). As Douglas Tallack explores through fiction, philosophy, art and film, the lobby is a site of fleeting drama, of 'meetings, collisions, gazes and glances', making it at once 'comic and disturbing' (2002: 141). What Walsh names as the 'lobby problem' Tallack also detects – an uncanny mix of the homely and the unhomely – and he describes the lobby as a strange stage set on which the ritual of arriving and checking in is played out, as well as a lot of waiting. Drawing in part on Kracauer's essay (1999 [1925]; see also Katz 1999), Tallack writes the modern hotel lobby as a space to wait and watch – and to be watched (hence its frequent appearance in detective novels and movies). Building from this observation, Tallack concludes that:

> The hotel lobby is a place to meet others but also to avoid the look of others; a place of seeing and being seen – but also of reserve and, as such, lounging in a lobby qualifies as a paradigmatic urban experience.
>
> *(2002: 146)*

And so it is perhaps understandable that Fredric Jameson, hunting for clues to postmodernism, might gravitate to a hotel lobby, if not to lounge then to gaze in awe at this particular hotel, imagined as he writes as 'a total space, a complete world, a kind of miniature city' (1984: 81). Famously, he finds in the lobby (or atrium as such spaces have now been routinely redefined and redesigned) 'a new collective practice, a new mode in which individuals move and congregate [as a] hyper-crowd' (Jameson, 1984: 81). Crucially, Jameson writes that the Bonaventure offers a kind of simulacrum of the city, a substitute or replacement for the LA that surrounds it. But it is the space itself that most fascinates and disturbs Jameson, from its mirror-glass exterior to its preponderance of escalators and elevators that seem to keep everyone in perpetual motion, and which seem to induce in Jameson a kind of motion sickness – stepping off, he finds himself at a loss to describe his arrival into the atrium, unable to discern its volume, all at sea in its 'milling confusion' (1984: 83). It is, in short, an experience of the postmodern sublime. Its architect, John Portman, declared that he 'wanted to explode the hotel' (quoted in McNeill, 2008: 384), and he certainly blew the mind of the postmodern adventurer.

Donald McNeill (2008) has provided a useful summary of writing on hotels that seeks to think of them in the context of the cities they inhabit, or perhaps seek to replace. His paper sketches one agenda for a geographical analysis of hotel space (we'll turn to a second agenda later) – seeing (urban) hotels as embodying twentieth- and twenty-first-century urbanism, whether used as motors for urban renewal, reflecting (or creating) consumer tastes, providing key nodes in new forms of mobility and 'circulation', or revealing some of the class and occupational hierarchies that underpin city life. The hotel is a kind of condensation or concentration of the city, a sign or symptom of broader urban restructuring and of the preoccupations of city planners, livers and dreamers. (Of course, we should be mindful of over-privileging 'the hotel' as this *ur-space* of modern/postmodern urbanism, and give some attention to other sites of rest, such as B&Bs and motels – the latter are perfectly described by Sarah Treadwell as 'filled with cheap deals, sour regrets, and nights of pleasure' (2005: 215).)

Tallack's discussion of seeing and being seen in hotel lobbies reminds us that hotels are, to borrow a phrase from Michael Herzfeld, spaces of 'conspicuous hospitality' (2012: 215) – precisely, places to see and be seen. While Tallack is concerned with the 'ordinary hotel guest', someone whose visibility is only a matter for themselves perhaps (it depends who they are sharing their room with), other guests (and hosts) are rendered more visible by the purpose of their stay. While McNeill (2008) notes that hotels are key sites where the business of cities takes place, a second research agenda is moving beyond this kind of 'business' to consider hotels as staging grounds for global geopolitics – a different kind of business. Sara Fregonese and Adam Ramadan (2015) have outlined this research agenda, and their review sits nicely alongside McNeill's to guide us through our thinking about hotels. Hotels, they write, are important geopolitical spaces, sites where the business of politics is performed (watching coverage of the recent Paris climate change talks after having read Fregonese and Ramadan's paper, I found myself endlessly wondering what was going on there in hotel bars, conference suites, bedrooms). 'Hotel geopolitics: a research agenda' provides an initial typology of the political uses of hotels, as sites of soft power, as soft targets for attack, as strategic infrastructure during conflict, as the space war reporters gather, and as sites for peace-making. Well-known hotel chains, from Hilton to Holiday Inn, are here redescribed as key sites in power plays and power struggles, in the brokering of peace or the theatre of war. As they conclude:

> Hotels are far more than simply detached spaces of depoliticised leisure and tourism, of corporate hospitality mediated by financial exchange. They are also *geopolitical* spaces, embedded within broader relations of conflict and peacemaking.
>
> *(Fregonese and Ramadan, 2015: 809; emphasis in original)*

Such hotels are also, as Ruth Craggs writes, 'spaces for performing political identities' (2012: 215) – spaces for the enactment of practices of hospitality, of staging welcomes and concocting convivial occasions (see also Craggs, 2014). International relations, Craggs reminds us, needs spaces for those relations to be performed, and the hotel has often been chosen as the ideal site for such hosting and guesting.

What emerges across this brief survey of hotel geographies is a clear reminder that spaces sometimes written off as only commercial and therefore instrumental and conditional – as far from 'pure hospitality' as it is possible to imagine – are actually filled up with countless other ways of relating (Bell, 2007a; Craggs, 2014). From the micropolitics of lounging in the lobby, looking and being looked at (or feeling lost and overawed), to the global geopolitics of diplomatic encounters in hotel spaces, and from the chance meetings among strangers in hotel bars to the planned and stage-managed encounters of world leaders sharing breakfast, hotels emerge as 'a tangle of ethical, (geo)political, commercial, and instrumental concerns' (Craggs, 2014: 98) that, in some sense, exceeds each of these different configurations of hospitality. We stay with hotels of a sort in my next discussion, though with a very particular form of hotel-space, in which very particular forms of hospitality are experienced.

Hospitelity: spaces of care in medical tourism

In this section, drawing on a recent research project,[2] I want to focus in on a particular emerging form of hybrid hospitable space in the context of medical tourism. For our purposes today, medical tourism can be defined as travel abroad for the purposes of accessing healthcare, and there are a number of different reasons why people are increasingly choosing to undertake these journeys, including cost, availability and quality of care (Connell, 2011). Medical tourism takes place across a whole range of different spaces, and is assembled when various complex flows interact (Holliday *et al.*, 2015), but here I want to turn attention to an iconic space of medical tourism – and also one that attracts quite a lot of critical commentary – the 'hospitel', or hotel-hospital hybrid. Sociologist Anthony Elliott sketches what he sees as the defining character of these spaces in his book *Making the Cut*: they are, he writes, forms of non-place – 'placeless, indistinguishable, indistinct. Like shopping malls and airports', he continues, 'private medical facilities and clinics are increasingly indistinguishable; they are, in effect, designed as "recuperative comfort zones"' which provide a 'sense of "global privatized enclosure"' in which the cocooned patient 'rarely interacts in any sustained way with other patients or staff', making medical tourism 'a kind of solitary ordeal' (2008: 104–105). Now, he might just have had bad experiences, but our own work (and that of others I'll refer to here) counters this construction of the solitary ordeal of the enclaved patient in a kind of medicalised non-place. Hospitels can in fact be intensely placeful, and intensely hospitable.

To be sure, as Audrey Bochaton and Bertrand Lefebvre (2009) note, there are significant changes in medical (and tourism) architecture, design and organisation condensed into the hospitel, crafting 'new places of care' or therapeutic landscapes. And if you only looked at the brochures and websites of places like Bumrungrad International Hospital in Bangkok – usually held up as the most iconic of these spaces, the Bonaventure of medical tourism – you might think that their plush interiors, non-specific 'international' hotel stylings and generically luxurious comforts do seem somewhat placeless. But more close attention to these spaces reveals a more complex picture. Such spaces are moreover, as Bochaton and Lefebvre put it, 'a paradoxical balance of medical, consumerist, and leisure space' (2009: 106).

First, and most simply, the extent of 'cocooning' that is experienced – and desired – is not quite as uniform as critics like Elliott suggest. One only has to step outside Bumrungrad to confront a more ordinary and distinctive 'Thai-ness', and certainly some medical tourists want to do this. Even for those who don't, the 'hermetically sealed' space of the hospitel is not the only place they experience: most will travel on ordinary flights alongside ordinary holidaymakers, business travellers and others; they will disembark, negotiate the airport and travel the city streets – even if in hybrid limo-ambulances. And many of the medical tourists want to experience the placefulness of the places they are staying in, not to be cocooned. Often, of course, this is part of the offer of medical tourism: 'surgery and safari'. In their ethnographic work on Thai hopsitels, Andrea Whittaker and Chee Heng Leng (2015) highlight the multiple experiences of medical tourists in and around hospitels. While much of their discussion centres on cross-cultural tensions between staff and patients, and between patients and patients, they also comment on the 'incompleteness' of the attempt to produce a pure, seamless hybrid of hotel and hospital. Here they summarise the tensions in attempting to accomplish this assemblage:

> the first part of the hybrid, that of a hotel, combines luxurious surroundings with convenient food and leisure activities. Single rooms and suites, all-day and overnight visiting … add to the sense of private space and hotel privilege. The second part, that of the hospital, is a space in large part determined by biomedical discourse and practices on the nature of health and disease, characterized by clinical spaces, liminal time, a lack of privacy for patients, technoscience and therapy.
>
> *(Whittaker and Chee, 2015: 292)*

This results, they conclude, in an uneasy and imperfect balancing act – a great example is the plush 'hotel' interiors, which British medical tourists we spoke to felt might be less hygienic than the sterile surfaces of a UK hospital. The lack of hand sanitising stations also caused concern, although the visible presence of cleaning staff was felt to be reassuring. Clearly, at different moments of their experience, medical tourists want to experience hotel-ness and hospital-ness in different proportions. Upon arrival, the hotel part of the hybrid eases nerves and connotes holiday luxury, but afterwards, perhaps, it's more important to feel like you're in a medical facility. But travel companions might complicate this, wanting a different type of experience during their stay, not wanting to while away their precious holidays in a clinical hospital.

Whittaker and Chee also note the uneasy balance of 'international-ness' and Thai-ness in the spaces they studied: Thai-ness was selectively desired and experienced, just as it was selectively constructed and offered. It was, for example, embodied in an assumed 'naturally caring' disposition of staff – used in marketing as a major part of the distinctive offer for medical tourism. But even this was experienced and responded to variably by medical tourists, with some critiquing the 'old fashioned' hierarchical staffing structure, and not everyone simply expecting and enjoying the 'subservient' care imagined as 'naturally Thai'.

Of course, the hospitality provided by hospitels is not the sum experience of care received by medical tourists. In our research, we found echoes of the discussions of informal hospitality-work undertaken by guests in commercial spaces (Lugosi, 2007): recuperating patients would support new arrivals, and constant use of social media between patients ensured that care was distributed among these communities of medical tourists (Jones *et al.*, 2014). At times, too, this spilled over into performing care-work for others, and we encountered striking moments of conviviality and care not just among medical tourists, but between them and other patients with whom they sometimes shared hospital spaces (Holliday *et al.*, 2015). Care is also undertaken by countless other intermediaries involved in medical tourism, from drivers to translators, travel companions and even, sometimes, by researchers (McDonald, 2011). And there are many moments of hospitality throughout the entire medical tourism journey, some of which we as researchers shared with participants, such as eating together in unfamiliar locations during recuperation. While to date there has been little interaction between work on medical tourism and that on hospitality, this initial exploration of the hospitel might suggest fruitful lines of enquiry to pursue in future work. To round off my discussion of geographies of hospitality, I am now departing the spaces of medical tourism, and turning to the shared dining table in other settings.

The art of eating together

> [O]nce they are done *in common*, eating and drinking normally go hand in hand with a
> remarkably diverse set of public or collective activities … The social, political, and cultural
> consequences of the common meal are extraordinarily varied.
>
> *(Hirschman, 1996: 547; emphasis in original)*

Commensality – the act of eating together at a shared table – has long been of interest to archae-
ologists, anthropologists and sociologists keen to trace those varied consequences and diverse
activities that Hirschman hints at here, and keen to unpack the practices and meanings of eating
together beyond the immediate household (Kerner *et al.*, 2015). In the kind of diplomatic occasions that manifest 'hotel geopolitics', the state banquet or 'informal' breakfast meeting testifies
to the power of sharing a meal table in terms of performing hospitality and lubricating politics
(Craggs, 2014). Summarising the anthropological reading of 'hospitable commensailty', Matei
Candea and Giovanni da Col write that it 'secures the maintenance of kinship and trade relations, and reinforces networks of mutual assistance; it increase intimacy, reinforces hierarchical
differences, frames class distinctions, helps to establish leadership, or serves as a pacifying device'
(2012: 9) – it also, they remind us, *materialises* hospitality, and through the sharing of food the
person 'is extended and dispersed' throughout the hospitable occasion (2012: 19). This interest
in eating together is not confined to intellectual projects: there is something of a resurgence of
enthusiasm for using food and eating as stimulants for social interaction and inclusion – a vivid
UK example being the Big Lunch project launched in 2009 and establishing itself as a new tradition for neighbourhoods up and down the country.[3]

However, my attention here is more specific, narrower: I am interested in artists using commensality as a form of artwork itself, in the staging of the sharing of food as a relational art
practice. More than simply 'art about food', this kind of art-eating reframes some of the anthropological interest in commensality, using shared food 'as a Trojan horse in order to address
related or even tangential topics' (Denfeld *et al.*, 2014: 10), raising questions about what and how
we eat, how to share each other's company, and through the often performative dimensions of
the staged shared meal, drawing our attention to the everyday business and busyness of cooking, eating, talking. Recent years have seen increasing interest among artists in debates about
hospitality (Tallant and Domel, 2012), as well as new forms of 'post-studio' and 'engaged' artistic
practice that seeks to move beyond the confines of the 'traditional' artwork and artworld, often
blurring the boundaries between art and activism. In this brief discussion, I will largely base my
thoughts around two examples, though many more are collected in books such as *Feast: Radical
Hospitality in Contemporary Art* (Smith, 2013) or *Experimental Eating* (Howells and Hayman,
2014), where among many instances we find a number that chime with the earlier discussion of
hospitality and geopolitics (albeit in a different register), including The American Reputation
Aid Society (a mobile kitchen dispensing archetypal American food to aid in mutual understanding), Enemy Kitchen (cooking and eating Baghdadi cuisine shared with military veterans) and
Conflict Kitchen (serving different national cuisines from countries in conflict with the US, for
example North Korea, Cuba, Afghanistan). These projects share an interest in grounding geopolitics in the mundane act of eating together, sharing food and stories, finding common ground.

My first example of an experiment in shared cooking and eating comes from the SoHo
district of New York city, and dates from the 1970s: Gordon Matta-Clark's *FOOD*, an artist-
run restaurant that at once built on Matta-Clark's ongoing experiments with urban space and
architecture, responded to a real need for a cheap place to eat in a neighbourhood-in-transition
colonised by artists and others in the wake of deindustrialisation (and a source of employment

for some who lived there), and came to serve as a stage for the performance of cooking and eating as works of art (for accounts, see Waxman, 2008; Hoare, 2013). Spawned of a growing DIY arts scene, *FOOD* was set up in 1971 by Matta-Clark and fellow artist Carol Gooden, and can be aligned with similar experiments in both relational aesthetics and communal gastronomy (Waxman 2008). *FOOD* pioneered having chefs on display (now a restaurant staple) and hosted many guest chef-artists (such as Robert Rauschenberg and Donald Judd) who staged themed feasts and cooked elaborate meals that married food with art and politics (including the politics of food). Every aspect of the food preparation process was performed, on display – including the washing of the dishes. While the looseness of the owners' grasp on the business of running a commercial restaurant meant that *FOOD* struggled to survive (at least until it later turned into a more conventional eatery), the point of *FOOD* was to try to posit an *alternative* to the usual way of producing and consuming food (and art). A film made by Matta-Clark, *A Day in the Life of FOOD*, captures something of the ethos and aesthetic of the venue in its early 1970s heyday, and a facsimile of the restaurant was staged at the Frieze New York art show in 2013.

FOOD's legacy can certainly be traced in many of the subsequent experiments in the art of eating together, including those staged by Lucy and Jorge Orta, who have used shared meals in a number of their art projects, including *All in One Basket* (using food waste from Les Halles market in Paris to make jams and pickles) and the massed sit-down dinners of their *70 x 7 The Meal* series, described as follows:

> 70 x 7 … is a pretext for multiple encounters of seven guests, invited to dine in surprising installations, complete with a set of limited edition Limoges porcelain, and a 'endless' tablecloth. Lucy and Jorge Orta have transformed the ancestral ritual of the meal into a series of dynamic encounters, bringing people from different horizons together, to meet, to discuss and debate … Each meal, in the form of an act, proposes a new educational, social, and environmental debate, and a pretext for new encounters for multiples of seven guests.
>
> *(Orta and Orta, 2006: 28–29)*

In the book *Collective Space* (2006) Orta and Orta propose a new iteration of the *70 x 7 The Meal* series, an immense feast (with at least 5,000 guests) spilling out of the gallery space of Tate Modern in London, across the Millennium Bridge, and onwards into the city streets. This variant of the meal is designed, they write, as 'a way to reclaim and reinforce the idea of belonging to the city' and to 'provoke a reflection on the loss of public space, and re-build a sense of civic pride, and sow seeds for future change' (Orta and Orta, 2006: 30). Although these outcomes are only hinted at, and the event itself remains speculative and unrealised, we can see a clear connection between *FOOD* and *70 x 7 The Meal*, as both bring people together in an artist-made environment (one a restaurant, the other an outdoor banquet) in order to share food but also to build something in common between the guests, a shared experience and a chance to reflect on themes and issues suggested by the setting and the food. In Orta and Orta's work, this is carried through to the design not only of the food, but also of the plates and tablecloths, all of which are united in their role as 'relational objects'. That's the watchword of this work, in fact: *relational*. Sitting down together to eat and talk produces new ways of relating (Lupton, 2011).

Conclusions

In this brief chapter I have sketched some lines of enquiry centred around geographies of hospitality. A selective itinerary through past work, largely by geographers, gave us some waymarkers for considering the sites and scales of hospitality, in both its commercial and social formations.

I then chose to pursue three quite distinctive lines: to think about hotels, mainly in terms of their relationship to the city and as stages for geopolitics and international relations; to then explore a particular and relatively new commingling of hotel-space with hospital-space, by discussing the 'hospitel' as experienced by medical tourists, a growing population that encounters hospitality in very interesting ways; and, lastly, to consider artists who use food and eating together in art projects, with a focus on the work of Gordon Matta-Clark and Lucy and Jorge Orta. While these might seem like a somewhat disparate selection, my aim has not been to offer a comprehensive assessment or programmatic agenda for researching geographies of hospitality, but instead to shed light on some interesting case studies that, each in their own different way, contribute to the broader ongoing project of critical hospitality studies.

Notes

1   I use the term 'geographical' quite loosely here, so my discussion includes 'honorary geographers' as well as those formally trained in or employed by geography departments.
2   Material for this section of the chapter is based on the ESRC research project 'Sun, Sea, Sand and Silicone: Mapping Cosmetic Surgery Tourism' (RES-062-23-2796). Further information on the project, and links to other outputs, can be found at www.ssss.leeds.ac.uk. Some of the ideas in this section were presented in a talk for the seminar series 'Exploring Hospitality in the Modern World' at the University of Nottingham in January 2015. Thanks to Mike Heffernan for inviting me, to all those who attended and shared stories, and to Mike and to Zoe Trodd and Graham Thompson for their hospitality.
3   For details, see www.thebiglunch.com.

References

Amin, Ash (2006) The good city, *Urban Studies* 43: 1009–1023.
Appadurai, Arjun (1990) Disjuncture and difference in the global cultural economy, *Theory, Culture & Society* 7: 295–310.
Barnett, Clive (2005) Ways of relating: hospitality and the acknowledgement of otherness, *Progress in Human Geography* 29: 5–21.
Bell, David (2007a) The hospitable city: social relations in commercial spaces, *Progress in Human Geography* 31: 7–22.
Bell, David (2007b) Moments of hospitality. In Germann Molz, Jennie and Gibson, Sarah (eds) *Mobilizing Hospitality: The Ethics of Social Relations in a Mobile World*, Aldershot: Ashgate, pp. 29–44.
Bell, David (2012) Hospitality is society, *Hospitality & Society* 1: 137–152.
Bell, David and Binnie, Jon (2005) What's eating Manchester? Gastro-culture and urban regeneration, *Architectural Design* 75: 78–85.
Bell, David and Valentine, Gill (1997) *Consuming Geographies: You Are Where You Eat*, London: Routledge.
Bochaton, Audrey and Lefebvre, Bertrand (2009) The rebirth of the hospital: heterotopia and medical tourism in Asia. In Winter, Tim, Teo, Peggy and Chang, T. C. (eds) *Asia on Tour: Exploring the Rise of Asian Tourism*, Abingdon: Routledge, pp. 97–108.
Broek Chávez, Frans van den and van der Rest, Jean-Pierre (2014) The hospitalities of cities: between the agora and the fortress, *Hospitality & Society* 4: 31–53.
Candea, Matei and Da Col, Giovanni (2012) The return to hospitality, *Journal of the Royal Anthropological Institute* 18: 1–19.
Chatterton, Paul and Hollands, Robert (2003) *Urban Nightscapes: Youth Cultures, Pleasure Spaces and Corporate Power*, London: Routledge.
Chauncey, George (1996) Privacy could only be had in public: gay uses of the streets. In Sanders, Joel (ed.) *Stud: Architectures of Masculinity*, New York: Princeton Architectural Press, pp. 224–267.
Connell, John (2011) *Medical Tourism*, Oxford: CABI.
Craggs, Ruth (2012) Towards a political geography of hotels: Southern Rhodesia, 1958–1962, *Political Geography* 31: 215–224.
Craggs, Ruth (2014). Hospitality in geopolitics and the making of Commonwealth international relations, *Geoforum* 52: 90–100.

Crang, P. (1994) It's showtime; on the workplace geographies of display in a restaurant in southeast England, *Environment and Planning D: Society and Space* 12: 675–704.

Denfeld, Zack, Kramer, Catherine and Conley, Emma (2014) Eating ahead: art, life and food. In Howells, Thomas and Hayman, Leanne (eds) *Experimental Eating*, London: Black Dog, pp. 10–23.

Derrida, Jacques (2001) *On Cosmopolitanism and Forgiveness*, London: Routledge.

Dikeç, Mustafa (2002) Pera peras poros: longings for spaces of hospitality, *Theory, Culture & Society* 19: 227–247.

Dikeç, Mustafa, Clark, Nigel and Barnett, Clive (2009) Extending hospitality: giving space, taking time, *Paragraph* 32: 1–14.

Elliott, Anthony (2008) *Making the Cut: How Cosmetic Surgery is Transforming our Lives*, London: Reaktion.

Fregonese, Sara and Ramadan, Adam (2015) Hotel geopolitics: a research agenda, *Geopolitics* 20: 793–813.

Gibson, Sarah (2003) Accommodating strangers: British hospitality and the asylum hotel debate, *Journal for Cultural Research* 7: 367–386.

Hall, Tom and Smith, Robin (2015) Care and repair and the politics of urban kindness, *Sociology* 49: 3–18.

Herod, A. (2010) *Hospitality in Early Modern England*, Oxford: Clarendon Press.

Herzfeld, Michael (2012) Afterword: reciprocating the hospitality of these pages, *Journal of the Royal Anthropological Institute* 18: 210–217.

Hirschman, Albert (1996) Melding the public and private spheres: taking commensality seriously, *Critical Review* 10: 533–550.

Hoare, Natasha (2013) Matta-Clark's FOOD, *The Gormand* 2: 34–41.

Holliday, Ruth, Bell, David, Cheung, Olive, Jones, Meredith and Probyn, Elspeth (2015) Brief encounters: assembling cosmetic surgery tourism, *Social Science & Medicine* 124: 298–304.

Howells, Thomas and Hayman, Leanne (eds) (2014) *Experimental Eating*, London: Black Dog.

Hubbard, Phil and Wilkinson, Eleanor (2015) Welcoming the world? Hospitality, homonationalism, and the London 2012 Olympics, *Antipode* 47: 598–615.

Jameson, Fredric (1984) Postmodernism, or the cultural logic of late capitalism, *New Left Review* 146: 53–92.

Jelloun, Tahar Ben and Bray, Barbara (1999) *French Hospitality: Racism and North African Immigrants*, New York: Columbia University Press.

Jones, Meredith, Bell, David, Holliday, Ruth, Probyn, Elspeth and Sanchez Taylor, Jacqueline (2014) Facebook and facelifts: communities of cosmetic surgery tourists. In Lean, Gareth, Staiff, Russell and Waterton, Emma (eds) *Travel and Transformation*, Farnham: Ashgate, pp. 189–204.

Katz, Marc (1999) The Hotel Kracauer, *Differences: A Journal of Feminist Cultural Studies* 11: 134–152.

Kerner, Susanne, Chou, Cynthia and Warmind, Morten (eds) (2015) *Commensality: From Everyday Food to Feast*, London: Bloomsbury.

Koch, Regan and Latham, Alan (2013) On the hard work of domesticating a public space, *Urban Studies* 50: 6–21.

Kracauer, S. (1999 [1925]) The hotel lobby, *Postcolonial Studies* 2, 3: 289–297.

Latham, Alan (2003) Urbanity, lifestyle and making sense of the new urban cultural economy: notes from Auckland, New Zealand, *Urban Studies* 40: 1699–1724.

Laurier, Eric and Philo, Chris (2006a) Cold shoulders and napkins handed: gestures of responsibility, *Transactions of the Institute of British Geographers* 31: 193–207.

Laurier, Eric and Philo, Chris (2006b) Possible geographies: a passing encounter in a café, *Area* 38: 353–363.

Laurier, Eric and Philo, Chris (2007) A parcel of muddling muckworms: revisiting Habermas and the early modern English coffee-houses, *Social & Cultural Geography* 8: 259–281.

Laurier, E., Whyte, A. and Buckner, K. (2001) An ethnography of a neighbourhood cafe, *Journal of Mundane Behaviour* 2, 2: 195–232.

Lugosi, Peter (2007) Consumer participation in commercial hospitality, *International Journal of Culture, Tourism and Hospitality Research* 1: 227–236.

Lugosi, Peter (2008). Hospitality spaces, hospitable moments: consumer encounters and affective experiences in commercial settings, *Journal of Foodservice* 19: 139–149.

Lupton, Ellen (2011) Food service: setting the table. In Casbon, Becca and Carey, Megan (eds) *Lucy + Jorge Orta: Food Water Life*, New York: Princeton Architectural Press, pp. 16–23.

McDonald, Emily (2011) Bodies-in-motion: experiences of momentum in transnational surgery. In Mascia-Lees, Frances (ed.) *A Companion to the Anthropology of the Body and Embodiment*, Chichester: Wiley-Blackwell, pp. 481–503.

McNeill, Donald (2008) The hotel and the city, *Progress in Human Geography* 32: 383–398.

Malbon, Ben (2002) *Clubbing: Dancing, Ecstasy, Vitality*, London: Routledge.

Orta, Lucy and Orta, Jorge (2006) *Collective Space*, Birmingham: ARTicle Press/ixia.

Rosello, Mireille (2001) *Postcolonial Hospitality: The Immigrant as Guest*, Stanford: Stanford University Press.

Schivelbusch, Warren (1993) *Tastes of Paradise: A Social History of Spices, Stimulants and Intoxicants*, New York: Vintage.

Seamon, David (1979) *The Geography of the Lifeworld: Movement, Rest and Encounter*, London: Croom Helm.

Smith, Stephanie (ed.) (2013) *Feast: Radical Hospitality in Contemporary Art*, Chicago: Smart Museum of Art, University of Chicago.

Still, Judith (2010) *Derrida and Hospitality: Theory and Practice*, Edinburgh: Edinburgh University Press.

Tallack, Douglas (2002) 'Waiting, waiting': the hotel lobby, in the modern city. In Leach, Neil (ed.) *The Hieroglyphics of Space: Reading and Experiencing the Modern Metropolis*, London: Routledge, pp. 139–151.

Tallant, Sally and Domela, Paul (eds) (2012) *The Unexpected Guest: Art, Writing and Thinking on Hospitality*, London: Art/Books.

Thrift, Nigel (2005) But malice aforethought: cities and the natural history of hatred, *Transactions of the institute of British Geographers* 30: 133–150.

Treadwell, Sarah (2005) The motel: an image of elsewhere, *Space and Culture* 8: 214–224.

Tufts, Steven (2006) 'We make it work': the cultural transformation of hotel workers in the city, *Antipode* 38: 350–373.

Walsh, Joanna (2015) *Hotel*, London: Bloomsbury.

Waxman, Lori (2008) The Banquet years: FOOD, a SoHo restaurant, *Gastronomica* 8: 24–33.

Weightman, Barbara (1980) Gay bars as private places, *Landscape* 23: 9–16.

Whittaker, Andrea and Chee, Heng Leng (2015) Perceptions of an 'international hospital' in Thailand by medical travel patients: cross-cultural tensions in a transnational space, *Social Science & Medicine* 124: 290–297.

4

Levinas, hospitality and the feminine other

Kim Meijer-van Wijk

Key themes

Introducing Emmanuel Levinas

Levinas and hospitality

Feminine hospitality

We could start this chapter by dishing up a vast array of interpretations and definitions, and refer to a number of debates in which the term hospitality takes centre stage. This would be done with the intention of illustrating the meaning and academic, societal or managerial relevance of hospitality. We will resist this temptation. We find that a philosophical understanding of hospitality is often eclipsed by endeavours to ground its academic or societal relevance. Instead, this chapter aims to convey a particular understanding of hospitality according to the French philosopher Emmanuel Levinas (1906–1995). We read this philosophy as a philosophy of hospitality according to, but not based upon, the reading of his colleague, dear friend and fellow philosopher Jacques Derrida (see Derrida, 1999). The purpose is to shed light on the fundamental question of why and how people are hospitable towards others.

We use the philosophy of Levinas to answer the central question from the perspective of the host/guest encounter. The argumentation is built up as follows: first, we will introduce Emmanuel Levinas through fragments of his life story that have led to the formation of his particular, and at times radical, philosophy. In this section, we will discuss the necessity of involving Levinas in the academic debate of hospitality. The second section addresses the link between Levinas' philosophy and hospitality. We will analyse chapters from *Totalité et Infini* (Levinas, 1961, 1969) and several collected philosophical papers (Levinas, 1987) that specifically address hospitality. The third and final section is devoted to the puzzling association of the 'femininity of hospitality' that Levinas considers is the 'primary hospitable welcome' (1969: 155).

DOI: 10.4324/9781315679938-5

43

To delve into Levinasian philosophy is challenging; his texts are written like poetry – repeatedly strengthening the same argument like 'waves on a beach' – (Derrida, 1978: 103). Nevertheless, we feel that this discussion will provide readers with a more fundamental understanding of the origin of hospitality and how it is linked to ethics.

Introducing Levinas

In the twentieth century, Levinas developed his radical thoughts on philosophy in order to 'disturb' the common philosophical order. Traditional Western philosophy at that time focused mainly on questions of being and humanity from an individual perspective, placing the self at centre stage. Wholly different than this traditional school of thought, Levinas' principal argument from the start has been that we cannot discuss philosophy or begin to speak of ethics if we focus on the self and thereby pre-exclude the Other.[1] Ethics begins when we encounter and welcome the Other. A consequence of this philosophical shift is that Levinas' magnum opus *Totalité et Infini* is read as 'an immense treatise *of hospitality*' by Derrida (1999: 21). In *Totalité et Infini* Levinas argues that the I should be open and welcome the Other, for whom she bears infinite responsibility. Welcoming the other is a prerequisite for ethics and it is exactly this intersubjective openness that caused Derrida to build his argument linking hospitality to Levinas' work. In *Adieu* (1999) – initially a eulogy for Levinas – Derrida introduced a novel reading of Levinasian philosophy as a 'philosophy of hospitality'. Since then, many scholars have built upon this interpretation (Derrida and Dufourmantelle, 2000; Katz, 2003; McNulty, 2006; Irigaray, 2008; Still, 2010a). However, instead of following Derrida's reading, we shall bring our focus back to its source as provided by Levinas. To understand the origin of Levinas' thinking, it is important to place this in the time frame of the twentieth century, during which the political and economic situation had a grave impact on Levinas' life and future work, in particular the Second World War. War can be considered as the absolute opposite of hospitality, and it was this experience of war that formed the beginning of *Totalité et Infini* as a philosophical plea for hospitality. We will start with a brief history of the life of Emmanuel Levinas.

Life and early career

Emmanuel Levinas was born in Kovno, Lithuania in 1906. Levinas came from a Jewish middle-class family and was the eldest of two brothers. He started studying philosophy at the University of Strasbourg in 1924. This is the place where Levinas met the philosopher Maurice Blanchot, with whom he developed a lifelong friendship. In 1928, Levinas attended Freiburg University to study phenomenology under Edmund Husserl[2] and, during this time, he also became acquainted with the work of Martin Heidegger.[3] Husserl and Heidegger were Levinas' principal influencers with regard to his early thinking. Moreover, Levinas dedicated his thesis to Husserl's work. *The Theory of Intuition in Husserl's Phenomenology* (Levinas, 1973) was the first French introduction of Husserl's philosophy. In this period (1932), Levinas married his childhood friend Raïssa Levi. Their daughter Simone was born before the war, and a second daughter and son were born after the war (Andrée Éliane and Michäel), although the second daughter died at a young age. Between 1930 and 1940, Levinas began to turn away from what he called the 'German thinking' of both Husserl and Heidegger. Their schools of thought focused too much on the *individual* (ego) and Levinas saw traditional Western philosophy as striving towards 'the perfection of our own being' (2003: 51). One could argue that this focus on the individual being risks excluding other human 'beings' that surround and affect us, and it is exactly this exclusion of the other that signifies much, but not all, of Levinas' future work.

The consequences of the Second World War

The course of Levinas' life took a significant turn during the Second World War. In 1939 he was naturalised as a French citizen and drafted into the army as an officer. At the end of 1939 he was sent to the front where he was taken as a prisoner of war. Due to his status as an officer, Levinas was sent to a military prison camp instead of a concentration camp. These were dire times for Levinas, who learnt that most of his family members (his parents, brothers and parents-in-law) had died during the pogroms in Kovno. His wife and daughter survived. As a result of an alleged message that Levinas sent to Blanchot during his captivity, Raïssa and Simone found refuge in Blanchot's apartment in Paris. They were then offered shelter in a convent near Orléans. The horrors of the war, the experiences during incarceration and the loss of his family had a profound impact on Levinas. During the Second World War Levinas experienced at first hand the monstrosities that follow when human beings devalue the life of other human beings into a subhuman state. To illustrate this point, Levinas shared an anecdote of how a wandering dog in the military camp would be the only living thing to recognise the imprisoned officers as human (also referred to as 'The last Kantian in Nazi-Germany', Levinas, 1990).

Presumably, it was the sum of Levinas' critique towards the prioritisation of the individual by traditional Western philosophers, plus the experience of human devaluation during the Second World War that resulted in his emphasis on the intersubjective relation for years to come. What went wrong in philosophy or the world for that matter? Was too much focus placed on the individual, or what Levinas calls the 'pure subjectivism of the I' (du subjectivisme pur du moi) (*Totalité et Infini*, 1969: 25; 1961: 11–12)? And did we, in an effort to understand the meaning of being – of subjectivity – set aside the hospitable welcoming of the Other? Levinas would probably affirm that there is no sense in thinking of morality or ethics – as philosophers do – from an individual perspective, no more than it makes sense for one to be hospitable alone. Hospitality is the encounter with the Other and so is ethics. During an interview in 1986 with François Poirié, Levinas argued that we have always been in a collective rather than an individual state: 'From the very start you are not indifferent to the Other. From the very start you are not alone!' (Poirié, 2001: 50). In the next section, we will extend this observation by discussing the link between Levinasian philosophy (particularly as described in *Totalité et Infini*) and the idea of hospitality.

Levinas and hospitality

In the preface of *Totalité et Infini*, Levinas says: 'This book will present subjectivity as welcoming the Other, as hospitality' (Ce livre présentera la subjectivité comme accueillant Autrui, comme hospitalité) (1969: 27; 1961: 12). By this statement, Levinas draws our attention to a new perspective on ethics. Following this understanding, ethics does not originate in reason, as many traditional Western philosophers of that time would have argued, but it precedes reason (Welten, 2011: 6). Ethics starts when we are called upon by the Other to take responsibility for her, much as hospitality begins after our doorbell has rung, and a stranger is standing on the doorstep. Might one understand from this introductory statement that Levinas intends to say that the very purpose of being lies in our being there for the Other and, more specifically, in our being hospitable towards that Other? Indeed, Levinas provides us with an 'ethics of hospitality' that gives philosophical primacy to the orientation towards the Other. Following this understanding, we will use the words 'ethics' and 'hospitality' interchangeably, as both relate to the relationship between the I and the Other. The intersubjective relationship for Levinas is constituted by language (*Totalité et Infini*, 1969: 39). It is through language that the I is urged to 'leave itself' (*Totalité et Infini*, 1969: 39) and move towards the Other who, during discourse, remains distant – transcendent.

The Other/L'Autrui

Let us further examine the ethical relationship by focusing on the mysterious Other Levinas is speaking of. When Levinas writes about the relationship, primacy is given not to the I, but to the Other. This is because the Other places an ethical appeal on me and thereby disrupts my 'order'. The Other that causes a disruption is a difficult, yet primary, element in Levinas' philosophy, and in many ways it is linked to the unanticipated encounter between a host and guest – the latter being a stranger at first. Yet, contrary to the dichotomous view of the host that provides and the guest that receives hospitality as presented in several studies of commercial hospitality (e.g. Lashley and Morrison, 2000), the understanding of this dichotomy according to Levinas is wholly different. Levinas (1987: 124) says that the host is already taken hostage by the guest long before her arrival. We will come back to the view of the host as hostage later in this chapter. First, we will elaborate on the meaning of the Other as guest. Therefore, we will start by examining the meaning and significance of the Other as radically different – or radical alterity – by reflecting upon Levinas, who writes:

> L'Absolument Autre, c'est Autrui. Il ne fait pas nombre avec moi. La collectivité où je dis « tu » ou « nous » n'est pas un pluriel de « je ». Moi, toi, ce ne sont pas là individus d'un concept commun.
>
> *(Totalité et Infini, 1961: 28)*

> The absolute other is the Other. He and I do not form a number. The collectively in which I say 'you' or 'we' is not a plural of the 'I.' I, you – these are not individuals of a common concept.
>
> *(Totalité et Infini, 1969: 39)*

In this section, Levinas introduces the Other as a Stranger (*l'Etranger*). Levinas means to say that the Other is literally different, irreducible, and thus not similar – or the same – to the I. We cannot, even if we wanted to, understand the Other as just another version of ourselves, which we then project onto her. The Other never lives up to our prejudice. Yet, although the Other is a stranger to me, I am always already a host to her. In an interview, Levinas describes our automatic responsibility to be hosts as follows: 'as if I had to do with the other before knowing him, in a past that has never taken place' (Poirié, 2001: 52). A scene between host and guest serves as a good example here.[4] When we are at home (*chez-soi*) and a stranger comes knocking, then, in a brief moment before we open the door, and even when we do open it, we are hesitant about the stranger standing on our doorstep. In a sense, we fear and even distrust this strange other. Is this a potential friend or hostile stranger? The eminent problem in this scene is exemplary of how our culture tends to deal with the unknown. Levinas terms this inclination to understand, determine and thereby capture others within our frame as 'totalising', as violence, even (1969: 40). The unknown brings unease, a violation of our integrity.

Consider how we deal with the refugees that have been spreading across Europe since 2012. These 'strangers' are met with much resistance. Are they friends (human beings worthy of refuge) or foes (IS-extremists, rapists)? Our (in)hospitality towards and underlying fear of strangers becomes painfully clear. Yet Levinas' philosophy of hospitality does not start with fear of the Other. As stated earlier, it begins even before fear arises; it starts with the I who is uniquely chosen – the chosen one – to be host to the Other. In contrast with the human inclination to 'resolve the unknown', Levinas presents the Other as completely transcendent and 'absolutely other' (1969: 40). Levinas does not settle the unease that comes with the unknown; he rather enforces it. Thus, if we open the door, it will be to welcome a stranger who we do not know, nor need to know, in order for us to engage in language. It is exactly this hospitable welcome of the strange other that Derrida (1999) argues happens without the condition of the knowing, that creates opportunity for the I to break out of its ego – or totality.

The breach/La rupture

Levinas is opposed to totalising systems of ego-thinking. His philosophy is meant to disrupt or 'breach' the inclination to frame others, or totalize them (1969: 40). With his presentation of the Other as stranger, Levinas appoints his philosophical ideas to the argument that the other may remain a stranger. We can let her be (Irigaray, 2008). This does not mean that we cannot enter into a relationship with her, nor does it relieve us of our obligation towards her. We have already stated earlier that Levinas' philosophy is challenging to understand. We have to disappoint readers who, up to now, believed that the Other is synonymous to the human other. By encountering the Other, Levinas does not necessarily suggest a human encounter with the Other as this can also be conceptual, without actual physical contact or even visual sight of the Other. Nevertheless, Levinas does speak of the face-to-face encounter, which is puzzling to say the least. Levinas' answer when asked about this idea was: 'The face is not of the order of the seen, it is not an object' (Poirié, 2001: 48). Levinas argues that we can either experience the face-to-face encounter as if we were photographers, seeing the face as object (looking at their hair, eyes and nose), or we can 'meet' the face and simply say 'good day!' (Poirié, 2001: 61). By doing the latter, we engage, we wish the Other well before even knowing her. This statement shows the primacy of ethics over the knowing.

Thus, the conceptual Other is always present, and so we are always already ethically obliged. Coming back to the face-to-face encounter, this is where the breach happens. The breach is caused by the void of the unknown. Remember how Levinas tells us to let the Other be completely other – or strange – if we do, then this void violently breaks through our totality. Our totality is breached because instead of reducing the other to an image that is constituted by ourselves (whereby we would stay in our totality) we break out of ourselves and our patterns of thought and move towards the infinite otherness of the Other. This is a somewhat troubling endeavour as the encounter with the other might change us – it calls us into question (Levinas, 1969: 43). Hence, this disruptive element – or trauma – central to Levinasian philosophy is analogous to the first welcome between I and the Other. In the following section we will discuss the welcoming movement that transforms the I into host, and the stranger into guest.

The face and its command/Le visage et son appel

The encounter with the Other not only imposes a breach on our totality, it also confronts us with an 'ethical appeal' which is the face of the Other. Again, we must not presume that this is always an empirical face, one that you can actually see. The word 'face' relates to the expression of the Other, which has an impact on myself. Levinas writes:

> La manière dont se présente l'Autre, dépassant l'idée de l'Autre en moi, nous l'appelons, en effet, visage. Cette façon ne consiste pas à figurer comme thème sous mon regard, à s'étaler comme une ensemble de qualités formant une image. Le visage d'Autrui détruit à tout moment, et déborde l'image plastique qu'il me laisse, l'idée a ma mesure.
>
> *(1961: 43)*

> The way in which the other presents himself, exceeding *the idea of the other in me*, we here name face. This *mode* does not consist in figuring as a theme under my gaze, in spreading itself forth as a set of qualities forming an image. The face of the Other at each moment destroys and overflows the plastic image it leaves me, the idea existing to my own measure.
>
> *(1969: 50–51)*

This quote shows that the face in no way lives up to my image of it. Instead, it expresses (*il s'exprime*) something and the openness with which I receive this expression can be considered as a welcoming movement that is a 'right and good movement' linked by Derrida (1999: 25) to hospitality. Coming back to the host–guest example I have, despite my hesitation, opened the door and engaged in conversation with the Other, whom I now welcome as guest. Of this gesture, Levinas says: 'Aborder Autrui dans le discours, c'est accueillir son expression où il déborde à tout instant l'idée qu'en emporterait une pensée' (To approach the Other in conversation is to welcome his expression, in which at each instant he overflows the idea a thought would carry away from it) (1961: 43; 1969: 51). Thus, the disturbance caused by the face-to-face encounter with the Other teaches me something new. It provides a new perspective that I could not have found myself. However, in order to learn – be taught – I must let 'the other into oneself, to one's space – it is invasive of the integrity of the self, or the domain of the self' (Still, 2010b: 13). Hence, the presence of the Other disturbs my order.

What is more, I must regard the Other as somehow higher than myself, coming from a height (Levinas, 1969: 79). The Other presents herself from an elevated – transcendent – position that we can compare with that of God. Levinas considers religion to be the relation with the Other. Hence, Levinas draws this comparison when he states that the Other 'resembles God' (1969: 293). Could I consider the Other as superior to myself? Levinas (1969: 216) argues that I should; the ethical relationship is asymmetrical. The Other is in charge and I am her subordinate. We can relate this asymmetry to an example in the hospitality industry. We should emphasise, however, that there is an eminent difference between behaviour governed by a specific function (i.e. waiting tables) and ethics. Nevertheless, we find asymmetry in many professional host/guest relationships that are based on the Dutch saying 'the guest is king', where the host is expected to act as a humble servant. Here, the host is a host on condition of getting financial compensation for his efforts (considering he is not a volunteer or philanthropist), which slightly complicates the matter of understanding his efforts as purely ethical. We can thus differentiate by asymmetry guided by ethics, or otherwise. The asymmetrical relation usually does not apply to guide human behaviour in everyday life (excluding parent–child/fan–idol/lover to lover relations) and it is certainly not a norm in our highly individualistic society. However, for Levinas the asymmetrical relationship is foundational for his philosophy. The Other is higher and deserves primacy, courteousness even. For Levinas, courtesy towards the Other is as if to say 'Apres vous' (Poirié, 2001: 49). With this understanding of the invasive nature of the encounter in Levinasian hospitality, the way that the face of the Other penetrates through my totality, my receiving of the Other and the asymmetrical nature of our relation, we can now begin to discuss the ethical appeal of the Other.

The appeal/le commandement

The face of the Other expresses itself in such a way that an appeal goes out from it. Levinas' philosophy is best known for this ethical appeal – or command – of the Other. In a way, the Other *is* the ethical appeal (Welten, 2011: 152). Here, we introduce yet another parallel between this philosophy and the idea of hospitality. We will discuss this similarity by analysing the meaning and consequence of the appeal. The ethical appeal is a 'command of hospitality'. It is as if the gaze of the Other places the burden of responsibility for the Other on 'the shoulders' of the I. Literally, her expression invokes our ability to respond (response-ability) to her being present. The encounter between the I and the Other can therefore never be neutral. It is not as if we need only open the door, see the other, let her expression affect – disturb – us and then go about our business. Following Levinas, the encounter would be rendered morally insignificant if it resulted in internal contemplation only. Therefore, Levinas stresses that we must act upon (respond to) the ethical appeal. Note that we do not act based upon a conscious decision to do so, our action of taking responsibility for the Other is what constitutes humanity.

We have already presented the ethical relation as asymmetrical. This asymmetry has implications for the ethical appeal. It implies that the Other may place the burden of responsibility on me but, conversely, I cannot demand her to also bear this burden in return. The responsibility I bear for the Other automatically exceeds her responsibility for me. I cannot simply copy and paste my responsibility onto her ('I'll scratch your back, if you scratch mine!') simply because the Other is radically different from myself – we is not the plural of I. I can only account for my own action. If it were any different, then the ethical relation would be reduced to an economic relation of trade (Welten, 2011: 154). As such, there is no moral obligation to reciprocity present in hospitality according to Levinas, who stresses that 'courtesy or ethics consists in not thinking that reciprocity' (Poirié, 2001: 49). Drawing the parallel to a general conception of hospitality asserted by Lashley and Morrison (2000), where hospitality is considered as the willingness to be hospitable without demanding something in return, we can see that the ethical relation according to Levinas is based on similar, yet not identical, precepts. On a more fundamental note, Levinas says that the encounter with the Other who expresses an ethical appeal to take responsibility is what places us on 'the right track'. It urges us to do 'good', or at least provides us with a trace to what is 'good'.

The subject as hostage/Le sujet comme otage

Taking the parallel one step further, the responsibility that we can take for the Other, the concrete action, is, for example, to let her share in our economy (our house and belongings). That could very well be, inviting the guest into our home in order to offer shelter and food. Here, Levinas refers to what is written in the Bible where hospitality is portrayed as feeding the hungry, giving clothes to the naked, water to the thirsty and providing shelter for the homeless (see Matthew 25: 34–36). Again, Levinas stresses that we are not indifferent to the, in his words, 'material misery' of the Other (Poirié, 2001: 52). Although there are other institutions that relieve our obligation to provide food and shelter for others (e.g. soup kitchens, homeless shelters), from an ethical point of view, Levinas states that we cannot be indifferent (Poirié, 2001: 52). Remember that before anything else – any claim or conversation – I am always automatically a host bearing responsibility for the strange Other, who is my guest. With this in mind, Levinas introduces the idea of the host (*hôte*) as hostage (*otage*) (Levinas, 1987: 124; Derrida, 1999). This, in fact, relates to the constitution of being as being for the Other. Therefore, the subject is a hostage. Due to the idea that we automatically bear responsibility, we cannot deny it and are being held hostage by it. The responsibility that we must take for the Other has no causal effect, it is not as though I am to blame for the material misery of the Other and therefore I have to solve it. I am always indebted to the Other. In his careful analysis of Levinas' philosophy, Derrida explains the idea of the subject-host as hostage as follows: 'the being hostage is the subjectivity of the subject as *Responsibility for the Other* (1999: 55). Thus, the I that is summoned by the Other to be host is held hostage by this very summoning. The I has no choice but to respond to this call. Levinas accords great value to the idea of the host considered as hostage and says: 'It is by reason of the stage of being hostage that there can be in the world pity, compassion, pardon and proximity (even the little there is)' (1987: 124).

The home/L'habitation

In order to clarify the idea of the host as hostage, we will discuss a specific situation in which this transformation can take place, the home. Before doing so, we will explain what Levinas means by this term. The home, or habitation, represents a separation from the world where man can be 'at home with himself' (d'un chez soi) (Levinas, 1969: 152; 1961: 162). While the home is a place where one can withdraw, or take 'empirical refuge', at the same time this home – or state of inwardness – also creates opportunity for the outside world to come in (Levinas, 1969: 154). It is only from within the seclusion of my house that I can be asked to open the door and be hospitable towards others. To further explain this inward/outward effect of habitation, Levinas (1969: 154) introduces the term 'dwelling', which signifies the state in which I contemplate the world in a state of recollection. This dwelling precedes the face-to-face encounter. In the shelter of my home, in the safety of it, I can start my movement to the outside world – the exterior. To this understanding, the Belgian philosopher Luce Irigaray (2008: 7) adds that dwelling is necessary for the movement from the self – the I – to the Other. For Irigaray, much value is accorded to the self and her dwelling as a condition to express hospitality to the other. Presumably, Levinas does not accord the same meaning to dwelling when primarily understood as a state of securing the position of the I. His philosophy concerns an orientation that begins with the I, but is always directed towards, or preceded by, the presence of the Other (Levinas, 1961: 215).

After clarifying Levinas' understanding of the home, we can now come to elaborate how the home can transform a host into hostage. Initially, the home belongs to the host. Due to this possession she is the only one – and uniquely so – who is obliged to, or could be asked to, share her home if needed. Mind that, in Levinas' philosophy, the host is always already obliged and called upon by the ethical appeal of the Other without any questions asked. Indeed, the home can be a place of refuge ideally situated to dwell, but it is also posited as an open invitation to strangers. Levinas says:

> car ma position de moi consiste à pouvoir répondre à cette misère essentielle d'autrui, a me trouver des ressources. Autrui qui me domine dans sa transcendance est aussi l'étranger, la veuve et l'orphelin envers qui je suis obligé.
>
> *(1961: 237)*

> for my position as *I* consists in being able to respond to the essential destitution of the Other, finding resources for myself. The Other who dominates me in his transcendence is thus the stranger, the widow, and the orphan, to whom I am obliged.
>
> *(1969: 215)*

A careful analysis of this quote shows us how Levinas connects the responsibility to care for the Other in a destitute state, here exemplified as that of a stranger, widow or orphan, to the I. Furthermore, the sentence mentioning 'finding resources' could very well relate to the possession of the home. This home, then, says Levinas, is essentially acquired to share with the strange Other. Here emerges the link between the home and the host-hostage transformation. This might be a startling way to think about the home. Do we not buy a house (and the high mortgage that comes with it) for our own enjoyment and that of our family? Here, in Levinas' terms, we would be mistaken. In looking at the word 'dominates' in the quote above, we see that the Other dominates us in their Otherness, in their destitution, thus obliging us to share our home if need be. We therefore find that the home provides hospitality in two ways. First, the home is 'hospitable for its proprietor' (Hospitalière à son propriétaire) (Levinas, 1961: 157; 1961: 169). It provides a place for the I to live and dwell. As Derrida says: 'a *hôte* received in his own home' (1999: 41). This can be thought of as interior hospitality. Second, it creates opportunity to be hospitable in responding to the ethical appeal of the Other. A response to this appeal could be to welcome the stranger into our home. Here we speak of exterior hospitality. Thus, the idea that we possess a home (as resource) in the first place and the responsibility to relieve the material misery of the Other together constitute a situation in which the I is taken hostage by the home. I cannot exclude myself from this permanent state of responsibility. The ethical appeal is already there, echoing in my home from the basement to the kitchen and the upstairs bedrooms, summoning my ability to respond from a height. To conclude, note that we must not understand the word 'hostage' with its common negative connotation of being held captive against your will. The ethical appeal of the Other and the sharing of our home with this Other, even if it transforms us from hosts to hostages, again is what makes us human.

We have shown how Levinas' idea of hospitality is radical and invasive of the self; hospitality is ethics. The face-to-face encounter with the Other – who remains a stranger – imposes an ethical appeal on us to take responsibility. What is striking about Levinas' idea of hospitality, as opposed to generally accepted ideas, is the thought that we are always already obliged to invite, care for and share with Others. We need not be asked to provide hospitality, paid for to provide it or otherwise. Levinas presents hospitality as an unavoidable feature of human nature, as its constitution, even. In the following section, we will further analyse a segment in Levinas' discussion of hospitality in the home that specifically relates the idea of hospitality as shown by the feminine Other: the hospitality of femininity. Though there are several passages in *Totalité et Infini* referring to the feminine (e.g. the 'Phenomenology of Eros'), we restrict our reading to one particular passage that deals explicitly with the question of hospitality imposed in this chapter. The passage called 'Habitation and the Feminine' (Levinas, 1969: 154; 'L'Habitation et le Féminin', Levinas, 1961: 164), is rather short, yet it has stirred up quite some discussion, predominantly among feminist philosophers. Contrary to the rhetoric in his other writing, Levinas remains somewhat ambiguous in describing feminine hospitality. Therefore, in response to Derrida's call for a 'long interrogatory analysis of this passage' (1999: 36), in the following section we shall endeavour to re-interpret the meaning of feminine hospitality.

Feminine hospitality

In *Totalité et Infini*, Levinas (1961: 155) discusses hospitality in the setting of the private home. As elaborated above, the home is the place where one lives and dwells in one's orientation towards the Other. Initially, Levinas describes the house as the place where the I can withdraw and be alone. However, in 'Habitation and the Feminine', Levinas (1969: 155) introduces another inhabitant of the home, namely the feminine other, or 'the Woman'[5] (*La Femme*). This passage is particularly interesting to analyse, since it specifically mentions the word 'hospitality', which is rarely the case in *Totalité et Infini* as Levinas tends to use the words 'welcome', 'receiving' and 'openness' when referring to hospitality. The question remaining is where does this Woman 'come from' and what is her position in Levinas' text? To answer these questions, let us examine the beginning of the passage where Levinas (1969: 154) uses the words 'intimacy' and 'familiarity' in relation to the being at home of the I (*le chez-soi*). The word familiarity is confusing here, as Levinas stated earlier that the I is alone in the home that automatically becomes an invitation for the Other, the stranger. Also, the word stranger does not correspond to familiarity. We are not familiar with strangers who Levinas says are 'already language and transcendence' – expressing an ethical demand from a non-empirical position (1969: 155). Hence, there must be another figure present in the home to whom Levinas is referring. He then goes on to explain how 'The intimacy with familiarity already presupposes is an *intimacy with someone*' (L'intimité que déjà la familiarité suppose est une intimité avec quelqu'un) (Levinas, 1969: 155; 1961: 165). Now it becomes more obvious that Levinas is referring to an actual person who is residing in the home. Moreover, this person – the Woman – is the one who brings about intimate familiarity in the home (Levinas, 1969: 154). Might we understand from this passage that the Woman is held responsible for producing the house as a home, as a sort of 'homemaker'? The answer to this question requires further examination.

Hospitality as discrete absence/Hospitalité comme absence discrète

The phrases with which Levinas introduces the Woman have been quoted many times before. However, it is vital to quote them again if we wish to understand the position of the Woman in Levinas' text:

> Et l'Autre dont la présence est discrètement une absence et à partir de laquelle s'accomplit l'accueil hospitalier par excellence qui décrit le champ de l'intimité, est la Femme. La Femme est la condition du recueillement, de l'intériorité de la Maison et de l'habitation.
>
> *(Levinas, 1961: 166)*

> And the other whose presence is discreetly an absence, with which is accomplished the primary hospitable welcome which describes the field of intimacy, is the Woman. The woman is the condition for recollection, the interiority of the Home, and inhabitation.
>
> *(Levinas, 1969: 155)*

We will analyse the words in this sentence that are necessary for understanding Levinas' idea of the Woman. These words are 'discreetly', 'absence', 'the primary hospitable welcome' and 'condition'. First, we have the word 'discreet' that has a double meaning in French (*discret/ discrete*) and English (discreet and discrete). If she is *discrete*, the Woman can be understood as being 'detached from others', whereas a *discreet* Woman would 'judge by means of silence' (Bevis, 2007: 321). It can be argued that Levinas is separating the Woman from the Other. This is because the Other is not discreet when expressing an ethical appeal to the I, breaking through totality, while the Woman signifies her presence more discreetly. She seems to have another 'function'. Second, she is also absent in that her language, as opposed to that of the Other, is silent (Derrida, 1999: 37). The Woman does not 'teach' the I (Derrida, 1999: 37), she is also not placed on a transcendent height similar to a deity (even though Levinas does use capital letters to indicate Woman). Thus, the Woman is a discreet absence, but foremost and third, she also embodies the primary hospitable welcome that Levinas argues is a 'welcome in itself' (1969: 157). Based on our reading of Levinas, we consider that the Woman is a welcome in itself because she facilitates the dwelling and individual recollection – or the interiority – of the I, thereby enabling the face-to-face encounter with the Other. She does this by means of discreet language, and thus different than the language with the Other – to 'open up the dimension of interiority' (Levinas, 1969: 155). Finally, we can argue that the discrete absence of the Woman – her language – is the condition for the I to be hospitable to the Other and, therefore, she represents hospitality. With this understanding of feminine hospitality, it is no surprise that Derrida argues the Woman is the 'anarchic origin of ethics' (1999: 44).

The Woman/La Femme

In the section above, we have seen that Levinas places the Woman in the home where she is a condition for hospitality. When reading 'Habitation and the Feminine', it becomes clear that the Woman 'lacks' many of the qualities possessed by the Other (Derrida, 1999). She comes short of the dimension of height, the ability to teach via language, and she does not express an ethical appeal. Does this mean that the Woman is somehow regarded as lower than the Other? Additionally, from an empirical viewpoint, it is not completely clear whether Levinas, by using the word Woman, is referring to an archetype or to an empirical woman. The confusion caused by this ambiguity has stirred up much debate, particularly among feminist scholars. Obviously, Levinas' postulation of the Woman as a discrete absence, securing intimate familiarity, gives rise to critique and 'grave misunderstanding' (Bevis, 2007: 323) by feminist scholars who, in their efforts to secure equality and universality (Borgerson, 2007), fear that Levinas not only places the Woman in a lower rank but indeed that he silences her altogether, which could even be seen as a totalising act. This concern becomes clearer when we review some of this criticism. Levinas is criticised by Luce Irigaray for leaving the feminine other without a face (such as the summoning face of the Other) and thus that his 'philosophy falls radically short of ethics' (1991: 113). Furthermore, Simone de Beauvoir (1993) accuses Levinas of privileging the masculine over the feminine, and regarding the feminine as a mere object that is needed for the man to become a subject. The woman, then, is a means to the end of man. Another critical issue raised by Borgerson (2007) is that Levinas reinforces rather than reduces the dualism between men and women. We take Villarmea's statement that Levinas does nothing to help women's emancipation (1999: 291) as a summary of the critical issues raised above.

Yet, if we follow Derrida's reading of Levinas, we find that a new meaning of femininity surfaces. On the one hand, as exemplified by critics of Levinas, we can interpret Levinas' writing as, in Derrida's terms, 'classical androcentrism' while, on the other hand, Levinas' idea of the Woman can also be interpreted as a 'feminist manifesto' (1999: 44). Let us then follow the latter as a more optimistic interpretation. The misunderstanding of Levinas' writing lies in the idea that the object of the text is indeed the empirical woman. The following quote by Levinas helps us to resolve this misunderstanding: 'Need one add that there is no question here of defying ridicule by maintaining the empirical truth or countertruth that every home in fact presupposes a woman?' (Faut-il ajouter qu'en aucune façon, il ne s'agit ici de soutenir, en bravant de ridicule, la vérité ou la contre-vérité empirique que toute maison suppose *en fait* une femme?) (1969: 158; 1961: 169). Here we see that Levinas anticipated the question that we, and many scholars with us, have raised. The idea of the feminine other is not to be understood as the empirical other woman. It is rather that Levinas introduces the feminine as a metaphor that indicates an appearance that precedes ethics or hospitality.

Derrida, in his meticulous analysis of this passage, concludes that the 'welcome in itself' is conferred to the 'feminine being', instead of 'empirical women' (1999: 44). Consequently, the feminine appearance serves as a condition for ethics. With this understanding, we begin to see how Levinas builds his argumentation of hospitality based upon several conditions. The feminine other – the Woman – is the first condition. She is another inhabitant of the home, thus part of the *chez soi*, that enables the dwelling of the I. Dwelling, that Levinas says is 'a coming to oneself' (1969: 156), takes place in the intimate familiarity of the home that is created by the feminine other. This dwelling serves as yet another condition for the I to welcome the Other in a face-to-face encounter, to be hospitable. Thus, the Woman is an essential element in Levinas' thinking on hospitality. She is not merely an object needed for the constitution of hospitality; it is rather that she precedes it.

Our analysis of the implication of the feminine other in 'Habitation and the Feminine' as asserted by Levinas follows the positive interpretation of a 'feminist manifesto' (Derrida, 1999). We take it that Levinas seeks to empower, rather than weaken, the position of the empirical woman by according such a fundamental and pre-original condition for hospitality to an appearance that is closely related, yet not similar, to it. This is not to say that the many critical, androcentric issues that have been raised are irrelevant. We simply do not follow that interpretation here as it is besides the point of our review into hospitality as ethics. Moreover, this is not a feminist inquiry. Indeed, we agree that critical inquiry into Levinas' writing can only help to further the scientific debate. We acknowledge the fact that Levinas mentions feminine features such as discretion, absence, intimacy and familiarity that come across as tiresome – according to general and might one say even totalising opinions of women – and old-fashioned female traits. Nevertheless, by interpreting Levinas' texts empirically, as if his philosophy merely discusses everyday situations between women and men, we have become preoccupied by what seems to us to be a 'straw man theory of Levinas' – deliberately presenting a weak argument to then knock it over with a stronger one. As mentioned before in this chapter, an overly empirical analysis of Levinas' philosophy often leads to misunderstanding. The Other is not the empirical other, the man standing across the street or the ice-cream vendor. Nor is the Woman a 'desperate housewife' (lighting the fire, providing cold beer and slippers, rolling her eyes) in our homes. Levinas asserts that these others are transcendent Others, without proper shapes or forms, present before anything else. Thus, Levinas' idea of femininity is inextricably interlinked to hospitality. This discussion functions to broaden the perspective of ethics as hospitality whereby the feminine other represents its fundamental condition.

Conclusions

In this chapter we have addressed the fundamental question of why and how people are hospitable towards each other by analysing the philosophy of Emmanuel Levinas. We have presented his 'philosophy as ethics' and concentrated foremostly on the face-to-face encounter between the I and the Other as radical alterity as described in *Totalité et Infini* (Levinas, 1961). Succinctly put, Levinas presents the ethical appeal of the Other as constitutional for the humanity of the I. His philosophy is often understood as a radical philosophy (Critchley and Bernasconi, 2002: 237). We have attempted to show the radical nature of his thinking by introducing Levinas' view of the host/guest, that is, the I/Other dichotomy and relation. We have interpreted the idea of hospitality as welcoming and openness towards the strange Other, without this welcoming being preceded by a conscious choice. Our analysis reveals that Levinas' idea of hospitality does not presuppose reciprocity, as my responsibility always exceeds that of the other. Furthermore, we have extended the view of hospitality by discussing its conditions with regard to the home, the dwelling and, finally, the fundamental condition for hospitality, enabled by the absent discretion of the Woman.

Levinas' philosophy of hospitality as ethics is fundamental in that it provides ethical groundwork for the human encounter; it is transcendental in that this encounter is experienced from a height, and it is metaphysical in that it provides an ethics of hospitality, *avant la lettre*, as an answer to the question: why be hospitable? This philosophy is difficult to comprehend as it rids you of the certainty of having understood what Levinas is actually saying. As soon as you picture the face-to-face encounter in your head, as though it were a movie scene, Levinas invites you to erase this image by presenting the untouchable and invisible Other almost as a deity. In trying to envision the home as one made of bricks and stone and a bright red front door, representing a threshold between the I and the Other that is used as a metaphor in many discussions of hospitality, Levinas pulls the rug from under your feet and presents it as a state of interiority, of dwelling. When you imagine the feminine other as an empirical woman, by the colour of her hair or the shape of her nose, Levinas' writing quickly convinces you otherwise. Levinas thus provides us with a philosophy that continually disturbs our mode of thought in the same manner that the Other in his philosophy disturbs the I, pulling us away from empirical science into philosophical interpretation. Challenging as it is, Levinas' philosophy invites us to rethink ethics as hospitality where taking responsibility for the Other is an inescapable yet basic feature of humanity. To conclude, we assert that in our shared ambition to further the study of hospitality it is essential to understand Levinas.

Acknowledgement

I would like to thank Dr Ruud Welten for his comments on earlier versions of this chapter.

Notes

1   According to Levinas' style of writing we capitalize the word Other in this chapter.
2   Edmund Husserl was a German philosopher who established the school of phenomenology.
3   Martin Heidegger was a German philosopher, well known for his works on existential phenomenology and philosophical hermeneutics (the interpretation of texts).
4   We use an empirical example here. Yet it must be noted that Levinas' view of hospitality does not depart from empirical encounters.
5   Levinas often uses capital letters to indicate Others who have elevated standpoints, such as the Other and, in this case, the woman.

References

Beauvoir, S. de (1993) *The Second Sex*, New York: Albert A. Knopf.
Bevis, K. (2007) Better than metaphors? Dwelling and the maternal body in Emmanuel Levinas, *Literature & Theology* 21, 3: 317–329.
Borgerson, J. (2007) On the harmony of feminist ethics and business ethics, *Business and Society Review* 112, 4: 477–509.
Critchley, S. and Bernasconi, R. (2002) *The Cambridge Companion to Levinas*, Cambridge: Cambridge University Press.
Derrida, J. (1978) Violence and metaphysics: an essay on the thought of Emmanuel Levinas. In *Writing and Difference*, London: Routledge & Kegan Paul, pp. 79–153.
Derrida, J. (1999) *Adieu to Emmanuel Levinas*, Stanford: Stanford University Press.
Derrida, J. and Dufourmantelle, A. (2000) *Of Hospitality: Anne Dufourmantelle Invites Jacques Derrida to Respond*, trans. R. Bowlby, Stanford: Stanford University Press.
Irigaray, L. (1991) Questions to Emmanuel Levinas. In Critchley, S. and Bernasconi, R. (eds) *Re-reading Levinas*, London: Athlone Press, pp. 109–118.
Irigaray, L. (2008) *Sharing the World*, New York: Continuum.
Katz, C. (2003) *Levinas, Judaism and the Feminine: The Silent Footsteps of Rebecca*, Bloomington: Indiana University Press.

Lashley, C. and Morrison, A. (eds) (2000) *In Search of Hospitality: Theoretical Perspectives and Debates*, Oxford: Butterworth-Heinemann.

Levinas, E. (1961) *Totalité et Infini: Essai sur l'extériorité*, The Hague: Martinus Nijhoff.

Levinas, E. (1969) *Totality and Infinity: An Essay on Exteriority*, trans. A. Lingis, Pittsburgh: Duquesne University Press.

Levinas, E. (1973) *The Theory of Intuition in Husserl's Phenomenology*, trans. A. Orianne, Evanston, IL: Northwestern University Press.

Levinas, E. (1987) *Collected Philosophical Papers*, Dordrecht: Martinus Nijhoff.

Levinas, E. (1990) The Name of a Dog, or Natural Rights. In *Difficult Freedom: Essays on Judaism*, trans. Seán Hand, Baltimore: Johns Hopkins University Press, pp. 151–155.

Levinas, E. (2003) *On Escape/De l'évasion*, trans., B. G. Bergo, Stanford: Stanford University Press.

McNulty, T. (2006) *The Hostess: Hospitality, Femininity, and the Expropriation of Identity*, Minneapolis: University of Minnesota Press.

Poirié, F. (2001) Interview with François Poirié. In Robbins, J. (ed.) *Is it Righteous to be? Interviews with Emmanuel Levinas*, Stanford: Stanford University Press, pp. 23–83.

Still, J. (2010a) Hospitality and sexual difference: remembering Homer with Luce Irigaray. In Tzelepis, E. and Athanasiou, A. (eds) *Rewriting Difference: Luce Irigaray and 'the Greeks'*, Albany: State University of New York Press, pp. 149–163.

Still, J. (2010b) *Derrida and Hospitality: Theory and Practice*, Edinburgh: Edinburgh University Press.

Villarmea, S. (1999) The provocation of Levinas for feminism, *European Journal of Women's Studies* 6: 291–304.

Welten, R. (2011) Emmanuel Levinas. In Ieven, B. and van Rooden, A. (eds) *De nieuwe Franse filosofie*, Amsterdam: Boom, pp. 149–162.

5

The philosophy of hospitableness

Elizabeth Telfer

> **Key themes**
>
> On being hospitable
>
> The good host
>
> Kind of guests
>
> Hospitableness as a moral purpose

When hospitality becomes an art it loses it soul.

(Max Beerbohm)

Hospitableness is the name of the trait possessed by hospitable people. It is clearly something to do with hospitality, so I shall begin with that. We can define hospitality, in its basic meaning, as follows: it is the giving of food, drink and sometimes accommodation to people who are not regular members of a household. Typically, givers, or hosts, provide these things in their own homes, and the point is that they are sharing their own sustenance with their guests. This notion may be stretched in various directions. For example, a firm is said to provide hospitality if it gives food and drink to visitors. But the central idea of the concept remains that of sharing one's own home and provision with others.

In doing so, a host accepts responsibility for the overall welfare of his or her guests. As the eighteenth-century gourmet and food writer Jean-Anthelme Brillat-Savarin says: 'To entertain a guest is to make yourself responsible for his happiness so long as he is beneath your roof' (1970: 14). If this is a host's task, it is concerned with more than food, drink and shelter; it means that a host must try to cheer up a miserable guest, divert a bored one, care for a sick one. Traditionally, the most important responsibility of all was for the guest's safety – hospitality was a kind of sanctuary, and the host was thought of as having undertaken a solemn obligation to make sure no harm came to his guest while under his roof. This idea is enshrined in many legends. In Wagner's opera

DOI: 10.4324/9781315679938-6

The Valkyrie, for example, Hunding the jealous husband cannot kill his enemy Siegmund while Siegmund is his guest – he has to wait until Siegmund leaves and then pursue him.

The nature and importance of hospitality has varied very much in different times and places, but this variation does not mean that there is no trait of hospitableness to discuss. Any trait will manifest itself in ways that differ according to prevailing conditions and conventions. For example, in a society with an institution of duelling, people can be courageous in ways impossible in a society with no such institution. In this discussion of hospitableness, I hope to unearth basic concepts that underlie differences such as these.

Brillat-Savarin's translator uses the phrase 'entertain a guest' – does this mean the same as 'provide hospitality'? There are contexts in which it is natural to speak of hospitality rather than entertaining, and giving a meal to a stranded traveller is hospitality but not entertaining, while giving smart dinner-parties seems like entertaining rather than hospitality. Where there is a difference, then, hospitality is associated with the meeting of need, entertaining with the giving of pleasure. But this difference is only a matter of nuance. Often the two words are equivalent, and I shall use 'entertaining' to mean the same as 'providing hospitality'.

So far I have spoken of hospitality as a private affair, based on a private home and given, not sold, to chosen guests. From this perspective, the idea of commercial hospitality seems like a contradiction in terms: the location of it is not a home, the hospitality is not given, the guests are not chosen. 'The American usage "hospitality industry" suggests an immediate paradox between generosity and the exploitation of the marketplace' (Heal, 1990: 1). But I shall argue that this contrast between true private hospitality and a false commercial imitation is too simplistic. For example, we shall see that the private host can be self-interested, the commercial one motivated by concern for his guests' welfare. We should not forget that an important forerunner of the modern hotel was monastic hospitality, which had features of both private and commercial hospitality; the hospitality was given for disinterested reasons, but the guests were un-chosen and the host was a religious institution, not a private person. In what follows, I shall start from the basis of private hospitality, but try to show as I proceed that commercial hospitality at its best shares many features of private hospitality, and that commercial hosts may possess the virtue of hospitableness.

The good host

How do we get from hospitality to hospitableness? A possible link might be the notion of a good host. But what is a good host? One might say (starting with the private host) that a good host is one who fulfils all the tasks of a host, and give a list of these tasks: he or she refills empty glasses, makes sure that guests are offered second helpings and so on. However, any such list cannot describe the *essence* of a good host, since it applies only to the conventions of a particular time and place. Perhaps we can derive a more general formula from the observation of Brillat-Savarin already quoted. If entertaining guests is making yourself responsible for their happiness so long as they are beneath your roof, a good host is one who does make his guests happy – or as happy as a host's efforts and ministrations can make them – while they are in his care.

Being a good host involves skills as well as effort. Some of these skills, like the tasks of a host, are clichés. For example, a good host can prevent a heated argument from becoming a quarrel. If we want a general formula for these skills, it must be this: what good hosts are good at is making their guests happy. In other words, they know what will please them and are able to bring this about.

Is being a good host equivalent to being hospitable? If we say after a party that the host was very hospitable, we may only mean that he or she was a good host – skilful and attentive. But being a good host is not really enough for being hospitable. For we would say that a host was not genuinely being hospitable if we discovered that he or she had an ulterior motive for being so attentive, one that had nothing to do with any desire to please the guests or any belief in an obligation to do so.

Genuinely hospitable behaviour, then, requires an appropriate motive. However, whether someone should be described as a hospitable *person* depends not only on his or her motive, but also on how often hospitable behaviour occurs. One can say, 'She's very hospitable when she entertains, but she almost never does'; such a person is scarcely a hospitable person. A hospitable person, I suggest, is someone who entertains often, attentively and out of motives appropriate to hospitality. (I shall discuss appropriate motives in the next section.)

Being a good host is not even necessary for being hospitable, since we can say, 'He is a very hospitable person, but not really a good host'. At first this seems paradoxical. One might think that the motives that prompt genuinely hospitable people to entertain would also prompt them to look after their guests properly. But the paradox disappears when we recall that a good host has to be skilful as well as attentive. Hospitable people are attentive, but they are not necessarily skilful and therefore may not be good hosts.

To sum up – and I am still talking about private hosts – a good host is not behaving hospitably unless he or she also has an appropriate motive. A person who regularly behaves hospitably is said to be a hospitable person; he or she will also be a good host, so far as attentiveness is concerned, but may lack the skill that would make him or her a good host without qualification.

How do these ideas apply to the commercial sector? The first question is: what *is* a host in the commercial sector? A firm that runs a chain of hotels might describe itself as in the hospitality business, and perhaps even as being hosts – certainly as 'hosting' events. But the professional people who are most nearly parallel to the private host are those who are directly in charge of the welfare of the guests: namely, the owners or managers of hotels or restaurants. These, after all, are the people who, if they seem to stamp their personality on what goes on, tend to be referred to, affectionately or otherwise, as 'mine host'.

Good commercial hosts of this kind, like their private counterparts, are good at securing their guests' welfare – 'guests' in the commercial context, of course, being people who have paid for their services, not people they have invited. What counts as welfare in this case will largely depend on what the customer is paying for, and may differ in some ways from what makes a private guest happy. For example, in a smart hotel customers may want and reckon they have paid for sophistication and elegance and/or privacy and discretion, whereas in a seaside family hotel guests may want informality and conviviality. Like his private counterpart, the commercial host will need to be attentive and skilful, but the skills required in elegant establishments may be beyond most amateur hosts (not all).

It should be noted that being a good host in the commercial sector is not the same thing as being a good hotelier or restaurateur. Quality as a host concerns only those aspects of the business that directly affect the guests, but the good hotelier or restaurateur has to be good at (or delegate to, and keep control of, those who are good at) all aspects of the business, including handling staff, managing the finances and the business' relationship with the wider community.

Can a commercial host be hospitable? On a superficial view this seems to be ruled out, on the ground that he or she always has an ulterior motive, namely the profit motive. But in the next section I hope to show that such a conclusion is too hasty.

Hospitable motives

I have said that if behaviour is to count as genuinely hospitable, it must have an 'appropriate' motive. What is appropriate? As an approach to this question, I shall begin with a list (which

I do not claim is exhaustive) of possible motives for offering hospitality, beginning as before with private hospitality.

First, there is a group of other-regarding motives. These include the desire to please others, stemming from general friendliness and benevolence or from affection for particular people; concern or compassion, the desire to meet another's need; and allegiance to what one sees as duties of hospitality, such as a general duty to be hospitable, a duty to entertain one's friends or a duty to help those in trouble. The first two types of motive in this group seem to embody the spirit of hospitality; someone who entertains from one of these motives is thought of as hospitable. However, there might be doubt about duty as a motive for genuine hospitableness, because it seems to be at odds with the idea of *warmth* contained in hospitality. If people entertain out of a sense of duty, are they being hospitable or merely dutiful? I suggest that they are being hospitable provided that what I call the spirit of the hospitality is generous. Suppose I am tired of entertaining, but out of a sense of duty invite new neighbours to dinner. If, when they come, I enter into the spirit of the occasion and want to please them, I am surely being hospitable. But if I continue to feel resentful, I am only being dutiful (though if the neighbours cannot tell the difference, perhaps I am still doing the right thing!).

A second group of motives may be called reciprocal motives. Examples of these are a desire to have company or to make friends, and the desire for the pleasures of entertaining – what we may call the wish to entertain as a pastime. I call these 'reciprocal' because they are not so purely 'other-regarding' as the first group, but they need not be purely self-regarding either. Someone who entertains to have company or to make friends is at the same time offering company or friendship to the guests. Similarly, hosts who entertain because they enjoy entertaining will normally bring pleasure to the guests as well as enjoying themselves, and one source of the hosts' pleasure will normally be the pleasure of their guests.

The latter kind of entertaining is also reciprocal in a stronger sense. Not only are hosts both giving and getting pleasure or company, they also entertain in the hope that the hospitality will be returned. This does not destroy the hospitable, other-regarding nature of such entertaining, because both parties have a kind of tacit agreement that they are jointly doing something of mutual benefit. The balance is delicate: if one party does all the entertaining, they are permitted to feel that their hospitality is being abused and they are being imposed upon, but if they are too calculating about an exact return they are thought to be self-interested rather than hospitable.

There can be purely self-regarding versions of these reciprocal motives. For example, there are hosts who entertain for pleasure and are essentially indifferent to the pleasure of the guests, since what they enjoy about entertaining – for example, cooking elaborate dishes – does not depend on whether guests enjoy themselves. Such hosts are not genuinely hospitable – though if their guests do enjoy themselves, they may either not see this or not think it matters. Similarly, a lonely person might invite people for the sake of their company and be indifferent to their welfare. For example, he spends so much time telling them his troubles that they have to go before he gets round to feeding them. Such a person is not hospitable. However, if he invites people purely to relieve his own loneliness but is genuinely solicitous of their welfare once they come, we surely think of him as hospitable.

What matters in assessing motives for hospitality, then, is not only the initial reason for inviting people, but also what we may call the spirit in which they are entertained: what moves the host when the guests are there? A host can redeem a self-regarding motive for an invitation by being concerned for the guests once they arrive.

A third group of motives for hospitality are not reciprocal because they spring from a desire to benefit the host rather than the guests. A common, fairly harmless motive of this kind is vanity: a desire to show off something, such as one's culinary skills or smart house. If hosts are moved only by vanity we think they are not being genuinely hospitable; hospitableness must have some regard for the guests. But in practice, of course, motives tend to be mixed. For example, a host may serve a particular dish out of vanity – that is, because she wants to impress the guests rather than because the she thinks they will like it – but otherwise be mainly influenced by a desire to please guests. We would still count the person as hospitable if the dominant consideration is the guests' pleasure, but the more the host is dominated by the desire to show off her skill or sophistication, the less hospitable she is.

Some self-interested motivations for offering hospitality (seduction, for example, and other forms of manipulating people through the pleasures of hospitality) are less harmless. Paradoxically, they tend to be dependent on actually pleasing the guest; unless the guest is pleased the manipulation does not succeed. But the host's motivation is ultimately self-interested. He is pleasing the guest for his sake, not theirs, and the situation is neither an other-regarding gift nor a reciprocal and equal exchange of benefit. Needless to say, such a person is not genuinely hospitable.

In the private sphere, then, hospitable motives are those in which concern for the guests' pleasure and welfare, for its own sake, is predominant, or where hosts and guests freely exchange hospitality for mutual enjoyment and benefit. And hospitable people, those who possess the trait of hospitableness, are those who often entertain from one or more of these motives, or from mixed motives in which one of these motives is predominant.

How do the motives of commercial hosts compare with these, and do they allow us to speak of them as acting hospitably? The first point to note here is that commercial hosts are not in a position to choose how often to entertain or to choose the guests, so we cannot speak of their motives in making these choices. However, we can ask about their motives in choosing this occupation in the first place, and in performing their various actions concerning the guests. It is natural to assume at first that both sets of motives must be self-interested. People choose to go into 'the hospitality industry' to earn a living, and the individual actions which constitute doing the job are motivated by the desire to keep the job, or to keep the business going if it is their own. But this is surely far too simple. People may take a job rather than be idle because they want a decent living, but they may choose this kind of job for motives resembling those of the hospitable private host: they enjoy making people happy by entertaining them. Again, they may duly perform their tasks because they want to keep their job, but if they try to perform them well, or do more than the job strictly requires, this can be because they genuinely want to please the guests or they have some notion of values of hospitality to which they aspire.

What about the profit motive? It is true that the need to make ends meet financially is a constraint within which commercial hosts work, but maximising profit need not be the main motive of those who sell commercial hospitality. (Of course it may be so in some cases, as may be other self-regarding motives, such as vanity in the case of the flamboyant restaurateur/chef, but one is not tempted to think that such hosts are hospitable.)

I conclude that, if a commercial host looks after his guests well out of a genuine concern for their happiness and charges them reasonably, rather than extortionately for what he does, his activities can be called hospitable. Admittedly, his guests are paying for what they get, but if we recall that there can be reciprocal motives for hospitality we can see this kind of hospitable behaviour as an extension of that idea. This kind of host gives generous, not minimal, service, because he wishes to please the guests. The guests pay, not by hospitality in their turn, but by a sum of money they see as low enough to be a good bargain and a foundation for friendly relations between host and guest. To say that a commercial host cannot be said to behave hospitably simply on the ground that he is paid for his work is like saying that doctors cannot be said to behave compassionately because they are paid for what they do.

The comparison with the doctor suggests another question: do we want to say that the commercial host who behaves hospitably in the context of his job is a hospitable *person*, possessing the trait of hospitableness? I think we would say that a host who was hospitable *only* in that context could not be called a truly hospitable person, any more than the doctor who shows compassion only at work is a truly compassionate person. But both may be fully possessed of the trait in question if they show it in private as well as professional life, and both may have chosen their particular profession precisely because they possess that trait.

Kind of guests

We can classify types of hospitality not only by motivation but also by kinds of guest. As we shall see, there is a correspondence between the two classifications, but it is by no means exact. I shall distinguish three kinds of guest: those in a relationship to the host not simply that of guest to host; those in need; and friends proper. Again, I shall start with non-commercial hospitality.

The relationship between host and guest can vary greatly. It can be either an official relationship which involves a duty of hospitality (for example, that between students in a university hostel and a warden who is expected to entertain them) or an unofficial connection, such as that between colleagues, neighbours, fellow parishioners, parents whose children are friends or, of course, relations – those whom people call their circle. I do not include in the term 'one's circle' people with whom the only relationship is one of friendship.

I shall not discuss official hospitality at length. A person could not have a trait of hospitableness based only on fulfilling official duties of hospitality, since these duties come and go with a particular post, whereas traits are a long-term disposition. However, officials can carry out official duties of hospitality in the same friendly spirit in which they might entertain those in their circle, and when they are thought of as hospitable it is because they do this. I shall therefore assume that hospitable officials can be regarded as extending their circle to include those they have an official duty to entertain, and not discuss them separately.

Possible motives for entertaining one's circle are enormously varied. One such motive – or ingredient in motivation, for motives can be mixed, as we said – is a sense of duty. In more formal societies, people have strict obligations to entertain, according to their status, others in their circle. These obligations are governed by rules, and are no less binding than the warden's obligation in our own society to entertain the students in her hostel. In our own society such rules are largely gone, but we are still apt to feel that entertaining one's circle is a good idea and perhaps a duty. This sense of duty does not only apply when a host has an official duty to entertain particular guests. People feel that they ought to entertain new neighbours or colleagues, or relations whom they have not seen for a while, on the looser ground that they think that they ought to express solidarity, or strengthen the bonds of family and community, and they see entertaining as a particularly good way of doing this.

Another kind of motive for entertaining one's circle, one which is hard to characterise, is something like the wish to be friendly, to offer some degree of personal relationship. Entertaining is a good way to be friendly because it involves the offer of a degree of intimacy, a share in the host's home life. This motive, as well as duty, can lead people to entertain those with whom their connection is essentially official. It is as if they were saying, 'Let's not be merely business partners, we are human beings as well'. Similarly, the warden might entertain students 'to show their humanity'.

Where someone frequently entertains his or her circle from one of the hospitable motives I distinguished earlier, he or she is one sort of hospitable person and has one sort of hospitableness. Entertaining one's circle cannot be sharply distinguished either from entertaining those in need or from entertaining one's friends. But there are some points to make about each of these other categories of guest that justify taking them separately.

A second kind of guest is the person in need of hospitality – either a need for food, drink or accommodation as such, or a psychological need of a kind which can be met particularly well by hospitality, such as loneliness or the need to feel valued as an individual. I shall give the name 'Good-Samaritan hospitality' to the activity of entertaining people because they seem to have such a need. Good-Samaritan hospitality can be shown to anyone, whether connected to the host or not. But the clearest cases of it are those where the guest is a stranger and the only possible reason for offering it is the perception of the guest's need. This kind of hospitality is perhaps the most fundamental kind of all. As I said earlier, in simple communities all travellers are strangers in need of food and shelter simply by virtue of being away from their own home, and there is usually felt to be a corresponding obligation of hospitality. Strangers who need hospitality in a modern urban setting, with its hotels and restaurants, do not need it simply because they are strangers. But there is still room for Good-Samaritan hospitality, as is shown by the true story of a couple who invited a complete stranger to come for Christmas because they had heard her on the radio talking about her dread of a lonely Christmas after a recent bereavement.

There are many kinds of motivation for Good-Samaritan hospitality, including consciously religious motivation, sense of duty and loving-kindness. In a particular case it may often not be clear, either to the hosts or to others, whether they are acting out of duty or loving-kindness. Phrases like 'We felt we had to do something' sound like duty, but may instead express the strength of a compassionate feeling. A person who, from any of these motives, regularly entertains others because they need it is a hospitable person – though the word 'hospitable' is too weak for especially saintly hosts.

The third group of guests are friends, by which I mean friends proper or intimates, rather than simply one's circle. People entertain their friends because liking and affection are inherent in friendship (Telfer, 1971); the liking produces a wish for the friends' company (as distinct from company in general), the affection a desire to please them. Liking and affection of course express themselves in other ways as well, but there is a special link between friendship and hospitality, one which I have already mentioned in connection with entertaining one's circle. Because it involves the host's home, hospitality (provided it is not too formal) is an invitation to intimacy, an offer of a share in the host's private life. When given to friends, who are already intimates, it has the effect of maintaining or reinforcing the intimacy.

However, there is a kind of paradox about entertaining the same people too often. If they reach a stage when they can 'drop in' and 'take pot luck', they scarcely count as guests and become 'almost part of the family'. Is turning friends into family the essence of this kind of hospitality, or does it go beyond hospitality? I think one might choose to say either. The important point is that there are two ways, each of which may have its place, in which I may try to please my guests. I can either make a special fuss of them, or deliberately avoid a special fuss and make them feel at home.

As always, attributing the trait of hospitableness to a person describes them as going beyond the average. Friends are not thought of as hospitable merely because they entertain each other, since this is to be expected. To count as hospitable in this sphere, hosts must be unusually ready to entertain their friends and unusually devoted to pleasing them. The same considerations as before apply about ulterior motives: if someone is always inviting his friends in to dinner simply to show off his cooking, he is not a hospitable person – but the friends may not mind, as long as the cooking is good.

Do we have a duty to entertain our friends? A hospitable friend is not normally acting *out of* a sense of duty. But it does not follow that there is no such duty. On the contrary, there are two reasons why we might assert that there is such a duty.

First, friends sometimes need hospitality. This reason is not based only on need, as with Good-Samaritan hospitality, since I may have a duty to entertain a friend in circumstances where I would not be obliged to do the same for a stranger. But we think of ourselves as having, even as having *undertaken*, special obligations towards our friends which we do not have towards strangers. We may also have a sense of an informal system of protection whereby everyone is looked after in this way by his or her friends.

Second, friends gain positive psychological benefits from hospitality. For example, if we share a meal with friends or have them to stay we include them in an informal ritual of fellowship; we strengthen their self-esteem by our readiness to share our own lives with them, and we rest and refresh them by waiting on them and by providing a pleasant atmosphere. In short, by our hospitality we can further our friends' psychological and physical well-being, and this is something that we have a duty to do. It is not such a pressing duty as meeting their needs, but it may be just as important, because prevention of loneliness, self-hatred and depression is better than cure.

As I have already said, we are not normally acting *out* of duty when entertaining friends. Sometimes, however, affection is not enough to motivate us. For example, we may be too wrapped up in our own troubles to feel affectionate, but we can still 'make an effort', as they say, and entertain friends out of duty. I argued earlier that entertaining can count as hospitable when its motive is duty, provided the spirit in which it is carried out is generous. However, there is a special problem about entertaining *friends* out of duty, in that it might be thought hypocritical: we are acting as though we have the usual motive for hospitality to friends when in fact we do not. Perhaps we can reply that if these are actions that we would not do for just anyone, they are the actions *of a friend*, and so they need not be seen as hypocritical even if they lack the spontaneity which normally goes with friendship.

How does this classification of types of guest apply to commercial hospitality? In the first instance it applies insofar as private hosts use commercial hospitality instead of their own homes to entertain private guests of all three kinds. So far I have written as though private hospitality is always in a private home, but that is not always the case. To the degree that the nature and the benefits of hospitality of all three kinds depend on the host's sharing his home life with his guests, such hybrid hospitality will lack some value. But in many situations it is perfectly appropriate to entertain guests away from home: the eponymous Good Samaritan looked after his beneficiary by taking him to an inn and paying for his accommodation there. One might even raise someone's morale more by entertaining him in a grand restaurant rather than at home, if what he needed was not intimacy but luxury.

In the second place, the relationship between guests paying for themselves and their commercial hosts falls into one of three patterns, which correspond roughly to the kinds of private guest I have distinguished. The first pattern corresponds to the official kind of entertaining inherent in some roles, but here the roles are the ordinary business ones of customer and provider. But, as I have said earlier, it is possible for a commercial host to carry out his or her role more or less hospitably. The second pattern arises in the situation where customers have special needs which they are hoping to meet through commercial hospitality. For example, they are escaping from chaotic troubles for a while in a quiet country hotel or looking for a confidant in the host of a pub. Although hosts in these situations are selling hospitality rather than giving it, they can still show or fail to show concern and compassion in meeting the guests' special needs and can still approach or fail to approach Good-Samaritan hospitality. The third relationship is that between commercial hosts and guests who are also their friends, as when regulars at a pub become friends of the landlord. Here, the problem is that a commercial host who is attentive to his friends in a way at all resembling the private entertainment of friends is likely to neglect his other customers. Perhaps a commercial host cannot be hospitable in a really friend-like, as distinct from friendly, way in his commercial setting.

So far I have written as though commercial hospitality is a kind of pale imitation of private hospitality, private hospitality necessarily being far superior. But this is by no means obvious. Here, for example, is Dr Johnson:

> There is no private house in which people can enjoy themselves so well as at a capital tavern. Let there be ever so great plenty of good things, ever so much grandeur, ever so much elegance, ever so much desire that everybody should be easy, in the nature of things it cannot be: there must always be some degree of care and anxiety. The master of the house is anxious to entertain his guests – the guests are anxious to be agreeable to him; and no man, but a very impudent dog indeed, can as freely command what is in another man's house, as if it were his own. Whereas, at a tavern, there is a general freedom from anxiety. You are sure of a welcome; and the more noise you make, the more trouble you give, the more good things you call for, the welcomer you are. No, Sir, there is nothing which has yet been contrived by man, by which so much happiness is produced as by a good tavern or inn.
>
> *(Boswell, 1934: 451)*

It is easy to feel some sympathy for this view. If we want to defend private hospitality against this attack we might point out that the mention of plenty, grandeur and elegance suggests that the host Johnson is thinking of is trying chiefly to impress the guests rather than please them. As we saw, this kind of hospitality is not really hospitable: genuinely hospitable hosts, aiming to please their guests, will not cause them this kind of anxiety. But Johnson might well reply that those genuinely hospitable but inept hosts who embarrass their guests by being over-solicitous about their welfare may be just as bad.

It might also be said that Johnson leaves out of account the role of what I called Good-Samaritan hospitality: going to the inn and calling for good things is enjoyable, but does not do much to relieve loneliness and friendlessness. However, a good commercial host, as we have seen, will try to befriend lonely customers, and can fulfil this kind of role for misfits who do not have friends. It is true that an important benefit of the hospitality of friends, as we saw, is that it makes its recipient feel wanted as an individual, and that being welcome as a good customer is not the same thing. But, for someone who has no proper friends, a genuinely friendly landlord, one who does not see him *only* as a customer, is a valuable substitute. Indeed, people sometimes feel in need of this kind of company precisely because it does not involve the demands of personal relationships.

This last point links with another criticism that might be made of Johnson, in that he fails to grasp that the pleasure of being privately entertained is not simply that of having agreeable food and drink, which might be better at the pub, but a complex pleasure which depends to a great extent on the fact that one is *in someone's home*. It is true that there can be a certain intensity about private entertaining which stems from this intimacy and heightens the experience. But a defender of Johnson can say that we do not always want this. For a relaxing evening that makes no demands, commercial hospitality, if it is hospitable in its own way, comes into its own.

Hospitableness as a moral virtue

I turn finally to the question of whether hospitableness is a moral virtue. As before, I shall first examine private hospitableness and then consider whether, if this is a virtue, the commercial host can also be said to have this virtue, or a similar one. To do this, I need to start by considering what a moral virtue is in general, and here I shall make use of the account of moral virtues given by Philippa Foot in her paper 'Virtues and Vices' (1978).

Foot claims that moral virtues possess three features. First, moral virtues are qualities that 'a human being needs to have, for his own sake and that of his fellows'. Second, they are qualities of will, rather than of intellect, situation or physique. Third, they are corrections of some common human tendency to either excess or deficiency of motivation. I shall consider the three types of hospitableness (hospitableness towards one's circle, Good-Samaritan hospitableness and hospitableness to friends) in the light of these criteria.

Foot suggests that, whereas courage, temperance and wisdom benefit both their possessor and others, justice and charity chiefly benefit others, sometimes at their possessor's expense: 'communities where justice and charity are lacking are apt to be wretched places to live' (1978: 2–3). Hospitableness resembles charity in that it benefits others rather than oneself. But would we say that a community without hospitableness is a wretched place to live, and that human beings therefore need to have this quality? It would be more plausible to say that the corresponding fault is one that human beings need to avoid. For example, if people are inhospitable to their circle, and do not entertain family, colleagues or new neighbours even when they really ought to do so, society is the poorer – even more so if people fail in Good-Samaritan hospitality and do not look after those in need in an emergency: such as for a motorist whose car is stuck in a snowdrift near one's house.

But there seems to be a gap between avoiding the fault of inhospitableness and being positively hospitable, doing more in this sphere than the average person. The trait of hospitableness seems to be only one way among others of being useful: a person can be just as generous, public-spirited, compassionate or affectionate whether or not he is positively hospitable. And whereas we might think that everyone ought to cultivate the broader qualities of generosity and compassion, it seems to be optional whether they show these qualities through hospitableness or in other ways. One cannot try to be every kind of good person.

I think that this optional feature applies even to hospitableness to friends. Admittedly, I argued earlier that there is a natural connection between friendship and hospitality that makes it likely that a good friend will also be a hospitable one. But, as before, we can distinguish between being inhospitable and not being positively hospitable. Failure to meet a friend's need for hospitality clearly makes someone inhospitable. But the obligation to benefit our friends in the kind of way hospitality benefits them seems to leave some room for choice: perhaps we can give our friends such benefits in other ways instead.

It might be objected at this point that, since anyone without friends is excluded from a network based on friendship, the trait of hospitableness to friends is not of general benefit. Admittedly, it is not of universal benefit, but a society where people are hospitable to their friends is presumably better on balance than one where they are not. However, what is of more general benefit than hospitableness to friends is a less exclusive kind of hospitableness, springing from other broad traits as well as affection, and extended to friends proper, those in one's wider circle and those in need. Hospitableness which is confined to friends is a useful trait, but because of its narrowness a less useful one than the kind of hospitableness – probably what most people mean by the word – which embraces others too.

If hospitableness is an optional way of realising broader virtues, why would a person choose this rather than other ways of doing good? One reason might be enjoyment: a person who enjoys entertaining has a disposition that will make it easy to be genuinely hospitable. Another possible reason is talent. Hospitableness is not fundamentally a matter of talent, as we saw, but people may be moved to seek it by the thought that they possess talents, interests or gifts of temperament that would enable them to be particularly useful in this way. A third reason is the possession of relevant gifts of fortune. For example, the owner of a large or beautiful house, or of a fine orchard or vegetable garden, has something special to offer, and perhaps special obligations too. But probably the most important reason why people choose to pursue the trait of hospitableness is that they are attracted by an *ideal* of hospitality, founded on a sense of the emotional importance of the home and of entertaining, and of the special benefits which sharing them can bring.

Foot's second criterion of a moral virtue is that it is a quality of will; she uses 'will' in a wide sense, to cover what is wanted and cared about as well as what is chosen. The purpose of this criterion is to distinguish moral virtues from physical and intellectual gifts and talents. My account of hospitableness meets this requirement in that it distinguishes hospitableness from being a good host, and depicts hospitableness as depending on devotion and a spirit of generosity rather than on skill.

It might seem that if moral virtues depend on wants and choices rather than talents they can be acquired by anyone who chooses. This is, however, not obvious; it may not always be possible to mould one's wants in the appropriate way. In the case of hospitableness, it might also be claimed that circumstances, rather than temperament, can prevent someone from becoming hospitable, because not everyone has the resources with which to entertain. (I have heard hospitableness called a middle-class virtue, presumably on these grounds.) But it is an oversimplification to say that people may not have the resources to entertain. Not everyone can provide lavish hospitality, or even conventional middle-class dinner parties, and admittedly homeless people cannot share their homes. But even a beggar can be hospitable by sharing food with a newcomer. Hospitality includes the sharing of one's own provisions, and the more needy a person is, the more generous and truly hospitable the sharing is.

The third feature of moral virtues, according to Foot, is that they help people to do what is difficult by correcting some excess or deficiency of motivation to which human beings in general are prone. All the kinds of hospitableness that we are considering pass this test, in that they counteract a common lack of motivation. Many of us do not entertain very much, not because we have chosen to pursue other ways of exercising virtues, but because we are too mean, lacking in compassion or coldhearted.

Conclusions

In this discussion of hospitableness as a virtue I have examined various kinds of private hospitableness – hospitableness to one's circle, Good-Samaritan hospitableness and hospitableness to one's friends – in terms of Foot's three criteria for moral virtues. I suggested that, whereas hospitableness conformed to the criteria of being a quality of will and of counteracting a common deficiency of motivation, it does not seem to fit the idea of being necessary for tolerable human life: what is needed for that is only avoidance of inhospitableness. I suggested that hospitableness can be seen as one way among others in which someone may choose to exercise various different more general virtues: benevolence, public-spiritedness, compassion, affectionateness. We might call it an optional virtue: we all ought to try to be compassionate, benevolent and affectionate, but we do not all need to try to be hospitable.

At this point we might ask whether hospitableness has the degree of unity that calling it an optional virtue suggests. It seems impossible to practise all kinds of hospitality: I may have to choose not only whether to try to be a hospitable person, but also what sort of hospitable person to try to be. Thus, I cannot entertain my friends if my house is always full of alcoholics 'drying out', and I cannot offer my home as a refuge for alcoholics if I am always occupied with my friends. There is even a potential conflict between friends and one's wider circle, in that if one always sees friends in a wider context, this seems to involve a dilution of friendship (but we did observe earlier that the kind of hospitableness which includes both groups is better than the kind which is confined to friends).

Given these difficulties, someone attracted by the ideal of hospitableness has a choice: they may decide to aim at one kind of hospitableness and not the others, or they might strive to be all-round hospitable people, balancing the claims of different kinds of hospitality. Two factors make this balancing easier. First, there can be claims of need among one's own circle of the kind that a Good Samaritan would acknowledge in any case. Second, the friends of hospitable Good Samaritans, if they are true friends, will sympathise with their Good Samaritan activities and perhaps help with them. A potentially alienating activity can thus become part of the friendship.

How does this account of hospitableness as an optional virtue apply to the commercial host? We have seen that he or she can be said to have the trait of hospitableness provided he or she is not hospitable only when on duty. If hospitableness is an aspect of various moral virtues, it can also be so in the commercial host, but there is a sense in which hospitableness is not an optional virtue for commercial hosts. In choosing that kind of job, they have in effect chosen hospitableness as one way in which they will try to show generosity, kindness and so on, since so much of their life is spent in contexts where hospitableness is called for.

References

Boswell, J. (1934) *Life of Johnson*, ed. George Birkbeck Hill, rev. L. F. Powell, vol. II, Oxford: Oxford University Press.

Brillat-Savarin, J. (1970) *La Physiologie du Gout*, trans. Anne Drayton as 'The Philosopher in the Kitchen', Harmondsworth: Penguin Books.

Foot, P. (1978) 'Virtues and vices'. In *Virtues and Vices*, Oxford: Basil Blackwell, pp. 1–18.

Heal, F. (1990) *Hospitality in Early Modern England*, Oxford: Clarendon Press.

Telfer, E. (1971) 'Friendship', *Proceedings of the Aristotelian Society* LXXI: 223–241.

6

The hospitality trades

A social history

John K. Walton

Key themes

Delete and replace with

The nature of hospitality and hospitableness

Hospitality dimensions and morphologies

Macro, meso and micro influences on hospitality

Comparative research and synthetics

> It is a sin against hospitality, to open your doors and darken your countenance.
>
> *(Proverb)*

Commercial hospitality has its roots in supplying to travellers, through the market, the basic human needs of food, drink, shelter and rest. This core of services has been embellished in various ways in different settings, through the provision of medical, sexual and entertainment options for customers. All of these aspects of hospitality go back a long way and have ebbed and flowed over time as well as varying between places. This chapter examines the rise of commercial hospitality in a British setting, while taking due note of the export and import of ideas and practices in response to international flows of travel and investment. It pursues the key themes through from medieval times, while taking note of enduring continuities alongside the changes, and resisting the temptation to view history as progress towards an ideal state which usually approximates disturbingly to current circumstances.

Accommodating travellers

The hospitality trades are as old as commerce, migration and pilgrimage, and there is evidence of specialised premises providing refreshment and accommodation in Roman times, as well as from the eighth century. Such services usually involved the supply of alcohol, although there were

DOI: 10.4324/9781315679938-7

also hostels that simply provided accommodation. Potential threats to public order and temptations to adulteration or false measures led authorities at local and national level to take an interest in regulating the trades even before taxation gave them a more immediate motive for inspection. The City of London had pretensions to licensing alehouses by the late twelfth century, and in 1266 the Assize of Bread and Ale sought to impose fair prices on Ale sellers nationally. A hierarchy of commercial outlets, from inns which provided stabling, through taverns which sold wine as well as ale, to humble cottage alehouses, was emerging in recognition of the differing needs of comfortably-off merchants and other travellers, urban refreshment-seekers and rural communities. Its development accelerated after the Black Death of the fourteenth century boosted living standards for the survivors by creating labour shortages. From the mid-sixteenth century onwards, accelerating population growth (with a hiatus in the later seventeenth century), expanding internal trade, intensifying state interest in the maintenance of order, and the productivity of labour, together with religious concern to regulate the morality of public behaviour, combined to make the hospitality trades increasingly important and visible (Clark, 1983).

The decline of older forms of hospitality to travellers also boosted this trend, while the post-Reformation disappearance of pilgrimage was more than balanced by the rise of secular forms of travel for enjoyment, interest and the pursuit of physical health, although the traffic flows changed, with Bath becoming more attractive than Canterbury. The church-ale, which raised money for parish purposes, also declined at about this time, as did the church as a social centre for parish gatherings. The duty of hospitality that had been assumed by the proprietors of substantial estates and country houses, which had fallen upon the wife as part of an extensive array of social obligations, was falling into decline in the later sixteenth century, while the dissolution of the monasteries removed another source of non-commercial catering for travellers (Heal, 1990). Informal 'open house' cottage hospitality to kin and even passers-by persisted at the wakes and feasts of northern England into the second half of the nineteenth century, but by that time those who commented on it saw it as anachronistic. Corporate bodies began to employ professional caterers, as in the case of Hull Corporation, where Isabel Langcaster, who died in 1637, 'left her late husband's servant all the spits and racks which she kept at the mayor's house' (Laurence, 1994: 150). Courts, guilds and colleges worked in similar ways. But above all, the ever-growing mercantile traffic on the roads and waterways of England, supplemented by nobility and gentry heading for London on legal business or shopping missions or to the spas to take a cure, was supplied with food, shelter and entertainment on a commercial basis. Substantial inns proliferated along all the main roads out of London, supplementing a much smaller number of medieval foundations, while alehouses became ubiquitous and increasingly attracted the suspicious attention of those in authority (Clark, 1983).

We know more about alehouses from the mid-sixteenth century because of the growing concern to license and control them. These were seen as harbouring vagrants and encouraging unruly amusements, gambling, sexual frolics, criminal conspiracies, Sabbath-breaking, distractions from church services and from work, defiance of authority and noisy, violent disorder. In 1495, justices of the peace were empowered to close alehouses and to require keepers to provide sureties for good behaviour. However, more effective legislation came in 1552, when an alehouse licensing system was formally vested in local justices, and holding an alehouse licence became a discretionary privilege rather than a legal right. Further legislation in 1563 and 1570 limited the number of taverns to be permitted in specific towns, and in the early seventeenth century successive attempts were made to tighten up the control of alehouses and of 'tippling' or sustained drinking for more than an hour at a time. A census of the drink trade in England and Wales in 1577 (with taxation in mind) found up to 24,000 establishments, as well as over 2,000 inns and 400 taverns. This was a ratio of perhaps one licensed premises to every 30 households, a good indication of the extent to which commercial hospitality had penetrated economic arrangements and everyday life by the middle of Elizabeth I's reign (Monckton, 1969; Clark, 1983: 41–43). At the local level, provision was sometimes even more lavish towards the mid-seventeenth century: twenty-five Essex townships had 107 known alehouses (52 unlicensed) in 1644, while in Lancashire thirty townships had 226 alehouses, as many as 143 being unlicensed. This was a ratio of one alehouse for every twenty households in the Essex villages, and one for every twelve in Lancashire, and it marked the sudden relaxation, in the Civil War period, of a long campaign to restrict the numbers of these meeting-places, which were often very small and informal (Wrightson, 1982: 168).

Alehouses were too important to be suppressed wholesale, and in the absence of effective local enforcement systems any attempt to do so would have been defied. Their roles in victualling, providing cooking facilities (customers often brought their own food), supplying a convivial pipe of tobacco from the early seventeenth century, offering lodgings to legitimate travellers and providing work for the old, the infirm and single women, thereby relieving potential distress without recourse to charity or the emergent parish poor-rate local taxation system, gave them powerful rhetorical and practical defences against their detractors. The focus of the campaigns of the early seventeenth century, backed up by the central government's Books of Orders which tried to suppress superfluous alehouses to preserve the barley supply in the frequent times of dearth which haunted these economically transitional years, was directed against the humbler alehouses where the village poor gathered, and which were thought capable of drawing others into debauchery and poverty.

Attacks came from the more literate and 'godly' of the villagers, an elite which was distancing itself from the more relaxed common culture of 'good neighbourliness', which tolerated occasional drunken silliness. It was often associated with Puritanism, a broadly defined tendency within the Church of England that combined introspective conscience-searching with the fear that the sins of others would provoke divine displeasure against the wider community, and which was in the ascendancy in many places, culminating in the Interregnum between 1649 and 1660 after the execution of Charles I. In the county town of Dorchester, for example, such groups saw 'a large proportion' of the population as 'in great need of reformation and discipline', especially the young, who might slip free from household discipline and follow dissipated paths, drinking, singing, engaging in idle chatter, being drawn into promiscuous sex which might beget bastards to be a charge on the community, disrupting church services when they went at all and neglecting their work (Underdown, 1992: 79–84). Drink damaged families and plunged them into deeper poverty. But efforts to suppress it proved unsustainable, driving it underground rather than preventing it altogether, and dividing communities, bringing gossip and ridicule to the doors of the reformers. Keith Wrightson has argued that '[a]t the level of the local community, the struggle over the alehouses was one of the most significant social dramas of the age' (1982: 167), and in the long run it was the bottom level of the emergent hospitality industry, among whom perhaps a quarter of the traders were women, which won out against its enemies.

Higher up the scale of provision, inns were growing impressively in scale and numbers during the century after the restoration of the monarchy in 1660. This was part of a wider pattern, as the middle ranks of commerce and the professions proliferated and prospered, and what Peter Borsay (1989) has called an 'urban renaissance' brought classical architecture (or at least frontages), luxury trades, public walks, dancing and display to provincial towns, which were becoming centres of polite society. The rise of the 'coaching inn' was part of this process. Borsay describes the 'great inns' of the 'elite of the innkeeping fraternity' as 'among the most spectacular examples of tradesmen's wealth'. A small town like Penrith, on the main road to Carlisle and Scotland, might have three or four such buildings, 'about three or four storeys high and of hewn stone', by 1731. At about the same time, the George at Northampton 'looks more like a palace than an inn', and the Bull at Stamford, on the Great North Road, 'would pass in Italy for a palace'. Borsay lists several other prime examples as 'the true palazzi of the English Augustan town' (1989: 210–211). Such inns had extensive stabling as well as accommodation for guests and their servants, and dining facilities on the grand scale. Henry Fletcher of the Royal Oak in Kendal, a smallish north-western market town, had a Red Room, a Green Room, a 'coffy house', a 'billyard room' and three parlours in 1743, when metropolitan houses had been following this path for a generation. As early as 1686 this northern market and manufacturing town was capable of supplying 279 guest-beds and 439 places for horses, although some of these would have been provided by small tavern and alehouse keepers who combined other trades with the sale of liquor and the furnishing of modest accommodation for travelling traders and country people (Walton, 1983).

Tiny market towns of 1,000 people or so, such as Kirkby Lonsdale and Appleby, could find beds and stabling for well over a hundred visitors on this basis (Marshall, 1975: 4–8). Inns also developed a trading role, as merchants met in private rooms and took the larger transactions away from the public eye of the market place, and the innkeepers acquired prosperity and prestige among the leading citizens of their towns. As the Royal Oak evidence hints in its relatively small way, the larger inns were offering sophisticated entertainments to their guests. As Borsay says, their association with the affluent made it 'natural that they should adapt to service the growth in polite leisure', providing theatres, music clubs, book clubs, assemblies for dancing and even (in the case of the Angel at Yeovil) a museum of antiquarian curiosities. The spa resorts, especially Bath, began to offer up-market lodging-houses as well as inns to accommodate their affluent visitors, and the development of a seasonal accommodation industry using purpose-built as well as adapted premises began at the seaside, with Brighton, Margate and Scarborough leading the way. The growth of urbane polite society, with its demand for news, political information and conversation, fuelled the parallel growth of the up-market coffee-house, which spread across the provinces from origins in Oxford, London and Bristol in the mid-seventeenth century (Borsay, 1989: 144–146).

By the mid-eighteenth century, the great inns, which provided stabling, horse and carriage hire and relatively sophisticated catering, were a cut above the generality of what had come to be called 'public houses', which had become common terminology for licensed premises. The term 'alehouse' was still used legally for all premises licensed by the justices of the peace to sell alcoholic drinks, but 'in everyday speech … it was now reserved for the smallest local drinking places, and often used more or less pejoratively alongside "pot-house"' (Jennings, 1995: 19). There were also unlicensed drinking-dens, known in Bradford as 'whisht' or hush-shops because their existence, although often tacitly tolerated by the authorities, was supposed to remain a secret. As the untrammelled urban growth of the late eighteenth and early nineteenth century took hold, such places began to revive and increase in numbers, although they were also on the increase in the wilder areas of poverty-stricken rural counties like Sussex, where (it was alleged) poachers and thieves shared out their proceeds.

Regulating excess

These developments on the lower rungs of the hospitality ladder worried the authorities just as the proliferation of alehouses had in an earlier period of population growth and economic turbulence. The century after 1660 had seen alehouses become more respectable, as the smaller and less salubrious ones were gradually squeezed out, the alehouse was no longer needed as an informal instrument of poor relief, and the larger places benefited from the increased purchasing power of prosperous times to approach the status of the inns. But gin-shops proliferated, especially in London, to alarm moralists and reformers from the early eighteenth century, and in the later eighteenth century unlicensed alehouses also revived, although the number of inns and public houses failed to expand in step with population, and in many counties a renewed round of campaigns by local authorities from the 1780s saw the suppression of many of the smaller local pubs in back-streets and isolated places. Magistrates feared sedition as well as crime and immorality. Strangers from a higher class would be easily recognised in this setting, and radical politics, illegal trade union activity and machine-breaking schemes could be pursued undisturbed when these became issues from the turn of the eighteenth and nineteenth centuries. But when legislation came, it favoured the developing fashion for free trade in all things rather than responding to authoritarian fears of subversion. The 'Beerhouse Act' of 1830 sought to buy support for a beleaguered Tory government by making the poor man's beer (this was a gendered rhetoric) cheaper and more accessible, boosting beer consumption at the expense of more damaging spirit-drinking, and benefiting growers of barley and hops. It allowed any householder to retail beer on payment of a two-guinea (£2.10) excise licence, subject to (among other things) 10 p.m. closing and maintaining order. This liberated beer selling from the control of the magistrates, and made it easier for political radicals to meet without fear of direct consequences. Four years later the cost of an on-licence was increased to three guineas (£3.15), but closing time was extended to 11 p.m., and not until 1869 did the magistrates recover their licensing powers. This was an important freeing-up and expansion of the lowest levels of the legitimate hospitality trades (Clark, 1983, chs 8, 11, 14; Jennings, 1995: 79–81).

Beer-house numbers grew very rapidly, offering a competitive challenge to established public houses. Within six months, over 24,000 excise licences had been issued, although the take-up rate varied widely, with ports like Liverpool well to the fore, and towns where pubs had been in short supply soon saw beer-houses in the majority of their licensed houses. Proprietors were drawn mainly from the ranks of skilled labour, and amenities varied widely. Many premises were small cottages knocked together, but others were purpose-built. Bradford's Red Lion was unusually well-appointed, with 'yew tree and Windsor chairs, long-seating, ale tables and bar fittings … plus bagatelle board and cottage pianoforte and various engravings, including Christ blessing little children and The Stolen Kiss'. Games played included dominoes, draughts, skittles, cards, shove-halfpenny and 'puff and dart', most of which were already available in the eighteenth century, although landlords had to be careful not to be caught permitting gambling. Basic food (bread and cheese or bacon and eggs) and lodging were often provided, and a significant minority of beer-houses were haunts of prostitutes, some of whom (as in Blackburn, where this was said to be the norm) were ostensibly employed as servants. Beer-houses might also play host to popular blood sports (pugilism, dog- and cock-fighting, rat-, badger- and fox-baiting) or offer singing-rooms, poses plastiques (strip-shows thinly disguised) or exhibitions, as in the Liverpool show which put customers under the influence of laughing-gas and invited the audience to laugh at the obscenities they uttered. They provided a safe haven for Chartist meetings and an accessible venue for friendly societies, which offered cheap mutual insurance. They became, in short, central to the social life of many working people, women as well as men, especially in the teeming early and mid-Victorian industrial towns (Jennings, 1995).

The lowest class of beer-houses, run by labourers in cottage parlours, overlapped with the cheap brothels and common lodging-houses that had long been a feature of every urban centre from the market town upwards, and often of those 'open villages' without a resident land-lord which housed rural labour forces for a wide area. Sleaford, a Lincolnshire market town with about 4,000 inhabitants at mid-century, had two cottage brothels in Back Lane behind the church, which were identifiable as such in the 1851 census, and other 'disorderly houses' elsewhere. Two of the prostitutes were witty enough to give 'free trader' as an occupation, responding ironically to the contemporary exaltation of untrammelled commerce in (almost) everything (Ellis, 1981: 17–18). Nearby Horncastle, of similar size but with an important river navigation running through it, had perhaps fifteen brothels in the 1830s and a maximum of twenty in the next decade, before a police campaign reduced their numbers; such establishments were not the sole prerogative of London or Liverpool. They were squalid, noisy and violent, attracting frequent intervention from police and neighbours, and we hear less of the quieter, more up-market 'accommodation houses' which serviced middle-class men (Davey, 1983: 32). The common lodging-house, offering a share of fire and mattress for a rock-bottom price, seems to have had its origins in the early eighteenth century, but it became the focus of a full-scale early Victorian moral panic, and remained a magnet for social investigators (whether reformers, sensation-seeking journalists or, in effect, well-connected tourists shown the sights by police patrols, like the French academic Hippolyte Taine in Manchester) throughout the nineteenth century and beyond. It was recognised to be the last resort of the impoverished before the ultimate humiliation of the workhouse, and part of its frisson was the idea that the honest and unfortunate poor would rub shoulders very closely, in the fetid and crowded sleeping accommodation, with thieves and prostitutes. But there was a parallel discourse, harking back to the 'low' sixteenth-century alehouse, which highlighted the irresponsible fun of being a member of the 'underworld', caring nothing for morals, cleanliness or appearances, and enjoying huge fry-ups in front of the communal fire while sharing stories of past escapes and depredations. Sanitary and police regulations at mid-century made life more difficult for lodging-house proprietors, but they met such an obvious need that there could be no question of suppressing them (Thompson and Yeo, 1971; Davey, 1983).

The established public houses had to respond to the new competition from the beer-houses, over and above their existing problems with specialist outlets for the sale of spirits (the famous 'gin palaces' which spread from London in the 1820s), with the 'chop houses' and other primitive restaurants (heirs to the earlier cookshops) which competed for another aspect of their trade, and with coffee stalls which began to attract working-class custom from the 1820s and 1830s. The pubs reacted partly by changing appearance and ground plan, looking less like ordinary houses displaying signs, and introducing plate glass, gas lighting (sometimes with spectacular effects) and more opulent internal decor (with extensive use of mirrors), as well as (by the 1850s and 1860s) adopting distinctive architectural flourishes on their corner sites, with turrets, arches and eclectic embellishments. Luxurious-looking surroundings became available to the poor for the price of a drink. Bars were opened out to accommodate greater crowds, and barmaid service from behind a counter, with overtones of glamour, replaced scurrying potboys and further enhanced efficiency, while the cooking of working men's food was rapidly abandoned. These changes were pioneered in London, but soon spread to the provinces (Girouard, 1984).

Additional competition for existing businesses came from the magistrates' increased willingness to license new pubs, which were at least under their control, to reduce the scope for beer-houses to spread, but much of this development took place in the spreading suburbs of the larger towns (Girouard, 1984). The 1830s and 1840s also saw the beginning of important changes in all of the 'three major roles' played by the pub in nineteenth-century Britain: transport centre, recreation centre and meeting place. The railways brought the demise of the coaching inn, which survived only at the limits of the system by 1860 (in the Lake District, for example, where tourists wanted to explore beyond railheads). Faster travel meant less demand for refreshments en route, although the great refreshment rooms at Rugby or Swindon struggled to serve trainloads of people at ten-minute refreshment stops before the advent of on-train catering on long-distance services, and railway food acquired its enduringly awful image, helped by Dickens's description of Mugby Junction. Quicker journeys also entailed fewer overnight stays, and these were increasingly channelled into a distinctive new building type, the railway hotel, which sprang up at termini and at tourist destinations from the 1840s onwards, reaching its apotheosis in the Gormenghast spires of the Midland Railway's St Pancras. Commercial travellers became railborne, drovers and their charges left the green-roads, and wayside inns lost their passing trade. Canal side pubs, which had catered for bargees, also suffered. On the other hand, pubs flourished around railway terminals and along the new routes for horse omnibuses and later trams which radiated from city centres, although as fewer (and poorer) people walked to work along these routes, the trade of houses between stops might be damaged.

The pub as a recreation centre flourished, as enterprising speculators tapped into rising demand and sought to lure customers away from cheaper back-street rivals. Hence the gaudiness, but some of the larger pubs also developed entertainments on the grand scale. The Eagle off London's City Road, rebuilt in 1839–40, 'set a new standard of splendour for public houses which was not to be equalled for many years', with its pleasure gardens (and garden orchestra), statues, fountains, cosmoramas, rope-dancers, ballet and much more. Suburban pubs offered huge dancing platforms and leafy promenading areas for families. The Music Hall emerged from such ventures, which were pioneered in Lancashire as well as London. For example, Bolton's Star offered assorted musical and comic turns and a museum by mid-century (Girouard, 1984: 35). At the more obviously disreputable end of the scale, the pub as masculine republic might be associated with pugilism or popular blood sports, or salacious mock trials full of double (and indeed single) entendres, but from the 1870s it also acted as one of the midwives of football as spectator sport, which proved altogether more respectable. The pub as meeting-place, meanwhile, continued to flourish, meeting the needs of a popular associational culture (friendly societies, political groups, trade unions, debating societies, botanists, enthusiasts for birds and animals) that usually had no alternative to the landlord's large room and payment of a 'wet rent' through consumption of his wares. The pub helped migrants to build a social life in strange surroundings and put workers in touch with employment opportunities. It was, however, in most cases a rival rather than a complement to the family, in terms of expenditure as well as sociability, and, as such, it remained a target for reformers' wrath.

The heyday of the urban pub came between the 1850s and the 1890s, when a range of speculators, from Birmingham jewellery manufacturers to London clergymen, sought to take advantage of increasing working-class spending power, especially in city centre locations. Specialised pub architects used pictorial effects in glass and tiling, and extravaganzas in carved wood and patent ceiling surfaces to create enticing environments. The pub resisted the threats and competition of the temperance movement (whose coffee palaces were financial failures, but helped to stimulate more commercial and less 'improving' ventures like Lockhart's Cocoa Rooms), and survived the casualties inflicted by magistrates and builders on popular suburban pleasure venues, and increasingly it diversified its offerings into snacks, soft drinks, Bovril and coffee, with ginger beer on draught. A frenetic burst of speculative building at the end of the century was followed by a rush of bankruptcies, and the peak of per capita alcohol consumption had already been scaled in the mid-1870s. By the Edwardian years the long decline of the pub had begun (Girouard, 1984; Crawford et al., 1986).

In some ways it had been foreshadowed by the withdrawal of the solid middle classes in the early Victorian years. The pubs of the second half of the century multiplied status gradations through small bars which segregated labour aristocrats or tradesmen from their poorer neighbours, and provided protected spaces for women to drink, making it easier for working-class women to visit the pub without necessarily compromising their respectability by late Victorian times. But they no longer accommodated the professionals or substantial employers who had still frequented the higher-class ones (though not the beer-houses or dram-shops) into the 1840s and perhaps the 1850s. At the top end of the scale, the rise of the gentleman's club creamed off the most affluent. These establishments proliferated in and around London's Pall Mall from the 1810s and 1820s onwards, pioneering new styles in classical architecture and making statements about power and wealth through their self-confident bulk, while boasting the most fashionable French chefs. They catered for men of particular tastes and opinions: the Reform for Whigs, the Carlton for Tories, the Athenaeum for artists and literary men, the Travellers', the United Service, the Oxford and Cambridge, and (for gamblers) Crockford's, among many others. They offered a masculine environment, with membership controlled by vote as well as subscription level, and their imposing libraries, smoking rooms, morning rooms and dining accommodation offered privileged enclaves for like-minded people, enabling aristocrats and affluent professional men to escape from their families as well as their social inferiors. Gentlemen could dine and stay overnight at their clubs, and unless they had raffish tastes and sought plebeian company, usually in a 'sporting' and betting context, there was no need to go further. The big provincial centres followed suit, although some early examples, like the autocratically-run John Shaw's punch club for Manchester merchants, were rather rough-and-ready, but, in its highest and most intimidating form, this was a metropolitan phenomenon (Stancliffe, 1938).

Eating and travelling as leisure activities

The Victorian years also saw the rise of the hotel, the restaurant and the sophisticated large-scale caterer. Inns and the larger public houses traded up to assume the more prestigious title 'hotel', which connoted a high standard of accommodation and catering and suggested a select clientele. Originally, hotels lacked public dining rooms, the food being served to guests privately, to order, in their suites, and from the 1820s some of London's best chefs were working on this principle (Mennell, 1985: 155). This definition was soon outmoded, however, and purpose-built premises in central London began by catering for those affluent families who no longer kept up a London house, and extended their range to London tourists, especially Americans, while the later nineteenth century saw a broader middle-class market catered for in extensive multi-storeyed buildings with smaller rooms.

The mid-Victorian years were the golden age not only of the railway hotels, but also of the grand hotel, at the seaside or in the Highlands, promoted speculatively by a limited company, as at Scarborough. Here, Cuthbert Brodrick's 'wondrous' eleven-storey Grand, completed in 1867, offered

> the advantages of a Boarding House with the luxury of complete appointments, good cuisine, prompt attendance, and strict selectness of a first-class Family Hotel. There is no good reason why Englishmen patriotic enough to patronise English watering-places should be deprived of the advantages enjoyed by those who go abroad.

This advertising leaflet makes clear that the hotel concept was a continental import, desirable but also exotic, which needed to be domesticated. Characteristically, the manager was M. Fricour, from the Hotel Mirabeau in Paris. Technology was called in to reassure (central heating, electric bells, steam kitchen lifts, 'hydraulic ascending room'), and when the table d'hôte was opened out to non-residents they were carefully vetted and their local address was checked. This was an up-market provincial example of a widespread set of developments, with troops of servants in hierarchical array, including imported chefs to provide sophisticated cuisine, some of whom went on to open pioneering restaurants wherever the market looked promising. The most opulent hotels took care of the reputation of their own restaurants. When the Savoy Hotel opened in the Strand, close to London's clubland, in 1890, the chef was the legendary Georges Auguste Escoffier (Mennell, 1985: 158). This was one example among many of the practice and person-nel of leading continental hotels being brought to England. When affluent families required large-scale catering for special occasions closer to home, meanwhile, specialist firms like Spiers and Pond were emerging to provide it.

Comfortably-off bourgeois society, like its aristocratic 'betters', increasingly preferred to eat at home, when the husband was not at his club, and the rituals of exchanging hospitality became increasingly demanding. Mrs Beeton's has become the classic advice manual, first published in 1861, but it was one of many competitors in a brisk Victorian market. Good servants, especially cooks, were at a premium, but domestic entertaining could also be sustained by hiring a chef, waiters and even place settings and table decorations, if the regular establishment of domestic servants and the supply of plate and cutlery were insufficiently impressive. This preference for the private and domestic over the public and unpredictable, except on great occasions, was a characteristic of the Victorian middle-class family which inhibited the growth of a restaurant and café culture on the European model. On the other hand, it boosted the grocer's licence for selling wine to be consumed at home, a Gladstonian innovation which was taken up most readily on the fringes of middle-class residential areas with few pubs, and which helped the emergence of a pattern whereby by the 1860s, the respectable classes were drinking at home, or not drinking at all.

As ladies began to sally forth to the new shopping streets and department stores that opened in London's West End and in favoured streets of provincial towns from the 1850s and 1860s onwards, however, some kind of respectable catering provision for them became necessary. So female safe havens developed, enabling ladies to refresh themselves without the embarrassment of being taken for prostitutes or pursued by strangers, in the form of department store cafés, confectioners' and tea rooms like those of Miss Cranston in Glasgow. Chains of refreshment houses also developed, aiming at a 'respectable' lower middle-class clientele of both sexes, as the 'white-blouse revolution' brought women into a widening range of city-centre employments. The Lyons corner houses, founded in 1894, quickly became famous as the reliable, cheap chain that most effectively met this need (Girouard, 1984: 206).

Other kinds of popular catering outlet, at a straightforwardly working-class level, were beginning to spread from the later nineteenth century, often complementing the pub rather than offering alternatives to it. The fish and chip shop, originating around 1870 (although fried fish and chipped or baked potatoes had been hawked around urban streets since at least the 1840s), spread rapidly through working-class areas, first as an after-the-pub snack, then as a provider of mid-day meals for factory workers and labour-saving fill-ups for families, with around 25,000 outlets in 1913 and an inter-war peak of nearer 35,000. These were almost all small-scale single-family enterprises, with only a few small chains (despite contemporary fears) and a handful of larger and more up-market restaurants, one of which (Harry Ramsden's of White Cross, Guiseley, in industrial Yorkshire, which opened in 1931) formed the basis for eventual multiplication of branches and stock market flotation in the 1990s. The problem was always the replication of standards and quality control (Mosey and Ramsden, 1989; Berry, 1991; Walton, 1992). Tripe and other offals also formed the basis of cheap restaurants, with a longer pedigree. Lancashire was a particular stronghold, and there were attempts to go up-market in the early twentieth century, as at Vose and Son's Tripe de Luxe Restaurant and Tea Room, which opened in Wigan in 1917 and featured panelled walls, furniture 'of the Early English style', and a Ladies' Orchestra (Houlihan, 1988: 6). Soon afterwards this trend was pursued by combines with chains of restaurants, most famously Parry Scragg and United Cattle Products, which survived into the 1970s. But most corner-shop tripe purveyors and fish fryers were drawn from the skilled working class, and in industrial and seaside Scotland and Wales, especially, the trade became a haven for Italian immigrants from the turn of the century, in tandem with ice cream and alongside the distinctive cafés which became popular meeting-places, generating some controversy in early twentieth-century Scotland because they brought young people of both sexes into contact in a relaxed setting, as well as providing gaming machines.

London's Italian community, centred on Soho, also joined French and other migrant groups to provide distinctive restaurants that were at the core of metropolitan bohemian society, but also set fashions that spread elsewhere (Sponza, 1988: 94–115; Colpi, 1991). Italians were also quick to move into the craze for milk-bars which provided another alternative to the pub in the 1930s. At an opposite extreme of cosy Englishness was the spread of the tea-room, often trying to re-create an imagined rustic cottage past, which became a feature of suburbs and market towns, and especially of the country roadsides and picturesque villages which became tourist and excursionist destinations for the cars and charabancs of the inter-war years. As we saw above, similar idioms could be introduced into tripe restaurants, and a thorough study of the tea-room vogue would be needed to tease out the varieties of context and ambience. J. B. Priestley, making his 'English journey' in 1933, met an ineffectual dabbler in various businesses who described his own venture into this field:'I tried it once. The wife was keen. In Kent. Good position, too, on a main road. We'd everything very nice … We called it the Chaucer Pilgrims – you know, Chaucer. Old style – Tudor, you know – black beams and everything. Couldn't make it pay … If you ask me what let us down, I'd say the slump in America. It was on the road to Canterbury – you see, Chaucer Pilgrims – but we weren't getting the American tourists. I wouldn't touch a tea room again, not if you gave me one.'

(1934: 6)

These small catering businesses had a high mortality rate, and survival usually required a second source of income in the family. Few fortunes were made: it was more a matter of hanging on and scraping a living. The tea-room as business venture attracted speculators of a more middle-class background than the fish and chip trade, with a very different ruling aesthetic and set of social pretensions (except where fish and chips acquired the pretensions of a restaurant). The pub, with its extensive hierarchy from back street to ostentatious drinking-palace, drew in a wider cross-section, although the rapid spread of the tied house system and the decline of the home-brew pub in the late nineteenth century altered the balance between independent businesses, tenants and managers. The new inter-war roadhouses on bypasses and arterial roads, built in 'Brewer's Tudor' and catering for the motor trade, added a new dimension, catering for modern needs in mock-medieval surroundings (Girouard, 1984; Crawford *et al.*, 1986).

The other sector of the hospitality trades that showed rapid expansion from mid-Victorian times to the 1930s was tourism, especially in the seaside resort, a distinctive kind of town prominent among the fastest-growing urban centres of the period. As the working-class seaside holiday originated in late Victorian Lancashire, with Blackpool the main beneficiary, and then developed a generation later in the West Riding and West Midland industrial districts, and as London's armies of white-collar workers and small traders found their way to the coast, so a new tier of cheap accommodation developed to service their needs during a short summer season. The established hotel and boarding-house trade, which catered especially for solid middle-class families for up to a month at a time, was augmented by cottage and terraced accommodation for working-class visitors who might stay for a few days or a week. Where 'respectable' landladies with capital and servants, usually spinsters or widows with annuities or investments to eke out, offered full board and sitting-rooms, their new counterparts were often working class, augmenting a family income, working round the clock for the summer and pressing their children into service too, and offering crowded, minimum accommodation with services (and therefore costs) cut to the bone for visitors who could only just afford the trip. Whether the visitors were Lancashire cotton workers, Yorkshire miners or, in the south-west, Swindon railway workers with a week's holiday and a privilege rail ticket, this added a new down-market dimension to the hospitality trades, and, where demand was high, as at Blackpool, new purpose-built 'company-houses', ordinary terraces with extra bedrooms, mushroomed around the railway stations. Thus was a precarious but lively new hospitality industry born, with its own folklore surrounding the rules by which landladies protected themselves and the extra charges they tried to levy for hot water or use of cruet (Walton, 1978, 1983, 1994).

This was not the only model for popular holidaymaking in the heyday of the British seaside. There were various forms of self-catering, including the 'bungalow towns' of converted tram-cars and railway carriages which colonised makeshift landscapes from the turn of the century, and the rise of the caravan from the inter-war years. Then there was the holiday camp, which also had turn-of-the-century origins but was being organised on a commercial basis, and also by trade unions, local authorities and the Co-operative movement, to supply cheap chalet accommodation and collective enjoyment to a clientele that was dominated, in the first instance, by white-collar workers. The almost-eponymous Billy Butlins arrived on the scene in 1936, and the camps enjoyed a post-war heyday in which some commentators were impressed by their vigour and cheerfulness, others horrified by what looked like exploitative regimentation (Hardy and Ward, 1984; Ward and Hardy, 1986). At their peak, however, they only accounted for around 5 per cent of domestic holiday 'bednights', compared with (in 1967) nearly 28 per cent spent 'staying with friends', a telling reminder of the continuing, unobtrusive importance of uncommercial hospitality in people's daily lives (Bramley, n.d.: Table 5).

Another 1967 statistic found that just over 15 per cent of 'bednights' were spent in licensed hotels, and the holiday hotel trade kept a resilient, conservative middle-class market, which resisted the swelling siren songs of 'abroad'. There had been little inter-war investment in seaside hotels, and hardly any in the post-war generation, but the desiderata of that generation which was moving into middle age in the post-war years were probably summed up by the popular travel writer S. P. B. Mais, writing about the Cawdor Hotel at Tenby in 1949. It was 'the ideal hotel', unpretentious, courteous, quietly efficient, with plenty of space at mealtimes, generous and 'exquisitely cooked' portions:

> The virtues of the Cawdor are legion. The stairs do not creak; the water is always hot; the lavatories are reading-rooms in little. There are no draughts; there are verandas on two floors; the doors stay shut; the windows open easily; there is a full-sized billiard room; there is a piano in the lounge; tea is not a pernickety drawing-room affair, but a solid sit-down business in the dining-room; the house is not old enough to be ghost or spider-ridden, not modern enough for chromium plate or fumed oak. Its smell is the smell of the Exmoor farmhouse in which I spent my heavenly childhood.
>
> *(Mais, 1949: 11–12)*

This was an ideal whose time would soon pass, and some of these virtues would not have looked like good business to a keen proprietor. Chloe Stallibrass and Julian Demetriadi have chronicled the decline of the seaside hotel during the third quarter of the twentieth century, although the census statistics are particularly fallible at the lower end of the market, where there were also many conversions from boarding houses to holiday flats and apartments. The problems posed by government policies, especially Selective Employment Tax, VAT and necessary but costly fire precautions in the early 1970s, played their part, but the wider context must also be considered, especially the rise of the Mediterranean (and then the longer-haul) package tour and the revolution it wrought in expectations about accommodation standards, which were difficult to meet in Victorian premises with complicated plumbing (Stallibrass, 1978; Demetriadi, in Shaw and Williams, 1997).

The decline of the seaside resort is one of several post-war British themes that need serious research. Others include the transformation of the pub, the rise of the wine bar and the revolution in eating out, which includes the movement of Chinese, Greek Cypriots and Turks into the fish and chip trade as well as the rise of Chinese, Indian, Italian and other ethnic restaurants. Furthermore the opening out of new tastes in food, wine and beer, and the proliferation of new kinds of fast food, with particular attention to the American chains like McDonald's, Burger King and KFC also need detailed research. Phenomena such as Pierre Victoire also need to be set in historical context. The development of themed hotel chains, and purpose-built resorts like Centerparcs, offers enticing research possibilities for those who are prepared to look behind the present, which anyone who wants to investigate present problems has of necessity to do. A particularly important theme, which has been touched on glancingly in this chapter, is the conditions of work in the hospitality industries, which have been examined critically not only for Burger King but also for smaller businesses and indeed their proprietors (Gabriel, 1988; Reiter, 1991). And when a whole (and compelling) academic thesis has been constructed around the 'McDonaldisation of society', while contemporary work on tourism and hospitality floods into print, the need to add a serious time dimension, with all the comparative elements that entails, becomes paramount (Alfino *et al.*, 1998; Ritzer, 1998). I hope this introduction to the history of hospitality will prove fecund in themes for others to follow.

Conclusions

The modern hospitality trades represent both a continuation and a break with traditions that extend through millennia. The caring treatment of travellers, together with mutual obligations between guest and host, were widely recorded through the early centuries of Roman Britain. Despite periods of expansion and decline there was a steady growth of trade between communities and consequently a growth in the number of people travelling. Initially, traditional values relating to the hospitable treatment of strangers enabled travellers to be accommodated in private dwellings. As the volumes of travellers grew, specialist inns emerged as places where travellers were accommodated, and the nature of the hospitality relationship began to change.

The eighteenth century witnessed an increased concern to reaffirm the moral obligations of hospitality. Some of these comments are contemporary with Samuel Johnson's declaration about the benefits of a good inn quoted in Telfer's chapter. Certainly, there has been an ongoing concern with the 'morality' of hospitality that has at times reflected the need to maintain the obligations of guests and hosts, and at other times has attempted to regulate the context of hospitality provision in the conduct of alehouses and the places where alcoholic drinks were provided for the poor.

Growing affluence and increased transport encouraged more travel and leisure eating for increasing numbers throughout the last couple of centuries. As people could eat more than they needed and could spend increasing amounts of leisure time on travel and eating away from home, hotels, guest houses and bed and breakfast accommodation, together with restaurants and cafés as we know them today, emerged to meet these needs.

References

Alfino, M., Caputo, J. S. and Wynyard, R. (1998) *McDonaldization Revisited*, New York: Greenwood.

Berry, Arthur (1991) *The Little Gold-mine*, Liverpool: Bullfinch.

Borsay, P. (1989) *The English Urban Renaissance*, Oxford: Clarendon.

Bramley, G. (n.d.) Tourism in Britain and some local economic effects (typescript in Lancaster University Library).

Clark, Peter (1983) *The English Alehouse: A Social History 1200–1830*, Leicester: Leicester University Press.

Colpi, Terri (1991) *The Italian Factor*, Edinburgh: Mainstream.

Crawford, A., Dunn, M. and Thorne, Robert (1986) *Birmingham Pubs 1880–1939*, Gloucester: Alan Sutton.

Davey, B. J. (1983) *Lawless and Immoral*, Leicester: Leicester University Press.

Ellis, Charles (1981) *Mid-Victorian Sleaford*, Lincoln: Lincolnshire Library Service.

Gabriel, Yiannis (1988) *Working Lives in Catering*, London: Routledge.

Girouard, Mark (1984) *Victorian Pubs*, New Haven: Yale University Press.

Hardy, Dennis and Ward, Colin (1984) *Arcadia for All: The Legacy of a Makeshift Landscape*, London: Mansell.

Heal, F. (1990) *Hospitality in Early Modern England*, Oxford: Clarendon Press.

Houlihan, M. (1988) *A Most Excellent Dish: Tales of the Lancashire Tripe Trade*, Swinton: Neil Richardson.

Jennings, Paul (1995) *The Public House in Bradford, 1770–1970*, Keele: Keele University Press.

Laurence, Anne (1994) *Women in England 1500–1760*, London: Weidenfeld and Nicolson.

Mais, S. P. B. (1949) *I Return to Wales*, London: Christopher Johnson.

Marshall, J. D. (1975) *Kendal 1661–1801*, Kendal: Titus Wilson.

Mennell, S. (1985) *All Manners of Food*, Oxford: Basil Blackwell.

Monckton, H. A. (1969) *A History of the English Public House*, London: Bodley Head.

Mosey, Don and Ramsden, Harry Jr, (1989) *Harry Ramsden: The Uncrowned King of Fish and Chips*, Clapham: Dalesman.

Priestley, J. B. (1934) *English Journey*, London: Heinemann.

Reiter, E. (1991) *Making Fast Food*, Montreal: McGill-Queen's University Press.

Ritzer, G. (1998) *The McDonaldization Thesis: Explorations and Extensions*, New York: Sage.

Shaw, Gareth and Williams, Allan (eds) (1997) *The Rise and Fall of British Coastal Resorts*, London: Mansell.

Sponza, L. (1988) *Italian Immigrants in Nineteenth-century Britain*, Leicester: Leicester University Press.

Stallibrass, C. (1978) The holiday accommodation industry: a case study of Scarborough, Ph.D. thesis, University of London.

Stancliffe, F. S. (1938) *John Shaw's Manchester*, London: Sherratt and Hughes.

Thompson, E. P. and Yeo, Eileen (eds) (1971) *The Unknown Mayhew*, Harmondsworth: Penguin.

Underdown, David (1992) *Fire from Heaven*, London: HarperCollins.

Walton, J. K. (1978) *The Blackpool Landlady: A Social History*, Manchester: Manchester University Press.

Walton, J. K. (1983) *The English Seaside Resort: A Social History 1750–1914*, Leicester: Leicester University Press.

Walton, J. K. (1992) *Fish and Chips and the British Working Class*, Leicester: Leicester University Press.

Walton, J. K. (1994) The Blackpool landlady revisited, *Manchester Region History Review* 8: 23–31.

Ward, Colin, and Hardy, Dennis (1986) *Goodnight Campers!*, London: Mansell.

Wrightson, K. (1982) *English Society 1580–1680*, London: Hutchinson.

7

Hospitality – a synthetic approach

Bob Brotherton

Key themes

The nature of hospitality and hospitableness

Hospitality dimensions and morphologies

Macro, meso and micro influences on hospitality

Comparative research and synthetics

This chapter is concerned with two distinct but interrelated issues. First, to bring to a decisive close the enduring debate regarding how to define hospitality, both conceptually and practically, and how the field of hospitality should be circumscribed. Second, to use this as the basis for developing a synthetic approach to the study of hospitality capable of embracing and making use of much, if not most, of the considerable volume of material now evident in the extant literature.

Hospitality – the state of play?

It is absurd that the issues of what hospitality is and how it should be defined are still contentious some forty years after 'hospitality' became the descriptor of choice, both in academia and among practitioners. Although the reasons for this may have been more a case of cosmetic spin than any real, substantial change in those early days there is no doubting the reality of it over time, with use of the terms 'hospitality management' and the 'hospitality industry' becoming the norm into the twenty-first century. This has resulted in a considerable body of literature, much of which is potentially valuable scholarly activity but is equally characterised by considerable repetition, circularity of argument, fundamental misunderstandings and misuse of basic terminology and concepts. Comments in the extant literature recording this lamentable failure are legion and really not worthy of extensive coverage here. However, the following

DOI: 10.4324/9781315679938-8

pronouncements by authors who, *inter-alia*, may be regarded as being in the vanguard of this shift illustrate that, regardless of the effort that has been expended, the end result has really been profoundly disappointing.

At the beginning of this process Middleton commented:

> There is a definitional problem arising from the term 'hospitality industry' which is not in common use in the United Kingdom … It may be surprising that, in the 1980's, one must contemplate educational programmes for the hospitality industry without agreement on what the industry comprises.
>
> *(1983: 51)*

At the same time Reuland and Cassee concluded that 'a thorough understanding of hospitality as a phenomenon is lacking because hardly any research has been done on this subject … Therefore, the concept and formation of a hospitality theory is still missing' (1983: 144). Even by the mid-1990s the situation was broadly the same according to Jones, who observed that 'the reality is that there is certainly no commonly shared paradigm of what we mean by hospitality' (1996: 6).

Some fifteen years later, in the editorial launching a new journal, Lynch and colleagues reflected:

> A considerable literature has been generated across a range of disciplines regarding definitions of and approaches to hospitality, but as this necessarily brief review makes clear, there is neither a single definition of hospitality … nor is there a unified theoretical framework within which hospitality studies are situated.
>
> *(2011: 5)*

Moving even nearer to the present Melissen (2014) states, quite correctly, that hospitality is a concept and that, as a concept, it may remain essentially the same in different contexts but equally may be manifested in different ways for differing reasons. However, this view is then accompanied by the observation that hospitality is a 'mystifying concept' (Melissen, 2014: 15) because its manifestations can be, and indeed usually are, idiosyncratic and highly dissimilar if not unique. As will be clarified later it is not a mystifying concept but rather one that is quite clear and consistent across differing contexts.

Thus, among this evolving and growing literature some authors have focused on the etymology, language and linguistics of 'hospitality' (O'Gorman, 2010), its varying manifestations and the differing contexts within which these arise (Lashley *et al.*, 2007) or have focused on a spiritual moral/ethical and/or religious prism (O'Gorman, 2005, 2007; Sherringham and Daruwalla, 2007). However, much, if not most, of this work reveals an almost total absence of any attempt to develop more 'grounded theory' through empirical enquiry. Only Brotherton (1989, 2003a, 2005) and Brotherton and Wood (2008) present results, derived from empirical enquiry, concerning how hospitality is perceived, and may be defined, by those most closely associated with it – namely its providers and receivers.

There are also those, for example Hemmington (2007) and Melissen (2014), who seem to have been seduced by Pine and Gilmore's experience economy work (1999, 2002) and seek to focus attention on hospitality as an experience designed, manipulated and managed by human activity. This, of course, is really yet another false dawn because anything may be described as an experience to a sentient human being and the only way to differentiate a 'hospitality experience' from any other human experience is to locate it within the context of a hospitality place, with all that implies. In addition is the ubiquitous tendency for commentators to use the adjective hospitable and the nouns of hospitableness and hospitality as entirely synonymous and perfectly interchangeable. It is, or indeed should be, axiomatic that they are not.

This begs the question of why these two distinct and dominant themes of focusing on diversity and difference and viewing hospitableness and hospitality as synonymous and interchangeable have been so ubiquitous. The former has essentially arisen due to a period of 'prometheus unbound' within which the old boundaries and certainties of hotel and catering and/or industrial hospitality management became challenged by wider and more critical thinking concerning the nature and relevance of the hospitality phenomenon in a more generalised series of contexts or settings. This has spawned, as Wood (2015) correctly identifies, a series of perspectives and approaches to these central questions that are loosely connected under the umbrella term 'hospitality studies'. This broad movement being characterised by a central concern to identify and comment on different forms and types of hospitality, within commercial and non-commercial contexts, to explore and adopt a range of social science perspectives, methodologies and techniques to investigate these, and to challenge the previous hegemony of the 'managerial' paradigm evident in the narrower field of hospitality management.

Though there is nothing inherently wrong in focusing on dissimilarity and difference to identify and explore the breadth and diversity of the hospitality phenomenon this has skewed the investigatory field and encouraged commentators to follow this direction of travel. As a consequence questions regarding what may be similar or the same about alternative hospitality morphologies have largely been ignored. The result has been the development of a rather atomistic body of literature lacking a unifying and solid conceptual anchor that could be used to provide a more universally accepted definition of hospitality and help circumscribe the field in a more logical and defendable manner.

Returning to the second theme, of viewing hospitable, hospitableness and hospitality as synonymous and interchangeable, this has really been something that should not have occurred in the first place and has been largely dysfunctional in helping to address the issues of being able to sensibly define and circumscribe the field of hospitality. If the field of hospitality is to have any real credibility it must be possible to identify what is legitimate to include within it and, by implication, what is not. As will be argued later, one of the most importance characteristics of hospitality, for both defining and circumscribing it, is the undeniable fact that it only occurs as a conscious human activity within the spatial construct of place and furthermore that this place is spatially constrained, predominantly to a single, localised venue. Though it may be reasonably argued that a hospitable environment, disposition, attitude, manner and behaviours are necessary for hospitality to exist, none of these, individually or collectively, are sufficient conditions for hospitality (Telfer, 1996, 2000; Brotherton, 2013).

It is perfectly possible to refer to people, places and wider environments as being hospitable, in that they are perceived as welcoming, friendly, aethestically pleasing, non-threatening or safe and demonstrate, either in their design and/or actions, that they reflect a concern with the well-being of those encountering them. However, they are not automatically providing hospitality as this constitutes something more than the existence of hospitableness. People may display hospitableness and be hospitable in a wide variety of circumstances that have nothing to do with hospitality per se. Both individuals and collective populations may be described as hospitable in that they display welcoming and friendly attitudes and behaviours and have a concern for the well-being of the other but this alone would not be sufficient to say they are providing hospitality.

Similarly, inanimate spaces and places, at a variety of spatial levels from local to national entities, may also be regarded as hospitable in that they are perceived to be conducive to the well-being of those who encounter them. It is quite normal to refer to inanimate environments and climates as being hospitable or inhospitable but no one would claim that they had received hospitality from such an encounter as the provision of hospitality is a human action. So, while hospitable attitudes, behaviours, environments and spaces may well be necessary for hospitality to exist they are not automatic indicators that it does. This really has quite profound implications for defining and circumscribing hospitality as this inability to distinquish between hospitableness and hospitality has contaminated a considerable proportion of the extant hospitality literature.

In relation to defining hospitality it should now be abundantly clear that hospitality can only occur within the context of a place and that the spatial dimensions of such places are necessarily constrained in the vast majority of cases. Of course it is possible to talk of nations being hospitable in providing hospitality to refugees and asylum seekers, an issue that has particular resonance within EU countries at the time of writing, but relatively speaking this is really a quite marginal activity at best and one that is designed as an interim stage in the process of accepting and assimilating immigrants into permanent residents and ultimately citizens of the country. Similarly, local residents and visitors are allowed free access to, and usage of, public spaces in urban and rural locations that they may regard as hospitable environments but within which hospitality is not provided, though obviously it may be if there are hospitality operators plying their trade within such locations. However, this would not constitute a transformation of these general public spaces into an overall space where hospitality is located, though it may make them more hospitable environments. The existence of places providing refreshment, such as kiosks, are nothing more than retail locations and places providing hospitality, such as cafés, restaurants and accommodation units, essentially comprise distinct places within the overall locality that not only confer temporary entry and usage rights, in the same way that the overarching spatial entity does, but in addition provide the additional physical and behavioural elements embodied within any type of hospitality morphology.

Hence, the starting point to construct a sensible, and universally applicable, definition of hospitality must be the type of spatial entity, or place, and the temporal dimensions relating to its occupancy and use. The essence of this, which has remained temporally constant and is spatially consistent, is that entry to this space is voluntary, temporally constrained and does not embody any transfer of ownership of any kind of resource or asset for future use or consumption. It is therefore a type of 'access and usage' or temporary rental transaction within which the obligations of the provider and user are known to each other. Thus, whatever term is used to describe the user/s – customers, clients or guests – they willingly pay a 'rent' for the privilege of occupying that space, being allowed to use its facilities and consume the services and products it offers. This rent may comprise a simple monetary transaction, for example paying the bill in a hotel or restaurant in a commercial context, or it may be embodied in the performance of appropriate social behaviours and obligations in non-commercial or private contexts (Brotherton, 2013).

Hospitality then only occurs within specific places of varying scales, forms and types but which all share the same basic structure and characteristics. These being that they are controlled spaces, in the sense that entry is not automatically free or guaranteed, they are places of temporary occupation and usage that do not transform the users into residents or resource/asset owners, and they provide hospitality products and services – food, drink, accommodation of varying types, entertainment, safety and security, service and so on – that are consumed on the premises during the temporary occupation by the receiver of these. This is a view nicely summarised by Sherringham and Daruwalla:

> The conditions accompanying this negotiated (service) transaction include the exchange between two or more parties of something of value, in the context of agreed conditions, time and place ... [involving the] temporary inhabitancy of a liminal space followed by their return across the boundaries, define hospitality.
>
> *(2007: 33)*

This should hardly be a revelation. It has been recognised for millennia that the hospitality guest has an intermediate or liminal status, he/she is neither a complete stranger/outsider or a fully integrated/permanent 'insider' member of the community. From the Caravanserais in the fifth century BC (Van Hoof *et al.*, 1996; O'Gorman, 2009) through monastic and manorial provision in the Dark Ages and early medieval times (Kerr, 2002, 2007; Gautier, 2009; O'Gorman, 2009) the provision of hospitality was normally limited to two to three days.

Hospitality places are commonly non-mobile, such as domestic homes, civic buildings, hotels, restaurants, bars and cafés, while others have varying degrees of spatial mobility, such as trains, airplanes, cruise ships, ferries and marquees. Whether they exist in a fixed location or have the ability to vary their spatial location they exhibit the same basic structure and characteristics described above. This combination of elements not only concentrates attention on the key aspects of hospitality that must be used to define it but also makes a major contribution to circumscribing it and to deciding what places, spaces and activities may be legitimately regarded as constituting the field of hospitality and what may not. Indeed, as Ritzer comments, 'It seems to me that it is the place that is one of the cornerstones of the hospitality industry' (2007: 136).

The view taken in this chapter suggests that the spatial incidence of hospitality is more constrained and limited than some commentators would contend, largely because this decisively solves the hospitable/hospitality conflation problem discussed earlier. It also clearly indicates that the processes and practices of hospitality exhibit particular types of exchange, which may be of a monetary or non-monetary form. In short, they may be economic or social transactions. This effectively validates, develops and refines earlier work focusing on hospitality as a distinct type of exchange (Brotherton, 1999a, 2002a, 2003a, 2005, 2006, 2013; Brotherton and Wood, 2000a, 2000b, 2008) and is also consistent with more general work on exchange reciprocity and culture (Fieldhouse, 1996).

Once again it is clear that a focus on the similarities and differences between hospitality situations, both temporally and spatially, is likely to be a productive way forward in developing more distinctive and robust theoretical and conceptual frameworks to guide empirical enquiry and strengthen the credibility of hospitality as a distinctive field of enquiry. Although forms and volumes of hospitality vary temporally and spatially their essence remains remarkably similar, if not constant (Finkelstein, 1989; Telfer, 1996; Sandoval-Strausz, 2007; Santich, 2007).

Finally, it is necessary to address another shibboleth existing within the contemporary hospitality literature. This is the issue of what may be loosely referred to as judgements regarding that mythical beast – the 'purity of hospitality'. With the notable exception of the insightful and significant contribution made by Wood (1994) the literature contains a veritable litany of misconceived comment and discussion relating to this issue that is invariably centred around value, and often class-based, pronouncements regarding the authenticity and purity of what tends to be referred to as 'true' or 'authentic' hospitality and the features that characterise this along with the presumed motives that explain its existence.

This is typified by Ritzer's piece entitled 'Inhospitable hospitality?' (2007) which encapsulates the essence of much of this debate. Ritzer (2007) suggests that contemporary commercial forms of hospitality provision have become inhospitable because they have become progressively more inauthentic due to the increasing emphasis placed upon rationalisation, standardisation, efficiency, control, predictability, homegenisation and commoditisation. There is, of course, a beguiling attraction in this view, but it is misconceived and the problem lies in the fundamental premise he uses to arrive at the 'inhospitable' conclusion, taking the rather naive, and incorrect, view that 'real' hospitality is unitary in form and provided solely from 'genuine', rather than 'ulterior', motives. Underlying Ritzer's view is the unstated, and subjective, assumption that a particular type of 'perfect' or 'pure' hospitality has existed and that this should be regarded as the 'ideal' to judge other forms against. This, of course, is perfect bunkum. The view that there is only one form of 'genuine' motive, which would appear to be something akin to one based upon perfect or pure altruism, is perhaps a morally attractive proposition but one that is illusory and based upon a romanticised and inaccurate conception of a type of 'golden age' of hospitality. Using Ritzer's criteria would patently render most forms of hospitality provision through the ages as inhospitable. Most hospitality has been provided on the basis of some kind of ulterior, instrumental motive.

Furthermore, to Ritzer the 'industrialisation' of commercial hospitality provision, characterised by the increasing incidence of the features referred to above, constitutes incontrovertible evidence that this type of hospitality is necessarily inauthentic. For this to be regarded as inauthentic it must be possible to define what constitutes authentic hospitality. However, this does not appear to be so easy. Indeed, Ritzer recognises that 'authenticity is a difficult concept and it is very hard to define exactly what we mean by it and to identify with any precision that which is authentic' (2007: 134). Although Ritzer concedes that it is very difficult to definitively establish what authenticity is, he then proceeds to contend that anything classified as routine and mechanical can be universally regarded as inauthentic. If the 'positive' form of the concept cannot be defined how is it possible to satisfactorily define the 'negative' or reverse form? The answer is, it is not, except via a path of reverse logic that would, logically, have to contend that if inauthenticity is defined as something based upon, and exhibiting, routine and mechanical features then to be regarded as authentic something must possess the reverse characteristics, it must be, perhaps among other things, spontaneous and organic.

Once again, there are obvious forms of hospitality provision that many, perhaps including Ritzer, might tend to regard as pure, true, real, genuine and authentic, but which exhibit similar degrees of routinisation and mechanical approaches to the organisation and delivery of the hospitality process as many contemporary commercial forms. For example, some commentators take the view that monastic and/or manorial hospitality provision in feudal societies constituted this 'ideal' authentic kind of hospitality but, in Ritzer's terms, these would be clearly defined as inauthentic as they exhibited considerable degrees of routinisation and very significant amounts of pre-planning and structuring. They were also highly discriminatory and hospitality was provided for ulterior motives such as the self-interest of religious believers, who engaged in obligatory 'good deeds' motivated by a desire to obtain rewards in the life to come (Santich, 2007). In addition, a significant proportion of formal hospitality provision in the ancient world was highly political in nature and motivation (Montanari, 1999) and the feudal elite of medieval times, who are often cited as examples of authentic providers, were primarily concerned to maintain their status, power and privileges by offering varying degrees of charitable largesse to the poor to deter social unrest and revolution and to their peers to establish and maintain their social standing (Mennell, 1985; Heal, 1990; Kerr, 2002). Goody suggests that, in such times; 'hospitality was a primary tool of politics' (1982: 141) and, according to Hollander (1981), nothing much seems to have changed with political elites still prone to using hospitality, at a state level, to manipulate the perceptions of 'important' visitors.

Even further back in time Sanchez-Moreno (2001) concludes that hospitality morphologies in the Iberian peninsular in the late-Iron Age exhibited strong politico-economic motives lying behind them. O'Gorman (2010) also suggests the predominance and importance of such motives in the ancient world. In a more contemporary context the findings of Traphagan and Brown (2002) indicate that, in Japan, commensality may be greater within the context of McDonald's than in more traditional Japanese hospitality morphologies. A cautionary note for those assuming that the same hospitality morphologies are perceived and used in the same way in different cultures!

Turning now to another revealing aspect of Ritzer's view, that of the addition of his personal and highly subjective opinion that the inauthenticity he sees being produced through such features is repellent to him. The fact that Ritzer dislikes hospitality provision that is based upon, and exhibits, routinisation, mechanical processes and behaviours reveals another common facet in this debate. The idealised and romanticised view of 'genuine' and 'authentic' hospitality is derived from a particular set of value judgements of what hospitality ought to be and this, in turn, is based upon a particular set of valorised social and cultural values. Indeed, such arbiters of cultural capital have a tendency to engage in snobbery and decry other types and forms of the phenomenon in question as inappropriate, inferior and inauthentic because they do not conform to their idealised concept. What Ritzer finds repellent may be exactly what others desire. For reasons of personal preference or because of lifestyle and time pressures many people may desire and value more limited hospitality. There are patently occasions when speed of service, value for money, limited provider–receiver interaction, convenience, even familiarity in knowing the 'script', are all positively valued by the guest, customer or consumer. All these facets serve the very purpose the receiver seeks to satisfy and, because of this, would recognise that the type of hospitality they receive under such conditions is different from that expected, and regarded as appropriate hospitality, under other conditions.

To bring this section to a close there now exists a clear definition of hospitality and a sound basis to delineate the hospitality field. All that remains is to consider the key dimensions of hospitality to operationalise the concept. Building upon Brotherton (2002a, 2003a, 2006, 2013) and Brotherton and Wood (2000a, 2000b, 2008) it is clear that all hospitality morphologies have five primary dimensions as follows:

- *The spatial dimension* – This identifies the places and spaces where all hospitality morphologies occur and the contention that these are 'situated' within particular combinations of societal forces, at particular times, which may be categorised as distinctive milieux.
- *The temporal dimension* – This focuses on the incidence of hospitality or the types of occasions hospitality morphologies are created for. It also recognises the 'temporary' nature of hospitality encounters and combines with the spatial dimension to highlight the notion of 'liminal space'.
- *The physical dimension* – This identifies the type of physical features and products associated with any given type of hospitality morphology. In combination with the spatial and temporal dimensions, this is central as it is the existence of what is often referred to as the 'holy trinity' – accommodation, food and/or drink – that helps to differentiate hospitality morphologies from others which can embody the previous dimensions.
- *The behavioural dimension* – This concentrates attention on the motives lying behind decisions to create various types of hospitality morphology and the human processes and interactions involved in the operation of such morphologies.

- *The transactional dimension* – This, in conjunction with the spatial and temporal dimensions, makes it clear that hospitality morphologies are characterised by temporary access and usage permissions not involving any transfer of resource or asset ownership to the consumer for future use or consumption.

Thus, any hospitality morphology is composed of these five primary dimensions. It is the empirical combinations and operational variations in these that give rise to many of the features normally associated with hospitality morphologies, namely conviviality, commensality, mutuality, sociability, transactional exchange and reciprocity. This is encapsulated within the idea of distinctive 'service cultures' created by alternative hospitality morphologies (Cuthill, 2007).

The question now is what is it that creates similarities and differences between observed hospitality morphologies over time and across space, and why? It is to these issues that the chapter now turns.

Hospitality – a way forward?

Given the view of what constitutes the essence of hospitality in the previous section there are certain corollaries. This view of hospitality clearly implies that certain conceptual and practical continuities will be evident, both spatially and temporally. Put simply, the essence will always be present wherever, whenever and whatever hospitality forms exist across time and space. However, it is not claimed that the manifestation of this essence, in terms of the more concrete forms hospitality takes in differing times and contexts, remains constant. Because hospitality is a human endeavour situated within the locus of human society, it is axiomatic that as such societies exhibit differing scales, structures, processes, values and foci in different time periods and contexts then the concrete manifestations of hospitality – 'hospitality morphologies' – similarly differ to reflect the milieu they exist within. Indeed Grignon (2001) makes a similar point in proposing that commensality as a phenomenon is universal but has a 'variety of shapes' and, as such, becomes amenable to the compilation of an 'inventory of commensality types'.

One way to focus on this juxtaposition of enduring essence and contextually dependent difference is to consider the former as the DNA of the hospitality genotype and the latter as the various phenotypes generated to provide 'species diversity'. In the same way that the human genome remains remarkably similar across different groups of human beings, yet exhibits obvious differences over time and across contexts, so too does hospitality (Brotherton and Wood, 2000a; Brotherton, 2002a, 2003b, 2006). Also important are the concepts of adaptability and phenotype plasticity (Mackenzie *et al.*, 1998). Both are concerned with survival and evolution. Adaptability is essentially an inherited trait that aids these and here it might be pertinent to suggest that 'hospitality memes' may exist which enhance the ability of the hospitality genotype to adapt, survive and evolve within different temporal and spatial milieux through the evolution of its phenotypes.

The term meme was first coined by Dawkins (1976) and is essentially the cultural equivalent of a gene. A meme is usually defined as a unit of cultural information, such as a cultural practice or idea, that is transmitted verbally or by repeated action from one generation to another and, in this sense, is an adaptive mechanism that, potentially, enables more rapid change and adaption. Though, of course, it may also prove to be a restraining factor in that custom and tradition can be inhibitors to innovation. Similarly, phenotype plasticity enables the hospitality species to vary in response to temporal and spatial variations which, in turn, facilitates species diversity, or the multiplication of hospitality morphologies. It is indisputable that the genesis of the hospitality genome is rooted in, and derived from, private, domestic and communal hospitality morphologies evident in early, primitive human societies and civilisations (Bell and Henry, 2001), and that this can still be evidenced in these types of societies that continue to exist in isolation within the modern world. Given this it should be possible to identify homologies within the variety of hospitality morphologies that have evolved from this common ancestor.

This raises some deceptively simple yet fundamental questions in relation to hospitality morphologies.

- What conditions are necessary and sufficient for hospitality to exist?
- What are the factors and forces that contribute to the evolution of hospitality?
- What are the particular effects of these forces and factors and why?
- How do they act to generate both similarity/continuity and difference/change in hospitality temporally and spatially?
- Why are particular types, or manifestations, of hospitality more, or less, prevalent and/or important in different temporal and spatial milieux?

The first question is really a matter of thresholds, distributions and choices in relation to the use of physical and human resources. In these respects it would not be unreasonable to propose that these resources constitute the basic parameters for hospitality to exist. Without both it is impossible to produce hospitality and without the latter there would be no demand for hospitality. Hence, they are fundamental to its existence. Without a sufficient quantity, or supply, of food and materials for shelter it would be impossible for anyone to provide hospitality. Therefore, if the quantity of physical resources increases, either by more extensive/efficient production or acquisition, especially in the form of surpluses, then the potential for more extensive hospitality provision does also. However, in the case of human resources, population growth per se does not automatically indicate the existence of greater potential or surplus. Indeed, although much has been made of the importance of hospitality in the early modern period (Heal, 1990) and beyond, some 75 per cent of Europe's increasing population was close to the subsistence level from the sixteenth to the late ninteenth century.

Use of the economists' concept of the production possibility frontier, or curve, may be helpful here. This indicates the total quantity of resources available to produce alternative combinations of products and/or services and demonstrates the principle of opportunity cost – that is, the amount of the alternative that has to be foregone in order to use these resources to produce hospitality. Of course, as the quantity of these resources increases over time, due largely to population and economic growth, the ability to generate a surplus rises and so does the potential for hospitality to be offered. Indeed, as Visser states, 'Civilisation itself cannot begin until a food supply is assured' (1991: 2), and the very existence of 'advanced civilisations' from the ancient world onwards only became possible because of food surpluses (Civitello, 2008). As societal evolution proceeds from the primitive to more advanced societies not only does the scale of resources available increase substantially but it also normally leads to a much higher proportion of this total output being available as surplus. Hence, the ability to make different choices concerning which forms of production and consumption are more, or less, desirable is enhanced. Therefore, it is reasonable to hypothesise a relationship between the size and scale of societies, their relative access to resources, and the volume and diversity of hospitality to be expected. Although this is likely to be a non-linear relationship, and one that will exhibit varying rates of change over time and volumes across different spatial locations (Mennell, 1985), it constitutes one of the basic reasons for differing quantities and forms of hospitality across time and space.

What is also important is a society's ability not only to discover and acquire resources but to exploit these resources in an effective and efficient manner. The potential embodied in a greater availability of resources is invariably realised through innovative ideas, technologies and techniques that enhance the productive capacity of these resources and/or the ability to convert these into enhanced inputs to facilitate a greater incidence and diversity of hospitality morphologies. However, there is no a priori causal link between an increase in resource potential and a consequent expansion in hospitality provision. This involves the type of opportunity cost choices outlined earlier. Such choices reflect societal values, preferences and priorities and, hence, are inextricably linked to the societal forces, or tectonics, that create and structure such influences. As these vary spatially and temporally the relative predominance and importance of alternative hospitality morphologies also varies and, given that resources and choices are not unlimited and equal in these contexts, a choice to increase one or more types of hospitality morphology is likely to lead to other types being diminished or crowded out. In this respect, although perhaps a broad generalisation, it is reasonable to contend that, relatively speaking, the volume and importance of private or domestic hospitality has declined over time, certainly in the Western world, while that of commercial hospitality has increased. Similarly, from the middle of the twentieth century, it is also evident that many societies have tended to value 'branded' commercial hospitality provision more than that of an individual or artisan nature. The consequence being that there has been a general crowding out of the latter by the expansion of the former. However, neither of these, more general or specific, trends are universal in the sense that exactly the same pace and extent of such shifts has been evident over the last sixty years or so in all societies and all societies are not at the same point now because many began from a different starting point at the outset of this process (Mennell, 1985; Slattery, 2009).

The question then arises what are these societal forces, or tectonics, that act to create and change hospitality morphologies temporally and spatially? In some respects the answer to this is quite a simple one. Hospitality does not exist in a vacuum and is therefore subject to the same tectonic forces that other forms of human activity are – that is, political, economic, social, cultural, environmental and technological. These forces combine and conspire, from local to global levels, to push and pull societies on evolutionary, and sometimes revolutionary, trajectories of change and development. They are not always equally important, temporally and/or spatially, to the outcomes of this process and neither are they equally influential over time or across space. Similarly, they may be centrifugal or progressive, or centripetal or conservative, in their effects.

In primitive societies the social structures and patterns are largely fixed due to physical and social isolation and the consequent dominance of the centripetal forces of habit, tradition, custom and so on. As societies develop they evolve and change due to the influence of centrifugal forces. Traditional hospitality forms become modified by social change – that is, the old 'rules' become less certain and rigid. Indeed, Olesen (1994) makes the point that a human activity, such as hospitality, conducted within a particular context or situation, needs not only to be studied within this context but also to be seen as something that is linked to larger and wider social forces. However, in any specific location and/or time period there may exist a decisive change in one force that makes it the 'key driver' of change in that context. In its most extreme form this would be regarded as a significant discontinuity, or indeed a revolution. Though these do exist within all the types of tectonic forces, and have quite dramatic consequences when they occur, they are relatively rare compared to the more evolutionary process associated with these forces. Nevertheless, many of these have profound and enduring effects on the nature of human societies that continue to be influential for decades, if not centuries, beyond their origins. At a societal level such revolutionary events and periods are well known but they also arise at more limited and specific spatial levels where they are particularly associated with individual agency.

At a societal level economic revolutions such as the agrarian and industrial revolutions that occurred in Europe and North America have all had significant national and international impacts on societies and hospitality morphologies, in particular through their effects on urbanisation, mobility and living standards. Similarly, political revolutions such as the American, Russian and French revolutions all created 'new' societies that, either rather quickly or over time, had quite transformative effects on hospitality. As Spang (2000) and Mennell and colleagues (1992) record it was the impetus of the new societal structures and republican values generated by the French Revolution that provided a major stimulus to the emergence of the restaurant as a new and distinct hospitality morphology, initially in post-revolutionary France and thereafter in other countries. However, although this revolutionary event undoubtedly created a major stimulus to the emergence of the restaurant there were also important antecedents. Mennell (1985), Mennell et al. (1992), Spang (2000), Keifer (2002) and Carlin (2008) all note that reforms to limit the monopoly powers of the 'guilds' in France and England in the sixteenth and seventeenth centuries enabled existing hospitality institutions, such as inns and taverns, to offer 'all-inclusive' fixed price menus or 'à la carte', individually priced menus.

Technological revolutions have also contributed to the emergence of new hospitality morphologies. As numerous authors, including Simmons (1984), Towner (1996), Van Hoof et al. (1996), Lane and Dupre (1997), Dittmer (2002), Powers and Barrows (2006) and Turkel (2009), have recorded revolutionary new transport technologies such as the railways, the automobile and commercial aviation have all led to growth and decline in both existing and new hospitality morphologies and continue to do so. Indeed, the more recent digital revolution is having widespread effects, in particular on the marketing and distribution systems associated with commercial hospitality but also on hospitality morphologies in terms of operational systems and customer interaction.

Although fundamental change to hospitality morphologies can clearly be influenced by such grand scale revolutions there are equally more localised and specific revolutions derived from significant changes to the structure, form and function of these morphologies themselves. Both Spang (2000) and Cocks (2001) comment that, in France and the USA respectively, essentially the same localised revolution led to a quite fundamental change in hospitality morphologies. There was a movement from 'service à la française' and 'table d'hôte' to 'service à la russe' and 'à la carte' in the early part of the nineteenth century in France and Spang (2000) makes the point that American and European accommodation provision separated out room and board in large high-end hotels in the nineteenth century. Along with the adoption of service à la russe and menus in the hotel dining rooms and the kitchen revolution, associated with Escoffier and many others, which began to simplify food production and menus to fit in with the adoption of service à la russe this had quite profound consequences. These hospitality morphologies and experiences were transformed from the more communal/collective forms of the past to a more private/individualistic experience. In turn these changes in food preparation, production and service heralded the age of waiters. Under the previous systems of table d'hôte, service à la française and the all inclusive American Plan, which also embraced the same foodservice features, there was no need for waiters because all the food was placed on the dining table at the same time and the diners all ate together communally so individual orders were non-existent. That said, such organisational and systemic changes do not always occur simultaneously across all hospitality morphologies, even those of the same basic type. For example, Turkel makes the point that, even in 1908, it was commonplace to find that 'about 90 percent of hotels were American plan, with cheap, unlimited food included in the room rate' (2009: xvi).

Equally one other, more 'localised', source of innovation which has generated 'revolutions' in hospitality morphologies should not be overlooked. This is the impact the agency of individual entrepreneurs has had. In both London and Paris the introduction of coffee and the establishment of coffee houses and cafés in the seventeenth century was largely the product of immigrant entrepreneurs from the eastern Mediterranean who developed a new hospitality morphology that had dramatic effects on the establishment and enhancement of civil society. Similarly, commenting on the development of the hotel industry in the USA, Sandoval-Strausz concludes that:

> The hotel as we know it today did not evolve randomly or naturally, nor did it develop as some sort of automatic response to structural needs. Rather, it was the deliberate creation of an identifiable group of people who lived in a specific place and time: the cities of the United States in the early days of the republic.
>
> *(2007: 1)*

Turkel (2009) also provides extensive evidence of the roles played by numerous hospitality entrepreneurs in the USA. Apart from the well-known story of the McDonald brothers and today's global McDonald's Corporation, Turkel highlights the contribution made by individuals such as George Pullman (the founder of Pullman railway sleeping and dining cars), Conrad Hilton and Kemmons Wilson (the founder of Holiday Inn), all of whom saw opportunities in exploiting changes in one or more of the wider tectonic forces and who created what we now recognise as global hotel brands. This confluence of societal level changes and individual agency has been, and continues to be, a significant source of new, revolutionary hospitality morphologies.

Despite change arising from revolutionary forces most change tends to be evolutionary rather than revolutionary, involving a confluence of forces from interrelated but alternative sources, the relative influence of each often being difficult, but not necessarily impossible, to ascertain or estimate. Slattery provides an example of this:

> the size, structure and growth of the hotel business in a country are functions of the prevailing economic structure. Thus, fundamental to comprehending the economic ascent of the hotel business is an understanding of the structural development of the economies in which hotels operate and which provide the fertility for hotel demand and supply to grow.
>
> *(2009: viii)*

Consequently, if the structural development and contemporary economic structures differ between countries then one would expect a lack of uniformity in the development and patterns of hotel business in these countries. Indeed, Slattery (2009) illustrates this by comparing Europe/North America with the rest of the world, noting that the ratio of the supply of hotel rooms to population size differs dramatically between these two. In the case of the former he suggests that this ratio is in the order of fourteen hotel rooms for every 1,000 citizens, whereas for the latter it is only one room for the same number of people. His explanation for this is the stage of economic development these two groups of economies have achieved, with Europe/North America clearly identified as advanced, tertiary economies and many of the rest seen as being underdeveloped and largely dependent on agriculture and extractive industries. This, of course, begs the question of what causes or drives such similarities and differences. Slattery (2009) suggests that the supply volume differences between the US and UK, that became increasingly pronounced over the twentieth century, can be accounted for by differential rates of structural change and development to a 'service-driven' economy and by differences in the political philosophies of the two countries (US – small government, UK – large government) that, in turn, facilitated or inhibited the rate of transition from a manufacturing-based economy to a service one.

In terms of the general evolution of hospitality morphologies it is also clear that the volume and frequency of travel and transient strangers has had a significant relationship with the dominant thinking concerning the most appropriate form of hospitality to meet prevailing conditions (Ohler, 2010). Increases over time in both the volume and frequency of travel have progressively led to the simultaneous increase in commercial forms of provision and the concomitant decline in domestic provision. As mobility in general increases individuals gradually become increasingly de-coupled from place and community. Over time mobility has increased due to expansion in local, regional, national and then international trade, industrial, political, technological and commercial revolutions, population growth and urbanisation, developments in transport technologies and individual/societal freedoms occasioned by greater degrees of political, economic and intellectual liberalisation (Bernstein, 2004).

Indeed, the unprecedented social changes, that began in early modern times but exploded during the eighteenth, nineteenth and twentieth centuries, associated with population growth (Flandrin, 1999; Morineau, 1999), industrialisation and urbanisation (Mennell, 1985; Beardsworth and Keil, 1997; Dittmer, 2002) and political/personal freedoms combined to generate levels of mobility previously unseen. Not only did the growth of cities and other urban areas generate intra-urban mobility but it also gave rise to significant levels of inter-urban mobility, in both national and international contexts. In turn, this facilitated an explosion in the incidence of the stranger and the concomitant issues associated with dealing with this phenomenon among communities previously unaccustomed to having to cope with such volumes. Indeed, when the need to deal with the stranger in terms of greater frequency, volume and diversity became a social reality existing forms of hospitality provision were found to be inadequate and this prompted the development of new morphologies and styles.

The reasons, or motives, which appear to have driven the evolution of hospitality include fear of the stranger who, historically, was imbued with mystical and magical attributes; explicit religious and/or superstitial commands or dictates (O'Gorman, 2005); the need to support commercial trading activity (Constable, 2003); those more associated with personal self-interest, such as to display wealth, power, cultural capital, conspicuous consumption, fashionability and to cultivate social status (Strong, 2002); and curiosity – that is, a desire to obtain and exchange news (Ohler, 2010).

Although historically the provision of private hospitality often tended to be a social, economic, political or religious obligation derived from prevailing societal conditions, now it is more a matter of individual discretion. This means that private hospitality, relatively speaking, has become less integral to a society's culture and more incidental. As societal cultures, generally speaking, have become less formalised and rigid in their structures and actions so liberalism, informality and casualisation have become more prominent, reflecting greater social and personal freedoms (Visser, 1991).

Conclusions

To bring together this discussion of the effects that macro/external and micro/internal forces have on hospitality morphologies is no easy task. However, one thing is clear, all hospitality morphologies across time and space are 'situated'. They exist within particular configurations of the actions and effects of the tectonic forces along with those of human agency. At specific times and in specific places or contexts there exist specific conditions which may be described as periods, ages, epochs or, indeed, milieux. These are identifiable temporal and/or spatial configurations that can be distinguished from those that precede and follow them. They are both the consequences of antecedent and contemporaneous structural conditions and human agency and form the antecedents of what is to follow. Hence, it is reasonable to contend that the boundaries between different milieux will be 'fuzzy' as they overlap, creating 'zones of transition' within which the 'present' milieu is not fully formed or the next is not yet established as the new one.

As Mennell (1985, 1992) observes, although the societal development of both England and France has been quite similar the culinary cultures, and consequent hospitality morphologies, that have emerged are quite distinctly different. Also, Teuteberg makes the pertinent point that

> with good reason it is thought that by way of dietary customs [substitute 'hospitality morphologies'?] demographic, economic, politico-judicial, sociocultural and even climatic and ecological phenomena can be combined in homogeneous categories which can be compared to each other outside of the bounds of time and space.
>
> *(1992: 115)*

Their specific configuration and conditions are derived from the recursive nature of the duality of structure and agency (Giddens, 1991) and the product of the dialectic relationship between the antinomic forces – centripetal (habit and tradition) and centrifugal (imagination and innovation) – existing at that time (Mennell, 1985), with the relative strength of the latter being subject to the moderating force of expectations (Brotherton, 2002a, 2005). Where the former is relatively stronger, Visser (1991: 42) suggests that attitudes based on 'neophobia' (the fear of the new) would be in the ascendency and coversely that 'neophilia' (the love of the new) would be the dominant driving force where the latter was stronger.

Thus there is an iteration between the general and the particular. It would be unrealistic to claim that a 'structural determinism' perspective explains all. Equally it would be indefensible to suggest that hospitality morphologies emerge and develop in isolation from the societal conditions they are situated within. To concentrate solely on either would be a mistake. Although general processes may have general effects they are also clearly capable of producing differing outcomes in different times and places as they interact with the specific conditions evident in each. That said it is axiomatic that such differences are unlikely to be unique in relation to each other. In short, commonalities will exist across these differing manifestations. Therefore, synthesis derived from the use of comparative methodology provides the necessary link. As Allen puts it, this is concerned with 'how the general and the particular are combined in explanation, how the particularity of place is preserved and modified within the generality of social change to produce different outcomes in different places' (1992: 107). For Giddens (1991) this illustrates the importance of agency where agents reflexively monitor their actions and external structures and subsequently rationalise them to develop transformations in both structures and agency. This is also similar to Elias's concept of 'figurations' (1978) that are 'contingent on the particular time and culture in which they occur, often changing in response to conflict and competition between social groups, and to wider socio-economic and political factors' (Germov and Williams, 1999: 302).

Exploring the synthesis available from such spatial and temporal similarities and differences, and the reasons for these, is really the sine qua non of comparative research in its many and varied forms (Brotherton, 1999b, 2000). Utilising either multiple case study and/or variable-based methods both convergence and divergence in hospitality morphologies can be systematically explored by adopting either 'positive' or 'negative' approaches. In the former 'common' outcomes are identified to establish which of the independent variables causing these are the same in each instance. Alternatively, the latter takes divergent outcomes and establishes the independent variables that create them in order to identify those variables having the greatest explanatory power across these divergent outcomes. However, to achieve this it is necessary to establish a sound comparative base capable of enabling the identification of both generic and context-specific causal factors (Brotherton, 1999b, 1999c, 2000) and to ensure that conceptual and metric equivalence are embedded in the research design to facilitate the valid transferability of results from one context to another (Brotherton, 2003b, 2008, 2015).

References

Allen, J. (1992) Introduction. Synthesis: interdependence and the uniqueness of place. In Massey, D. and Allen, J. (eds) *Geography Matters: A Reader*, Cambridge: Cambridge University Press in association with Open University Press, pp. 107–111.

Beardsworth, A. and Keil, T. (1997) *Sociology on the Menu: An Invitation to the Study of Food and Society*, London: Routledge.

Bell, S. and Henry, J. F. (2001) Hospitality versus exchange: the limits of monetary economics, *Review of Social Economy* 59: 203–228.

Bernstein, W. J. (2004) *The Birth of Plenty*, New York: McGraw-Hill.

Brotherton, B. (1989) Defining hospitality, tourism and leisure: perspectives, problems and implications, *International Association of Hotel Management Schools, Autumn Symposium*, The Queen's College, Glasgow.

Brotherton, B. (1999a) Towards a definitive view of the nature of hospitality and hospitality management, *International Journal of Contemporary Hospitality Management* 11: 165–173.

Brotherton, B. (1999b) Comparative research. In Brotherton, B. (ed.) *The Handbook of Contemporary Hospitality Management Research*, Chichester: John Wiley, pp. 143–172.

Brotherton, B. (1999c) Case study research. In Brotherton, B. (ed.) *The Handbook of Contemporary Hospitality Management Research*, Chichester: John Wiley, pp. 115–141.

Brotherton, B. (2000) The comparative approach. In Brotherton, B. (ed.) *An Introduction to the UK Hospitality Industry: A Comparative Approach*, Oxford: Butterworth-Heinemann, pp. 1–22.

Brotherton, B. (2002a) Towards a general theory of hospitality. Presented and work-in-progress abstract published in *Proc. Eleventh Annual CHME Hospitality Research Conference*, Leeds Metropolitan University.

Brotherton, B. (2003a) The nature of hospitality: hotel guest associations and metaphors. Presented and work-in-progress abstract published in *Proc. Twelfth Annual CHME Hospitality Research Conference*, Sheffield Hallam University.

Brotherton, B. (2003b) Is your mirror the same as mine? Methodological issues in undertaking and interpreting cross-cultural studies, *Tourism Today* 3: 26–37.

Brotherton, B. (2005) The nature of hospitality: customer perceptions and implications, *Tourism and Hospitality Planning & Development* 2: 139–153.

Brotherton, B. (2006) Some thoughts on a general theory of hospitality, *Tourism Today* 6: 8–19.

Brotherton, B. (2008) *Researching Hospitality and Tourism*, London: Sage.

Brotherton, B. (2013) Hospitality and hospitality management. In Wood, R. C. (ed.) *Key Concepts in Hospitality Management*, London: Sage, pp. 59–63.

Brotherton, B. (2015) *Researching Hospitality and Tourism*, 2nd edn, London: Sage.

Brotherton, B. and Wood, R. C. (2000a) Conceptualising hospitality – the next frontier? Presented at the Ninth Annual CHME Hospitality Research Conference, Huddersfield University.

Brotherton, B. and Wood, R. C. (2000b) Defining hospitality and hospitality management. In Lashley, C. and Morrison, A. (eds) *In Search of Hospitality: Theoretical Perspectives and Debates*, Oxford: Butterworth-Heinemann, pp. 134–156.

Brotherton, B. and Wood, R. C. (2008) The nature and meanings of hospitality. In Brotherton, B. and Wood, R. C. (eds) *The SAGE Handbook of Hospitality Management*, London: Sage, pp. 37–61.

Carlin, M. (2008) 'What say you to a piece of beef and mustard?' the evolution of public dining in medieval and Tudor London, *Huntingdon Library Quarterly* 71: 199–217.

Civitello, L. (2008) *Cuisine and Culture: A History of Food and People*, 2nd edn, Hoboken, NJ: John Wiley.

Cocks, C. (2001) *Doing The Town: The Rise of Urban Tourism in the United States, 1850–1915*, Berkeley: University of California Press.

Constable, O. R. (2003) *Housing the Stranger in the Mediterranean World*, New York: Cambridge University Press.

Cuthill, V. (2007) Sensing and performing hospitalities and socialities of tourist places: eating and drinking out in Harrogate and Whitehaven. In Germann Molz, J. and Gibson, S. (eds) *Mobilizing Hospitality: The Ethics of Social Relations in a Mobile World*, Aldershot: Ashgate, pp. 83–100.

Dawkins, R. (1976) *The Selfish Gene*, Oxford: Oxford University Press.

Dittmer, P. R. (2002) *Dimensions of the Hospitality Industry*, 3rd edn, New York: John Wiley.

Elias, N. (1978) *The Civilising Process*, Oxford: Blackwell.

Fieldhouse, P. (1996) *Food and Nutrition: Customs and Culture*, 4th edn, Cheltenham: Stanley Thornes.

Finkelstein, J. (1989) *Dining Out: A Sociology of Modern Manners*, Oxford: Blackwell.

Flandrin, J. L. (1999) The early modern period. In Flandrin, J. L., Montanari, M. and Sonnenfeld, A. (eds) *Food: A Culinary History from Antiquity to the Present*, New York: Columbia University Press, pp. 349–373.

Gautier, A. (2009) Hospitality in pre-viking Anglo-Saxon England, *Early Medieval Europe*, 17: 23–44.

Germov, J. and Williams, L. (1999) The hyper-rational social appetite: towards a synthesis of food trends. In Germov, J. and Williams, L. (eds) *A Sociology of Food and Nutrition: The Social Appetite*, Victoria, Aus.: Oxford University Press, pp. 301–310.

Giddens, A. (1991) *Modernity and Self-Identity: Self and Society in the Late Modern Age*, Cambridge: Polity Press.

Goody, J. (1982) *Cooking, Cuisine and Class: A Study in Comparative Sociology*, Cambridge: Cambridge University Press.

Grignon, C. (2001) Commensality and social morphology: an essay of typology. In Scholliers, P. (ed.) *Food, Drink and Identity: Cooking and Eating in Europe Since the Middle Ages*, Oxford: Berg, pp. 23–33.

Heal, F. (1990) *Hospitality in Early Modern England*, Oxford: Clarenden Press.

Hemmington, N. (2007) From service to experience: understanding and defining the hospitality business, *Service Industries Journal* 27: 747–755.

Hollander, P. (1981) Political hospitality, *Society* 19: 66–78.

Jones, P. (1996) Hospitality research – where have we got to?, *International Journal of Hospitality Management* 15: 5–10.

Keifer, N. M. (2002) Economics and the origin of the restaurant, *Cornell Hotel and Restaurant Administration Quarterly* August: 58–64.

Kerr, J. (2002) The open door: hospitality and honour in twelfth/early thirteenth-century England, *Journal of the Historical Association* 87: 322–335.

Kerr, J. (2007) 'Welcome the coming and speed the parting guest': hospitality in twelfth-century England, *Journal of Medieval History* 33: 130–146.

Lane, H. E. and Dupre, D. (1997) *Hospitality World: An Introduction*, New York: John Wiley.

Lashley, C., Lynch, P. and Morrison, A. (2007) Ways of knowing hospitality. In Lashley, C., Lynch, P. and Morrison, A. (eds) *Hospitality: A Social Lens*, Oxford: Elsevier, pp. 173–191.

Lynch, P., Germann Molz, J., Mcintosh, A., Lugosi, P. and Lashley, C. (2011) Editorial – theorizing hospitality, *Hospitality & Society* 1: 3–24.

Mackenzie, A., Ball, A. S. and Virdee, S. R. (1998) *Instant Notes in Ecology*, Oxford: BIOS Scientific.

Melissen, F. (2014) The concept of hospitality. In Melissen, F., Van der Rest, J. P., Josephi, S. and Blomme, R. (eds) *Hospitality Experience: An Introduction to Hospitality Management*, Groningen/Houten: Noordhoff, pp. 11–36.

Mennell, S. (1985) *All Manners of Food: Eating and Taste in England and France from the Middle Ages to the Present*, Oxford: Blackwell.

Mennell, S. (1992) Divergences and convergences in the development of culinary cultures. In Tueteberg, H. J. (ed.) *European Food History: A Research Review*, Leicester: Leicester University Press, pp. 278–288.

Mennell, S., Murcott, A. and Van Otterloo, A. H. (1992) *The Sociology of Food: Eating, Diet and Culture*, Newbury Park, CA: Sage.

Middleton, V. (1983) Marketing in the hospitality industry. In Cassee, E. and Reuland, R. J. (eds) *The Management of Hospitality*, Oxford: Pergamon, pp. 51–68.

Montanari, M. (1999) Food systems and models of civilisation. In Flandrin, J. L., Montanari, M. and Sonnenfeld, A. (eds) *Food: A Culinary History from Antiquity to the Present*. New York: Columbia University Press, pp. 69–78.

Morineau, M. (1999) Growing without knowing – production, demographics and diet. In Flandrin, J. L., Montanari, M. and Sonnenfeld, A. (eds) *Food: A Culinary History from Antiquity to the Present*, New York: Columbia University Press, pp. 374–382.

O'Gorman, K. D. (2005) Modern hospitality: lessons from the past, *Journal of Hospitality and Tourism Management* 12: 141–151.

O'Gorman, K. D. (2007) The hospitality phenomenon: philosophical enlightenment?, *International Journal of Culture, Tourism and Hospitality Research* 1: 189–202.

O'Gorman, K. D. (2009) Origins of the commercial hospitality industry: from the fanciful to the factual, *International Journal of Contemporary Hospitality Management* 21: 777–790.

O'Gorman, K. D. (2010) *The Origins of Hospitality and Tourism*, Oxford: Goodfellow.

Ohler, N. (2010) *The Medieval Traveller*, 2nd edn, Woodbridge: The Boydell Press.

Olesen, V. (1994) Selves and a changing social form: notes on three types of hospitality, *Symbolic Interaction* 17: 187–202.

Pine, B. J. and Gilmore, J. H. (1999) *The Experience Economy*, Boston: Havard Business School Press.

Pine, B. J. and Gilmore, J. H. (2002) Differentiating hospitality operations via experiences, *Cornell Hotel and Restaurant Administration Quarterly* June: 87–96.

Powers, T. and Barrows, C. W. (2006) *Introduction to the Hospitality Industry*, 6th edn, Hoboken, NJ: John Wiley.

Reuland, R. J. and Cassee, E. (1983) Hospitality in hospitals. In Cassee, E. and Reuland, R. J. (eds) *The Management of Hospitality*, Oxford: Pergammon, pp. 143–163.

Ritzer, G. (2007) Inhospitable hospitality? In Lashley, C., Lynch, P. and Morrison, A. (eds) *Hospitality: A Social Lens*, Oxford: Elsevier, pp. 129–139.

Sanchez-Moreno, E. (2001) Cross-cultural links in Ancient Iberia: socio-economic anatomy of hospitality, *Oxford Journal of Archaeology* 20: 391–414.

Sandoval-Strausz, A. K. (2007) *Hotel: An American History*, New Haven: Yale University Press.

Santich, B. (2007) Hospitality and gastronomy: natural allies. In Lashley, C., Lynch, P. and Morrison, A. (eds) *Hospitality: A Social Lens*, Oxford: Elsevier, pp. 47–59.

Sherringham, C. and Daruwalla, P. (2007) Transgressing hospitality: polarities and disordered relationships? In Lashley, C., Lynch, P. and Morrison, A. (eds) *Hospitality: A Social Lens*, Oxford: Elsevier, pp. 33–45.

Simmons, J. (1984) Railways, hotels, and tourism in Great Britain 1839–1914, *Journal of Contemporary History* 19: 201–222.

Slattery, P. (2009) *The Economic Ascent of the Hotel Business*, Oxford: Goodfellow.

Spang, R. L. (2000) *The Invention of the Restaurant: Paris and Modern Gastronomic Culture*, Boston: Harvard University Press.

Strong, R. (2002) *Feast: A History of Grand Eating*, London: Jonathon Cape.

Telfer, E. (1996) *Food for Thought: Philosophy and Food*, London: Routledge.

Telfer, E. (2000) The philosophy of hospitableness. In Lashley, C. and Morrison, A. (eds) *In Search of Hospitality: Theoretical Perspectives and Debates*, Oxford: Butterworth-Heinemann, pp. 38–55.

Towner, J. (1996) *An Historical Geography of Recreation and Tourism in the Western World, 1540–1940*, Chichester: John Wiley.

Traphagan, J. W. and Brown, L. K. (2002) Fast food and intergenerational commensality in Japan: new styles and old patterns, *Ethnology* 41: 119–134.

Turkel, S. (2009) *Great American Hoteliers – Pioneers of the Hotel Industry*, Bloomington, IN: Author House.

Van Hoof, H. B., McDonald, M. E., Yu, L. and Vallen, G. K. (1996) *A Host of Opportunities: An Introduction to Hospitality Management*, Chicago: Irwin.

Visser, M. (1991) *The Rituals of Dinner*, London: Penguin Books.

Wood, R. C. (1994) Some theoretical perspectives on hospitality. In Seaton, A. V. (ed.) *Tourism: The State of the Art*, Chichester: John Wiley, pp. 737–742.

Wood, R. C. (2015) *Hospitality Management: A Brief Introduction*, London: Sage.

8

Dinner sharing

Casual hospitality in the collaborative economy

Szilvia Gyimóthy

> **Key themes**
>
> The business model of social dining platforms
>
> Commodifying homes as commercial hospitality arenas
>
> Casual hospitality and the illusion of social dining
>
> Exclusive dining societies

> This is a technology platform that brings people together. Sharing a meal, sharing stories, sharing laughs with new people in someone's house is deeply personal, authentic, and intimate … it also happens to be the original social network.
>
> *(Rothman, 2014)*

Within the last few years, the peer-to-peer marketplace has expanded both in terms of geographical scale and organizational forms (Rifkin, 2000; Botsman and Rogers, 2010; Dredge and Gyimóthy, 2015) The social web or Web 2.0 and mobile technologies have paved the way for digital platforms intermediating between individuals from any corner of the world (Felländer *et al.*, 2015), and have given rise to collaborative economic phenomena like peer-to-peer rentals, ridesharing, and social dining (also known as dinner sharing). Social dining intermediaries such as EatWith, Feastly, MealSharing or Voulez-Vous-Diner facilitate visitors connecting with locals and enjoying home-cooked meals in private homes. From a technotopian perspective, it is digital technology that genuinely connects people. As one of the sites claims, they reconfigure conventions of eating out, by bringing "local chefs with a passion for cooking and entertaining together with locals and travelers looking for an exciting new dining experience" (EatWith 2015a). Bonding with and sharing moments of intimacy with strangers is framed as new or alternative tourism, which thrives on and is conditioned by social networking technologies (Germann Molz, 2013).

DOI: 10.4324/9781315679938-9

The most compelling narrative about the sharing economy is the return to "the original social network" and to a long-gone, closely knit community lifestyle, offering an alternative to our contemporary, alienated and individualistic society. As the epigraph above illustrates, dinner sharing businesses appropriate the values and moral philosophy of welcoming guests in a domestic setting, but stretching and infusing new meaning into notions of private hospitality. By claiming to re-invoke deeply personal and authentic relationships, collaborative businesses are disposed towards a specific moral mission, which is challenging and standing in sharp contrast to industrial tourism and inhospitable corporate agendas (Ritzer, 2007; Germann Molz, 2013). Meal sharing experiences are frequently assessed as better than commercial meals, and guests claim that they "get so much more out of these dinners than in a fancy restaurant" (St. Louis, 2014). Implicitly, collaborative tourism discourses carry normative ideas about the "original" way to travel, or the right way to consume and to interact with locals (Germann Molz, 2013).

We should nevertheless address and question the implied truthfulness underlying this moral agenda. Digitally networked communities are not simply upscaled versions of Tönnies' Gemeinschaft; people are unlikely to engage spontaneously in intimate relationships with altruistic private hosts. Modern tourists are temporary flâneurs with a loose attachment to the places they visit, or as Bauman notes, they are "being *in* but not *of* the place" (in Franklin, 2003: 208). Visitors have no commitments, other than to consuming a pleasurable experience, and they are not locked in the everyday ordering structures of local life. These transient individuals do not have the same rights and obligations as permanent citizens and there are no standard rules regulating their interactions with the host community (Franklin, 2003). This is a defining feature of the "tourist syndrome" (Franklin, 2003), resulting in frail and shallow relationships which tourists enter into wherever they go.

But how do the new technological advances facilitate interconnectedness among strangers on a large geographical scope? How are host–guest exchanges mediated through digital infrastructures, and how are various conditions of hospitality (trust, openness, and equality) warranted and operationalized? This chapter attempts to problematize the emergent social practice of dinner sharing, by disentangling the business model of the largest digitally facilitated social dining platform (EatWith), and the mechanisms enabling the carefree hosting of strangers and meeting locals. Second, the narrative strategies of commodifying homes as commercial arenas are analyzed to highlight co-existing ulterior and altruistic aspects of digitally mediated hospitality. Third, Bauman's notion of cloakroom communities is invoked to reveal the "illusion of the social" in social dining. These three analytical departures will contribute to deconstruct the exclusive dining societas framed as equitable host–guest experiences and add further to the critique of the collaborative economy (Dredge and Gyimóthy, 2015).

The business model of social dining platforms

Sharing meals is by no means a new host–guest experience. The quest for unmediated and authentic encounters with locals has long been identified as one of the main drivers of postmodern tourism and has existed since the mid-twentieth century (Welk, 2004). Hosting strangers in private homes on commercial terms is equally a deep-rooted phenomenon; the first bed and breakfasts and chambre d'hôtes going back to as far as the nineteenth-century in Europe. In France, table d'hôtes (referring to simple meals prepared by the B&B hosts) have become staple items of rural vacations in the post-war period. All staying guests would sit around the same table and small-talk while sharing dinner and listening to their hosts telling about their region or recommending activities in the neighborhood. In fact, experiencing an area like/with the locals was perfectly possible before the Internet. Nevertheless, some decades ago, finding the most convivial host and the coziest cottage was a logistically complicated affair, fraught with information asymmetries (and perhaps even risks). Owing to the social networking technologies available today, it is much easier to find such experiences. New collaborative economic platforms and intermediaries offer an immediate and comparable overview of potential hosts, and it is possible to retrieve recent and reliable recommendations from a number of independent peer review sites (Hamari *et al.*, 2015). Also, the production, transaction, and distribution costs of an online company mediating between potential guests and hosts are minimal (Rifkin, 2015; Sigala, 2015), thus lowering the entry barriers for new enterprises and allowing innovative initiatives.

One of these enterprises is EatWith, an Israeli start-up from 2010, which was triggered during dining with a local family on a holiday in Crete. Delighted by the ambiance and meal experience with private hosts, the founders Guy Michlin and Shemer Schwarz designed a business model opening up "more authentic and delicious" local dining experiences as alternatives to tourist trap restaurants. However, the narrative focus is on cosmopolitan cuisine rather than simple dishes from grandma's kitchen. Competitive strengths are defined according to the uniqueness of the one-off menus offered by creative chefs and the exclusivity of private venues offering an "intimate setting" (EatWith, 2015a). Within five years, the company has grown to include fairly diverse dining events in over 150 cities around the world from San Francisco to Rome.

EatWith's website features over 300 private hosts offering a variety of meals such as paellas in Madrid, Anatolian mezes in Istanbul or Nordic fusion cuisine in Berlin. Some are celebrity chefs, while others are passionate amateurs, each carefully inspected by EatWith in advance and approved with an "EatWith Verified Host" badge. Potential guests are guided through a simple, three-step purchase process (browse-book-enjoy). The all-inclusive, prix-fix menus are listed by location and date on the website, explained with ample visual material and up-to-date ratings. It is possible to filter results according to price range, party size, meal type, and cuisine. Meal prices vary between 25 and 65 euros per person, of which EatWith retains 15 percent for covering transaction and administration costs. After selecting a location and a chef, guests book and pay for their dinner online, including the tip. Payments are transferred to respective hosts 24 hours after the dinner event. There are no monetary transactions at the dining event itself; the disguised payment handled by the company also adds to the illusion of a private hospitality exchange. Yet, as is demonstrated below, the domestic dining experience is conditioned and modulized in every detail.

Guarantees, disclaimers and modulized matchmaking

Arguably, it can feel awkward to sign up for a dinner at a stranger's house using a mobile app. EatWith is a typical digital intermediary and claims to take great measures to ensure safe and successful transactions between hosts and guests. The vetting procedure entails a personal visit to each prospective chef, checking out parameters such as food quality, cleanliness, and the interpersonal skills of the host. The identities of guests are also verified, and only registered users aged 18 or older are entitled to use the services offered in the platform. On taking a closer look, responsibilities, as far as possible, rest with the parties involved.

> Participating in food events such as home meals, personal chef cook services, dinner parties or other user's activities as a result, directly or indirectly, from using EatWith ("Food Event"), is entirely at your own risk ... EatWith has no control over the conduct of any Hosts, Guests or any other User and recommends respective users to examine the terms and

details prior to any booking and confirmation … We do not accept any liability for any loss, damage, cost or expense that you may suffer or incur as a result of or in connection with your participation in any Food Event conducted by a User or a third party.

(EatWith, Terms of Service, 2015b)

There is no explicit insurance policy protecting anyone hosting a meal, and guests may only get a refund in the event of misconduct during food events, *should* the company decide in its sole discretion. Apart from this, the company disclaims all warranties regarding the correctness of information provided by the hosts, including the availability, reliability, or quality of food served during dining events. Further, EatWith explicitly disclaims being in the food vendor business and reverts all responsibility to the hosts regarding compliance with laws and regulations. Such disclaimers elegantly bypass the lack of control of food hygiene, personal security, and tax declarations, which points at multiple problems in operating and regulating footloose commercial enterprises across the blurred boundaries of private and commercial hospitality.

In order to reduce the uncertainties connected with hosting strangers at home, the company requests guests to provide their real names and email addresses. These contact forms containing personal details (also including allergies and dietary requirements) are forwarded to the hosts, giving them the opportunity to check out profiles before confirming the reservation. Furthermore, it is possible to sneak peek the composition of a dinner party, checking out fellow guests' photos, nationality, occupation, and city of residence. Another dinner-sharing platform, the Cornwall-based Social Dining Network even prompts users to indicate their co-dining group preference (fine diners, vegetarians, seafood lovers, fitness fanatics, or singles, among others). The modular design evokes the algorithms of contemporary digital dating apps, ensuring near or perfect matches between hosts and their guests beforehand. Finally, trust is also embedded in the standardized peer rating system; following the logic of other online market valuation platforms, like Tripadvisor. Affiliated chefs are evaluated by their patrons subsequent to their visit along three parameters (overall experience, food quality, and cleanliness). This crude meritocratic system may lead to a ranked hierarchy among popular hosts in the same location, simplifying the selection process.

In the modular business model of social dining, hospitality itself is conditioned and reduced into a number of transparent parameters, elegantly organized into a searchable and bookable menu. As Marek Korczynski and Ursula Ott (2006) so aptly point out, the menu operates as a mediator and a buffer between the individual autonomy of customers and structures of power. The enticing website listings of dinner events appeal to guests' sense of freedom to choose the optimal dinner experience. The ritualized, selected, and standardized presentation of welcoming, creative chefs (and even co-diners) upholds the enchanting myth of guests' sovereignty. Guests are simultaneously reminded of and exempted from culturally established hospitality practices; for instance, they are encouraged, but not obliged to bring small gifts for their hosts. The alleged "intimate and authentic" encounter among strangers is mass-customized. In this way, hospitality becomes a calculated equation, where trust between hosts and guests is conditioned along carefully designed algorithms. However, private dinners cannot be standardized entirely, and as the next sections demonstrate, there is room for improvisation.

"Dine in a chef's home!" Homes as commercial hospitality arenas

Having deconstructed the business model of dinner sharing, we can now turn our attention to the role of the hosts and their homes. Contemporary sociologists have addressed the commodification of personal sphere, identifying complex rationales within various lifestyle enterprises

(Andersson-Cederholm and Hultman, 2010; Andersson-Cederholm, 2015). Through studies of contemporary practices in tourism and hospitality small and medium-sized enterprises, these authors highlight the hybridity of their business motives (driven by commercial and social objectives) and argue that the domestic arena itself has become a key competitive argument. In this section we will explore the narrative strategies through which chef's homes and private lives are staged in EatWith's market communication. Throughout the website and other media, three broad themes emerge to define the dinner-sharing host: personal bonds, professional pride, and local ambassadorship. These are discussed below.

> We take great pride in finding and vetting the most creative chefs. You'll get to enjoy getting to know them and the story behind their dishes.
>
> *(EatWith 2015a)*

EatWith puts an emphasis on contrasting social dining to dining in commercial restaurants, suggesting an opportunity to develop personal relationships with hosts. Potential guests may immerse themselves in the personal stories of affiliated chefs before the dinner event takes place. The website presentations describe the sample menu, but also provide a biographic summary of each host, revealing giveaways about their lifestyle, preferences, and hobbies. Consider the following disclosure:

> To find a perfectly ripe avocado or mango, to pick mushrooms in the forest to a Sunday dinner and to make our own Granola makes us happy! We do not eat food because we are hungry, we eat because we love cooking, eating and throwing dinner parties! ... Like everyone else we love NY and go there over the weekend only to eat and feel the pace. At the moment we are into Bikramyoga so do not be surprised if we try to get you to start.
>
> *(Julia, Sweden)*

By reading about Julia's passion for food, yoga, and for New York, we get an impression of her attitudes (hedonist, novelty, and pleasure-seeker), personality (extrovert, social, and perfectionist) and even economic status (able to afford a weekend trip to New York). Arguably these miniature biographies are crafted to appeal to visitors, who can, in a voyeuristic manner, familiarize themselves with private details and pretend to be an acquaintance of the host by the time of arriving at the food event. The tidbit stories facilitate and reinforce the grazing behavior of contemporary tourists, who are in search of "untried tastes and un-experienced sensations" (Franklin, 2003: 208). Yet those virtual pre-familiarizing practices are not entirely reciprocal or symmetric: guests only share brief and functional information about themselves as they register. Being paying customers, they are not required to charm their hosts; the personal data is solely used to verify their identities as safe clients. This also underlines the transitory, grazing character of the dinner-sharing experience; once guests have consumed a delightful dinner and the satisfaction fades, they will move on to their next experience. Hence, the deeply personal bonding alluded to in the promotional material is highly situated and illusory.

EatWith also presents some of its hosts in brief (3–5 minutes long) promotional video clips, distributed on multiple social media platforms. These videos have an autobiographical character, featuring the hosts as first person narrators, and are built around similar narratives of culinary playfulness and experimentation. One confessionary video vignette features a young Dutch woman moving to Barcelona to realize her dream of living as a chef. Although she is an electrician by profession, her dedication to cooking and hosting is evident:

> Since I can remember I always loved to be in the kitchen. Cooking comes so naturally to me and I wonder why it took so long to figure out what to do in with my life. I love how food can bring people together … it's what makes me happy.
>
> *(Yorinde, Barcelona)*

Yorinde's story is very similar to that of the other showcased cosmopolitan gastronauts from around the world. Many of them have moved to a new country to pursue their burning passion for food, and the culinary dedication seems to outweigh the fact that most chefs are autodidact. The honest narratives of the skilled and experienced amateurs are presented through everyday practices, and further strengthen the rhetoric ploy to convey the genuineness and sincerity of a private host. For example, as a typecast Italian mamma expresses, while the camera follows her on her daily grocery tour:

> When I wake up in the morning I immediately think about shopping. I bicycle to the market and I buy vegetables, seasonal food and specialties … I go back home and here start my happy day, because my love is in my cuisine. *Amo cucinare!*
>
> *(Barbara, Rome)*

In various ways, these video testimonies emphasize the gratifying experience of bringing people together and share the enjoyment of culinary delights:

> A friend of me told about EatWith. I came home and search the web, and when I saw it I was so happy because I realized that this is my job now! People come here and meet each other from all over the world. Immediately they are friends. It is very funny and interesting. The best compliment I have ever received is: My heart is full now.
>
> *(Barbara, Rome)*

> To get to see their faces and see their eyes light up when they take the first bite … that just priceless … that long mmmm-sound, that's what I love. That's what I cook for!
>
> *(Coreen, San Francisco)*

The gratification gained from guests' compliments resonates well with Telfer's notion of hospitableness (2000), identifying it as a benevolent, compassionate action, driven by the desire for being with, pleasing, and entertaining others. However, hosts do get decent compensation for their efforts, and hence they simultaneously represent ulterior and altruistic motives of hospitality (Lashley, Introduction to this volume). This highlights the hybrid nature of the dinner sharing, which is governed partly by capitalist market logic and partly by social capital and collaborative values (Rifkin, 2015). As Bauman (2002) foresaw it in his book, *Society under Siege*, modes of travel and hospitality have become reconfigured. Individuals are providing food and drinks to strangers in a domestic context, and their fleeting relationship extends beyond the narrow and sanitized scope of commercial service encounters. Nevertheless, the commercial exchange itself exempts the guests from reciprocating the favor, and it is not known whether the participants at a dinner event could establish lasting social bonds in the future.

Third, the featured chefs are also portrayed as "typical locals," living an almost cartoonish "good life" in a "relaxed vibe." They are knowledgeable about the "right" places in the city and visitors are encouraged to take the role as extras for a single evening performance enacted on a private scene:

> We welcome you to our central Barcelona apartment with a wonderful rooftop terrace to enjoy an amazing assortment of fusion tapas inspired by my Italian heritage and Nuria's Catalan family. Depending of the season we will offer you a tasting menu of more than 15 type of tapas gourmet exploring several flavors and culinary techniques ... The secret is indeed the natural and fresh product. Our "dealer" is Santa Caterina market ... probably the best in town! ... Come and have a good time with me and my lady, meeting other locals and travelers, and we'll be happy to share a lovely evening and recommend you our favorite places in town.
>
> *(Ascanio, Barcelona)*

The quote above indicates that Ascanio and his girlfriend not only take pride in being private hosts (willingly sharing their rooftop terrace), but also act as patriotic ambassadors for Barcelona itself. This kind of civic public diplomacy—that is, when residents take over municipal hospitality duties in one-to-one encounters—is the ultimate ambition of most city branding managers. Civic hospitality is not driven by extrinsic motives, but rather by a deep-rooted identification and affective relationship with the city of residence. As Barbara's quote below demonstrates:

> I am Barbara I live in Rome I was born in Rome. I love to cook and I love welcoming people. That's why I cook for travelers who come here from around the world. I come from a typical Roman family who lives here for 9 generations ... I love everything about Rome because it is romantic, lively and unique.
>
> *(Barbara, Rome)*

Being a ninth generation Roman citizen, Barbara is fully subscribing to Rome's touristic imagery and she is permanently enacting the generous local host. She is living the "Rome brand," making her living by selling her culture and lifeworld as a spectacle, being romantic, lively, and unique herself. Cultural commodification in the wake of tourism has been described by scholars, yet, so far, private homes (at least in the Western world) have been considered a territory beyond the reach of tourists. With the rise of the collaborative economy, domestic and everyday settings are becoming colonized and commercialized along the standard narratives of tourism marketing. These kind of endeavors are referred to as lifestyle enterprising arenas, constituting an in-between space of the private and the public (Andersson-Cederholm, 2015). Erika Andersson Cederholm and Johan Hultman (2010) studied the social dynamics of host–guests relationships in B&Bs and demonstrated that their hybrid nature (being commercial and personal at once) results in ambiguity as well as a constant negotiation of physical, social, and emotional boundaries. The illustrations in this section feature proud and self-confident hosts, with seemingly no dissonance or incongruity between their private and commercial selves. This does not necessarily imply that they fully identify with their roles as EatWith chefs; nevertheless, it would require other types of data to explore how they handle interactions and settle ambiguities during social dining events.

Casual (contingent) hospitality and the illusions of social dining

Let us turn our attention to the communitarian aspects of dinner sharing, and the raising market awareness of the social linking value of food. In her video, Yorinde talks about the joy of turning her home into an international travelers' lounge:

> What I like about hosting dinners is that people are coming from all over the world; there are young people, old people, there are couples and there are people travelling alone. There is such an interesting mix of people. People who come in are kind of shy and timid and then they open up and make friends ... in my living room! That's awesome, right?
>
> *(Yorinde, Barcelona)*

It is one giant leap into the unknown to make friends with strangers, even in a comfortable, private setting. But how does making friends happen? Facing the Other is an ambivalent feeling, as Bauman (2001) notes, and he refers to Kant by describing it as a "sublime" experience. It is "a mixture of fear and awe", being both attracted to and repelled by the strange and unfamiliar (Franklin, 2003: 214). For an illustration of coping with those awkward moments, excerpts are presented from a blogger's footage:

> This week, I did something that would probably make most New Yorkers think I was crazy. I ate dinner in a stranger's apartment with seven people I'd never met before using meal-sharing website. I was skeptical when I arrived and definitely concerned about making conversation with total strangers for the next two hours ... While we waited for the other four guests, Simon [the host] directed us to his terrace, which offered a great view of lower Manhattan. Getting to know people was a little weird at first, especially since I was by myself ... As we started to eat, it was a little difficult to get conversation started. We were all trying to be polite, so we mostly chatted about our careers ... Up next was a soup d'oignon, better known as French onion soup. At this point, our conversation had turned to international travel. There was an awkward pause when one of the guests said she doesn't travel, but I still enjoyed learning about parts of the world I've never been, like Amsterdam and Tasmania. Once we were done eating, Simon left the kitchen and joined us at the table. Exchange rates, jet lag, and Australian football were the main topics of conversation ... The entire evening lasted about two hours. By the end, I was surprised by how comfortable I felt around my fellow diners.
>
> *(Kircher, 2015)*

The concerns described above resonate with the ambivalence that Bauman describes on "meeting the other." The blogger calls the dinner sharing experience bluntly "crazy" (rather than sublime), which reveals mixed feelings towards being in the immediate proximity of strangers in a private, yet unfamiliar space. Note how this casual dining community attempted to adhere to the script of a social dinner among friends/colleagues; and how sentiments and moods developed within two hours, starting from skeptical and feeling weird to becoming polite and at last comfortable. During the course of the evening, the participants gradually recognized the individuality of each other, through the shared stories of work and travel, yet conveniently avoiding private topics. This kind of casual and noncommittal conversation is referred to as sociability by Georg Simmel (1950), describing a superficial and playful form of social exchange, where individuals pretend as if they were in close friendship with each other. As one of the hosts notes, the spatial context of the domestic setting plays a significant role in allowing for spontaneous connections and proper conversation:

> I started cooking and the love of cooking when I realized that it was a way of getting people together. And so I started hosting these elaborate parties ... It is so much more fun when you are doing it for people you don't know because you don't know what's going

to happen. What is really fun about hosting EatWith dinners for me is bringing people together in a kind of environment that allows for connections and allows for communication. It goes so much beyond "oh I saw this movie last week…" It is about the art of conversation. I feel like we could get a lot better at that. Some of it got lost in our super attention-deficit society. Actually sit down and talk to this person you don't know. I consider it a successful event when the connections people have made is moved to the future in some way—whether it is for work, for fun or even romantically.

(Rebecca, San Francisco)

Talking over dinner with strangers may mimic the practices of close friendships and acquaintances, yet it is very different from lasting, closely knit communities. Dinner sharing events are mere substitutes for communities, summoning people with similar interests (food, travel, leisure) for a short stretch of time. Bauman calls these "cloakroom/peg or two-hour communities" (2001: 31), similar to crowds attending a theatre performance. People go to the cloakroom to hang up their coats before the play and when it is over, they pick up their belongings, leave in different directions and perhaps never come together again. Social dining events can be regarded as an ephemeral spectacle for cloakroom communities, during which interests "which divide them are temporarily laid aside, put on a slow burner or silenced altogether" (Bauman, 2001: 200). The success of EatWith underscores the longing for genuine communities, which the company simulates and promises to replicate ("the original social network" in the opening quote), but which are, according to Bauman (as well as to the host Rebecca), no longer available. In the absence of real personal relationships, people settle for quick-fix solutions, effectively delivered by contemporary tourism (Franklin, 2003).

Exclusive dining societies, pretended Otherness

Finally, we must address one of the pervasive claims of the collaborative economy, namely the communitarian and pro-social myth. According to the assertions of Botsman and Rogers (2010) and others (Stokes *et al.*, 2014), the new economy embraces openness, inclusivity and the commons; it reallocates wealth across the value chain, and it carries the seeds of a more fair, just, and equal society. Social dining platforms present similarly alluring promises, as in the following video promotion from EatWith:

EatWith is a great place to meet a lot of amazing people. Everybody is here for a reason. You come here seeking something or looking to grow in some way. The more you open to interactions the more doors will open to you. Most people who come to these dinners are more curious and looking for new experiences. You meet scientists, people from Wall Street, artists, musicians, foodies everything … Food is a really really equalizing experience. You have this experience when you are mutually enjoying something together and then you are a little bit more sensitive to each other. In the beginning we didn't know what to think but then we have realized what it meant to other people. What a great way to step into a city and meet some locals get some recommendations.

(EatWith, 2015a)

In deconstructing this excerpt, we get an impression of an exclusive foodie society, which makes it difficult to substantiate the "equalizing experience" claim of dinner sharing. The hosts (at least the ones promoted by EatWith) are presented as resourceful hipsters and expats, who engage in social dining not out of necessity, but as a leisure pastime. The guests are equally well-off international travelers situated in the top tiers of the knowledge and creative economy. Looking at the price range of the dinner events, it can be seen that they are far from available and affordable to all. Collaborative phenomena reproduce, rather than level out the growing inequalities in our contemporary society, and as one critic notes, "it trades on cultural homogeneity and established social networks … Where it builds new connections, it often replicates old patterns of privileged access for some, and denial for others" (Cagle, 2014). The romantic utopia of better, equitable and unmediated encounters between locals and tourists never existed in the first place—what we have observed above is but a comfortably familiar bonding between affluent and mobile individuals, with a bit of "local flavor."

Taking a closer look at the featured locations, it can be noted that the spreading of the social dining events is spatially uneven. Dinner sharing consumer practices take place in larger cities, mostly in chic neighborhoods, confirming Bauman's notion of a segregated world:

> The world is divided up into those places where tourists are carefully ushered into and through, and those places they are prevented from seeing. Tourists only *flow* into certain places.
>
> *(Franklin, 2003: 207)*

The inequality and social bias embedded in this particular example is echoed in the first indicative studies capturing the uptake of the collaborative economy. In the UK, two-thirds of the population is claimed to engage in collaborative activities, but there is a significant demographic bias among those participating (Stokes *et al.*, 2014) towards economically active, urban residents occupying managerial, professional, and administrative jobs. Dinner sharing is not a survival phenomenon, rather, it is driven by and benefits people with high cultural, digital, and networking capital, looking for just the right balance between "pretended otherness" and reassuring familiarity (Franklin, 2003: 213).

Conclusions

This chapter has explored the emergent notion of dinner sharing to illustrate how hospitality is contextualized anew in the collaborative economy. The business models, discourses, and practices of dinner sharing highlight a hybrid socio-economic phenomenon, which is governed both by and beyond commercial agendas. Consequently, it promotes a hybrid form of hospitality that bridges private, cultural, and commercial domains, and embraces (or cross-appropriates) moral, economic, social, and cultural norms from each. As the peer-to-peer marketplace moves into the domestic arena, it exploits the cultural associations of private hospitality, while downplaying the commercial aspects of social dining. Homes and home-cooked meals around the dinner table are consequentially vouched for being the "natural" environment for authentic meetings with locals from other cultures. EatWith and similar business initiatives subscribe to the communitarian dream of moral or alternative tourism (Germann Molz, 2013), claiming to re-embed dis-embedded personal relationships.

These moments of shared intimacy with strangers are but a staged and illusory endeavor. The analytical sections aimed to problematize some of the persistent truisms of the collaborative economy and revealed contradictory values and meanings emerging from cross-appropriated, casual social dining practices. The hospitality of platform businesses can be defined as modular, noncommittal and elitist. It is modular because the host–guest relationship is mediated by interactive social networking technologies, where search algorithms condition and commodify trust between strangers. Second, dinner sharing is non-committal, because the mutuality of the private encounter only lasts as long as the dinner event, reducing sociality to playful and non-binding sociability. Social dining is a spectacle for cloakroom communities (Bauman, 2000) and as Bauman foresaw it more than a decade ago: *"from now on the communities—more postulated than imagined—may be only ephemeral artifacts of the ongoing individuality play, rather than the identities determining and defining forces"* (2000: 22). Third, the hospitality of dinner sharing is elitist, as the cultural encounters take place between like-minded and privileged members of the creative middle class, rather than low-income people.

We are just beginning to grasp the significance of the collaborative economy, implying that most research on the subject (including this chapter) has so far been speculative or exploratory. There is a need for more rigorous, empirical studies to fully understand the economic and social aspects of phenomena like dinner sharing, and the ways in which they stretch the scope of contemporary hospitality.

References

Andersson-Cederholm, E. (2015) Lifestyle enterprising: the "ambiguity work" of Swedish horse-farmers, *Community, Work & Family* 18, 3: 317–333.

Andersson-Cederholm, E. and Hultman, J. (2010) The value of intimacy—negotiating commercial relationships in lifestyle entrepreneurship, *Scandinavian Journal of Hospitality and Tourism* 10, 1: 16–32.

Bauman, Z. (2000) *Liquid Modernity*, Cambridge: Polity Press.

Bauman, Z. (2001) *Community—Seeking Safety in an Insecure World*, Cambridge: Polity.

Bauman, Z. (2002) *Society under Siege*, Cambridge: Polity.

Bauman, Z. (2003) *Liquid Love: On the Frailty of Human Bonds,* Cambridge: Polity Press.

Botsman, R. and Rogers, R. (2010). *What's Mine is Yours: How Collaborative Consumption is Changing the Way We Live*, New York: HarperCollins.

Cagle, S. (2014) The case against sharing: on access, scarcity and trust, at https://thenib.com/the-case-against-sharing-9ea5ba3d216d. Accessed May 5, 2015.

Dredge, D. and Gyimóthy, S. (2015) The collaborative economy and tourism: critical perspectives, questionable claims and silenced voices, *Tourism Recreation Research* 40, 3: 286–302.

Eatwith (2015a) Bring people together one meal at a time, at http://www.eatwith.com/brand/about/. Accessed December 12, 2015.

Eatwith (2015b) Terms of service, at http://www.eatwith.com/brand/terms-of-service/. Accessed December 12, 2015.

Felländer, A., Ingram, C., and Teigland, R. (2015) *Sharing Economy: Embracing Change with Caution*, Näringspolitisk Rapport #11, Stockholm: Entreprenörskapsforum.

Franklin, A. (2003) The tourist syndrome: an interview with Zygmund Bauman, *Tourist Studies* 3, 2: 205–217.

Germann Molz, J. (2013) Social networking technologies and the moral economy of alternative tourism: the case of couchsurfing.org, *Annals of Tourism Research* 43: 210–230.

Hamari, J., Sjöklint, M., and Ukkonen, A. (2015) The sharing economy: why people participate in collaborative consumption. *Journal of the Association for Information Science and Technology*, DOI: 10.1002/asi.23552.

Kircher, M. M. (2015) I ate dinner at a strangers place using an app and I'd totally do it again. *Techinsider*, at http://www.techinsider.io/eatwith-app-lets-you-eat-cheap-with-strangers-2015-10. Accessed December 12, 2015.

Korczynski, M. and Ott, U. (2006) The menu in society: mediating structures of power and enchanting myths of individual sovereignty, *Sociology* 40, 5: 911–928.

Rifkin, J. (2000) *The Age of Access: The New Culture of Hypercapitalism, Where all of Life is a Paid-For Experience*, New York: Putman.

Rifkin, J. (2015) *The Zero Marginal Cost Society: The Internet of Things, the Collaborative Commons, and the Eclipse of Capitalism*, New York: Palgrave Macmillan.

Ritzer, G. (2007) Inhospitable hospitality. In Lashley, C., Lynch, P., and Morrison, A. (eds.) *Hospitality: A Social Lens*, Oxford: Elsevier, pp. 129–139.

Rothman, S. (2014) Our investments in EatWith: the dinner table as the original social network, at http://www.greylock.com/our-investment-in-eatwith-the-dinner-table-as-the-original-social-network/. Accessed December 1, 2015.

Sigala, M. (2015) Collaborative commerce in tourism: implications for research and industry, *Current Issues in Tourism*, DOI: 10.1080/13683500.2014.982522.

Simmel, G. (1950) *The Sociology of Georg Simmel*, Glencoe, IL: The Free Press.

St. Louis, R. (2014) Would you eat in a strangers home?, at http://www.bbc.com/travel/story/20140422-dine-with-strangers-in-their-home.

Stokes, K., Clarence, E., and Rinne, A. (2014) Making sense of the UK collaborative economy, at http://www.nesta.org.uk/publications/making-sense-uk-collaborative-economy. Accessed May 5, 2015.

Telfer, E. (2000) The philosophy of hospitableness. In Lashley, C. and Morrison, A. (eds.) *In Search of Hospitality: Theoretical Debates and Perspectives*, Oxford: Butterworth-Heinemann, pp. 38–55.

Welk, P. (2004) The beaten track: anti tourism as an element of backpacker identity construction. In Richards, G. and Wilson, J. (eds.) *The Global Nomad. Backpacker Travel in Theory and Practice*, Clevedon: Channel View, pp. 77–91.

9

Religious perspectives on hospitality

Conrad Lashley

Key themes

Social psychology and religion

Religion

Religious forms

The morality of hospitableness

> This is my simple religion. There is no need for temples; no need for compli-
> cated philosophy. Our own brain, our own heart is our temple; the philosophy
> is kindness.
>
> *(Dalai Lama)*

The study of religions suggests that the requirement to be hospitable to strangers and welcome all, irrespective of social status or stigma, is a worldwide defining feature of 'good' behaviour. This chapter explores the religious context of a sample of religions through time and across the globe. Although the narrative of who or what God or the gods are varies according to different social and economic settings, there are consistencies in moralities that human societies espouse. This suggests that the hospitality obligation is reflected in the religious views of hunting and gathering, as well as agricultural and industrialised societies.

While the chapter adopts a largely anthropological stance, it starts with a brief discussion of social psychological insights into the power of group membership in defining identity. Group membership is typically used to describe the individual and his/her differentiation from others. Religious affiliation is often one of the memberships cited, along with gender, age, sexual orientation and so forth, that is used in defining the self. Religion and its various codes of conduct and moralities perform an important role in describing 'us and them'. 'Faith binds' is not just an empty rhetoric of the faithful; it forms an important bond between people within, and across, societies.

DOI: 10.4324/9781315679938-10

111

The obligation to overcome the fear of out-group members and to welcome strangers is a powerful theme across religions. However, the obligation to be hospitable to strangers is only part of the story. Acts of hospitality are also required to distribute goods where some society members have more than others. Also, hospitality is advocated as support to those who have little, and is more than charity given at the whim of the donor – this is a requirement whereby the needs of the needy are addressed.

Social psychology and religion

While this chapter principally explores the nature of religion and the links between religion and the morality of hospitality, it is important to set the study within the context of social psychology. Individuals define themselves through the groups to which they belong, or to which they believe they belong. Group membership is a defining feature of society, as individuals identify who they are through their group membership: ethnicity, gender, age, religion, region, city, sports club supporter and so on. Each of these groups has a group identity that defines it, and the expectations of what group members should be like and do. Religious groupings, in particular, include observations about how good group members perform. These religious observations all have something to say about hosts' obligations to guests.

Individuals belong to two types of groups. The first are large groups of the sort mentioned earlier. They provide a sense of identity, but individuals can never know all fellow group members. These are called secondary groups. In other words, a person may declare they belong to a national group, say the Dutch, without knowing all the other people who make up the nation – the Dutch people. However, they do influence individuals in how they act, and what they consider to be right or wrong.

Membership of groups can result in all sorts of positive and negative behaviour – supporting the football team, and being in conflict with supporters of other teams; saluting the flag and fighting others who salute other flags. Much human conflict can be explained in terms of inter-group relations – war between nations, racism, ageism and sexism, for example, all involve individuals who belong to one specific group holding stereotyped views about members of other groups. Social psychologists talk about 'in-group' (groups to which individuals belong) and 'out-group' (groups to which individuals do not belong) relationships. Typically, people have positive perceptions of the group(s) to which they belong, and have more negative perceptions of groups to which they do not belong.

The second type of group, known as primary groups, are where members are all known to each other and have face-to-face relationships. Typically, these have about 10–12 members – any larger and they break up into smaller groups. These are sometimes called psychological groups (Huczynski and Buchanan, 2001) because they exist not only in interactions between members, but through the perceptions of members of themselves and other group members, and members of other groups. Huczynski and Buchanan describe psychological groups as 'people who consider themselves to be part of an identifiable unit, who relate to each other in meaningful fashion who share dispositions through their shared sense of collective identity' (2001: 277). Primary groups can have a powerful influence in creating bonds with other group members, and in ensuring a collective pressure on individual behaviour and beliefs. Within a religious context, primary groups have the role of creating the sense of belonging associated with religious practice, and of rejecting those who are deemed to transgress these practices.

The study of social psychology provides an insight into the inter-personal and group identity dimensions of religious beliefs and institutions. At a societal level, religions help create a shared sense of belonging to individuals who may never know all group members because the secondary group is so large. They then shape behavioural practices, including dress codes, language and rituals expected of group members. On a personal level, the collective practice of ceremony and moral worthiness are both used to assess the individual and provide a set of guidelines – of what to do and think.

On religion

It is said that humans began to evolve about two million years ago, but emerged in the modern human forms about 200,000 years ago (Howell, 2015) and, for most of this history, humans existed in varying forms of hunting and gathering, or foraging, society. Early systems of farming, such as herding and slash and burn, began to emerge around 10,000 years ago. For most of this agricultural period, land ownership and access to land was a key for human societies. The ownership and control of land became a deeply influential issue in the development of power relations in communities. Industrial societies started to develop with intensity in the 1800s, though this was a culmination of trends in trade and the making of things that had been developing over centuries.

Throughout this history, all human societies, no matter how large or small, embraced some form of religion (Lambek, 2008). The nature of the beliefs and the practices involved vary considerably. Indeed, views about the nature and purposes of religions are also the subject of considerable controversy. That said, there are some common features and contents that all religions appear to include. In the context of this chapter, they all have something to say about the nature of the host and guest, particularly how the host should treat the guest, and how the guest should behave to the host. A common feature across all societies is that there is a duty to welcome, to protect and to nurture the guest. Examples of these different observations about the duty to be hospitable will be discussed later.

Before discussing the moral obligation to be hospitable, it is necessary to discuss the role and purpose of religion. As might be expected with a subject that requires believers to have faith, there are many views about the role and purpose of religion. Karl Marx (1961 [1887]), for example, famously observed of the nineteenth-century experience that 'religion is the opium of the people'. By this, he meant that religion serves a purpose in keeping people obedient and unquestioning of the structures of power and exploitation surrounding them. While in the contemporary context there may be fewer 'addicts' than in Marx's day, religious faith continues to hold powerful sway over the lives of many human beings. Indeed, many contemporary conflicts seem to have some religious dimension.

The study of religion does not require a belief in, or rejection of, basic religious tenets. Some writers talk about a religious agnosticism, in other words studying religion as a human phenomenon without necessarily addressing the issues of proof of the existence of deity or deities. I take the view, informed by anthropology and sociology, of looking at these various religious forms as a way of understanding the ubiquitous nature of the requirement to welcome guests (out-group members).

The word 'religion' in Western European languages probably derives from Latin translations from Hebrew and Greek. For Tyler, religion 'is the belief in spiritual beings' (2008: 8). Though, this begs the question: what are spiritual beings? I prefer Smart's definition (1966: 10), which lists eight features of religions:

1   Ritual or practice;
2   Doctrinally all philosophical;
3   Mythical narrative;

4   Experiential and emotional;
5   Ethical and legal;
6   Social organisation;
7   Material or artistic;
8   Political and economic.

Smart's features enable a comparison between religions and religious systems by providing a set of issues or themes that need to be considered if one is to discuss and attempt to draw similarities and differences between them. For the purpose of this chapter, the treatment of strangers has much to do with doctrinal, ritualistic, ethical and legal dimensions of religion.

Many early scholars, when comparing religions around the world, were guilty of assuming that the Judeo-Christian tradition was the mirror image of evolutionary superiority arising from Social Darwinism (Bowie, 2006). To many nineteenth-century observers, the people living in Africa, Australia and the Americas were devoid of religion. There was an implicit assumption that religions could be defined as 'world' religions or as 'primal' religions. While some of the assumptions may now be seen to be somewhat racist, and the categories actually difficult to sustain in reality, they do present an interesting way of looking at the nature of religion and its purpose.

World religions are said by Bowie to include the following features: they are based on written scriptures; they include the notion of salvation from outside; they are universal or have universal potential; they can substitute or supplant primal religion; and they often form a separate sphere of activity (2006: 23). Primal religions, on the other hand, are said to be oral and lack written texts; they are this worldly in orientation; they are usually confined to a single language or ethnic group; they form the basis from which many world religions emerged; religions and social life are inseparable; and there is no separation between the sacred and the everyday experiences of the group (Bowie, 2006: 23). Reverting back to the insights gained from social psychology referred to earlier, religions can be said to provide a belief system that supports group identity. As Lambek summarises:

> In so far as religion forms the cultural ground (or 'worldview') of a society or serves to articulate its major concerns, it is intimately linked to such matters as human conception, kinship, and the life cycle, to the environment, ideas of human sociality, affinity, and exchange, conceptions of and conditions of human dignity, creativity and human well being.
>
> *(2008: 9)*

Within a modern context, the work of Max Weber has been extremely influential in drawing a link between certain religious ideas and the development of capitalism. In his famous work 'The Protestant ethic and the spirit of capitalism' (Weber, 2008) he suggests that there was a link between religious ideas and participation in the pursuit of wealth. Weber identified a problem in preindustrial societies where labourers would not be engaged in the pursuit of wealth for its own sake, but would often work for as much time as it took to earn enough to subsist, and then have leisure time. Thus, in Weber's view, paying high wages did not result in more output, but less, because people would work for as little as possible to maximise their leisure time. The Protestant perspective made a virtue of work for its own sake, suggesting that this was the will of God. Weber saw the pursuit of output, wealth and hard work as being consistent with the Protestant ideologies and ideas that emerged at the time. Weber shows that certain branches of Protestantism had supported worldly activities dedicated to economic gain, seeing them as endowed with moral and spiritual significance. This was not a goal in itself; rather they were a by-product of other doctrines of faith that encouraged planning, hard work and self-denial in the pursuit of worldly riches.

In my view, religion meets a need in people to have some understanding of the world in which they live, and the world before and the afterlife. Hunting and gathering societies have been the dominant social form throughout human history, and by studying these societies some authors suggest that religion originates in dreams that create an 'other world'. This world can include lost loved ones, and an imaginary life encompassing rational and irrational impulses and observations. Religion also provides narrative and explanations to questions about human existence, as well as about the purpose of life and what goes beyond (Morris, 2006). Before scientific explanations of the world began to emerge, religion provided a narrative that seemed to work and explain the nature of the environment in which humans exist (Lambek, 2008). It is interesting, for example, that monotheism originated only after the emergence of farming and settled communities based on agriculture and agricultural trade, and presumably personal land ownership.

Religious forms and hospitality

This chapter does not claim to provide a thoroughly systematic discussion of religion and religious forms. It does attempt to provide examples spanning both time and space, showing that belief systems practised by people across societies include some requirement to look after and protect the guest. This section gives insight into various religious forms as a way of showing how different belief systems have emerged around the globe and, from this, require adherents to welcome strangers.

Given the full length of human history, it is important to start with a discussion of hunter and gatherer, or foraging, societies. While Western agricultural forms of production probably began to emerge about 10,000 years ago, hunters and gatherers represent the longest period of social organisation and economic existence. As the name suggests, hunters and gatherers survive by foraging from the available vegetable and livestock. It is suggested that early humans foraged without hunting or fishing. It is also said that foraging preceded active hunting. This may have included pillaging the carcasses of dead animals killed by other creatures or that had died of natural causes. The development of tools to hunt in the form of spears and bows and arrows emerged later. Typically, men hunt while women forage or gather, though this is not universally true. There are examples of communities where the gender roles are less strictly defined. The key point here is that communities who live as hunters and gatherers live off the land without actively engaging in food production in a farmed way.

The religious beliefs of hunters and gatherers are largely understood through studies of the few remaining communities that still exist on hunting and gathering. Their beliefs are said to be beliefs that all objects, whether they be animate or inanimate, possess a supernatural power. Religious practices are principally concerned with protecting individuals and groups from these powers. Animism is another form where these forces are said to possess powers that can do harm or good. Hunter-gatherer religions, though different from current 'world religions', often incorporate narratives about the nature of human existence and the forces that shape human experiences. Most importantly, they set out moral codes that define what is expected of community members – defining good and bad actions. Typically, they have something to say about receiving the stranger.

Traditional Australian Aborigines are said to have occupied the continent for at least 40,000 years, with little evidence of fundamental societal change over that period. Anthropologists and other social scientists have identified high value being given to generosity and the willingness to share. There is clearly importance placed on hospitality and sharing with others as an indicator of morality and goodness. Hunting and gathering as a socio-economic system probably requires cultural importance to be placed upon magnanimity. Individual greed is condemned because it is perceived as being counterproductive to the overall social good. The ethics of generosity are given high importance. Though land appears to be 'owned' by individuals, access to it is shared among many. Interestingly, notions of trespass or denial of access seem to not exist, or at least are overwhelmed by a predominant morality of hospitality and generosity. So here we can see that hospitality and hospitableness are predominant social values even in what appear to be the most simple of societies.

In North America and Canada, aboriginal tribes also existed in forms of hunting and/or fishing, and gathering. In these tribes, given a wider array of animal and plant life than their Australian counterparts, hospitality overlapped the redistributive nature of hospitality with ritualised feasting in the tradition of potlatch. The word comes from Chinook Jargon and means to give away, or a gift. In north-west America and Canada, aboriginal Indian tribes engaged in a form of hospitality that involved generosity and giving from individuals with high social status. Typically, this form of hospitality involved feasting and dancing, and the distribution of goods according to the social status of the donor. Usually it was practised in the winter months, as the milder months were used for securing goods for the family, clan or village and returning to share them with friends and neighbours. The redistributive function of food and goods involved high status individuals giving to others in the clan or group. Status and prestige were raised according to the amount given away by hosts. Hence, the status of different family groups was not perceived by the amount of wealth acquired but by the amount of resources given away. Hospitality through feasting and ceremonies provides an indicator of social status and standing. The rituals of speechmaking and feasting were important aspects of tribal life. The greater the rank of the donor, the more was given away in the form of the hospitality provided through feasting. As with contemporary societies, hospitality provided by hosts was used to signify special occasions such as births, marriages, deaths and initiation into secret societies. Even more trivial events might be celebrated and recognised with potlatch, because an important purpose was to recognise the wealth and status of the host.

The comparison with current neo-liberal Western culture celebrating personal ownership is revealing. Indeed, when the British and French colonialists arrived, potlatch, practised by the indigenous tribes, was outlawed because it was deemed to be irrational and a sign that the indigenous populated was 'unstable'. The Potlatch Ban was passed by the government in 1885 and lasted until 1951. Fundamentally, the Christian occupiers could not understand the potlatch notion of working hard with the sole purpose of giving the gains to other people.

Adding to this global insight into the need to be hospitable, Hinduism and Confucianism, based principally on the Indian sub-continent and in China, both require adherents to be hospitable. Hindu ideas and teachings are said to have emerged some 5,000 years ago, alongside systematic agriculture. Offering hospitality to strangers is a fundamental feature of beliefs and culture. The unexpected guest was to be particularly honoured. The unpredicted guest was called *atithi*, which translates literally as 'without a set time'. A popular proverb says: 'The uninvited guest should be treated as good as God.' Tradition teaches that even the poorest should offer at least three things: sweet words, a sitting place and refreshments (at least water). 'Even an enemy must be offered appropriate hospitality if he comes to your home. A tree does not deny its shade even to the one who has come to cut it down' (Mahabharata, 12.372).

Confucianism, based upon the writings of Confucius, emerged in China in the sixth to fifth century BC. While it may not conform to the norms of many religions in advocating an afterlife and the existence of heaven, it does present a guide to living. This somewhat humanist approach is widely followed across China and South East Asia. The key observations about hospitality require individuals to share with others and welcome strangers into their own space. The notion of openness and humanity, together with sharing and generosity, inform the host's obligations to all guests.

Heal (1984) demonstrates the central importance of hospitality and hospitableness in the period from 1400 to 1700 in Britain. Writing about hospitality in early modern England, Heal reveals that the duty to offer hospitality to strangers was a deeply held belief: 'Whilst hospitality was often expressed in a series of private actions and a particular host, it was articulated in a matrix of beliefs that were shared and articulated publicly' (1984: 2). Heal (1990) also points to the significance of hospitality, and particularly, the treatment of travellers as an important value in early modern England. Julian the Hospitaller's name was frequently invoked as an example of good host-like behaviour: 'His qualities of charitable giving and selfless openness to the needs of others were those constantly commended in late medieval and early modern England whenever hospitality was discussed' (Heal, 1990: vii). Julian was acknowledged as the patron saint of travellers and innkeepers in the Catholic faith. Many of the apocryphal stories about Julian's welcome and generosity were used as exemplars to others. One of the most famous reported that Julian gave up his own bed to a leper. The expression of hospitality at that time had much in common with classical Rome (Heal, 1990). A powerful ideology of generosity was formulated in an *ius hospitii*, but was based on practical benefits. It assisted in the integration of strangers and, through the inclusion of guests-friends, formed a necessary part of the system of clientage based upon mutual obligations found in feudalism in medieval Europe. In both Rome and early modern England, 'good entertainment provided a necessary part of the everyday behaviour of leading citizens' (Heal, 1990: 2).

Heal highlights a number of roles that hospitality played at the time. Apart from values relating to the treatment of strangers and travellers, hospitality formed an important part of the local political economy. The redistribution of food and drink to neighbours and to the poor helped to maintain social cohesion. Feasts played an important part in ensuring that mutuality and social obligation were met in medieval England, and the 'open door' was given high social value. Hospitality assisted in maintaining power relationships based on elite families. By feeding neighbours, tenants and the poor, the feudal lords were able to expect a mutual obligation from the recipients. Most importantly, the stranger was to be received and offered shelter, food and drink, as it was required of both defined cultural behaviour and the teachings of Christianity. These suggested that Christ would come to the host's door dressed as a beggar, and if Christ were then denied hospitality, hosts would have all their property taken away.

The Christian religion still advocates hospitality as a key plank in the behaviour of the faithful. Several of the teachings of the New Testament also highlight hospitable treatment of Christ and the disciples. However, the requirement to be hospitable to strangers goes beyond the immediate treatment of Jesus and the disciples. It is claimed that the faithful demonstrate their faith when they honour the poor and the needy. Luke (14: 13) advocates giving to the poor, the needy, the lame and the blind as way of demonstrating faithful behaviour. In the gospel of Matthew, the behaviour of those who do will be most favourably blessed, 'For I was hungry and you gave me something to eat, I was thirsty and you gave me something to drink, I was a stranger and you invited me in, I needed clothes and you clothed me, I was sick and you looked after me' (Matt. 25: 34–36). Luke says, 'When you give a banquet, invite the poor, the crippled, the lame, the blind, and you will be blessed' (Luke 14: 13). Furthermore, the faithful are instructed to 'love your neighbour as yourself' (Matt. 22: 39). At these and other points, the Scriptures clearly show that offering hospitality to strangers is a basic requirement of the Christian faithful.

Writing from a more contemporary religious perspective, Nouwen (1998) begins his discussion of hospitableness by contrasting the English understanding of 'hospitality' with that of Germany and the Netherlands. He suggests that in both the latter cases, the word for hospitality translates as indicating freedom and friendship for guests. This insight informs his definition of hospitality as 'primarily the creation of a free space where the stranger can enter and become a friend' (Nouwen, 1998: 49), of allowing room spiritually, physically and emotionally for the guest. He states that genuine hospitality involves generous giving without concern for return or repayment. In the context of some of the chapters in this book, it is not concerned with reciprocity. Hosting, he writes, is about listening, about allowing people to be themselves and about giving them room to 'sing their own songs, speak their own languages, dance their own dances ... not a subtle invitation to adopt the lifestyle of the host, but the gift of a chance to find their own'; it is 'about inviting guests into our world on their terms' (Nouwen, 1998: 78).

Through these and other texts, it is possible to see that Christian writers are advocating hospitality to strangers as a defining feature of good human behaviour and a Christian requirement. However, the need to be hospitable goes beyond Christianity. The Old Testament advocates the customary sharing of meals as a way of distributing excess to the poor and the needy. The practice of hospitality in settings where it was unlikely that the guest could repay the host was fundamental. Indeed, many biblical stories advocate generosity by hosts in contexts where they could not expect repayment. For example, Abraham generously received three strangers who turned out to be angels. At another point, Lot was spared the destruction of Sodom and Gomorrah because he had offered hospitality and protection to two visitors who turned out to be angels. Through the stories of the Israelites, it is argued that their experiences of movement and being strangers in foreign lands meant they developed an intensive awareness of the need for hospitality and the need to offer food, drink and accommodation to strangers and those in need.

Those writing from an Islamic perspective (Meehan, 2013) claim that only the Muslim faithful understand the need to be hospitable. It is claimed that non-believers will only offer hospitality with an expectation of worldly gain. The true believer offers hospitality to strangers to honour God. Mohammed is quoted as saying, 'Let the believer in Allah and the day of judgment honour his guest' (Meehan, 2013). It is required that all must be welcomed and treated with respect, whether they are family or non-family members, believers or non-believers. Stories are related about the behaviour of Mohammed as being hospitable to strangers and never dining alone. One parable has Mohammed feeding three strangers who turn out to be angels after they have been shown generous hospitality. Another popular story has hosts feeding guests with the host's own food because they have little to share. These acts of generosity in either sharing or giving all they have to a stranger are claimed to be an exclusive perspective of the faithful, but in reality can be seen to be a feature of all these religions. Indeed, the story of guests turning out to be God, gods or angels is a common theme in all these religious parables. Acts of extreme generosity to the stranger result in excessive reward, while the failure to be hospitable results in the poor hosts having their goods taken away.

These examples of the duty to be hospitable are an aspect of religious adherence but these qualities are not unique to people of faith. There is a strong tradition of atheism in human history. The Greek philosopher Epicurus (341–278 BC), for example, asks some important questions. His ideas have regularly been distorted, attacked or dismissed by the religious establishment, because he makes a powerful critique of religion. Writing around the cusp of the fourth and third century BC, he asks, if the gods exist why do bad things happen? To paraphrase his argument, he says if the gods are all seeing, all merciful and all-powerful, why do bad things happen to people? Either the gods cannot see the bad things that happen, hence they are not all seeing, or if they can see bad things happening but cannot be bothered to do something about them, they are not all merciful. If they can see the bad things happening, and would like to do something about them but are not able, they are not all powerful. 'So why call them gods?', asks Epicurus. While most of his contemporaries believed that the gods existed and lived on

Mount Olympus, Epicurus offered an atheistic critique of religion that still has relevance today. Epicurus's Golden Rule, 'Treat others as you would like to be treated' in particular has relevance to our discussion of how hosts should behave to guests. Strangers entering new spaces are likely to feel anxious and uncertain, and they need to be made to feel safe and at ease.

Humanism offers a way of thinking about the world that does not require belief in God or the gods. The application of the 'scientific gaze' is fundamental to humanism. Reason and objective reality can explain the questions human beings want to ask about the human condition. Rather than a specific doctrine, it is more a general stance or attitude that upholds human reason, ethics and justice. It is an optimistic attitude to life, whose ultimate goal of human development is doing good and leaving the world a better place for future generations. As a doctrine, it acknowledges the worth of all humans and their ability to determine between good and bad, right and wrong, through the recognition of human qualities, especially rationality. Essentially, humanism recognises the value of all human beings, and proposes that all human beings can address all the world's problems and issues.

In these circumstances, hospitableness to others is an act of both generosity and recognition of the commonality of human needs. The guest's needs are fundamental, and the host has an obligation to protect and shelter the guest as needed in his/her own terms. The qualities of hospitableness, also genuine hospitality (Telfer, 1996, 2000), radical hospitality (Derrida, 2002) or altruistic hospitality, embrace the following: the desire to please others; general friendliness and benevolence; affection for people; concern for others and compassion; the desire to meet another's need; a desire to entertain; a need to help those in trouble; a desire to have company or to make friends; a desire for the pleasures of entertaining.

Conclusions

While the emergence of the word hospitality to describe a cluster of industry activities providing food, drink and accommodation services provided a catchy collective noun, it also presented researchers with the opportunity to explore universal meanings of hospitableness. This chapter has outlined some of the religious observations about the need to be hospitable to strangers and travellers, but also to those who are poor and in need of help. Being hospitable is what good people do on one level, but it also performs a redistributive function, whereby those who have more give to those who have less. In some societies, social status is increased by that which is given, rather than what is acquired.

This chapter has provided examples of religions from around the world and across various human social forms, including hunting and gathering, farming and industrialised societies. While the moral codes and religious narratives vary, a constant theme is that welcoming the stranger, providing shelter, food and drink to strangers and those in need is a constant strand in the definition of moral human behaviour. To paraphrase Derrida (2002), hospitality is society.

References

Bowie, F. (2006) *The Anthropology of Religion: An Introduction*, Oxford: Blackwell.
Derrida, J. (2002) *Acts of Religion*, London: Routledge.
Heal, F. (1984) The idea of hospitality in early modern England, *Past and Present* 102, 1: 66–93.
Heal, F. (1990) *Hospitality in Early Modern England*, Oxford: Clarendon Press.
Howell, E. (2015) How long have humans been on earth?, at http://www.universetoday.com/38125/how-long-have-humans-been-on-earth/. Accessed 11 November 2015.
Huczynski, A. A. and Buchanan, D. A. (2001) *Organizational Behaviour: An Introduction*, London: Prentice-Hall.

Lambek, M. (2008) *An Anthropology of Religion*, Oxford: Blackwell.

Marx, K. (1961 [1887]), *Capital: A Critique of Political Economy*, vol. 1, Moscow: Progress (originally published in German).

Meehan, S. (2013) Hospitality in Islam: the joy of honouring guests, *Understanding the Ethics of Islam*. Available at http://eislaminfo. blogspot.com/2012/12/hospitality-in-islam.html. Accessed 20 June 2016.

Morris, B. (2006) *Religion and Anthropology: A Critical Introduction*, Cambridge: Cambridge University Press.

Nouwen, H. (1998) *Reaching Out: A Special Edition of the Spiritual Classic including Beyond the Mirror*, London: Fount (an Imprint of HarperCollins).

Smart, N. (1966) *Dimension of the Sacred: An Anatomy of the World's Beliefs*, London: HarperCollins.

Telfer, E. (1996) *Food for Thought: Philosophy and Food*, New York: Routledge.

Telfer, E. (2000) The philosophy of hospitableness. In Lashley, C. and Morrison, A. (eds) *In Search of Hospitality: Theoretical Perspectives and Debates*, Oxford: Butterworth-Heinemann, pp. 38–55.

Tyler, E. B. (2008) Religion in primitive culture. In Lambek, M. (ed.) *A Reader in the Anthropology of Religion*, Oxford: Blackwell, pp. 23–33.

Weber, M. (2008) The Protestant work ethic and the spirit of capitalism. In Lambek, M. (ed.) *A Reader in the Anthropology of Religion*, Oxford: Blackwell, pp. 48–56.

10

Hospitality and social ties

An interdisciplinary reflexive journey for a psychology of hospitality

Marcia Maria Cappellano dos Santos, Olga Araujo Perazzolo,
Siloe Pereira and Isabel Baptista

> **Key themes**
>
> Hospitality/welcoming
>
> Social ties
>
> Identity and alterity
>
> Psychology of hospitality

There is no house or interior without a door and window.

(Jacques Derrida)

A brief foray into studies in the most diverse fields of knowledge, time and space is sufficient for coping with the wide range of relational practices that have been considered as illustrative of the hospitality phenomenon. At the same time it is possible to identify in those practices – political, ethical, social, cultural, commercial-economic, and legal, among others – what led scholars in philosophy, psychology and anthropology to include hospitality within their scope and investigative processes. Through these theoretical lenses hospitality is analysed, and transaction and reciprocity establish themselves as key features of the study of hospitality when present in actions taken by individuals placed at relational poles, reflecting welcoming cognitive-affective dispositions and desires from one another, and indicating potential for the establishment or strengthening of social ties. However, this does not exclude the possibility of the occurrence of eventual self-centred relationships of welcoming, opening space to situations of inhospitality and movements that can reflect, in the reverse direction, the weakening of social ties. It is interesting to remember that the Latin form *laqueus*, the etymological origin of the word 'tie', designates a slipknot, which unties easily. Thereby, the weaving of the tethers of social ties requires, as noted by Santos, 'genuine relationships of acceptance, in which individuals recognize, interact and host each other, alternately transforming themselves into *the other*, directing their look to the *other*'s look' (2014: 13).

DOI: 10.4324/9781315679938-11

With this understanding, the reflections that follow embark on the paths of psychology, psychoanalysis, philosophy, tourism and anthropology, with characteristic outlines and features of each of these areas, allowing, however, that approximations are built among them, since they are mainly sustained by the understanding of hospitality through and in the relationship with *the other*.

This reflexive journey is based on work that has been developed since 2009 by the Research Group Tourism: Human Development, Language and Educational Process, from the University of Caxias do Sul, Rio Grande do Sul, Brazil, in which hospitality has been the object of theoretical and methodological research in the intertwining of these areas.

The processes of perception and interpretation of the other

From the perspective of psychological science, in seeking to understand the complex phenomenon of hospitality, possible contributions from different analytical biases are identified, even when taking those that focus on fundamentally intra-psychic aspects of individualistic tendencies, since the ties established with *the other*, individual and collective, are the essence of the human being. That being so, psychology is applied through the dynamics of ontogenetic and epistemic approaches in an effort to understand hospitality in a context that recognises the kaleidoscopic nature of human and social phenomena. In this sense, it may be said that psychology always considers *the other* and takes into account the plural constitution in the formation of the psychological universe. It does so by articulating representations of reality, socio-psychological tensions resulting from systemic interactions and the set of linguistic signs that weave together social ties. Two assumptions become relevant at the heart of such considerations: the first is that the individual constitutes and develops themselves in the relationship and through it; the second is that the relational interaction happens through hospitality, the effect of the dynamics of the welcoming. Thus, psychology is considered a *locus* of knowledge for hospitality and a possible field for research on the topic. Therefore, contributions from the fields of, among others, social, cognitive and systemic psychology, and from psychoanalysis become relevant.

In social psychology, three nodal themes that offer elements for understanding the phenomena operating in hospitality practices may be considered: social cognition, the formation and changing of attitudes, and group processes (Fiske *et al.*, 2010).

Social cognition

Social cognition refers to the phenomenon by which subjects process the information gathered from the environment, in the context of social relations, modelling their own behaviour from indicative perceptions of adequacy or inadequacy. Therefore, it assumes skills to identify socially relevant and expected behaviours, as well as the ability to adopt alternative behaviours in different contexts, including those involving cooperation and altruism, essential for living together in society and, hence, for building social ties (Adolphs, 2001; Emery and Clayton, 2009).

Also, as part of social cognition, the process of understanding our own mental states (emotions, needs, intentions, etc.) as well as other people's is an example of the intersection of knowledge involving neurobiological substrates and theoretical propositions that integrate studies with individuals and groups, in search of clarification of relational phenomena. The basic assumption is that neuro-cerebral mechanisms intervene in social reasoning through specialised structures of self-perception and perception of *the other* (Ferreira, 2010). Research in this area has been presented to explain common failures in social relations and hospitality practices in situations where social cognition is verified as impaired, such as with people with autism, schizophrenia or poisoning by chemical substances, among other disorders (Heatherton and Wheatley, 2010). The progressive expansion of knowledge in the field of neuroscience, much of which consolidates theories that have long been formulated, before being considered evidence of biological preponderance based on behaviour, ratifies the integration of biological, psychological and social aspects in an inseparable combination of the constituent factors of human phenomena.

Social cognition also includes social perception. Studies on this subject indicate the tendency to make complex and extensive judgements about others, even when information is restricted and there is little objective data. In the process of knowing the other, we build a theory on how this person is, giving him/her characteristics, as it seems likely, from a store of 'personal knowledge' (Fiske and Taylor, 1991). Thus, social perception integrates the set of human skills in the service of relational demands and protection of self, so that a rapid evaluation of the other will influence decisively the welcoming or rejection, according to the expectation created by the behavioural characteristics of that other. From this angle, it is appropriate to consider, in the perception of the other, a significant margin of 'error' or perceptual and cognitive distortion, particularly given that, as a rule, these processes are beyond the control of the perceiver.

The primary perception of individuals, groups and institutions has a profound effect in establishing the quality of relationships in the process of mutual acceptance, in the installation or not of hospitality space. This process becomes even more complex when taking into account the tendency of people to meet the expectations of those who perceive them. By different means of communication, the perceiver builds their perception of the subject, and the way the subject is perceived corresponds to this perception. This logic applies to perceptions in a positive or negative valuation in relations between parents and children, in social relationships, among protagonists in the commercial field, in work processes, in the creation of political images and so forth. In addition, it would explain the different perceptions that every person has of themselves in different contexts, reflecting on successes and failures in building ties that approximate people and groups.

Given the importance of these factors for the quality of the composition of the social fabric, the effort being carried out in psychology to develop intervention methodologies to enhance skills and minimise preconception effects in the perception of the other is significant. Relevant interventions could contribute to the development of reflective processes of interaction, beyond training actions that tend to favour reinforcements that automate behaviour, which usually do not touch the psycho-affective essence of the formation of ideas about how the other is.

As an illustration of these methodologies, we will refer to the action research conducted in a community with tourism potential, located in the north-east region of Rio Grande do Sul state, Brazil. There, a skill was developed and implemented that mobilised intervention processes for hospitality and for collective involvement in actions focused on tourism (Perazzolo, Pereira, Santos and Ferreira, 2014). It is emphasised here that the narratives of the subjects that were part of representative segments of the community revealed, in the stage preceding the intervention, differences and internal conflicts, which indicated the commitment of the disposition for cooperation, for joint decisions and reflections, for the reception of people and for the cooperative planning of tourism development.

The methodological proposal had hospitality or welcoming as one of the founding elements of tourism. According to the researchers, the origin of tourism is 'the human drive (*trieb* in German) for knowledge, which Freud (1976a) called the epistemophilic drive' (Perazzolo, Pereira, Santos and Ferreira, 2014: 66). In other words, tourism comes from the human impulse to embark in the direction of new knowledge. So this is where welcoming is installed as a relational phenomenon and a catalyst for learning, to the extent that 'it requires a willingness to get out of oneself, to create and transit through an area that is also of the other, that involves welcoming and being welcomed' (Perazzolo, Pereira, Santos and Ferreira, 2014: 68). This is, therefore, an essential condition for tourism to occur. In the same way, the subject who genuinely welcomes the other is also driven by the desire to know. Similarly, he/she would correspond to a tourist who does not move. It would be, in the words of the authors, a *'tourist of the other'* (Perazzolo, Pereira, Santos and Ferreira, 2014: 68).

On the other hand, the process of intervention was guided by the theory of thought developed by Bion (1994), which provides an explanation of development by means of learning through experience, and through relationships. The heart of his conception of man is 'marked primarily by the mental growth from endless transformation processes leading to new patterns of thinking, which implies the involvement of the whole personality' (Perazzolo, Pereira, Santos and Ferreira, 2014: 71). From this perspective, discussions in systematised group meetings involved the strategy of intervention, in which the slippage of meaning occurred, increasing complexity of thinking, awareness to host the other within oneself and the development of collective relations based on mutual welcoming. Underlying this option, it was supposed that the construction of social projects in which tourism would stand out in the socio-economic profile of the community could be enhanced.

The results of the reflexive processes of interaction, described in detail in the research, stated, according to the researchers' terms, the occurrence of significant changes in the formulation of the concepts, but also in behavioural and affective spheres. The researchers emphasise that it can be assumed that 'the effective transformation of willingness to welcome requires that a trial time full of feelings may mediate the reflections and initiate enhancer behaviours of cooperative practices, which are motivated by the desire and commitment to welcome' (Perazzolo, Pereira, Santos and Ferreira, 2014: 74). These behaviours signal the strengthening of social ties of and in the community.

Attitude formation and change

Another important concept in the examination of the conditions for welcoming and, therefore, of the constitution of hospitality is the concept of attitude, which consolidates the thinking, feeling and acting triad, and involves perception as well as behaviour. When an attitude is formed, it tends to become rooted and durable, making changes complicated, reflecting on the relational dimension (Fiske *et al.*, 2010). Thus, the form of thinking about a particular person, group or situation will reflect the way of feeling and behaving towards others. This phenomenon is also the basis of prejudice of any kind. Negative attitudes tend to cause behaviours marked for rejection, such as, for example, hostility to immigrants. In other words, a positive or negative attitude affects how people, tourists, buyers/sellers, brands and so forth are welcomed.

The theories about the tendency of the mind to seek constant balance, backed up by studies on cognitive consistency (Festinger, 1975), offer explanations about resistance to changing perceptions and attitudes. The maintenance of feelings and thoughts in relation to the other help people maintain a state of balance and constancy in order to obtain mental comfort. Breaking down established beliefs creates tensions that initiate processes for the restoration of homeostasis, organising new perceptions and attitudes, or causing psychological discomfort, such as mental pain (Bion, 1984). To avoid this discomfort, one tends to keep units of coherent and consistent ideas, feelings and behaviours, a process that could explain difficulties in making changes in the welcoming mood in personal, social and commercial areas, among others.

Group processes

Another axis of interest of social psychology concerning group phenomena also requires some consideration. It should be noted that in this area, explanatory, conceptual and dynamic systems have long been built, theorising about the relations of interdependence of parties in a group context, constituting an organised, self-regulated and semi-permeable totality. The different lines approximate contributions, such as Kurt Lewin's field theory (1975), Maturana and Varela's systemic propositions (2002) and theoretical and practical systemic approaches of intervention with families and groups (Bowen, 1989). A group is, as a rule, designed as a unit, greater than the sum of its parts, with its own identity and culture, involved and constrained by a field that maintains cohesive members, making demands and behaviour mutually interdependent. This would explain the changes in behaviour of people in different groups (family, leisure, professional, religious, etc.), changes which derive from the game of internal and external forces, creating tensions that require constant adjustment in the search for balance.

The idea of hospitality at the level of the social group unit derives from these premises. A welcoming collective body is brought about by the subjective construction of ideas and representations shared by a group of people. This creates a unit with its own profile, whose characteristics have an impact on the nature of affections that set the tone for the relations and on behaviours that harmonise, or not, towards common goals. A collective body that welcomes itself and the other is constituted by means of cultural knowledge and circulating values, in the way it establishes exchanges, by how it takes and offers services that supply and keep alive the social body, and the management of resources, knowledge and exchanges that occur in the internal and external environment of the social body (Santos, Perazzolo and Pereira, 2014).

Psycho-relational dimensions of hospitality

In addition to the extensive reading of hospitality that social psychology provides, the cognitive, systemic and psychoanalytical approaches also offer elements to build a *psychology of hospitality*. From the early days of psychology, several theories have pointed to the relational dimension as the core of human life. Since the development of psychoanalytic theory by Freud (1976a), it has been difficult to deny the importance of relationships in the origin and organisation of the psyche associated with social interactions. As proposed by Freud, the relational experiences of the first years of life are constitutive of the matrices of the further development and take place within a scenario where *the other* – via family ties and regulatory echoes of society – features with the *self* – the history of uniqueness. Representatives of the English, French and American schools of psychoanalysis ratify the importance of progressive differentiation *I-you*, and the insertion of the third, the *he*, in building the sense of social plurality – *we and they*.

In the English school, the character and identity formation of individuals occurs through the creation and settlement of an internal world by representation of people. This would occur through predictable relationships (such as those with the mother/caretakers in the early stages of life) and unpredictable relationships (like the interactions of chance that occur throughout life). Theorists such as Melanie Klein (1974) and Wilfred Bion (1984) are important representatives of this sociological model of the mind. Hospitality, from this perspective, would be the means of the constitution of the subject, to the extent that hosting and being hosted marks the essential dynamic of the construction of the subject, which, by nature, is plural.

With regard to the American school, there are the contributions of Kohut (1959), considered the precursor of the psychology of the *self*, as it is recognised in the universe of psychoanalysis.

The author outlines his understanding of man, paying particular attention to the processes of introspection and empathy, with an emphasis on lived experience, therefore moving beyond the *instinctivist* model developed by Freud. This means that, in human development, in the constitution of the *self*, a relationship matrix is presumed, a *self* in the world.

The French school, on the other hand, of which Jacques Lacan (1978) is an important representative, highlights the experience of absence and deprivation, originally lived in the triangular relationship (father, mother, son) and in paternal interdiction. The psychic inscription of the name of the father, in other words the acceptance of the speech that reflects the voice of the *great other* (echo of social speech), marks the constitution of the subject through the access to culture, setting the regulatory limits, enabling order and its maintenance in the social group.

It is in the centre of the experience of absence and deprivation that *the other*, the third, enters the psycho-relational dynamic, allowing the constitution, or not, of a structure capable of recognising what is different of the self and the relevance of social regulatory systems, of the laws of coexistence. From this perspective, the *other* is always the third, the one who breaks the primarily specular duality (which originates from the mother–child relationship), enabling the triangulation of psychic structure and giving meaning to the *I*, to the *you* and, finally, to the *he*, also in plural versions of the pronouns. In other words, without the *he*, the *you* is just a reflection of the *I*. This cutting experience – that is, the experience of the admission of a third party in the psycho-relational universe of subjects – is riddled by repression, as proposed by Freud (1976a). This process will generate the on-going discomfort of the abdication of the *trieb*, inducing subjects to find ways to adapt their demands to social norms and to move in search of desire, lost and forgotten in its primary form.

This would explain the human search for knowledge and would characterise the inspiration that activates the historical development of humankind and of societies. Without the experience of absence/deprivation, which installs the *he*, the *I* inhabits the space of the narcissism in which the *other* is disregarded. It is necessary to insert the *other*, the *great other* (the symbolic unfolding of the third, the culture), so that a distinct desire may be recognised and an effective and supportive relational system of hospitality and reciprocity established. In this process, the basis of the relationship and the construction of social ties would be sedimented. Lévi-Strauss (2009), in the field of anthropology, can also be referred to as a theorist who shares the idea that the deprivation experience, particularly the one concerning the incest prohibition, is marked by the passage of the state of nature to the state of cultural subject. That is to say that the individual is placed at the point of intersection between nature and culture.

It is noted that the social ties bind the individual to their culture, through listening to the speech of the *great other* and through the response that this process generates. This means that the nature of the ties changes according to the demands of each period, of each socio-relational niche in which the individuals are placed. Therefore, if the culture, according to contemporary thinkers, talks about the values of hyperconsumption, about the blindness to the emptiness and to the ephemeral (Lipovetsky, 2005), about the weakening or liquidity of human bonds (Bauman, 2004), about the spectacularisation of life (Debord, 1997), marks of these aspects tend to be inserted in the dynamics of the constitution of the social body. It will be highlighted that the scenario of hyper-individualisation indicates an obvious constraint in the disposition for the welcoming of *the other*, paradoxically intensifying the specular phenomenon in which the *I* and *the other* are, or need to be, equal. In this sense, hospitality may advertise itself as an inspiring paradigm of change in the systems of relations at the macrosocial level.

Another important dimension to be mentioned in the context of the contribution of psychology to the understanding of the hospitality phenomenon refers to reflections, which are situated on the border of evolutionary thought and ethology. In this space, the importance of the relations can be recognised in the adaptive root of the species. The theory of fetalisation, or neoteny (originally proposed by Louis Bolk, 1926), proposes that the biological incompleteness, the phylogenetic opening of the species, explains the human need to be with like others, in a cooperative relationship of mutual care. This perspective harmonises with the idea of caring for the other as a human commitment (Heidegger, 1989; Levinas, 2004), although it is acknowledged that contrary answers, of rejection and aggression, integrate the set of human reactions to fear, to anger, to the need to adapt and to maintain living conditions.

Thus, in the history of the human species, taking care of the other in the survival process was intrinsically associated with the maintenance of relations and with mutual attention throughout life, unlike other hominids, who separated themselves from their groups of origin in sexual maturity, and this is probably is why they are extinct (Lewin, 1999). The relationship fills the place left open by the overcoming of the idea of biological determinism, and constitutes the privileged way for the promotion of essential learning for human development, from birth to death. A man needs to learn almost everything, and that constant demand to know would explain the restless and gregarious nature as a dynamic axis of the constitution of the social subject; the development of skills for mutual welcoming, providing life, new and progressive knowledge, favoured conditions for the establishment of links that allow the insertion of the *other* inside the very man, inaugurating opening to the internal and external diversity. The known cases of wild children, supposedly raised in an animal environment and who did not laugh, speak or interact (Lévi-Strauss, 2009) when they were found, allow reflections on the importance of alterity in the construction of the *self* and of humanity as a product of human relationships. In reflections about the ways that human productions and thinking may take, the concept of rhizome (Deleuze and Guattari, 2010) has contributed to the understanding of the unpredictability of the developments and directions of these possible paths.

Regarding the importance of reciprocity in relationships, psychology studies on newborn competencies, even considering the limited repertoire of behaviours of an essentially biological base, indicate characteristics of propensity, which are innate for bonding. These studies reinforce the assumption that this is one of the most effective and necessary competencies for development. As Bowlby (1978) said, the human baby is born equipped with behavioural systems that provide the foundation for the later development of attachment or binding behaviour. The work of Bowlby, besides contributing in different ways to the theoretical structure on child development, inspired research on the civilising process, such as that developed by Elias and Scotson (1994). These assumptions indicate that human relationships are not options, but conditions of life, and these relations happen through hospitality.

Other relevant contributions to the understanding of mutual welcoming mechanisms come from studies that focus on primary bonds, characteristic of the mother–baby relationship, such as those by Winnicott (2006) and Bion (1984), which address the maternal ability to interpret demands and peculiarities of the newborn and give them the answers they need. This moment marks the beginning of the communication and interplay that will allow the baby to move forward in a relational dynamic that will occur throughout life. The competencies that rule the primary relationships – in which one of the protagonists of the asymmetric dialogue, the baby, demands to be listened to and answered on their needs, and the other, the mother, makes herself available and wishes to listen, to interpret and meet the identified needs – do not run out, therefore, in childhood or in maternal action. On the contrary, they are developed and may be transformed, depending on the circumstances, throughout life, in welcoming exchanges, when the protagonists may alternate at the poles of the relationship. In the context of a *psychology of hospitality*, therefore, it is considered that the need for care and for welcoming the other is, in theory, common to all individuals, as well as the ability and the desire to welcome. This reveals the phenomenon that connects and transforms people and groups in different conditions of relational symmetry and synchrony (Perazzolo, Pereira and Santos, 2014).

Accordingly, the relations are likely to be characterised as (a) asymmetrical, when it is verified basic difference in the level of dependency (for example, son–mother, immigrant\native, student–teacher, etc.), (b) symmetrical, when there is, in principle, equivalence and ability to exchange demands in equal conditions (for example, the interrelationships occurring in the world of playfulness, cooperation, trade, etc.), or (c) ammetrical, when self-centred demands prevail and deafen one or both poles of the relationship, and so the relation is not carried out.

With regards to the synchrony, it is considered that welcoming, facilitator of the hospitality phenomenon, may occur at a time when the relationship settles as a fact, making almost visible the 'in *between*' space, which is formed by the mutual action of welcoming. However, it may also occur before the meeting, when there is previous answering to the supposed needs of an individual or groups, a process that is easily understood in the commercial universe, when the actions preceding the reception of clients, for example, derive from the prior interpretation of their needs. The relation of welcoming may occur even after the meeting, when relational experiences alter the process of future welcoming (Perazzolo, Pereira and Santos 2014b).

The dynamics of hospitality, as it occurs in primary relations, assumes that the demands of the other are accepted, thought about and returned in the form of answers – or action – enhancing the process of identification, welcoming and transformation of mutual expectations in a continuous interplay. The conditions of being welcomed and welcoming alternate, in the relationship, and it is in this process that the 'in *between*' space of the hospitality is established. In essence, it is translated into an empathic exercise that requires abdication of previous assurances of the demands of the other and displacement of the very demands of the phenomenal centre of desire. This process features a relational unit envisaged by the recognition of the two poles, which may take the singular form, but also the form of a group, social or collective body. These views, as previously mentioned, form part of the concept of Welcoming Collective Body, a model developed by Santos, Perazzolo and Pereira (2014), which presents a theory of collective hospitality and a methodology of analysis of welcoming characteristics at institutional and social level. It refers to a

> body that personifies the representation evoked by its name, which gives form and identity to the communities. The proposition, derived from studies about welcoming in four communities with tourist potential in the northeast of the state of Rio Grande do Sul/Br, rests on the understanding that the social body of a group/community is structured from the interconnection of at least three vertices: exchanges/services; knowledge/culture; managing organism. The layout of this triangulation defines the space in which the phenomenon of welcoming and the hospitality practices are organised and developed.
>
> *(Santos, Perazzolo, and Pereira, 2014: 55)*

At this point, it is pertinent to consider that these approaches are in addition to other assumptions of a metaphysical nature. In the same way, they join the contributions of studies on biopsychic processes involving organic responses to the perception of the other, which recognise neurochemical flows that provide conditions for reciprocity (Shamay-Tsoory, 2011). It is worth taking into account the possibility of two primary destinations in a human approach: hospitality and inhospitality, or the rejection/refusal of the other – a process that is expressed by different manifestations of withdrawal and aggressiveness. The recognition of an opposite disposition to hospitality, as plausible and feasible as this, points out that the coexistence of both need to be considered when addressing the nature and challenges of relationships. In summary, a meeting would, then, have two possible outcomes: one, facilitator of successive approximations, thinking development and mutual change through affective and cooperative ties; and two, facilitator of the withdrawal, due to the rejection and/or contempt for learning experiences that others may make available, or due to the defence against the perception of the risk for the *I/we, mine/ours*. The ambivalence, on the other hand, would mark the coexistence of both valences operating in the same relational dynamics. Thus, it may be said that as well as having the same etymological root, the words 'hospitality' and 'inhospitality' also have the psychological root, which feeds contradictory emotions such as love, hate or both in the complex relational plot.

Given these considerations, the understanding of the hospitality phenomenon may be expanded if the knowledge produced in the field of psychology in dialogue with assumptions, among others, of a philosophical, sociological and anthropological nature is taken into account. The theory of the Gift (Mauss, 2005), for example, that sustains the give-receive-return triad, does not exclude giving and not receiving in return. On the contrary, it increases the perspective of a human disposition to the other, founded in the early interactions that weave together the social ties. In the socio-economic context, scholars have already highlighted the need for a more comprehensive definition of hospitality. Statements, for example, that hospitality 'may be conceived as a set of behaviours originating from the very base of society' (Lashley and Morrison, 2004: 5) are compatible with the idea of an intrinsic demand, psychologically built for hospitality which embraces phenomena involving exchanges, learning experiences and also economic and social development.

This brief summary of contributions from psychological science confirms the complexity of the phenomenon of hospitality in the uniqueness/identity interplay and, at the same time, the configuration of an equally complex conceptual universe. These fields have contributed to ideational approaches and withdrawals that focus on the *I-other* contextualised in different dimensions, such as ethics, politics and the social. In this sense, the term 'hospitality' evokes an ancestral duty increasingly contemporary, associated with the welcoming practices of alterity that generate social ties, which, immediately, convoke a substantial reflection on the human condition. Thinking about what human beings should do involves, indeed, reflecting on what they are (Flahault, 2011). That is, what defines the nature of the human being, or yet, to what extent does the hospitality relationship affect the processes of personal development? What kinds of changes are caused in the consciousness of the individuals?

In adopting principles of an anthropology of alterity to Levinas' matrix this type of question can be answered, sustaining the idea that hospitality is a structural feature of the human identity, which corresponds to what Francis Jacques (1982) designated as 'relational subjectivity'. This position leads to the other side of the welcoming situation, to the experience of a 'subjective rupture' lived by the one who welcomes.

Hospitality and personal identity

It is known that the knowledge produced in the social and human sciences in the last decades on the processes of human development provide the grounds for a relational humanism, which forces us to question the idea of a self-founder and self-sufficient subject. The concept of personal identity becomes inseparable from the concept of alterity, although the arguments tend to differ relatively to the definition of that *other* and, above all, to the place occupied in interpersonal relationships.

In this case, and in accordance with a Levinasian line of inspiration, the notion of hospitality is used to describe an interpersonal relationship linked to the primacy of alterity, defending that it is in the presence of the *other*, recognised and respected as a truly *other*, that the identity finds the secret of its temporal fecundity.

For Levinas (1988, 1990), the identity is the result of a historic construction that begins in the relation with the inhabited world, a world that is desirably enjoyed, appropriate and represented. It is important to emphasise this aspect, since a decisive demarcation in relation to the idealistic conceptions of identity is being questioned. By situating the process of personal achievement in the sensitive and pleasant connection with the inhabited world, Levinas refuses to reduce the person to subjectivity, defending a human identity in 'flesh and blood', rooted in a concrete world, and with which it establishes hospitality ties.

In this way, for Levinas, as Freud already proposed (1976b), 'the Self is not a being that always remains the same, but it is the one whose existence consists in identifying itself, rediscovering its identity through everything that happens to it' (1988: 24). That is how the *self* reveals itself to be identical in the course of time and through all its changes, even when, in dialogue with its intimate alterity, it has the illusion of being another one, a denied illusion, in a divisive way, in the 'face-to-face' situation – that is, before the testimony of radical alterity given by someone else.

In this sense, the real *other* is effectively another person, someone equally capable of inner life, which is to say, someone able to possess the world subjectively, to represent it and to communicate it. That is what the consciousness discovers when it welcomes the interpellation of another human being, someone who also has a face. On the face of every person, there are mysteriously unique marks of a personal identity, of another freedom, another story of life, and that is why 'we are always late to meet the other' (Levinas, 1990: 140). The wrinkles marking the face of the elderly, for example, indicate precisely the extent of our delay.

The obedience to the 'law of the face' becomes thus constitutive of the identity, explaining hospitality as an experience that largely transcends the simple reception of the strange. Hospitality happens when the reception 'gives way' to the entry of the new, thereby producing changes in the welcoming subject, no matter how risky this experience may prove to be. There is no true openness and exposure to the other without such dimension of risk being present.

In fact, the real risk to identity lies in the temptation of the person becoming retracted in themselves, with 'doors and windows closed' to the other and, thus, deprived of their vital stimulus. This closing logic leads to distortions in the process of formation of the identity, producing a subjectivity condition that is favourable to the expression of narcissistic identities and to the emergence of mixophobic social cultures. Instead, the hospitality experience, as a subjective welcoming of the alterity, serves to counter this tendency and to dissolve any illusion of self-sufficiency. A truly autonomous identity is an identity that lives the fullness of the interdependence condition; it is an identity capable of dealing with uncertainty and the unpredictable.

According to Derrida (1997), the total exposure to the unexpected defines pure or unconditional hospitality. By definition, hospitality contains in itself a latent threat of hostility. However, authentic hospitality begins precisely there, in the availability to welcome the other – the unknown, the strange, the unexpected – leaving any personal fear aside. Paradoxical as it may seem, the persistent subordination to the imperative of unconditional hospitality, in every historical circumstance, is what allows the practice of hospitality to materialise with all its regulations.

As Daniel Innerarity (2001) has observed, reality itself tends to behave like an 'autonomous guest' and often an inconvenient one. Welcoming with hospitality means opening up to the unknown and the unexpected, and this unexpected often manifests in the form of annoyance, disappointment and breakdown of expectations. On the basis of the process of identity construction, it is not the simple exercise of the will, but a vital and permanent tension between freedom and alterity, between intention and opposition, between security and risk. In this process, the intersubjective linking relations, intrinsically enigmatic, play a critical role.

An example of this tension in Levinas' argument (1988) is paternity. 'Paternity remains a self-identification, but also a distinction within identification – a structure unforeseeable in formal logic' (Levinas, 1988: 245). Children, at the same time 'ours' and 'not-ours', always come from beyond the possible and beyond the projects. As such, they establish a close relationship that is untranslatable in ordinary language, and that helps explain the meaning of personal fulfilment.

Conclusions

The paths travelled so far come to reiterate not only the complexity of the hospitality phenomenon, but, or even because of that, the importance of the complementarity of different perceptions in the search for their understanding. It is in this sense that thinkers who emphasise aspects of the uniqueness of subjects in their relations of constitutive interdependence of identity and hospitality were called here to dialogue.

It was this understanding that directed the exercise carried out here, which systematises the contributions that came primarily from psychology, like those attributed to Freud, Bion, Kohut and Bowlby – which allow us to outline some grounds for what might be called a *psychology of hospitality*. This is a psychology that points to the recognition of the *other* as *one other*, in their uniqueness, which, when or if recognised, creates fertile ground for the chain of transformation of the *self* and the *other*, which characterises relational processes of welcoming. These same contributions refer to the dialogue with thinkers of the philosophical and anthropological universe, especially Levinas, Derrida and Lévi-Strauss, which allowed us to highlight the significant transforming potential originating from the exposure of the *self* to the *other*, when there is no previous knowledge, and from which one never gets away. This is the intrinsic relationship between identity and alterity, and between hospitality and development of social ties.

References

Adolphs, R. (2001) The neurobiology of social cognition, *Current Opinion in Neurobiology* 11: 231–239.
Bauman, Z. (2004) *Amor Líquido*, Rio de Janeiro: Jorge Zahar.
Bion, W. R. (1984) *Attention and Interpretation*, London: Karnac Books.
Bion, W. R. (1994) Estudos psicanalíticos revisados, 3rd edn, Rio de Janeiro: Imago.
Bolk, L. (1926) *Das Problem der Menschwerdurg*, Jena: Von Gustav Fischer.
Bowen, M. (1989) *La terapia familiar en la práctica clínica*, vol. II, Bilbao: Desclée de Brouwer.
Bowlby, J. (1978) Attachment theory and its therapeutic implications. In Feinstein, S. C. and Giovacchini, P. L. (eds) *Adolescent Psychiatry: Developmental and Clinical Studies*, New York: Jason Aronson, pp. 5–33.
Debord, G. (1997) *A sociedade do espetáculo: comentários sobre a sociedade do espetáculo*, Rio de Janeiro: Contraponto.
Deleuze, G. and Guatari, F. (2010) *O anti-Édipo: capitalismo e esquizofrenia*, São Paulo: Editora 34.
Derrida, J. (1997) *Adieu - À Emmanuel Lévinas*, Paris: Éditions Galilée.
Elias, N. and Scotson, J. L. (1994) *The Established and the Outsiders*, New York: Sage.
Emery, N. J and Clayton, N. S. (2009) Comparative social cognition, *Annual Review of Psychology* 60: 87–113.
Ferreira, M. C. (2010) A Psicologia Social contemporânea: principais tendências e perspectivas nacionais e internacionais, *Psicologia: Teoria e Pesquisa* 26: 51–64.
Festinger, L. (1975) *Teoria da dissonância cognitiva* (Psyche), Rio de Janeiro: Zahar.
Fiske, S. T. and Taylor, S. E. (1991) *Social Cognition: From Brains to Culture*, 2nd edn, New York: McGraw-Hill.
Fiske, S. T., Gilbert, D. T. and Lindzey, G. (2010) *Handbook of Social Psychology*, vol. 2, 5th edn, Hoboken, NJ: John Wiley.
Flahault, F. (2011) *Où est passé le bien commun?*, Paris: Mille et une nuits.
Freud, S. (1976a) *Inibição, sintoma e ansiedade (1926–1929)*, Edição Standard Brasileira das Obras Completas de Sigmund Freud, vol. 20, Rio de Janeiro: Imago, pp. 93–201.

Freud, S. (1976b) *Psicologia de grupo e a análise do ego* (1921), Edição Standard Brasileira das Obras Completas de Sigmund Freud, vol. 18, Rio de Janeiro: Imago, pp. 91–179.

Heatherton, T. F. and Wheatley, T. (2010) Social neuroscience. In Baumeister, R. F and Finkel, E. J. (eds) *Advanced Social Psychology: The State of the Science*, New York: Oxford University Press, pp. 575–612.

Heidegger, M. (1989) *Ser e tempo*, 3rd edn, Petrópolis, RJ: Vozes.

Innerarity, D. (2001) *Ética de la Hospitalidad*, Barcelona: Península.

Jacques, F. (1982) *Différence et Subjectivité*, Paris: Aubier Montaigne.

Klein, M. (1974) *Inveja e gratidão: um estudo das fontes do inconsciente*, Rio de Janeiro: Imago.

Kohut, H. (1959) Introspection, empathy and psychoanalysis, *Journal of the American Psychoanalytic Association* 7: 450–483.

Lacan, J. (1978) O seminário sobre a carta roubada. In *Escritos*, São Paulo: Perspectiva, pp. 17–67.

Lashley, C. and Morrison, A. (eds) (2004) *Em busca da hospitalidade: perspectivas para um mundo globalizado*, Barueri, SP: Manole.

Lévi-Strauss, C. (2009) *As estruturas elementares do parentesco*, 5th edn, Petrópolis, RJ: Vozes.

Levinas, E. (1988) *Totalidade e Infinito*, Lisboa: Edições 70.

Levinas, E. (1990) *Autrement qu'être ou au-dela de L'Essence*, Paris: Kluwer Academic.

Levinas, E. (2004) *Entre nós: ensaios sobre a alteridade*, 4th edn, Petrópolis, RJ: Vozes.

Lewin, K. (1975) *Teoria dinâmica de personalidade*, São Paulo: Cultrix.

Lewin, R. (1999) *A evolução humana*, São Paulo: Atheneu.

Lipovetsky, G. (2005) *A era do vazio*, Barueri, SP: Manole.

Maturana, H. R. and Varela, F. J. (2002) *A árvore do conhecimento: as bases biológicas da compreensão humana*, 2nd edn, São Paulo: Palas Athena.

Mauss, M. (2005) *Sociologia e antropologia*, São Paulo: Cosac & Naify.

Perazzolo, O. A., Pereira, S. and Santos, M. M. C. (2014) Sincronia e simetria: proposições tipológicas para o acolhimento, XI Seminário da Associação Nacional de Pesquisa em Pós-Graduação em Turismo, Ceará: Universidade do Estado do Ceará, pp. 1–11.

Perazzolo, O. A., Pereira, S., Santos, M. M. C. and Ferreira, L. T. (2014) Acolhimento e desenvolvimento socioturístico: para uma psicopedagogia do laço social. In Santos, M. M. C. and Baptista, I. (eds) *Laços Sociais: por uma epistemologia da hospitalidade*, Caxias do Sul: EDUCS, pp. 65–82.

Santos, M. M. C. (2014) A metáfora laços sociais e a hospitalidade. In Santos, M. M. C. and Baptista, I. (eds) *Laços Sociais: por uma epistemologia da hospitalidade*, Caxias do Sul: EDUCS, pp. 13–17.

Santos, M. M. C, Perazzolo, O. A. and Pereira, S. (2014) A hospitalidade numa perspectiva coletiva: O corpo coletivo acolhedor. In Santos, M. M. C. and Baptista, I. (eds) *Laços Sociais: por uma epistemologia da hospitalidade*, Caxias do Sul: EDUCS, pp. 49–63.

Shamay-Tsoory, S. G. (2011) The neural bases for empathy, *Neuroscientist* 17: 18–24.

Winnicott, D. W. (2006) *Os bebês e suas mães*, São Paulo: WMF Martins Fontes.

11

Hospitalities
Circe writes back*

Judith Still

> **Key themes**
>
> Animals
>
> Carol Ann Duffy
>
> Derrida
>
> Homer
>
> Sexual difference

A guest never forgets the host who had treated him kindly.

(Homer)

Homer's *Odyssey* is one of the key intertexts for thinking about hospitality in the Western world; hospitality has always, apparently, declined since the days of Homer.[1] Hospitality is particularly necessary in the aftermath of war, a time of travel, of exile, perhaps of home-coming. Different episodes in the *Odyssey* can be interpreted along a continuum from a hospitality of excess to bonds of mutual protection for chieftains or heads of household, bearing in mind that these rationally agreed compacts are sealed with feasting and gift exchange that always has the possibility of slipping into sacrificial superabundance. At the same time the details of the Homeric text are sufficiently complex and ambivalent to cover a range of failures of hospitality as well as hospitality itself.[2] The narrative of the home-coming Odysseus or Ulysses has been evoked in a wide range of contexts since the mythical bard Homer first sang of his experiences, and the re-tellings (including James Joyce's famous work) themselves get re-told and re-analysed. I would argue that the relationship between literature and philosophy as a shadowy duelling duo is always already inscribed in thinking about hospitality; philosophy pays attention to the ethical responsibility of the host, but literature is hospitable to different meanings – conjuring up the ambiguity of both host and guest.

In *Derrida and Hospitality* (Still, 2010), I focused not only on Odysseus as guest, but also on Telemachus as guest (and host), and the suitors as guests and hosts. I referenced the story of Circe in the *Odyssey* as an example of the typical Homeric female host who is 'amorous and thus liable to hold our hero back' (Still, 2010: 58), but did not pay particular attention to the details. Yet the representation of the nymph encapsulates the ambiguities and tensions of hospitality – if we read it carefully – and so I shall return to it here. Theory as philosophy tends to imagine the host in a position of power – and this is true in many situations, but power is complex, and hospitality involves openness even to dangerous guests. While Circe is quasi-divine entertaining mortals, she is also a female entertaining men. Consideration of the vulnerability of the open host (for example, to rapacious guests) does not often entail specific consideration of women in themselves as opposed to women as the property of men. The bond of traditional hospitality is set up between men however much empirically there may be many exceptions to any such rule, and however much women may service the infrastructure of hospitality. *The Odyssey*, after all, gives one of the clearest warnings in any text about the dangers of listening to tempting sirens. The host may become the hostage of the guest even though it is the guest's subordination to the host that is the classic philosophical starting point. I shall be analysing Circe via a wonderful poem by the British Poet Laureate Carol Ann Duffy about a female persona who, the reader will remember, has a reputation, established by a former lover, for turning men into swine (Duffy, 1999, 47–48). Characteristically, Duffy uses the first person singular, a female voice. As her persona contemplates her cooking pot, she dramatises the way that women's voices are rarely heard, remarking to her companions: 'Look at that simmering lug, at that ear, / did it listen, ever, to you, to your prayers and rhymes, / to the chimes of your voices, singing and clear?' This may be an imperfect woman – but we might recall that Odysseus may be a hero but is not exactly a perfect man. Where sirens are concerned he notoriously wanted to have his cake and eat it. Duffy's Circe keeps hogs, and enjoys cooking up pork dinners for, and with, female friends; but the relationship between men and pigs in this poem is kept on the level of language, cunning figures of speech drawing on the everyday to suggest porcine similarities rather than supernatural metamorphoses.[3]

Defining hospitality: a few of the questions

It is very difficult to define hospitality – personally I would talk about a structure of welcoming difference, but certainly not everyone would agree with that. Some thinkers would claim that hospitality *is* ethics, and *is* definitional of humanity. I do not want to spend too long on definitions – but will just pose a few questions:

- Who and to whom? (Who can be a guest, who can be a host?) If the guest is unexpected – who will the guest be?
- *Semblables*: What does that term imply?[4] Can we only offer hospitality to those whom we recognise as being like ourselves? Do we only recognise hospitality when it is offered by those with whom we can identify?
- Is the structure of hospitality one of reciprocity? Or does reciprocity lead to economic exchange which erodes true hospitality?[5]
- Is violence, including sexual violence, contingent or structural to hospitality?
- Is hospitality defined by the content of the relationship, for example the offer of food or a bed for the night?
- How should the guest show *reconnaissance* (recognition and gratitude)? Is the telling of tales integral to the situation?
- What or who supports the infrastructure of hospitality – the question of service: who prepares the food and makes the bed?
- Material: who is the food and who is (in) the bed?

I shall pause on a quotation from Jacques Derrida, the foremost thinker of hospitality in recent times. The key point is that he is challenging another great thinker of hospitality, and good friend, Emmanuel Levinas, over the boundaries of hospitality. Levinas seems to be struggling to have the most open understanding possible of the hospitable relationship – but claims that it is *between men*. His preferred term – which he distinguishes from *semblable* – is brother. Here we must remember that he was born in 1906, and even more importantly perhaps, is writing in French. Nevertheless for some feminists today (including myself) this term can seem symptomatic of a problem – of a focus on humanity that potentially does violence to sexual difference. One of Derrida's responses to this is to open up hospitality to animals – and the argument can be made that this is ethically right in itself and/or that it is only by including animals that we can be sure that we are not excluding some human beings:

> Hospitality – if there is any – must, would have to, open itself to an other that is not mine, my hôte, my other, not even my neighbor or my brother (Levinas always says that the other, the other man, man as the other is *my* neighbor, my universal brother, in humanity. At bottom, this is one of our larger questions: is hospitality reserved, confined to man, to the universal brother? For even if Levinas disjoints the idea of fraternity from the idea of the 'fellow [*semblable*],' and the idea of neighbor [*prochain*] or of proximity from the idea of non-distance, of non-distancing, of fusion and identity, he nonetheless maintains that the hospitality of the hôte as well as that of the hostage must belong to the site of the fraternity of the neighbor). Hospitality, therefore – if there is any – must, would have to, open itself to an other that is not mine, my hôte, my other, not even my neighbor or my brother, perhaps an 'animal' – I do say animal.
>
> *(Derrida, 2002: 363)*

So can we humans be hospitable to other animals, can animals be hospitable to us? These two final questions in the quotation from Derrida unsettle both hospitality and the setting of the borderline between animal and human. How is hospitality understood such that *either* by definition it is between two human beings *or* by definition an open welcoming that cannot specify the guest in advance? As Anne Dufourmantelle quotes Derrida: "'If you don't do justice to hospitality toward animals, you are also excluding gods'" (Derrida and Dufourmantelle, 2000: 142) This relates, furthermore, to the notion of not-quite-human humans, those to whom we need not offer hospitality (nor feel that they offer us hospitality) because they do not meet the criteria we have set; they are outside the borders set up which, in limiting hospitality, are thought to enable it. A question puts some flesh on the bones of the politico-ethical debate concerning the limited hospitality (at best) of the auto-immune sovereign state: how are those considered *not* to be (good) citizens or brothers framed, those such as women, savages, slaves or animals? One answer is that sovereign man is deemed (say, by Kant) to be master of himself (*ipse* and *potes*) as woman, servant, slave cannot be. Women may be framed as goddesses or as servants or slaves, or indeed animals.

Circe

Homer's *Odyssey*, that *Urtext* of hospitality, celebrates hospitality between men and condemns inhospitality to men – although even this masculine hospitality is not unproblematic, the reader always has to ask 'in whose voice' is the tale told? But it also, perhaps, shows a range of (auto-immune) worlds which are very inhospitable to women and/or to those of a different ethnicity and/or to animals; these various categories are those who are not brothers, not *semblables*. The

Odyssey shows women serving – serving up food or serving for sex – the hostess is an ambiguous figure in many languages. So women and animals (serving as food) are represented first as part of the infrastructure of hospitality. But semi-divine Circe is a host in the *Odyssey*, and, rather different, in Carol Ann Duffy's poem of that name. Duffy goes on implicitly to pose the question – what kind of tenuous community can we imagine for women in the face of general inhospitality to women? But even her new community of 'nymphs', hospitable to those excluded or exploited by the larger society, is not only marked by loss but also perhaps founded on sacrifice – on violence towards new victims whether men or pigs. There is no suggestion then that even utopias can sacrifice sacrifice (in other words that implies that violence is structural rather than contingent to hospitality).

Duffy then takes on the *Odyssey* and rewrites one episode radically in the voice of Circe. In the original this tale is told by Odysseus, rather than by the narrator, as an example, I would suggest, of sticky or smothering feminine hospitality. Odysseus is hoping to persuade his latest host King Alcinous *not* to seek to keep him as a woman sneakily would, not to offer him his daughter in marriage *but rather* to offer him, as a fraternal guest-friend, precious objects and a ship to set him freely on his way. And indeed he is successful in this.

Boldly taking the accusation made against this solitary witch figure, Circe, that she domesticates male guests and turns them into inferior (if tasty) penned animals, Duffy presents a witty celebration of hospitality *between women* (or at least females) where indeed men are (like) animals – the material infrastructure of hospitality, something which is particularly funny because the reader knows this is rarely the case except where there is an extreme hierarchy of servitude. I should say 'females' because the *Odyssey* seems clear that hospitality is very dangerous for mortal women (either as hosts or guests) – exceptions are only made for those named as divine or semi-divine, for the possibility of entertaining gods in disguise (like angels in the Old Testament) is a key driver of ancient hospitality. But Circe is not quite a goddess (she is not like Athena) she is just a nymph.

Circe's domestication of her foreign guests could of course be read as a forced assimilation or as servitude – guests who become guest workers or even slaves. An interesting parallel might be right-wing French republicanism, for example, which has been known to suggest that all French school children should be grateful to be offered delicious pork for their school dinner, even if they are Jewish, Muslim or vegetarian – and that women in veils should be grateful to be liberated by being banned from public places or even physically attacked and the veil torn from them. Yet to see this as a parallel is to accept King Odysseus's story that Circe is the one in the position of power, and thus he is justified in using any trick against her – and the sovereign is always justified even when he is in exile. If the reader recognises the vulnerability of the hostess, if only to emotional abuse, then the speculative interpretation of her forms of response, and forms of violence, in social intercourse – even forms hardly to be recommended - might be more open.

Duffy's poem 'Circe' is from *The World's Wife* – the title of her collection suggests that the world is the master who can welcome into or exclude from his domain, while his property, his wife, is a handmaiden to his endeavour – Duffy gives us Frau Freud, Mrs Darwin, even Mrs Lazarus speaking back to this tradition. But in the case of a quasi-deity the title is just Circe, and in any case Mrs Odysseus would be the patient Penelope. Circe is 'just' one of the many females Odysseus has sex with – the equally defamed Calypso is another example of a creature who is described in the *Odyssey* as a clinging hostess who keeps her man her prisoner.

As I have suggested, hospitality, from entertaining friends at home to the hospitality industry, typically involves the offer of food and/or a bed – and so the politics of food and bed are part of it. Women frequently serve as an indispensable part of the infrastructure of hospitality, and yet are poorly rewarded, if not expendable, as individuals. In this *Urtext* of hospitality, Homer's *Odyssey*, we could consider the ambiguous position of vulnerable women. Penelope's maids, for example, who served as bed companions for her princeling suitors, invasive and greedy guests in her house, are hanged by her son when her husband Odysseus finally returns to his rightful place. The reader is not quite sure whether these maids were forced or willing, and Odysseus does refer to rape. The patriarchal narrative context is one in which even the noble-born Trojan women taken by the victorious Greeks have little choice but to submit to their new lot as bed slaves. Even if the Ithacan maids were 'willing' to acquiesce to the powerful guests' demands, and disloyal to their house, hanging might be seen as a harsh sentence – it is a more ignominious death of course than that meted out to the men shot by Odysseus's arrows in spite of their treatment of Odysseus both as absent King and husband, and present beggar asking for hospitality.

In the *Odyssey* Circe could be seen, if I read against the grain, as a woman alone invaded by unexpected male guests. She does have some handmaidens but if her surprise guests are thieves, murderers or rapists – and in fact if you look at the behaviour of the Greeks in Troy, they are all three – the handmaidens may be of little service, and indeed (like Penelope's maids) they are of little help when Odysseus turns his sword on her. Circe responds to uninvited male visitors by domesticating and thus transforming them – but the story (*his* story which goes down in history), the tale told by Odysseus, makes this witchcraft. She gives his men a herb which turns them into docile animals. Only at the point of his sword does she give in (a hostage?), abandon her plan to better him and take him to her bed – at the point of his sword. Odysseus and his companions become Circe's happy guests until they remember home, and their *difference*.

Duffy turns the tables, however, on this famous traveller's tale with a life-enhancing portrait of a ball-breaking carnivorous survivor – in Homer the dish offered by Circe is meat-free, but Duffy has her serve the chauvinist pigs right. This brings out some of the discomfort or unease which a heuristic reading of Homer might gloss over.

> I'm fond, nereids and nymphs, unlike some, of the pig,
> of the tusker, the snout, the boar and the swine.
> One way or another, all pigs have been mine –
> under my thumb, the bristling, salty skin of their backs,
> in my nostrils here, their yobby, porky colognes.
> I'm familiar with hogs and runts, their percussion of oinks
> and grunts, their squeals. I've stood with a pail of swill
> at dusk, at the creaky gate of the sty,
> tasting the sweaty, spicy air, the moon
> like a lemon popped in the mouth of the sky.
> But I want to begin with a recipe from abroad
>
> which uses the cheek – and the tongue in cheek
> at that. Lay two pig's cheeks, with the tongue,
> in a dish, and strew it well over with salt
> and cloves. Remember the skills of the tongue –
> to lick, to lap, to loosen, lubricate, to lie
> in the soft pouch of the face – and how each pig's face
> was uniquely itself, as many handsome as plain,
> the cowardly face, the brave, the comical, noble,
> sly or wise, the cruel, the kind, but all of them,
> nymphs, with those piggy eyes. Season with mace.

Well-cleaned pig's ears should be blanched, singed, tossed
in a pot, boiled, kept hot, scraped, served, garnished
with thyme. Look at that simmering lug, at that ear,
did it listen, ever, to you, to your prayers and rhymes,
to the chimes of your voices, singing and clear? Mash
the potatoes, nymph, open the beer. Now to the brains,
to the trotters, shoulders, chops, to the sweetmeats slipped
from the slit, bulging, vulnerable bag of the balls.
When the heart of a pig has hardened, dice it small.
Dice it small. I, too once knelt on this shining shore
watching the tall ships sail from the burning sun
like myths; slipped off my dress to wade,
breast-deep, in the sea, waving and calling;
then plunged, then swam on my back, looking up
as three black ships sighed in the shallow waves.
Of course, I was younger then. And hoping for men. Now,
let us baste that sizzling pig on the spit once again.

Duffy's poem celebrates cooking (for friends), an activity which we could interpret *here* as showing women as the agents, rather than the objects, of transformation and metamorphosis – as indeed the sorceress nymph Circe is through her offer of refreshments to visitors. Duffy's Circe wants 'to begin with a recipe from abroad'. The listener might hear 'a broad', a woman as the origin of the design for the meal. Although usually not recognised as such, cooking is a form of technology, if we consider how the term has functioned in Derrida's writing, in particular technology as the *articulation* of nature and culture. Women's *work*, I would argue, is culturally central and yet (or, therefore) downgraded as natural. Cooking is part of *domestic labour*, and notably of the technique of hospitality – a cultural practice that, at best, however labour-intensive, will *seem* natural and effortless. This quotidian even proletarian female practice of serving up economical and relatively simple food for family, or here friends, is not the famous artistic creativity of the master *chef* – although, of course, fashions in consumption may perfectly well adopt any peasant or poor cuisine so long as it can be sold with a high profit margin to *distinguish* the discerning quality of those who purchase it. Duffy – as a writer – turns the preparation of pork into poetry, conjuring up the imagined voice of the witch lingering over her double meanings. Herbs, used by Circe for magical transformation in the *Odyssey*, in the modern poem can become violent instruments we imagine using on a yobby liar – mace – or the healing process after betrayal – thyme. The salty skin of the living pig, or the dead one (crackling), might also refer to the taste of a lover's body – salty from sea water or the exertion of sex.

For a different perspective on women as hostesses, I could turn to another tale of metamorphosis into a pig: Marie Darrieussecq's 1996 dystopian fiction *Truismes*, translated as *Pig Tales* (1997), which suggests the ambiguity of *sex work* in particular – is it a job? Is it an extra to a job? Can it be acknowledged? And while her protagonist explicitly becomes more or less like an animal, this also has a relationship, if a less explicit one, to the mechanical nature of what she is doing. It is important, in other words, that women's work is patriarchy made invisible, made natural.

Duffy's poem could be understood as the preparation of a cannibal feast; the pot and the spit are classical cannibal accoutrements, and there is a foregrounding of the linguistic play of cannibalism in the double meanings of flesh, hardened heart and so on.[6] This could encourage a readerly response of nausea (a desire to vomit from the mouth rather than take anything into the mouth), for instance as 'the sweetmeats slipped / from the slit, bulging, vulnerable bag of the balls' reminds readers of oral love and sex, with 'eating' literalised in the poetic image. Hospitality can be physically intimate – which might imply pleasurable or might mean alarming or disgusting. Taking something (a foreign body) in (to yourself) is the synecdoche of hospitality. In Darrieussecq's novel, pork products arouse particular disgust and nausea as the narrator's body identifies with the pig. But, even if the reader gags, old Circe has the magic power of transformation, and nereids and nymphs to share her thoughts, beer and cheek with, while Darrieussecq's protagonist eventually finds solace in a community of pigs.

Duffy treats the love of men, as opposed to pig meat, as something nostalgic. Nostalgia is a major theme in the *Odyssey* but largely in the vein of Odysseus's longing for home (his kingdom) – Homer lavished little care on the women or men his wily trickster uses and abuses en route when he is desperate for a meal and a bed for the night. In Duffy's poetic revenge fantasy, amorous lyricism is present, but reserved for hopeful youth – *now*, for the disillusioned mistress, tongue is to be firmly in cheek. Duffy's Circe, older and wiser, a more domestic goddess, has entertained many men, some better than others, but all with 'piggy eyes'. The reader could interpret that as greedy eyes, men, perhaps like the tricky Odysseus who are ultimately out for what they can get from hosts or hostesses. Darrieussecq's *Pig Tales* outlines the brutality of men towards women in far greater detail – while here Duffy focuses on the empowerment of the older, more cynical woman, who recollects the closed ears and lying tongues as she turns them into tasty food for her female guests – and food for thought. Mature women are of course seldom treated kindly in patriarchal myths and stories – especially when they enjoy themselves not only with memories and friends, but also with sensual delights, lip-smacking food and beer. A poem that celebrates the pleasure of an old(er) woman in her own voice is a rare treat to be savoured especially for the female consumer of the text.

What does carnivorousness, what does cannibalism signify in terms of a democratic or hospitable society? Does the poem end with a new community of *semblables* with their own exclusions or does the nostalgia for sexual and ethnic difference, for the migrant or the traveller, maintain a generous fracture in the community? Does the sensual oral pleasure in the play of poetic language allow us to think about eating well together by acknowledging our frightening desire to bite as well as lick and kiss – unafraid of the response of nausea or gagging?

A final question is that of the relationship between philosophy and literature. Fiction has examined the position of the guest more often than philosophy, which tends to focus on the responsibility of the host, assumed to be in the position of power.[7] Post-colonial fiction has taken the perspective of the migrant, for example – and Duffy's Circe wants 'to begin with a recipe from abroad', the foreign is brought in orally – raising the question of foreign food, foreign culture as part of a hybrid world that was globalised up to a point even in Homer's day. Life-writing as often addresses the pleasures and tribulations of being a guest as being a host; Rousseau is an early example (see Still, 2011, 1993). Duffy here imagines a hostess, not quite in the long tradition of mythical women like Philomela who get revenge on an abusive man by serving up a cannibal feast, but rather one who gets pleasure from feasting with other women – perhaps her lovers serving as food for gossip to be picked over.

As a coda, returning to Derrida's question about hospitality to other animals, I should like to present a quotation from a more recent source, a 2013 introduction to Critical Animal Studies – in my view this is an area that needs more feminist work, but equally critical hospitality as well as feminism can learn from current work in this field. It is good to remember the reality of female animals (here, sows) as well as figuring animals in literature.

Most, if not all, contributors to critical animal studies would agree that, particularly since the seventeenth century, modern Western ways of knowing nonhuman animals, inseparable from violent techniques practiced on them, have turned animals into 'stone', that is, into inert objects, useful and disposable things: *reproductive machines* is the term ethicist Peter Singer uses when discussing the fate of sows in today's industrialized hog farming, where the goal is to use all available manufacturing techniques to 'produce' as many as possible pigs per sow per year, and to fast-track those pigs, those 'products', to slaughter weight (Singer, *Liberation*, 126).

(McCance, 2013: 2)

Eating pigs is thought in some cultures to be the closest you can get to eating human flesh while still restricting permissible sacrifice to animals. I would suggest that Duffy's poem subtly raises the question with regard to a hospitable society: who or what can we eat? It is not only that the pigs are sentient beings too, or that these particular pigs might once have been men, but that greedy pleasure in food (and indeed lust) is often represented as piggish – thus Circe and the nymphs, even as they embrace life, also *risk* being named as swine and brought towards death. The animal–human boundary is more porous than philosophers would like, and any exclusion from the community may end with the return of what has been repressed.

Conclusions

Duffy's response to Homer has a female host entertaining female guests – a very rare occurrence in classical tales of hospitality, and especially rare in Homer's epic tale of Odysseus's long journey home from war. In Duffy's 'Circe', men enter the scene only indirectly as memories – or, just perhaps, as pork. This is a witty rejoinder to the story King Odysseus tells to King Alcinous, which not only entertains but also incidentally instructs his host by showing examples of failures of hospitality and hopefully demonstrating his own worth as a guest. Odysseus is making a gesture of gratitude to Alcinous by relating his tale of woe, but is perhaps thereby less grateful to Circe, for example, by making her into fodder for his narrative about a witch who turns men into swine, and indicating how she can be dominated by a bold and resourceful man in spite of her magic tricks. This raises the difficult question of reciprocity in the affective and material economy of hospitality. Furthermore, it raises the question whether hospitality need be open to otherness or is simply an exchange between *semblables*, 'people like us'. Derrida suggests that only by including animals can we be sure that we are not excluding certain categories of human (not that this is the only reason for nibbling at the animal–human borderline). The exclusion or betrayal of women is re-cast or memorialised in Duffy's poem by the figural play that represents men as pigs. Odysseus, even in his own story a lying, thieving and violent guest, frames many inhospitable races as cannibals – a political accusation frequently made about people not like us (Barker *et al.*, 1998). Duffy's joyous re-inscription of a cannibal feast as everyday culinary magic worked on pork both hints at all the elements of doubt that should hang over accusations of cannibalism, and also blurs the boundary between eating your own species and consuming other species. Some communities may be thought to be simply more hospitable than other communities, as illustrated in Homer's epic poem, but Duffy's small contribution to the long intertextual history Homer has spawned shows the complexity of hospitality to insiders and to outsiders – and the spectre of cannibalism reminds the reader how hard it is to sacrifice sacrifice.

Notes

★ 'Circe' from *The World's Wife* by Carol Ann Duffy (Copyright © Carol Ann Duffy, 1999), is reproduced by kind permission of Picador and Rogers, Coleridge & White Ltd.

1   See my *Derrida and Hospitality* (Still, 2010), in particular the section 'Homer' pp. 52–67 in Chapter 2 'Patriarchs and their Women, some inaugural intertexts of hospitality: the *Odyssey*, Abraham, Lot and the Levite of Ephraim', pp. 51–92.

2   In *Taking on the Tradition*, Michael Naas evokes *The Odyssey* in a chapter on hospitality; he raises the key questions of threshold and the name, and makes some very interesting points although he does not quite follow the details of the text – for instance he implies that Polyphemos invites Odysseus in as his guest which is not the case (2003: 155–156). Naas then uses the story of Polyphemos as a parable for states with (fierce) border controls and close inspection of passports – clearly a critical question for our times (2003: 156ff.). However, by the time Odysseus is asked his name the Cyclops has already killed four and eaten two of his crew; it is not clear that the others would have been spared whatever name/passport had been given (*The Odyssey*, book IX). I shall refer to book numbers (in Roman numerals) for ease of comparison between editions.

3   See my *Derrida and Other Animals* (Still, 2015) for an earlier version of this analysis of Duffy, and also analysis of a number of other authors who draw on the Circe episode including Plutarch and La Fontaine.

4   Much has been written on this term. I shall just give one reference: Cheah and Guerlac (2009) relate the *semblable* to the brother, seeing the politics of fraternity as a politics of sameness and thus of exclusion or autoimmunity, of autochthony and the nation/national citizenship (referring *inter alia* to Derrida, 2005: 57–58). They point out that as the world is ever more globalised the fantasmatic integrity of national borders and homogeneity of the nation is ever more delusional – there should be a different model: the friend as the other in oneself, and the other as friend, which might allow democracy to come.

5   Commentators on Derridean hospitality are usually much exercised by the distinction between conditional (familiar, rule-bound) and unconditional or absolute hospitality. Bennington (2016) indicates a structure of Derrida's thought that would mean, I could extrapolate, that absolute hospitality would be the end (aim) of hospitality. Absolute hospitality, I would suggest then, functions to poke (befriend?), prod, upset the laws of hospitality (maybe a *demi-hospitalité* in Bennington's or Derrida's vein) – which tell us that absolute hospitality would be the end (ruin) of hospitality (see note 7 below). He writes:

> The ongoing paradox or aporia is that the dignity *most digne de ce nom* is thereby the dignity that is *less* that full-blown sovereign dignity, and rather (on the model of the *demi-deuil* that turns out to be the only mourning *digne de ce nom*, or the *demi-démocratie* that Laurent Milesi once suggested to me was the appropriate way to think of the 'démocratie à venir' (the very concept that in *Rogues* prompts Derrida to promise one day a 'long justification' of his use of the idiom *digne de ce nom*)) – rather the dignity most worthy of its name, as good as it gets, is a *demi-dignité*. That *demi-dignité* is always less than sovereign, and the 'digne de ce nom' structure would always be a sign of that. Any X *digne de ce nom* would on this hypothesis be situated in the tension towards the Idea and somewhat pulling back against that tension which it cannot simply ignore.
>
> *(Bennington, 2016: 57)*

6   *The Odyssey* is full of examples of cannibalism. In Book X, which focuses on Circe, Odysseus moves quickly from the model host Aeolus to his experiences in the land of the huge cannibal Laestrygonians where he loses the crew of all his ships bar his own – harpooned like fish to make a loathsome meal.

7   Philosophy responds to

> a conjugal model, paternal and phallogocentric. It's the familial despot, the father, the spouse and the boss, the master of the house who lays down the laws of hospitality. He represents them and submits to them to submit the others to them in this violence of the power of hospitality, in this force of ipseity.
>
> *(Derrida and Dufourmantelle, 2000: 149)*

In the face of the traditional power of the host, ethical philosophy then tries to imagine a radical abdication of power. However, that is less something that Derrida promotes than some of his readers have presumed. Bennington more advisedly suggests that the key 'slogan' of deconstruction is: "'la différance infinie est finie,'", and that this is

> a claim about a principle of internal ruin in the Kantian Idea, which elsewhere I have tried to capture in the formula 'the end is the end:' as Derrida is extremely clear about in the work on hospitality, if one ever reached the *telos* prescribed by the Idea, then the result would not be the end in the sense of fulfilment but the end in the sense of catastrophe, as a supposedly achieved justice turned out to be the end of justice, a supposedly achieved democracy the end of democracy, and so on.
>
> *(Bennington, 2016: 56)*

References

Barker, F., Hulme, P. and Iversen, M. (eds) (1998) *Cannibalism and the Colonial World*, Cambridge: Cambridge University Press.

Bennington, G. (2016) Derrida's dignity. In Phillips, J. (ed.) *Derrida Now: Current Perspectives in Derrida Studies*, Cambridge: Polity Press, pp. 41–63.

Cheah, P. and Guerlac, S. (2009) Introduction. In Cheah, P. and Guerlac, S. (eds) *Derrida and the Time of the Political*, Durham, NC and London: Duke University Press.

Darrieussecq, M. (1997) *Pig Tales: A Novel of Lust and Transformation*, trans. Linda Coverdale, London: Faber and Faber.

Derrida, J. (2002) Hostipitality. In Anidjar, G. (ed.) *Jacques Derrida: Acts of Religion*. New York and London: Routledge, pp. 356–420.

Derrida, J. (2005) *Rogues: Two Essays on Reason*, trans. P. Brault and M. Naas, Stanford, Stanford University Press.

Derrida, J. and Dufourmantelle, A. (2000) *Of Hospitality: Anne Dufourmantelle Invites Jacques Derrida to Respond*, trans. R. Bowlby, Stanford: Stanford University Press.

Duffy, C. A. (1999) *The World's Wife*, London: Picador.

Homer (1946) *The Odyssey*, trans. E. V. Rieu, Harmondsworth: Penguin.

McCance, D. (2013) *Critical Animal Studies: An Introduction*, Albany, NY: SUNY Press.

Naas, M. (2003) *Taking on the Tradition: Jacques Derrida and the Legacies of Deconstruction*, Stanford: Stanford University Press.

Still, J. (1993) *Justice and Difference in the Works of Rousseau*, Cambridge: Cambridge University Press.

Still, J. (2010) *Derrida and Hospitality: Theory and Practice*, Edinburgh: Edinburgh University Press.

Still, J. (2011) *Enlightenment Hospitality: Cannibals, Harems and Adoption*, Oxford: The Voltaire Foundation.

Still, J. (2015) *Derrida and Other Animals: The Boundaries of the Human*, Edinburgh: Edinburgh University Press.

12

On the hospitality of cannibals

Ruud Welten

Key themes

Hospitality as metaphor

Psychoanalytic approach of hospitality

Hospitality and hostility

Cannibalism

Better sleep with a sober cannibal than a drunken Christian.

(Melville)

In one of the first chapters of Melville's *Moby Dick*, Ishmael is looking for a place to sleep. His irrepressible desire to sail the ocean has brought him to Nantucket, port of departure to whaling vessels, in search of a captain willing to employ him. He only just manages to secure a bed in the Spouter-Inn, where the innkeeper suggests that he share a bed with a harpooner. What? Share a bed with a stranger, another man at that?

> No man prefers to sleep two in a bed. In fact, you would a good deal rather not sleep with your own brother. I don't know how it is, but people like to be private when they are sleeping. And when it comes to sleeping with an unknown stranger, in a strange inn, in a strange town, and that stranger a harpooneer, then your objections indefinitely multiply.
>
> *(Melville, 1992: 17)*

Who is this harpooner, who hasn't arrived yet? The innkeeper's stories give rise to ominous premonitions. The harpooner is late, he chuckles, because he is out in the streets selling shrunken heads hunted in New Zealand ('great curios, you know').

DOI: 10.4324/9781315679938-13

Ishmael is reluctant to share a bed with a person engaging in 'Cannibal Business'. Yet he doesn't have much choice: he accepts the offer, awaiting the return of the cannibal with trepidation. Ishmael is already in bed when the heavily tattooed 'cannibal' enters the room, only to frighten him even further. From the corner of his eye Ishmael can see the heads, the magical objects the cannibal apparently worships, and more importantly, the terrifying, black, lacerated face of his bedfellow. 'The next moment the light was extinguished, and this wild cannibal, tomahawk between his teeth, sprang into bed with me.' The cannibal notices Ishmael and, also in fear, yells at him. 'Who-e debel you? ... you no speak-e, dam-me, I kill-e.' Ishmael cries out for the innkeeper, who hurries in and eventually manages to calm him down: 'Don't be afraid now', said he, grinning again, 'Queequeg here wouldn't harm a hair of your head.' Pacified at last Ishmael reconciles with the situation, accepts that Queequeg can be trusted and concludes: 'Better sleep with a sober cannibal than a drunken Christian' (Melville, 1992: 26). The opening lines of the next chapter are endearing: 'Upon waking next morning about daylight, I found Queequeg's arm thrown over me in the most loving and affectionate manner. You had almost thought I had been his wife' (Melville, 1992: 28) and further on: 'Thus, then, in our hearts' honeymoon, lay I and Queequeg – a cosy, loving pair.'

Nothing less than the initiation of an intimate friendship between two men from two radically different cultures who are going to have to depend on each other for months, the honeymoon of Ishmael and Queequeg is crucial to the further development of *Moby Dick*. Primarily, however, the honeymoon of Ishmael and Queequeg is a story about hospitality. Ishmael is looking for a place to sleep, for an inn, and almost like in the Christmas story, he is relegated to the *backspace* of the inn, where all's well that ends well.

With regard to 'hospitality', the *host* is the stranger whose customs we do not understand. He attracts us or repels us, not infrequently simultaneously. The encounter between Ishmael and Queequeg takes us to the extremes of hospitality: on the one hand to the refusal to accept an obscure offer to share a bed with a repelling stranger, on the other to a story that ends in the awakening from a deep sleep like a 'cosy, loving pair', in the arms of that same, snoring stranger. We know that these extremes meet in hospitality, not since Derrida, but since Cicero at least: 'Someone who, strictly speaking, was a *perduellis*, an enemy, used to be called a *hostis* – a softening by understatement of a harsh reality for what our ancestors called a *hostis*, we now call a *peregrinus*: a stranger' (Cicero, 2005: 39). He refers to the stem of the word hospitality – *host* – which is clearly recognisable in English and French. The French *l'hôte* refers to both the guest and the host and, more importantly, both contemporary languages also show the double bind of hospitality: the word *hostile* contains the same stem. Hospitality always refers to the still undecided relationship between strangers.

Melville describes a situation that confirms, even surpasses Derrida's undecidedness: who is the guest, and who is the host in this case? Is it the innkeeper? Or is Ishmael Queequeg's guest, or perhaps the other way around? The latter would be problematic: to Queequeg, Ishmael is an *unannounced* guest and hence a guest that is not a guest, which is precisely why Derrida would say that he *is* a guest indeed (a guest is not someone we expect, but a guest is someone we receive *nonetheless*, like an asylum seeker or a refugee, which of course implies nothing at all about the nature of the reception). So, who is the host? Is the other friend or foe? Is he really a cannibal, or isn't he? (A question which, as we shall see, never fails to arise when cannibals are involved.) Is this double bind – this fear of violence, this hope of mercy – perhaps the distinguishing characteristic of *hospitality/hostility*? The fact that Ishmael *doesn't know* what his reception will eventually result in is crucial to the story. He has to rely on the frightening stories of the innkeeper and on his own misgivings. The suspicion that his bedfellow is a cannibal drives the extremes to extremes and this, as we shall see, is crucial to Melville.

Cannibalism as a psychoanalytical metaphor

The warm, semi-homoerotic bed scene that ends the chapter contrasts sharply with the minimum of hospitality and the menacing misgivings at its beginning. It is no coincidence that the two men meet each other in bed. The bed is both the symbol of hospitality (see Bed and Breakfast and Hotel pictograms) *and* the place where one invites the other to make love. It is the ultimate place of seduction, of reception. The sexual act, due to its physical proximity and fusion as well as the conception that may result from the reception of sperm, may very well be the ultimate form of hospitality. This invites a psychoanalytical interpretation of *Moby Dick* – the sperm whale (the whale is a mammal, after all). On the one hand, we have the conjunction hospitality/sexuality; on the other we have sexuality/cannibalism. There are interesting similarities between sexuality and cannibalism. Both involve physical advances that end in physical communion. Both involve delay, ritual foreplay and ecstatic climaxing. But perhaps the most strikingly similar is their physical character: their physical hospitality and physical reception. Sexuality and cannibalism both aim for total hospitality, for the assimilation of one body by another.

Cannibalism is always a desire of the mouth, an oral desire that cannot be explained by hunger unless the cannibalism involved is survival cannibalism. It is not the flesh of the other that nourishes, but their eroticised body (Safouan, 2001). Of all human activity, the sexual act alone allows the eating of the other to the extent that it involves their bodily fluids. In his review of Dennis O'Rourke's documentary *Cannibal Tours*, Dean MacCannell associates cannibalism with the ritual fellatio found among the Sambia tribe in New Guinea (he refers to the work of anthropologist Gilbert Herdt, who describes sexual practices among New Guinea cannibals that are not driven by passion, but by cultural regulations that curb the sex drive. Young boys fellate adolescent young men, who become heterosexual only at a later age; MacCannell 1990: 20). Here, as in Moby Dick, the sperm is of crucial importance. 'A Squeeze of the Hand', the chapter in which the bonds of friendship among the seamen are tightened while they extract the sperm of a dead whale strengthens the homo-erotic metaphor struck up in the honeymoon chapter. In *Moby Dick* the sperm, in the shape of a sperm whale, takes the place of homo-erotic desire. The fertilising sperm represents the hospitality that marks the conception of new life; the sperm in Moby Dick stands for the homo-erotic pleasure of absolute fraternisation, another form of absolute hospitality.

It is not a far-fetched interpretation of 'A Squeeze of the Hand':

> Squeeze! squeeze! squeeze! all the morning long; I squeezed that sperm till I myself almost melted into it; I squeezed that sperm till a strange sort of insanity came over me; and I found myself unwittingly squeezing my co-laborers' hands in it, mistaking their hands for the gentle globules. Such an abounding, affectionate, friendly, loving feeling did this avocation beget; that at last I was continually squeezing their hands, and looking up into their eyes sentimentally; as much as to say, – Oh! my dear fellow beings, why should we longer cherish any social acerbities, or know the slightest ill-humor or envy! Come; let us squeeze hands all round; nay, let us all squeeze ourselves into each other; let us squeeze ourselves universally into the very milk and sperm of kindness.
>
> *(Melville, 1992: 456)*

145

The 'squeeze of the hand' stands for male masturbation, which places the obsession with the sperm whale in *Moby Dick* in an altogether different light. As a biographer of Melville writes,

> In whaleships, to be sure, men found a degree of provisional privacy sufficient for mutu-ally desired sexual acts. The diaries the marine drummer Philip C. Van Buskirk kept a few years later suggest that in the navy mutual masturbation was commonplace (sodomy much less so).
>
> *(Parker, 1996: 207)*

The sperm – the sperm whale – is a Lacanian object of desire – the cause of a desire that cannot be known or accessed. In psychoanalysis, all things said and written have meaning – though not the meaning the subject attributes to them. It's not so much that Melville uses veiled language to talk about homoerotic desires, but rather that the language and the literature generate a homo-erotic discourse, a discourse on 'sperm whales'.

The great hunt for the sperm whale transforms into a hunt for sperm, which represents pleasure and ecstasy rather than fertility. Not so much, therefore, a book about Captain Ahab's hunt for Moby Dick as a metaphor for men hankering after women (Warren, 1984). The obsessed hunt for the big whale psychoanalytically symbolises the libido – a sperm-oriented homoerotic libido. Reviewing *Moby Dick*, Jean-Paul Sartre pointed out that the hunt for Moby Dick is driven by hate rather than love: 'Le sujet romanesque de Moby Dick est tout juste à l'envers de celui d'une passion dans le désert: non pas l'amour d'une bête pour un homme, mais la haine d'un homme pour une bête' (Sartre, 1970: 636). Ahab wants revenge, destruction, not love or eroticism.

There is debate among Melville's biographers as to whether the author of Moby Dick was a homosexual (Miller, 1975: 25–53; Bergman, 1991: 143–149; Crain, 1994). However the terminology may be confusing, because it is anachronistic. In his article 'Lovers of human flesh: homosexuality and cannibalism in Melville's novels', Caleb Crain (1994) writes that the word 'homosexuality' didn't appear in the British language until 1892. Words that suggested it covered a range of connotations, from 'friendship' to 'sodomy'. The word 'homosexuality' involves the recognition that such a thing exists, which was unthinkable in nineteenth-century America. It was taboo, unmentionable: like cannibalism was in civilised society. That is to say, cannibalism as a survival strategy was known among sailors, but they didn't call it that. We don't call someone that eats human flesh after a plane crash a cannibal either. A cannibal would be someone who ritually eats human flesh. Such a cannibal, incomprehensibly differ-ent from us, was the other. Cannibalism and homosexuality were seen as practices so 'horrible and bestial' that they could not be expressed directly in positive terms ('sodomy' implies moral abjectness).

Sexuality and cannibalism both involve the physical relationship with the other. However, there is also an important difference between the two. Unlike the cannibalistic act, the sexual act leaves the other alive – though philosophers like Georges Bataille and Roland Barthes called orgasm 'la petite mort'. Death, in this view, is not the *worst* thing that can happen to a person, but rather the *best*, since life has no greater physical pleasure to offer. In this view, the sexual act is one that extends the warmest of welcomes, one of physical hospitality, one that may lead to utter destruction, like that of the mate of the black widow spider, who is attacked and eaten when the mating is done. Again, hospitality – *host/hostile* – shows both its sides in a single act. It is only too easy to see *only* the violence in that. Anthropologists describe a range of different kinds of cannibalism, recognising an important difference between cannibalism to destroy the enemy (as a trophy) and ritual cannibalism (Lindenbaum, 2004).

Cannibalism is about physical communion with the other by oral fixation as well, like that of bear fanatic Timothy Treadwell in Werner Herzog's documentary *Grizzly Man*: obsessed with the desire to live among bears, he's eventually slain and eaten by a grizzly (Herzog, 2005). Treadwell wants to become one with the Alaskan outdoors, he wants to be like the bears, he wants to *be* a bear, and this tragic longing leaves him no alternative but to submit to the radical hospitality of nature: he realises this – literal – communion by dying. The documentary leaves no room to doubt whether his death was self-chosen. Nothing would have hurt Treadwell more than to die like a man among men. He was no big game hunter, like Ahab, but a man looking for absolute communion, which can be realised only through absolute hospitality. In a sense, Derrida is wrong when he says that absolute hospitality is impossible or even 'inconceivable and incomprehensible' (2002: 362). It would be correct to say that absolute hospitality is very possible but inevitably leads to death. Just like the physical act of making love, the act of cannibalism *is* radical hospitality – total reception and admission of the other.

The cannibal as a colonial metaphor

Metaphors refer to a meaning implicitly, so without making the referral ('like') explicit. According to Lacan (1991/2001), metaphors replace one signifier by another and thus create new signification effects. Lacan understands metaphors as entirely linguistic indicators of what Freud calls 'condensation'. Behind the metaphoric 'condensation' characteristic of his patient's dreams, Freud suspected displacement phenomena caused by neurosis. In dreams, neurotic repression is lifted. Things people keep compartmentalised while they are awake, manifest in a 'condensed' form while they dream. Linguistic metaphors mirror this condensation. The notion is of great importance to literature: we can no longer assume that what we read is merely the result of the writer's conscious intentions. The text tells us more than the writer intends to say. *Moby Dick* is a sea of metaphors. The story doesn't say what it wants to say and tells us more than it means to. Yet *Moby Dick* resists psychoanalytical interpretation at the same time, and it does so actively: the story obsessively wants to be complete, comprehensive and all-encompassing. It doesn't want to miss a thing. In chapter 35, 'The Mast-Head', for instance, the crow's nest is described metaphysically. The ocean is the universe; its view of the ocean sublime. The sailor in the crow's nest can't afford to miss something: it's like the pulpit sung of in chapter 8. 'The world's a ship on its passage out, and not a voyage complete, and the pulpit is its prow' (Melville, 1992: 45). The story *has to* convey everything there is to convey about whales (chapter 32, 'Cetology') and oceans. The cannibal metaphor, the one that we're interested in, is only one among many. However, the metaphor of the sperm whale, or that of the honeymoon, demonstrates that despite Melville's obsession with comprehensiveness, the text cannot but generate new meanings that presuppose suppressed premises or prescience.

What's important to the interpretation of the cannibal metaphor is that the suppressed premises are colonial. Rather than the biology or the anthropology of the cannibal, they involve an imagery that metaphorically generates him. In literature – from early modern to contemporary – the cannibal may well be the most important metaphor for the other available. Modernism is associated with the discovery of new worlds and thus of other cultures. Physical journeys involve a physical metaphor of the other. The cannibal is this physical 'other' par excellence, because rather than my recognition, my culture or my customs, the cannibal metaphor involves my body, being eaten by the other. The cannibal is also the ultimate other because his eating habits are incomprehensible from a Western point of view. Biologically speaking, a cannibal is as human as I am, but his behaviour is unpredictable – he may strike at any time. In the range of 'others' that I may encounter in the world, the cannibal is the most incomprehensible. It's not just that he's savage and uncivilised but, socialised the way that I am, I can only understand his eating habits, ritual or otherwise, as murder or the slaughter of me for food. The life of the metaphoric cannibal I am referring to doesn't equal the life of the 'real', anthropologic cannibal.

The metaphor always generates a cannibal who is uncivilised, yet more 'authentic', more 'natural' than the colonialist. He is the alter ego of the Western, civilised man. Characteristically, the cannibal metaphor, which was first famously introduced by Montaigne in his essay 'On cannibals', was never recorded straight from the cannibal's mouth, but only emerges in the writings of the 'civilised'. Colonialism and cannibalism have always been closely linked. To the colonialist, the cannibal legitimises his actions. In that respect, the cannibal is the enemy. Dean MacCannell points out that the cannibal metaphor generates a new metaphor:

> The ex-primitives in *Cannibal Tours*, for their part, appear unable to get a metaphor past their lips in either direction. Their way of assimilating the German colonist was to eat his brains. It is noteworthy in this regard that Americans also eat their former enemies, the Germans, but only metaphorically, of course: as frankfurters, and hamburgers.
>
> *(1990: 22)*

Primarily, the attitude towards cannibals is one of *hostility*, but it turns into hospitality every time: the cannibal is welcomed as the 'authentic' human being – not the empirical person, but the spectre, the metaphor of a man unlike us, a man who must be submitted to mission work and development aid in the name of humanity. Or has become a commoditised tourist attraction, as in *Cannibal Tours* (O'Rourke, 1988). Again, this is the unfamiliar other of Derrida's and Cicero's double bind. For the other is enemy and example at the same time. The cannibal is un-alienated, after all: he is *the noble savage*.

In his essay on cannibals, Montaigne writes about peoples that have recently been discovered at the time:

> These nations then seem to me to be so far barbarous, as having received but very little form and fashion from art and human invention, and consequently to be not much remote from their original simplicity. The laws of nature, however, govern them still, not as yet much vitiated with any mixture of ours: but 'tis in such purity, that I am sometimes troubled we were not sooner acquainted with these people, and that they were not discovered in those better times, when there were men much more able to judge of them than we are.
>
> *(2002 [1580])*

The basic idea is very modern indeed: the other, which we've prematurely depicted as barbaric, turns out to be original and authentic on closer inspection. He lives in a world as yet unaffected by the barbarity of the Western world. The argument resurfaces time and again in literary history, particularly in the work of Melville. 'May not the savage be the happier man of the two?', Melville muses in his debut, *Typee* (1996: 29). The noble savage must be cherished – a standard known to prevail only after all savages, noble or otherwise have been either eradicated or 'infected' by civilisation themselves. The cannibal is man in his primitive stage, in Freud's oral phase (1909): as yet unaware that satisfaction can be mediated by language or culture, he strives for immediate gratification. He wants oral gratification, exploring his surroundings by mouth like a baby. This is exactly why the cannibal is *innocent*, or rather hasn't lost his innocence yet, which *we* have. Cannibals are not punished for the murder they commit; similarly, we do not punish tigers for killing their prey. These are natural creatures; honest, authentic creatures. The Western world, formerly known as 'civilised', is now called 'barbaric', whereas the former barbarians reveal to us the origins of humanity.

The Philippines, 1971. A tribe called the Tasaday, which has been living without any contact with the outside world for eight centuries, is discovered. The Tasaday become famous: visiting celebrities include Charles A. Lindbergh and Gina Lollobrigida. Associated Press and the National Geographic Society come to shoot documentaries. One year after the 'discovery', the Philippine government decides to protect the tribes' primitive state by banning all colonists, tourists and ethnologists. However, as Jean Baudrillard describes in *La précession des simulacres*, the contact with anthropologists has immediately resulted in the onset of 'instant decay, like mummies exposed to the open air' (2010: 7). The story of the noble savage is somewhat more complicated than we might suspect. Anthropologists gave short shrift to Rousseau's noble savage myth (Chagnon, 2013). The Deconstructivist theses about hospitality especially became even more complex than they already were. The example of the Tasaday demonstrates that hospitality, the reception of the Western, outside world by a formerly hermitically sealed community, may lead to the latter's destruction. A destruction that according to Baudrillard leads to a shock reaction: the 'Westerners' recognise that they are responsible for the murder of the Tasaday and decide to leave the tribe alone. But there is no turning back. The colonialists may now recognise they are colonialists, however they've already created and confirmed a colonial situation: for the Tasaday are now dependent on the colonialists' decision. (Like the Indians of the Brazilian rainforests were dependent on Sting to become authentic Indians.) The Westerners have 'discovered' the Tasaday, as if they were a new species, and taken the same decision with regard to the Tasaday as they would have taken with regard to rainforests and species threatened with extinction. The other has become the object of the colonialists' actions and the relationship, the objectification is irreversible.

It is conceivable that this is the real reason why the cannibal's existence rests on conjecture rather than empirical evidence. In *Typee*, Melville writes:

> It is a singular fact, that in all our accounts of cannibal tribes we have seldom received the testimony of an eyewitness to the revolting practice. The horrible conclusion has almost always been derived either from the second-hand evidence of Europeans, or else from the admissions of the savages themselves, after they have in some degree become civilized.
>
> *(1996: 234)*

The noble savage is always beyond our reach. Like the rainbow, he yields when we approach. He lived once, in a remote spot, and after having set out to find him, our arrival is only just preceded by his loss of authenticity, as anthropologists and tourist always, tragically, find. Looking for cannibals, we're always too late. The cannibals have become extinct, have been converted or have been civilised, have been made the objects of touristic commodification or are simply done eating. Yes, but what exactly did they eat? Following the above-mentioned psychoanalytical interpretation of the cannibal metaphor, wanting to see the cannibal implies voyeurism, the desire to spy on the other, to invade his physical intimacy. We're now nearing the touristic desire for absolute transparency. Like the colonist traveller, modern tourists want 'a look behind the scenes' of the other. And what scenes more strange than those of the cannibal? The touristic demand for transparency – the demand to see everything – exposes civilised Europeans as voyeurs whose gaze destroys that which they want to see. The cannibal is constantly backing out of perspective of the Westerners. In *Cannibal Tours*, the tourists that visit New Guinea are too late (O'Rourke, 1988). They find only the descendants of cannibals, making a living by telling stories to tourists. The closer we get to the cannibals, the more the metaphor eludes us, to become merely an object of discourse. The invisibility of the cannibal is his ultimate revenge on the colonial gaze. Nineteenth-century travellers, modern tourists and even anthropologists sooner or later realise that their visiting cannibals will not dull the myth, but rather strengthen it. The cannibal is a Western metaphor, a myth. Not because man-eaters don't exist, but because noble-savage-man-eaters can only exist in the perspective of 'civilised' cultures. The cannibal is an invisible host.

In this sense, Queequeg is a product of the imperialist imagination cultivated by Melville. *Thanks to* Queequeg, Ishmael can be cast a civilised man – Queequeg as a projection that owes its existence to civilised literature. This is beyond Derrida's 'impossible' hospitality – which doesn't involve an ethics of hospitality (a tautology anyway according to Derrida) but rather the attitude towards the other on the basis of an overly imaginative, culturally predetermined context. 'Hospitality, is culture itself and not simply one ethic among others' (Derrida, 2005: 16). Here, 'hospitality' no longer refers to an attitude, but to the mental receptivity towards the other.

The relationship between Ishmael and Queequeg, who develop a close friendship in the following chapters, represents the overcoming of fear of the other: the fear of the cannibal. 'Yet see how elastic our stiff prejudices grow when love once comes to bend them', says Ishmael once his fear of Queequeg has turned to love (Melville, 1992: 90). Is the honeymoon of Ishmael and Queequeg a symbol of the bridging of unbridgeable cultural differences? Yet in a sense, they never succeed in creating a synthesis. For Queequeg remains what he is, a cannibal, and Ishmael expects no conversion or 'integration'. And it's not as if they *understand* each other. Queequeg's 'Ramadan', which is described in chapter 17 and involves his meditating stolidly standing with his arms thrown up to heaven, a small idol, 'Yoyo', balanced on top of his head, is absurd to Ishmael. Melville's obviously made a mix of non-western spiritual rituals (the combination Ramadan-meditative posture-idol leaves a lot of room for interpretation: what religion is this?). Nevertheless, Ishmael is doing his utmost to be tolerant: 'I did not choose to disturb him till towards night-fall; for I cherish the greatest respect towards everybody's religious obligations, never mind how comical' (Melville, 1992: 90). Ishmael's attitude towards the strange religion is thoroughly Western and modern. His hospitality is conditional:

> I have no objection to any person's religion, be it what it may, so long as that person does not kill or insult any other person, because that other person don't believe it also. But when a man's religion becomes really frantic; when it is a positive torment to him; and, in fine, makes this earth of ours an uncomfortable inn to lodge in; then I think it high time to take that individual aside and argue the point with him.
>
> *(Melville, 1992: 94)*

Ishmael is *so* over proselytising: he's just looking for the best way to relate to Queequeg – even though the relationship remains strained while Queequeg is a cannibal. In many respects, the story of Ishmael and Queequeg mirrors Melville's autobiographical fascination with the other; a fascination clear from the books that precede *Moby Dick*.

The man who lived among the cannibals

In his own time, Melville wasn't famous for *Moby Dick* (which was published unsuccessfully in 1851 and recognised as a masterpiece only in the 1920s) but for *Typee: A Peep at Polynesian Life*, which was published in 1846. It earned him the reputation of 'the man who lived among the cannibals' (Bryant, 1996). In *Typee*, Melville is Tommo the traveller recounting all he has seen and gone through. The book tells us how Tommo arrives on the largest of the Marquesas Islands in the Southern Pacific Ocean, Nuka Hiva (Melville spelled it 'Nukuheva'), and is based on Melville's experiences in the Taipivai valley (or, Americanised, 'Typee Valley') in the east of Nuka Hiva. Earlier visits to the Marquesas Islands (or 'French Polynesia') had fostered unbridled phantasies about cannibals and the alleged promiscuity of the islanders. James Cook visited the south of the island in 1774 and the French went ashore in 1791. In November 1813, the Massachusetts navigator David Porter declared that he had conquered Nuka Hiva in the Marquesas Islands in the name of the United States and founded the hamlet of Madisonville (a conquest, incidentally, which was never ratified by the United States Congress, which is why the village never became an American colony) (Melville, 1996: 11). In 1842, the Marquesas Island passed into French hands. Robert Louis Stevenson, the Scottish writer of *Treasure Island*, went ashore on Nuka Hiva in 1888, and as of 1891 Paul Gauguin roamed Tahiti and the neighbouring island looking for noble savages to immortalise through the paintings that would make him famous after his death (Welten, 2015). Near the end of his life, Gauguin relocated to Hiva Oa, an island that was (mistakenly) known for its cannibals at the time, to flee the colonialist grip the French had by that time established on Tahiti. Even today, reports – legitimate or otherwise – of the cannibalistic practices of Polynesian tribes feature in the touristic imagination. A visit to an island that accommodates cannibals guarantees a trip off-the-beaten-track.

In 1841, Melville boarded the whaler *Acushnet*, on its way to the Marquesas Islands. The *Acushnet* anchored in Polynesia, where Melville was involved in a mutiny. He was imprisoned in Tahiti, but escaped and wandered the islands for two years. *Typee* romanticises the – nevertheless actually true – story of his visit to 'Nukuheva'. It is the story of Tommo's flight from the whaler *Dolly* to the island and an attempt at an anthropology of the islanders in an age when anthropology had yet to be invented. Autobiography, anthropology and geography alternate in the text. Along with Toby, who breaks his contract with the captain, Tommo goes ashore on the island, obsessed with the desire to see cannibals – an obsession that drives him into the arms of the natives, who subsequently won't let him go.

In Melville's debut, the Derridian double bind of hospitality is even more obvious than in his later *Moby Dick*. For quite a long time, Tommo and his companion Toby – the latter flees halfway through the book – are kept guessing whether they have arrived in the land of violent cannibals known as the Typee or in that of another man-eating tribe, the Happar. The question 'Typee or Happar?' runs through the narrative like a chorus. Actually, the question actually denotes: 'Where am I?' Or: 'Am I dealing with cannibals here?' Or: 'Isn't this much hospitality suspect?' (In another book, *Mardi*, Melville exclaims, 'how annoying is sometimes an over-strained act of hospitality!' (1998: 270).) Curiosity about cannibals is bound to involve this type of ambivalence. The most important question is: are these malicious cannibals, or aren't they? 'Typee or Happar?' 'Friend or foe?', '*Hostile* or *hospitable*?' Tommo and Toby find themselves in a situation that remains undecided:

> Typee or Happar? The point was one of vital importance, as the natives of Happar were not only at peace with Nukuheva, but cultivated with its inhabitants the most friendly relations, and enjoyed besides a reputation for gentleness and humanity which led us to expect from them, if not a cordial reception, at least a shelter during the short period we should remain in their territory.
>
> *(Melville, 1996: 50)*

Hospitality constantly raises the question whether malice is involved. For we know nothing of the host's intentions, we only have his behaviour to go by, and that may be kind and courteous while a threat actually exists.

> I shuddered when I reflected that there was no longer any room for doubt; and that, beyond all hope of escape, we were now placed in those very circumstances from the bare thought of which I had recoiled with such abhorrence but a few days before. What might

not be our fearful destiny? To be sure, as yet, we had been treated with no violence; nay, had been even kindly and hospitably entertained.

(Melville, 1996: 76)

The cannibals thus appear hospitable, unlike Hollywood zombies that look as if they will strike given the opportunity. The quote ('treated with no violence') also reveals that rapprochement involves an expectation of violence, as well as surprise ('*even* kindly and hospitably') about the welcoming reception. Tribal Chief Mehevi is praised for his hospitality several times ('the hospitable Mehevi' (Melville, 1996: 95)) and the cannibal girls are 'at the same time wonderfully polite and humane' (Melville, 1996: 77). The Typee are constantly described in terms of kindness and hospitality: 'All the inhabitants of the valley treated me with great kindness' (Melville, 1996: 113). And Tommo cannot stop mentioning 'the numberless proofs of kindness and respect which I received from the natives of the valley' (Melville, 1996: 118). 'Sometimes I rambled about from house to house, sure of receiving a cordial welcome wherever I went' (Melville, 1996: 151). Yet kindness and hospitality are at the same time suspect:

> The natives, actuated by some mysterious impulse, day after day redoubled their attentions to us. Their manner towards us was unaccountable. Surely, thought I, they would not act thus if they meant us any harm. But why this excess of deferential kindness, or what equivalent can they imagine us capable of rendering them for it? We were fairly puzzled. But, despite the apprehensions I could not dispel, the horrible character imputed to these Typees appeared to be wholly undeserved.
>
> *(Melville, 1996: 118)*

Tommo's companion Toby is convinced that such a degree of hospitality can only signify postponement of the cannibalistic practice that awaits him: 'Why, they are cannibals!' Tommo also often voices doubts, since he knows very well 'that these very men, kind and respectful as they were to me, were, after all, nothing better than a set of cannibals' (Melville, 1996: 118). *Typee* unremittingly testifies to the 'puzzling' nature of the cannibals' hospitality. It's never entirely clear what the intentions of the hosts are.

The imaginary cannibal

Likely, literature about cannibals can't but be anything but colonialist literature, since it portrays the other as a primitive savage. It would be naive to think that Tommo the individual has nothing to do with 'the system' of colonialism, or that Robinson Crusoe can only be understood as a totally autonomous individual (Sartre, 1964: 47–48). Edward Said is clear on the subject: 'Robinson Crusoe is virtually unthinkable without the colonizing mission that permits him to create a new world of his own in the distant reaches of the African, Pacific, and Atlantic wilderness' (1993: 64). Karl Marx repeatedly rejects such Robinsonades, written by authors that seem to believe that placing a man on a deserted island creates an opportunity to understand homo sapiens from scratch. Imagine *not* understanding Robinson, who is thrown back upon the most elementary of human needs, on the basis of the society that has produced him. Robinson Crusoe is a myth, because his arrival on the island is supposed to be a new beginning even though he has already and irreversibly been civilised (Casarino, 2002). And yet, despite the obvious similarities, Tommo is no Robinson. Why not? Because Tommo has to rely on *hospitality*. In Robinson Crusoe, one Friday Robinson meets a stranger, whom he calls Friday. The other is incorporated in a system Robinson lived in before he ever set foot on the island. Robinson is not received by

Friday, the latter is annexed. Tommo and Toby can't afford such colonialism. They are lucky not to be served as a meal. In other words: the host – the Typee – calls the tune.

Westerners that wonder whether they have ended up among cannibals start out from the assumption that the others might be cannibals to begin with. In other words, the cannibal isn't a man whom they encounter, only to find out later that he kills people and eats them – as we have seen, this rarely happens – but rather a man they do not know at all, though they have heard the terrifying stories that are told about him. Where do these stories come from? Cannibalism is mentioned in the literature of the conquistadores, like Hernan Cortes' *Letters from Mexico* (2001). But here, as we have seen before, cannibalism refers to something unspeakable: 'they are cannibals, of which I send Your Majesty no evidence because it is so infamous', Cortes writes to his king (2001: 146). In a footnote, the publisher writes that Cortes never actually met any cannibals, though he used them as an argument for catching slaves. To conquistadores, mentioning cannibals had a clear function: it not only gave them an excuse to forcefully civilise the locals, do missionary work or confiscate slaves, but was also considered proof that they had indeed reached the new world. The cannibal discourse is not primarily descriptive, it is primarily legitimative. Where Melville is concerned, it is clear from his references that he was familiar with the travel reports of, for instance, James Cook. These were published in the late eighteenth century and cannibalism plays an important part in them. Even in Cook, the cannibal is already a metaphor for the savage, uncivilised man who might – worst case scenario – eat other people. Whether any cannibal ever really did remains uncertain, especially since subsequent representations of Cook's travels are filled with cannibal rhetoric. Even in Cook, the interest in other cultures clearly boils down to curiosity about the possible existence of cannibals. In New Zealand and Hawaii, Cook and his men are known to have prepared human flesh and served it to the natives. If the natives were to accept it, then that would prove that they were actually cannibals. Cook was murdered in Hawaii in 1779 after unresolved cultural miscommunications. Parts of his body were presented to local natives as well, to see how they would react. Are they cannibals, or aren't they? (Melville refers to the incident. Toby doesn't trust the food they are served. Is it human flesh? '"But, I say, Tommo, you are not going to eat any of that mess there, in the dark, are you? Why, how can you tell what it is?" "By tasting it, to be sure," said I, masticating a morsel that Kory-Kory had just put in my mouth; "and excellently good it is, too, very much like veal." "A baked baby, by the soul of Captain Cook!"' (Melville, 1996: 95).)

Typee is not merely a travel report on the adventures of 'the man who lived among the cannibals': Melville joins the discourse on cannibals. As Edward Said famously writes in *Orientalism*:

> In the system of knowledge about the Orient, the Orient is less a place than a topos, a set of references, a congeries of characteristics, that seems to have its origin in a quotation, or a fragment of a text, or a citation from someone's work on the Orient, or some bit of previous imagining, or an amalgam of all these.
>
> *(1978: 117)*

Similarly, the 'empirical' cannibal doesn't precede the descriptions and stories that supposedly mirror an anthropological phenomenon, but rather emerges from a system of knowledge, 'through the grapevine', which generates a strong imagery. *Typee* is therefore neither a travel report nor a novel: it is something in between. The cannibal is a figment of popular fiction, a tourist attraction generated by a discourse; a product of the colonial imagination and of the tourist gaze (Urry, 1990/2002).

Here, 'colonial' does not only (or at all) refer to an econopolitical subjugation, but to the systematic subjugation of the other to images created by Westerners. Melville is well aware of this and Melville-interpreters opine, not undeservedly, that postcolonial literature begins with *Typee* and *Moby Dick* (Sanborn, 1998). They are colonial literature that simultaneously resists colonial prejudice.

> Are these the ferocious savages, the blood-thirsty cannibals of whom I have heard such frightful tales! They deal more kindly with each other, and are more humane, than many who study essays on virtues and benevolence, and who repeat every night that beautiful prayer breathed first by the lips of the divine and gentle Jesus.
>
> *(Melville, 1996: 203)*

The pictures colonial literature paints of cannibals are highly prejudicial. Tommo repeatedly *catches* himself being prejudicial. When he describes his encounter with Kory-Kory, a native, his reluctance to consider him the absolute other is discernible. He compares Kory-Kory's tattooed face with faces he saw before:

> His countenance thus triply hooped, as it were, with tattooing, always reminded me of those unhappy wretches whom I have sometimes observed gazing out sentimentally from behind the grated bars of a prison window; whilst the entire body of my savage valet, covered all over with representations of birds and fishes, and a variety of most unaccounta-ble-looking creatures, suggested to me the idea of a pictorial museum of natural history, or an illustrated copy of Goldsmith's Animated Nature.
>
> *(Melville, 1996: 83)*

Toby appears to be reducing Kory-Kory to a colonial object, yet feels embarrassed about it at the same time:

> But it seems really heartless in me to write thus of the poor islander, when I owe perhaps to his unremitting attentions the very existence I now enjoy. Kory-Kory, I mean thee no harm in what I say in regard to thy outward adorning; but they were a little curious to my unaccustomed sight, and therefore I dilate upon them. But to underrate or forget thy faith-ful services is something I could never be guilty of, even in the giddiest moment of my life
>
> *(Melville, 1996: 83)*

It's Kory-Kory's hospitality and humanity that cause Toby to apologise.

So the undecidedness that is so typical of an encounter between strangers affects the 'civilised' guest as well. What does the encounter with the white man mean from the perspective of the cannibal? In 'Hostpitality', Derrida (2002: 359) reminds us of the work of anthropologist Alfred Métraux, who described how white guests were being received as the dead returning, like 'révenants'. In *Cannibal Tours* (O'Rourke, 1988) a native, presented as the descendant of 'real cannibals', shares how his ancestors saw German colonialists arriving by boat on the river and mistook them for the spirits of their ancestors. The *révenant* is the one who returns: not exactly a stranger, since he is a member of the community, even though he has comes from 'the other side'. Their reception by the cannibals was therefore also a feast of recognition. It is not just colo-nialists and tourists that conjure up the other from their own imagination: cannibals approach the other in the exact same way. The imagery is generated on both sides. This complicates the hospitality and cannibalism issue: who (or what) is being received is not an empiric man, not even the other, but an *image*. The civilised man imagines the other as a cannibal. That cannibal is imaginary. And an imaginary cannibal cannot be a host: the other is a figment of the imagination and as such, he is bound to meet expectations. What is being received (by either side) is not a living man, but an image, a projection. When Tommo and Toby run into people on the island for the first time, Melville reverses the cannibal question: 'I verily believe the poor creatures took us for a couple of white cannibals who were about to make a meal of them' (Melville, 1996: 69). Melville uses his own unfamiliarity with cannibals to describe how the other may perceive him. The other does not see him as a colonialist or tourist, but rather as a white cannibal.

Typee is definitely a product of a colonial imagination; yet it wants to be an eye-witness account at the same time. In *The Sign of the Cannibal: Melville and the Making of a Postcolonial Reader*, Geoffrey Sanborn wonders whether the subtitle of *Typee* – that is, *A Peep at Polynesian Life* – doesn't already suggest that 'Playboy-mansion images of Polynesian women' were going to be presented (1998: 79). True, Tommo shows himself sensitive to the charms of the natives, both the ladies and the men: in chapter 18 we catch him skinny-dipping with the local girls and his affection for Fayaway, a pretty native girl, appears to portend the paintings Paul Gauguin made in Tahiti.

Colonial literature is an art of prejudice, ready-made imagery and tourist gazing. The cannibal is doomed to be authentic forever: first for the conquistadores, then for the colonialists, then for the tourists. How can these prejudices be negated? Well, reverse them! 'Better sleep with a sober cannibal than a drunken Christian'. Who is the civilised? Who is the savage?

> the wide difference between the extreme of savage and civilized life! A gentleman of Typee can bring up a numerous family of children, and give them all a highly respectable cannibal education, with infinitely less toil and anxiety than he expends in the simple process of striking a light; whilst a poor European artisan, who through the instrumentality of a lucifer performs the same operation in one second, is put to his wit's end to provide for his starving offspring that food, which the children of a Polynesian father, without troubling their parents, pluck from the branches of every tree around them.
>
> *(Melville, 1996: 112)*

Chapter 17 compares the details of civilised and savage life, and the first is outdone by the second every time. Civilised life harbours many kinds of jealousy, rivalry and deceit, which is why Melville speaks of 'civilized barbarity' (1996: 125). The Typee, by contrast, don't even have a word for virtue and have been fortunate enough to evaded the 'the root of all evil': money (Melville, 1996: 126). Melville writes: 'Civilization does not engross all the virtues of humanity' (1996: 202). Yet labelling the reversal of colonial imagery 'postcolonialism' is too easy. Perhaps *Typee* confirms, rather than negates, the myth of the noble savage. And wasn't the myth of the noble savage the main trope of colonial literature? Perceiving the other as a savage, using the other to project a model of authenticity, is part and parcel of colonialism. Postcolonialism doesn't *follow* colonialism (as Montaigne's 'On cannibals' demonstrates) but *accompanies* it, like its conscience – which is perhaps precisely what literature is supposed to do.

Conclusions

Once the savages and cannibals are brought to the table, there's no way back: the radical difference between us and them that is so characteristic of travel reports has been established. Only the negation of the difference, a negation on a first-person basis, has a chance of reversing it. Tommo describes how Mehevi stares at him: 'Never before had I been subjected to so strange and steady a glance; it revealed nothing of the mind of the savage, but it appeared to be reading my own' (Melville, 1996: 71). Melville is searching for the connection between people, in the way they look at each other, love each other, for instance in the relationship between Ishmael and

Queequeg. But perhaps this will land us in a vicious circle. Perhaps such face-to-face-relationships are symptomatic of what Marx called Robinsonades. Is this relationship an encounter or is it, as a relationship, already embedded in a culture of travel, expectation, colonialisation and so on? This undecidability – 'fairly puzzled' – leaves the cannibal to roam forever on the margins of our culture. The hospitality that characterises the encounter between Ishmael and Queequeg is a metaphorical hospitality, one that invites openness to the other, but only to a certain extent, which is why even Melville, despite his efforts, could not dissociate himself from colonialism.

References

Baudrillard, J. (2010) *Simulacra and Simulation*, Ann Arbor: University of Michigan Press.

Bergman, D. (1991) *Gaiety Transfigured: Gay Self-Representation in American Literature*, Madison: University of Wisconsin Press.

Bryant, J. (1996) Introduction. In Melville, H., *Typee: A Peep at Polynesian Life*, London: Penguin Classics.

Casarino, C. (2002) *Modernity at Sea: Melville, Marx, Conrad in Crisis*, Minneapolis: University of Minnesota Press.

Chagnon, N. (2013) *Noble Savages: My Life Among Two Dangerous Tribes – The Yanomamö and the Anthropologists*, New York: Simon & Schuster.

Cicero, (2005) *On Duties*, Book I, XII, Loeb Classical Library, XXI, Cambridge, MA and London: Harvard University Press.

Cortes, H. (2001) *Letters from Mexico*, New Haven: Yale University Press.

Crain, C. (1994) Lovers of human flesh: homosexuality and cannibalism in Melville's novels, *American Literature* 66: 25–53. Available at http://www.steamthing.com/cannibals. Accessed 12 May 2016.

Derrida, J. (2002) Hostipitality. In Anidjar, G. (ed.) *Jacques Derrida: Acts of Religion*. New York and London: Routledge, pp. 356–420.

Derrida, J. (2005) *On Cosmopolitanism and Forgiveness*, New York: Routledge.

Derrida, J. and Dufourmantelle, A. (1997) *De l'hospitalité*, Paris: Calmann-Lévy.

Freud, S. (1909) *Drei Abhandlungen zur Sexualtheorie*. Available at http://www.psychanalyse.lu/Freud/FreudDreiAbhandlungen.pdf. Accessed 12 May 2016.

Herzog, W. (dir.) (2005) *Grizzly Man*, Lions Gate Films.

Lacan, J. (1991/2001) *Le séminaire livre VIII. Le transfert*, Paris: Seuil.

Lindenbaum, S. (2004) Thinking about cannibalism, *Annual Review of Anthropology* 33: 475–498.

MacCannell, D. (1990) Cannibal tours, *Visual Anthropology Review*, 6, 2: 14–24.

Melville, H. (1992) *Moby Dick. Or, The Whale*, London: Penguin Classics.

Melville, H. (1996) *Typee: A Peep at Polynesian Life*, London: Penguin Classics.

Melville, H. (1998) *Mardi and a Voyage Thither*, Evanston, IL: Northwestern University Press.

Miller, E. H. (1975) *Melville*, New York: George Braziller.

Montaigne, M. de (2002 [1580]) On cannibals. Available at http://ocw.mit.edu/courses/literature/21l-449-end-of-nature-spring-2002/readings/lecture4.pdf. Accessed 1 July 2016.

O'Rourke, D. (dir.) (1988) *Cannibal Tours*, documentary film.

Parker, H. (1996) *Herman Melville: A Biography*, vol. 1: *1819–1851*, Baltimore and London: Johns Hopkins University Press.

Safouan, M. (2001) *Les séminaires de Jacques Lacan*, Paris: Librairie Artème Fayard.

Said, E. (1978) *Orientalism*, New York: Pantheon.

Said, E. (1993) *Culture and Imperialism*, New York: Vintage Books.

Sanborn, G. (1998) *The Sign of the Cannibal: Melville and the Making of a Postcolonial Reader*, Durham, NC: Duke University Press.

Sartre, J.-P. (1964) Le colonialisme est un système (1957), *Situations*, V, Paris: Gallimard.

Sartre, J.-P. (1970) 'Moby Dick d'Herman Melville', in: *Les écrits de Sartre. Chronologie Bibliographie commentée*. Paris: Gallimard.

Urry, J. (1990/2002) *The Tourist Gaze*, London: Sage.

Warren, R. (1984) 'Deeper than Sappho': Melville, Poetry, and the Erotic, *Modern Language Studies* 14, 1: 70–78.

Welten, R. (2015) Paul Gauguin and the complexity of the primitivist gaze, *Journal of Art Historiography*. Available at https://arthistoriography.files.wordpress.com/2015/06/welten.pdf. Accessed 12 May 2016.

13

An Asian ethics of hospitality

Hospitality in Confucian, Daoist and Buddhist philosophy

Martine Berenpas

Key themes

The ethics of Asian hospitality

Hospitality in Confucianism, Daoism and Buddhism

A comparative study in hospitality

The last couple of decades have witnessed an enormous interest in comparative thinking and a revival of interest in Chinese philosophy. Comparative philosophy is aimed at the search to identify similarities and differences between Western and Eastern philosophical traditions in order to elaborate on modern socio-political problems such as gender inequality, ecological civilisation and immigration issues. Especially in a time of rapid globalisation and problems that exceed national borders, it is nowadays necessary to leave the beaten track and explore new streams of thought.

In the case of hospitality studies, it seems more than obvious that we should not only include a Western analysis of hospitality, but also explore other perspectives as well. Rather than pursue an understanding of hospitality that can only be understood from a Western perspective, we should extend our understanding to other cultures to gain a much fuller and more diverse look at the nature and practice of hospitality. This chapter will try to fill the gap by discussing hospitality in the three major Chinese philosophical systems: Confucianism, Daoism and (Chinese) Buddhism. As Lashley notes in Chapter 9, the requirement to be hospitable has been an important theme of human moral systems across the globe. It is therefore not a surprise that the three major Chinese philosophical traditions revolve around the question of how to be virtuous in a life with others.

Chinese civilisation appears to have embodied ideals present in the thought of Confucius, Daoism and Buddhism. Although other influences such as the legalist movement, the logicians and neo-Confucianism should not be neglected, I will limit the scope of this chapter to these

DOI: 10.4324/9781315679938-14

three early philosophical systems. I will concentrate on *The Analects* (Confucius), *The Daodejing* (Laozi, Daoism) and early Chinese Buddhism, as formed during the Medieval Period (fourth–seventh century). The main focus of this chapter will be to answer the questions of how these traditions see hospitality as a virtue and how they treat the stranger. Answering these questions will help us to understand the locus and limits of hospitality. The three different Chinese traditions will lead to an 'Asian ethics of hospitality', in which filial piety and closeness to the other are the most important metaphysical assumptions.

To understand the Asian approach to hospitality, it is important to identify the moral assumptions on which Confucianism, Daoism and Chinese Buddhism are grounded. Important questions concern whether these moral assumptions are based on cultural, social and religious norms that might hinder a universal approach to hospitality. It is one thing to be hospitable to someone who is close to us, but it is another thing to be hospitable to a stranger. A main theme that I will raise, therefore, is whether Confucianism, Daoism and Buddhism are able to ground the moral responsibility to be hospitable to the stranger from outside of Chinese civilisation. As Julia Kristeva notes in her book *Strangers to Ourselves*, the ethical challenge of hospitality is to be 'able to live with the others, to live *as others*, without ostracism but also without levelling' (1991: 2).

The question of whether the three major Chinese philosophical traditions are able to ground a universal approach to hospitality is closely tied to the form of humanism they promote. Humanism is a broad category of ethical, metaphysical, epistemological and political philosophies in which human interest, values and dignity are described. Confucianism, Daoism and Chinese Buddhism are all grounded in a particular form of humanism, which determines the moral compass of their philosophy (McNaughton, 1974; Havens, 2013).

The dominant Chinese conception of humanism is the Confucian theory of *Ren* (*Jen*; 人), also known as the *Mandate of Heaven*. This mandate is a self-existent moral law that is nurtured by human virtue. For Confucius, man's destiny depends upon his own good words and deeds. This leads to a strong emphasis on a virtuous society based on a just government and harmonious human relations. In the first part of this chapter, I will outline the Confucian ethics that I will classify as a classical form of virtue ethics that fosters harmony, filial piety and tradition. Although humanism and appropriate conduct towards others are at the heart of the Confucian system, I will argue that Confucianism fails to construct a universal ethics of hospitality. Due to its moral particularism, it is not able to yield the universal duty to be hospitable to the stranger.

The Daoist movement primarily targets Confucian particularism, arguing that it leads to viciousness and violence. Daoist philosophy as practised in the *Daodejing* emphasises the withdrawal from the world that is characterised by a belief in a false reality of right and wrong. Daoism focuses on 'emptying' the mind in such a way that it can act accordingly to the unifying source of the world, Dao. The Daoist movement rejects political and moral control in favour of an inner-worldly way of thinking. Because Daoism sees Dao as oneness, it is very suspicious of language. Daoism argues that language, and especially the naming of things and persons, violates the oneness of Dao and moves human life further away from the ultimate truth. Daoism promotes a provisional, relational model of meaning in which concepts and terms are interrelated. In the second section, I will outline Daoist philosophy and its language critique. The Daoist critique on language has implications for the way we conceive hospitality. When language is artificial and moves us away from the truth, rules and regulations that govern the way we need to treat the stranger become undesirable. By relating Daoist philosophy to Jacques Derrida's notion of hospitality, I will outline the paradoxical nature of 'unconditional hospitality' in which both hospitality and its opposite are unified.

The last Chinese tradition I will explore in the light of hospitality is early Chinese Buddhism. When Buddhism arrived in China, it was mixed up with popular beliefs and practices such as Confucianism and Daoism. The goal of Chinese Buddhism was to gain the wisdom that things do not possess a self-nature. More than Daoism, Buddhism rejects language in favour of a bodily experience of the world. I will highlight the importance of the term 'ganying' for understanding Buddhist hospitality. The virtue of ganying is universalised beyond kinship and beyond nationality, and, as such, serves well for unconditional hospitality in which the stranger is accepted as a stranger. At the end of this chapter, I will compare the three traditions and will identify filial piety as one of the core characteristics of Chinese culture.

Being hospitable to one's relative: Confucianism and ethical particularism

Confucius (551–479 BC), the latinised version of K'ung Fu-Tzu, was born a couple of centuries before Socrates' teachings on ethics and rhetoric, and is one the most influential sages of Chinese culture. The primary sources of Confucius's teachings are the *Lun Yu* or the *Analects*, also referred to as 'the selected sayings'. The *Analects* have had a tremendous impact on Chinese philosophy. David Hinton even argues that: '*The Analects* have had a deeper impact on more people's lives over a longer period of time than any other book in human history' (2013: 42).

Confucianism is essentially a humanistic philosophy, which diverges from views in the supernatural to explain phenomena in favour of reason and rationality (Havens, 2013: 40). Confucius places *Ren*, translated as humanity or humankind, at the heart of his philosophy and focuses on practical human life. The perfect man, or the sage, is defined by four virtues: *ren* (humanity), *li* (ritual propriety), *zhi* (practical wisdom) and *yi* (moral conduct). *Ren* is the most important virtue. The perfect man is to Confucius the 'man of *ren*', who 'wishes to establish his own character, he also establishes the character of others, and wishing to be prominent himself, he also helps others to be prominent' (*Analects*, 6:28). *Ren* is the virtue of balancing aspects of the self and aspects of society, and is expressed by conscious acts (*chung*) of altruism (*shu*). The virtue *Ren* is centred on the relations that man has with others. McNaughton defines *Ren*, therefore, as 'the natural warm human feelings for others, graded according to one's relation to them' (1974: 27).

The fundamental concern of Confucianism is learning to be human. Humankind is like an untouched block of wood, which needs moral training in order to be virtuous. The dominant theme of Confucian teaching is the equal emphasis on knowledge and action. One needs to put his virtue into practice in order to be genuinely virtuous, because 'A man with clever words and an ingratiating appearance is seldom a man of humanity' (*Analects*, 1:2), but moral training through knowledge of rituals and tradition is equally important. Confucianism does not focus on a meta-ethical universal theory of humankind, but focuses on the individual who realises his life among others. Confucian ethics is therefore solidly rooted in society and in social relations. *Ren* can only exist within a social construct and can only be fully developed within the sphere of relations around the individual. *Ren* promotes sympathy and reciprocity which are essentially for emotional control and, ultimately, for establishing social harmony. Filial piety is therefore one of the most important virtues to promote *ren*. In *Analects* 1:6, Confucius says that 'young men should be filial when at home and respectful to their elders when away from home. They should be earnest and faithful. They should love all extensively and be intimate with men of humanity.'

To be virtuous is, to Confucius, tied to Chinese tradition and culture. Respecting one's ancestors and honouring the Zhou dynasty (4000–1000 BC) were important aspects of cultivating the virtue of *li* (ritual propriety, rite, role, ritual). In Confucianism, *li* is aimed at humans finding their appropriate place in relation to tradition and cosmology. In *Analects* 1:12, Confucius argues that 'Among the functions of propriety (*li*) the most valuable is that it establishes harmony. The excellence of the ways of ancient kings consists of this. It is the guiding principle of all things great and small.'

When the virtue of *li* is pursued by humans, the virtue of *yi* becomes apparent. *Yi* is commonly translated as 'rightness' or 'justice', and involves the moral disposition to do good by expressing appropriate conduct towards others. *Yi* has, in contrast to the abstract notion of *li*, a merely practical orientation. *Yi* represents the accumulated effort of following rules and being able to choose the right moral conduct in a given (changing) situation. In *Analects* 17:23, Confucius argues that without the guidance of *yi*, a man with a favourable disposition turns out to be acting against the Way: 'When the superior man has courage but no righteousness, he becomes turbulent. When the inferior man has courage but no righteousness, he becomes a thief.'

The last virtue that Confucius distinguishes in the *Analects* is the virtue of *Zhi*, which is best translated as 'practical wisdom'. Practical wisdom is needed in order to correctly judge social situations and obey the rituals and roles that different social relationships prescribe. It is important to note that *Zhi* is not merely an epistemic notion, but has a moral connotation as well. For Confucius, no part of human life is free from morality. Every aspect of human life is participating in and appraised by the Way as outlined in the *Analects*. The virtue of *Zhi* should therefore be interpreted as 'the wisdom of having a proper mind'; it is not only having knowledge but also acquiring this knowledge in harmony with the Way.

Confucius's focus is not on abstract terms and concepts, but evolves around the practical human life. It focuses on specific human virtues that endorse the Confucian way. In terms of classification, Confucius's ethics can be classified as a virtue ethics. In line with Alasdair MacIntyre's definition of virtue ethics (1981), Confucius's ethics has a strong emphasis on human life as a whole, whose character provides the virtues with a particular *telos* (1981: 204). Furthermore, classical Confucianism seems to match with 'ancient virtue culture' in which 'moral thinking and action is structured according to some version of the scheme of the classical', where 'the chief means of moral education is the telling of stories. They provided a moral background to contemporary debate' (MacIntyre, 1981: 121). In the case of Confucianism, this moral background is the Zhou dynasty and the *Book of Odes*, which is used in the *Analects* as a symbol for this period. The *Book of Odes* is therefore frequently quoted in the *Analects* to justify Confucius's moral theory.

Confucius endorses such virtues as diligence, reliability and persistence together with cooperation, loyalty and responsibility to one's community and organisation. The grounding tenet of *ren* is the relationship between two people such as father–son, friend–friend and citizen–king. Confucius's main idea is that if these interpersonal relations are well regulated, society as a whole will be in good order. Responsibility to the other, an important ethical precondition for hospitality, is in Confucianism defined in terms of social status and filiality, and is, as such, limited to particular individuals. Although Confucius seems to argue that *ren* should embrace all, moral responsibilities seem to be tied to one's specific relation with the other. Confucius is very clear in seeing filial piety and brotherly respect as the root of *ren* (*Analects*, 1:2), and underlines the importance of moral duties for practical social life.

Filial piety was an integral part of Chinese culture, and was therefore embraced by Confucius as one of the most important moral duties. We will see later that even Daoism and Chinese Buddhism accommodate to a lesser degree this cultural background of Chinese civilisation. The idea that filial piety will harmonise social relations and, as a consequence, will lead to a stable society, is the motivation for Confucius's moral particularism. Confucius argues that to be virtuous is 'knowing the right way to act' in different situations. Each situation requires different moral acts. Moral particularism argues that there are no moral principles and that moral judgments are dependent on the particular situation. Although there are some objections to stating that Confucius promotes moral particularism,[1] it is clear that his philosophy is family-centred.

When we try to answer the question of whether Confucius's philosophy does justice to the stranger, it is clear that it immediately runs into trouble. Filial piety and strict obedience to one's superiors jeopardise the responsibility one has to welcome the stranger in an act of unconditional hospitality. Yu Hai (2005) argues that xenophobia and the legitimization of discrimination against other races in China is largely due to the Confucian tradition:

> The Confucian tradition, which has shaped Chinese culture, emphasizes a dichotomy between 'Hua Xia' (an ancient name for China) and 'Man Yi' (neighbouring barbarians), saying by way of Confucius 'They do not share the same blood as we do, so they must be different from us in nature'.
>
> *(2005: 2)*

Confucius's emphasis on filial piety only poses a problem when there is an apparent conflict between moral duties. Confucius is very clear in saying that if there is a conflict of duties between taking care of our families and helping others, our obligations to our family come first. In *Analects* 3:18, Confucius argues:

> In our village there is someone called true person; when his father took a sheep on the sly, he reported him to the authorities. Confucius replied, 'Those who are true in my village conduct themselves differently. A father covers for his son, and a son covers for a father. And being true lies in this'.

Here we see in a clear way what is especially disturbing in Confucian ethics; its demand for absolute loyalty to one's superior leads to choices in particular situations that make the outsider, the one who has no relatives on whom he can count, particularly vulnerable. What Confucius seems to promote is conditional hospitality, in which the moral duty to be hospitable depends on the relation I have with the other.

Although unconditional hospitality, in which every individual has the moral duty to be hospitable to every other human being, is closed off by Confucius particularism, it does not mean that we do not have the moral obligation to be hospitable. Being hospitable is at the core of Confucian ethics, but is hierarchically classified. Confucius does underline the moral duty to be hospitable to others when this does not conflict with our moral duties towards family or immediate superiors. In *Analects* 12:2, Confucius argues:

> In your public life, behave as though you are receiving important visitors; employ the common people as though you are overseeing a great sacrifice. Do not impose upon others what you yourself do not want, and you will not incur personal or political ill will.

If we apply this to the stranger from outside Chinese civilisation, Confucius argues that we should not try to force him to blend in, or to force him to adopt the same cultural beliefs and practices. Although this is an important step in respecting the other as other, it fails to ground the moral duty to be hospitable to him.

Confucius's particularism grounds hospitality in some sense, but fails to ground hospitality to the ones who most need it; it fails to protect the refugees, the strangers without citizenship. In a world where all human beings must live on the territory of nations, we need to be aware that having a nationality is a gateway to other rights. This is especially true in a Confucian society, where moral duties are grounded in filial piety and loyalty. Hannah Arendt points to the way this system neglects the outsider, the stranger, the stateless who lacks the very 'right to have rights'. The key to the stateless stranger's status is the loss of 'his place in a community', 'his political status' and 'the legal personality which makes his actions and part of his destiny a consistent whole' (Arendt, 1951: 301).

The status of the stranger is in Confucianism unsecure, and is dependent on whether the duty to be hospitable to him conflicts with other duties to relatives and society. If hospitality is about welcoming the stranger, the vulnerable other, into our lives, the Confucian tradition seems not to be our best option. We will see that Daoism and Chinese Buddhism both reject the Confucian emphasis on the practical life and instead focus on a universal theory of (human) life. As such, they go beyond kinship and national identity and are more open to accepting the stranger.

The innate violence of hospitality: Daoist philosophy and the contamination of language

Daoism is named after the central principle of Dao as the origin of the world, which pervades the tradition of Chinese philosophical writings and rituals. Daoism originated in China, but has encompassed over time so many different beliefs, practices and traditions that it is very difficult to define exactly what Daoism is. Most scholars argue that Daoism focuses more on the nature of Dao and less on how Dao functions than other Chinese schools of thought (Wing-Tsit, 1963: 136; Burik, 2009: 90). The use of Dao as the Way, or the Path, is not limited to Daoism; all major Chinese traditions use Dao to describe the path that humankind should follow. Specific for the texts that are nowadays considered as 'Daoist texts' is that they see Dao not as a system or as a standard for human conduct, but classify it as the spontaneous, eternal and nameless unity of all. Early Daoism saw Confucianism as the main reason for all the problems that arose in the late Warring State period. Like Confucius, Daoism tries to get back into a state of *wu-wei* (state of moral perfection). The way to achieve this *wu-wei* state is, however, fundamentally different than in Confucianism.

Although Daoism does not denote a specific school but rather covers a whole range of doctrines, a growing body of literature suggests that the *Chung Tzu* and the *Lao Tzu* (*Daodejing*) form the core collections of writings that can be called 'Daoist' (McNaughton, 1974: 42). In this chapter, I will concentrate on early Daoism and will therefore use the *Daodejing* as a primary source.

The fundamental difference between the *Daodejing* and the *Analects* is that, in the *Daodejing*, Dao is not interpreted as a method for human moral conduct, but as the ultimate origin of being. Dao is interpreted as 'oneness', as eternal, spontaneous, nameless and simplicity. As a way of life, Dao denotes spontaneity, naturalness, weakness and non-action (*wu-wei*). *Wu-wei*, as the paradox of trying not to try, is the effort of letting nature take its own course. *Wu-wei*, the action of inaction, is the central paradox of Daoism and, as a concept, is second in importance only to the Dao itself which embodies it.

An important aspect of the state of *wu-wei* is emptying the mind. Edward Slingerland defines *wu-wei* as follows:

> To attain Laozian *wu-wei*, you need to *undo* rather than do, gradually unwinding your mind and body, shedding book learning and artificial desires. The goal is to relax into a state of perfect nondoing (*wu-wei*) and unselfconsciousness, like settling into a nice warm bath.
>
> (*2014: 99)*

Daoism is suspicious of language, which, to Daoism, makes human life artificial. The sage in Daoism is man who 'manages affairs without action' and 'spreads doctrines without words' (*Daodejing*, 2).

The suspicion of language has to do with the original oneness of Dao, which gets lost in the process of individuality and naming. For Daoist philosophy, relationality is prior to identity and individuality because relationality expresses the nature of Dao as oneness. This relationality means that there is no literal meaning of a term; all terms, concepts and notions rely on each other and cannot be properly understood independently (Burik, 2009: 106).

Language plays an important role in classical Chinese philosophy. Classical philosophers such as Confucius and Mozi were, however, less interested than Western philosophers in the representative function of language, and more preoccupied with the pragmatics of language. Confucianism was, for example, interested in language as the ultimate tool to guide social behaviour and establish social harmony. Tanaka argues that all references of Dao need to be understood in terms of language:

> Each philosopher's formulation of the 'best' way to prescribe our social behaviour has come to be known as Dao. A Dao is a way to guide our behaviour in social contexts. Given that it is language that guides our behaviour, a Dao is a language, whatever the form it takes, for the guidance.

> *(2004: 194)*

Daoist philosophy's approach to understanding Dao and language as such is remarkable, because the Daoists were interested in the limits of language as guidance. In the *Daodejing*, these limits of language are often expressed in the embracement of opposites. Several passages draw attention to the unifying structure of opposites in which 'to bend is to become straight' and 'to be empty is to be full' (*Daodejing*, 22). What the *Daodejing* wants to show is that language's ability to guide us is limited, and that we should be aware that all language is provisional.

What does this suspicion of language and the exposure of the limits of language mean for hospitality? Can we be hospitable to anyone if there is no distinct language vocabularium or moral guide that can force us to be hospitable? In order to answer these questions, it is interesting to compare the Daoist's focus on the limits of language with Derrida's postmodern project of deconstruction and Derrida's particular view on hospitality.

Drucilla Cornell argues that Derrida's project of deconstruction can best be called the 'philosophy of the limit' (1992: 1). Cornell argues that Derrida's intention is not to undermine the importance of philosophical practices, but to expose the limits of language and, as such, of any system. The exposure of the limits of language demonstrates 'how the very establishment of the system implies a *beyond* to it, precisely by virtue of what it excludes' (Cornell, 1991: 1).

Derrida has written extensively about language, grammatology and logocentrism. He was also politically engaged and wrote on topics such as hospitality. His view on hospitality can help to enlighten us as to what the Daoist approach to hospitality would be. In *Adieu to Emmanuel Levinas*, Derrida poses the question of whether hospitality is an 'interruption of the self' (1997: 51). This deconstructive approach to hospitality is a hospitality in which the self is being interrupted by the other. This is only possible if the self and the other are ultimately related to each other and do not exclude each other; this is why Derrida (1997: 51) argues that in hospitality the self imposes the interruption upon itself.

For Derrida, absolute hospitality is an 'ethics without law and without concepts' (1997: 111). Any law or concept would make hospitality conditional and subject to rules and regulations that would undermine its universal structure. Language is not able to do justice to unconditional hospitality; it enables distinctions, dichotomies and rules, and, as such, imposes conditions. Just as in Daoist philosophy, Derrida emphasises the 'wholeness' or interrelatedness of terms and concepts.

Unconditional hospitality is structured as a universal singularity that precedes actual hospitality, or hospitality as enforced by laws and custom. For Daoist philosophy this implies an embracing of opposites, since both the conditions for such hospitality and for its impossibility are unified in this notion of absolute hospitality. As chapter 37 of the *Daodejing* says: 'Tao [Dao] invariably takes no action, and yet there is nothing left undone'; unconditional hospitality is indifferent to morality, but forms the precondition for our moral duty to be hospitable.

Daoist suspicions of language affirm a life without a focus on wisdom or knowledge. For Daoists, a truth derived from linguistic analysis becomes meaningless and serves humans little. Instead, they focus on man's inner nature and promote an inner-worldly way of viewing reality. Although Daoism pays much attention to the inner self of a person, it is not meant to exclude the external. Although early Daoism advocates going beyond the given structures of the world in the quest for transcendence and salvation, it also tries to accommodate Chinese cultural background by introducing a notion of filial piety. For early Daoism, following the Dao means also to be at peace with one's ancestors. Mugitani (2004) argues that filial piety in Daoism is not concerned merely with the biological parent–child relation. Loyalty or obedience would actually obstruct living according to Dao because this would promote a belief in reality as fixed and stable, something that Daoism rejects.

The Daoist philosophy of hospitality is a 'trying not to try', in which we refrain from representing, classifying or naming the stranger, and welcome him in a state of *wu-wei* which reveals the ultimate oneness of Dao. In the next section, we will see this notion of unconditional hospitality being taken up by Chinese Buddhism and incorporated in its notion of *ganying*.

Mutual resonance and its demand for hospitality: hospitality in medieval Chinese Buddhism

When Buddhism first arrived in China via the Silk Road, it was mixed up with traditional beliefs and practices. Due to its resemblance to Daoism, concepts and terms from Buddhism were matched by Chinese thinkers and evolved to two different schools of Chinese Buddhism: the school of dhyana (concentration) and the school of prajna (wisdom). These schools evolved independently from the evolution of Indian Buddhism. As Liebenthal has aptly argued, 'The so-called schools were originated by the Chinese and had no relation to Indian controversies. The Chinese asked all the questions and Indian Buddhist revelation supplied the answers' (1955: 74).

The Buddhists regarded the ultimate reality as transcending all being, names and forms, and as empty and quiet in nature. The Buddhist goal is to enter the state of *wu-wei*, which, in Chinese Buddhism, is the unifying experience of nirvana where one is free from negative Karma. Buddhists also express reality as the unifying truth as *dharma*. *Dharma* is the ultimate reality that is beyond our complete knowing, but is accessible through the Buddha. *Dharma* liberates the enlightened man from Karma and suffering.

The basic beliefs of Buddhism are the Four Noble Truths and the Eightfold Path. The first noble truth is the admission that life is suffering. The second noble truth is that the cause of suffering is desire, greed, ignorance and attachment. The third noble truth is to end desire, greed, ignorance and attachment. The fourth noble truth tells how to end these vices. In the Eightfold plan, Buddhism lays out its soteriological strategy: right understanding, right views, right speech, right effort, right livelihood, right behaviour, right concentration and right meditation.

Buddhism started in India as a religion advocating departure from family life, but it ended in China praising the virtue of filial piety. In a sense, Buddhism in its original form was never accepted in China; Indian Buddhism was more interpreted to fit Chinese culture than vice versa. Buddhism in India embraced the virtue of the celibate life, and it magnified misery and suffering inherent in family life. When these ideas were introduced into China, it was inevitable that it would be adapted to the Chinese tradition.

Not only did the Chinese thinkers adapt Buddhism in such a way that it was in line with the virtue of filial piety; it seems that the Chinese also tried to adapt the problem of causality to fit into their own culture. The problem of causality is one of the most important in the Buddhist schools. All Buddhist schools think of plurality of causes and effects instead of the one-to-one relationship between cause and effect. There is ample evidence that the original Indian idea of divine power became mingled with the traditional Chinese concepts of 'stimulus and response' (*Ganying*). *Ganying* is treated both as a general condition of life based on impersonal causes and, more personally, as the mutual resonance of individuals and things.

Although the Chinese word *ganying* does not match any particular Sanskrit term, it frequently occurs in Chinese Buddhist texts. *Ganying* is seen as the principle that underlies the interaction between Buddha and a disciple. The disciple is said to *gan* (stimulate) the Buddha, to which the Buddha's compassionate *ying* (response) resonates. *Ganying* does not involve magic or supernatural activity per se; it most often refers to the manifestation of an enlightened person, who is triggered by a group of believers. *Ganying* thus involves at least two persons who are in a state of *wu-wei*. *Ganying* can therefore, in my opinion, best be translated as 'mutual resonance'; it is the resonantal or symbiotic interaction of stimulus and response.

Ganying has received little attention from modern scholars, due, in part, to its inclusion in writings that did not belong to the Indian Buddhist tradition. Furthermore, the concept of *ganying* has both scientific and philosophical overtones, and is a compound binomial expression. *Gan* is semantically related to affect, feeling or stimulus and may syntactically function as a verb, substantive, adverb or adjective. The term *ying* is commonly translated as 'response', 'reflex' or 'effect'. *Ying* may also function as a verb, noun, adverb or adjective depending on the relative position of the word within a sentence. *Ganying* subsequently may be translated as 'action and reaction', 'stimulus and response' or 'affect and effect'.

In Buddhism, *ganying* refers to a symbiotic response through feelings and affections. It unfolds the interrelatedness of all things and exposes their ultimate shared origin. Mutual resonance is the presence (being) that resonates its non-presence (non-being). We saw this earlier in Daoism; in this view, opposites are dissolved.

In Buddhism, hospitality is intimately related to the divine. The way one treats a guest says much about one's relation with the divine. Lawrence Babb argues, for example, that 'the entire sequence has one overall purpose: to make the [god or] goddess feel like a welcome guest' (1975: 43). In this sense, mutual resonance is a form of hospitality, and hospitality in Buddhism is a form of worship.

Ganying promotes 'inductivity', 'sympathy', 'compassion' and 'co-respondance' which result from a natural feeling of responsibility that is beyond moral laws and concrete rules or regulations. The hospitality that *ganying* induces recognises the universe as 'the on-going evolving harmony expressed as the quality of life achieved by the insistent, co-creating particulars' (Ames, 2008: 42).

Because *ganying* is in touch with the true nature of the world, it expresses the myriad of things and can operate at several levels simultaneously. Second, *ganying* expresses at the same time the relationship between the realm of humans and heaven (*tian*). James Benn describes *ganying* as a sincere act that justifies one's intentions: 'It is understood that human actions and emotions can and do cause cosmic response and transformation. Acts that are the most sincere because they are selfless will cause the cosmos to respond in accordance with the petitioner's intention' (2007: 7). Hospitality seen in this way is not only a mutual resonance between host and guest, but moreover an act of hospitality between host and heaven. The hospitality of the host resonates with heaven's unconditional hospitality, which empowers and justifies the host's act.

Conclusions

In this chapter I have outlined the three major Chinese philosophical traditions in the light of hospitality. I have set out the foundations of each tradition and explored these foundations in relation to hospitality. We have seen that all three traditions are focused on the question of how to lead a good life. For Confucianism, this life is doing the right thing in a particular situation. Recognising what the right thing to do is, to Confucius, a matter of training and experience. Only the virtuous man who has trained himself extensively recognises what is needed in a particular situation. To Confucius, it is important that we change our innate nature through observing rituals and traditions and by having the right mindset. An important aspect of Confucianism is appropriate conduct for concrete human relations.

When we explore the nature of hospitality in Ancient Chinese philosophy, we need to understand the foundations of Chinese culture. The phenomenon of filial piety is, I would argue, crucial to our understanding not only of Confucianism, but of Chinese civilisation throughout time. In September 2015, the *Wall Street Journal* published an article titled 'Why China is turning back to Confucius'. It showed how China's central party wanted to reintroduce the concept of filial piety to establish harmony within its society. Filial piety grounds governmental rules and regulations, and, as such, makes it extremely relevant for understanding the Asian perspective of hospitality. In the Asian world, it is the family that is at the centre, not the individual. The most important philosophical traditions are therefore less interested in the moral duty of an individual, but more focused on one's moral duty in the light of one's relation to another person.

Filial piety is a virtue of respect for one's father, elders and ancestors. For Confucius, filial piety is the foundation and the highest standard for ethical conduct. Filial piety harmonises human relations and, as a consequence, leads to a stable and prosperous society. Man's first and foremost moral duty is to be hospitable to one's elders, ancestors or father. Hospitality in Confucius is first and foremost a conditional hospitality, which is tied by rules and regulations. Confucius does recognise the duty to be hospitable to the person from outside our community, but this seems to be more the kind of hospitality that implies not doing him harm based on the rule that one should not do to another what one does not like oneself. Based on this rule, we can argue that, to Confucius, we should be hospitable to the stranger, not because *we owe it to him*, but because we would want to be accepted if we were the stranger. When, however, this moral duty to be hospitable to the stranger interferes with our obligations to our elders, father or ancestors, we should choose filial piety over helping a stranger.

The moral particularism that Confucius seems to promote is one of the main critiques of the Daoist movement. The Daoists contributed all the particular problems suffered by Chinese society during the Warring State period to the focus on rules, regulations and traditional rituals. Daoism pursues the state of *wu-wei*, a state of being one with Dao. One's moral duty should be 'trying not to try' and letting go of all linguistic distinctions such as laws, rules and regulations. Unlike Confucius, in Daoism less, rather than more, culture is needed. Confucius's humanism is that of a crude human nature which is in need of cultivation. Man becomes virtuous by observing rules such as filial piety and by gaining experience through social practice. The Daoist movement argues that cultures have messed people up. To Daoism, human nature is essentially good; all we need to do is let go of everything artificial and follow our innate dispositions.

The philosophical target of Daoism is language. Daoism argues that moral predicaments like 'right' and 'wrong' alienate us from our own nature because they focus on the external, social use of language instead of on our inner nature. In the light of hospitality, Daoists seem to argue against any form of conditional hospitality that is based on distinctions, rules or traditions. What the Daoist movement seems to aim at is what Derrida has defined as 'unconditional hospitality'. Unconditional hospitality is hospitality at its purest. However, as Derrida notes, unconditional hospitality can never be obtained in practical human life. In order for unconditional hospitality to be fulfilled, a complete openness would be required, yet the very introduction of host and guest is already a violation of this openness. Recognising the stranger is already conditional and, as such, already alienates man from his innate nature.

What Daoism does contribute to the debate on the nature of hospitality is that conditional hospitality is, in its nature, artificial and cannot really guide us. But, as Derrida indicates, conditional laws are necessary in order for unconditional hospitality to be manifested. We need to recognise the stranger, for example, as a stranger in order to be hospitable. What Daoism does suggest is that our duty to be hospitable should be universalising, eternal and without constraints; we should be hospitable to everyone, at all times, in all standards. In our daily lives, however, we can only realise a fraction of this ideal; the ethical dilemma shows the impossibility and ambiguity of its metaphysical foundation.

A nice parable that illustrates this ethical dilemma is that of Hundun at the end of the *Zhuangzi*, one of the core Daoist teachings. In the parable, Hundun (Chaos) invites his two neighbours, named Shu (brief) and Hu (sudden), to visit him. The guests repay Hundun's generosity by drilling seven holes (for seeing, hearing and breathing) in his face to make him more 'human', but, at the end, Hundun dies. The parable shows not only that chaos as the process that drives existence cannot be grasped, but also how language can lead to a blindness. Shu and Hu cannot see Hundun as Hundun, but see him as 'lacking something'. The problem with Shu and Hu is that they cannot go beyond the linguistic categories by which they have learnt to interpret the world. Daoism points to something that is very valuable for an ethics of hospitality; it should not be tied by (cultural) linguistic distinctions that make us blind for seeing the other as he is.

Daoism foregrounds the absolute priority of unconditional hospitality but shows us at the same time the impossibility of it. Unconditional hospitality is hospitality in its purest form, but, in its purest form, it is also the least attainable, because it embodies both hospitality and its opposite. Conditional hospitality is, therefore, the only act realisable for humans; it is the simple fact that if we choose to help a stranger, we exclude by this choice all the others in need of our help. Daoism recognises the paradoxical nature of morality and hospitality, and argues that language, in a sense, is not the ultimate method that brings us truth. However, in order for man to live his life with others, we need to live at the level where things are presumed.

We see the ethical dilemma of unconditional and conditional hospitality again in Chinese Buddhism. Chinese Buddhism was influenced by Confucianism and Daoism and adapted to Chinese culture. Chinese Buddhism is, like Daoism, fundamentally nondualistic and emphasises the mutual sameness and interpretation of the ultimate and the human practical realm. In the light of hospitality, one term that helps us determine the Buddhist approach to hospitality is *ganying*. *Ganying* as mutual resonance promotes the welcoming of the other, the alien, the wanderer and the refugee. It enacts the commitment to take the other not as an enemy, but as a friend, setting aside the intimations of hostility in 'hospitality'. Chinese Buddhism embraces in this sense the concept of unconditional hospitality in which the host recognises himself in the other, recognises the interdependency of everything.

To conclude, an Asian ethics of hospitality should recognise one's moral duty to be hospitable to one's father, ancestors and family. Filial piety is at the heart of the Chinese tradition and cannot be taken for granted. Asian hospitality is, however, not limited to filial piety. Daoism and Chinese Buddhism go beyond the ties of kinship, and both recognise unconditional hospitality as hospitality in its purest form and argue for an awareness of linguistic artificial distinctions that are necessary for practical life but lead to moral blindness and narrowness. An Asian perspective on hospitality is therefore foremost an ethics of sympathy for humankind (*ren*): humankind that respects family living, while at the same time participating in nature's wholesome equilibrium and harmony.

Note

1 When one assumes that Confucius embraces a form of moral particularism, it is very difficult to explain its tremendous influence on the Eastern world.

References

Ames, R. T. (2008) Paronomasia: a Confucian way of making meaning. In Jones, D. (ed.), *Confucius Now: Contemporary Encounters with the Analects*, Chicago: Open Court, pp. 37–48.

Arendt, H. (1951) *On the Origins of Totalitarianism*, New York: Schocken Books.

Babb, L. (1975) *The Divine Hierarchy: Popular Hinduism in Central India*, New York: Columbia University Press.

Benn, J. (2007) *Burning for the Buddha: Self-Immolation in Chinese Buddhism*, Honolulu: University of Hawai'i Press.

Burik, S. (2009) *The End of Comparative Philosophy and the Task of Comparative Thinking*, Albany : State University of New York Press.

Cornell, D. (1992) *The Philosophy of the Limit*, New York: Routledge.

Derrida, J. (1997) *Adieu to Emmanuel Levinas*, Stanford: Stanford University Press.

Hai, Y. (2005) *Racism and Xenophobia in China*, Fudan University.

Havens, T. (2013) Confucius as humanism, *CLA Journal* 1: 33–41.

Hinton. D. (2013) *The Four Chinese Classics: Tao Te Ching, Analects, Chuang Tzu, Mencius*, Berkeley: Counterpoint.

Kristeva, J. (1991) *Strangers to Ourselves*, trans. L. S. Roudiez, New York: Columbia University Press.

Liebenthal, W. (1955) Chinese Buddhism during the 4th and 5th centuries, *Monumenta Nipponica* II, 1: 44–81.

MacIntyre, A. (1981) *After Virtue*, Notre Dame, IN: University of Notre Dame Press.

McNaughton, W. (1974) *The Confucian Vision*, Ann Arbor: University of Michigan Press.

Mugitani, K. (2004) Filial piety and authentic parents in religious Daoism. In Chan, A. K. L. and Tan, S. (eds) *Filial Piety in Chinese Thought and History*, London: RoutledgeCurzon, pp. 110–121.

Slingerland, E. (2005) *Trying not to Try: The Art and Science of Spontaneity*, New York: Crown.

Tanaka, K. (2014) The limit of language in Daoism, *Asian Philosophy* 14: 191–205.

Wing-Tsit, C. (1963) *A Source Book in Chinese Philosophy*, Princeton: Princeton University Press.

14

Observing hospitality speech patterns

Leanne Schreurs

Key themes

Speech acts

Threats to face

Pragmatic messages

Linguistic forms

> Visits always give pleasure – if not the arrival, the departure.
>
> *(Proverb)*

It has been argued that verbal social interactions have greatly influenced hospitality experiences (Robinson and Lynch, 2007a: 238). From a linguistic perspective, the study of hospitality has surprisingly been limited to date (see, for instance, Robinson and Lynch, 2007b, for a discussion of this issue). As a preliminary study, in this chapter a qualitative analysis will be conducted of individual examples of speech acts (Searle, 1969: 16) that are thought to be typical of hospitality settings. A novel will be analysed on the linguistic forms that constitute the act of greeting and inviting, as well as the meanings of the forms and the circumstances within which the speech acts were performed. The findings serve to illustrate how the use of language could shape hospitality experiences.

In order to gain a general understanding of the sophisticated nature of human communication (Diver *et al.*, 2012: 446), it will be considered how one and the same linguistic form may lead to different interpretations. Important in this regard is that a literal sentence meaning may differ from the speaker's utterance meaning (Searle, 1978: 207). The example in (1) is a dialogue between two flatmates. They are both at home, when, suddenly, the doorbell rings. Then, they shout to one another:

DOI: 10.4324/9781315679938-15

(1) – The doorbell is ringing!

– I'm in the bathroom!

– Okay![1]

Although by the literal meaning of the sentences in (1) it is only revealed that the doorbell is ringing, and that the person addressed is in the bathroom, they will most certainly be understood as the utterances indicated in (2):

(2) – Would you mind opening the door?

– I'm sorry but I can't.

– I'll go then.

Clearly, the conveyed information in (1) is neither a mere statement about the ringing doorbell, nor is it about the addressed person being in the bathroom. The reason for uttering the sentences is a request to open the door, and a subsequent rejection. As such, the acts of communication are performed by the utterance of a sentence, namely, making a request and rejecting it successively (Austin, 1976: 6). Hence it appears that speakers, when uttering a sentence, may not only refer to the literal meaning of the specific sentence, but also convey a pragmatic message (cf. Searle, 1978: 208; see, for instance, Harris and Monaco, 1978 for a discussion of the pragmatic implications of a message).

The pragmatic message of an utterance is expressed by means of speech acts, such as making a request. The difficulty pertaining to speech acts in general, and to indirect speech acts (Searle, 1975: 60; cf. the example in (1)) in particular, is that they are objectively unverifiable categories. Curiously enough, that means that the literal meaning of 'The doorbell is ringing!' does not entail any sort of request, nor does 'I'm in the bathroom!' involve any kind of rejection. Therefore, the intentions of the speakers in (1) will only be achieved when the hearers understand that, under certain conditions, the utterances count as a request or as a rejection respectively (Searle, 1969: 49; Austin, 1976: 8). Hence, the success of the performance of a particular act partly depends on the hearer's ability to make a guess at the intended message (Diver, 2012: 479). The request in (1) is successfully brought off, albeit it is not responded to with compliance. However, it is not unlikely that a speaker might make a request, but fails to do so because his interlocutor takes it as a mere observation, for example in (1) after a long time of the doorbell not working properly. Therefore, speakers need to secure the *uptake* of the pragmatic message (Austin, 1976: 117).

In contrast to speech acts, the linguistic forms that constitute these acts are most certainly objectively verifiable. In fact, they are the only observable indications that speakers can account for (Diver, 2012: 451). Consequently, the meaning of an invariant linguistic form may lead to different interpretations and thus to various communicated messages (Dreer, 2007: 58). Furthermore, it has been argued that certain linguistic forms may affect a speaker's *face* (Brown and Levinson, 1987: 61) – that is, the public self-image all speakers are thought to have, and from which two basic needs follow in communication. On the one hand, it is argued that speakers need to feel appreciated by others (*positive face*); on the other hand, speakers supposedly want their actions to be unimpeded by others (*negative face*) (Brown and Levinson, 1987: 61). In this chapter, it will be argued that interaction between the meaning of the linguistic forms and the enhancement of positive and negative face could be particularly relevant to communication in hospitality situations.

Since the content of face will differ between cultures (Brown and Levinson, 1987: 61), there is probably no such thing as 'standard hospitable language usage'. Hence, in order to gain a deeper understanding of how the meaning of a specific linguistic form may lead to the interpretation of hospitable language usage, only a look can be taken at typical hospitable speech acts. Unlike Derrida, who studied the notion of *absolute hospitality* (Derrida and Dufourmantelle, 2000: 25), and others, who focused on hospitality as 'the business of furnishing food or lodging or both to paying visitors who are typically called guests' (Heffernan, 2014: 11), in this chapter, hospitality will be analysed as far as communication is concerned. Hereafter, communication in hospitality will refer to situations that belong to the domestic domain (Lashley, 2008: 74).

In daily life, hospitality concerns encounters between strangers, friends and relatives, that is to say, 'people who are not regular members of a household' (Telfer, 2000: 39), in the home. The speech acts that are performed in these encounters will be analysed on the linguistic forms that are used to constitute these acts. To this purpose, a novel was chosen since it has been argued that 'literature tends to slight hospitality at its best' (Heffernan, 2014: 333; see also Lashley *et al.*, 2007 for a discussion of this issue). In literature, the plot is commonly motivated by conflict and love. As the example in (4) shows (see p. 174), on the one hand, hostility and hospitality are related notions (Heffernan, 2014: 2). On the other hand, there also seems to be a kinship between love and hospitality. To love someone implies to receive the other without conditions. However, the dark side of both hospitality and love is that one risks betrayal in receiving a guest and in taking a lover (Heffernan, 2014: 333). This is exactly what happens to the protagonist of the novel under analysis when she makes a lover of her guest. The results of the analysis are restricted to the specific novel and, therefore, cannot be taken as an independent proof of the influence of the individual linguistic form and its meaning to the pragmatic message. Nevertheless, the findings serve to illustrate how certain linguistic forms, used in a particular set of speech acts, may contribute to the message in hospitality situations.

First, the key theoretical concepts of this study, based on the examples in (1) and (2), will be briefly explained in the remainder of this chapter. Second, the method employed to conduct a qualitative analysis of two of the most salient examples of hospitality situations will be described. Third, the results obtained from the analysis will be presented. Fourth, a general discussion will follow regarding the issue of the conveyed message being more or something else than is actually said. The linguistic forms that contribute to the message in hospitality situations will receive particular interest. Finally, a summary and conclusion will be formulated, including the limitations of the study, and recommendations will be given for further research.

Some theoretical considerations

To speak a language implies the performance of speech acts (Searle, 1969: 16). Several speech acts are performed by the production of a sentence. In this chapter, the term 'speech act' will refer to the illocutionary act (Searle, 1969: 24). For example, the illocutionary act in (1) is the act of making a request. Moreover, the perlocutionary force (Searle, 1969: 25) of the illocutionary act is taken into account, since this force will be relevant to the positive and negative face of speakers in general and, thus, to hospitality experiences in particular. In the example in (1), the perlocutionary act is the effect of making the person addressed open the door (Searle, 1969: 25; see, for instance, Márquez Reiter and Placencia, 2005 for a summary of speech act theory). The example in (1) contains the speech acts of requesting and rejecting, and illustrates how the utterance of a sentence implicates an action. The utterances that 'do' something have been confronted with the utterances that just report on something. The latter class of utterances are defined as 'constatives', and may be assessed as either being true or false. The observation that the doorbell is ringing, for example after a long time of not working properly, may be true. The former class of utterances, or 'performatives', rather than being true or false, may be 'happy' or 'unhappy' (Austin, 1976: 14). In (1), the performative is assessed as 'unhappy', since the request was not brought into effect.

Moreover, with regard to performative utterances, the example in (1) has illustrated that a speaker does not need to utter the words 'I request' or 'I reject', in order to indicate that he is actually making a request or rejecting it. Rather than being straightforward, the use of linguistic forms of which the literal meaning differs from its conveyed meaning (*indirectness*; Brown and Levinson, 1987: 134) may serve the same purpose. Indeed, under certain circumstances, this may be a preferable *communicative strategy* (Dreer, 2011: 21). Important in this regard are the notions of positive and negative face. As has already been argued, speakers want others, their interlocutors, to approve of their personality. The use of polite address terms, for instance, may enhance a speaker's positive face.[2] In addition, speakers wish to have freedom of action; they do not want to be impeded by others.

Most importantly, the social necessity to attend to both positive and negative face is considered to be a universal phenomenon in human communication. If face is a common notion that can be lost and enhanced (*mutual vulnerability of face*; Brown and Levinson, 1987: 61), speakers will generally cooperate in order to maintain face. Therefore, they try to avoid speech acts that imply a possible threat to one or both faces (*face-threatening acts*; Brown and Levinson, 1987: 60). To make a request is a negative face-threatening act, since the speaker clearly imposes his will on the hearer. In addition, to reject a request may constitute a positive face-threatening act, since the need of the speaker who makes the request is openly ignored (Brown and Levinson, 1987: 62).

Now, the interlocutors in (1) are confronted with two opposing tensions. The first will be the speaker's need to ask the person addressed a favour. In this case, the speaker wants the hearer to open the door. The second will be not to offend the person addressed. The speaker needs the hearer to open the door, without giving him a feeling of being constrained. In return, for obvious reasons, the person addressed needs to decline the request. In addition, he preferably has to do so without being impolite. The example in (1) contains a commonly used strategy to deal with these tensions, namely conventional indirectness (Brown and Levinson, 1987: 132). The literal meaning of the sentences differs from the speaker's utterance meaning, but the latter meaning is considered to be contextually unambiguous. In (1), the speakers distance themselves from the speech acts of requesting and rejecting by use of linguistic forms that literally only report on the ringing doorbell and on the interlocutor being in the bathroom. These forms apparently do not constitute a threat to either of the faces. As a result, the purpose of communication is achieved with a minimum threat of 'losing face'.

In comparison to the example in (1), the literal meaning of the linguistic forms in (2) is more clearly related to the pragmatic conveyed message. Still, this example contains formulas to reduce the threats to both faces. The request 'Would you mind opening the door?' is in fact only a question, as opposed to the imperative 'Open the door!', which constitutes an order, and, as such, is more of an overt threat to the negative face of the interlocutor. Again, to a large extent, the circumstances determine the interpretation of conveyed information. In comparison to the utterances in (1) and (2), the utterance of 'Open the door!' may be a highly negative face-threatening act at first sight. However, in cases of great urgency, it is a perfectly understandable utterance that will probably not offend anyone (Brown and Levinson, 1987: 96). Indeed, when bringing in a victim of a car crash, the non-urgent 'Would you mind opening the door?' could possibly constitute a threat to the victim's life.

Methodology of the case study

To illustrate how, under certain circumstances, the interpretation of specific linguistic forms may lead to hospitality experiences, several situations in a novel that are considered to be typically hospitable have been observed. The Colombian Spanish novel *La marquesa de Yolombó* 'The marchioness of Yolombó' (Carrasquilla, 1974 [1928]) describes the life in a little village in Colombia, at the end of the colonial period. The story revolves around the protagonist Bárbara Caballero, who breaks with the traditional role of the woman around the home. In a society ruled by men and *machismo*, the exploration of gold mines, an activity typical of the region in which the story takes place, makes her very rich. She becomes famous for her exceptional life style, her money, her aversion to the common practice of slavery and also for the title of marchioness, which was given to her by the king of Spain as a reward for her dedication and loyalty to the Spanish court. Unfortunately, her success leads to her misfortune, as she is betrayed by her brand new husband who turns out to be a criminal with his eye on her fortune.

Aside from the fact that the novel is considered by some to be one of the most famous examples of Colombian literature (Aristizábal, 2006), it is of interest because of the description of several hospitality situations, that is to say, everyday life situations in which a visitor, being a stranger or not, is welcomed by the person who is being visited. In addition, the novel contains a variety of different linguistic forms, such as five forms of address and two types of verb mood, where in contemporary English it is most common to only use one ('you' and the indicative mood respectively). In order to conduct a qualitative analysis, two of the most salient dialogues in hospitality situations were first identified. Next, from the dialogue two types of speech acts were selected that seem to be characteristic of hospitality situations, namely the greeting and the invitation. Then, the linguistic forms that constitute these acts were observed, as well as the meanings of the forms and the circumstances within which the speech acts were performed.

Qualitative analysis of two hospitality situations

The dialogue in (3) illustrates an encounter between two inhabitants of Yolombó. The speakers are the guests of high-class, Don[3] José María, and his host of mid-class, Don Rufo. José María is a rich, elderly widower who is looking for a new wife because 'yo no puedo dormir solo porque me da mucho frío' (I can't sleep alone because I get cold) (Carrasquilla, 1974: 166). He has seen Rufo's beautiful, teenage daughter walking through the village. Now, José María knocks on his door to ask for her hand in exchange for some jewellery:

(3) – ¡Ah de la casa! – grita en cuanto arrima.

– Buenos días, señor Don José María – contesta Don Rufo saliendo al corredor,

muy hospitalario y atento – ¿Por qué no se desmonta y se cuela?

– Con mucho gusto, si lo permite el amigo.

– ¡Tanté no permitirle! Más que fuera

(Carrasquilla, 1974: 158)

– Hey, anybody home? – he screams, while arriving at the house.

– Good morning, Mr Don José María – Don Rufo answers while coming to the corridor, very hospitable and polite – Why don't you get off the horse and come in?

– With pleasure, if you allow me to do so, my friend.

– How will I not allow you! Of course I do.

According to the narrator, the utterances of the host in (3) are 'muy hospitalario y atento' (very hospitable and polite). Now the speech acts performed in (3) will be analysed, as well as the linguistic forms involved.

In (3), the host expresses a greeting and an invitation. The greeting, 'Buenos días, señor Don José María' (Good morning, Mr Don José María), consists of two parts. After a quite common greeting, wishing the other person a good day, a succession of two formal address terms can be observed, *señor* (mister) and *don*, followed by a double proper name, indicating that the speaker in question is being very polite. The invitation, 'Por qué no se desmonta y se cuela?' (Why don't you get off the horse and come in?), may be characterised as extremely indirect, presenting an interrogative sentence structure – a question – that additionally contains a negation. However, it is very clear that, just as has been observed in the discussion of (1) and (2), the host does not expect a literal answer to the question, but instead expects the guest to accept or reject the invitation, which is indeed the case as he answers 'Con mucho gusto' (With pleasure).

Observing another similar dialogue of a hospitality situation, the dialogue in (4a) also contains an invitation speech act. Yet, the linguistic forms of this dialogue are even more remarkable than the ones presented in (3). Conversation (4a) represents a dialogue between an inhabitant of Yolombó and a visitor to the village, Fernando de Orellana, presumably a Spanish nobleman, who has reached the village of Yolombó only recently. His joviality and courtesy make him a beloved man in just a few days. More importantly, he is considered to be a good match for Bárbara Caballero, the marchioness of Yolombó. In (4a), José María tries to convince Fernando to stay as his guest until the rainy season is over.

(4a) – ¿Para qué viniste aquí, paisano de mil demonios?

– ¡Ni lo sé, Don Chepe![4] [...]

Y se levanta y se lleva el pañuelo a los ojos y se pasea. Don Chepe se alza, a su vez, le toma por los molledos y le regaña con cariño, disfrazado de rabia:

– ¡De aquí no te vas, gitano del demonio, hasta que a nosotros nos dé la gana! Estás prisionero. ¿Lo oyes?

(Carrasquilla, 1974: 488–489)

– Why have you come here, compatriot of a thousand devils?

– I have really no idea, Don Chepe! [...]

And he gets up and brings his handkerchief to his eyes as if to dry them. Now Don Chepe stands up, grabs him by his arm and falls out with affection, disguised as fury:

– You aren't going anywhere, gipsy of the devil, not before we want you to! You are our prisoner, do you understand?

In (4a) we see a statement, 'De aquí no te vas' (You aren't going anywhere), followed by a term of abuse, 'gitano del demonio' (gipsy of the devil). By the former utterance the speech act of prohibiting is performed, whereas the latter constitutes the speech act of insulting. Although both acts are not very hospitable at first sight, the narrator reveals that this is only apparent, as he previously explains that the host 'le regaña con cariño, disfrazado de rabia' (falls out with affection, disguised as fury). Again, it is clear that the message intended is an invitation to stay, although the meaning of the linguistic forms is something totally different. Fortunately, the guest gets the message, which is illustrated by the remainder of the dialogue:

(4b) – Pero ¿cómo me quedo aquí más tiempo? ¡Eso es abusar de la hospitalidad!

– ¡No digas pendejadas ni vengas a injuriarnos con reparos! Mi casa, la del Capitán, las de mis hijos, son tus casas.

(Carrasquilla, 1974: 489)

– But how can I stay here even longer? That would be an abuse of your hospitality!

– Don't talk nonsense nor offend us with objections! My house, the Captain's house, my children's houses, are all yours.

In sum, the linguistic forms used in the examples in (3) and (4a) vary from very polite to apparently extremely impolite. In both examples, the speech act of inviting is performed. Moreover, the literal meaning of the linguistic forms that are used in the examples does not have a one-to-one relationship with the pragmatic message that is conveyed.

Typical hospitality speech patterns

Speech acts were analysed, as well as the linguistic forms that constitute these acts, in the dialogues that were performed in two different hospitality situations. The utterance of the host in (3) was described as 'very hospitable and polite', whereas in (4a) the host 'falls out with affection, disguised as fury'. So, speakers may employ different communicative strategies in order to be hospitable. Since greetings and invitations seem to be particularly relevant to hospitality situations, these two aspects will be further discussed.

Greetings

The speech act of greeting is typically performed to enhance the positive face of interlocutors (Haverkate, 1994: 88). Moreover, greetings are considered to be a universal phenomenon. All cultures make use of greetings in communication (Haverkate, 1994: 84), although the way of greeting will differ among cultures (see, for instance, Hofstede *et al.*, 2010 for a discussion of cultural differences). As such, they are particularly relevant to the communication in hospitality situations. Speakers may have several reasons to perform a greeting. In the hospitality situation in (3), the greeting, ¡Ah de la casa! (Hey, anybody home?) is most probably uttered to attract the interlocutor's attention (Haverkate, 1994: 85). In addition, greetings may be performed to confirm the hierarchical position between the speakers, which is commonly defined by their social position and the grade of intimacy between them (Haverkate, 1994: 85). In (3), the positive effect of the greeting, 'Buenos días' (Good morning), is intensified by the formal titles of address, *señor* (mister) and *don*. Since there are neither kinship nor friendship ties between the speakers, and, also, considering the difference in social class, the use of these linguistic forms in the given circumstances is perfectly understandable.

In (3), both the wish in 'Buenos días' (Good morning) and the terms of address *señor* (mister) and *don* serve to enhance the positive face of the interlocutor. However, generally, the use of address terms may be problematic when the speaker, accidentally or intentionally, misidentifies the interlocutor (Brown and Levinson, 1987: 67). This is the case when a speaker addresses his interlocutor in an embarrassing way, for example by using a proper name where mister and/or *don* is expected. The speaker, then, is being too familiar, and may insult his interlocutor implying that the social distance between them is smaller than it is felt by his interlocutor (Brown and Levinson, 1987: 230). Nonetheless, in the greeting in (3), the combination of the specific terms seems to be used in order to avoid misunderstanding, and can therefore be taken as an enhancement of the positive face of the guest.

Invitations

Similar to greetings, invitations are also considered to be polite speech acts, as they express the intention of the speaker to carry out an action for the interlocutor's benefit (Haverkate, 1994: 106). However, contrary to the greeting above, which is meant as an enhancement of the positive face of the interlocutor, invitations also imply an intrusion in the behaviour of the interlocutor. As such, the speaker imposes on the hearer's negative face, as it interferes in his freedom of action. There is a risk that interlocutors may not wish to receive an invitation, for instance when the person addressed is in a hurry, or when the hearer belongs to a higher social class than the speaker, as is the case in the example in (3) (Brown and Levinson, 1987: 99). Consequently, the person addressed is confronted with a dilemma. To accept the invitation implies a threat to his own negative face, whereas to decline the invitation will probably signify a threat to the speaker's positive face. Now, based on the mutual vulnerability of face, it is assumed that speakers will generally cooperate in maintaining their mutual faces (Brown and Levinson, 1987: 61). Hence, to be truly hospitable, the speaker that conveys the invitation needs to consider the threats to both faces. Both in (1) and in (3), we have seen that the speakers do so by using linguistic structures that literally express other speech acts differing from what they in fact pragmatically imply.

And so, the intended message of the invitation in (3) is dressed up as a negative question. This communicative strategy is used to propose an activity to the interlocutor (Matte Bon and Sánchez Paños, 1995: 319). Negative questions are commonly used by speakers to indicate what they know about their interlocutor's needs (Brown and Levinson, 1987: 122). They have certain linguistic characteristics to redress the imposition of the face-threatening act of, in the specific case, the invitation. First, the verb form is the indicative mood, which is commonly seen as the unmarked or neutral form of the verb (Dreer, 2007: 45), as opposed to the imperative, which would imply a more direct threat to the interlocutor's negative face (Brown and Levinson, 1987: 99). Second, the invitation in (3) has a negation in the structure, leaving no opportunity for the guest to change his actions. The host is just asking a question, and it is up to the guest whether to take it as the invitation implied by it or not. Third, the conjugation of the verbs in third person singular, as opposed to the second person singular denoting a familiar form, indicates the polite form of the verb. As such, the verb conjugations can be taken as an enhancement of the interlocutor's positive self-image.

Similar to the example in (3), in (4a) the linguistic structures that are used literally express other speech acts than their pragmatic implications. In contrast, surprisingly enough, the linguistic forms in (4a) constitute a serious threat to the interlocutor's positive and negative face at first sight. In this example, a prohibition is performed by means of a statement, 'De aquí no te vas' (You aren't going anywhere), not leaving any freedom of action to the guest at all. Moreover, even an insult is observed in 'gitano del demonio' (gipsy of the devil). Yet, it was still considered to be an example of a hospitality situation, which followed from the remainder of the dialogue in (4b).

Now, the use of apparent terms of abuse in social relationships that are characterised by certain intimacy, such as *gordito* (fatso) used by women to address their husband, is in some cultures a quite common communicative strategy to assert such intimacy (Brown and Levinson, 1987: 229; Fitch, 1998: 43; Hofstede *et al.*, 2010: 391). A speaker may even threaten the positive face of his interlocutor by being too polite, as it implies that the social distance between them is greater than is felt by the interlocutor (Brown and Levinson, 1987: 229–230). In the hospitality situation in (4a), the term of abuse denotes intimacy, and is therefore taken as an enhancement of the hearer's positive face. Moreover, by the speech act of prohibiting, the speaker in fact insists that the hearer may impose on his negative face (Brown and Levinson, 1987: 99). Hence, the prohibition to leave is an enhancement of the positive face of the hearer, and is interpreted as an invitation to stay. Important in this regard is that no other face wants are threatened, which is clearly dependent on the circumstances. Obviously, in the hospitality situation in (3), the performance of the speech acts of prohibiting and insulting would have been highly offensive.

Conclusions

In summary, in this chapter, two examples of hospitality situations taken from a novel were identified. A qualitative analysis of the speech acts that were performed in both examples was conducted. Linguistic forms that constituted the speech act of greeting and inviting were focused on, as these acts seem to be particularly relevant to hospitality situations. The dialogues once again illustrated that speakers do not need to say 'I greet' or 'I invite' in order to perform a greeting or an invitation. Indeed, they showed that there may not be a one-to-one relationship between the meaning of linguistic forms and the pragmatic message they convey. Still, the message may be perfectly understandable. In addition, it was found that the linguistic forms used in the hospitality situations varied from very polite to apparently extremely impolite.

The examples indicated that hospitality could be related to different linguistic systems interacting with the context. On the one hand, speakers are thought to have the need to not be impeded by others. On the other hand, they too want to be appreciated by others. Therefore, they avoid potential threats to their mutual negative faces, as well as enhancing their positive face, which seems to be relevant to hospitality as far as it concerns communication. Both the examples in (3) and (4a) illustrated that the linguistic forms that may intervene in hospitality situations possibly are address terms, since they affect an interlocutor's positive face. Moreover, different sentence structures, such as the interrogative structure with a negation in (3), seem to be relevant to hospitality situations, as they clearly influence the negative face of speakers.

It can be concluded that, although each and every linguistic form has its own invariant meaning, the context highly contributes to the pragmatic message that is conveyed. Indeed, with regard to indirect speech acts, as in the examples in (3) and (4a), the context seems to be crucial for a hearer in order to understand the pragmatic message, since the sentence he literally hears and understands means something else. Contextual factors such as the social status of the speakers and the social relationship between them, for example whether they are strangers to each other or not, seem to be decisive in the choice of one or another linguistic form. To call a stranger a 'bastard' in order to be hospitable is quite unthinkable, whereas the example in (4a) has shown that, in intimate social relationships, the use of a term of abuse may be taken as a sign of appreciation.

Yet, the considered relationship between speech acts and the linguistic forms that constitute these acts, as well as the relationship between the circumstances of a speech act and the message it conveys, need to be empirically validated. A discourse analysis of the specific novel may be conducted. The distribution of specific linguistic forms over speech acts on the one hand, and of speech acts over specific social relationships on the other, may shed light on the interaction of the meaning of a linguistic form and the pragmatic message it conveys. The type of communicative situation, for example whether it is a conflictive situation or not, may also be relevant in this regard, since it is not very probable that the use of insulting address terms will be taken as a sign of appreciation in conflictive situations. In addition, the findings derived from the qualitative analysis based on the novel need to be tested in reality, for example by means of experiments in which speakers are asked to rank a number of specific linguistic structures on their degree of hospitality. It is hoped that this will be useful in showing that, although we cannot speak about standard hospitable language usage, hospitality and language are inextricably entwined.

Notes

1 I am indebted to Bob de Jonge for this example, but he claims that its origin is elsewhere. Unfortunately we have not been able to find the original source to give it full credit here.
2 This is very well expressed in a Dutch TV commercial for the fast food chain McDonald's. It shows a little boy ordering a meal for the whole family. The lady behind the counter addresses him as 'sir'. When the parents ask their son whether he managed to order the meal, he answers, very cheerfully: 'She called me "sir"!' To have been addressed with a respectful title of address seemed to impress him more than to have successfully ordered the meal. See www.youtube.com/watch?v=d9J6KNba4vU. Accessed 24 March 2016.
3 The title *Don* is used before a first name to express politeness or respect towards the person addressed (Real Academia Española, 2001). Its function is somewhat comparable to the use of 'Sir'.
4 The proper name 'Chepe', when used in intimate social relationships, is a nickname for 'José'.

References

Aristizábal, A. (2006) Libros clave de la narrativa colombiana (III). La marquesa de Yolombó. Available at http://cvc.cervantes.es/el_rinconete/anteriores/diciembre_06/27122006_01.htm. Accessed 24 March 2016.

Austin, J. L. (1976) *How to do Things with Words*, 2nd edn, Oxford: Oxford University Press.

Brown, P. and Levinson, S. C. (1987) *Politeness: Some Universals in Language Usage*, New York: Cambridge University Press.

Butt, J. and Benjamin, C. (2000) *A New Reference Grammar of Modern Spanish*, 3rd edn, New York: McGraw-Hill.

Carrasquilla, T. (1974) *La Marquesa de Yolombó*, Bogotá: Instituto Caro y Cuervo.

Derrida, J. and Dufourmantelle, A. (2000) *Of Hospitality*, trans. R. Bowlby, Stanford: Stanford University Press.

Diver, W., Huffman, A. and Davis, J. (2012) *Language: Communication and Human Behavior: The Linguistic Essays of William Diver*, Leiden: Brill.

Dreer, I. (2007) *Expressing the Same by the Different: The Subjunctive vs the Indicative in French*, Amsterdam: Benjamins.

Dreer, I. (2011) The distribution of linguistic forms and textual structure. In Jonge, B. de and Tobin, Y. (eds) *Linguistic Theory and Empirical Evidence*, Amsterdam: Benjamins, pp. 18–44.

Fitch, K. L. (1998) *Speaking Relationally: Culture, Communication, and Interpersonal Connection*, New York: Guilford Press.

Harris, R. J. and Monaco, G. E. (1978) Psychology of pragmatic implication: information processing between the lines, *Journal of Experimental Psychology: General* 107, 1: 1–22.

Haverkate, H. (1994) *La Cortesía Verbal: Estudio Pragmalingüístico*, Madrid: Gredos.

Heffernan, J. A. W. (2014) *Hospitality and Treachery in Western Literature*, New Haven: Yale University Press.

Hofstede, G., Hofstede, G. J. and Minkov, M. (2010) *Cultures and Organizations: Software of the Mind*, 3rd edn, New York: McGraw-Hill.

Lashley, C. (2008) Studying hospitality: insights from social sciences, *Scandinavian Journal of Hospitality and Tourism* 8, 1: 69–84.

Lashley, C., Lynch, P. and Morrison, A. J. (2007) *Hospitality: A Social Lens*, Amsterdam and Oxford: Elsevier.

Márquez Reiter, R. and Placencia, M. E. (2005) *Spanish Pragmatics*, Basingstoke: Palgrave Macmillan.

Matte Bon, F. and Sánchez Paños, I. (1995) *Gramática Comunicativa del Español; P. 1: De la Lengua a la Idea. – P. 2: De la Idea a la Lengua*, new rev. edn, Madrid: Edelsa.

Real Academia Española (2001), *Diccionario de la Lengua Española*, 22nd edn, Madrid: Editorial Espasa Calpe.

Robinson, M. G. and Lynch, P. A. (2007a) Hospitality through poetry: control, fake solidarity, and breakdown, *International Journal of Culture, Tourism and Hospitality Research* 1, 3: 237–246.

Robinson, M. G. and Lynch, P. A. (2007b) The power of hospitality: a sociolinguistic analysis. In Lashley, C., Lynch, P. A. and Morrison, A. J. (eds) *Hospitality: A Social Lens*, Amsterdam and Oxford: Elsevier, pp. 141–154.

Searle, J. R. (1969) *Speech Acts: An Essay in the Philosophy of Language*, Cambridge: Cambridge University Press.

Searle, J. R. (1975) Indirect speech acts. In Cole, P. and Morgan, J. L. (eds) *Syntax and Semantics*, vol. 3: *Speech Acts*, Academic Press, New York, pp. 59–82.

Searle, J. R. (1978) Literal meaning, *Erkenntnis* 13: 207–224.

Telfer, E. (2000) The philosophy of hospitableness. In Lashley, C. and Morrison, A. (eds) *In Search of Hospitality: Theoretical Perspectives and Debates*, Oxford: Butterworth-Heinemann, pp. 38–55.

Part II
Experiencing hospitality

15

Hospitality, migration and cultural assimilation

The case of the Irish in Australia

Barry O'Mahony

> **Key themes**
>
> Social mobility
>
> Irish theme pubs
>
> Consuming hospitality
>
> Host–guest relationships

I'm sure I don't know half the people who come to my house. Indeed, from all I hear, I shouldn't like to.

(Oscar Wilde)

The colonisation of Australia by Europeans began in 1788, when a fleet of 11 ships carrying just over 969 English convicts and military personnel landed at Botany Bay. After some anxious times in this unfamiliar land, the colony began to prosper and, over the next two hundred years, attracted large numbers of migrants from many lands. This steady growth resulted in a stable society that, while still evidencing its British beginnings, is a considerable multicultural mix. Migrants and their descendants now hold important governmental and business positions across the country. There is also complete freedom of worship and a wide acceptance of a range of cultural practices. Within this context, the Irish were the second largest ethnic group in the early days of the colony, but at that time were predominantly low status convicts or, later, working-class free settlers.

During their transportation to Australia and their subsequent incarceration in the colony, Irish convicts were subject to significant ill-treatment and had few, if any, social advantages. Later, when convict labour was replaced by a migrant labour scheme, the predominantly Anglican community was even less accepting of the Irish. Further tensions appeared as a result of post-famine migration, with some particularly cruel newspaper reports directed at Irish famine orphans, and again during the First World War, when the Irish Catholic Archbishop,

DOI: 10.4324/9781315679938-17

Daniel Mannix, played a key role in the referendum that rejected conscription. Indeed, as late as the 1950s, Irish nationals suffered discrimination in employment and were predominantly confined to roles as working-class citizens. This chapter focuses on three selected periods in Irish–Australian history to explain how the Irish involvement in the cultivation, distribution, preparation and consumption of food and beverages, along with their engagement with the hospitality industry, mitigated these tensions and played a substantive role in smoothing political and religious differences between the English and the Irish in Australia.

Period one: cultivation

Colonisation of Australia, or, more precisely, New South Wales, began with the landing of what is now known as the First Fleet. For the first three years only those convicted of crimes in England were transported, and the majority were either Londoners or the poor of English cities. Hughes (1988) has compiled a skills audit of these first settlers and asserts that none were trained in the intricacies of farming (see Table 15.1). 'Other trades' includes domestic servants, tailors and a silk dryer but, remarkably, not one farmer was taken to the new colony. Not surprisingly, then, the first attempts to establish the food supply were not successful, even though a number of plants and seeds were loaded in England and farm animals had been taken on board during the Fleet's stopover at the Cape of Good Hope.

Five and a half months after arrival, the Governor, Arthur Phillip, reported on the state of food production in a private letter to Under-Secretary Nepean. His dissatisfaction with the current skills base was evident: 'if fifty farmers were sent out with their families they would do more in one year in rendering this colony independent of the mother country, as to provisions, than a thousand convicts' (Phillip, 1788). In October of the first year, Phillip reported that early efforts at cultivation continued to meet with poor returns despite an optimistic report by Captain Watkin Tench who wrote in 1788 that:

> there seems to be no reason to doubt that many large tracts of land around us will bring perfection whatever shall be sown in them. To give this matter a fair trial some practical farmers capable of such an undertaking should be sent out; for the spots we have chosen for experiments in agriculture, in which we can scarce be supposed adepts, have hitherto but ill repaid our toil.
>
> *(2009: 71)*

Table 15.1 Skills audit of the convicts on the First Fleet

Trade	Number of persons
Seamen	8
Carpenters, shipwrights and cabinet makers	6
Shoemakers	5
Weavers	5
Watermen	4
Ivory turners	3
Brickmakers	2
Bricklayers/masons	2
Other trades	47

Source: Hughes (1988: 74).

Their toil would continue to go unrewarded, and the years 1788 to 1792 bear testimony to a time of deep despair in which 'the colonists were afflicted by semi-starvation, scurvy, dysentery, and infections' (Wood, 1988: 163). A secure food supply remained beyond their reach, and 'they were almost totally dependent on the supply of food brought with them, and additional supplies sought in long return voyages to the Cape of Good Hope and Batavia' (Wood, 1988: 163). Lack of nutrition led to a reduction in working hours and there was little progress in agriculture (Walker and Roberts, 1988).

Governor Phillip appealed to Lord Sydney to send famers, predicting that 'in the third year from the time the settlers arrive there will be a market well supplied with grain, poultry, hogs and goats, all of which has been a great increase, but killed, from wanting corn to support them' (Phillip, 1790a). In June 1789, he received word from Lord Grenville (Secretary of State) that the *Guardian*, a convict transport ship, was being despatched to Sydney with 'about twenty-five convicts who are either artificers or persons accustomed to agriculture' (Grenville, 1789a: 121). Just off the Cape of Good Hope, however, the *Guardian* collided with an iceberg. Most of those on board were despatched in life boats and sadly four out of five of these were lost at sea. The badly damaged ship made it back to port and, although 'all 25 gardening convicts had remained on board and helped bring the *Guardian* safely back to the Cape' (Rees, 2001: 183), none continued to New South Wales because the Captain had petitioned for their pardon in reward for their willingness to assist during the disaster (Collins, 1798; Rees, 2001).

When the Second Fleet arrived, a number of the convicts on board were found to be incapable of work. Collins describes them as 'very improper subjects for an infant colony because many were invalids or old people' (1798: 124). Governor Phillip was not impressed:

> the sending out of the disordered and helpless clears the gaols and may ease the parishes from which they are sent … [but] … the settlement, instead of being a colony which will support itself, will, if the practice is continued, remain for years a burthen to the mother-country.
>
> *(1790b: 195)*

In November 1790, Lord Grenville responded, advising that a Third Fleet would be ready to leave England within a month and that the number of convicts being transported was about to rise because of the overcrowded 'state of the hulks [and] … the number of felons under sentence of transportation, not only in this Kingdom, but in Ireland' (Grenville, 1789b). In April 1791, the *SS Queen* departed from Cobh in Cork with 133 male and 23 female convicts on board. In contrast to the Second Fleet, which transported a high number of females, the first transport from Ireland had a majority of male prisoners (84 per cent) on board (Hughes, 1988; National Archives of Ireland).

Shortly after their arrival in September 1791, the Irish were among those convicts clearing land and sowing seed at Rose Hill (west of Sydney). These agricultural efforts were more successful than any previous attempts. When the next crop was harvested, Governor Phillip reported to Home Secretary, Henry Dundas (in March 1792) that the maize that had been harvested was better than expected, particularly in view of the dry weather. He also remarked that the crop was sown late in the year, confirming that Irish convicts were involved in its cultivation.

The 'turn around' from famine to plenty that occurred in a few short years is remarkable, particularly when one considers that prior to this 'the colony came very close to failure from malnutrition' (Wood, 1988: 163). The plausible proposition that I present here is that Irish convicts, many of whom were used in subsistence farming, were able to make the land fertile and productive because they brought the specific farming skills that were needed in the colony at that time. These agricultural skills allowed the Irish to prosper in the new colony. Referring to the Irish during the period between 1792 and 1795, Hirst asserts that 'a well-disposed country worker transported to Australia and assigned to a settler found it very easy to adapt to what was required of him' (1983: 32). This was also evident in later years. For example, historian Patrick O'Farrell's edited volume of *Letters from Irish Australia* highlights the case of Robert Boyd, a convict still under sentence who writes, optimistically, to his wife, declaring that:

> I am happy to inform you that I am master of sixteen head of cattle which I have bought at different (sic) times with money earned after doing my government work and had you been with me I could have had trice as many, so that you may very clearly see what an opportunity there is for well conducted persons.
>
> *(Boyd, 1837, cited in O'Farrell, 1984: 17)*

The success of individuals such as John Lacey, who, following emancipation in 1810, went from a small grant of land to become the owner of 1,080 acres of prime farm land, are a testimony to their accomplishments (Costello, 1987). Indeed, Costello (1987) relates countless individual success stories of Irish prosperity on the land.

Despite these collective steps forward in agriculture, however, a class distinction soon began to crystallise within the colony. Once self-sufficiency had been achieved and the food supply was secure, differences between the Irish and their convict working-class companions surfaced.

Whereas the English and Scots convicts were all Protestants, the Irish were nearly all Catholics. If, in both cases, these religious alliances were merely nominal, they represented a profound divergence in cultural background and orientation, world view, historical experience and sense of values. The Reformation and the politics that followed it had created a gulf across which English Protestant and Irish Catholic beheld each other with incomprehension, hatred and fear (O'Farrell, 1985: 3).

The partial acceptance that allowed the Irish to achieve success was based on needs which had been met by the farming skills that they brought with them to the colony, the importance of farming to the New South Wales economy, and the shortage of labour at that time. Thus, the acceptance of the Irish was confined to their role in supporting the emerging economy, and this conditional acceptance continued for some time. For example, the leading newspaper the *Sydney Atlas* published the following in 1848:

> So long as Catholics confined themselves to religion we shall do not more than smile at their nonsensical mummeries, or pity their senseless superstition but should they engage in 'politics', remorseless resistance, indeed attack, would ensue.
>
> *(Sydney Atlas, 4 May 1848)*

O'Farrell explains that 'politics meant any attempts to change or challenge the colonial *status quo*' (1985: 20). Under this type of scrutiny it was clear that, even fifty-seven years after the arrival of the first Irish convicts, many of the opportunities available in colonial life were not open to them. Consequently, as the next phase will show, when the farming skills that Irish migrants brought to colonial Australia were no longer valued, the hospitality industry provided them with the opportunity to engage in the Australian economy without coming into conflict with the English.

Period two: distribution and preparation

When convict transportation to New South Wales ended in 1840, the colony sought to replace convict labour by introducing assisted passage schemes. A lack of women in the colony also led to 'ardent recruiting activity in the British Isles' (Haines, 1998: 48). Women from England, Wales and Scotland proved less responsive than the Irish and, in fact, the Irish were the only group of emigrants to colonial Australia in which males and females were evenly matched. Fitzpatrick quantifies this, stating that 'whereas men greatly outnumbered women among newcomers from Britain, Europe, and America, the female percentage of Australia's Irish-born population was 48 in 1861, 50 in 1871, 49 in 1891, and 50 in 1901' (1998: 163–164).

Arrivals also increased as a result of the Great Famine in Ireland, during which 'at least 800,000 people, about 10 per cent of the population, died from hunger and disease between 1845 and 1851' (Lee, 1989: 1). The famine left many children orphaned and most ended up in workhouses. As a result, Earl Grey developed a scheme to relocate orphaned girls to Australia so they could escape poverty in Ireland (Costello, 1987). 'Aged from 14 to 19 they had been chosen from the various work-houses and the girls' discipline, education and general appearance was found to reflect great credit on [these institutions]' (Costello, 1987: 129). Indeed, when the first of the Irish orphan girls arrived in Melbourne in late 1848, Government officials reported that all of their employers were very pleased with them. However, attacks on the Irish in the newspapers were common (Rule, 1998) and soon after their arrival an editorial in the *Argus* in Melbourne described them as 'the most useless, ignorant and wasteful lot of females that ever set foot on these shores' (*Argus*, 30 May 1850).

Irish males arriving in Melbourne were also in a tenuous position. They were unable to farm in Victoria because Crown land had not been available for sale. Instead, small allotments were released for housing and wealthy pastoralists squatted on Crown land, dominating agriculture. Effectively farmers without land, the Irish were described by Murtagh (1959) as unprotected proletariats. The social struggles that took place from the 1860s to the 1880s meant that they continually came into conflict with the financially successful pastoralists (Parnaby, 1983).

One avenue by which many of the Irish achieved social improvement without coming into conflict with the protestant majority was via the hospitality industry. In fact, MacDonagh notes that 'they were grossly over-represented ... in the liquor industries and trades' (1986: 165). Irish women in particular focused their domestic service skills on the commercial hospitality industry, operating and maintaining order in hotels and public houses. These skills were sought after because the long distances between pastoral lands and major markets required sustenance along the way, and the demand for hospitality services also grew in direct proportion to increases in the population and because traffic to and from the goldfields of Victoria provided a steady stream of customers (Serle, 1963). Higgs explains that, at the time, 'bar work was one of the few areas available to unskilled men and women' (1991: 70). More importantly, bar maids could earn almost double the annual wage of their counterparts in domestic service (Kirkby, 1989). In addition, 'with relatively small capital outputs, a woman could erect a humble inn with the potential to expand as the colony grew' (Higgs, 1991: 70). Indeed, many of the early inns and hotels were extremely rudimentary, constructed of wooden palings with whitewashed canvas walls. These were gradually improved and expanded when it became a licensing condition to have at least six bedrooms for guests (O'Mahony and Clark, 2013).

Like their farming counterparts in early New South Wales, for many Irish migrants the hospitality industry provided the opportunity to achieve social and financial success, especially in Victoria. O'Mahony (2007) documents the case of Michael Lynch and his sisters Anne and Margaret, all of whom prospered in the colony. Arriving in Melbourne with no resources, within a decade they owned and operated a string of inns and hostelries in Footscray (west of Melbourne) and were able to purchase large land holdings when the first sale of Government land took place in 1851 (Carstairs and Lane, 1988; Selaf, 1989). An analysis of the liquor licensing records of the period highlights countless other Irish men and women who were licence holders in the Footscray region. These include John Murphy, licensee of Raleigh's Punt Hotel in nearby Essendon; Pat Meagher, who owned the Stanley Arms in Footscray and later sold it to Michael Ryan; and the Point Hotel in Kensington which was owned by Patrick O'Toole and later by James Murphy (in 1883), who then sold it to a Mrs O'Connell in 1890 (*Footscray Advertiser*, 26 July 1890). Personal accounts of the Irish-Australian experience contained in letters back to Ireland, published by historian David Fitzpatrick (1995), also show that Irish migrants arriving in Victoria in the mid-1800s arrived during a period of expansion, which occurred first in the town of Melbourne then later in the rest of the District. The demand for food, beverages and accommodation at this time created exceptional opportunities in the hospitality industry, which provided the impetus for the Irish entry into the sector.

By redirecting their efforts away from farming and into hospitality, they were no longer a threat to the pastoralists, mainly because the 'liquor trade', as bar work was termed at the time, was considered an unsavoury business by the Protestant upper classes and thus became what O'Mahony (2007) refers to as 'uncontested space'. On a broader scale, however, their involvement in the 'provision of food, drink and accommodation represents an act of friendship, [and] it creates symbolic ties between people which establish bonds between those involved in sharing hospitality' (Lashley, 2000: 11). This sharing of hospitality, therefore, provided an opportunity for the Irish and the English to gain a better cultural understanding of each other, particularly when the hospitality that they provided was served in hotels and inns that were also the family home. Thus, the Irish were sharing their private space with guests and providing cultural insights into their home environment, albeit for commercial purposes (McWhannell and Lynch, 2000). During this period, the Irish made a significant contribution to the style and essence of the hospitality industry in Australia. In the next period, which involved extensive research with patrons of Irish theme pubs in Melbourne, the vestiges of these Irish values and the characteristics of early hospitality were both confirmed and celebrated over 150 years later.

Period three: consumption

This phase of the study explores the remarkable rise in the popularity of Irish theme pubs in Melbourne and involved a survey of 300 Irish theme pub patrons and a series of in-depth follow-up interviews with twenty-four of those surveyed. Key quotes from these respondents are presented to highlight tier perceptions of the theme pub environment.

While the Irish theme pub is not exclusive to Australia, the findings of this study show that Irish theme pubs in Melbourne are different to those experienced elsewhere. In the UK, for example, the theme pub has been found to be more of a branding exercise, and many of the major elements found in Irish theme pubs in the UK are not evident in Melbourne, for instance live Irish music (Knowles *et al.*, 2000). According to respondents in this study, a high degree of cultural authenticity in Irish themes pubs in Melbourne is perceived. Although many Irish theme pubs in Melbourne are not owned by Irish landlords, owners do attempt to reproduce Irish culture and respondents in this study felt that they were succeeding. The Quiet Man pub in

Flemington in the city's west is a particularly good example because it is surrounded by high-rise housing commission flats, shabby shops and pawnbrokers. Customers are clearly not attracted by these surroundings and data collected from customers of this pub show that many perceive that they are engaging with a recreated Irish environment. One way that this is accomplished is through the employment of young Irish visitors on working holidays who are employed for their Irish accent, attitude and the cultural contribution that they can bring to the theme pubs. In fact, the manner and friendliness of these staff was one of the reasons cited for why Irish theme pubs are so popular. Most respondents felt that the Irish were exceptionally good at portraying this friendliness and, as such, this represented a major attraction.

Many respondents also believed that Irish theme pubs provided an insight into Irish culture. Those with knowledge of Irish history, culture or literature were aware of the relevance of the artefacts and images that they encountered in these pubs, while for others the resonance with Irish culture was based on their knowledge of the history of the Irish in Australia. The manner in which these pubs are decorated, the extensive use of wood and old-fashioned furnishings, was portrayed as distinctly Irish. Thus, it is argued that the decor is, in fact, a cultural bridge that leads one to question what Irish culture actually is perceived to be. Other respondents believed that Irish theme pub owners have managed to harness a number of tangible and intangible cultural elements that are recognised by their customers. In fact, all of the respondents in this study identified at least one cultural attribute in the pubs that they had visited. Des explained that 'it tries to be based, as much as it can be, to an Irish pub and especially designed so that when they come in it is recognised as an Irish pub'. This seems to have had the desired effect on patrons, as Jack articulated when he stated that:

> I think if I were blindfolded and taken into a pub and it's revealed to me I could tell immediately that it is an Irish pub. So in saying that I think that, yes, I think that they have tapped into something that's recognisable. Whether it is fair dinkum Irish or not is a bit hard to say.

One of the attractions of the 'whole package' is the way that Irish pubs expose people to Irish culture in a form that they can relate to and enjoy. This serves to improve the image of the Irish as a race and also increases the popularity of the Irish theme pub. The notion of linking the consumption of food and beverages and the surroundings in which they are consumed with the 'consumption of culture' is not new. Indeed, Bell and Valentine (1997) proposed that, when consuming ethnic cuisine, one might consider oneself to be, if only momentarily, immersed in the culture from which that food is derived.

The majority of respondents were also of the opinion that the Irish were fun and fun-loving, and that Irish theme pubs were places to go to when you wanted to have a laugh. One of the strongest themes that emerged from the interviews was that the Irish are perceived to know how to enjoy themselves. All respondents were asked if they had fun at the Irish theme pubs that they had visited and they unanimously answered that they had. Moreover, most respondents reported that Irish theme pubs were safe environments, even if there were levels of drunkenness that occurred there. This was an acknowledgement that people get drunk in Irish theme pubs but that this drunkenness does not degenerate into unacceptable behaviour. As a result, it is contended that Irish theme pubs have done more to erase the negative images and stereotypes of the past and to create a lasting and accurate picture of the Irish character. In this sense, Irish theme pubs can claim some credit for the fact that 'the Irish stereotype has lost its associations of drunkenness, ignorance and violence, to be replaced by sociability, creativity and a highly developed sense of humanity' (Bishop, 1999: 8).

To the respondents in this study, Irish theme pubs were perceived to be friendly and welcoming establishments with an open and inclusive atmosphere. According to respondents Lauren and Kevin, this inclusiveness is a reflection of the Irish attitude to life and it is this, among other things, which makes Irish theme pubs so much more than just hotel bars. Indeed, Siobhan, who was born in Ireland, contrasted the intimacy of Irish theme pubs with another quality hotel bar, in this case using the Sheraton hotel as an example. Siobhan believes that creating a sense of community is essential to the creation of atmosphere. In Ireland, she asserted, the pub is a very important aspect of community life. She went on to explain that pubs in Ireland were centres for debate, and that 'in Ireland we discuss everything ad nauseum in the pub'. She clarified that 'it's not necessarily what's being discussed but how it's being discussed and how it's being argued amongst people in the pubs'. She reported that it wouldn't be unusual in Ireland to join somebody else's discussion in a pub, and that this occurs in Irish theme pubs in Melbourne as well.

The atmosphere of an Irish theme pub was also found to be a highly valued element of the experience, albeit an abstract, intangible and elusive component. Respondents' descriptions reveal that atmosphere can involve a number of sub-components, for example it is 'relaxed but cheerful' (Stephanie), 'without tension ... welcome ... friendly ... [and] ... pressure free' (Chris), 'it's not intimidating for a woman or for women going out ... [and] you can actually sit there and talk with your friends and not feel threatened that someone's going to come and ... try some pick up lines' (Stephanie). Several other female respondents also remarked that the atmosphere in Irish theme pubs is gender inclusive, respectful and mannerly, and that this was important to them.

Respondents also believed that the *craic*, or fun, sums up the Irish attitude to life, and some reported that this was what they tried to engage with when visiting an Irish theme pub. In order to access and celebrate this aspect of Irish culture, Irish theme pub customers were prepared to change their behaviour to fit in with the values and attitudes that they perceived to be Irish. This is in keeping with Griffin's assertion that 'the physical environment does play a role in the design of human behaviour' (1990: 1). He goes on to advise that people will produce certain learned behavioural responses to certain types of environments. These environments, he concludes, 'ensure that people raised in our western culture will tend to exhibit predictable behavioural patterns when situated within them' (Griffin, 1990: 1).

For many respondents in this study, visits to Irish theme pubs were perceived to be a celebration of Irish culture. Rosemary, for example, sees visits to Irish theme pubs as 'an opportunity to slip into another culture without having to spend the money on the air ticket to get there'. Jack also felt that he was immersing himself in Irish culture, so much so that when he visits P. J. O'Brien's on days when the pub is quiet he looks around to see if 'George Bernard Shaw is actually round in that snug over there whipping out a scene or two'. Jack also believes that there is a cultural resonance involved because:

> a lot of Australian culture is inexorably linked with Irish culture and an understanding of Australian culture has actually got to go back to its grass roots and, in this case, it's partly Irish, partly English, partly Scottish with a flavour of internationalism.

Historically, he stated 'Irish pubs have had a consistent, strong attraction in Australia because ... it's just a familiar thing for a lot of Anglo-Celtic sort of people'. He contends that, even if Australians are not of Irish descent, because they have been surrounded by neighbours and friends who are, they can recognise and understand Irish culture. Another respondent, Ron, who is of Scottish background, felt that he had an intuitive understanding of Irish culture, claiming 'I know these people, I know the history, I know the place, even though I haven't been there'.

Despite an apparent knowledge of Irish culture, Jack, like many of the respondents in this study, had never been to Ireland. Indeed, most of the respondents that expressed strong and interesting views about Irish culture had not been to Ireland. David explained this, noting that he had no Irish links but that he felt an affinity with the Irish-Australian experience. His understanding of this experience was 'of typically but not exclusively coming from convict stock, coming from an underclass, coming from a religious minority'. He recalled his knowledge of Peter Lalor (who led the rebellion on the Victorian Goldfields) and Archbishop Daniel Mannix, reflecting that, because he had never been to Ireland, his perceptions of Irishness are based on his knowledge of those Irish people who were part of the early Australian landscape. Thus, there is a cultural resonance based on ingrained notions of Irish hospitality, culture and humour.

This cultural resonance is based on innate notions of Irish-Australian hospitality as opposed to purely Irish hospitality. For example, the propensity for providing a friendly welcoming atmosphere was identified by several respondents as an Irish cultural attribute, but when probed further it was clear that their perceptions had been fashioned by their knowledge of the Irish in Australia. This association between respondents' perceptions of Irish culture and Irish-Australian history has a number of important implications, mainly because of the history of the Irish involvement in early Australian pubs as described earlier in this chapter.

Conclusions

While the hosting of Australians in Irish theme pubs represents full acceptance of both the Irish and Irish values within Australian society, this integration occurred over a long period of time. Indeed, tension, struggle and adversity mark the history of the Irish in early Australia, and the fact that Irish assimilation occurred at all is significant. Kiernan, for example, advises that 'whereas much Irish national culture may be assimilated, this cannot be the case with Catholicism, as no one would seriously argue that Catholicism can be assimilated into Protestantism' (1984: 5). This is notable because tension in the relationship between the English and the Irish in colonial Australia generally centred on religious differences. There is also a pattern to the manner in which the relationship ebbed and flowed. For example, there were degrees of acceptance by both parties in the early years that included non-acceptance, partial acceptance and, later, full acceptance. Partial acceptance was evident during times of struggle, such as the early attempts to achieve self-sufficiency on the land and the need for a labour force. Once these national impediments had been overcome, however, tension emerged again.

By engaging in the cultivation, distribution and consumption of food and drink, however, the Irish were able to achieve social and financial improvement without coming into conflict with the English. This is significant because there are some similarities between the Irish experience and the manner in which Italian, Greek and Chinese migrants have integrated into Australian society. In his book, *Buongiorno Australia*, for example, historian Robert Pascoe (1987) describes the experience of Italian migrants as fruit and vegetable producers in Victoria. They moved from cultivation into distribution though fruit and vegetable markets and family-run shops in Australian cities and suburbs. This pattern also emerges within the Greek community. For example, Greek migrants have had extensive involvement in the fishing industry and are also well represented in the distribution of seafood within the fish markets and in fish and chip shops throughout Australia. According to Symons (1982), the Chinese community also began life in Australia in a similar manner. In the 1800s, for instance, they were disproportionately represented in market gardening but by the end of the century many had made the transition from cultivation into distribution and were to be found as merchants and shopkeepers in Sydney and Melbourne (Bannerman, 1998).

In concluding this chapter, therefore, it is worth reiterating that the acceptance of the Irish and, more specifically, Irish working-class Catholics into Australian society has been a lengthy process, and social inclusion for the Irish was a battle that was hard fought and won. The role of the hospitality industry was critical to their assimilation and continues to provide a vehicle for social inclusion today. Thus, the popularity of Irish theme pubs in the city and suburbs of Melbourne reflects the progress of Anglo-Irish relations in Australia, and the efforts of the Irish within the food and beverage sector have played a substantive role in smoothing the differences between the English and the Irish, thereby allowing the creation of a 'new' and better society.

References

The Argus, 30 May 1850.

Bannerman, C. (1998) *Acquired Tastes: Celebrating Australia's Culinary History*, Canberra: National Library of Australia.

Bell, D. and Valentine, G. (1997) *Consuming Geographies: We are Where We Eat*, London: Routledge.

Bishop, P. (1999) *The Irish Empire: The Story of the Irish Abroad*, London: Boxtree.

Carstairs, J. and Lane, M. (1988) *Pubs, Punts and Pastures: The Story of Irish Pioneer Women on the Salt Water River*, St. Albans, Vic.: St. Albans Historical Society.

Collins, D. (1798) *An Account of the English Colony in New South Wales: With Remarks on the Disposition, Customs, Manners, & c. of the Native Inhabitants of That Country*, London: T. Cadell (Libraries Board of South Australia, Facsimile Edition, 1971).

Costello, C. (1987) *Botany Bay: The Story of the Convicts Transported from Ireland to Australia, 1791–1853*, Cork: Mercier Press.

Fitzpatrick, D. (1995) *Oceans of Consolation: Personal Accounts of Irish Migration to Australia*, Melbourne: Melbourne University Press.

Fitzpatrick, D. (1998) 'This is the place that foolish girls are knowing': reading the letters of emigrant Irish women in colonial Australia. In McClaughlin, T. (ed.) *Irish Women in Colonial Australia*, Sydney: Allen & Unwin, pp. 163–181.

Footscray Advertiser (1959) *Footscray's First 100 Years: The Story of a Great Australian City*, Footscray, Vic.: The Advertiser in association with Footscray City Council.

Grenville, W. W. (1789a) Letter from the Right Hon. Lord Grenville to Governor Phillip (19 June 1789), *Historical Records of Australia*, Series 1, Vol. 1, p. 121.

Grenville, W. W. (1789b) Letter from the Right Hon. Lord Grenville to Governor Phillip (24 December 1789), *Historical Records of Australia*, Series 1, Vol. 1, p. 133.

Griffin, T. (1990) The physical environment of the college classroom and its affects on students, *Campus Ecologist* 8, 1: 1–5.

Haines, R. (1998) 'The priest made a bother about it': the travails of 'that unhappy sisterhood' bound for colonial Australia. In McClaughlin, T. (ed.) *Irish Women in Colonial Australia*, Sydney: Allen & Unwin, pp. 43–63.

Higgs, B. (1991) But I wouldn't want my wife to work there! A history of discrimination against women in the hotel industry, *Australian Feminist Studies* 14, Summer: 69–81.

Hirst, J. B. (1983) *Convict Society and its Enemies: A History of Early New South Wales*, Sydney: Allen & Unwin.

Hughes, R. (1988) *The Fatal Shore*, New York: Random House.

Kiernan, C. (1984) Introduction. In Kiernan, C. (ed.) *Ireland and Australia*, Dublin: Mercier Press.

Kirkby, D. (1989) Women's work as barmaids, *Lilith* 6, Spring: 96.

Knowles, T., Howley, M. and Joudallah, B. (2000) The preservation of the UK public house: past, present and future. Proceedings of the Council of Australian University Hospitality and Tourism Educators Conference, Adelaide.

Lashley, C. (2000) Towards a theoretical understanding. In Lashley, C. and Morrison, A. (eds) *In Search of Hospitality: Theoretical Perspectives and Debates*, Oxford: Butterworth-Heinemann, pp. 1–17.

Lee, J. (1989) *The Modernisation of Irish Society 1848–1918*, Dublin: Gill & Macmillan.

MacDonagh, O. (1986) The Irish in Australia: a general view. In MacDonagh, O. and Mandle, W. F. (eds) *Ireland and Irish-Australia: Studies in Cultural and Political History*, London: Croom Helm, pp. 155–174.

McWhannell, D. and Lynch, P. (2000) Home and commercialised hospitality. In Lashley, C. and Morrison, A. (eds) *In Search of Hospitality: Theoretical Perspectives and Debates*, Oxford: Butterworth-Heinemann, pp. 100–117.

Murtagh, J. G. (1959) *Australia: The Catholic Chapter*, Melbourne: The Polding Press.

National Archives of Ireland, Official Papers, CSO OP vol. 1, 1788–1831.

O'Farrell, P. (1984) *Letters from Irish Australia 1825–1929*, Sydney: New South Wales University Press and Belfast: Ulster Historical Foundation.

O'Farrell, P. (1985) *The Catholic Church and Community: An Australian History*, Sydney: University of New South Wales Press.

O'Mahony, B. (2007) Uncontested space: case studies of the Irish involvement in the hospitality industry in colonial Victoria, *International Journal of Culture, Tourism and Hospitality Research* 1, 3: 203–213.

O'Mahony, G. B. and Clark, I. (2013) From inns to hotels: the evolution of public houses in colonial Victoria, *International Journal of Contemporary Hospitality Management* 25, 2: 172–186.

Parnaby, J. E. (1983) Charles Gavan Duffy in Australia. In MacDonagh, O., Mandle, W. F. and Travers, P. (eds) *Irish Culture and Nationalism, 1750–1950*, London: Macmillan, pp. 56–68.

Pascoe, R. (1987) *Buongiorno Australia: Our Italian Heritage*, Richmond, Vic.: Greenhouse.

Phillip, A. (1788) Letter from Governor Phillip to Undersecretary Nepean (9 July 1788), *Historical Records of Australia*, Series 1, Vol. 1, p. 56.

Phillip, A, (1790a) Letter from Governor Phillip to Lord Sydney (13 February 1790), *Historical Records of Australia*, Series 1, Vol. 1, p. 158.

Phillip, A. (1790b) Letter from Governor Phillip to the Right Hon. W.W. Grenville (14 July 1790), *Historical Records of Australia*, Series 1, Vol. 1, pp. 195–197.

Phillip, A. (1792) Letter from Governor Phillip to Home Secretary Dundas (2 October 1792), *Historical Records of Australia*, Series 1, Vol. 1, p. 374.

Rees, S. (2001) *The Floating Brothel*, Sydney: Hodder Headline Australia.

Rule, P. (1998) 'Tell father and mother not to be unhappy for I am very comfortable': a sketch of Irish women's experiences in colonial Victoria. In McClaughlin, T. (ed.) *Irish Women in Colonial Australia*, Sydney: Allen & Unwin, pp. 123–141.

Selaf, G. (ed.) (1989) *Footscray: A Pictorial Record of the Municipality from 1859–1988*, Melbourne: City of Footscray.

Serle, G. (1963) *The Golden Age: A History of the Colony of Victoria, 1851–1961*, Melbourne: Melbourne University Press.

The Sydney Atlas, 4 May 1848.

Symons, M. (1982) *One Continuous Picnic*, Adelaide: Duck Press.

Tench, W. (2009 [1788]) *Watkin Tench's 1788*, ed. T. Flannery, Melbourne: Text Publishing.

Walker, R. B. and Roberts, D. C. (1988) Colonial food habits: 1788–1900. In Truswell, A. and Wahlqvist, M. (eds) *Food Habits in Australia*, Melbourne: Rene Gordon, pp. 40–59. Available at http://apjcn.nhri.org.tw/server/markwpapers/mark_books/foodhabits.html. Accessed 2016.

Wood, B. (1988) Food and alcohol in Australia: an historical overview: 1788–1938. In Truswell, A. and Wahlqvist, M. (eds) *Food Habits in Australia*, Melbourne: Rene Gordon. Available at http://apjcn.nhri.org.tw/server/markwpapers/mark_books/foodhabits.html. Accessed 2016.

16

Women experience hospitality as travelers and leaders

Judi Brownell

Key themes

Women's communication style

Servant leaders

Needs of women travelers

Positive change in the hospitality workplace

Women's voices have not always been heard. The stories they tell have often been whispered, shared with other women in private, quiet places. Historically, many women had no career goals of their own, but derived satisfaction from serving and caring for their families, friends, and communities. This was particularly true in the United States during the 1950s, when new products for the home came on the market and women drew their identities from roles as wife and mother. The media contributed to this image of women at the center of domestic activity (Brownell and Walsh, 2008). Respectable women stayed in the home, served as needed, cared for their husband and children. They were sensitive to others' needs, often suppressing their own strong emotions to please their loved ones. And they always listened.

During the following decades, changes began that would dramatically affect both the family and the hospitality workplace. As the US economy moved from manufacturing to service, women were not only in demand but were choosing to work outside the home. While gaining increased independence, they continued to be the primary caregiver and homemaker. The jobs they obtained were largely limited to positions of service and support; gender stereotypes regarding the suitability of women for employment persisted, and constrained the types of work women were offered.

As the twenty-first century approached, increasing numbers of women began to move into positions of greater responsibility and opportunity. Gender-linked assumptions regarding their potential and effectiveness, however, remained. Perhaps one of the most significant stereotypes

DOI: 10.4324/9781315679938-18

that continue to hinder women's career development relates to their communication style. Characterized as weak, passive, and ineffective, women have struggled over the years to gain recognition and credibility for their accomplishments. Gender stereotypes persisted; relatively few women were able to overcome this barrier and move beyond middle management into hospitality leadership positions.

This chapter focuses on women in hospitality in the United States. We propose that the characteristics that traditionally have been viewed as hindering a woman's ability to fully experience the world and hold leadership roles are, in fact, key to their potential to make unique contributions to hospitality. Women's voices have gained strength and clarity as they have realized the promise and power of their gender-linked communication styles and accompanying competencies. We suggest here that women embrace the affective side of communication that, as we will discuss, distinguishes their ways of traveling and leading. In this chapter we demonstrate that recognizing and embracing these characteristics results in satisfaction as a traveler and effectiveness as a hospitality leader.

While women have come a long way over the last few decades, the goal is no longer to develop a more masculine style to compete with men for senior positions in the workplace. Gender differences will always exist; gender will always influence perceptions, shape experiences, and direct behavior. Men and women view the world from different perspectives, hold different assumptions and make sense of events through gender-specific lenses. They also communicate differently. Here, we focus on what these differences mean for how women can directly shape their hospitality experience; first by increasing their satisfaction as a guest and then by relying on their gender-linked communication strengths to lead hospitality organizations. We propose women's voices as a theme, envisioning a future characterized by increased satisfaction and credibility in the hospitality experience. Women achieve these two outcomes by embracing and applying their gender-linked strengths—most notably, emotional awareness and sensitivity and empathic listening.

This chapter begins with a brief overview of gender differences in communication, focusing on the two specific communication competencies that give women a distinct advantage. These two competencies, emotional sensitivity and listening, are then examined as they shape women's travel experience and as they facilitate women's leadership effectiveness. Women are traveling alone in rapidly increasing numbers, and our first discussion focuses on how the travel experience is enhanced when women recognize and seek settings that elicit the emotions that are key to their satisfaction. Next, our focus turns to the hospitality workplace where we review several of the traditional gender-linked challenges women have confronted. We then explain how two key gender-linked communication competencies, emotional sensitivity and listening, position women to become effective Servant Leaders. We further suggest that, as women assume leadership in hospitality, they are well-positioned to create environments that are not only satisfying to travelers but also inclusive and respectful of women employees in the hospitality workplace.

Women communicate

Boys and girls grow up with different social experiences, different expectations, and from an early age begin to exhibit distinctly different communication styles (Pearson, 1995). While a variety of gender-linked communication behaviors have been identified and studied, we concentrate on those associated with the affective domain as they are particularly relevant to our discussion of women's hospitality experience. Specifically, we focus on emotional sensitivity and responsiveness, and listening. These behaviors have significant implications for women traveling, serving, and leading.

Women high in emotional intelligence

We know that women have stronger emotional, personal responses to their experiences than do men (Sinclair *et al.*, 2010). A focus on feelings and emotions characterizes what Bloom and his colleagues (1964) call the affective response. These sensitivities have more recently been captured in a set of competencies referred to as EI, or Emotional Intelligence (Goleman, 1996). Individuals with a high EI are aware of their own emotions and particularly sensitive to feelings expressed by others. Such individuals are skilled at interpreting nonverbal cues and using this information to guide their thinking and actions. Individuals who are high in the social awareness component of EI are most likely to support and develop others.

Emotional Intelligence appears to be stronger for women than for men—that is, women pay more attention to and respond more readily to the affective elements of a situation (Simon and Nath, 2004). Studies indicate that women process information more comprehensively, assimilating a variety of nonverbal cues in responding to their environment (Pan and Ryan, 2007). As a result of gender differences in information processing and decoding capacities, men and women do not perceive their physical surroundings in the same manner (Ganesan-Lim *et al.*, 2008).

Women also use emotion in making choices to a much greater degree than do men (Raman *et al.*, 1995). Because they are more sensitive to contextual elements and can access their emotional responses more readily, women depend more heavily on affect and, subsequently, they use it more extensively in making judgments about the quality of their experiences. Men, on the other hand, are more outcome-focused and consider fewer cues in their assessments (Iacobucci and Ostrom, 1993). While in the past women were reluctant to acknowledge their dependence on the emotional component of their experience, particularly in business settings, the affective response is now recognized as a powerful and often neglected aspect of service and effective leadership.

Women high in empathic listening

Closely related to Emotional Intelligence is empathic listening. There is little question that women and men exhibit different listening preferences and strategies. Women, as noted earlier, are more likely than men to recognize emotions and to demonstrate empathy. Tannen (1990) points out that women are socialized to hear a language of connection and intimacy, whereas men speak and hear a language of status and independence. The storytelling typical of a man's communication style is often about gaining attention and recognition.

In addition, women are more likely to share their personal concerns and respond with sensitivity to the needs and feelings others express. Women demonstrate their interest by asking probing questions to draw out their partner, and then demonstrate concern with clear nonverbal responses. In face-to-face encounters, women typically use more eye contact and significantly more facial expression than do men. Women's style is empowering in its other-centered focus; the speaker feels valued and understood (Arliss, 2001; Brownell, 2013).

Since effective listening requires the interpretation of meaning, men and women hear messages consistent with their personal interests and motives. As Tannen again explains, "We all want to be heard, but not merely to be heard. We want to be understood—heard for what we think we are saying, for what we know we meant" (1990: 48). Women's communication preferences differ from men's in other significant ways as well. For instance, men more frequently interrupt than do women. Men spend much more of their talk time telling stories, often enhancing them for entertainment value. It is not unusual for men to emphasize the humorous aspects of an event. Women, on the other hand, personalize their message, often emphasizing the emotional aspects (Brownell, 1992; Pearson, 1995). A women experiencing and retelling the same event is likely to focus on how it made them feel, emphasizing their frustration, concern, or excitement.

As women begin to travel widely and as they move into leadership positions, they too will have stories to tell, stories that reinforce positive images of successful women and that highlight the value of women's gender-linked communication competencies. Women's more emotional experience when on a journey becomes significant as increasing numbers of women begin to travel.

Women experience travel

While women have long been responsible for planning family travel, there has been a recent and steady increase in the number of women traveling alone (Khan, 1999). Since the Wyndham Hotel Group pioneered its programs and resources for women travelers in 1995, women have become an increasingly larger share of the business travel market. Currently, nearly half of all US business travelers are female, and that number is projected to increase throughout the coming decades (Barletta, 2006; U.S. Travel Association, 2014). As hospitality organizations confirm the significant impact this expanding market has on their bottom line, increased attention is being placed on better understanding how women experience travel.

Although some may argue that men and women want essentially the same things from their travel experience, recent research suggests otherwise (Smith and Carmichael, 2006; Newth, 2009). As we have discussed, emotions have a significant effect on women's perceptions and judgments. Attending to the affective component of the traveler's experience is key to satisfying guests, particularly women on the road.

Since women use emotion in their decision making to a much greater degree than their male counterparts (Pan and Ryan, 2007), creating an environment that elicits positive affect is likely to have a significant impact on women's travel choices and subsequent satisfaction. By better understanding the female business traveler, whose preferences are more strongly influenced by how the travel experience makes them feel, women's distinctive needs and preferences can be addressed.

Women business travelers in the US

The majority of women traveling alone are on business. A recent survey described the typical woman business traveler as a baby boomer who has a bachelor's degree, is married with no children at home, and who takes at least four trips a year. These women view business travel as necessary to their career advancement. When Newth (2009) examined women travelers on the dimensions of experience, income, rank, age, and education, she found that variations in personal characteristics, needs, and behaviors could be clustered into one of three distinct demographic groups which she labeled connective, empowered, and productive.

Women are not only traveling more frequently, they are traveling differently than their male counterparts. Over half of room nights spent by women are associated with multi-night stays for meetings, conferences, or conventions. Importantly, women more frequently include personal time as part of their business trip: 44 percent incorporate leisure experiences into their travel and over 20 percent of women business travelers add vacation days to extend their stay (NYU Tisch Center, 2003). Clearly, women seek and create experiences that provide positive emotional responses.

One of the most comprehensive surveys of women business travelers, *Coming of Age: The continuing evolution of female business travelers,* was conducted through the Tisch Center at New York University in collaboration with Wyndham Hotels (NYU Tisch Center, 2003). In this recent study, 596 women were asked a range of questions pertaining to their travel preferences and experiences. Researchers found that women travelers seldom took their families on business trips. The majority of respondents felt little stress or guilt about traveling and being away from home. Nearly 80 percent of the women surveyed indicated that they viewed travel as essential to their job and few saw it as disrupting family life. The women who responded felt that business travel not only contributed to their professional advancement but also provided the freedom from daily routines that enabled them to renew and re-energize. As in similar surveys, results indicated that women business travelers frequently incorporated relaxation and leisure time into their business trips (Brown, 2003). Much research supports the notion that positive affect—consumption emotions such as comfort and pleasure—is directly related to guest satisfaction, and this appears to be particularly true for women travelers (Barsky and Nash, 2002; Bigne et al., 2008).

There seems to be no doubt that guests vary in the degree to which cognitive and affective aspects influence their hotel selection and overall judgments regarding the quality of their stay (Joseph and Newman, 2010). Only recently have women been clear in expressing their dissatisfaction with the traditional, male-focused travel experience and in identifying ways in which their travel can be enhanced.

The hotel experience

To determine the specific affective experience women seek, literature on women business travelers from the last two decades was analyzed. Four distinct affective states were identified as recurring themes. From this review, it appears that women are most satisfied when their hotel experience elicits the following four emotions: feelings of safety, feelings of comfort, feelings of empowerment, and the feeling of being valued (Brownell, 2011).

Feelings of safety

Above all, women want to feel safe. John Portman and Associates, for instance, conducted a survey of what women want when they travel (Carbasho, 2002). This study of 13,000 women from Fortune 1,000 companies confirmed what numerous previous studies of women's travel needs had revealed: women wanted to know that the hotel was concerned with keeping them safe when away from home (Kamberg, 2001; McCoy-Ullrich, 2002). Unlike male travelers who were satisfied with information about fire exits and in-room safes, women were more concerned with their personal safety from intruders or assaults (Newell, 2009). Examples of specific measures hotels have taken include well-lit hallways, covered parking, and dead bolts on doors (Coleman, 2002).

Feelings of comfort

Women are more concerned about getting a good night's sleep than are their male counterparts. The National Sleep Foundation and Hilton Hotels conducted a joint study and discovered that nearly 20 percent more women than men are concerned with travel-related sleep issues. Nearly 80 percent of women surveyed believed that sleep is itself a valuable use of time while 30 percent of their male counterparts saw sleep as "a waste of time" (Hamilton, 1999). Women take sleep seriously and are twice as likely to bring their own pillow when they travel.

Women seek relaxation and comfort from their hotel experience. Women travelers have inspired such innovations as Westin's Heavenly Bed, which features multiple layers of sheets, a down comforter, and a pillow-top mattress (Swift, 2000). Numerous attributes of the hotel room environment itself—heat, light, sound, color—contribute to perceptions of comfort and relaxation, with increasing numbers of hotels striving to create a spa-like ambience (Baker and Cameron, 1996; Hinkin and Tracey, 1998).

Feelings of empowerment

When Newth (2009) studied women business travelers, the one thing all women in her sample had in common was the desire to feel empowered. Surveys reveal that women seek business travel to broaden their horizons, contribute to their professional advancement, and provide freedom from daily routines. Nearly 80 percent of women surveyed indicated that they viewed travel as essential to their job, and few saw it as disrupting family life. Studies indicate that women travelers, regardless of their profile, find travel empowering. When on the road, opportunities to exercise on site, request room service, or take advantage of the executive lounge give women a sense of well-being and enjoyment.

Room service and the convenience of in-room facilities play an important role in helping women on the road achieve a sense of independence and well-being (Sharkey, 2002). A 2001 study, for instance, found that over 75 percent of women order room service at least once a day when traveling compared to 54 percent of men (Carbasho, 2002). In a 2003 study (Brown), the top-ranked "must haves" for women business travelers included mini-bars (71 percent) and spa services on the premises (47 percent). In addition, women seek hotels with an on-site fitness center (Coleman, 2002). When women business travelers were surveyed by Kempinski hotels, workout facilities were ranked first among the features of an "ideal" accommodation (Hart, 1993).

Feelings of being valued

Beyond standard services, women also appreciate an array of amenities that make them feel pampered and valued. A recurring theme that has emerged in recent surveys is that women on the road do not feel that the travel industry values them. Hotels have begun to respond to this concern by providing up-graded amenities, brand-name bath products, make-up mirrors, fresh flowers, and flavored coffees and teas. Women also enjoy large windows, light colored walls, and stylish room furnishings (Swift, 2000; Coleman, 2002).

Without doubt, women find travel satisfying when their emotional needs are met. Addressing these needs can be accomplished in any number of ways. For those seeking to satisfy women travelers, changes can be implemented in each of three categories—amenities, facilities, and services—to enhance one or more of the four desired affective components of a traveler's experience. We suggest, however, that it is not a particular amenity or service or facility that all women want; rather, women travelers respond more holistically to their service and surroundings (Gobe and Zyman, 2010). Positive hotel experiences for women travelers engage their senses and make them feel safe, comfortable, empowered, and valued.

Hotels respond to the women business traveler

The informed selection of both tangible and intangible elements—colors, sizes, lighting, and other features—can create environments that contribute to eliciting a particular emotion. It seems clear that a holistic approach to increasing guest satisfaction by addressing affective as well as cognitive elements of the travel experience is likely to result in higher levels of satisfaction for women travelers (Verhoef et al., 2009). Since the emotion-eliciting items within the service environment can be managed, women travelers' satisfaction can be increased by focusing on the fit between the specific emotions that drive satisfaction and the characteristics of the particular hospitality experience (Han and Back, 2007; Cambern and Goulder, 2009). Those seeking to please women travelers have nearly unlimited options in addressing their emotional needs.

The industry's response to women travelers has been accelerating as more properties explore ways to increase satisfaction through enhancements in amenities, facilities, and services. An increasing number of hotels are developing spa-like, relaxing environments designed especially to meet women's preferences (Aggeles, 2010). San Francisco-based Kimpton Hotels and Restaurants began its *Women in Touch* program to celebrate women travelers by anticipating their needs (Cambern and Goulder, 2009). The Pan Pacific San Francisco supplies its female guests with a personal escort to their room. In Illinois, both Loews and Wyndham hotels set aside networking tables in their restaurants for solo women who prefer to dine with others (McCoy-Ullrich, 2002). W Hotels provides its female travelers with *Wonder Woman* packages designed to make their stay more relaxing. Crown Plaza has made the 11th floor of its hotel women only, and has further addressed women's preferences by providing covered parking close to the lobby entrance of other properties (Gioia, 2007). In Miami, Don Shula's Hotel & Golf Club has created the Patrician floor of 18 rooms exclusively for women, and experiences an average of 95 percent occupancy. The property also keeps a complete history of female guests so that it can better anticipate their needs upon return.

In spite of significant progress, additional questions remain. Among them:

1   How do women's experiences and preferences compare to hotel managers' perceptions of women travelers' needs?
2   Is there a hierarchy of women business travelers' needs that hotel managers would be well-advised to consider?
3   What services, amenities, and facilities have the most direct influence on women's affective responses? Is there a threshold related to various affective states?
4   Can the women business traveler market be further segmented? What variables most directly affect women's needs and preferences?
5   What impact does women's travel have on work and family balance? On career advancement? Are there different consequences for men's and women's travel?

Not only have women spoken out regarding their travel preferences, they are also capitalizing on their gender-linked communication preferences as they move into positions as hospitality leaders. Empathetic listening and emotional sensitivity combine to make women particularly effective leaders in the hospitality workplace, a setting that has traditionally posed challenges for female employees. While for decades our notion of leadership was largely male-dominated, the last decades have witnessed a growing recognition of the power of women's communication competencies in creating highly effective service environments. The emotional self-awareness and sensitivity that we recognize in woman travelers also serves women well as they extend their influence to become Servant Leaders who are well-prepared to address issues requiring emotional sensitivity and understanding.

Women experience the hospitality workplace

We begin by highlighting aspects of the hospitality environment that have long created challenges for women employees and guests. Gender influences interpersonal dynamics and this is particularly true in strong and sexualized hospitality environments. Workplace cultures are created through the rituals that are enacted, the company policies that are enforced, and the stories that are repeated to new organizational members. Norms used to guide action, as well as long-established expectations both contribute to a culture that has not always been respectful of women. Hospitality implies meeting needs, having a good time, doing whatever it takes to satisfy. Images of the industry include wine glasses and moonlit patios, whirlpools, and breakfast trays. Symbols of romance, of feeling good, of access, predominate (Brownell, 1992).

Often the amount of contact between individual employees can at least partially explain gender behavior in what Gutek and her colleagues (1990) termed a "sexualized" work environment. In hospitality, many employees work in close proximity to one another. Their shifts are long and irregular, often including evening and nighttime hours. The duties of hospitality workers are likely to take them into settings traditionally associated with sexual behavior—bedrooms, bars, and lounges. In other instances, employees work poolside in a casual, informal atmosphere. In addition, hospitality employees are often hired, in part, because of outgoing personalities and physical attractiveness. In many instances their required dress accentuates gender differences and sexuality (Brownell, 1992).

The characteristics of hospitality organizations also make them challenging environments for women when they are serving guests. "Good service" is largely a subjective assessment, defined by individual perceptions and expectations. Often, the guest becomes a "partial employee," managing a set of expectations regarding how he or she will be treated. Expectations for women, who have traditionally been perceived as service providers or as sexual objects, may not be in keeping with their understanding of what their job entails. Problems also arise when employees are asked for specific services on the basis of their gender. In such cases, employees must manage "moments of truth," specific decisions that have an impact on meeting the guest's expectations.

The way in which hospitality leaders respond to inappropriate gender-related behaviors is critical in shaping the hospitality experience for the women who work there. Much of the literature on gender differences in communication suggests that women in leadership positions would benefit from adopting a number of more masculine behaviors. Training programs have emphasized that women's communication styles disadvantage them, and that the behaviors typical of men's interactions would assist women as they seek to gain credibility, claim their equal status, and continue to develop professionally.

Here we suggest that it is precisely women's gender-linked communication preferences and competencies that ultimately will enable them to achieve their goals—whether by clearly defining the emotions that constitute a positive travel experience or by demonstrating their effectiveness as hospitality leaders through listening and responsiveness. The following section describes a leadership style that highlights women's natural communication competencies and that facilitates their ability to have a positive and lasting impact in addressing the challenges women confront in the hospitality workplace.

Women experience leadership

Servant Leadership is an emerging framework from which to appreciate the power of women's gender-linked communication preferences. The Servant Leader is uniquely equipped to empower hospitality employees and serve the unique needs of women travelers. Such leaders demonstrate the sensitivities and competencies required for effectiveness in a diverse workplace. The essence of Servant Leadership is that the leader is motivated by a desire to serve and empower others. Such leaders are well-positioned to respond to the preferences of women travelers and to support and nurture women at work (Greenleaf, 1977; Avolio and Gardner, 2005; Brownell, 2010).

The principles of Servant Leadership are particularly relevant when leaders seek to distinguish themselves by their employee-centered practices (Russell and Stone, 2002; Barbuto and Wheeler, 2006). Servant Leaders rely on their emotional sensitivities and engage in continuous self-reflection and active listening (Ciulla, 1995; May et al., 2003; Washington et al., 2006). Such behavior is critical as it influences choices and shapes subsequent interpretations of events (Russell, 2001). A woman's ability to listen empathically and to include affective as well as cognitive dimensions in problem solving positions her well to navigate challenging organizational environments. Through genuine consideration for the employee's welfare, Servant Leaders effectively resolve conflict, promote inclusiveness, and engage in numerous activities that directly shape and enhance employees' workplace experience (Kouzes and Posner, 1995).

Servant Leaders are distinguished by how they behave. Their focus of concern, motivation, and means of influence can be distinguished from more well-known leadership styles. Among the defining activities of a Servant Leader are active listening, stewardship, and a strong commitment to both human development and building community (Spears, 1998). The Servant Leader is accountable to those she serves. Servant Leader practices are powerful in facilitating excellent service by empowering employees and encouraging them to take personal responsibility for their decisions and behavior.

Assessment instruments have also provided support for a number of characteristics shared by Servant Leaders (Russell and Stone, 2002; Mayer et al., 2008; Rennaker, 2008). One survey examines Patterson's seven-component theory of Servant Leadership (2003) which assesses humility, trust, and empowerment, among other factors (Dennis and Bocarnea, 2005). Typically, instruments also address such factors as stewardship (Barbuto and Wheeler, 2006) and service orientation.

Women's communication style provides them with a powerful opportunity to create strong service cultures that encourage respectful behavior in today's workplace. One of the most relevant and distinctive outcomes is the development of an inclusive environment for women at work. The Servant Leader views employees as responsible organizational citizens and then focuses on supporting and responding to the needs she identifies (Blanchard, 1995; Graham, 1995). The trust Servant Leaders place in others allows them to take initiative in performing their jobs. It also inspires employees to become "exemplary followers" who are more likely themselves to demonstrate empathy and concern for their guests (Banutu-Gomez, 2004). Numerous researchers have recognized that the trust resulting from Servant Leadership practices encourages organizational citizenship behavior and the sense of community so central to a productive workplace (Ehrhart, 2004: 62).

The Servant Leader philosophy is also directly aligned with the activities required to satisfy women travelers. Servant Leaders practice leadership as hospitality (Bennett, 2007). The assumption, "I am a leader, therefore I serve," is embedded in the concept of the woman's role, one to whom the guest's welfare is entrusted (Sendjaya and Sarros, 2002). The Servant Leader sees herself as a steward of the organization and a facilitator of healthy organizational practices (Block, 1993; Russell, 2001).

As definitions of customer service turn to customer care, Servant Leadership becomes increasingly relevant. Servant Leaders understand, appreciate, and care for their guests (Schueler, 2000). Employees, inspired by the example their leader sets, are also more likely to provide generous and genuine care to travelers. When employees take personal responsibility for addressing each guest's needs, when they serve out of a personal commitment to provide value and assistance, service becomes authentic and quality increases. This customization of service translates into high emotional satisfaction, particularly for women on the road (Spears, 1996; Autry, 2004; Covey, 2006).

A Servant Leader's scope of concern extends beyond the guest and the organization and into the larger social and physical environment. These leaders feel a profound responsibility to participate in and contribute to the communities to which they belong, thereby extending their reach to all stakeholders (Banutu-Gomez, 2004). Servant Leaders' fundamental philosophy of stewardship ensures their commitment to protect both people and resources.

Experiencing the future: women's voices

We have seen that the gender differences that have long been thought to disadvantage women are now recognized as critical to effective hospitality leadership. Women who embrace a model of Servant Leadership are well-positioned to meet the needs of women travelers, empower women in the hospitality workplace, and create socially conscious organizational cultures that value service and community engagement.

Women in hospitality leadership will undoubtedly listen to the voices of women travelers who are more freely making their travel preferences known. While there was a time when women on the road simply accepted the standard travel practices, their growing comfort with requesting changes to the status quo is likely to result in higher quality experiences for all travelers. The travel experience itself is important to women, especially when traveling alone. Servant Leaders who are responsive to women travelers' needs will ensure that their travel is safe, comfortable, empowering, and that they feel valued.

Servant Leaders are also well-positioned to address the gender issues surrounding women in the hospitality workplace. Their emphasis on listening and emotional awareness enables them to readily recognize and address the gender-related challenges women confront. As increasing numbers of women move into leadership positions, the situation for women employees is likely to dramatically improve. As Servant Leaders, we can expect that women will empower their employees, listening with empathy to voices that have not always been heard. Women leaders are well-prepared to understand individual concerns and then provide the support and resources required to give women working in hospitality the necessary confidence and competence as they develop in their careers. As the workplace becomes more diverse, these behaviors will have an even greater impact.

Leadership positions also open opportunities for women to create more inclusive, respectful, and socially conscious organizational cultures. As they welcome women travelers and encourage women in the workplace, Servant Leaders also extend their influence to care for the welfare of their neighborhoods by providing service beyond the walls of their organizational settings. Women have always been at the heart of the family, and as leaders their sensitivities and other-centered focus facilitate their involvement in service activities that benefit a larger community.

Conclusions

As we look to the future, we recognize women's emerging influence in shaping the hospitality experience. It becomes clear that women have unlimited potential to serve as a positive force in transforming service environments. The hospitality workplace, which has always presented challenges for women traveling, working, and leading, is built on assumptions and expectations that must change. Women are speaking out about the experiences they seek from travel and are leading hospitality organizations by trusting their emotional competence and their listening effectiveness. Women are giving voice to their preferences and abilities; their satisfaction and success results from embracing their distinctive perspectives and competencies, both on the road and in the board room.

If women's ways of traveling and leading are to continue to impact the hospitality experience, women in all positions must be prepared to confront challenges with the courage of their convictions. While women in hospitality are making progress, the journey has been slow and the path often winding and uphill. The number of women leaving the hospitality industry is still too high; the number of women reaching senior leadership positions is still too low. This situation has been intensified by women's assumptions that their gender-linked communication behaviors were less effective in the workplace than a man's more direct and assertive style. It is the affective side of communication that distinguishes women's ways of traveling and leading. By recognizing and embracing their strengths in emotional intelligence combined with effective listening, women are well-positioned to become courageous Servant Leaders who enhance the experiences of their guests, employees, and communities.

References

Aggeles, T. (2010) Hospital's new women's unit designed for spa ambience, *St. Petersburg Times*, May 11, tampabay.com. Available at http://license.icopyright.net/user/viewFreeUse.act?fuid=MTEz MTAwMzY%3D. Accessed November 7, 2015.

Arliss, L. (2001) *Gender Communication*, Englewood Cliffs, NJ: Prentice-Hall.

Autry, J. A. (2004) *The Servant Leader: How to Build a Creative Team, Develop Great Morale, and Improve Bottom-line Performance*, New York: Three Rivers Press.

Avolio, B. and Gardner, W. L. (2005) Authentic leadership development: getting to the root of positive forms of leadership, *Leadership Quarterly* 16, 3: 315–338.

Baker, J. and Cameron, M. (1996) The effects of service environment on affect and consumer perceptions of waiting time: an integrative review and research proposition, *Journal of the Academy of Marketing Science* 24, 4: 338–349.

Banutu-Gomez, M. (2004) Great leaders teach exemplary followership and serve as servant leaders, *Journal of American Academy of Business* 4: 143–161.

Barbuto, J. E. Jr. and Wheeler, D. W. (2006) Scale development and construct clarification of servant leadership, *Group & Organization Management* 31, 3: 300–326.

Barletta, M. (2006) *Marketing to Women: How to Increase your Share of the World's Largest Market*, Chicago, IL: Dearborn.

Barsky, J. and Nash, L. (2002) Evoking emotion: affective keys to hotel loyalty, *Cornell Hospitality and Restaurant Administration Quarterly* 43, 1: 39–46.

Bennett, J. B. (2007) Engaged, but not heroic, academic leadership, *Academic Leadership: The Online Journal* 2, 4: 235–244.

Bigne, E., Mattila, A. S., and Andreu, L. (2008) The impact of experiential consumption cognitions and emotions on behavioral intentions, *Journal of Services Marketing* 22, 4: 303–315.

Blanchard, K. (1995) Servant leadership, at Appleseed.org, http://www.appleseeds.org/Blanchard-Serv-Lead.htm. Accessed December 2, 2015.

Block, P. (1993) *Stewardship: Choosing Service or Self-Interest*, San Francisco: Berrett-Koehler.

Bloom, B. S., Engelhart, M. D., Furst, E. J., Hill, W. H., and Krathwohl, D. R. (1964) *Taxonomy of Educational Objectives: The Classification of Educational Goals*, New York: David McKay.

Brown, K. (2003) Second groundbreaking survey challenges stereotypes surrounding women business travelers, NYU Press Release, October 28.

Brownell, J. (1992) Gender and communication in the hospitality industry. In Arliss, L. P. and Borisoff, D. J. (eds.) *Women and Men Communicating: Challenges and Changes*, Fort Worth, TX: Harcourt Brace Jovanovich, pp. 193–216.

Brownell, J. (2010) Leadership in the service of hospitality, *Cornell Hospitality Quarterly* 3: 363–378.

Brownell, J. (2011) Creating value for women business travelers, Cornell Center for Hospitality Research Report, Ithaca, NY: Cornell University.

Brownell, J. (2013) *Listening: Attitudes, Principles, and Skills*, 5th edn, New York: Allen and Bacon.

Brownell, J. and Walsh, K. (2008) Women in hospitality. In Brotherton, R. and Wood, R. (eds.) *Handbook of Hospitality Management*, London: Sage, pp. 107–128.

Cambern, A. and Goulder, M. (2009,) Increase in female business travelers prompts hotels to add amenities, *Columbus Dispatch*, April 16. Available at http://www.dispatch.com/live/content/business/stories/2009/04/16/Female_Business_Travelers.ART_ART_04-16-09_A8_G2DI9KN.html. Accessed November 7, 2015.

Carbasho, T. (2002) Survey offers insight into what female business travelers seek, *Pittsburgh Business Times* 22, 7: 24. Available at http://proquest.umi.com/pqdweb?index=18&did=164199881&SrchMode=3& sid=1&Fmt=3&VInst=PROD&VType=PQD&RQT=309&VName=PQD&TS=1273681099&clien tId=8424&aid=1. Accessed May 10, 2015.

Ciulla, J. B. (1995) Leadership ethics: mapping the territory, *Business Ethics Quarterly* 5, 1: 5–28.

Coleman, A. (2002) Should women receive special treatment?, *Director* 56, 5: 45.

Covey, S. R. (2006) Servant leadership, *Leadership Excellence* 23, 12: 5–8.

Dennis, R. S. and Bocarnea, M. (2005) Development of the servant leadership instrument, *Leadership & Organization Development Journal* 26, 8: 600–615.

Ehrhart, M. G. (2004) Leadership and procedural justice climate as antecedents of unit-level organizational citizenship behavior, *Personnel Psychology*, 57, 1: 61–94.

Ganesan-Lim, C., Russell-Bennett, R., and Dagger, T. (2008) The impact of service contact type and demographic characteristics on service quality perceptions, *Journal of Services Marketing* 22, 7: 550–561.

Gioia, J. (2007) Catering to the woman traveler, *Herman Trend Alert*, October 3.

Gobe, M. and Zyman, S. (2010) *Emotional Branding: The New Paradigm for Connecting Brands to People*, New York: Allworth Press.

Goleman, D. (1996) *Emotional Intelligence: Why it Can Matter More than IQ*, New York: Bantam Books.

Graham, J. W. (1995) Servant leadership in organizations: inspirational and moral, *Leadership Quarterly* 2, 2: 105–119.

Greenleaf, R. K. (1977) *Servant Leadership: A Journey into the Nature of Legitimate Power and Greatness*, New York: Paulist Press.

Gutek, B. A., Cohen, A. G., and Konrad, A. M. (1990) Predicting social-sexual behavior at work: a contact hypothesis, *Academy of Management Journal* 33, 3: 560–577.

Hamilton, C. (1999) You are getting sleepy: do women make better business travelers than men?, *CMA Management* 73, 7: 38.

Han, H. and Back, K. (2007) Assessing customers' emotional experiences influencing their satisfaction in the lodging industry, *Journal of Travel & Tourism Marketing* 23, 1: 43–56.

Hart, W. (1993) What women want, *Cornell Hotel and Restaurant Administration Quarterly* 34, 5: 39–46.

Hinkin, T. and Tracey, J. B. (1998) The service imperative: factors driving meeting effectiveness, *Cornell Hospitality and Restaurant Administration Quarterly* 39, 5: 59–67.

Iacobucci, D. and Ostrom, A. (1993) Gender differences in the impact of core and relational aspects of services on the evaluation of service encounters, *Journal of Consumer Psychology* 2, 3: 257–286.

Joseph, D. L. and Newman, D. A. (2010) Emotional intelligence: an integrative meta-analysis and cascading model, *Journal of Applied Psychology* 95, 1: 54–78.

Kamberg, M. L. (2001) Travel industry sets sights on women travelers, *Women in Business* 53, 6: 30.

Khan, S. (1999) Aiming to please: women business travel industry introduces more services for female customers, *USA Today*, June 10, O1B.

Kouzes, J. M. and Posner, B. Z. (1995) *The Leadership Challenge: How to Keep Getting Extraordinary Things Done in Organizations*, San Francisco: Jossey-Bass.

McCoy-Ullrich, D. (2002) Alone on the road: travel industry responds to women's security needs, *American Woman Road & Travel*, February 1, 5–7.

May, D. R., Chan, A., Hodges, T. D., and Avolio, B. J. (2003) Developing the moral component of authentic leadership, *Organizational Dynamics* 32, 3: 247–260.

Mayer, D. M., Bardes, M., and Piccolo, R. F. (2008) Do servant leaders help satisfy follower needs?, *European Journal of Work and Organizational Psychology* 17, 2: 180–197.

Newell, A. (2009) Do female business travelers have different needs? Survey says: Yes, at http://www. theglasshammer.com/news/2009/06/05/do-female-travelers-have-different-needs.

Newth, F. (2009) The new strategic imperative: understanding the female business traveler, *International Business & Economics Research Journal* 8, 11: 51–64.

NYU Tisch Center Survey (2003) *Coming of Age: The Continuing Evolution of Female Business Travelers*, New York: New York University.

Pan, S. and Ryan, C. (2007) Gender, framing, and travelogues, *Journal of Travel Research* 45: 464–474.

Patterson, K. A. (2003) Servant Leadership: a theoretical model, Dissertation, Regent University, Virginia Beach, VA.

Pearson, J. C. (1995) *Gender and Communication*, Dubuque, IA: Wm. C. Brown.

Raman, N., Chattopadhyay, P., and Hoyer, W. (1995) Do consumers seek emotional situations: the need for emotion, *Advances in Consumer Research* 22: 537–542.

Rennaker, M. A. (2008) Listening and persuasion: examining the communicative patterns of Servant Leadership, Dissertation, Regent University, Virginia Beach, VA. AAT 3309285.

Russell, R. F. (2001) The role of values in servant leadership, *Leadership & Organization Development Journal* 22, 2: 76–84.

Russell, R. F. and Stone, A. G. (2002) A review of servant leadership attributes: developing a practical model, *Leadership & Organization Development Journal* 23, 3: 145–157.

Schueler, J. (2000) Customer service through leadership: the Disney way, *Training & Development Journal* 54, 10: 26–31.

Sendjaya, S. and Sarros, J. C. (2002) Servant Leadership: its origin, development, and application, *Journal of Leadership & Organization Studies* 9, 2: 57–64.

Sharkey, J. (2002) One woman's account of two hotel experiences, *New York Times*, July 30, p. C7.

Simon, R. and Nath, L. (2004) Gender and emotion in the U.S.: do men and women differ in self-reports of feelings and expressive behavior?, *American Journal of Sociology* 109: 1137–1176.

Sinclair, M., Ashkanasy, N., and Chattopadhyay, P. (2010) Affective antecedents of intuitive decision making, *Journal of Management and Organization* 16, 3: 382–398.

Smith, W. W. and Carmichael, B. A. (2006) Domestic business travel with a focus on the female market, *Journal of Travel and Tourism Marketing* 21, 1: 65–76.

Spears, L. (1996) Reflections on Robert K. Greenleaf and Servant Leadership, *Leadership & Organization Development Journal* 17, 7: 33–35.

Spears, L. (1998) *Character and Servant Leadership: Ten Characteristics of Effective, Caring Leaders*, Indianapolis, IN: Spears Center for Servant Leadership.

Swift, S. (2000) Hotels, airlines catering to women travelers, *Indianapolis Business Journal* 21, 5: 20–25.

Tannen, D. (1990) *You Just Don't Understand: Women and Men in Conversation*, New York: William Morrow.

U.S. Travel Association (2009) U.S. travel forecasts. UStravel.org., October 27, at http://www.ustravel.org/sites/default/files/page/2009/09 /ForecastSummary.pdf. Accessed January 21, 2011.

Verhoef, P. C., Lemon, K., Parasuraman, A., Roggeveen, A., Tsiros, M., and Schlesinger, L. (2009) Customer experience creation: determinants, dynamics and management strategies, *Journal of Retailing* 85, 1: 31–41.

Washington, R. R., Sutton, C. D., and Field, H. S. (2006) Individual differences in servant leadership: the roles of values and personality, *Leadership & Organization Development Journal* 27, 8: 700–716.

17

Hospitality employment

The good, the bad, and the ugly

Shobana Nair Partington

Key themes

Nature of hospitality sector

Bad and ugly employment

Good practices

Characteristics of the workforce

Adam Smith in his seminal work *The Wealth of Nations* (1776) advocated the inequality of the labour market by explaining that 'labour belongs to the labourer'. Even though the common wages of labour depend on the contract between the labour and the master (known as 'employer' in the modern economy), it is not surprising to find that employers had stronger power in this relationship. Adam Smith's views are still relevant in today's modern economy. Although we no longer rely on the manufacturing sector that was dominant during the eighteenth century, the problems that existed because of the power struggle between employers and workers that led to poor pay and working conditions can still be discussed today in relation to the hospitality sector.

The hospitality sector is one of the largest and fastest growing sectors of the global economy that is highly labour intensive (International Labour Organisation, n.d.) and offers varied opportunities for people in diverse sub-sectors (Baum, 2007). The sector has grown from strength to strength, has continued to be strong and resilient during the economic downturn and is a fundamental contributor to economic recovery, creating millions of jobs (United Nations World Tourism Organization, 2015). In the UK, it is the fourth biggest sector in employment terms. In 2014, employment in the UK hospitality sector stood at 2.9 million jobs, representing 8.8 per cent of total UK employment (Oxford Economics, 2015).

Despite the tremendous growth in the hospitality sector, it continues to have a negative image. The sector is considered to be part of the secondary labour market that faces low wages, high

DOI: 10.4324/9781315679938-19

turnover, part-time or temporary work, limited promotional opportunity and career development. The sector is also often described as being busy and fast-paced, requiring employees to be flexible and able to adjust to new challenges in order to address ever-growing customer needs. This is not necessarily negative and can be considered as a pull factor for workers interested in this industry (Mkono, 2010). At one end of the sector, hospitality employment faces challenges in response to the characteristics and nature of the work; at the other end, the characteristics of the sector attract workers, creating good employment opportunities. In recent years, a number of studies have highlighted some of the positive elements of hospitality employment. Sadly, 'the bad and the ugly' aspects of hospitality employment dominate the literature in this area and outweigh 'the good', which further entrenches the negative image of the sector. Leading from this premise, this chapter first describes the characteristics and nature of the sector. This is followed by a discussion on the specific employment practices that can be considered the 'good, bad and ugly'. Finally, workforce characteristics and the challenges faced by the sector are discussed.

Characteristics and nature of the hospitality sector

It is important to recognise how the trends and characteristics of the sector have shaped the types of employment and skills that the sector requires. The hospitality sector generally consists of accommodation and food service activities. The Standard Industrial Classification (2007) of economic activities for this sector includes hotels and similar accommodation; holiday centres and villages; youth hostels, other holiday and other collective accommodation; recreational vehicle parks, trailer parks and camping grounds; other accommodation; licenced and unlicensed restaurants; cafés, take-away food shops and mobile food stands; event catering activities; other food services; licensed clubs, public houses and bars. The definition provided by People 1st (the Sector Skills Council for the Hospitality, Leisure, Travel and Tourism industries) (2013) is also central to this discussion, as the reports developed by People 1st are referred to throughout this chapter. Ten sub-industries make up this sector: hotels; restaurants; pubs, bars and nightclubs; food and service management; hospitality services; events; gambling; self-catering accommodations, holiday parks and hostels; visitor attractions; and tourists services. It is the most diverse sector, comprising a range of different industries, but all with their roots in the food, drink and accommodation services.

The size of establishments can be considered as one of the key influences on the employment characteristics of the hospitality sector (Lucas, 2004). The hospitality sector continues to be dominated by micro-sized establishments (employing ten employees or fewer) and only a small proportion consists of large organisations. Almost half (46 per cent) employ fewer than five people, while only one per cent of businesses employ more than 100 people (People 1st, 2013). Therefore, it is important to recognise the importance of the micro/small-sized organisations for this sector and the challenges that come with it. The reason for this high prevalence of micro-sized and owner-managed establishments can be explained mainly by the low barrier of entry into this sector, whereby relatively limited capital and fewer skills are required to set up a business (Hughes, 1992). Consequently, the hospitality sector attracts a large number of unqualified operators whose motivations for entry are often 'cited as a twin desire for greater control over personal working environments and a job that involves social interaction with others' (Wood, 1997: 341).

Dominance of small businesses in this sector automatically leads to unavoidable challenges in relation to lack of career path for staff, informal approaches to employment practices in relation to recruitment, performance appraisal and training. However, employment practices in small organisations are not necessarily bad, just different to formal approaches used by large organisations, as highlighted by Cobble and Merrill:

> employee-employer relations may be personal and collaborative rather than adversarial, formalised and highlight bureaucratic. The employment relationship is not the classic one described by Marx, nor is it even the conventional us-versus-them world view that often prevails in large bureaucratically-run enterprise.
>
> *(2009: 159)*

Authors such as Lockyer and Scholarios (2004) advocate that there are best practices that can be captured from the informal approaches used by smaller businesses in the hospitality sector, especially in relation to employee recruitment. Even though the sector is dominated by small industries, a significant proportion of the workforce (42 per cent) is employed by large organisations that employ more than 250 employees (People 1st, 2013). Therefore, the best way forward in terms of the impact it can have on the workforce is to focus on larger employers to ensure that they recognise their responsibility in delivering good practices and the part they play in portraying the image of the sector.

The main growth of the hospitality sector over the period 1998–2014 in the UK appeared to be in licensed and unlicensed restaurants and cafés, food service activities, and hotels and similar accommodation (Oxford Economics, 2015), which are typically small businesses employing fewer than ten staff. There has been a noticeable decline in event catering, public houses and bars, and licenced clubs. Public house owners cited the cheaper availability of alcohol in supermarkets and off licenses, the smoking ban and the trend towards wine drinking as a few of the factors contributing to the decline in the trade (Hickman, 2008). However, according to People 1st (2013) the decline over recent years in the pubs, bars and nightclubs workforce is beginning to stabilise, as many of these businesses continue to diversify their offering through food and dining, and so on.

The employment relationship in this sector embodies a triadic power relationship between employers, workers and customers, whereby the customer directly impinges on how workers carry out their work, which in turn has implications for the rules of employment (Lucas, 2004). This can be challenging as customer expectations can be viewed as evolving, complex and demanding (Duncan *et al.*, 2013). The focus of the hospitality sector is on exceeding customers' expectations. Therefore, providing the highest level of service is one of the greatest challenges facing these employees, especially as they have to manage emotions and provide a friendly service at all times. This can be stressful and emotionally draining. Hochschild first described this as emotional labour by defining it as 'the management of feelings to create a publicly observable facial and bodily display' which is 'sold for wage and therefore has exchange value' (1983: 7). Emotional labour among hospitality employees has been well documented, as employees are expected to express feelings such as enthusiasm, friendliness and cheerfulness despite negative emotions that they may experience (Pizam, 2004; Wong and Wang, 2009; Shani *et al.*, 2014).

The sector is arguably very labour-intensive and, despite advancements in technology, approaches used to substitute labour with technology in this sector are limited. Its productivity is reported as being significantly less than comparable sectors such as construction, manufacturing and retailing (People 1st, 2015b). The factors blamed for this low productivity level include lack of sufficient skills, high staff turnover that deviates training investment, poor staff retention and poor career path or progression. The sector has often been associated with high staff turnover and there is continuous debate in this area on whether it is good or bad. The latest report by People 1st (2013) noted that the labour turnover rate across the hospitality and tourism sector continues to fall, with the latest data showing a turnover rate of 20 per cent, a significant fall from 31 per cent for the whole sector in 2009. This could be a result of the aftermath of recession, where employees are reluctant to move jobs. However, People 1st (2013) argues that employers are beginning to recognise the problems of staff turnover in terms of the cost to the business and are trying to introduce initiatives to retain their staff.

The growth in the sector means there is a continued need for new staff. People 1st (2013) reported that 16 per cent of employers in this sector had a vacancy, compared to 12 per cent across the UK economy. In terms of vacancies that they considered hard to fill, 6 per cent of employers had these vacancies, slightly higher than the UK average of 4 per cent. There are significant variations in job postings by occupation, with the highest numbers of roles available for restaurant managers and a variety of chef occupations. Acknowledging the diverse characteristics of the sector, the next two sections focus specifically on aspects of hospitality employment that could be considered 'good, bad, and ugly'.

Employment in the hospitality sector: 'the bad and the ugly'

Hospitality employment is repeatedly characterised as low paid, low skilled, part-time and seasonal, with poor management and lacking a clear career path (Walmsley, 2004). Authors such as Karatepe and Uludag (2007) and Wong and Ko (2009) describe the long and unsociable hours faced by hospitality employees as non-conducive for a healthy work–life balance. All these factors and the negative image of this sector can be considered to be the main contributing factors to high staff turnover and poor retention in the sector.

Hospitality is Britain's fourth-largest sector, worth more than £60bn a year (Oxford Economics, 2015), but it is concerning that the sector has continued to be identified as the lowest paid sector in the UK. The Office for National Statistics (2014) reported that the accommodation and food service sector had the lowest gross weekly earnings of £316 for full-time employees compared to the average for all sectors and services of £518. Low pay dominates this sector and it was placed under the Trade Boards as far back as the 1940s, and sadly is still recognised as being low paid even fifteen years after the implementation of the National Minimum Wage (NMW). Discussion regarding wages rarely ventures beyond this as the focus tends to be on wages at the lower end of the occupational spectrum, even though there is great variation depending on occupation (Walmsley, 2015). The high proportion of micro- or small-sized firms in the hospitality sector, and the lower skills associated with this sector, can partly explain the reason for the low pay experienced by workers. The low pay is also further entrenched by the type of employees that are attracted to this sector, such as young workers, women and migrants.

In order to tackle low pay in the UK, the latest initiative that has been introduced by the government is Living Wage. Living wage is an hourly rate promoted by the Living Wage Foundation (LWF) to encourage employers to pay above the legally binding minimum wage (Department for Business Innovation & Skills, 2015). The living wage is determined by the LWF based on the amount an individual needs to earn to cover the basic costs of living, and acknowledges that living costs vary in different parts of the country. Currently, the living wage is on a voluntary basis, but by April 2016 this will be compulsory for all employees aged 25 years or older and companies will be required to pay a minimum of £7.20 an hour. This will rise to £9 an hour by 2020. Similarly to when the NMW was introduced, the hospitality sector, along with retail and support services, has been identified as a sector that will be hit hard by this new rate.

Smaller businesses are expected to be hit harder than larger companies, and, as an overwhelming majority of the hospitality sector is small businesses, this is worrying for employers.

The British Hospitality Association (BHA) (2015) has already expressed its concern: as a quarter of the hospitality workforce is on the minimum wage and a significant further proportion earn between the NMW and the new 'Living Wage' rate, the introduction of the Living Wage will have considerable impact on this sector, especially when the costs of maintaining differentials are also taken into account. Similar arguments were presented by the BHA when the NMW was introduced, and, since its introduction, there has been a consensus notion of the limited impact it has had on the sector (Adam-Smith et al., 2003). The NMW was accommodated by employers without many changes to their employment practices and hence, according to Adam-Smith et al. (2003), one should not overstate the importance of the effect statutory intervention has on the employment relationship.

Given the diverse size and characteristics of the sector, the types of employment are varied, ranging from unskilled porter to highly skilled manager, and depend on the types of customers served and types of workers required. However, the majority of staff employed in the sector are generally regarded as semi- or unskilled (Lucas, 2004; Riley, 2011). A past employers' survey found that employers in the hospitality sector only value generic skills such as the ability to follow instructions, willingness to learn and the ability to be flexible and adaptive (Hospitality Training Foundation, 2000). Employers were also found to be sceptical of qualifications, as they did not view these as a guarantee of the skills they require from employees. However, in recent years the sector has placed more emphasis on soft skills and has recognised the additional skills that are needed, and problems in recruiting (People 1st, 2013).

People 1st (2013) identified that the skills that are currently difficult to recruit can be grouped into three areas: job-specific skills, which include culinary skills for chefs; inter-personal skills or softer skills such as communication, customer service and team working; and management and leadership skills. Customer handling skills was reported as the area most commonly needing improvement and the top skills concern for the future, followed by management and leadership. However, Lashley (2009) has argued against the simplistic approach to identifying the skills needed, as there are different skill clusters within each skill that employers seek, and each operates under different labour market conditions that need to be considered. With the greater emphasis now being placed on soft skills, there needs to be strengthening of the conceptualisation of soft skills to determine if they are worthy of the 'skilled' label (Hurrell et al., 2013).

The hospitality sector is notorious for its reputation as a poor trainer (Pratten, 2003). People 1st (2013), however, argues that employers in this sector spend a substantial amount of money on training mainly because of the high number of staff that need to be trained in an on-going cycle of replacement, but fail to reap the benefits as the staff do not remain in the organisation long enough to be proficient. This leads to employers' reluctance to invest in training for their workers beyond induction, as they are unlikely to reap the benefits if the trained workers do not stay with them long enough. The persistent problem of recruitment and retention has been well explored in studies relating to the hospitality sector (e.g. Ohlin and West, 1994; Iverson and Deery, 1997). The constant challenge faced by employers is the recruitment of the right calibre and skilled staff, particularly in finding candidates who have been trained in the specific skills the kitchen requires, and this problem may be perpetuated by the negative perception held of the sector in terms of low pay and long hours. This suggests that the hospitality sector needs to undertake a more active recruitment policy. Yet, recruitment methods are far from being actively pursued. Studies such as that by Lockyer and Scholarios (2004) have highlighted the general lack of systematic selection procedures for the hotel sector, particularly in smaller hotels, and Lashley and Chapman (1999) have cited the poor quality of recruitment practices as the main cause of high staff turnover in the sector.

Lately, large hotels have also come under attack, accused of exploiting their workers, mainly their housekeeping staff (Roberts, 2015). These hotels deny responsibility for the working conditions of these employees who work in their hotels, as cleaning is outsourced, but such reports further cloud the image of this sector, especially when a headline in the *Guardian* reads 'Britain's hotel workers – bullied, underpaid and with few rights' (Roberts, 2015). The reliance on sub-contractors to deliver services in the hospitality sector has been growing year by year in an attempt by companies to reduce costs. Companies find that by outsourcing they are able to 'leverage vendor competencies in highly specific areas while also eliminating the distraction of having to manage peripheral functions' (Davidson *et al.*, 2011: 502). It is, however, worrying when hotels lose control in areas that could be considered the heart of the service, such as housekeeping.

Earlier studies have highlighted a concerning view that owner managers of small firms were aware of the potential trade-off between high labour turnover and higher wages (Rainnie, 1989). This group employed disadvantaged or marginal labour groups who would be more stable in employment terms at low pay levels. As argued by Lucas and Wood (2000), the excess supply of marginal workers drawn from groups such as women, young workers, casual employees, students, part-timers and migrant workers, who have little bargaining power, further drives down the pay in this sector. Authors such as Sachdev and Wilkinson (1998) have also argued that the skills required to work in the hospitality sector are seriously undervalued and that has contributed to the depression of pay in this sector. Recent studies, however, have highlighted the importance of soft skills in the hospitality sector that should not be undervalued (e.g. Burns, 1997; Warhurst and Nickson, 2007).

Considering the bad press faced by this sector, it has continued to grow globally, and has supported the UK economy during recession. Therefore, it is important to highlight the aspects of employment that can be regarded as good and as attractive to potential employees.

Employment in the hospitality sector: 'the good'

The core UK hospitality sector had seen employment rising steadily since the late 1990s, up until the onset of the recession in 2008–2009 (Oxford Economics, 2015). However, the hospitality sector has still been identified as one of the main drivers of the UK economy throughout the economic downturn (People 1st, 2015a). People join the sector mainly because of its accommodating characteristics, the wide range of jobs available and the diverse human capital requirements (Szivas *et al.*, 2003). This suggests that the sector has 'attractive opportunities, and is not just the occupation many will follow in the absence of anything else' (Janta *et al.*, 2011: 1008).

The hospitality sector has often been described as having the highest levels of turnover in the UK, experiencing a turnover rate of 20 per cent in recent years, and it has a much younger workforce than average (Michel, 2014). This is expected as the sector relies on high numbers of students, overseas visitors and people temporarily working while between jobs. For many establishments, the seasonal take-up of student workers is desirable, as the establishments do not want staff to stay on for a prolonged period. They want staff during busy periods and do not need them during the quiet winter season. More importantly, flexible hours also make these jobs particularly attractive to students who can juggle education with their jobs. As highlighted by Lucas (2004), there is a coincidence of needs between employers and students, which creates a 'win-win' situation for both groups.

The sector relies mainly on core staff, full-time, part-time and increasingly casual and outsourced staff in an attempt to minimise labour costs. The Travel and Tourism Survey in the UK found that around one-third of staff working in guest houses, hotels, restaurants and pubs are employed on zero hour contracts, well over 60 per cent of these staff regularly work 20 hours or more and with more than three-quarters of these routinely employed for 40 hours per week (CLH News, 2014). This demonstrates a regular income for this group of workers and this arrangement may suit groups of workers, such as students and women workers with childcare responsibilities. Davidson and colleagues propose that, in light of the increasing use of casual and agency workers in the sector, there could be 'the emergence of a dual labour market where there is likely to be considerable competition for the best people, with human resource management concentrating on talent management and recruitment [of core staff]' (2011: 511). They argue that such staff members are likely to see improvements in pay, benefits and working conditions.

Studies such as that of Mkono have also attempted to defend careers in the hospitality sector, describing the portrayal of hospitality work in previous studies as being unbalanced: '[it] has seemed to suggest that hospitality employees and managers never enjoy their work; that they are constantly trying to escape its drudgery' (Mkono, 2010: 857). There is a significant proportion of hospitality workers and managers who have chosen to work in the sector for decades and sometimes for their whole working lives, and who are often overlooked by researchers. Mkono (2010) found that the Zimbabwean hotel managers liked their career, and the reasons for this included the interaction they have with people from various countries, cultures and lifestyles; working in a 'nice' environment; perks; challenging and stimulating work; glamour/prestige; the global nature of the sector and associated mobility; opportunities for networking with various groups of people; growth opportunities; the dynamic and exciting nature of the sector; the ability to apply individual creativity; and, finally, working with a diverse workforce.

Other studies have highlighted enjoyable and positive attributes of working in the hospitality sector, which include intrinsic rewards associated with helping customers and a sense of accomplishment on completion of a challenging task (Weaver, 2009). Authors such as Harbourne have also strongly argued against the bad image of the hospitality sector:

> there is a tremendous amount of job satisfaction, skill levels are high, and as for unsocial hours – well, that is just a term dreamt up by people working nine to five who cannot conceive of the benefits of travelling to work before the rush hour and having free time during the daylight hours of the afternoon.
>
> *(1995: 37)*

Harbourne found that the main sources of satisfaction for workers were from opportunities to meet people, teamwork with colleagues, workplace atmosphere and a degree of control workers had over the way they perform their jobs.

Contributing to this discussion, Riley and colleagues (2002) identified a number of characteristics that make employment in the hospitality sector attractive. First, the sector accommodates people of a variety of skills. Second, the constant fluctuation in consumer demand means lack of routine for the workers as improvisation and flexibility are seen to be an important part of the job. Third, the boundaries between work and leisure time are often obscured whereby it is argued that the working hours can constitute leisure when customers, many of whom are friends or acquaintances, are entertained. Some workers may also spend their leisure time at their workplace. Fourth, a large proportion of the jobs in this sector have direct contact with customers, and it is an attractive feature for workers who like dealing with customers. Finally, the flexible nature of the employment to match fluctuations in seasonal and periodic tourism demand can be argued to suit certain type of workers, such as students and women workers, who can fit the jobs around their education or childcare duties.

Consideration of pay in the hospitality sector often starts with a negative observation and this is highlighted as a main concern as it has been argued that a large number of the jobs in the sector are

213

dominated by low pay. However, caution has to be taken when condemning the sector for low pay, as the full remuneration package, instead of just basic pay, should be reviewed since jobs in this sector have access to non-monetary and informal rewards. Authors such as Alpert (1986), Wood (1997) and Riley *et al.* (2002) argue that, in some occupations, basic pay is often supplemented by fringe benefits such as food and lodging, tips and 'fiddles', and this should not be ignored. Larger hotels were found to provide free staff uniforms (and sometimes dry cleaning), free meals while on duty and benefits, including overnight stays, pension, sick pay schemes, private medical insurance and discounts on gym membership (Nickson, 2013). However, Lucas (2004) has highlighted that workers in the hospitality sector enjoy fewer benefits than those in other sectors.

Having considered the areas of good, bad and ugly practices in the hospitality sector, it is important to now review the workforce characteristics and the challenges the sector needs to be aware of in relation to employment.

Workforce characteristics and challenges

Supply and demand for labour in the UK has undergone major changes in recent decades. These changes were accelerated mainly as a result of government policy in the 1980s which promoted labour market deregulation and encouraged flexible work in an attempt to boost economic growth and increase efficiency. On the demand side, there has been a dramatic rise in flexible and temporary employment, often at the expense of more stable jobs, as employers keep their core workforces lean while seeking to resource in response to peaks in demand (Recruitment and Employment Confederation, 2015). On the supply side, the increase in female and youth labour, coupled with a growing migrant and multicultural population, has led to an increasingly diverse workforce.

The hospitality sector relies heavily upon the numerical flexibility of its workforce to overcome the problem of demand fluctuation, and young, female and migrant workers tend to fulfil this need of the sector. During the 1980s, involvement of young and women workers in the British hospitality sector increased due, in part, to the expansion of the fast food industry (Reiter, 1996; Lucas and Ralston, 1997). This trend continued to rise, and the flexible nature of employment, particularly for bar and waiting staff, also attracted women returnees, who need to work part-time to fit in with family demands, and students, who have to combine employment with their full-time education commitments (Hakim, 1996; Lucas and Ralston, 1997; Curtis and Lucas, 2001).

Currently, 34 per cent of the hospitality workforce is aged under 25, compared to 12 per cent across the economy (People 1st, 2015a). These workers consist mostly of young people combining further and higher education studies with working at weekends and evenings. This trend, however, is now considered worrying because of the demographic changes currently faced in the EU with a decreasing number of young people. The demographic trends projected over the long term by the European Commission (2015) reveal that Europe will turn 'increasingly grey' in the coming decades, and by 2030 the EU working age population will have shrunk by 13 million. Fotakis and Peschner have highlighted the severity of this demographic change in the EU:

> During the next 20 years, the developed world will experience the massive exit of the 'baby-boom' generation which is already under way. Although the incoming generations are better educated, which is a positive development in terms of employment perspectives, they are considerably smaller in size.
>
> *(2015: 39)*

For the hospitality sector, which has seen high growth in recent years, with a prediction that it would require almost 524,000 more staff by 2020, this is alarming news as this sector has traditionally targeted and employed younger workers, and this might no longer be a sustainable recruitment strategy (People 1st, 2015a). The on-going struggle to attract UK workers will continue to increase the need for migrants. The sector has historically relied heavily on migrant workers, mainly to take hard-to-fill vacancies. Migrant workers are also attracted to these jobs, as the relative pay is higher than that offered in their home countries and some see these jobs as a way to improve their language skills and thus help them progress in their career. However, according to Janta *et al.* (2011), even migrant workers plan to eventually move out of this sector because of the poor working conditions, supporting the notion proposed by Szivas and Riley that 'tourism employment might play the role of "any port in a storm" ... "a refuge sector"' (1999: 748) or as Wildes accurately described it – 'a mere stopover to something better' (2007: 7). In short, some authors such as Lucas (2004) argue that workers only remain in the sector out of fear of unemployment and that the most talented workers will leave the sector to work in other sectors.

A number of studies have found that employers prefer migrant workers to British workers mainly because of their better work ethic, a positive attitude towards work and a higher skill level (Devine *et al.*, 2007; Lyon and Sulcova, 2009; Janta *et al.*, 2011). However, these studies also noted some of the challenges posed in managing migrant workers. These include managing the working relationship between local and migrant workers so as to be mindful of cultural differences, communication concerns between migrant workers and local workers and customers, and local workers feeling threatened by the presence of migrant workers in terms of their job security. Baum (2012) also further highlighted the challenges in terms of the role that employees played in conveying destination image. Using the example of Ireland, he emphasised that an intangible conflict may exist between the image engendered by the new multicultural workforce and the traditional emphasis Ireland has placed on the friendliness of Irish people as part of its tourism destination marketing campaign.

Even though a number of studies have shown the benefits migrant workers bring to the sector, it is concerning to think that, as long as the migrant workers are able to fill these vacancies, employers do not see the necessity to change their practices to improve working conditions in the sector. Sadly, migrant workers may indirectly help to continue to entrench certain employment practices that are favourable to employers (Janta *et al.*, 2011), and as Baum exerts, 'the widespread recruitment and use of migrant labour in the tourism industry of developed countries has acted to the detriment of real change within the sector's workplace' (2007: 1394). However, the changing face of the EU's demographics, in terms of the falling number of young people, could also mean that the sector may have to reconsider its employment strategy. Employing older workers, women with children or improving retention are approaches that need to be seriously considered. Recruiting outside Europe is an option, but that can only happen if significant political changes are made to allow greater migration into the UK, particularly for what are deemed to be lower skilled roles (People 1st, 2015a).

Conclusions

The changes in the demographics of the EU population are fundamental to the future directions of employment in the hospitality sector. With the forecast decrease in the number of young workers that this sector heavily relies on, there has to be a more creative way of recruiting staff and managing the flexibility that is required in order to attract women to return back to work and pursue their career after periods of childcare. The sector needs to recognise the changing landscape of the labour market and be proactive in developing recruitment and retention strategies that will create a sustainable workforce. What is worrying is the continuous bad press received by this sector over the last decade in terms of its pay and working conditions. Hospitality scholars have continued to highlight the negative *image of the* sector. Jobs in the hospitality sector are associated with low pay, unsocial hours, low job security, low skills and limited promotional and career development opportunities, all of which are seen to contribute towards high turnover rates.

The recruitment and retention challenges for this sector will likely continue to intensify unless the core characteristics of the sector are effectively challenged and the employer brand for the overall sector improves (Hughes and Rog, 2008). The image of a sector can be argued to be a key labour market player, as it may attract suitable workers to the sector but also has the power to deter suitable workers and attract unsuitable workers (Riley *et al.*, 2002). Historically, the service element of hotel work has been blamed for the low image of the sector (Corcoran and Johnson, 1974). Despite some of the poor working conditions in the sector, satisfaction and attractiveness motivate individuals to take up jobs in the sector (Janta *et al.*, 2011), making it the world's largest sector in terms of employment.

Although the projected image of the sector may not be accurate, it is crucial, as it can play a key role in recruitment of new, and retention of existing, employees (Baum, 2006). It is promising to see that a few studies recently have started to attempt to highlight positive features of this sector, rather than dwelling on its negative image. The jobs in the sector are seen to be fast paced, sociable and flexible, and to require certain types of skill sets that are suited to some people. It is important to celebrate the aspects of employment that continue to attract a large workforce to this sector and highlight factors that contribute towards employees remaining in this sector.

It is fair to say that enough has been written and said about the hardships of working in the hospitality sector, and too little has been said about the favourable side of working in this sector. The key elements of this sector that create a buzz and charm should not be sidelined, and more research is needed in reviewing the projected image of the sector to ensure a well-balanced perspective. If 'the good' outweighs 'the bad and the ugly', the sector can continue to attract quality workers and develop future leaders for the sector.

References

Adam-Smith, D., Norris, G. and Williams, S. (2003) Continuity or change? The implications of the National Minimum Wage for work and employment in the hospitality industry, *Work, Employment and Society* 17, 1: 29–47.

Alpert, W. T. (1986) *The Minimum Wage in the Restaurant Industry*, London: Praeger.

Baum, T. (2006) *Human Resource Management for Tourism, Hospitality and Leisure: An International Perspective*, London: Thomson Learning.

Baum, T. (2007) Human resources in tourism: still waiting for change, *Tourism Management* 28: 1383–1399.

Baum, T. (2012) Migrant workers in the international hotel industry, International Migration Paper 112, Geneva: International Labour Organization. Available at http://www.ilo.org/wcmsp5/groups/public/---ed_dialogue/---sector/documents/publication/wcms_180596.pdf. Accessed 10 December 2015.

British Hospitality Association (2015) We require a constructive dialogue with George Osborne, *BHA News*, 9 July 2015, at http://www.bha.org.uk/bha_news/we-require-a-constructive-dialogue-with-george-osborne/. Accessed 16 October 2015.

Burns, P. M. (1997) Hard-skills, soft skills: undervaluing hospitality service with a smile, *Progress in Tourism and Hospitality Research* 3, 3: 239–248.

CLH News (2014) Horizon brighter for UK tourism & leisure sectors, says MHA, *CLH News*, 1 July 2014, at http://catererlicensee.com/horizon-brighter-for-uk-tourism-leisure-sectors-says-mha/. Accessed 10 December 2015.

Cobble D. S. and Merrill M. (2009) The promise of service worker unionism. In Korczynski M. and Macdonald C. (eds) *Service Work: Critical Perspectives*, Routledge: New York, pp. 153–174.

Corcoran, J. and Johnson, P. (1974) Image of four occupations, *Hotel, Catering and Institutional Management Association Journal*, June: 13–19.

Curtis, S. and Lucas, R. (2001) A coincidence of needs? Employers and full-time students, *Employee Relations* 23, 1: 38–54.

Davidson, M. C. G, McPhail, R. and Barry, S. (2011) Hospitality HRM: past, present and the future, *International Journal of Contemporary Hospitality Management* 23, 4: 498–516.

Department for Business Innovation & Skills (2015) Policy paper: National Living Wage, at https://www.gov.uk/government/publications/national-living-wage-nlw/national-living-wage-nlw. Accessed 10 November 2015.

Devine, F., Baum, T., Hearns, N. and Devine, A. (2007) Cultural diversity in hospitality work: the Northern Ireland experience, *International Journal of Human Resource Management* 18, 2: 333–349.

Duncan, T., Scott, D. G. and Baum, T. (2013) Mobilities of hospitality work: an exploration of issues and debates, *Annals of Tourism Research* 41, April: 1–19.

European Commission (2015) *The 2015 Ageing Report: Economic and budgetary projections for the 28 EU Member States (2013–2060)*, Brussels: European Commission.

Fotakis, C. and Peschner, J. (2015) *Demographic Change, Human Resource Constraints and Economic Growth: The EU Challenge Compared to Other Global Players*, Luxemburg: European Commission.

Harbourne, D. (1995) Issues in hospitality and catering, *Management Development Review* 8 1: 37–40.

Hakim, C. (1996) Working students, students in full-time education with full-time and part-time jobs, Working Paper WP8, London: Department of Sociology, London School of Economics.

Hickman, M. (2008) The big question: why are so many pubs shutting down, and is their decline bad for society?, *The Independent*, 6 March, at http://www.independent.co.uk/news/uk/home-news/the-big-question-why-are-so-many-pubs-shutting-down-and-is-their-decline-bad-for-society-792022.html. Accessed 12 November 2015.

Hochschild, A. R. (1983) *The Managed Heart: Commercialization of Human Feeling*, Berkeley: University of California Press.

Hospitality Training Foundation (2000) *Skills and Employment Forecasts 2000: For the Hospitality Industry*, London: Hospitality Training Foundation.

Hughes, H. L. (1992) *Economics for Hotel and Catering Students*, 2nd edn, Leckhampton: Stanley Thomas.

Hughes, J. C. and Rog, E. (2008) Talent management: a strategy for improving employee recruitment, retention and engagement within hospitality organization, *International Journal of Contemporary Hospitality Management* 20, 7: 743–757.

Hurrell S. A., Scholarios, D. and Thompson, P. (2013) More than a 'humpty dumpty' term: strengthening the conceptualization of soft skills, *Economic and Industrial Democracy* 34, 1: 161–182.

International Labour Organisation (n.d.) Hotels, catering and tourism sector, at http://www.ilo.org/global/industries-and-sectors/hotels-catering-tourism/lang--en/index.htm. Accessed 30 December 2015.

Iverson, R. D. and Deery, M. (1997) Turnover culture in the hospitality industry, *Human Resource Management Journal* 7, 4: 71–82.

Janta, H., Ladkin, A., Brown, L. and Lugosi, P. (2011) Employment experiences of Polish migrant workers in the UK hospitality sector, *Tourism Management* 32, 5: 1006–1019.

Karatepe, O. M. and Uludag, O. (2007) Conflict, exhaustion, and motivation: a study of frontline employees in Northern Cyprus hotels, *Hospitality Management* 26: 645–665.

Lashley, C. (2009) The right answers to the wrong questions? Observations on skill development and training in the UK's hospitality sector, Tourism and Hospitality Research 9, 4: 340–352.

Lashley, C. and Chapman, A. (1999) Labour turnover: hidden problem, hidden cost, *Hospitality Review* 1, 1: 49–54.

Lockyer, C. and Scholarios, D. (2004) Selecting hotel staff: why best practice does not always work, *International Journal of Contemporary Hospitality Management* 16, 2: 125–135.

Lucas, R. (2004) *Employment Relations in the Hospitality and Tourism Industries*, London: Routledge.

Lucas, R. E. and Ralston, L. M. (1997) Youth, gender and part-time employment: a preliminary appraisal of student employment, *Employee Relations* 19, 1: 51–66.

Lucas, R. E. and Wood, R. C. (2000) Work patterns and employment practices. In Brotherton, B. (ed.) *An Introduction to the UK Hospitality Industry: A Comparative Approach*, Oxford: Butterworth-Heinemann, pp. 93–120.

Lyon, A. and Sulcova, D. (2009) Hotel employer's perceptions of employing eastern European workers: a case study of Cheshire, UK, *Tourism, Culture and Communication* 9, 1/2: 17–28.

Michel, M. (2014) Recruitment strategy needed to tackle £2.7 million turnover cost, *Big Hospitality*, 14 October, at http://www.bighospitality.co.uk/Business/Recruitment-strategy-change-needed-to-tackle-2.7m-turnover-cost. Accessed 8 September 2015.

Mkono, M. (2010) In defence of hospitality careers: perspectives of Zimbabwean hotel managers, *International Journal of Contemporary Hospitality Management* 22, 6: 858–870.

Nickson, D. (2013) *Human Resource Management for the Hospitality, Tourism and Events Industries*, 2nd edn, Oxford: Butterworth-Heinemann.

Office for National Statistics (2014) *Patterns of Pay: Estimates from the Annual Survey of Hours and Earnings, UK, 1997 to 2013*, at http://www.ons.gov.uk/ons/dcp171766_353368.pdf. Accessed 10 December 2015.

Ohlin, J. B. and West, J. J. (1994) An analysis of the effect of the fringe benefit offerings on the turnover of hourly workers in the hotel industry, *International Journal of Hospitality Management* 12, 4: 323–336.

Oxford Economics (2015) *The Economic Contribution of the UK Hospitality Industry*, Oxford: Oxford Economics. Available at http://www.bha.org.uk/wordpress/wp-content/uploads/2015/09/Economic-contribution-of-the-UK-hospitality-industry.pdf. Accessed 10 December 2015.

People 1st (2013) *State of the Nation Report 2013*. Available at http://www.people1st.co.uk/getattachment/Research-policy/Research-reports/State-of-the-Nation-Hospitality-Tourism/SOTN_2013_final.pdf.aspx. Accessed 16 October 2015.

People 1st (2015a) Will recruiting younger people will become thing of the past? Available at http://www.people1st.co.uk/getattachment/Research-policy/Research-reports/Monthly-insights-reports/151014-recruiting-young-workforce.pdf.aspx. Accessed 8 September 2015.

People 1st (2015b) *The Skills and Productivity Problem*. Available at http://www.people1st.co.uk/getattachment/Research-policy/Research-reports/The-Skills-and-Productivity-Problem/Report-The-Skills-and-productivity-problem-Oct-15.pdf.aspx. Accessed 10 December 2015.

Pizam, A. (2004) Are hospitality employees equipped to hide their feelings?, *International Journal of Hospitality Management* 23, 4: 315–316.

Pratten, J. D. (2003) The training and retention of chefs, *International Journal of Contemporary Hospitality Management* 15, 4: 237–242.

Rainnie, A. (1989) *Industrial Relations in Small Firms: Small isn't Beautiful*, Routledge, London.

Recruitment and Employment Confederation (2015) *Building the Best Job Markets in the World: The Expert View*, London: Recruitment and Employment Confederation. Available at https://www.rec.uk.com/__data/assets/pdf_file/0018/200691/Building-the-best-jobs-market.pdf. Accessed 12 November 2015.

Reiter, E. (1996) *Making Fast Food: From the Frying Pan into the Fryer*, 2nd edn, London: McGill-Queen's University Press.

Riley, M. (2011) *Human Resource Management in the Hospitality and Tourism Industry*, 2nd edn, New York: Routledge.

Riley, M., Ladkin, A. and Szivas, E. (2002) *Tourism Employment: Analysis and Planning*, Clevedon: Channel View.

Roberts, Y. (2015) Britain's hotel workers – bullied, underpaid and with few rights, *Guardian*, 30 May.

Sachdev, S. and Wilkinson, F. (1998) *Low Pay, Working of the Labour Market and the Role of the Minimum Wage*, London: Institute of Employment Rights.

Shani, A., Uriely, N., Reichel, A. and Ginsburg, L. (2014) Emotional labor in the hospitality industry: the influence of contextual factors, *International Journal of Hospitality Management* 37: 150–158.

Smith, A. (1999 [1776]) *The Wealth of Nations, Books I–III*, ed. A. Skinner, London: Penguin.

Standard Industrial Classification (2007) *Standard Industrial Classification of Economic Activities (SIC) 2007*, Cardiff: Companies House. Available at https://www.gov.uk/government/uploads/system/uploads/attachment_data/file/455263/SIC_codes_V2.pdf. Accessed 10 November 2015.

Szivas, E. and Riley, M. (1999) Tourism employment during economic transition, *Annals of Tourism Research* 26, 4: 747–771.

Szivas, E., Riley, M. and Airey, D. (2003) Labour mobility into tourism: attraction and satisfaction, *Annals of Tourism Research* 30, 1: 64–75.

United Nations World Tourism Organization (2015) *UNWTO: World Tourism Barometer*, 13, 1. Available at http://dtxtq4w60xqpw.cloudfront.net/sites/all/files/pdf/unwto_barom15_01_january_excerpt_1. pdf. Accessed 10 December 2015.

Walmsley, A. (2004) Assessing staff turnover: a view from the English Riviera, *International Journal of Tourism Research* 6: 275–287.

Walmsley, A. (2015) *Youth Employment in Tourism and Hospitality: A Critical Review*, Oxford: Goodfellow.

Warhurst, C. and Nickson, D. (2007) Employee experience of aesthetic labour in retail and hospitality, *Work, Employment and Society* 21, 1: 103–120.

Weaver, A. (2009) Perceptions of job quality in the tourism industry: the views of recent graduates of a university tourism management programme, *International Journal of Contemporary Hospitality Management* 21, 5: 579–593.

Wildes, V. (2007) Attracting and retaining food servers: how internal service quality moderates occupational stigma, *Journal of Hospitality Management* 26, 10: 4–19.

Wong, J. and Wang, C. (2009) Emotional labour of the tour leaders: an exploratory study, *Tourism Management* 30, 2: 249–259.

Wong, S. C. and Ko, A. (2009) Exploratory study of understanding hotel employees' perception on work–life balance issues, *International Journal of Hospitality Management* 28, 2: 195–203.

Wood, R. C. (1997) *Working in Hotels and Catering*, 2nd edn, London: Routledge.

18

Consuming hospitality

Peter Lugosi

Key themes

Hospitality as play

Hospitality as safety and shelter

Hospitality as imposition

Hospitality identification

Consumption refers to a broad set of practices, processes and outcomes (Holt, 1995; Miller, 1995; Bell and Valentine, 1997; Paterson, 2006). Consumption involves the reception, interpretation and use (i.e. transformation and incorporation) of objects, actions, spaces, sights, sounds, smells and events. Consumption may therefore have physical, embodied and material dimensions, but it may also have symbolic, psychological and emotional ones in terms of what is being consumed, when, how and the resulting consequences (Miller, 1995; Shove *et al.*, 2009). Consumption may be considered as experience, involving different sensations and emotional states (Holt, 1995; Paterson, 2006). Consumption also involves acquiring, assigning and manipulating meanings attached to objects and experiences (Miller, 1995; Paterson, 2006). Interpreting and assigning meaning to the acts, objects and spaces of consumption is also used to classify the people, places and organisations involved (Bourdieu, 1984; Bell and Valentine, 1997).

Within the context of the following discussion, the 'consumer' does not consider consumption a passive or a unidirectional process of reception or interpretation. Consumption requires people to engage, invest and to perform the practices of consuming (Warde, 2005). It is also important to acknowledge at the outset that hospitality is co-created through a series of spatial, material, performative and representational practices involving the simultaneous input of producers and consumers (cf. Lugosi, 2014a; Ritzer, 2015). Consumer input may be restricted to perception, but it often involves actions and practices beyond psychological processes; it requires

DOI: 10.4324/9781315679938-20

consumers to mobilise various competencies and resources (Lugosi, 2008). This chapter, however, focuses on the consumption or reception of hospitality rather than the broader process of production or co-creation.

This chapter distinguishes between different forms of hospitality according to the underlying logics that shape how and why it emerges, and considers the diverse implications for those involved in its consumption. For example, some forms of hospitality consumption are chosen because they bring benefits for their consumers. I argue that hospitality may be consumed as play, which has hedonic benefits. It may be consumed to ensure safety and well-being. The consumption of hospitality may also underpin social organisation and group cohesion. However, I also consider how hospitality can be imposed and used coercively as a form of control, or within the process of domination. I explore how hospitality can be used in the process of identification as individuals engage in consumption practices to articulate their sense of selves, as well as their belonging to or difference from others. I also consider how hospitality consumption may be used to ascribe or impose identities and position on others in attempts to control and dominate.

The function of choice is an important consideration in the following discussion of hospitality consumption. Choices require knowledge and capabilities to appreciate different options regarding what to consume, when, and how, and having the resources and opportunities to decide between options. Hospitality-related consumption choices involve freedom *from* constraints or threats and freedom *to* act and experience, suggesting permission and entitlement. Arguably, no choice regarding the consumption of leisure is totally without constraint (Rojek, 2010). However, as the discussion below illustrates, choices concerning consumption involve differing degrees of freedom from and to depending on the contexts and underpinning logics of hospitality, as well as the capacities of consumers.

Hospitality as play

Conceiving hospitality as play suggests that consumption is a liminal or liminoid activity (Turner, 1974, 1982, 1992). The term 'liminoid' refers to moments of time out of ordinary time in contemporary consumer culture, during which people abandon or at least challenge certain norms and obligations, albeit for short periods (see also Turner, 1992; Lugosi, 2007; Sherringham and Daruwalla, 2007). Visiting restaurants, bars and nightclubs, for example, reflects leisure (non-work) consumption.

The opportunity for liminoid consumption is often a central feature of commercial hospitality, tourism and leisure. Hotels are frequently treated as spaces of disinhibition, where consumers can indulge desires, for example illicit interactions (Pritchard and Morgan, 2006; Harper, 2008; Ho, 2008; Berdychevsky *et al.*, 2013). Bars and nightclubs are spaces for social interaction and hedonistic consumption of alcohol and other (legal and illegal) substances (Malbon, 1999; Andrews, 2005, 2009; Lugosi, 2009). Cafés and bars can act as sites for sociality and intellectual encounters, and occasionally as spaces for deviant behaviour and the exchange of revolutionary ideas (cf. Katovich and Reese, 1987; Barrows and Room, 1991; Kneale, 1999; Laurier, 2008; Warner *et al.*, 2013). Restaurants and other foodservice outlets can offer gastronomic experiences, encounters with new and 'strange' cultures, and, to some, the reinforcement of family values and a release from the burdens of domestic work (cf. Shaw and Dawson, 2001; Long, 2004; Germann Molz, 2007; Lugosi *et al.*, 2016).

Conceiving hospitality consumption in commercial contexts as freedom from normative pressures and freedom to engage in hedonistic behaviours has a number of implications. For commercial hospitality, leisure and tourism operators, it is a central feature of their business propositions for their clientele. The ability to construct appealing offerings and deliver positive experiences therefore represents financial opportunities (Pine and Gilmore, 1999; Gilmore and Pine, 2002; Morgan *et al.*, 2010). However, these can also represent operational challenges and risks for organisations. Liberated consumers engaging in hedonistic consumption may lead to the harassment of staff and having to deal with people not conforming to social norms (Guerrier and Adib, 2000; Poulston, 2008; Lugosi, 2014a). Deviant behaviour among some customers can jeopardise the experience of other consumers and tarnish the image of organisations leading to loss of business. Disinhibited consumption may thus need to be controlled and allowed with specific restrictions set upon it. For example, venues can impose limits on the amount that can be consumed, who they allow into a venue, what are tolerable levels of deviant behaviour and the sanctions for people exceeding them (Lugosi, 2014a).

Hospitality as safety and shelter

A well-established theme in discussions of historical and contemporary hospitality is safety (Burgess, 1982; Derrida, 2001; Lashley, 2008; Fourshey, 2012). Notions of shelter, safety and security within hospitality can be viewed as freedom from the threat of physical, psychological or emotional harm (see, e.g., Lee, 2013). Receiving and consuming hospitality among migrants, refugees and children without families is seen as crucial to ensuring their short-term survival, as well as their long-term well-being, (re)integration and socialisation into society (Doty, 2006; Sirriyeh, 2013; Kravva, 2014; Sredanovic and Lelleri, 2015). Places of shelter and food provision are also important for helping homeless people, albeit often temporarily (Bolland and McCallum, 2002; Arnold, 2004; Hogeveen and Freistadt, 2013).

Natural and man-made crises often prompt hospitable responses. For example, terrorist attacks, severe weather conditions such as snow falls and rains have caused injuries, trapped people in cities and destroyed their homes, and the acceptance of hospitality provided by residents and businesses enabled people to overcome the impacts of the resulting social, psychological and economic shocks (cf. Knable, 2002; Anjaria, 2006; Lugosi, 2014b). Hotels have become safe spaces during a number of armed conflicts around the world (Fregonese and Ramadan, 2015). Social and economic crises have also forced people to seek support in obtaining food from sources such as food banks and religious institutions (Loopstra and Tarasuk, 2012; Lambie-Mumford, 2013; Kravva, 2014). However, as a number of critics have noted, hospitality is often a short-term response to the symptoms of broader social problems, for example political instability, economic inequality and segregation, without necessarily addressing their root causes (Loopstra and Tarasuk, 2012; Lambie-Mumford, 2013; Kravva, 2014).

The consumption of hospitality, and engaging in hospitality-related transactions, can, however, help to articulate stronger and more sustained notions of community, which serves to resist threats. For lesbian, gay, bisexual, transsexual/transgender (LGBT) consumers, for example, food, drink and retail settings have often been 'safe' spaces, allowing them to express their sexuality while negating risks of violence and persecution (David, 1997; Brown, 2000; Lugosi, 2009). Consuming within such hospitable spaces has also enabled LGBT consumers to maintain a sense of economic and social visibility in society rather than being contained in hidden, marginal social spaces (Skeggs, 1999; Moran *et al.*, 2001; Binnie and Skeggs, 2004). Economic visibility in the marketplace may help to empower LGBT consumers because commercial service providers who cater for their needs see them as lucrative segments. Social visibility through hospitality consumption also serves to 'normalise' and legitimise the presence of LGBTs in hetero-centric societies. However, it is important to be mindful that visibility is dependent upon people's ability to pay and thus be legitimate consumers; so social acceptance is not open to all and is not an uninhibited consumer choice (Lugosi, 2009). Increased visibility within consumer spaces may also have the contrasting effect of prompting further surveillance and violence (Moran and Skeggs, 2004).

Hospitality as well-being

A theme closely related to and emerging out of notions of safety is well-being. Well-being is itself a contentious concept, which can refer to physiological, emotional and physical dimensions, and academics have argued over its definition and measurement (Dodge *et al.*, 2012). However, on a more general level it refers to a state involving positive affect and satisfaction, in which there is a balance between social, psychological and physical challenges, and resources (Dodge *et al.*, 2012). It has been argued that, historically, hospitality was often provided and consumed as part of charitable behaviour to help ensure the well-being of the socially disadvantaged (Heal, 1984; Bennett, 1992). Hospitality could therefore be considered directly socially functional, as it was given to those who depended on it – that is, the hungry, poor, sick, disabled and displaced. However, Bennett's work (1992) suggests that hospitality could also be indirectly functional, as hospitable events were used by the wealthy to raise funds to support the socially marginalised and disadvantaged.

Arguably, the consumption of recreational hospitality continues to fulfil similar functions in contemporary society. The notion of recreation (re-creation) implies liberated and liberating consumption, which can have social and psychological benefits (Rojek, 1995). It can be an outlet for venting social and psychological tensions, thus supporting individual and collective well-being. Hospitality spaces also support well-being and health by enabling people to receive care and facilitating social connectedness, reducing social exclusion. Beyond addressing short-term safety needs in response to crises, the consumption (and provision) of hospitality can contribute towards longer-term community cohesion and resilience. For example, Lugosi (2011) noted that community hospitality initiatives such as the Eden Project's 'Big Lunch' events sought to bring neighbours together and (re)build a sense of local community through the collective consumption of food and drink (www.thebiglunch.com/about/). Similarly, the Macmillan Cancer Support charity launched the 'Coffee Morning' initiative, where people could raise money for the charity through participating in hospitable social events (http://coffee.macmillan.org.uk/). Within such non-commercial settings, consumption serves a broader sense of collective self-interest and well-being.

The mobilisation of hospitality for promoting community and sociability is in response to the increasing fragmentation of society and the recognition that social isolation has negative impacts on physical and mental health (Coyle and Dugan, 2012; Luo *et al.*, 2012; Steptoe *et al.*, 2013; Melton, 2014). It has been argued that consuming in hospitality spaces, such as day and health centres for the elderly and for people suffering from serious illnesses, can help their recovery and improve their health (cf. Cheang, 2002; Rosenbaum, 2006; Rosenbaum *et al.*, 2007; Glover and Parry, 2009; Rosenbaum *et al.*, 2009; Simpson-Young and Russell, 2009; Rosenbaum *et al.*, 2014). The ability to access hospitality and hospitable spaces can thus be seen as a social and psychological resource. Commercial hospitality spaces can also serve community needs and improve well-being in other ways. In the United Kingdom, for example, within rural, isolated and socially excluded communities, public houses have taken over the provision of postal, grocery and community health services, where existing commercial and governmental bodies have withdrawn, while also maintaining their more general role in facilitating social interactions (Sandiford and Divers, 2011, 2014; Muir, 2012; Cabras and Mount, 2016).

It is worth commenting on the role of hospitality consumption within organisational and work settings, which can support the functioning of organisations and the well-being of their stakeholders (Lugosi, 2014b). Work-related meals, such as business lunches, are used to build contacts, make good impressions on potential colleagues and clients, and display power through the food ordered and the knowledge of drinks such as wines (Dienhart and Pinsel, 1984; Adams et al., 2000; Roger, 2003; Jay, 2006). Discussions of inducting new employees make references to the importance of offering drinks and food (e.g. Connelly, 2005), pointing out that opportunities to consume together are key aspects of the welcome. Research also showed how rituals of food preparation and consumption in the workplace help to reinforce group identity and interdependence (Lee, 2001; Valentine, 2002; Driver, 2008; Thomson and Hassenkamp, 2008). Practices of food and drink consumption within organisations can also help to cope with the stresses of work (Stroebaek, 2013).

Studies have shown how work relationships extend into non-work contexts, through such hospitality consumption as drinking after work, eating together at lunch and socialising with colleagues outside the workplace (cf. Flores-Pereira et al., 2008; Altman and Baruch, 2010; Strangleman, 2010; Mitchell et al., 2014), and there is increasingly a blurring of the divide between work and leisure. Importantly, research suggests that people who engage in work-related drinking benefit in the form of higher incomes (cf. Peters and Stringham, 2006; Peters, 2009; Ziebarth and Grabka, 2009).

The preceding discussion suggests that consuming hospitality ensures social cohesion in the workplace and it should therefore be seen as a positive part of organisational life. However, it is important to stress that hospitality within organisations may be used more divisively. Rituals and routines of hospitality consumption, for example during work-related meals or social functions, also help to articulate boundaries, hierarchies and various regulatory regimes (Rosen, 1985; Di Domenico and Phillips, 2009). Hospitality is not equally available to everyone and it always has the potential to exclude some and place the interests of some parties over others. Decisions regarding who is invited, what they are entitled to, how they should conduct themselves and how they should reciprocate reflect the instrumental nature of hospitality to position and control.

Hospitality as imposition

It is important to acknowledge that the reception and consumption of hospitality is not freely chosen by all. However, imposition exists on a continuum, with milder and more severe forms. At the milder end is hospitality having to be consumed because people are caught in ongoing, obligatory transactions with hosts analogous to gift relations (Burgess, 1982; Mauss, 1990). As Derrida (2000) has suggested, hospitality does not exist in pure, altruistic forms – giving implies the requirement both to accept and to reciprocate (see also Derrida and Dufourmantelle, 2000; Komter and Leer, 2012; Kosnik, 2014). The refusal to accept hospitality when offered may be considered an insult to the giver (Hobbs, 2001; Pitt-Rivers, 2012). Similarly, failure to show gratitude and to reciprocate can lead to tensions and, on occasion, open conflicts. The acceptance of hospitality also represents a power relationship where rules have to be observed, for example etiquettes of drinking and eating (Visser, 1991; Curro, 2014). Accepting hospitality suggests being obligated to perform the role of the guest in transactions of hospitality.

Imposed hospitality can also take different forms. For example, during travel and tourism, consuming food, drink and shelter may be done out of necessity rather than personal choice. Such consumption contexts may have limited choices regarding what is available, and few or no alternative providers to choose from. This may be the case in some resorts and transport hubs (i.e. stations, airports and seaports), and on airplanes, trains and cruise ships, and on organised tours, particularly when a third party has the power to decide where, when and how hospitality is consumed (cf. Dann, 2000; Weaver, 2005; Harrison and Lugosi, 2013).

Hospitality is also imposed on people in institutional contexts where, by default, freedoms are constrained, for example in hospitals, care homes, schools and state-provisioned housing (Johns *et al.*, 2010; Wingate-Lewinson *et al.*, 2010; Edwards, 2013). Within such contexts, the providing institutions have considerable control over where people must take shelter, what food and drink can be consumed, when, where and how (Wingate-Lewinson *et al.*, 2010; Edwards, 2013; Johns *et al.*, 2013). Furthermore, hospitality in such institutional contexts is determined by broader factors, such as the budget allocated to provide shelter and sustenance, and the motivation behind the hospitality – that is, rehabilitation, health promotion, care and welfare provision (Bland, 1999; Hartwell and Edwards, 2003; Hendy *et al.*, 2005; Edwards, 2013).

Organisationally or institutionally imposed hospitality takes more severe forms in prisons, secure mental institutions and detention centres housing, for example, migrants and refugees (cf. Valentine and Longstaff, 1998; Pugliese, 2002; Smith, 2002; Gibson, 2003; Rozakou, 2012; Brisman, 2013). Such contexts reflect what Goffman called 'total institutions' (1968: 4). Within total institutions, there is clear role and power distinction between the providers and recipients of hospitality. Behavioural norms, mobility and use of space are strictly imposed upon 'captive guests' (i.e. refugees, detainees, prisoners and patients). In short, the practices of hospitality consumption are defined by the total institution, which is itself a proxy agent of larger state institutions. States enact political ideologies and project power through imposed consumption of hospitality.

Hospitality as identification and positioning

The discussion of hospitality as representing freedom, choice and imposition points to broader issues concerning the identities of those who consume it. Social scientists argue that identities are not determined solely by genetics, nor should identities be seen as stable, fixed properties of individuals (Lugosi, 2013). Identities are fluid, undergoing constant re-construction. Importantly, the notion of self-as-process implies that identities are never finalised projects. Instead, they are rearticulated through our thoughts, behaviours, embodied actions and speech acts. Notions of the self are shaped by the environment, levels of technology and social relations (Hall and Du Gay, 1996). Authors have argued that it is more useful to think about selves through the notion of *identification* (e.g. Bhabha, 1990, 1996; Hall, 1996). Who we think or feel we are is shaped by how we identify with or against others. Any notion of self and identity is thus relational and subject to contestation and change. However, it is also useful to highlight the tensions between identity and identification as being a choice, and identity as being ascribed by others.

The consumption of hospitality is one of many domains of social activity through which identity is constructed, adopted and ascribed. Sociologists, anthropologists and geographers often argue that the consumption of hospitality is a conscious choice by people to articulate a sense of belonging to a group, establish some political tie or distinguish themselves from others (Sloan, 2004; Cuthill, 2007; Lashley *et al.*, 2007; Lugosi, 2013; Craggs, 2014; Fregonese and Ramadan, 2015). It is also possible to argue that the notion of free choice is a fallacy. Our choices regarding where, when and how we consume hospitality, such as which restaurant we patronise or who we socialise with, are shaped by such factors as gender, ethnicity and class habitus (Williams, 2002; Sloan, 2004, 2013). Nevertheless, people with greater access to social, cultural and economic capital (Bourdieu, 1984), and those who have entitlements to mobility, for example because they are legal citizens in a state, have a greater choice over how identities are constructed and articulated through the consumption of hospitality.

Even within such consumption of hospitality, identities remain contested and open to manipulation and re-articulation. The reshaping of identities may emerge as people physically consume hospitality, and as their consumption is mediated and represented by others. For example, consuming in a restaurant or hotel may reflect one type of identification with an immediate social group (cf. Sloan, 2004, 2013; Bell and Valentine, 1997; De Solier, 2013; Getz et al., 2014). However, as those embodied experiences are mediated through social media, their implications for notions of identity can change. For instance, people viewing and commenting on such consumer experiences via social media may have alternative perspectives on the people involved and the activities, which may reinforce or contest identity claims (Lampel and Bhalla, 2007; Watson et al., 2008; Lugosi et al., 2012; Osman et al., 2014). Commercial organisations may also capture and analyse social media representations of hospitality consumption to create new taxonomies of consumers, segment markets and target consumers with marketing promotions (Lugosi et al., 2012; Sigala et al., 2012). Identification and the articulation of identity through hospitality consumption are thereby subject to commercial exploitation.

The projection and imposition of identity and position through hospitality consumption takes many forms, some more insidious than others. Craggs (2012), for example, argued that hotels in colonial Africa were sites for assigning status to various ethnic groups. Creating segregated spaces and events within hotels were mechanisms through which Europeans continued to assert their 'dominant' status. Food and drink-related events were used to create shared spaces of consumption that temporarily brought together different ethnic groups. However, such events continued to be used to articulate the inferiority of the 'other' and the superiority of the colonisers, with allowances made for a privileged few African elites to be deemed 'worthy'. Importantly, because hotel spaces were used to designate and segregate, they also became the focus of resistance (Craggs, 2012). Actively engaging in multi-racial dining became a form of politicised consumption through which racist policies and beliefs could be visibly challenged.

The relative freedom to choose how identities are constructed and how identification is performed can be contrasted with those who do not have such entitlements. This may include people who do not have access to or cannot mobilise appropriate forms of capital, but the notion of ascribed identity has different dimensions for those consuming imposed hospitality – that is, prisoners, the homeless, undocumented migrants and refugees (Pugliese, 2002; Gibson, 2003; Darling, 2009; Rozakou, 2012; Hogeveen and Freistadt, 2013; Kravva, 2014). The imposition of hospitality becomes part of institutional or state strategies to strip people of their former identities as they are 'contained' within institutions. Importantly, the construction of identity through imposed hospitality arguably has longer term effects as migrants and refugees are treated as individuals who need to reciprocate for the 'generous' hospitality they have received (cf. Healey, 2014). The perceived obligation to show gratitude to the 'host' may continue to construct notions of identity after they have left the spaces of migrant 'care' and containment.

Conclusions

This chapter has considered different drivers and rationales for consuming hospitality and the implications these may have for groups and individuals. The discussion has suggested that the underpinning logics of hospitality may fundamentally shape what forms it may take, how it is consumed and by whom. Consuming hospitality may thus provide opportunities for some people, for example to connect, grow, heal, escape or demonstrate status. For others, hospitality and the need to consume it in specific ways may be a threat, particularly as it is used to classify and to restrict movement or choice. In principle, this suggests there is a clear distinction between freedom and constraint. However, it is important to remain mindful of the fact that no hospitality-related choice is completely unrestricted because it always takes place within a social context. So even if consumption is supposedly freely chosen, choices are always shaped by the resources available to people, whether it is in the form of economic capital, knowledge or competence. Some hospitality-related decisions are, however, much more overtly controlled and governed by others. Imposing the consumption of hospitality, and the forms that it can take, offers a way to exercise and project power.

Distinguishing between different forms of hospitality consumption based on its underlying logics opens up a number of lines of enquiry. It points to the need to examine the resources and competencies that shape the (perceived) choices of those who receive and consume hospitality. It also helps to consider why and how hospitality consumption may become a threat to some or an opportunity to others in different contexts. Examining the underlying logics of hospitality consumption may also help to reveal why it is produced or mobilised in very specific ways by individuals, organisations and states. However, within any such study of hospitality consumption it is also important to avoid treating it as passive reception. Those receiving and consuming hospitality are part of the co-creation process, and even within imposed forms of hospitality they have some agency in shaping how they accept it, how they participate, how they are controlled through it and how they are defined by it.

References

Adams, R. T., Adams, A. A., and Seff, R. A. (2000) *60 Minutes to Success: The Ultimate Guide to Power Lunching*, Lincoln, NE: iUniverse.
Altman, Y. and Baruch, Y. (2010) The organisational lunch, *Culture and Organization* 16, 2: 127–143.
Andrews, H. (2005) Feeling at home: embodying Britishness in a Spanish charter tourist resort, *Tourist Studies* 5, 3: 247–266.
Andrews, H. (2009) 'Tits out for the boys and no back chat': gendered space on holiday, *Space and Culture* 12, 2: 166–182.
Anjaria, J. S. (2006) Urban calamities: a view from Mumbai, *Space and Culture* 9, 1: 80–82.
Arnold, K. (2004) *Homelessness, Citizenship, and Identity: The Uncanniness of Late Modernity*, Albany: State University of New York Press.
Barrows, S. and Room, R. (1991) *Drinking: Behavior and Belief in Modern History*, Berkeley: University of California Press.
Bell, D. and Valentine, G. (1997) *Consuming Geographies: We Are Where We Eat*, London: Routledge.
Bennett, J. M. (1992) Conviviality and charity in medieval and early modern England, *Past and Present* 134, February: 19–41.
Berdychevsky, L., Poria, Y. and Uriely, N. (2013) Hospitality accommodations and women's consensual sex, *International Journal of Hospitality Management* 34: 169–171.
Bhabha, H. K. (1990) Interview with Homi Bhabha: the third space. In Rutherford, J. (ed.) *Identity: Community, Culture, Difference*, London: Lawrence & Wishart, pp. 207–221.
Bhabha, H. K. (1996) Culture's in-between. In Hall, S. and du Gay, P. (eds) *Questions of Cultural Identity*, London: Sage, pp. 53–60.
Binnie, J. and Skeggs, B. (2004) Cosmopolitan knowledge and the production and consumption of sexualized space: Manchester's gay village, *Sociological Review* 52, 1: 39–61.
Bland, R. (1999) Independence, privacy and risk: two contrasting approaches to residential care for older people, *Ageing and Society* 19, 5: 539–560.
Bolland, J. M. and McCallum, D. M. (2002) Touched by homelessness: an examination of hospitality for the down and out, *American Journal of Public Health* 92, 1: 116–118.
Bourdieu, P. (1984) *Distinction: A Social Critique of the Judgement of Taste*, London: Routledge.

Brisman, A. (2013) Fair fare? Food as contested terrain in US prisons and jails. In Lefler, L. J. (ed.) *Southern Foodways and Culture: Local Considerations and Beyond*, Knoxville, TN: Newfound Press, pp. 67–146.

Brown, M. (2000) *Closet Space: Geographies of Metaphor from the Body to the Globe*, London: Routledge.

Burgess, J. (1982) Perspectives on gift exchange and hospitable behaviour, *International Journal of Hospitality Management* 1, 1: 49–57.

Cabras, I. and Mount, M. (2016) Economic development, entrepreneurial embeddedness and resilience: the case of pubs in rural Ireland, *European Planning Studies* 24, 2: 254–276.

Cheang, M. (2002) Older adults' frequent visits to a fast-food restaurant: nonobligatory social interaction and the significance of play in a 'third place', *Journal of Aging Studies* 16, 3: 303–321.

Connelly, L. M. (2005) Welcoming new employees, *Journal of Nursing Scholarship* 37, 2: 163–164.

Coyle, C. E. and Dugan, E. (2012) Social isolation, loneliness and health among older adults, *Journal of Aging and Health* 24, 8: 1346–1363.

Craggs, R. (2012) Towards a political geography of hotels: Southern Rhodesia, 1958–1962, *Political Geography* 3, 4: 215–224.

Craggs, R. (2014) Hospitality in geopolitics and the making of Commonwealth international relations, *Geoforum* 52: 90–100.

Curro, C. (2014) A 'Gift from God'? Georgian hospitality between tradition and pragmatism, *Hospitality & Society* 4, 3: 293–310.

Cuthill, V. (2007) Sensing and performing hospitalities and socialities of tourist places: eating and drinking out in Harrogate and Whitehaven. In Germann Molz, J. and Gibson, S. (eds) *Mobilizing Hospitality*, Aldershot: Ashgate, pp. 83–100.

Dann, G. (2000) Overseas holiday hotels for the elderly: total bliss or total institution? In Robinson, M., Long, P., Evans, N., Sharpley, R. and Swarbrooke, J. (eds) *Reflections on International Tourism: Motivations, Behaviour and Tourist Types*, Sunderland: Centre for Travel and Tourism in association with Business Education Publishers, pp. 83–94.

Darling, J. (2009) Becoming bare life: asylum, hospitality, and the politics of encampment, *Environment and Planning D: Society and Space* 27, 4: 649–665.

David, H. (1997) *On Queer Street: A Social History of British Homosexuality 1895–1995*, London: HarperCollins.

De Solier, I. (2013) Making the self in a material world: food and moralities of consumption, *Cultural Studies Review* 19, 1: 9–27.

Derrida, J. (2000) Hostipitality, *Angelaki: Journal of Theoretical Humanities* 5, 3: 3–18.

Derrida, J. (2001) *On Cosmopolitanism and Forgiveness*, London: Routledge.

Derrida, J. and Dufourmantelle, A. (2000) *Of Hospitality*, Stanford: Stanford University Press.

Di Domenico, M. and Phillips, N. (2009) Sustaining the ivory tower: Oxbridge formal dining as organizational ritual, *Journal of Management Inquiry* 18, 4: 326–343.

Dienhart, L. and Pinsel, M. E. (1984) *Power Lunching: How You Can Profit From More Effective Business Lunch Strategy*, Chicago: Turnbull and Willoughby.

Dodge, R., Daly, A., Huyton, J. and Sanders, L. (2012) The challenge of defining wellbeing, *International Journal of Wellbeing* 2, 3: 222–235.

Doty, R. L. (2006) Fronteras compasivas and the ethics of unconditional hospitality, *Millennium-Journal of International Studies* 35, 1: 53–74.

Driver, M. (2008) Every bite you take … food and the struggles of embodied subjectivity in organizations, *Human Relations* 61, 7: 913–934.

Edwards, J. S. (2013) The foodservice industry: eating out is more than just a meal, *Food Quality and Preference* 27, 2: 223–229.

Flores-Pereira, M. T., Davel, E. and Cavendon, N. R. (2008) Drinking beer and understanding organizational culture embodiment, *Human Relations* 61, 7: 1007–1126.

Fourshey, C. C. (2012) Karibu stranger, come heal thy host: hospitality as historical subject in Southwestern Tanzania, 1600–1900, *African Historical Review* 44, 2: 18–54.

Fregonese, S. and Ramadan, A. (2015) Hotel geopolitics: a research agenda, *Geopolitics* 20, 4: 793–813.

Germann Molz, J. G. (2007) Eating difference: the cosmopolitan mobilities of culinary tourism, *Space and Culture* 10, 1: 77–93.

Getz, D., Robinson, R. N., Andersson, T. D. and Vujicic, S. (2014) *Foodies and Food Tourism*, Oxford: Goodfellow.

Gibson, S. (2003) Accommodating strangers: British hospitality and the asylum hotel debate, *Journal for Cultural Research* 7, 4: 367–386.

Gilmore, J. H. and Pine, J. (2002) Differentiating hospitality operations via experiences: why selling services is not enough, *Cornell Hotel and Restaurant Administration Quarterly* 43, 3: 87–96.

Glover, T. D. and Parry, D. C. (2009) A third place in the everyday lives of people living with cancer: functions of Gilda's Club of Greater Toronto, *Health & Place* 15, 1: 97–106.

Goffman, E. (1968) *Asylums: Essays on the Social Situation of Mental Patients and Other Inmates*, Harmondsworth: Penguin Books.

Guerrier, Y. and Adib, A. S. (2000) 'No, we don't provide that service': the harassment of hotel employees by customers, *Work, Employment and Society* 14, 4: 689–705.

Hall, S. (1996) Introduction: who needs identity? In Hall, S. and du Gay, P. (eds) *Questions of Cultural Identity*, London: Sage, pp. 1–17.

Hall, S. and du Gay, P. (eds) (1996) *Questions of Cultural Identity*, London: Sage.

Harper, S. (2008) 'When you walk through these doors, you can be anything you want': authenticity, fantasy and neoliberal ideology in Hotel Babylon, *Journal of British Cinema and Television* 5, 1: 113–131.

Harrison, D. and Lugosi, P. (2013) Tourism culture(s): the hospitality dimension, *Tourism Recreation Research* 38, 3: 269–279.

Hartwell, H. J. and Edwards, J. S. (2003) A comparative analysis of 'plated' and 'bulk trolley' hospital food service systems, *Food Service Technology* 3, 3–4: 133–142.

Heal, F. (1984) The idea of hospitality in early modern England, *Past and Present* 102, February: 66–93.

Healey, R. L. (2014) Gratitude and hospitality: Tamil refugee employment in London and the conditional nature of integration, *Environment and Planning A* 46, 3: 614–628.

Hendy, H. M., Williams, K. E. and Camise, T. S. (2005) 'Kids Choice' school lunch program increases children's fruit and vegetable acceptance, *Appetite* 45, 3: 250–263.

Ho, S. L. (2008) Private love in public space: love hotels and the transformation of intimacy in contemporary Japan, *Asian Studies Review* 32, 1: 31–56.

Hobbs, T. R. (2001) Hospitality in the First Testament and the 'Teleological Fallacy', *Journal for the Study of the Old Testament* 26, 1: 3–30.

Hogeveen, B. and Freistadt, J. (2013) Hospitality and the homeless: Jacques Derrida in the neoliberal city, *Journal of Theoretical and Philosophical Criminology* 5, 1: 39–63.

Holt, D. B. (1995) How consumers consume: a typology of consumption practices, *Journal of Consumer Research* 22, 1: 1–16.

Jay, R. (2006) *The Art of the Business Lunch: Building Relationships between 12 and 2*, Franklin Lakes, NJ: Career Press.

Johns, N., Edwards, J. S. and Hartwell, H. J. (2013) Hungry in hospital, well-fed in prison? A comparative analysis of food service systems, *Appetite* 68: 45–50.

Johns, N., Hartwell, H. and Morgan, M. (2010) Improving the provision of meals in hospital: the patients' viewpoint, *Appetite* 54, 1: 181–185.

Katovich, M. and Reese, W. (1987) The regular: full-time identities and membership in an urban bar, *Journal of Contemporary Ethnography* 16, 3: 308–343.

Knable, C. R. (2002) September 11, 2001: recovering hospitality at ground zero, *Cornell Hotel and Restaurant Administration Quarterly* 43, 5: 11–26.

Kneale, J. (1999) 'A problem of supervision': moral geographies of the nineteenth-century British public house, *Journal of Historical Geography* 25, 3: 333–348.

Komter, A. and Leer, M. V. (2012) Hospitality as a gift relationship: political refugees as guests in the private sphere, *Hospitality & Society* 2, 1: 7–23.

Kosnik, E. (2014) Work for food and accommodation: negotiating socio-economic relationships in non-commercial work-exchange encounters, *Hospitality & Society* 4, 3: 275–291.

Kravva, V. (2014) Politicizing hospitality: the emergency food assistance landscape in Thessaloniki, *Hospitality & Society* 4, 3: 249–274.

Lambie-Mumford, H. (2013) Every town should have one: emergency food banking in the UK, *Journal of Social Policy* 42, 1: 73–89.

Lampel, J. and Bhalla, A. (2007) The role of status seeking in online communities: giving the gift of experience, *Journal of Computer-Mediated Communication* 12, 2: 434–455.

Lashley, C. (2008) Studying hospitality: insights from social sciences, *Scandinavian Journal of Hospitality and Tourism* 8, 1: 69–84.

Lashley, C., Lynch, P. and Morrison, A. (eds) (2007) *Hospitality: A Social Lens*, Oxford: Elsevier.

Laurier, E. (2008) Drinking up endings: conversational resources of the café, *Language & Communication* 28, 2: 165–181.

Lee, D. S. (2001) The morning tea break ritual: a case study, *International Journal of Nursing Practice* 7, 2: 69–73.

Lee, M. K. (2013) Captivity and hospitality in the New Americas, *Hospitality & Society* 3, 1: 43–55.

Long, L. M. (2004) *Culinary Tourism*, Lexington: University Press of Kentucky.

Loopstra, R. and Tarasuk, V. (2012) The relationship between food banks and household food insecurity among low-income Toronto families, *Canadian Public Policy* 38, 4: 497–514.

Lugosi, P. (2007) Queer consumption and commercial hospitality: communitas, myths and the production of liminoid space, *International Journal of Sociology and Social Policy* 27, 3/4: 163–174.

Lugosi, P. (2008) Hospitality spaces, hospitable moments: consumer encounters and affective experiences in commercial settings, *Journal of Foodservice* 19, 2: 139–149.

Lugosi, P. (2009) The production of hospitable space: commercial propositions and consumer co-creation in a bar operation, *Space and Culture* 12, 4: 396–411.

Lugosi, P. (2011) The role of hospitality in supporting community and wellbeing, *Hospitality Review* 13, 4: 3–4.

Lugosi, P. (2013) Food, drink and identity. In Sloan, D. (ed.) *Food and Drink: The Cultural Context*, Oxford: Goodfellow, pp. 20–50.

Lugosi, P. (2014a) Mobilising identity and culture in experience co-creation and venue operation, *Tourism Management* 40: 165–179.

Lugosi, P. (2014b) Hospitality and organizations: enchantment, entrenchment and reconfiguration, *Hospitality and Society* 4, 1: 75–92.

Lugosi, P., Janta, H. and Watson, P. (2012) Investigative management and consumer research on the internet, *International Journal of Contemporary Hospitality Management* 24, 6: 838–854.

Lugosi, P., Robinson, R. N. S., Golubovskaya, M., Foley, L. and Harwell, J. (2016) Experiencing parenthood, care and spaces of hospitality, *Sociological Review* 64, 2: 274–293.

Luo, Y., Hawkley, L. C., Waite, L. J. and Cacioppo, J. T. (2012) Loneliness, health, and mortality in old age: a national longitudinal study, *Social Science & Medicine* 74, 6: 907–914.

Malbon, B. (1999) *Clubbing: Dancing, Ecstasy, Vitality*, London: Routledge.

Mauss, M. (1990) *The Gift: The Form and Reason for Exchange in Archaic Societies*, trans. W. D. Halls, New York and London: W. W. Norton.

Melton, G. B. (2014) Hospitality: transformative service to children, families, and communities, *American Psychologist* 69, 8: 761–769.

Miller, D. (ed.) (1995) *Acknowledging Consumption*, London: Routledge.

Minca, C. and Ong, C. E. (2015) The power of space: the biopolitics of custody and care at the Lloyd Hotel, Amsterdam, *Political Geography*, DOI:10.1016/j.polgeo.2015.03.001.

Mitchell, R., Boyle, B., Burgess, J. and McNeil, K. (2014) 'You can't make a good wine without a few beers': gatekeepers and knowledge flow in industrial districts, *Journal of Business Research* 67, 10: 2198–2206.

Moran, L. and Skeggs, B. (2004) *Sexuality and the Politics of Violence and Safety*, London: Routledge.

Moran, L., Skeggs, B., Tyrer, P. and Corteen, K. (2001) Property, boundary, exclusion: making sense of hetero-violence in safer places, *Social and Cultural Geography* 2: 407–420.

Morgan, M., Lugosi, P. and Ritchie, J. R. B. (eds) (2010) *The Tourism and Leisure Experience: Consumer and Managerial Perspectives*, Bristol: Channel View.

Muir, R. (2012) *Pubs and Places: The Social Value of Community Pubs*, 2nd edn, London: Institute for Public Policy Research.

Osman, H., Johns, N. and Lugosi, P. (2014) Commercial hospitality in destination experiences: McDonald's and tourists' consumption of space, *Tourism Management* 42: 238–247.

Paterson, M. (2006) *Consumption and Everyday Life*, Abingdon: Routledge.

Peters, B. L. (2009) The drinkers' bonus in the military: officers versus enlisted personnel, *Applied Economics* 41, 17: 2211–2220.

Peters, B. L. and Stringham, E. (2006) No booze? You may lose: why drinkers earn more money than non-drinkers, *Journal of Labor Research* 27, 3: 411–421.

Pine, B. J. and Gilmore, J. H. (1999) *The Experience Economy*, Boston: Harvard Business School Press.

Pitt-Rivers, J. (2012) The law of hospitality, *HAU: Journal of Ethnographic Theory* 2, 1: 501–517.

Poulston, J. (2008) Metamorphosis in hospitality: a tradition of sexual harassment, *International Journal of Hospitality Management* 27, 2: 232–240.

Pritchard, A. and Morgan, N. (2006) Hotel Babylon? Exploring hotels as liminal sites of transition and transgression, *Tourism Management* 27, 5: 762–772.

Pugliese, J. (2002) Penal asylum: refugees, ethics, hospitality, *Borderlands e-journal* 1, 1, at http://www.borderlandsejournal.adelaide.edu.au/vol1no1_2002/pugliese.html.

Ritzer, G. (2015) Hospitality and prosumption, *Research in Hospitality Management* 5, 1: 9–17.

Roger, B. (2003) Corporate hospitality: executive indulgence or vital corporate communications weapon?, *Corporate Communications: An International Journal* 8, 4: 229–240.

Rojek, C. (1995) *Decentring Leisure: Rethinking Leisure Theory*, London: Sage.

Rojek, C. (2010) *The Labour of Leisure: The Culture of Free Time*, London: Sage.

Rosen, M. (1985) Breakfast at Spiro's: dramaturgy and dominance, *Journal of Management* 11, 2: 31–48.

Rosenbaum, M. S. (2006) Exploring the social supportive role of third places in consumers' lives, *Journal of Service Research* 9, 1: 59–72.

Rosenbaum, M. S., Sweeney, J. C. and Massiah, C. (2014) The restorative potential of senior centers, *Managing Service Quality* 24, 4: 363–383.

Rosenbaum, M. S., Sweeney, J. C. and Windhorst, C. (2009) The restorative qualities of an activity-based, third place café for seniors: restoration, social support, and place attachment at Mather's – more than a café, *Seniors Housing & Care Journal* 17, 1: 39–54.

Rosenbaum, M. S., Ward, J., Walker, B. A. and Ostrom, A. L. (2007) A cup of coffee with a dash of love: an investigation of commercial social support and third-place attachment, *Journal of Service Research* 10, 1: 43–59.

Rozakou, K. (2012) The biopolitics of hospitality in Greece: humanitarianism and the management of refugees, *American Ethnologist* 39, 3: 562–577.

Sandiford, P. J. and Divers, P. (2011) The public house and its role in society's margins, *International Journal of Hospitality Management* 30, 4: 765–773.

Sandiford, P. J. and Divers, P. (2014) The English public house as a 21st century socially responsible community institution, *International Journal of Hospitality Management* 41: 88–96.

Shaw, S. M. and Dawson, D. (2001) Purposive leisure: examining parental discourses on family activities, *Leisure Sciences* 23, 4: 217–231.

Sherringham, C. and Daruwalla, P. (2007) Transgressing hospitality: polarities and disordered relationships? In Lashley, C., Lynch, P. and Morrison, A. (eds) *Hospitality: A Social Lens*, Oxford: Elsevier, pp. 33–45.

Shove, E., Trentmann, F. and Wilk, R. (eds) (2009) *Time, Consumption and Everyday Life: Practice, Materiality and Culture*, Oxford: Berg.

Sigala, M., Christou, E. and Gretzel, U. (eds) (2012) *Social Media in Travel, Tourism and Hospitality: Theory, Practice and Cases*, Farnham: Ashgate.

Simpson-Young, V. and Russell, C. (2009) The licensed social club: a resource for independence in later life, *Ageing International* 34, 4: 216–236.

Sirriyeh, A. (2013) Hosting strangers: hospitality and family practices in fostering unaccompanied refugee young people, *Child & Family Social Work* 18, 1: 5–14.

Skeggs, B. (1999) Matter out of place: visibility and sexualities in leisure spaces, *Leisure Studies* 18: 213–232.

Sloan, D. (ed.) (2004) *Culinary Taste*, Oxford: Elsevier.

Sloan, D. (ed.) (2013) *Food and Drink: The Cultural Context*, Oxford: Goodfellow.

Smith, C. (2002) Punishment and pleasure: women, food and the imprisoned body, *Sociological Review* 50, 2: 197–214.

Sredanovic, D. and Lelleri, R. (2015) The 'Emergency North Africa' in the Bologna area: visions and tensions of hospitality in operators' discourses, *Hospitality & Society* 5, 2–3: 203–220.

Steptoe, A., Shankar, A., Demakakos, P. and Wardle, J. (2013) Social isolation, loneliness, and all-cause mortality in older men and women, *Proceedings of the National Academy of Sciences* 110, 15: 5797–5801.

Strangleman, T. (2010) Food, drink and the cultures of work: consumption in the life and death of an English factory, *Food, Culture and Society* 13, 2: 257–278.

Stroebaek, P. S. (2013) Let's have a cup of coffee! Coffee and coping communities at work, *Symbolic Interaction* 36, 4: 381–397.

Thomson, D. and Hassenkamp, A. M. (2008) The social meaning and function of food rituals in healthcare practice: an ethnography, *Human Relations* 61, 12: 1775–1802.

Turner, V. (1974) *Dramas, Fields, and Metaphors: Symbolic Action in Human Society*, Ithaca, NY: Cornell University Press.

Turner, V. (1982) *From Ritual to Theatre: The Human Seriousness of Play*, New York: PAJ.

Turner, V. (1992) *Blazing the Trail: Way Marks in the Exploration of Symbols*, Tucson: University of Arizona Press.

Valentine, G. (2002) In-corporations: food, bodies and organizations, *Body and Society* 8, 1: 1–20.

Valentine, G. and Longstaff, B. (1998) Doing porridge: food and social relations in a male prison, *Journal of Material Culture* 3, 2: 131–152.

Visser, M. (1991) *The Rituals of Dinner: The Origins, Evolution, Eccentricities and Meaning of Table Manners*, Harmondsworth: Penguin.

Warde, A. (2005) Consumption and theories of practice, *Journal of Consumer Culture* 5, 2: 131–153.

Warner, J., Talbot, D. and Bennison, G. (2013) The cafe as affective community space: reconceptualizing care and emotional labour in everyday life, *Critical Social Policy* 33, 2: 305–324.

Watson, P., Morgan, M. and Hemmington, N. (2008) Online communities and the sharing of extraordinary restaurant experiences, *Journal of Foodservice* 19, 6: 289–302.

Weaver, A. (2005) Spaces of containment and revenue capture: 'super-sized' cruise ships as mobile tourism enclaves, *Tourism Geographies* 7, 2: 165–184.

Williams, A. (2002) *Understanding the Hospitality Consumer*, London: Butterworth-Heinemann.

Wingate-Lewinson, T., Hopps, J. G. and Reeves, P. (2010) Liminal living at an extended stay hotel: feeling 'stuck' in a housing solution, *Journal of Sociology and Social Welfare* 37, 2: 9–34.

Ziebarth, N. R. and Grabka, M. M. (2009) In vino pecunia? The association between beverage-specific drinking behavior and wages, *Journal of Labor Research* 30, 3: 219–244.

19

Hospitality and prosumption

George Ritzer

> **Key themes**
>
> Hospitableness
>
> Inhospitality
>
> Prosumption, smart prosuming machines
>
> McDonaldisation

Almost a decade ago, I was asked to give a talk on the hospitality industry drawing on my work on McDonaldisation (Ritzer, 1983, 1993, 2015a), postmodern theory (Ritzer, 1977) and globalisation (Ritzer and Dean, 2015), especially the 'globalisation of nothing' (Ritzer, 2012). I have continued to write about those topics, and there are many ways in which I could expand on the application of those ideas to the hospitality industry. However, what I will do here is further develop and apply a new strand of my work on the '*prosumer*' to the hospitality industry (Ritzer and Jurgenson, 2010). My interest in this topic derives, in part, from a brief section on 'putting the customer' to work in early editions of *The McDonaldization of Society*. There are many examples of this in the fast-food industry (such as customers being expected to clean up after themselves), as well as in the hospitality industry more generally. Such consumers who produce are one broad type of prosumer and the one that will be of primary interest here. The other type is the producer who consumes (e.g. who uses raw materials in producing a finished product). Those who work in the hospitality industry are such prosumers. For example, they produce a variety of services for their customers as they consume information, overtly and covertly, about what services are available and which services the customers want and how they would like to have them delivered. While the focus here is on consumers who produce, we will also reflect on corresponding changes in producers who consume in the hospitality industry. Before we can get to all of this, I need to explain my thinking on the prosumer.

Defining and conceptualising prosumption

As a term, prosumption is formed out of the combination of the concepts of *production* and *consumption*. In fact, prosumption is defined as the interrelated process of production and consumption. For much of recent history, especially since the Industrial Revolution, the popular and academic focus within the economy has been on production (e.g. Marx, 1967 [1887]; Veblen, 1964 [1914]). More recently, especially after the end of the Second World War, the focus began to shift to the increasingly dominant process of consumption (e.g. Baudrillard, 1998 [1970]; Galbraith, 1964). While these are certainly important processes and worthy of continuing attention, the focus on one or the other has tended to obscure the fact that *both* are better seen as processes of prosumption. That is, much production takes place in the process of consumption; there can be no consumption without some production (e.g. of that which is to be consumed such as a home-cooked meal; of the meaning of, for example, a home-cooked meal as opposed to one eaten in a fast-food restaurant or in a five-star restaurant). Similarly, much consumption is associated with the process of production (e.g. of the raw materials and labour-time needed to produce an automobile, and of the meanings of the work involved and of the automobile that is produced). Thus, prosumption (*not* production or consumption) is seen here as the generic process – one that subsumes production and consumption. Indeed, the latter, as we will see, should be viewed as extreme sub-types of prosumption.

Figure 19.1 offers a view of prosumption not as a single process (or phenomenon), but rather as a wide range of processes existing along a continuum. The poles of the continuum involve production redefined (a bit awkwardly, but more accurately) as 'prosumption-as-production' (p-a-p) and consumption as 'prosumption-as-consumption' (p-a-c). This means, among other things, that production and consumption, at least in their pure forms devoid of prosumption, do not exist on this continuum. There is no such thing as either pure production (without at least some consumption) or pure consumption (without at least some production); the two processes always interpenetrate. In the middle of the prosumption continuum, production (-as-consumption) and consumption (-as-production) are more or less evenly balanced; it is there where something approaching balanced (between p-a-p and p-a-c) prosumption exists (see Figure 19.1). Although they are usually seamlessly intertwined, we also need to distinguish between the 'consumption' and 'production' phases[1] of p-a-p, as well as of p-a-c (see Figure 19.2).

Prosumption-as-production involves those (typically workers) who consume what is needed in order to be able to produce goods and services with what they have consumed. In this, we are distinguishing between the time during, and the process in which, p-a-ps consume and produce. It takes prosumers-as-producers[2] time and energy both to produce and to consume during the prosumption process. For example, in putting hubcaps on a car in the assembly process, it takes time and energy not only to put the hubcaps on the car (the production phase), but also to retrieve them from where they are stored (the consumption phase). This distinction seems trivial, but it is important to the general conceptualisation of prosumption.

Prosumption-as-production	Balanced presumption	Prosumption-as-consumption

Figure 19.1 The prosumption continuum

Production and consumption phases	Balanced production and consumption	Consumption and production phases

Figure 19.2 The prosumption continuum with phases of production and consumption

The same distinction between phases needs to be made for prosumption as consumption, and in this case it is of much greater consequence, especially in today's world. However, it is difficult to conceive of p-a-cs as producers. My earliest thinking on this issue was in my work on the McDonaldisation of society (Ritzer, 2015a), in a discussion of the ways in which fast-food restaurants are 'putting customers to work'. Just as p-a-ps must consume, p-a-cs (prosumers-as-consumers) must produce as 'producing consumers' (Dujarier, 2014) or 'working customers' (Rieder and Voss, 2010). Of course, the process of putting customers to work was not invented by the fast-food restaurant. Customers have *always* worked in restaurant settings (e.g. in the most traditional of restaurants by, for example, reading and ordering from menus), but there has been a long tradition of refining and expanding that work. For example, the late nineteenth- and early twentieth-century cafeterias led consumers to perform a wide range of tasks on their own such as retrieving trays, utensils and napkins, lining up and wending their way through a line where they obtained the food they desired, and then paying at the cash register at the end of the line (Hardart and Diehl, 2002). In traditional restaurants these tasks are performed by paid employees such as wait-staff and bus-persons.

There are a series of broader senses in which p-a-cs are producers (or working customers). P-a-cs are producing awareness of, and desire for, various products (e.g. a meal at a cafeteria, a Big Mac at McDonald's) long before they ever enter a setting in which they can consume them. Traditionally, this awareness is produced when p-a-cs encounter someone who has consumed something that they conclude they would like to have. In the contemporary context, this production of desire is even more likely to occur in encounters with advertisements about various products (Baudrillard, 1998 [1970]; Schudson, 1986). However the desire is produced, p-a-cs then must produce the actions required to get them to the brick-and-mortar location (or the website) where the products are available for sale. Once there, the initial desire needs to be reproduced (or possibly altered) and translated into the more specific steps needed to actually obtain and purchase the product. While all of this is accomplished in cafeterias or fast-food restaurants, much additional work is required when consumers use the drive-through windows at fast-food restaurants. Among the required tasks are ordering the food at one point in the drive-through lane and picking it up at another, driving away with food and unwrapping it (likely in the car) and then disposing of the debris (engaging in the work of garbage disposal and saving the fast-food restaurant the expense involved in having paid employees do that work).

Much the same process occurs in other brick-and-mortar contemporary consumption settings such as, for example, Wal-Mart. First, a desire for a specific product (and there are many) on offer at Wal-Mart needs to be created by p-a-cs. More importantly, at least from Wal-Mart's perspective, a desire to purchase that product there rather than from a competitor also needs to be created. Second, there is work involved in the trip, often lengthy, to Wal-Mart and the negotiation of the parking lot and entrance to the store. Third, once in the usually huge and labyrinthine store, p-a-cs must obtain carts and make their way through it to find what they came for. Inevitably, they will find and pick up other products that they did not have in mind before they arrived. Fourth, when they are done, they must pay for their purchases, increasingly by doing all of the work themselves at self-checkout lanes. Then, the purchases must be transported to (usually) one's car and then home, where additional work is needed to unload, unpack and perhaps construct (as in the case of IKEA's famous Billy Bookcase) the final product. Various steps are then required to use, and in some cases use up, that which was purchased. Throughout this phase of the process p-a-cs are doing much (re-)definitional work as they reassess the feelings that led to the initial desire to obtain the product. Once the product is gone (used up, disposed of or relegated to a storage area), a final assessment occurs which may (or may not) lead to the same or similar purchases. If the assessment is a positive one, the process may begin again.

The above is little more than a brief sketch of the many acts that can be seen as being involved in the production phase of p-a-c. Given that, in what sense is there a consumption phase of p-a-c? In what senses are p-a-cs consumers? These are much easier questions to answer since p-a-cs are what we usually consider consumers and it seems abundantly clear that they are engaged in the process of consumption. Much of what has been described above as production (e.g. the acts involved in using and using up products) is closely related to, if not indistinguishable from, consumption, or in the terms used here, the consumption phase of p-a-c. However, a distinction can be made between the steps taken to produce consumption and those involved in the consumption process itself. In most cases, these are simply different ways of looking at the same steps. For example, one produces the various steps involved in eating a bowl of cereal (getting the cereal box from the cabinet and the milk from the refrigerator, retrieving a bowl and a spoon, combining the cereal and milk in a bowl) at about the same time one actually consumes (eats) that cereal. Whether or not they are separated in time or place, the production and consumption phases need to be distinguished in order to make it clear that both occur in p-a-c (and p-a-p).

Prosumption in the hospitality industry

Given this conceptual background, we turn now to a discussion of prosumption in the hospitality industry. The conventional view in the hospitality industry (and in many other contexts, industrial and otherwise) is that people are involved in it as either producers or consumers of hospitality. Those who work in the hospitality industry (producers, workers) are expected to provide contexts that are welcoming and where hospitality is most likely to be on offer (say, a cruise ship, a theme park, a casino-hotel), as well as to be those trained to be hospitable and involved in creating and maintaining a hospitable environment. The consumers are expected to consume that hospitality within those contexts, as well as in activities created and run by the relevant employees. The consumers are not expected to produce much, if any, of the hospitality and the producers are not expected to consume very much except, perhaps, feedback from customers on how welcome they are being made to feel.

However, from the point of view of this analysis, this approach is based on, and fatally flawed by, the creation of a clear binary distinction between producers and consumers of hospitality. *Both* consumers and producers are – indeed have always been – prosumers of hospitality. This is true whether they are to be found at the p-a-p or p-a-c ends of the prosumption continuum, or anywhere in between. The degree to which they prosume hospitality, the degree to which they produce (p-a-p) and consume (p-a-c) it, varies depending on their position on the continuum, but *all of them* are involved in prosumption. Those at the p-a-c end do more of what is traditionally thought of as consumption than production, and the reverse is the case for those at the p-a-p end; consumption and production are more evenly balanced for those in the middle. It would be useful to examine the full range of prosumption processes in the hospitality industry and, more generally, to take a whole new look at the industry from that perspective. However, such an analysis would require far more than a single chapter. In any case, my main interest is *inhospitality*, not the hospitality industry in general. The primary concern here is a more limited analysis of the ways in which looking at the industry from the perspective of prosumption contributes to our understanding of the inhospitality that increasingly dominates it, especially some of its most recent manifestations.

We begin with p-a-c. Those whom we have traditionally thought of as consumers (even though they have always been prosumers) in the hospitality industry have increasingly and more clearly become prosumers (p-a-cs) of hospitality. Most generally, this means that, instead of having services performed for them by workers (p-a-ps), p-a-cs (guests) are increasingly producing those services, or at least some aspects and portions of them, more-or-less on their own. This represents a severe challenge to the traditional notion of hospitality as involving, indeed necessitating, others (p-a-ps) helping, entertaining, protecting and serving their guests. Hospitality is typically seen as a one-directional process from the person being hospitable to the consumer of that hospitality. In other words, the consumer is generally seen as a passive recipient of hospitality.

Take, for example, the characteristics of 'genuine hospitality' identified in a bank of questions on the topic created by Blain and Lashley (2014). Most of those characteristics put the burden for hospitality on the producer, on the production of hospitality. For example, 'I do whatever is necessary to ensure that guests have a good time', 'I enjoy taking responsibility for the wellbeing of guests', 'It means the world to me when guests show their approval of my hospitality', 'I seek out opportunities to help others' and so on. However, those who make these kinds of statements are not just producers of hospitality, they are also consumers, especially of what their guests are doing and feeling (as well as recent developments in the hospitality industry). From the point of view of prosumption, the need for those in the hospitality industry to consume information about guests should receive more attention in that industry, as should techniques that would help them enhance guests' experience based on that information.

More importantly, far more attention needs to be devoted to the guests as prosumers of their experiences. In the terms of a related perspective on prosumption, guests need to be seen as *co-creators* of hospitality and hospitable experiences (Prahalad and Ramaswamy, 2004). Indeed, it could be argued that they play a greater role in creating hospitable experiences than those who work in the industry. Their satisfaction depends, in part, on creating hospitable experiences in the ways that those in the industry expect them to be created. More importantly, it hinges on their ability to create all sorts of activities and meanings that serve to make their experiences more meaningful, as well as meaningful in ways that those in the industry might not have anticipated. The focus in the hospitality industry needs to be on creating contexts in which p-a-cs can freely create all sorts of meaningful experiences for themselves with the help, of course, of hospitality workers and the hospitality setting. Perhaps above all, the contexts created in the hospitality industry should not restrict that creative process. Further, in their efforts to be hospitable, those who work in the industry should not restrict the efforts by p-a-cs to create what they consider to be hospitable experiences.

In other words, the hospitality industry adopts a far too passive image of its p-a-cs. The p-a-ps in the industry seek to create hospitable experiences for p-a-cs rather than encouraging them to be actively involved in their creation. P-a-cs should also be encouraged to create such experiences on their own, or at least to go beyond those created by the p-a-ps. The passive view of p-a-cs in the hospitality industry is challenged by the concept of the prosumer which assumes that consumers (p-a-cs) are *always* active producers of what they consume. It is also challenged in other bodies of work such as studies of audiences in general and fans in particular, as well as in recent works on brands.

One example in terms of audiences is Stuart Hall's work on encoding and decoding (1980). Broadcasting structures, such as those associated with television, emit 'encoded' messages embedded in specific programmes. However, to have an effect, these programmes and their meanings must be 'decoded' by the audience. In other words, the audience must do interpretative work in order to understand the meanings of a TV programme and for those meanings to have an effect on them. Indeed, the objective fact of TV discourse (p-a-p) and the subjective interpretive work of the audience (p-a-c) cannot be clearly separated from one another; they are dialectically related. Thus, Hall rejects the idea, associated with the Frankfurt School, of the power of the media and their control over the audience.

According to Dallas Smythe, under monopoly capitalism 'all non-sleeping time of most of the population is work time' (1977: 123). Included in the 'work' done during this period is 'essential marketing functions for the producers of consumers' goods' (Smythe 1977: 123). Advertisers are seen as buying the marketing services of the audience. Audiences work for advertisers by creating the demand for their products. They 'learn to buy particular "brands" of consumer goods, and to spend their income accordingly' (Smythe 1977: 126). In so doing, they 'complete the production process of consumer goods' (Smythe 1977: 126).

Within media studies, but specifically focused on 'fans', is the work of Henry Jenkins (2006). In his early work on textual poachers, Jenkins (1992) takes on the idea that fans are 'brainless consumers'. Textual poachers, following de Certeau (1984), are seen as those who extract from texts that which they find useful or pleasurable, and use those extracts to create texts of their own. However, the term 'poachers' better reflects the media realities of the early 1990s than those of today. That is, the media owned and controlled the means of producing texts, and fans had to poach them in order to produce their own texts. However, in the age of the Internet the media have much less control over those means of producing texts, and fans exercise greater control over them and are able to produce texts largely on their own (e.g. on blogs, Facebook pages and Twitter).

In the process of writing *Textual Poachers*, Jenkins (1992) developed the broader idea of participatory and convergence culture which informs much of his more recent work. Participatory culture is one where fans (a main concern in Jenkins's work) are not mere spectators but active participants; fandom is a specific form of participatory culture. In convergence culture, the interaction of the powers of the media producer and the media consumer has unpredictable consequences. His primary interest is to counteract the idea of the passive media spectator with the ideas of spectators performing work and as consumers engaged in active participation. This is especially the case with new technologies empowering audiences who are demanding the right to participate.

This process is also clear in the case of brands, where consumers play a major role in producing the shared meanings that are the brand; they do not simply accept the brand messages created by marketers and advertisers. Thus, in a real sense, prosumers produce the meaning that surrounds brands such as McDonald's, BMW and Nike. Arvidsson refers to these prosumer (although he doesn't use this term) creations as an 'ethical surplus' or a 'social relation, a shared meaning, an emotional involvement that was not there before' (2005: 237).

All of this work is in tune with the view that people (guests) are not passive consumers of hospitality, but are its active co-creators. Specifically, p-a-cs play an active role in being helped, entertained, protected and served by others. Instead of focusing on how to do these things for their customers, the hospitality industry needs to become more active in finding ways to get p-a-cs more involved in being helped, entertained, protected and served. The more active involvement of prosumers (p-a-ps) in hospitality will not only enhance these processes, but lead prosumers (p-a-cs) to be more satisfied with them because they will see the active role they are playing in them. Furthermore, more active involvement by p-a-cs will lead to the discovery and institutionalisation of new forms of hospitality; p-a-cs can be a good source of innovation. A traditional, one-directional, top-down model of hospitality becomes increasingly inappropriate, if not impossible, as consumers are seen as prosumers.

Furthermore, there are an increasing number of situations in the hospitality industry where there is no other, or at least the role of the other is greatly reduced. If there is no other (no service provider), then there can be no real hospitality. The only possible source of this hospitality is the p-a-c. While being totally on one's own as a p-a-c is rare, p-a-cs are certainly increasingly on their own in settings in which we have traditionally expected to be treated hospitably by p-a-ps.

In her typology of 'consumer work', Dujarier (2014) labels this the 'self-service work' performed by prosumers. Examples include:

- automated systems for answering phone calls at hospitality settings, where the caller is required to make a series of choices rather than having an employee make the choices for them;
- self check-in kiosks at motels, airports and so on;
- self-service in fast-food restaurants;
- self-serve buffets on cruise ships, in casinos, chains of restaurants based on buffets;
- self-service breakfasts at motels including toasting one's own bagels, making one's own waffles;
- being asked to clean up after oneself before one's airplane lands;
- playing slot machines (and other automated gambling games), where the gamblers (consumers) produce their own games, as well as the payouts from those games.

In all of these examples, the prosumer produces outcomes, does work, which was formerly done for them. That work was often performed in a hospitable manner, or at least was an occasion in which hospitality could be offered and displayed. If the opportunities to perform these tasks are eliminated, so too are expressions of hospitality emanating from hosts to guests. The hospitality that is offered in these contexts is inauthentic. It likely comes from such sources as computerised voices, canned messages on video screens and employees who are more likely than not following scripts. As p-a-cs, people can, at least theoretically, make such greetings seem more genuinely hospitable. However, those efforts are likely to be greatly limited, if not doomed to failure, without interacting with a fully functioning human being (p-a-p).

A related problem involves the creation of settings – what I have called 'cathedrals of consumption' (Ritzer, 2010) – where the hospitality is frequently artificial, inauthentic and built into the structure rather than being extended by others (p-a-ps). Examples of this are legion, such as being told to 'have a nice day' as one leaves many of these cathedrals of consumption or when one has highly scripted interaction with costumed characters at Disney World. More generally, settings such as Disney World are supposed to be structured to be welcoming so there is supposedly little need for anything but the scripted interaction with costumed characters. Nevertheless, visitors are prosumers and they are busy in those contexts creating many things about what goes on there, including the sense that they are welcome. Unfortunately, this is largely a one-sided construction; the p-a-cs are on their own with little or no help from p-a-ps.

While these structures are artificially hospitable, there are aspects of them, or of other structures, that are downright inhospitable. The truth is that p-a-cs are not welcome in, for example, fast-food restaurants, or at least they are not welcome to stay very long. In the hopes that p-a-cs would leave quickly, McDonald's famously created chairs designed to make customers uncomfortable after 20 minutes. More telling is the inhospitable drive-through window. It is designed to prevent anything but the most fleeting and scripted hospitality (if one can call it that). In fact, it is designed to keep not only those troublesome p-a-cs – and any need to be hospitable – out of the restaurant, but also the garbage they create which, in the case of the drive-through window, they take with them as they leave. By the way, in so doing, the consumers of the restaurant's products also become the producers of garbage disposal; they become prosumers (p-a-cs) in yet another way.

While there is a general trend in the direction of inhospitality, there are also profound differences among and within hospitality settings in terms of the degree of (in)hospitality offered.

To put this in sociological terms, *hospitality settings are highly stratified*. In addition, within any given setting there is considerable stratification in terms of the services received and the ways in which they are offered. The basic point is that the less well-off are those who are more likely to use the kind of self-service systems described above and, as a result, are likely to receive little or no hospitality from p-a-ps. Even when they are in more traditional settings (restaurants such as Olive Garden) where services are offered by other humans, they are likely to receive little in the way of hospitable treatment.

In contrast, the well-to-do are less likely to be in contexts where self-service is the norm. Rather, they are likely to be in settings where services are provided to them and in a highly hospitable manner. Compare a fast-food restaurant to a three-star Michelin restaurant, a cruise on a Princess (or, heaven forbid, a Disney) cruise ship to one on a Seabourn ship, a casino in downtown Las Vegas to the one in the Mandarin Oriental on the Strip. There is also internal stratification within many hospitality settings where those who can afford it still receive a great deal of hospitality; things are done for them rather than them being asked to do the tasks themselves. Examples include private rooms in elite restaurants, separate, high-stakes gambling rooms in casinos, concierge floors and service in hotels, and first-class compartments on airlines and cruise ships.

In fact, as hospitality declines and disappears, at least for those who are not societal elites, most consumers will forget, or never come to know, hospitality as it has existed in various settings. For example, how many airplane passengers remember, or have even experienced, the hospitality that was at one time offered to passengers in an economy class cabin? Who remembers that economy passengers generally felt the need to 'dress up' in order to fly economy (or any other) class? Furthermore, many have come to the view that the lower prices (or is it greater profits) that they have been led to think are associated with less (or no) hospitality are preferable to better service. As that kind of thinking spreads, where does that leave the hospitality industry?

The fact is that there has always been an elitism built into that industry (and most others). Most people in the world, even in the developed world, rarely, if ever, experience the offerings of the hospitality industry. As a result of ongoing changes, especially the rise of smart prosuming machines (see below), we can expect what we have traditionally considered to be hospitality to be offered to an ever smaller, increasingly elite, population. Whatever we may think about elitism, this means less work in the hospitality industry, or at least less work for those with the interpersonal skills and knowledge base historically associated with those who work in that industry (concierges, wine stewards) and who offer hospitality.

The inhospitality of the hospitality industry reaches its logical extreme on the Internet. No hospitality is expected or possible when the p-a-c uses the online reservation systems for airlines, hotels and motels, or buys an array of products from Amazon.com and other online 'cathedrals of consumption'. The p-a-c, of course, does all of the work associated with those reservations and purchases and, more generally, with all online systems. For example, choice of airlines, airline routes, prices, seating (and much more) are left to p-a-cs operating on their own, as is all of the work involved in actually making the choices. The systems, of course, are not constructed to be hospitable. In fact, they are constructed to be as daunting to the prosumer, as inhospitable, as possible in order to ward off requests or questions from those who use the system. There is no helping hand on those systems let alone tangible assistance. Gone (at least in most cases) are the helpful employees in travel agencies (as well as in local bookstores or hardware stores). In addition, it is difficult to contact human beings about issues or problems with those online systems, and, even if one could, they are unlikely to be hospitable. The same is the case with online casinos and other gambling systems. Without any human beings to deal with, it is impossible for the p-a-c to receive, or even expect, much in the way of hospitality, if any at all.

Smart machines and the new prosumer

While prosumption is a primal process (Ritzer, 2014), it has taken new forms and acquired much greater significance today, in part, as a result of various technological changes (Ritzer, 2015b). As a result, we can think in terms of a 'new prosumer'. Furthermore, businesses (and other organisations such as the government and, for example, its use of citizens to fill out their own census forms rather than having the work done by census takers) seem to have grown more aware of this phenomenon and are creating conditions to expedite and exploit it. Businesses (and others entities such as the government) are, in the main, *not* doing this with an explicit notion of the prosumer in mind, but they are aware of the specific manifestations of prosumption in the operations in which they are involved. As we have seen, the many recent examples of prosumption in the hospitality industry make it clear that it, too, is operating, at least implicitly, with a sense of the new forms of prosumption and their significance to the industry.

One thing we will see more of in general, and specifically in the hospitality industry, is the use of more 'smart prosuming machines' (Ritzer, 2015b). This is part of the trend away from human to non-human technology. This trend is important in itself and, more specifically, for what it means for the hospitality industry. Before we get to that, we need some introduction to these machines and their relationship to prosumption.

Smart machines and prosumers-as-producers

Smart machines and automation alter, and in many ways improve, the process of prosumption-as-production. In many cases, they make p-a-p easier by conceptualising and performing tasks that are quite onerous to human workers such as welding and painting cars on automobile assembly-lines. However, they also can be seen as deskilling work by taking skills from humans and building them into the technology. Thus, there are pluses and minuses as far as the implications of these changes for p-a-p are concerned. At the extremes, however, smart machines (Kelly and Hamm, 2013) can, and increasingly will be able to, replace human workers (the p-a-ps). In fact, the literature on producers, or in our terms p-a-ps, has been primarily concerned with the issue of job loss as a result of their introduction and the subsequent expansion of smart machines (Brynjolfsson and McAfee, 2014).

Smart machines will themselves become p-a-ps through the use of sensors that will, for example, ascertain that there are problems with a particular phase of the production process (a part does not meet specifications; the paint on the car is the wrong colour or applied unevenly) or even with a finished product. Eliminated in these cases, at least in part, is the need for human p-a-ps to make these judgements (involving further deskilling) and because of the reduced need to take time to attend to such matters, fewer human employees will be needed. Reductions in the number of workers are also occurring, and will occur more frequently in the future, as smart machines literally do the work themselves without human intervention. Such robotisation has already occurred in many production settings, including, among others, BMW's automobile assembly line in Munich where robots put fenders on cars, weld and paint the cars, and so on.

Overall, the increasing sophistication and utilisation of smart machines in p-a-p has been going on for some time and has been the subject of much analysis, albeit *not* from the perspective of prosumption. When we look at it from that point of view, we can see that both the production and consumption phases of p-a-p are affected by smart machines and automation. In the case of automobile production, today's robots both pick up (consume) a fender needed by the car under construction and put the fender on the car (produce). An understanding of prosumption adds greater nuance to our understanding of what is transpiring since both the consumption and production phases of p-a-p are profoundly altered by smart machines and automation.

More directly relevant to the hospitality industry is the use of smart machines in the banking industry, where ATMs do the work rather than tellers. Then there are the self-checkout systems in supermarkets, where p-a-cs do all of the work of unloading their carts, scanning their purchases and then their credit cards, bagging their purchases and then carrying them to their cars. The same is true at self-service petrol stations. All of this reduces the need for p-a-ps and changes the nature of the work for those who remain.

Of more recent vintage are the various kinds of kiosks used by p-a-cs in lieu of interacting with, and making arrangements with, service workers (p-a-ps). This is most obvious in such kiosks in the airline and hotel industries, but they are proliferating elsewhere including the fast-food industry. In some cases the p-a-c encounters such kiosks on entry to the restaurant, and in others, most notably Chilis (and Applebees), there are wireless, tabletop, touch-screen tablets (manufactured by Ziosk) at the table where p-a-cs order food and drink, and can even scan their credit cards to pay the bill, without interacting with waitpersons. In order to prevent p-a-cs from growing bored, they can even play games on those computer terminals (at an additional cost). Chilis insists it is still in the business of 'service' and offering hospitality. The chain contends that the terminals will never replace human servers, but one is forced to wonder about such an assertion in the long run. There are already automated sushi restaurants where p-a-cs make their selections on their own from a conveyor belt with various options passing before them. Bills are calculated automatically on the basis of the different types of plates used; there are even sushi restaurants where p-a-cs can deposit their used plates and have their bill calculated automatically.

Of course, we are in the infancy of the development of smart machines, especially in the hospitality industry. As they grow increasingly sophisticated, they will acquire a greater ability to 'think' on their own and to take on more tasks now being handled by human p-a-cs. Thus, it is easy to predict that smart machines will do more things, gain more control over people and eventually replace many – perhaps even all – of them in the workplace. It is clear that we will see greater use of smart machines in the obvious areas of the material production of automobiles. They will also be employed to an increasing degree in the service industries in general and the hospitality industry in particular. They will perform some hospitality functions on their own and, in other cases, supplement the work of human hospitality workers. However, given the greater complexity of hospitality work compared to the work in the automobile industry, it is difficult to see smart machines playing anywhere as great a role in the hospitality industry. We have mentioned above various technologies already in use in the hospitality industry (e.g. self-check-in technology) that can be seen as smart machines. In some cases they do replace humans, but *what they cannot do is offer the genuine hospitality that can be offered by p-a-ps in the hospitality industry*. We will see further incursions of smart machines into the hospitality industry, and they will be programmed to offer something closer to traditional hospitality (we can even envision robots simulating the work of those in the industry), but it is impossible to think of that as anything like what we have traditionally thought of as hospitality. While genuine human hospitality will continue to be offered by p-a-ps to elite p-a-cs, and may even be enhanced, we will need to rethink what we mean by hospitality for the vast majority of p-a-cs. It may well be that, for most, hospitality will be a thing of the past – what most p-a-cs will deal with increasingly is the inhospitality industry.

In the end, looking at producers as p-a-ps in the hospitality industry (and everywhere else) in general, and specifically in their relationship to smart machines, does not really add a great deal to our understanding of what is happening, and is likely to happen, to them. This is because much of this has been studied and thought about under the heading of the automation of production. Where adding prosumption to this analysis is most illuminating is in the case of what we traditionally think of as consumption (p–a–c). It is p–a–c that is now in the process of being altered dramatically, including, and maybe especially, in the hospitality industry, by smart prosuming machines.

Smart machines and prosumers-as-consumers

Much more attention has been paid to producers (or in our terms, p–a–ps) than to consumers (p–a–cs) because of the long-term 'productivist bias' in the social sciences. More specifically, the possibility of a major change in the nature of work, and, more extremely, of substantial job loss, has had far greater priority than changes wrought in the consumption process (although these two sets of changes are, as we've seen, closely connected). Furthermore, the focus on production has led to earlier, quicker and more dramatic applications of smart machines to p–a–p. It is clear that, as a result of the development and use of such machines, much work can be performed more quickly and efficiently, yielding greater profits. It has not been nearly as clear that increased use of smart machines in p–a–c will lead to greater profits. It is also the case that it is far easier to bring in smart machines to change what p–a–ps do than it is in the case of p–a–cs. Because p–a–ps are generally paid employees, employers can more easily implement whatever innovations they deem necessary with little or no resistance from employees. However, p–a–cs are not employees; they are not being paid. Businesses, especially those in the hospitality industry, cannot afford to anger or alienate them by imposing smart machines (or at least too many of them, too often and in the wrong contexts) on them. The implementation of such technology in p–a–c has to be done much more subtly. Furthermore, these kinds of changes need to please, or at least seem to please, p–a–cs (the consumers in the hospitality industry), while there is no such requirement in the case of p–a–ps (those who are employed by the industry). Thus, the introduction of smart machines in p–a–c tends to be done covertly or to be made to seem highly appealing by, for example, offering quicker service and/or lower prices. While the changes in p–a–c may seem less important than changes in p–a–p, *it is in p–a–c that the biggest changes are being made, and are likely to be wrought, by the increasing number and sophistication of smart prosuming machines.*

The human p–a–c is beginning to be controlled, and perhaps eventually replaced, by smart machines or, more specifically, *smart prosuming machines.* Critical here is the development of increasingly powerful sensors (using nanotechnology) that can be attached to objects worn by ('wearables') or otherwise associated with, p–a–cs.[3] Take, for example, driving on toll roads and the hospitality workers who staff the toll booths. Instead of producing money to pay the toll needed to consume more miles on a toll road (and being greeted by the toll taker), e-tolls allow people to glide by or through toll-taking areas and have the charge debited electronically to their E-Z pass accounts. This is made possible by smart technology at toll areas and transponders in cars. On some roads, no humans work any longer in toll-taking areas. Thus, drivers who do not have an E-Z pass or the correct change will automatically be sent a bill or ticketed. Transponders also allow cars, as well as other types of vehicles (e.g. tractor trailers) subject to different charges, to be identified automatically. This is a domain in which the replacement of human hospitality workers by smart presuming machines has already occurred and will expand in the future. It is also a domain in which the p–a–cs have already acquiesced by obtaining and using those transponders. The only hospitality those p–a–cs are likely to experience is an automated display thanking them and suggesting they 'have a nice day' as they drive through.

Universal product codes (UPCs) have already dramatically altered the nature of prosumption in a wide range of cathedrals of consumption, and they have the potential to change it much more in the future. For example, instead of p–a–cs unloading products to be scanned at the checkout counters at supermarkets, Wal-Mart or IKEA, the UPCs associated with those products can be read directly by the computer as one checks out. Alternatively, the shopping cart can be equipped with a transponder that reads the UPCs during the process of shopping. Final bills can be tabulated automatically and be ready for shoppers as they leave the store, or the bills can be e-mailed to them. It will soon be possible for a p-a-c to shop in a supermarket (and elsewhere) without encountering hospitality workers, let alone any hospitality.

3-D printers involve smart technology that consumes information (e.g. blueprints) and raw materials (e.g. plastics), and uses them to automatically produce an increasingly wide variety of end-products (Anderson, 2012). To the degree that our homes or other settings become production locales is the degree to which people will no longer need to venture into settings of consumption where hospitality is possible.

Perhaps the best example of the use of smart prosuming machines in the hospitality industry is, not surprisingly, to be found in Disney theme parks and its 'magic bands'. According to Disney's website:

> MagicBands are innovative all-in-one devices that you can use to enter Disney theme parks, unlock your Disney Resort hotel room, use the FastPass+ entrance for attractions and entertainment experiences you selected, charge purchases to your room, and link Disney PhotoPass photos to your Disney account.

Visitors receive a 'MagicBand' when they stay at a Disney Resort hotel, or are a Walt Disney World Passholder. Those who are not staying at a Disney Resort hotel and/or are not a Passholder receive a card when they purchase park admission. They can also purchase a 'MagicBand' at Disney theme parks and the Downtown Disney area. As a result of 'MagicBands', visitors will be less likely to encounter hospitality workers on entering the park, on checking into hotels on the grounds, in gaining entry to their hotel rooms, on entering and paying for various attractions and so on. The result will inevitably be fewer hospitality workers and fewer opportunities to offer – or experience – hospitality.

The bands can also be used to enhance inauthentic hospitality experiences. For example, hidden sensors can be used to allow an employee dressed up as Mickey Mouse to greet children by name and wish them 'Happy Birthday'. The bands can be used to track visitors as they move through the park, which attractions they enter, and what they purchase. Such information has ominous implications in terms of surveillance, but more prosaically it can be used to sell more souvenirs, food and attractions to visitors. While wearables like Disney's 'MagicBands' have not yet proliferated widely in the hospitality industry, it is highly likely that they will. They are naturals for cruise ships and casino-hotels, among other places. Those cathedrals of consumption already have multi-purpose key cards that can be used not only to enter one's cabin or room, but also to pay for various amenities during one's stay. It is but a short step from those cards to something like Disney's 'MagicBands'.

Smart prosuming machines and the irrationality of rationality

There are, of course, numerous advantages to the rise of smart prosuming machines in general and more specifically in the hospitality industry. However, these non-human technologies can also be discussed under the heading of the 'irrationality of rationality' (Ritzer, 2012). Clearly, the prosuming machines discussed above are highly rational technologies. However, like all forms of rationalisation, they produce, and are accompanied by, a wide range of irrationalities. For example, they can fail to operate properly, causing, at the minimum, inconvenience (e.g. getting a ticket because one does not have the correct change needed at an automatic toll booth which offers no other way to pay the toll).

It may well be in the hospitality industry that these irrationalities reach their logical extreme. Among other things, they threaten to reduce the need for people in the industry, to reduce the need for those who remain to be hospitable and to threaten the industry as a whole, at least as it is now constituted. These threats exist not only because smart prosuming machines do more and more things on their own, but also because prosumers (p-a-cs) themselves are increasingly operating without any assistance. Irrationalities such as these do not mean that we need to be reactionaries standing against the increasing autonomy of p-a-cs, or Luddites opposing and rejecting smart prosuming machines. Clearly, they bring with them many advantages, but we should not ignore the irrationalities associated with them, as well as with many other aspects of our increasingly rationalised (or in my terms, McDonaldised) society.

While smart prosuming machines will increase in number and diversity and become more important in coming years, human prosumers will not disappear. They will continue to work, albeit in smaller numbers, in settings dominated by p-a-ps, although more as monitors and minders of those prosuming machines. P-a-cs will continue to consume (really prosume), but the nature of that process will be altered radically by smart prosuming machines. Most generally, the synergistic employment and exploitation of p-a-ps, p-a-cs *and* prosuming machines will lead to a radically different economic system that has the potential for unprecedented profitability because, primarily, of the decline of paid human employees, including those in the hospitality industry and who offer hospitality.

Conclusions

The whole notion of the hospitality industry, and of hospitality in general, needs to be re-evaluated in the era of the new prosumer and smart prosuming machines. It seems clear that the traditional notions of hospitality hearken back to an earlier era, and ongoing changes are forcing us to reconsider hospitality (and much else). Among the issues pointed to by this analysis are:

- the decline of settings that offer hospitality;
- the decline of employment opportunities for hospitality workers;
- the decline in the opportunities to offer hospitality for the hospitality workers that remain;
- a decline in interest in hospitality on the part of consumers;
- the automation of hospitality and whether what such automated systems offer is 'true' hospitality;
- the increasingly stratified nature of the hospitality industry.

Overall, given the increasing affluence of the developed world, and of the elites in all parts of the world, the hospitality industry will survive. However, it will increasingly be bifurcated into a small number of settings that offer elites the kind of hospitality we traditionally associate with the industry and a vast majority of settings that offer what is best described as inhospitality to most of the rest of us.

Notes

1   While the traditional terms of production and consumption are employed here for the sake of simplicity and clarity, these phases should also be seen as being subsumed under the heading of prosumption. In addition, while these phases are depicted as if they are separate and distinct, in fact that they almost always occur in conjunction with one another.

2   Throughout this chapter I will use p-a-p (prosumption-as-production) and p-a-c (prosumption-as-consumption) to designate prosumption processes and p-a-ps (prosumers-as-producers) and p-a-cs (prosumers-as-consumers) for those who engage in those processes.

3   They can also even be inserted in the body of the prosumer, although that is highly unlikely in the hospitality industry. A bit more likely is the insertion of sensors in employees (p-a-ps). One Silicon Valley scientist says: 'The reason we are talking about wearables is because we are not at implantables yet', but 'I'm ready. Others are ready' (Ortutay, 2014: 3d). Implanted prosuming machines would serve to turn prosumers into a new type of cyborg (Haraway, 1991).

References

Anderson, C. (2012) *Makers: The New Industrial Revolution*, London: Random House.

Arvidsson, A. (2005) Brands: a critical perspective, *Journal of Consumer Culture* 5, 2: 235–258.

Baudrillard, J. (1998 [1970]) *The Consumer Society: Myths and Structures*, London: Sage.

Blain, M. and Lashley, C. (2014) Hospitableness: the new service metaphor? Developing an instrument for hosting, *Research in Hospitality Management* 4, 1&2: 1–8.

Brynjolfsson, E. and McAfee, A. (2014) *The Second Machine Age: Work, Progress and Prosperity in a Time of Brilliant Technologies*, New York: Norton.

de Certeau, M. (1984) *The Practice of Everyday Life*, Berkeley: University of California Press.

Dujarier, M. (2014) The three sociological types of consumer work, *Journal of Consumer Culture*, DOI: 10.1177/1469540514528198.

Galbraith, J. K. (1964) *The Affluent Society*, New York: Houghton Mifflin.

Hall, S. (1980) *Culture, Media, Language*, London: Unwin Hyman.

Haraway, D. (1991) *Simians, Cyborgs and Women: The Reinvention of Nature*, New York and London: Routledge.

Hardart, M. and Diehl, L. (2002) *The Automat: The History, Recipes and Allure of Horn & Hardart's Masterpiece*, New York: Clarkson Potter.

Jenkins, H. (1992) *Textual Poachers: Television Fans and Participatory Culture*, London: Routledge.

Jenkins, H. (2006) *Convergence Culture: Where Old and New Media Collide*, New York: New York University Press.

Kelly, J. E. and Hamm, S. (2013) *Smart Machines: IBM's Watson and the Era of Cognitive Computing*, New York: Columbia University Press.

Marx, K. (1967 [1887]) Capital. In *Capital: A Critique of Political Economy*, vol. 1, New York: International Publishers.

Ortutay B. (2014) Super nerd: stares a tiny price to pay for trying Google Glass, *Sarasota Herald Tribune*, 15 March, 1D, 3D.

Prahalad, C. K. and Ramaswamy, V. (2004) *The Future of Competition: Co-Creating Unique Value With Customers*, Cambridge, MA: Harvard Business School Press.

Rieder, K. and Gunter Voss, G. (2010) The working customer: an emerging new type of consumer, *Journal Psychologie des Alltagshandelns/Psychology of Everyday Activity* 3, 2: 2–10.

Ritzer, G. (1977) *Postmodern Social Theory*, New York: McGraw-Hill.

Ritzer, G. (1983) The McDonaldization of society, *Journal of American Culture* 6: 100–107.

Ritzer, G. (1993) *The McDonaldization of Society*, Thousand Oaks, CA: Pine Forge Press.

Ritzer, G. (2010) *Enchanting a Disenchanted World*, 3rd edn, Thousand Oaks, CA: Pine Forge Press.

Ritzer, G. (2012), 'Hyperconsumption' and 'hyperdebt': a 'hypercritical' analysis. In Brubaker, R., Lawless, R. and Tabb, C. J. (eds) *A Debtor World: Interdisciplinary Perspectives on Debt*, New York: Oxford University Press, pp. 60–80.

Ritzer, G. (2014) Prosumption: evolution, revolution or eternal return of the same?, *Journal of Consumer Culture* 14: 3–24.

Ritzer, G. (2015a) *The McDonaldization of Society*, Thousand Oaks, CA: Pine Forge Press.

Ritzer, G. (2015b) The 'new' world of prosumption: evolution, 'return of the same', or revolution?, *Sociological Forum* 30, 1: 1–17.

Ritzer, G. and Dean, P. (2015) *Globalization: A Basic Text*, Malden, MA: Wiley-Blackwell.

Ritzer, G. and Jurgenson, N. (2010) Production, consumption, prosumption: the nature of capitalism in the age of the digital 'prosumer', *Journal of Consumer Culture* 10, 1: 13–36. Schudson, M. (1986) *Advertising: The Uneasy Persuasion*, New York: Basic Books.

Smythe, D. (1977) Communications: the blindspot of Western Marxism, *Canadian Journal of Political and Social Theory* 1: 120–127.

Veblen, T. (1964) *The Instinct of Workmanship and the State of the Industrial Arts*, New York: Augustus M. Kelly.

20

Liquid hospitality

Wine as the metaphor

Sjoerd Gehrels

Key themes

Hospitality

Wine

Liquid hospitality

Innovation in hospitality

The invitation to contribute a chapter about 'liquid hospitality' is exciting because it touches a concept that has not really been explicitly explored in the literature before. Hospitality has been extensively described and explained from simplistic straightforward notions up to elaborate theoretical discussions resulting in conceptual models to direct further research. Examples of adjectives used with the term hospitality include genuine, authentic, commercial, private, academic, social, reciprocal, redistributive, altruistic, contemporary, good and humanitarian. Expressions using 'liquid' as the adjective, and one way or another connected to hospitality, wines and beverages include -happiness, -pleasures, -images, -investments, -asset management, and -assets. The combination of 'liquid' with hospitality seems almost untraceable except for 'liquid southern hospitality', which was left as a guest comment on TripAdvisor from people visiting the FireFly distillery in South Carolina.

The first association with liquid hospitality that comes to mind is 'wine' as the liquid symbolisation of hospitality. In order to construct a concept of 'liquid hospitality', first a specific hospitality definition is provided in this chapter to prelude on how wine can be seen as a metaphor for liquid hospitality. Wine as a representation of liquid hospitality has been so much present in my professional and personal life that elements of ethnographic research infuse the narrative. Furthermore, the chapter offers a variety of connections between wine and elements of hospitality. It is not the intention in this chapter to provide an all-encompassing grounded theory about 'liquid hospitality', but to trigger associating with the term. Wine, not just defined

DOI: 10.4324/9781315679938-22

as an agricultural product to be tasted and drank, but instead taken as a major element within hospitality culture, offers directions for further exploration under the heading of 'liquid hospitality'. This has been virtually untouched until now although there are examples that link wine to something more. Perdue (1999) nicely summarises the value of wine by saying that wine tastes good, it enhances food, provokes conversation and warms gatherings of family and friends where it is served.

The benefits of wine consumed in moderation have been well known for thousands of years in nearly every civilisation. In the Bible, Psalms 60:3, there is reference to wine as something important: 'Thou hast shewed thy people hard things; thou has made us drink the wine of astonishment'. This chapter consists of a small investigation into a workable hospitality definition, then an exploration of wine and its associations, finally leading to the construction of wine as 'liquid hospitality'. In terms of the ethnographic component in this chapter I have used slices of materials composed in earlier unpublished personal dissertation studies about 'wine management' and 'teaching wine management'. In doing so, I have taken the author's space to relate previous research findings to my own personal experiences of having been a sommelier and a wine management lecturer for almost a decade. It is the aim of this chapter to sensitise the reader to the developing concept of wine as representation, the metaphor, of liquid hospitality.

Hospitality

Hospitality has historically been considered a virtue. Practically every country and every culture in the world has an understanding of hospitality. Before the Common Era, Hindus already had community subsidised refugee homes where tired travellers could be nurtured (Gehrels, 1995). In Western culture, Christian communities founded the so-called 'hospitia' that had a similar function. In France, the Hôtel-Dieu still provides care for the poor. Hospitality was seen as a religious duty because the pauper who asked for help could in principle be the reborn Christ who should be received as The Lord himself. In some monasteries the abbot had his quarters next to the entrance in order to see the guest in need of care knocking on the gate. Hospitality, originally, was about nurturing the stranger without making money from the activity and always in essence dealt with interaction between people.

The story of the 'Innkeeper of Pidalgo' by Dutch author Godfried Bomans (Vijver, 1996) illustrates the true nature of hospitality:

> Of this innkeeper they told, he insisted to only take the profits needed to keep himself and his wife alive, while he spent the extra profits for purchasing new pans and finely crafted skimmers. If a guest ate very much, he even refused any compensation saying that the sight of such an eater was reward enough for him. At large events, he stood rubbing his hands in the doorway in delight while his eyes looked kindly on his grateful guests. Once upon a time at a gunmen's meal, they saw him weep for joy.

Clearly, hospitality lived in this way, although offered in the context of a business, comes close to what Lashley refers to as 'altruistic hospitality' (2015: 5).

French philosopher Jacques Derrida made a distinction between unconditional hospitality, which he considered impossible, and hospitality which in his view was always conditional (O'Gorman, 2006). Derrida defined hospitality as inviting and welcoming the 'stranger'. He envisioned this as taking place on different levels: the personal level where the 'stranger' is welcomed into the home, and the level of individual countries. The term 'hospitality' is derived from two Latin stems, 'hospes' having the meaning of 'guest' or 'stranger' and 'hostis' meaning 'stranger' or 'enemy' (Gehrels, 1995). The ambivalence of the matter is that 'hospitality' is about welcoming the stranger, while 'hostis' developed into 'hostility' (towards the stranger).

An experience of hospitality occurs when people meet and engage. Explained in a traditional simplistic and commercial setting such as in the hospitality industry (Figure 20.1), the experience is constructed by the tangible product being shared, the environment in which the interaction takes place and the behaviour of the people involved.

The product consists principally of food, drink and accommodation while the environment includes the location, exterior, interior and the effect of other people in the vicinity. Behaviour as offered by the hospitality provider is constructed by personality (traits), value systems, culture, other motivational components, knowledge and skills. Expectations of customers or guests are affected by their needs, goals and objectives, directed by their personality, value systems, culture and the knowledge with which they enter the interaction. The encounter between offer and demand results in a 'moment of truth'. Ample evidence in the literature suggests that the price paid for the hospitality experience has an influence on the perception of those involved (Kandampully and Suhartanto, 2000; Hellstrand, 2010; Chong, 2015). A more sophisticated view on hospitality was developed by Lashley and Morrison (2000) who looked at the concept from the point of view of a broad range of social sciences.

The resulting model in Figure 20.2 (Lashley, 2015) demonstrates that hospitality is a phenomenon that can be identified in three partly overlapping domains. The Venn diagram presents the area of hospitality and the possibility of managing experiences in the overlap of private, social and commercial activities. The social domain relates to the culturally influenced societal context in which hospitality is shared. The domestic domain is connected to the provision of hospitality in peoples' private dwellings where they invite and entertain people. The commercial domain

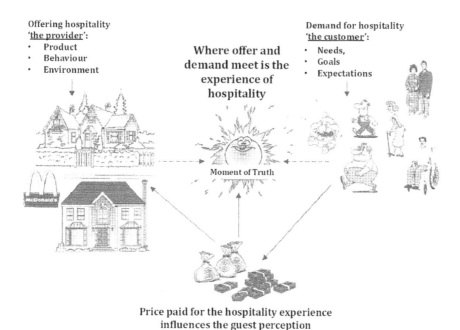

Figure 20.1   Hospitality industry model

Source: Gehrels (1995).

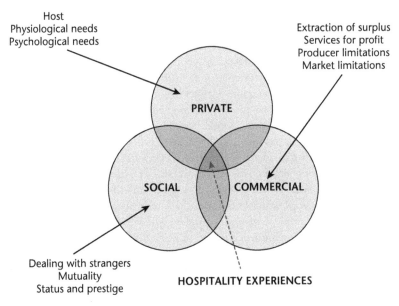

Host
Physiological needs
Psychological needs

Extraction of surplus
Services for profit
Producer limitations
Market limitations

PRIVATE

SOCIAL   COMMERCIAL

Dealing with strangers
Mutuality
Status and prestige

HOSPITALITY EXPERIENCES

Figure 20.2   Hospitality experiences model
Source: Lashley (2015: 4).

concerns the provision of hospitality as an economic activity providing food, drink and accommodation for financial gain as depicted before in Figure 20.1. To follow Lashley's hospitality experiences model, 'Liquid Hospitality ⇔ Wine' will be examined in the context of the three domains: social, private and commercial. In order to emphasise the relevance of considering wine as a metaphor for liquid hospitality, in the remainder of this chapter the terms 'wine' and 'liquid hospitality' are used interchangeably.

Liquid hospitality in the social domain

Wine is one of the elements in life that has always been considered a sophisticated hospitality-related beverage par excellence and the ideal accompaniment to food (Romani and Gistri, 2008). Somebody regularly enjoying wine is referred to as an oenophile (Collins, 2004), which may have a peculiar sound to it. Wine is a complex beverage; it contains many natural components that scientists are still discovering new facts about it. Wine appreciation and therefore wine consumption in the world is substantial. Klosse (2014) defines wine as an important element within gastronomy and therefore a source of pleasure. Wine and therefore liquid hospitality are connected to the art of living and enjoying the beautiful things in life.

In 2013, world wine consumption was at a level of 238.7 million hectolitres. The United States now has the biggest internal wine-consuming market in the world with total of 339 million cases of wine in 2013. This was above France's 296 million cases, Italy's 288 million, Germany's 274 million and China's 144 million (which made it the world's fifth largest consumer of wine). The UK came in sixth, drinking a total of 133 million cases (Lyons, 2015). Some countries such as Argentina, Chile, Brazil, South Africa and Romania saw a rise in 2013 of wine consumption compared to 2012, while others such as the US and China had a slight decrease.

How can one begin to explain the enormous appeal of fermented grape juice? How is it that this product of crushed grapes, yeast and time in a barrel has so fascinated people worldwide for many generations? How is it that a single bottle of wine can fetch hundreds of thousands of dollars at auction? Why are so many traditions, in so many cultures, centred on the consumption of wine? Wine is unique, and no other consumable product comes close to the appeal of wine. Wine has many meanings and carries great symbolism. And most importantly, for the purpose of constructing this chapter, wine unites people, thereby constituting or at least assisting in the creation of hospitality encounters. Part of the reason is that wine is beyond the ability of humans to fully understand it.

As people attempt to relate their personal experiences to others, they make connections with those who are struggling to define their own personal experiences. There is a sense of togetherness needed to share experiences that occurs when a bottle of wine is shared. A newly opened bottle will be different a day, a week or a month from now as it would have been different a day, a week or a month ago. Experts encourage us to allow a freshly poured glass to breath, because wines live in their bottle. They soften and harden, they mature, and once that wine is consumed it is one less bottle in the supply of that particular vintage.

Historical context

French historians (Brusse, 1989) seem to be convinced that Adam was already drinking wine in paradise. He took too much wine and appeared not to be able to limit his consumption. As history reveals it was God who in an attempt to divert Adam from drinking brought in Eve. If Eve had then kept to picking grapes, instead of apples, evil would never have ruled the world after the seduction of Adam by the snake. For perhaps a more reliable description of history there are quite accurate findings on where wine culture started. Faber and Lems (1995) put some historic facts about the development of wine growing in perspective. Fossils of wine leaves have been found and dated to originate from the beginning of the Tertiary period some 60 million years ago. Real structured wine growing has been estimated to have started between 5,000 and 4,000 years before Christ in the Caucasus, although early traces of wine growing have also been located in the south of Spain. From the Caucasus wine growing spread in several directions: west (Turkey), south-west and east (Arabia).

The eastern direction of wine growing never fully developed mainly because of the influence of Islam, which forbids the consumption of alcohol. About the consumption of alcohol in Islam it is said: 'In both [wine and gambling] is great sin, and (some) utility for men; but the sin of them is greater than their usefulness' (Abbas and Atwell, n.d.) and in other texts a direct relation between alcohol and Satan is defined. For Muslims, drinking of wine would most certainly not be attractive as the text in the Koran implies that whoever drinks wine is a disbeliever and therefore should be punished with 40 to 80 lashes. In the south-west, the country between the rivers Euphrates and Tigris, the heavy clay soil was not really ideal for wine growing. The best natural opportunities for wine growing appeared to be in the coastal countries of the near east (Turkey, Syria, Lebanon, Israel, Egypt).

Many stories in the Bible are proof of the importance of wine for society in Israel and Palestine. Most notably, the wedding at Cana in Galilee stands out, the occasion where Jesus turned water into wine (John 2:1–12). This magical conversion allowed the wedding guests to continue their celebration and this connects to wine as a metaphor of liquid hospitality. From these areas in the Middle East wine growing spread to Greece. Particularly in ancient Greece the knowledge and standing of wine and wine growing achieved great sophistication although in Egypt traces were also found of early techniques to explore grape cultivation. Drinking wine was an important element in ancient Greek society. It is, however, interesting to note that wine in Greek culture was always diluted with water; consumption of pure wine was considered to be for barbarians. Another point of study is the wide range of wines that were cultivated in ancient Greece.

The Greeks brought wine culture to different countries in Europe such as France, Spain and even as far as parts of Northern Africa. After the Greeks brought culture and knowledge of wine growing to the world, the Romans expanded wine to different parts of the world. Italy in 2000 BC was called 'Oinotria' by the Greeks, which literally means 'the land with vines growing on posts'. The Romans were not at first particularly interested in the making and drinking of wine. Wine was supposed to be a beverage for the gods and ordinary people were best not to consume it. At the end of the first millennium BC a major change in the Roman attitude towards wine occurred under Emperor Augustus. The first 'great growths' of wines originate from the centuries after that in which wine became a part of sophisticated culture.

The Romans when conquering France brought under Caesar a lot more vines and so Gaul became a very important centre of the wine world. In particular, the expansion of the Roman Empire brought wine culture to Germany, the Benelux countries, Hungary, Bulgaria, Romania and even as far as the southern half of England. As has become clear after two millennia, it was especially in France that wine culture grew to the importance it sustains in present times. A factor that most certainly had an influence on the popularity of wine was the poor condition and shortage of drinking water especially in the major cities. In Paris in the second half of the eighteen century a wine consumption of 350 litres per year for the Paris male inhabitant was normal (Garrier, 1998). This implied a daily consumption of almost a litre (!) of wine per person. The development of wine as a companion for food in its modern context started in the nineteenth century.

In the seventeenth century wine was transformed from a simple, bulk commodity to one distinguished by vineyard, vintage, grape varietals and the time-bound element of cellaring, and was increasingly consumed in society. This laid the foundations for the emergence of wine connoisseurship and a conspicuous link with elite social profiling. In the 1970s, the New World wine industries in South Africa, Chile, Australia and New Zealand democratised the cultural and social value of sophisticated wine consumption. Democratisation enabled connoisseurship for middle-class individuals with variable wine tastes (Howland, 2013).

It was under the influence of the English aristocrats, who dined to drink wine and not the other way around (Mennell, 1985), that the culinary tradition started in France. France and its famous wine culture combined with gastronomy inspired many wine growers around the world, particularly in the twentieth century, to produce wines from the famous grape varieties that are now so well known. The ever-growing elite image of wines like Bordeaux and Burgundy and the constant rise in prices put wines produced worldwide from grape varieties Cabernet Sauvignon, Chardonnay and Pinot Noir in the spotlight. Château Mouton Rothschild 1945, Bordeaux, Grand Cru Classé at a sales price of €5,000 per bottle (Gehrels, 2005) illustrates the enormous value accumulated in these wines.

In a philosophic evaluation of food (and drinks) as elements of culture Telfer (1996) considers food and wine to be (minor) forms of art. Following Telfer's notion, the concept of liquid hospitality materialised in its wine metaphor as being important in society as a higher good is worthy of consideration. Wine consumption and appreciation have been growing significantly since the Second World War (Paulissen, 1973). As reasons for consumers' growing interest in wines, Paulissen mentions first the strong growth of tourism whereby people travel to wine producing countries and thus learn to appreciate wines even more and, second, the strong increase in advertising for wines.

Another good indicator that illustrates the importance of wine in society is the retail industry. Looking at wines and their presence in retailing provides a relevant indication of investment in space and costs by entrepreneurs and appreciation by customers. A relationship seems apparent between holidays and wine. The memory of the holiday experience is reinforced by drinking wines tasted when engaging in vacation experiences. There is a recognisable focus on wine as culturally important for society as a whole and as specifically so for the individual. In the next section, wine as liquid hospitality in the private domain will be considered.

Liquid hospitality in the private domain

As mentioned, one of the major stimulators of wine as part of daily life has been the retail sector. The policy implemented by many of the leading supermarkets to offer a broad range of wines from around the world, supported by advertising and special promotions, has tremendously added to the importance of wine in daily culture. Dimensions that can be identified in peoples' appreciation of taste and liquid hospitality in the private domain based on research in the retail sector are as follows (Gehrels, 2004):

- *Common patterns and rituals.* In the morning a glass of orange juice with breakfast, coffee at the office, tea in the afternoon, a beer or glass of wine after work and in the evening. Fresh fruity or light rosé and white wines on a sunny terrace. Wine; sweltering summer nights, in the garden or on the balcony, enjoying life goes together with a good glass of wine. A full-bodied red wine if the weather is slightly off and to give warmth on gloomy autumn and winter days. The tastes that accompany daily life give a feeling of security.
- *The need to try out new things.* If a lot of elements in daily life are highly predictable this creates the need for new experiences and excitement. The need for new experiences is also realised in cooking and enjoying new dishes and trying new and unknown wines.
- *The human desire to expand on knowledge and experiences.* Closely following the second dimension, there seems to be a significant human desire to enrich life in terms of expanding knowledge and experience. Courses in cooking and wine are for that reason gaining in popularity. This dimension influences the development of taste itself. Especially bitter tastes are interesting to develop while sweet tastes become somewhat boring after an initial appreciation.
- *Enjoying for the pure sake of it.* Taking time for one-self. Enjoying easy sweet, smooth and creamy tastes such as milk chocolate. Drinking wines like Alsatian Pinot Blanc and Pinot Gris with a richness and a slight hint of sweetness is comparable, and they are appreciated in the same way.
- *Being together in an atmosphere of cosiness.* Dining together with family and/or friends around Christmas and other festivities. Enjoying a sports event on television, celebrating a special occasion, having a wine and cheese moment and many more fall into this dimension. Easy 'eatable' or 'drinkable' types of taste are related to this dimension of pure liquid hospitality.
- *Health: a basic need for almost everyone.* Health is experienced as one of the most valuable assets of human kind. This need to stay healthy is illustrated in the search for healthy food products, vitamins and so on. A wealth of research can be found that points to a correlation between a regular daily (but moderate) consumption of, in particular, red wine and a lower chance of suffering heart diseases.

The famous 'French Paradox' whereby people living in southern France eat a lot of fat and drink a lot of wine but on average are among the longest living people in Europe inspired authors such as Montignac (1996) to preach new ways of living. Looking at the causes of a presumed positive influence that alcohol and wine in particular have on human health, a few indicators were found (Stuttaford, 1997). First, alcohol (i.e. ethyl alcohol) has a positive effect on the platelets in the blood and lowers their stickiness. The clumping together of platelets is one of the important factors in causing coronary thrombosis, which eventually can lead to a heart attack. Conversely, a very heavy alcohol intake increases the overall level of blood fats such as cholesterol and triglyceride that assist in the development of heart diseases.

Second, there is research that suggests a positive effect of the so-called antioxidants in red wine, in particular, on too great a development of free radicals in the blood. The chain reaction resulting from the spreading of the free radicals, in the wrong circumstances, can be destructive to the human body. Diseases that seem to be related to the effect of free radicals are cataracts, macular degeneration of the retina, blindness and even cancer.

Human taste and appreciation in its many dimensions are connected to the relationship between culture, wine and health specifically in the private domain where liquid hospitality manifests. At the same time it supplies a foundation for the particular place wine as liquid hospitality has in contemporary culture. In fact, wine can be seen as distinctive product in human civilisation. Overstreet (1999) refers even to a wine lifestyle that by accumulating knowledge, experience and confidence, and learning by experimentation brings people closer to the goal of living and entertaining effortlessly. In doing so, wine as liquid hospitality in the private domain is an essential indicator symbolising quality of life. In the next section of the chapter, wine as liquid hospitality in the commercial domain is investigated.

Liquid hospitality in the commercial domain

Wine as a product has been an essential part of hospitality and the hospitality industry for centuries. In a hospitality setting, wine complements culinary experiences (Aune, 2002) and contributes to socialising, relaxation and learning (Barber, 2005). Wines are purchased for many reasons, and in different hospitality settings, such as hotels, bars, pubs or restaurants (Barber, 2009). Wine is an integral part of the restaurant business and the selection of wines must be consistent with the restaurant concept and compatible with the style of food served at the restaurant (Huiskamp, 2001).

The economic importance of liquid hospitality for the hospitality industry is obvious. Hotels with food and beverage outlets in different categories generate between 15 and 22 per cent of their gross revenues from the sales of beverages. With an estimated percentage of between 20 and 60 per cent of the beverage sales consisting of wine sales, total wine sales account for between approximately 4 and 13 per cent of total gross revenue of hotels (Gehrels, 2004). For restaurants the percentage of wine sales of total sales is estimated at around 20 per cent where total revenues from beverages vary from 25 to 33 per cent of total sales. It is clear that the sale and consumption of wines is of significant importance for the hospitality industry specifically when looking at the continuing growth in wine's popularity.

As mentioned, the hospitality industry – that is, the commercial hospitality domain – tends to produce substantial revenues on wines. Selling wine in a restaurant is an important income producer if it is done in the correct way. Therefore, it is important to recognise that wine is not just another liquid product, but a moment of liquid hospitality. It is culture, history, sensuality and opulence that people share when they enjoy wine. The liquid hospitality moment of celebrating wine needs to be respected by paying attention to the details that honour it, with correct glassware, correct temperature, correct quantity, and with skill and professional attention from the people who serve it. It is also difficult to present wine if the ambiance of the location does not offer guests the small but significant details that they normally don't have at home.

In an attempt to provide a better understanding of the way guests choose wine in a restaurant, Corsi and colleagues (2012) came up with interesting findings. Grape varietals are key choice drivers, followed by the awards obtained by a wine and its price. Less important are a wine's region of origin and tasting notes offered on the wine menu. The least important choice factor is food-matching suggestions.

To offer genuine liquid hospitality, basic questions similar to the ones asked when offering hospitality in general need to be answered. Who are the guests/customers that engage in the moment? What do they expect from the liquid hospitality being offered? What is their perception of the commercial domain they enter into? Are their expectations really fulfilled? The growing awareness and importance of liquid hospitality in the commercial domain is illustrated by statements of practitioners in the Dutch hospitality and retail industries.

A Michelin three-star chef:

People are tasting better every day. Ingredients are getting better, as well as personal taste. Essential is personal perception. A person tastes by using his brains and his wallet at the same time of course.

Purchasing manager of a major retailer:

Not so long ago, less than a quarter of the Dutch population consumed foreign cheeses, this number has now increased to half the population. There is a significant trend to try more new tastes. The willingness to explore and develop taste is very present.

A culinary journalist, more critical:

Nowadays tastes are piled up. This makes it very difficult to distinguish between the individual ingredients. Obviously, something needs to be done against 'taste blurring'. If the famous chefs, the food industry and the culinary journalists join forces, it might develop in the right direction in due time.

Director of a taste research company:

Tasting is the way to get experience and knowledge about gastronomy, in other words 'exposure'. This is not yet happening enough in the Netherlands if one compares it with the situation in France, Belgium and some of the English-speaking nations. Funny enough we teach children in school about mathematics and music but we do not teach them to discover taste. Why don't we develop regular classes in tasting in (primary) schools?

Awareness of taste among guests in the commercial hospitality domain has an impact on expectations placed on the providers in hotels and restaurants. This assumption is supported by Borchgrevink and Susskind (1998) who found that customers in mid-priced, casual-theme restaurants expect service employees to be knowledgeable about the wines they serve. Furthermore, they concluded that these expectations should at least be met and preferably exceeded. Managers of this type of restaurant should then be encouraged to train their service staff. This recommendation is further stressed given that service employees' credibility and competence are positively related to restaurant guests' purchases of recommended wines.

Finally, a completely different take on liquid hospitality in the commercial domain is offered by Overton and Banks (2015) when they talk about the phenomenon of 'conspicuous wine production'. Wine production is a global industry which has grown significantly over the last few years, particularly in the case of New World wines such as from Chile, North America, South Africa, China and India. Wine production has become part of national development strategies with symbolic value. In some cases, such as in China, the state encourages the country's wine production as a means for reshaping national identity. Similarly, individual entrepreneurs in New Zealand, Thailand and Chile invest in wine properties to gain status. This development started in the USA a few decades ago when people from film and theatre started wineries in California. Wine has become an iconic product that assists in repositioning national and individual images, and contributes to building identity and the status of countries and individual people. Having defined liquid hospitality in the commercial domain, in the final section of this chapter I pull together conclusions on wine as a metaphor of liquid hospitality.

Conclusions

Examples can be found in the hospitality literature that illustrate the importance of wine as liquid hospitality for contemporary society. Wine is a nutritious, physiologically active, complex beverage that can feed bodies, influence health and behaviour, and engage peoples' intellects (Baldy, 1997). Tasting wine is a way of life and the human race tastes everything that comes into contact with the senses, be it works of art, the present moment, the reality of existence: objects, people, the arts, love, life. This notion puts wine among subjects like culture, fine art, sports and intellectual activities. A growing number of world citizens associate wine with a gracious more relaxed, sociable lifestyle, while demographic studies have shown that wine drinkers are better educated and earn more than non-wine drinkers. The latter position could, however, very well be explained by the fact that wines of quality are fairly expensive and thereby wine drinkers automatically will have more finances at their disposal. People want to know more about wine for social and professional reasons and want to be able to discuss wine intelligently, assuming wine knowledge to be a valuable social skill and that knowledge of and appreciation for good food and wine is an asset.

Drinking wine can be considered as a celebration of life, good food and special company (Zraly, 1999), and one of the great pleasures of the world, while its enjoyment is enhanced by an understanding of its varieties, flavours and styles. Wine as an expression of liquid hospitality is an adventure and a lifestyle (Overstreet, 1999). Wine as a carrier of liquid hospitality is both a lifestyle and an attitude, a casual expertise, an effortless enjoyment, subtlety without confusion, hedonism without excess, serious (but not too serious) fun for grown-ups, and finally one piece of a bigger puzzle wherein the finer things in life become part of one's everyday experience. It is this kind of explicit strategic philosophising that has become more obvious in relation to wine, emphasising its value for (parts of) society. The opening and sharing of a bottle of wine brings a broader sense of enjoyment and understanding of life. It represents one of the most sophisticated, interesting hobbies. Wine is a catalyst for camaraderie, travel and adventure; it is exciting and stimulating, inspiring and challenging. It is a subject of incredible depth and range, yet is also amazingly accessible.

Wine is made to be appreciated and celebrated. Wine improves the disposition, restores the spirit, dispels sorrow, generates laughter, overcomes timidity while it evokes friendship, stimulates conversation and appetite, adds zest to a meal and aids in convalescence (Lamb and Mittelberger, 1980). Dovaz (1999) refers to some of the famous wine brands as 'vintages of the century' thereby positioning these particular wines in combination and at the same stage as world famous historical events. An example of this bringing forward of wine as a marker of world history is the following representation of the year 1945 – Burgundy wine, Clos de Lambrays and the end of the Second World War, the Noble prize for medicine awarded to Alexander Fleming and the right to vote for women in France. Wine generates revenues for the hospitality industry and retail businesses, and provides income to people in these sectors to those directly involved or indirectly connected.

Although it is important to understand the nature of wine, properly assessing its product characteristics and pairing wines with food, there seems to be a dimension missing in the dominantly technical approaches. The omission in wine research appears to be in the field of wine's liquid hospitality value and the meaning wine has for people as an element of human interaction. Sociologists who have studied wine or wine culture are few (Undheim, 2010). Therefore, looking at wine in the context of connecting people could be an area of research for further exploration. Wine is important for people and as a consequence it is also important for hospitality. Examples come alive when hotel management school graduates recall having met each other as quite different personalities through engaging in wine tasting. One said: 'I would never have become friends with some of my fellow students, if it had not been for the wine society we were members of.' Another interesting example involves two graduates who started a relationship after graduation. This, as their close friend said, 'would never have happened if they had not been so passionately working together to organize the wine tastings of our wine association'. Can one believe this, wine as a dating tool?

Then, on a more serious note, a wine merchant to whom I talked recently mentioned the funeral of his father:

> My father passed away last year way in his nineties. He had started to appreciate wines at a later age after my brother married the daughter of a French wine grower. We were very sad and met as close family next to his coffin before the actual ceremony took place. There I realised that the most honouring tribute to my father would be to sit together and contemplate his life while sampling an extraordinary wine, and so we did.

This well-known wine authority said: 'We have shared our memories and special moments in which dad featured, honouring his life while sharing a precious Corton 1984.' The examples given here can be seen as illustrations of wine as a metaphor for liquid hospitality. To finish this chapter the words of Goethe speak for themselves in the context of wine being a driver for liquid hospitality: 'Wine rejoices the heart of people and joy is the mother of virtue.'

Retrospective considerations

Looking in this chapter at the concept of liquid hospitality represented by wine as the metaphor triggers retrospective considerations. The question can legitimately be asked: 'Is it correct to position wine as the symbol for liquid hospitality?' There are obviously members of the professional and academic communities who will plea for a wider take on the matter. Why would 'cocktails' or 'spirits' not be considered as liquid drivers for hospitality and socialising of people? I can imagine the bartender community protesting at this exclusive argument of wine as metaphor of liquid hospitality, and they would probably have a point. And what of beer as a contemporary multi-functional beverage bringing people together to celebrate life and come more regularly to the gastro-arena? While we are at it, let us not forget the barista school of thought that would definitely be able to argue that it is coffee that serves in a variety of preparations to provide all-day liquid hospitality. Indeed, there are no fully objectively chosen validations for only mentioning 'wine' in the context and metaphor of 'liquid hospitality'. From the perspective of its rich history and culture, however, wine can be justified as the metaphor to frame the concept of liquid hospitality. Having served as a sommelier and wine management lecturer, it became clear to me that people, guests and graduates after many years still recall interactions with and about wine as expressions of hospitality encounters. Having said this, any counter argument should be stimulated to further develop a definition of liquid hospitality perhaps expanding the 'liquid' element to other beverages. I hope this chapter may serve the purpose of continuing research and discussion about the concept of liquid hospitality.

References

Abbas, N. and Atwell, E. (n.d.), The Qurany Concepts Tool: Chapter Name: Al-Baqra Verse No:219, University of Leeds, at http://www.comp.leeds.ac.uk/nora/html/2-219.html. Accessed June 2016.

Aune, L. (2002) The use of enchantment in wine and dining, *International Journal of Contemporary Hospitality Management* 14, 1: 34–37.

Baldy, M. W. (1997) *The University Wine Course*, San Francisco: The Wine Appreciation Guild.

Barber, N. (2005) Wine label design, information and bottle packaging: influence on wine buying behaviours, Masters thesis, Purdue University, West Lafayette.

Barber, N. (2009) Wine consumers information search: gender differences and implications for the hospitality industry, *Tourism and Hospitality Research* 9, 3: 250–269.

Borchgrevink, C. P. and Susskind, A. (1998) Beverage communications at mid-priced, casual-theme restaurants: guest experiences and preferences, *Praxis–The Journal of Applied Hospitality Management* 1, 2: 92–116.

Brusse, J. (1989) *De Matige Drankgids: Hoe blijf ik Bacchus de baas?*, trans. Y. Charpak and A. van Hoang, Kampen: La Riviere & Voorhoeve.

Chong, K. W. (2015) The influence of price structures on experience quality and behavior intention in hospitality industry, *International Journal of Marketing Studies* 7, 6: 137–144.

Collins, S. (2004) *Dictionary of Wine Odd Bins*, London: Bloomsbury.

Corsi, A. M., Mueller, S. and Lockshin, L. (2012) Let's see what they have…: what customers look for in a restaurant wine list, *Cornell Hospitality Quarterly* 53, 2: 110–121.

Dovaz, M. (1999) *Vins du Siècle*, Paris: Assouline.

Faber, L. and Lems, E. (1995) *Wijn! Wijn!! Wijn!!!*, Utrecht: RMO/Kosmos-Z&K.

Garrier, G. (1998) *Social and Cultural History of Wine*, Paris: Larousse-Bordas.

Gehrels, S. A. (1995) *Gastvrijheid en Distributie*, Meppel: EduActief.

Gehrels, S. A. (2004) Wine management in Dutch culinary restaurants, Masters dissertation, Oxford Brookes University, Oxford.

Gehrels, S. A. (2005) Wine in a cultural context. In Van der Hoek, K. W. and Heinhuis, E. (eds) *Babylon United: Opstellen over Gastvrijheid en Cultuurverschillen*, Leeuwarden: Christelijke Hogeschool Nederland, International Hospitality Management, pp. 41–56.

Hellstrand, P. (2010) Price impact on guest satisfaction, *Hospitality.Net.*, 6 January, at http://www.hospitalitynet.org/news/4044870.html. Accessed November 2015.

Howland, P. J. (2013) Distinction by proxy: the democratization of fine wine, *Journal of Sociology* 49, 2–3: 325–340.

Huiskamp, R. (2001) *Great Restaurant Concepts: An In-depth Analysis of Five Noteworthy European Success Stories*, Wervershoof: Food & Beverage.

Kandampully, J. and Suhartanto, D. (2000) Customer loyalty in the hotel industry: the role of customer satisfaction and image, *International Journal of Contemporary Hospitality Management* 12, 6: 346–351.

Klosse, P. (2014) *The Essence of Gastronomy: Understanding the Flavour of Foods and Beverages*, Boca Raton, FL: CRC Press.

Lamb, R. B. and Mittelberger, E. G. (1980) *Celebration of Wine and Life: The Fascinating Story of Wine and Civilization*, San Francisco: The Wine Appreciation Guild.

Lashley, C. (2015) Hospitality and hospitableness, *Research in Hospitality Management* 5, 1: 1–7. Available at http://www.stendenaihr.com/media/77/NL/algemeen/original/RiHM5.1.April%202015.pdf. Accessed April 2016.

Lashley, C and Morrison, A. (2000) *In Search of Hospitality: Theoretical Perspectives and Debates*, Oxford: Butterworth-Heinemann.

Lyons, W. (2015) Who's driving world wine consumption?, *Wall Street Journal*, 28 January. Available at http://www.wsj.com/articles/whos-driving-world-wine-consumption-1422461583. Accessed November 2015.

Mennell, S. (1985) *All Manners of Food: Eating and Taste in England and France from the Middle Ages to the Present*, Oxford: Basil Blackwell.

Montignac, M. (1996), *Ik ben slank want ik eet*, Valkenswaard: Artulen.

O'Gorman, K. D. (2006) Jacques Derrida's philosophy of hospitality, *Hospitality Review* 8, 4: 50–57.

Overstreet, D. (1999) *Overstreet's New Wine Guide*, New York: Clarkson Potter.

Overton, J. and Banks, G. (2015) Conspicuous production: wine, capital and status, *Capital & Class* 38, 1: 197–210.

Paulissen, M. (1973) *About Wines: A Guide for Fans and Amateurs*, Amsterdam: H. J. Paris.

Perdue, L. (1999) *The Wrath of Grapes: The Coming Wine Industry Shakeout and How to Take Advantage of It*, New York: Avon Books.

Romani, S. and Gistri, G. (2008) Wine consumption practices and meanings as depicted in Italian TV fiction. Paper presented at 4th International Conference of the Academy of Wine Business Research, Siena, 17–19 July.

Stuttaford, T. (1997) *To Your Good Health! The Wise Drinker's Guide*, London: Faber and Faber.

Telfer, E. (1996) *Food for Thought: Philosophy and Food*, London: Routledge.

Undheim, T. (2010) What is sociology of wine?, *Sociology of Wine*, at http://sociologyofwine. com/2010/10/13/what-is-sociology-of-wine. Accessed 27 December 2015.

Vijver H. (1996) *Ethiek van de gastvrijheid*, Assen: Van Gorcum.

Zraly, K. (1999) *Windows of the World Complete Wine Course*, millennium edn, New York: Sterling.

21

Hospitality, territory and identity

Reflections from community tourism in Aventureiro Village, Ilha Grande/RJ, Brazil

Helena Catão Henriques Ferreira and Aguinaldo César Fratucci

Key themes

Hospitality

Hospitality in protected areas

Identity and territory

Community tourism

In hospitality, the chief thing is the good will

(Greek proverb)

It is not uncommon nowadays to see the growth of a type of nature-oriented tourism, focused on so-called 'simpler' social relations and modelled on solidarity, which we believe is 'primitive' or 'traditional', and linked to the idea of community. Today, representations of nature have become associated with those living in a healthy environment, in clear opposition to those inhabiting the big cities, which are seen as full of tensions and dangers, pollution and hostility. Thus, protected areas around the world have come to be perceived as 'pieces of paradise'.

There has also been an increasing concern within urban populations for an environment that differs from theirs, a rural and natural world considered as 'pure' and 'regenerating'. In contrast to previous decades when the image of rurality was still negative and associated with backwardness, in the late 1960s the Western world began to look critically upon the urban-industrial lifestyle. The non-urban environment and life in rural spaces was viewed more positively. Since then, this conception has been re-edited, reinvented and absorbed by the tourism market itself as a signal of distinction (Bourdieu, 2002) and differentiation from the tourist product.

As Bauman states, the word 'community' suggests safety and cosiness in the face of the 'unrelenting times' in which we live, 'times of competition and disdain for the weaker ones, when people around hide the game and just a few are interested in helping us, when in reply to

DOI: 10.4324/9781315679938-23

our cries for help we hear warnings to stay on our own' (2003: 8). It is in this context that the word 'hospitality' becomes more valued, and this is what is searched for as one gets to know new lands and people, mainly during free time from the world of work, when one can enjoy the social contract – which seems to be denied in more formal and urban relations.

Godbout (1997) argues that, although this complex social phenomenon cannot be seen exclusively from the perspective of the gift in the sense coined by Mauss (2003) in his *Essay on the Gift* (*Essai Sur le Don*, 1923), hospitality involves gift giving and generosity. Therefore, the gift would be the relation of a basic exchange between social actors, which is never exclusively economic but also made up of affective, emotional elements such as kindnesses, rites and so on – that is, moral and spiritual values. For Godbout (1997), although the gift is a characteristic of 'primitive' societies, it is also important for the modern individual, who would be constantly involved in these relations. Thus, the intersubjectivity and the sociability would be related to a permanent cycle of giving-receiving-returning. The main idea of the notion of the gift for Mauss is that this cycle, which he calls a 'system of total instalments' (2003: 191), although made of obligations, establishes itself in a voluntary manner, through the gifts that, in each specific case, present themselves in a proper way.

This chapter will reflect on the dynamics of hospitality with local populations and their relationship with tourist organisations and the impact of tourists on their living space, mainly those considered as traditional, such as Vila do Aventureiro, Ilha Grande, Rio de Janeiro, on Brazil's south-east coast. The aim is, especially, to understand (taking the notion of hospitality as starting point and reference) how environmental and tourism incursions into their domain relate to representations of place, how preservation of nature and *locus* of pleasure and leisure have been perceived by the inhabitants, from this sociability established with new local demands.

The work is based on the results of ethnographic field research, using direct observation and in-depth interviews with local social actors, state and NGO representatives, researchers and tourists, as well as participation in community meetings related to the creation of Aventureiro's Sustainable Development Reserve (RDS).

Aventureiro village is located in the south-west of Ilha Grande, in the bay of the same name, and lies within the territory of Angra dos Reis city, in the state of Rio de Janeiro. Ilha Grande is located between coordinates 23° 5' and 23° 14' S and 44° 5' and 44° 23' W, in the tourist region called Costa Verde, on Rio's south coast. Comprising 193 km², it is the largest island in Ilha Grande Bay, with great potential for tourism development, thanks to its natural and cultural characteristics, and its privileged location among the main urban centres in the country (Rio de Janeiro, São Paulo and Belo Horizonte) (Figure 1).

In the thirty-three years between the creation of Praia do Sul Biological Reserve (REBIO) in 1981 and Aventureiro Sustainable Development Reserve (RDS) in 2014, its population dwelt in a forbidden place, as its ancestral territory had been incorporated into the territory protected by the Biological Reserve. The Biological Reserve (SNUC, 2002) is one of the most restrictive types of protected areas of conservation in Brazil, where housing is not allowed, and not even people, except those linked to the administrative agency and researchers, with the permission and previous monitoring of that agency.

Aventureiro residents are considered to be one of the 'traditional caiçara populations' of the state of Rio de Janeiro, remnants of those who would have inhabited extensive coastal strips of Brazil in the past. The 'caiçara' identity is characterised as a category attributed to those inhabitants by agents outside of the location (environmentalists, researchers and tourists), and it has been known since the creation of the Biological Reserve. Those recognised as caiçara populations are the ones who lived on the Brazilian coastline (from Rio de Janeiro State to the north of Santa Catarina State), comprising a mix of indigenous, white and black people, associated with

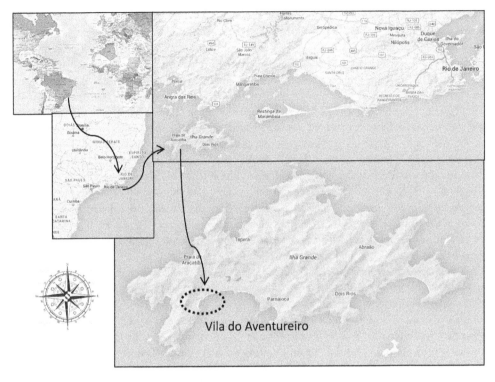

Figure 21.1   The location of Vila do Aventureiro, Ilha Grande, RJ, Brazil

shifting cultivation practices (with a soil rotation system aiming at recovering agricultural areas), small-scale fishing (practised with traditional technologies) and extractivism (hunting, shellfish and forest species collection).

According to Cristina Adams (2000), the word 'caiçara' originates from the Tupi-Guarani language and means 'man from the coast'. It would have originally designated stakes that surrounded villages and also corral branches fixed on the water to capture fish and afterwards used to denominate the dwellings made on the beach to protect canoes. Later on, it came to identify Cananéia inhabitants in São Paulo, and finally gave name to all individuals from Brazilian coastline communities, from Paraná (or north of Santa Catarina) to Rio de Janeiro. Adams reports that, while some authors consider caiçara culture as a subculture of caipira culture (a bush culture specific to Brazil), others believe that 'caiçaras and caipiras have their own identities, with unique lifestyle and culture' (2000: 105). For Adams (2000), as the coastline was the first Brazilian area to be populated, there were common elements to all coastal populations arising from similar influences on their cultural foundations. Thus, traditions and characteristic elements of Tupi-Guarani indigenous groups were, from the beginning, mixing traditions and elements of Portuguese culture. Several instruments and indigenous techniques were integrated into their culture, such as the planting system (itinerant, burning-based and fallow lands), cassava plantation, flour production, combined crops with cassava, the use and technique of canoe factoring, methods and techniques of fishing, and net manufacturing, among many others. Likewise, indigenous meals came to incorporate elements brought from the Portuguese, such as wheat, white rice, English potatoes and some other vegetables previously unknown to them (Ferreira, 2004).

Arruda (2000) also observes the indigenous influence on the forms of work organisation and sociability. In caipira culture (and in caiçara too), families represent units of production and consumption based on reciprocity, as shown in mutual aid and their joint action during religious feasts. Portuguese colonisation was based on the exploitation of products valued in the international market and population increased around these exploitations. However, Brazilian economic cycles migrated from one region to another, with the replacement of one product by another. When a region lost economic importance it would be abandoned, leaving in its place small population clusters relatively isolated and scattered, making their living from an economy based on self-production. Thus, caiçara populations were formed in the interstices of large economic cycles of the colonial period and strengthened when the activities focused on exploitation declined (Diegues, 1996). These populations always kept some connections with larger and closer cities to varying degrees, depending on them to sell excess products from their farming or fishing and also to buy products non-generated in the community.

Adams (2000) mentions Setti's observation that the inhabitant of Ubatuba sees himself as a caiçara once he is named as such, but that this is not a definition that originated in the community itself. The term 'caiçara' does not comprise a native category of Aventureiro, for local inhabitants are accustomed to calling themselves 'Aventureiro's children'. But nowadays, the natives somehow have incorporated this category.

Identity and territory

Caiçara identity, attributed by external agents, has been gradually assumed by Aventureiro's inhabitants, although ambiguously. This problem was due mainly to social relations established at the creation of the Biological Reserve (1981), since when it became necessary to defend the right of its permanence in native territory. Subsequently, a new cycle of valuing caiçara identity has been verified from representations tourists make on the life of the natives. Caiçara, then, has come to mean 'person of the land' and distinguishes natives from immigrants and tourists, consolidating itself as a sign of authenticity.

Cuche (2002) understands that social identity represents, in one single moment, a process of inclusion and exclusion. She delimitates the group (who is and is not part of it) and distinguishes it from other groups. In this perspective, the various conceptions of culture influence what is understood as cultural identity. If it is conceived as a 'second nature', identity is regarded as a mark that would define the individual once and for all and from which he cannot escape (Cuche, 2002); identity would be an essence, on which the individual or the group would not have any influence. On the other hand, under a subjectivist point of view, 'ethno-culture is a sense of binding or an identification with an imaginary collective, to a lesser or greater degree' (Cuche, 2002: 181). This view, however, would include a reductionist perspective of identity, taking it as a matter of deliberate choice by the individual. Although this interpretation has the merit of understanding the possibility of identity variation, it leaves room, on the one hand, for an unrealistic and excessively ephemeral conception of its collaboration. Cuche (2002) shows, on the other hand, the importance of perceiving the relational character of identity. In this case, it would be the context that would explain why, in one moment, an identity can be rejected and in another assumed. 'The construction of an identity is made within social contexts that determine the position of the agents and, for this reason, orient their representations and choices' (Cuche, 2002: 182).

From this relational perspective of identity, according to Barth (2000), different identities are built as social groups get in touch as result of their interactions – which would explain why caiçara identity, first unknown and then representative of the devaluation and dispossession suffered by the population in question, became, at a certain moment, important in the fight for territory.

The dispossession process mentioned here is related to the conception of territory by Raffestin (1986), according to which it is the social actor who, by taking over a space, turns it into his own territory. In this sense, we can detect the presence of several types of territorialisation over a single physical area (Haesbaert, 2011). At Aventureiro, as far as the natives are concerned, the territory is related to a living space, to memory and affection, and a sense of belonging. The space territorialised by them was seen as a place of agricultural practices, of the farm, and it was in relation to this that a family was constituted. With the installation of a biological reserve encompassing this territory, a new territoriality came to dispute both the appointment and the uses of this very space. It also becomes a place of nature preservation. In place of farms, new social actors represented by both governmental and non-governmental environmentalists see the forest in terms of regeneration and endangered species. Then, from the moment when tourism is also territorialised, conceptions of walking tracks, diving waters, landscape for enjoyment, and space arise and are seen as a 'piece of paradise' (Ferreira, 2004). For Barel (1986), each and every territory has its own codes, representations and borders. With new visions brought to Aventureiro's space and mainly with the new regulations that come to exist on it, one may consider that there was a retraction of native territory, which would indicate a process of dispossession, even if people have actually remained in the area. They were not able to develop agriculture in their customary mode or carry out extractivist activities, and their presence there became unstable and permanently transient, as contradictory as this might seem (Ferreira, 2004).

However, in the clash between these overlapping territories (Fratucci, 2014), there is a redefinition of each of them. The native territory is transformed through its relations with territories of preservation and tourism. Besides physical changes in their borders, one observes a process of inculcation or incorporation of values. Thus, new conceptions related to nature arise. Consumption habits are incorporated, changes of values occur, such as monetisation of life, changes related to the old sociability are turned into solidarity. With the insertion of competitiveness relations, demanded mainly by tourism, the perception of native territory through the elements valued by environmentalism and tourism such as fauna, flora and landscape may be mentioned as evidence of this incorporation. Dominated groups who naturalise these representations without realising the relation of forces to which they are subjected somehow legitimise the symbolic power of dominant representations, but they are also re-elaborated by the values and representations of the community itself (Ferreira, 2004).

Solidarity, hostility and hospitality

According to Darbon (1997), while solidarity is related to a set of behaviours that have to do with an identity principle that shapes a specific social group, and according to which the idea of belonging on the part of its members, and of exclusion on the part of non-members, is included, hospitality, in contrast, evokes opening to alterity, even though these limits are constantly redefined and renegotiated. Godbout (1997), however, understands that bonds of kinship (and by extension, bonds of community) can be a perfect place for many ways of help to be put into action, and that welcoming a member of the family who is in difficulties would illustrate the first form of hospitality. In this case, solidarity would not oppose hospitality, but would rather be closely linked to it as one of its attributes. Godbout also highlights two possible statuses for the person received: group member or foreign. To welcome members strengthens the sense of belonging to the network. However, it is important to consider that, even for hospitality that occurs among close family members, there is a border demarcation between the one who receives and the one who is received. Hospitality establishes a temporary difference of status, somewhere between belonging and alterity. This view is important when we consider that a community, much as it is cohesive, is not totally homogeneous. There is always a hierarchisation and a negotiation process in the game of social relations connected to it. From this point of view, hospitality is based on alterity and differences that exist even in family or community groups.

The passage from exteriority to interiority of a group is the act or action of crossing its social and cultural borders, involving authorisation or an invitation to experience hospitality (Raffestin, 1997). In this sense, it would be a characteristic mechanism of margins, border regions, whether material or not, from which it would be possible to cross borders without violence. It would be the space of friendliness (Raffestin, 1997). The enclosed space of safety would open to a foreign world, always considered hostile. Hospitality, therefore, would have found a place where it would be possible to articulate the known world with the unknown. Raffestin (1997) proposes that hospitality goes far beyond the dynamics of the relation between the one who receives and the one who is received and, therefore, can be conceived as the knowledge of the practice that establishes itself with the other through itself. Hospitality would be founded on the idea that a man is linked to another man. The one who receives in the sedentary position is in fact an immigrant, a foreigner who waits, and the one who is received in the nomadic position is the virtual image of the other (Raffestin, 1997). There is a minimisation of difference to allow friendliness, whereas conflict is triggered when differences are emphasised. Hospitality involves a regulating function and that promotes friendliness and allows the weakest to preserve a minimum of autonomy in a difficult environment.

Hospitality establishes bridges between those who are different. Many conflicts take place due to misunderstandings fed by different conceptions and practices of public and space, rhythms of life rooted in behaviours taken as natural by a certain group, but reproved by others. Spaces of dialogue are helpful in improving hospitality between groups, once harmony is established at the expense of difference (Raffestin, 1997).

The life of Aventureiro's inhabitants has always been marked by practices of solidarity, whether in the organisation of traditional feasts and rituals, in collective action for building houses or in farm work, fishing and boat transportation. However, from the early 1980s, this population that had lived far from contact with outside people started to receive periodic visits from state agents, due to the creation of a biological reserve. It is worth noting that these contacts were not friendly and full of warmth. If hospitality is a social relation, one assumes that it takes place in the two senses and, therefore, may come from the one who arrives (raising similar reactions from the receptor). And, in the same way, it would occur with its counterpart, whether inhospitability or even hostility. These contacts put the inhabitants in a chronic situation of illegality because they inhabit a space that environmental legislation has come to determine as uninhabitable. Many conflicts have started since then, and the atmosphere of hostility between both parties has dominated the relations established. Old habits have been questioned and banned by state agents, and this has deeply marked the perception of residents about the protected area, creating trauma, sorrow and resentment.

Several adaptive processes to the new situation have taken place. In accordance with broad discussions at the international level focusing on the rights of traditional populations regarding their territories and the installation of protected areas from the creation of the National System of Units of Conservation (SNUC) in 2000, the relation with native populations became regulated. The new sensitivity to traditional communities has resulted in indigenous populations being relocated to parks and biological reserves in areas similar to their original homelands.

These new areas are usually fully protected, resulting in the maintenance of these populations in their habitat. NGOs and other social agents monitor these communities, as 'areas of dislocation' or processes of 'conservation unit re-categorisation'.

Tourism appears in this sense as an economic activity of increasing importance for these populations deprived of their traditional livelihood. In parallel, these areas of 'preserved nature', increasingly rare in the contemporary world, come to be objects of desire for urban populations, generating growth of a specific tourist demand. If, on the one hand, this means another problem with which the state has to deal, on the other, ongoing interaction processes of these actors/ social agents have been determining cultural exchanges and intercultural processes (Canclini, 2015) that keep within them certain conceptions of hospitality; once cultural borders are crossed, permanent negotiations are established in search of accommodating conflicts or even aiming to their resolution, and 'acceptance' of the 'other' happens, even on a provisional basis and subjected to setbacks.

Community tourism at Aventureiro

The kind of tourism that came to be practised at Vila do Aventureiro and which has been changing over time, mainly through the contact of the native population with tourists, is known today as community, or community-based, tourism (Costa et al., 2009). Over the last decades, Ilha Grande has become one of the main tourist destinations in the state of Rio de Janeiro. Local tourist activity intensified from 1994 on, when a maximum-security prison, installed in mid-twentieth century on the oceanic part of the island, was closed. It is worth noting that, historically, Ilha Grande hosted several other penal institutions, thanks to its strategic location in relation to both the continent and sea routes.

At Aventureiro, the process of tourism growth occurred in a diverse and slower manner than in the rest of the island, for when the touristification of Ilha Grand received a large boost, Aventureiro's area was already part of a Biological Reserve. In Aventureiro tourist accommodation has not been developed, apart from the many campgrounds and some bed and breakfast units, known in the native language as 'little rooms', for they are in fact rooms that comprise part of the resident's house and are rented to tourists (because of the environmental legislation in force, it is not possible to build new houses in the location).

What characterises this as community tourism is the fact that the residents themselves are in charge of its management – that is, the organisation of the activity (according to a native *ethos*) and the administration of small businesses (campgrounds, bars and tourist transportation) are the responsibility of the community itself, which has made social mobility possible for families (Costa et al., 2009).

It is worth noting that today many and diversified experiences are categorised as community or community-based tourism, and it is not possible to generalise these experiences within a homogeneous field of action and investigation. However, some characteristics are common and remain constant to this varying type. One is the fact that community tourism is related to the paradigm of sustainability, which, since the 1990s, has inspired actions turned to sustainable development in the world. In this sense, there is a concern with a development model that is not committed exclusively to the economic sphere, but is also concerned with environmental, social and cultural issues (Ferreira and Tomé, 2014). Another point to be highlighted refers to the fact that this development could be framed as a local and endogenous type (Bartholo et al., 2009), based on the value of local nature, human and micro-economic capital, which is becoming a trend of tourist activity, providing the opportunity to promote inclusion, contribute to the confrontation of poverty and minimise social inequalities (Ferreira and Tomé, 2014).

This kind of tourism has also been associated with local populations' 'protagonism' (one of the main characteristics of Aventureiro's tourism) and their cultural tradition of hospitality, welcoming and reciprocity. Bauman states that the word community evokes a 'warm and cozy place' (2003: 7) and 'all we miss and need to live safely and confidently' (2003: 9).

As for the issue of hospitality at Aventureiro, it should be highlighted, above all else, that hospitality, once it is interwoven with the sociability of a certain group, is also related to the values and ways of life of that group, and, therefore, varies in the way it is conceived. Certain forms of 'receiving the client', in the manner that is understood locally to be adequate, for instance, may not be part of 'well receiving' according to the 'canons' of a more standardised tourism and Western and capitalist logics. Hospitality is carried out on its own terms and the attention to the tourist is limited by what he/she considers convenient. Native solidarity displayed in times of need and in hospitality is more widely practised than in urban communities. Hospitality through rendered information also makes itself present with intensity. In this case, there are trust issues involved. As the inhabitants have lived, and somehow still live, in a situation of instability and conflict, all that is said at the beginning of a relationship with someone who is 'outside' is weighted with much care. Researchers can feel the change in the behaviour of people of the community once they understand that the interlocutor can be trusted. From an attitude that is initially suspicious, they become extremely collaborative and friendly. Tourists themselves also experience a change of behaviour in relation to them. When they first arrive, they are treated with reserve and estrangement, like 'the stranger', and many times as 'a necessary evil'. But as they return, a relation of proximity takes shape, mainly when visitors respond to this hospitable sociability, becoming interested in local issues and the people of the community, remembering their names and so on, thus twisting the logic that says that the one who receives is always the one who gives and the one who is received is always the one who receives, and making of his presence the gift (Darbon, 1997). Depending on the level of proximity and involvement with their problems, visitors come to be considered by the community as friends.

However, one can observe moments when the borders are well defined, mainly regarding time and space markers. Demands seen as 'off-hour' or 'out of touch', such as visitors waking up residents in the middle of the night to 'buy some beer' (Ferreira, 2004) are rejected. As the tourist's physical space invades the domestic space (campgrounds are in families' backyards and 'little rooms' are part of the houses themselves), it is necessary to clearly define symbolic spaces from use in order to preserve the family's intimacy.

During traditional feasts, although tourists today may take a very active part, many times helping with the organisation, some moments are reserved for the community, such as religious and social roles (carrying the litters of saints in the feasts, coordinating celebrations along with or in the absence of the priest, providing assistance to the priest during the feast, among others), being the host (promoter and coordinator elected during the feast for next year), collecting resources and so on.

Aventureiro's inhabitants perceive tourism ambiguously: it produces economic autonomy but at the same time provokes social and cultural changes that lead to challenges. One of them is what they identify as the decrease in solidarity among people. Competitive logic that characterises contemporary tourist activity, by which those who have a more market-oriented view offer differentiated services to tourists, is sometimes seen as unfair, as if they want to conquer all tourists. For Raffestin (1997), the monetisation of life forces back classical hospitality, giving precedence to economic exchange relations.

Aventureiro's natives also complain about the near-ending of joint efforts (exceptions being special situations such as those in cases of emergency or in the organisation of feasts, work in the church and so on) associated with working on the farms or the 'mullet trawl' (practised with trawl nets, with the help of women, children and elderly), even though they are aware that the end of this practice is not directly associated with tourism, but with the decline in fish numbers, which is mainly the result of industrial fishing and high traffic of motor boats.

Relations with those 'outside', in this case state agents, environmentalists, researchers and tourists, helped the group to 'define its identity, built up on belonging to a location' (Carneiro, 1998: 62). Local traditions, so valued by a certain type of tourist and seen not as a reproduction of the past but re-contextualised as a new reading of the present, combine with the creation of 'a specific space and, at the same time, a welcoming space' (Cara, 1996, quoted in Ferreira, 2004: 54).

Irving points to the 'essential condition' for community-based tourism being the 'encounter between identities' (2009: 116). In the organisation of this type of tourism, an ethical commitment is necessary in order to take into consideration respect for hosts and their culture, so that a 'real interchange among subjects' is made possible (Irving, 2009: 116), and this would be in accordance with the spirit of the gift, where this 'encounter' would be translated by giving, receiving and re-attributing (Mauss, 2003). In this sense, the 'quality of the visitors' experience is related to the host's quality of life' (Irving, 2009: 117).

Sustainable Development Reserves (RDSs), community tourism and hospitality

Community-based tourism is considered as a possible and adequate form of economic activity within protected areas such as the Sustainable Development Reserve or Extra-activist Reserve (Sustainable Use Conservation Units), since they are based on the protection of traditional communities, their environment and practices. The inclusion of these categories in the National System of Units of Conservation was due to the struggle of these traditional populations for their rights in the context of environmentalism.

Following a process that had begun in January 2008, the Aventureiro Sustainable Development Reserve was created in May 2014. Since 1981, with the creation of Praia do Sul State Biological Reserve which encompassed the area of Vila do Aventureiro, the local population had been suffering threats of forced removal. In 2000, an environmentalist NGO presented an investigation request at the Brazilian Prosecutor's office asking for the removal of local inhabitants. This had a huge impact on the community, which for a long time had been living insecurely. In order to defend themselves before the Prosecutor's Office, residents created the Association of Residents and Friends of Aventureiro – AMAV. This association became a channel of claims before the state but, at the same time, helped them to start and organise local tourism.

During the Carnival of 2006, after a disastrous operation of the Angra Legal project, which withdrew tourists from Aventureiro and prevented residents from receiving visitors, the Association started a court case at the Prosecutor's Office requesting the area's re-categorisation. After much negotiation, in January 2008 the state government started the re-categorisation process.

It was not an easy case. Over two years, monthly meetings were held with the Environment State Secretariat, the community, NGOs and even some tourists. There was no agreement on reorganisation. Within the environmental state agencies there was a deep disagreement between at least two segments: one group considered it absurd 'to lose' a Biological Reserve area, while another struggled for re-categorisation of the area as a Sustainable Development Reserve (RDS), in order to reconcile caiçara population interests with nature conservation. Among members of the community there was also a clash of interests. One group wanted re-categorisation so that the area would be regulated solely by the more flexible APA de Tamoios legislation. Another group thought that the caiçara population would have more guarantees under an RDS categorisation, as APA legislation could leave room for more aggressive economic interests and other exogenous forces to intervene, in which case they would probably lose their rights. A letter signed by 66 out of just over 100 residents asking for re-categorisation as an RDS was sent to the R.J. State Legislative Council, which spent four years analysing the proposal. This instigated a new cycle of clashes of interests but the categorisation was finally approved in May 2014. Since then, there have been attempts to create an RDS Advisory Council, with representatives of several agencies and Aventureiro's community. However, due to the state's difficulties in conducting the process and weak community organisation, the process has ground to a halt.

The category of Sustainable Development Reserve, a unit referred to in article 18 of SNUC, is a kind of protected area created to reconcile nature conservation with the culture of a traditional community ancestrally linked to territory, as well as to ensure sustainable use of natural resources (SNUC, 2002). Its activities must be regulated by a management plan, put together by the Advisory Council, but open to public participation. In it, several areas and appropriate uses for each one must be defined and categorised, and the traditional community activities must always be contemplated by the plan. In the case of Aventureiro RDS, due to the importance tourism has acquired for the local population over recent years, the development of a community-based tourism project is also expected.

It is possible to identify through community-based tourism thinking the strengthening of the idea of cultural heritage, 'traditionality', ancestrality and constituted community. The tourist product is something of an invented and fanciful world, built on an imagined native 'community'. Thus, normative precepts are established on how social links must look among all involved in community tourism activities and how they must be organised.

In this case, tourism must be inspired and guided by relations of cooperation, co-operativism, solidarity and hospitality. Although they encompass commercial relations, these must express themselves as exchange, interaction, discovery and feedback. Some local communities that feel tourism has invaded their territory end up resisting it. One of the important elements in planning areas for tourism is the calculation of a touristic load – establishing not only the volume of visitors an environment is capable of receiving, but also considering the population living space and quality of life in which hospitality is offered (Camargo, 2006).

For Grinover (2006, 2007), hospitality is implicit in the fields related to the state, the commercial area, urban structures and also interaction with family. It presupposes the entry, the inclusion of a visitor into an organised system in which rules of use must be respected through articulation between public and private, in relations between social groups, families and values on which communities rely.

The quality perceived in relation to goods and services in the tourism of a location has an impact on the tourist's perception of hospitality, generating a sense of welcoming or, instead, of hostility. Dencker and Bueno (2006) states that when tourist developments exclude local populations, they are interpreted as hostile, causing conflicts with the locals and in their relations with tourists. Thus, hospitality can only be offered to visitors if practised within the community itself.

In this context, local identity becomes a major issue. Grinover (2006) states that it is not possible to give the visitor the opportunity to appropriate, read and interpret the space if the inhabitant does not develop a commitment to it. In order to acquire its own identity, a place needs to value its experiences, stories, narratives, myths, culinary traditions, memories and so on, not as nostalgic identities, but to open it to interculturality.

Conclusions

Hospitality appears as an important factor in community-based tourism in areas of traditional populations. In one sense, it is part of the tourist product itself offered in this type of tourism, as there is an expectation from visitors that they will find closer personal relations, humanised care and contact with local culture. It is a social relationship and therefore a two-way road, welcoming and acceptance, with a need for the host to understand the perspectives of guests but also for guests to understand and respect the needs of their hosts. It is a process of permanent negotiation on worldviews and know-how, in which there is always some possibility that both parties can learn from the other and adapt.

The affirmation of local identities, built very closely in the with the notion of territory, although much more as a symbolic than a physical space, and also constantly rebuilt in this contact with the 'other', becomes important, so that the tourism project of a certain area reflects both the desire and the possibilities of its own population regarding the visitor's welcoming. The exercise of mutual hospitality can also contribute to valuing local culture and protecting traditional customs. Hospitality involves both opening and closing, whereby groups expand and shrink as individuals move across boundaries.

At Aventureiro, hospitality expresses itself in the offering of family space for tourist accommodation, in simple food, similar to that which is consumed at home, in the offer of helpful information about footpaths, the sea, the climate and customs of the place, as well as immediate aid to those injured or ill. Also, in the many stories told and retold to visitors who, at the same time help, with their questions, to construct a local memory. And in the permission to help at feasts and, from time to time, to join in some collective tasks, such as pulling a fishing net or unloading a boat.

Cultural heritage, which is also inspired in the look of the 'other', has brought back to Aventureiro flour mills, the valuing of festivities, medicines and traditional food, the importance of canoes, farm nostalgia, fishing memory and, finally, the opportunity to build a particular tourism project, more validated in its own culture and, for this reason, in the desire of welcoming the other, the stranger, the tourist.

References

Adams, C. (2000) *Caiçaras na Mata Atlântica*, Annablume: FAPESP, São Paulo.

Arruda, R. (2000) Populações tradicionais e a proteção dos recursos naturais em unidades de conservação. In Diegues, A. C. (ed.) *Etnoconservação: novos rumos para a proteção da natureza nos trópico*, São Paulo: Ed. Huicitec.

Barel, Y. (1986) Le social et ses territoires. In Auriac, F. and Brunet, R., *Espaces, jeux et enjeux*, Paris: S.L. Fondation Diderot Fayard.

Barth, F. (2000) *O guru, o iniciador e outras variações antropológicas*, Rio de Janeiro: Ed. Contra Capa.

Bartholo, R., Sansolo, D. and Bursztyn, I. (2009) Turismo para quem? Sobre caminhos de desenvolvimento e alternativas para o turismo no Brasil. In Bartholo, R., Sansolo, D. and Bursztyn, I., *Turismo de base comunitária: diversidade de olhares e experiências brasileiras*, Rio de Janeiro: Letra e Imagem.

Bauman, Z. (2003) *Comunidade: a busca por segurança no mundo atual*, Rio de Janeiro: Jorge Zahar.

Bourdieu, P. (2002) *O Poder Simbólico*, Rio de Janeiro: Bertrand Brasil.

Camargo, L. O. (2006) Hospitalidade sem sacrifício? O caso do receptivo turístico. *Revista Hospitalidade* 3, 2, Editora Anhembi Morumbi, pp. 11–28.

Canclini, N. G. (2015) *Diferentes, desiguais e desconectados: mapas da interculturalidade*, Rio de Janeiro: Editora UFRJ.

Cara, R. B. (1996) El turismo y los procesos de transformación territorial. In Rodrigues, A. B. (ed.) *Turismo e geografia: reflexões teóricas e enfoques regionais*, São Paulo: Ed. Huicitec.

Carneiro, M. J. (1998) Ruralidade: novas identidades em construção, *Revista Estudos, Sociedade e Agricultura* 11, Rio de Janeiro: CPDA.

Costa, G., Catão, H. and Prado, R. (2009) Praia do Aventureiro: um caso *sui generis* de gestão local do turismo. In Bartholo, R., Sansolo, D. and Bursztyn, I., *Turismo de base comunitária: diversidade de olhares e experiências brasileiras*, Rio de Janeiro: Letra e Imagem.

Cuche, D. (2002) Cultura e identidade, *A noção de cultura nas Ciências Sociais*, Bauru: EDUSC.

Darbon, S. (1997) La 'grand famille' du rugby: entre l'hospitalité et solidarité. In Gotman, A., *Comunications: L'hospitalité*, Paris: Seuil.

Denker, A. F. and Bueno, M. S. (eds) *Hospitalidade: cenários e oportunidades*, São Paulo: Pioneira Thomson Learning.

Diegues, A. C. (1996) *O mito moderno da natureza intocada*, São Paulo: Editora Huicitec.

Ferreira, H. C. H. (2004) *Redefinindo territórios: preservação e transformação no Aventureiro – Ilha Grande/RJ*, CPDA/UFRRJ, Dissertação de Mestrado, Rio de Janeiro.

Ferreira, H. C. H. (2010) *A dinâmica da participação na construção de territórios sociais e do patrimônio ambiental da Ilha Grande/RJ*, Tese de Doutorado, Rio de Janeiro: CPDA/ UFRural RJ.

Ferreira, H. C. H. and Tomé, M. (2014) Turismo comunitário: Possibilidades de inclusão social pelo turismo. In Costa, C., Brandão, F., Costa, R. and Breda, Z., *Turismo nos países lusófonos. Conhecimento, estratégia e território*, vol. I, Lisboa: Escolar Editora.

Fratucci, A. C. (2014) Turismo e territories: relações e complexidades, *Caderno Virtual do Turismo* 14, 1: 87–96.

Godbout, J. (1997) Recevoir c'est donner. In Gotman, A., *Comunications: L'hospitalité*, Paris: Seuil.

Grinover, L. G. (2006) A hospitalidade urbana: acessibilidade, legibilidade e identidade, *Revista Hospitalidade* 3, 2, São Paulo: Editora Anhembi Morumbi.

Grinover, L. G. (2007) *A hospitalidade, a cidade e o turismo*, Série Turismo, São Paulo: Aleph.

Haesbaert, Rogério (2011) Concepções de território para entender a desterritorialização. In Santos, M. *et al.* (eds) *Território, territórios: ensaios sobre o ordenamento territorial*, Rio de Janeiro: Lamparina, pp. 43–71.

Irving, M. A. (2009) Reinventando a reflexão sobre Turismo de Base Comunitária. In Bartholo, R., Sansolo, D. and Bursztyn, I., *Turismo de base comunitária: diversidade de olhares e experiências brasileiras*, Rio de Janeiro: Letra e Imagem.

Mauss, Marcel (2003) Ensaio sobre a dádiva. *Sociologia e Antropologia*, São Paulo: Cosac Naify.

Raffestin, C. (1986) Écogénèse territoriale et territorialité. In Auriac, F. and Brunet, R., *Espaces, jeux et enjeux*, Paris: S.L. Fondation Diderot/Fayard.

Raffestin, C. (1997) Reinventer l'hospitalité. In Gotman, A., *Comunications: L'hospitalité*, Paris: Seuil.

SNUC (2002) *Sistema Nacional de Unidades de Conservação*, Lei N° 9 985, 2000 e Decreto N° 4 340, 2002, MMA, Brasília.

22

Fluid hospitality in
Adventures of Huckleberry Finn

Bastienne Bernasco

> **Key themes**
>
> Narrative hospitality
>
> Host–guest interaction
>
> Hospitality in classic novels
>
> The morality of hospitality

> It's not the quantity of the meat, but the cheerfulness of the guest, which makes the meal.
>
> *(Edward Hyde, 1st Earl of Clarendon)*

This chapter aims to contribute to the project of hospitality studies by examining a classic novel that was originally written for children and published in America in 1884. It offers a unique and much-debated reflection on a culture in which slavery was an established legal practice, supporting the agricultural, pre-industrial economy of America before the Civil War. The central theme is the companionship between a boy and a slave at odds with a society that is marked by slavery and the systematic exclusion of fellow human beings. Hospitality, which has been called a defining feature of human morality (Lashley, Introduction to this volume), seems ineffectual in a society where slavery is institutionalized by law—where, ironically, Southern hospitality used to be an element of the regional branding. Still (2010) discusses the tension between the law of hospitality as a moral principle and the societal codes of hospitality. She notices that tension and even terror will be the result if the law of hospitality, "cementing human interdependency," does not relate to the personal and socio-political context (Still, 2010: 20). The projected analysis of hospitality in this classic novel will therefore be used to understand morality and humanity in the society in which Huck and Jim live.

DOI: 10.4324/9781315679938-24

Adventures of Huckleberry Finn

> Once there was a thick fog, and the rafts and things that went by was beating in tin pans so the steamboats wouldn't run over them. A scow or a raft went by so close we could hear them talking and cussing and laughing—heard them plain; but we couldn't see no sign of them; it made you feel crawly, it was like spirits carrying on that way in the air. Jim said he believed it was spirits; but I says: "no, spirits wouldn't say, 'dern the dern fog'."
>
> *(Twain, 1996 [1884]: 163)*

This passage in Mark Twain's novel *Adventures of Huckleberry Finn*, set at the time of Twain's youth around 1830, shows refugees Huck and Jim. Huck, the boy, and Jim, the slave, observe other people passing on the river, who appear to them like disembodied sounds or spirits. It is an uncanny scene, which evokes doubts of whether this society can appear to be human or somehow hospitable to people who are separated from it.

Huck and Jim travel across the Mississippi on a raft, each escaping from their lives in the small town of St. Petersburg, each heading for liberty. This river version of the all-American road movie promises a familiar narrative scheme: we expect an epic journey, away from somewhere, which will transform the central heroes, or at least deliver them at some happier place, some ultimate destination. Hospitality should sustain the travelers with the offer of shelter and food and a temporary home away from home. Indeed, the book brings forth a wide variety of host–guest encounters. What is the nature of these encounters? How does hospitality appear to Huck and Jim? And how does it affect each of them as they move along?

Before discussing the hospitality within the novel, a brief outline of the plot will be given. Then, as we enter the world of the novel, we identify the particular act of hospitality that is observed by engaging with the literary text—the exchange between the author and narrator as host and the reader as guest, as they create, enter, and navigate the fictional world.

The plot

Huckleberry Finn is the 14-year-old son of a drunkard and the friend of 13-year-old Tom Sawyer, the main character in an earlier book by Twain. He lives in the town of St. Petersburg on the Missouri shore of the Mississippi river. Huck is raised at the home of the Widow Douglas. His father, a tramp, takes him away to a shanty in the woods. Huck manages to escape and wanders off. He meets the runaway slave Jim and decides to join him in his attempt to reach freedom by traveling southbound along the river to the Illinois shore. They travel by night, using a raft and a canoe. Along the way, Huck and Jim get caught up in a variety of events, which bring them into contact with people on the river and in the towns along the shore. They fail to reach the free states, and Jim is caught and locked up on a farm owned by Tom Sawyer's aunt and uncle. Tom Sawyer arrives on the farm and Huck and Tom release Jim. It is then revealed that Jim is already a free man, as he has been given his freedom by his owner, Miss Watson. In the final scene, Huck announces that he will strike out on his own.

Huck's world

Despite the distance in space and time and the strangeness of the Native American dialects, *Adventures of Huckleberry Finn* is still an inviting book. Let's cross the threshold of the book at its opening pages, as its curious guest. Mindful of Ricoeur, we experience reading as inhabiting a shared space, as "a way of living in the fictive universe of the work" (Ricoeur, 1991: 27). We will attempt "the *act of reading* that completes the work, transforming it into a *guide* for reading, with its zones of indeterminacy, its latent wealth of interpretation, its power of being reinterpreted in new ways in new historical contexts" (Ricoeur, 1991: 27). Such an open attitude defines our method of enquiry. As we read, we enter into the hospitable exchange between the text as host and ourselves, its readers, as its guests.

Who is our host? Mark Twain is the author of the book, and we are aware that he is master of the narrative. With a sophisticated gesture, Twain hands over the book in his Notice before the first chapter, issuing a warning to any reader who expects a traditional children's book: "Persons attempting to find a motive in this narrative will be prosecuted; persons attempting to find a moral in it will be banished; persons attempting to find a plot in it will be shot" (1996 [1884]). Obviously, the writer is the inventor, creator, and director of the book, but, at the same time, allows no interference by the reader—we should accept the book just as it is. Twain simply breathes life into his characters and he gives us the boy Huckleberry Finn as the narrator *within* the book. It's Huck who addresses us in the opening sentence. "You don't know about me, without you have read a book by the name of 'The Adventures of Tom Sawyer', but that ain't no matter" (Twain, 1996 [1884]: 3). Immediately, we feel that we are *here with Huck*, sharing the same space. With the author at one remove, Huck is our guide to the world we are about to enter, as if he steps up from the side of the road and strikes up a conversation with a passing stranger. This way, Huck invites us to cross the threshold to Huck's life *in the world*, which is different from Huck's former life—which was *in a book*. Before the end of the second paragraph, Huck has picked up Twain's story and starts to disclose events from his own perspective.

But where exactly are we *here with Huck?* Huck refers to events in the past, but does not at this point reveal where, when, or why exactly he delivers his story to us. We have to wait until the end of the book, when Huck claims that he has actually written the book that is now completed: "there ain't nothing more to write about and I am rotten glad of it" (Twain, 1996 [1884]: 363). In effect, by claiming to be the sole author of his biography, the narrator-host demands his reader-guest suspends disbelief. If we decide to stay with Huck and trust his version of events, we join him in the world as he has experienced it, which is a world we are strangers to.

Huck in St. Petersburg

If Huck is our host, where is Huck's home? We know he was born in St. Petersburg. Notions of home may help in assessing Huck's *relation* to this town. Ideally, home is a place where we are born, fed, sheltered, protected; a dwelling where we are entitled to stay, a place where we can be our authentic selves. It is a place we identify with and a place where our roots lie. The concept of home is closely linked to hospitality, as only the individual who claims a place as his home can be host to his guests. The host is able to control the guest entering his territory. The etymology of the word hospitality contains a complex duality. As shown in a study by Hattink and Lub (2015), it embraces the root words for guest and host: *hostis* (from Latin), *xenos* (from Greek) or *ghosti* (from Proto-Indo-European), meaning either guest or stranger; and on the other hand *potis* (from Latin), *despótes* (from Greek) or *poti* (from Proto-Indo-European), meaning master (of the home). Conversely, what is home to the master of the place is a strange space for the guest who enters; he has left the place he is familiar with and needs to familiarize himself with the world that is not his home. The relative positions occupied by host and guest as they engage in their relationship, are modified by their orientation towards what is native and foreign territory to them.

Huck has no real home in St. Petersburg. He tells us that the Widow Douglas has adopted him as if he is her son "and allowed she would sivilize me" (Twain, 1996 [1884]: 4). Huck knows that the purpose of the Widow's hospitality is to reform him—to change him into someone who accords with the culture of this place. The Widow and her sister, Miss Watson, attempt to reform Huck by teaching him about religion and Providence—the celestial support available to any Christian. His Christian hosts may rely on Providence, but Huck, as critical guest, understands the hidden message—that Providence will exclude people like himself. He receives hospitality on the condition that he can't be himself. So who is there for Huck to rely on?

In the house of these pious ladies, mealtime conventions are forced on Huck.

> Supper: the widow rung a bell for supper, and you had to come to time. When you got to the table you couldn't go right on eating, but you had to wait for the widow to tuck down her head and grumble a little over the victuals, although there weren't really anything the matter with them.
>
> *(Twain, 1996 [1884]: 4)*

The comic word *grumbling* delivers Huck's interpretation of this religious ritual of prayer before food, which to Huck, as a guest, is incomprehensible.

The widow reads to Huck the biblical story of Moses in the Bulrushes—like Huck, a foundling. He understands immediately that the distant event of this boy discovered in the river Nile loses all meaning if the storyteller denies the gifts of hospitality to the real guest here before her.

> Here she was a bothering about Moses, which was no kin to her and no use to anybody ... Yet finding a power of fault with me for doing a thing that had some good in it. And she took snuff, too; of course that was all right, because she done it herself.
>
> *(Twain, 1996 [1884]: 5)*

While Huck rejects Moses' story as irrelevant, the reader is tempted to see meaning in this denial and to consider the similarities between Huck and Moses. Moses, the son of a Hebrew slave, is adopted by the daughter of the Pharaoh after he orders all newborn Hebrew boys to be killed, to reduce the population of the Israelites—an enslaved minority. When he is a grown man, Moses is sent back to Egypt by the God of the Hebrews, to demand the release of the Israelites from slavery. During his journey, Moses is called to receive the Ten Commandments and to teach the laws of God to his people, forging a new nation (Machinist, 2000). The kinship between Moses and Huck is strong. Like Moses, Huck is a motherless, and therefore rootless, boy, selected by an all-controlling maker, the author of the book, to be his central persona. Like Moses, Huck will be engaged in liberating the enslaved. Could this likeness tell us that Huck is *delivered* to this community like a cuckoo into a foreign nest—and that Huck, like Moses, has a mission and a message? Will Huck's impact on people—including his reader/guest—be more effective *because* he is a stranger to the place he inhabits?

Staying at the house of the Widow Douglas, Huck is made restless by his controlling host. "All I wanted was to go somewheres; all I wanted was a change" (Twain, 1996 [1884]: 5). Every night, as soon as it gets dark, he escapes from his room and joins his friend Tom Sawyer who is waiting for him.

Huck does not really enter home territory with Tom and the town boys as they gather at the local cave. Tom Sawyer is in charge of the adventure, borrowing the rules of his favorite "pirate books and robber books" (Twain, 1996 [1884]: 12). Tom's gang is bound by rituals and threats; the boys' family members will be killed if secrets are told. Soon enough, the gang discover Huck has no family, other than a drunken father who has disappeared. Huck tells us "they talked it over and they was going to rule me out" (Twain, 1996 [1884]: 12). When Huck creatively offers Miss Watson as a substitute, he is then allowed to come in and sign the bond with his blood. This ritual exchange of finger blood marks the boys' commitment to the adventure. Huck, however, is about to distance himself from this world of make-believe. "We played robber now and then about a month, and then I resigned … We hadn't robbed nobody, we hadn't killed any people, but just pretended" (Twain, 1996 [1884]: 17). He begins to question Tom's stories and fantasy apparitions. Huck concludes that "all that stuff was just one of Tom Sawyer's lies" (Twain, 1996 [1884]: 20). The moment defines Huck's distancing from boyhood, the realm of play and imagination. By rejecting Tom's Quixotic perspective on the world, which holds that truth appears *from the imagination*, Huck crosses over to the adult, realist perspective of the world where truth appears *from experience*.

Huck's father

Huck has never known his mother. In the St. Petersburg universe, mothers have been replaced by aunts and teachers. The well-meaning Widow Douglas, the zealous Miss Watson, and several other women raise children without providing the love of a mother. And Huck's father is the worst kind of parent, a drunk and a vagrant. One day, Huck finds out that he is back in town by noticing his tracks in the snow. The trail reveals "there was a cross on the left boot-heel made with big nails, to keep off the devil" (Twain, 1996 [1884]: 23). Anxious, Huck seeks out Jim, the slave who has been brought to live at the house by Miss Watson, expecting to get his advice. Taking his cue from the spirits inside a hairball, Jim advises him:

> de bes' way is to let de ole man take his own way. Dey's two angels hoverin' roun 'bout him. One uv' em is white en shiny, en 'tother is black. De white one gits him to go right, a little while, den de black one sail in en bust it all up. A body can't tell yit, which one gwyne to fetch him at de las'. But you is all right. You gwyne to have cosidable trouble in yo' life, en cosidable joy. Sometimes you gwyne to git hurt, en sometimes you gwyne to git sick; but every time you's gwyne to git well agin.
>
> *(Twain, 1996 [1884]: 25)*

Jim's advice reveals the experience of a man who has learnt to deal with the unpredictable behavior of his master, and remains optimistic. It also reveals Jim's attitude towards fate, the unpredictable force that may be seen as the non-Christian version of Providence. From his perspective as a life guide, Jim reassures Huck that he will be all right. It is a useful lesson: If the parent lacks a moral compass, the son must rely on himself.

Sure enough, the father materializes when Huck returns to his room after dark: "my breath sort of hitched—he being so unexpected" (Twain, 1996 [1884]: 26). However, a few days later, having exhausted the town's hospitableness, Huck's father ("Pap") takes his son away to an old log hut on the Illinois shore. Huck briefly enjoys the freedom, "laying off comfortable all day, smoking and fishing, and no books nor study" (Twain, 1996 [1884]: 33), but he soon realizes this is no life for him. Pap's erratic violence, hitting Huck and locking him up for three days, gets the better of Huck. The situation climaxes in a horrifying scene, in which Pap returns home, gets delirious, chases Huck, calls him "The Angel of Death" and nearly kills him before falling into a drunken sleep. Huck decides to escape from this dangerous home and take to the woods: "just tramp right across the country, mostly night times, and hunt and fish to keep alive, and to get so far away that the old man nor the widow couldn't find me any more" (Twain, 1996 [1884]: 35). Huck suffers, and we feel his anguish: "I slipped the ramrod down to make sure it was loaded, and then I laid it across the turnip barrel, pointing towards pap, and set down behind it to wait for him to stir. And how slow and still the time did drag along" (Twain, 1996 [1884]: 39).

Pap is contrasted with Jim, who is a father himself. At a later stage of their journey on the raft, Huck wakes up and observes Jim sitting there, "moaning and mourning to himself" (Twain, 1996 [1884]: 206). Huck knows what is ailing Jim. They have failed to reach Cairo where Jim was supposed to buy his freedom so that he would be able to pick up his wife and children.

> He was thinking about his wife and children, away up yonder, and he was low and home-sick; because he hadn't ever been away from home before in his life; and I do believe he cared just as much for his people as white folks does for their'n. It don't seem natural, but it is so.
>
> *(Twain, 1996 [1884]: 206)*

His empathy with Jim's feelings and his insight that black people love their children just as much as white people do, show Huck's deepening acknowledgement of Jim, as a human being as well as a friend.

Finally, Huck decides to escape his father's prison home by a highly dramatic ploy resonant of Shakespearean tragedy. After killing a pig and trailing a sack of flour through the pig's blood across the ground to the river bank, he drowns the sack—substitute for his body—and effectively stages his own murder before taking off in his father's canoe. This brutal act—hacking the animal to death with an axe, using its blood to appear as his own blood—signals the desperation of a boy left to his own devices. This theatrical murder of his self has profound implications for the boy aged 14. Here, at the onset of his journey into adulthood, Huck crafts a new existential loneliness. He is the only one who knows he is still alive. Others will think he is dead. A motherless child, an outsider without a home, a prisoner and then a refugee, he is now severed from life as a human being.

Huck and Jim on Jackson's Island

Huck then takes his canoe up to Jackson's Island. His existence here resembles that of an American Robinson Crusoe. The island is a hospitable place where he knows no one ever comes, where he can rest and reflect. "I laid there in the grass and the cool shade, thinking about things and feeling rested and rather comfortable and satisfied" (Twain, 1996 [1884]: 48). Huck explores the island and, like Robinson, "I was boss of it; all belonged to me, so to say" (Twain, 1996 [1884]: 51). But the loneliness creeps up on him, and when he hears a man's voice he decides "I can't live this way; I'm agoing to find out who it is that's here on the island with me; I'll find it out or bust" (Twain, 1996 [1884]: 53). By the light of the moon, Huck, now master of the island, notices a human being lying there. The man appears in the night, lit by a fire, asleep. At first dawn, he bounces up at Huck's exclamation: "Hello, Jim!" (Twain, 1996 [1884]: 53). Jim's initial reaction is to kneel down before Huck, and beg him not to do him any harm.

This island encounter between the white boy and the black man is remarkably similar to the iconic meeting between Robinson Crusoe and the man who arrives on the island after him. We recall the scene:

> When he espied me he came running to me, laying himself down again upon the ground, with all the possible signs of a humble, thankful disposition, making a great many antic gestures to show it … In a little time I began to speak to him; … first, I let him know his name should be Friday, which was the day I saved his life: I called him so for the memory of the time. I likewise taught him to say Master; and then let him know that was to be my name.
> *(Defoe, 1919 [1719]: 142)*

The newcomer approaches Robinson and immediately offers himself as a servant and a slave. Accepting the other person as his gift, the host confirms his ownership and mastery. But is this hospitality? According to Derrida (Derrida and Dufourmantelle, 2000), the essence of the relationship between host and guest is that they recognize each other's status and role of host and guest. By demanding his name and identity, the host will establish the lawful claim of the guest to his hospitality (Derrida and Dufourmantelle, 2000: 27). Robinson Crusoe, the man who has appropriated the island since his arrival, does not even ask for the new man's name—and so ignores his right to hospitality. To refer to Derrida's explanation of the host–guest encounter, Crusoe's act involves a negation of the other being as a "subject in law" who can "respond on his own behalf" (Derrida and Dufourmantelle, 2000: 27). The language of the subjected person is ignored. And the name that replaces his own, Friday, is the name of a Christian time frame. Thus, we find that Robinson's hospitality consists of the most radical subjection of his guest—a manifestation of the domination and power enclosed in the word.

Huck walks in the trail of Robinson. His meeting with Jim, too, is a meeting of unequal individuals: a boy bearing two names encounters a man with only one name. Jim is not a citizen; he is known as someone's property—Miss Watson's Jim. Huck might have grown into a respectable citizen, if the town's educators had had their way. But despite their obvious differences, Huck does not show any signs of mastery over Jim. Instead, Huck sweeps away all differences when he acknowledges they are companions from now on: "I was ever so glad to see Jim. I warn't lonesome, now" (Twain, 1996 [1884]: 54). Huck and Jim have each settled and appropriated Jackson Island: they have each found and explored the island as their hiding place. And where Jim kneels before Huck, this is for a different reason: he mistakes Huck for a ghost—the boy who has died and appears in a spectral form.

Huck and Jim share information on how they got here and they compare how they managed to avoid being discovered. Jim confides in Huck that he ran off, and that he had to hide since he decided to escape from his owner and Huck shows his understanding: "Well, that's so. You've had to keep in the woods all the time, of course. Did you hear 'em shooting the cannon?" (Twain, 1996 [1884]: 57). Jim's answer, in turn, reveals his awareness of Huck's plight: "Oh, yes. I knowed dey was arter you. I see um go by heah; watched um thoo de bushes" (Twain, 1996 [1884]: 57).

Huck's reunion with Jim restores him as a human being. Jim is now the only one who knows him as a living person. To the rest of the world, Huck remains *un-alive*. From here on, he will conceal his identity to anyone he meets. For this purpose, he invents an endless range of false names and disguises. Usually, Huck is the one to venture out of their hiding place, with Jim staying behind, guarding the raft, sleeping, waiting for Huck to return, and even disappearing from the action altogether—often for quite long periods. But Jim is not just a shadowy presence. As Huck and Jim rest at their home camp at the Jackson Island cave, Jim asserts himself as Huck's active protector, the adult caring for the child. Their dialogue contains a friendly reminder of Huck's dependence on Jim—and a subtle reference to the power wielded over white children by the slaves who care for them.

> "Jim, this is nice," I says. "I wouldn't want to be nowhere else but here. Pass me along another hunk of fish and some hot corn-bread." "Well, you wouldn't a ben here, 'f it hadn't a ben for Jim. You'd a ben down dah in de woods widout any dinner, en gittn' mos' drownded, too, dat you would, honey."
>
> *(Twain, 1996 [1884]: 61)*

With Mrs Loftus

When Huck prepares to take the canoe into town to get some news, Jim suggests he dresses up as a girl. Huck knocks at the door of "a little shanty that hadn't been lived in for a long time" (Twain, 1996 [1884]: 72). Peeping through the window, Huck knows the woman he sees there is a newcomer, and he reckons that "if she has been in such a little town two days she could tell me all I wanted to know" (Twain, 1996 [1884]: 72). We see Huck in his girl's frock in the door frame. "'Come in,' says the woman, and I did. She says: 'Take a cheer.' I done it. She looked me all over with her little shiny eyes, and says: 'What might your name be?' 'Sarah Williams'" (Twain, 1996 [1884]: 73). The exchange between host, Mrs. Loftus, and guest continues in this comic frame. But the host suspects Huck's identity is false and tests her guest by asking her twice to repeat her name. After finding out Huck is a boy, she concludes he is "a runaway 'prentice— that's all" (Twain, 1996 [1884]: 78). She offers him protection on the condition that he tells her everything. Huck smartly relates the story of how he ended up here—by escaping from a mean farmer. In return, the host discloses useful information: her husband is off to Jackson Island with a gun, hoping to get the three hundred dollar reward for the runaway slave. By keeping his cover, Huck gets at the truth: this host is out to get him, not to protect him. Sending him on his way, the host apparently thinks she has cleverly unmasked her guest and made him harmless. This exchange between host and guest, who both expect to get useful information, makes it clear that Huck needs to mask his real identity—otherwise the host would surely have handed Huck and Jim over for the reward.

Home on the raft

On the raft, Jim and Huck resume their journey and glide along the river. Jim builds a snug wigwam on top and they hang up a lantern. This is their floating home on the Mississippi, a secure place from which they contemplate their nightly existence: "It was kind of solemn, drifting down the big still river, laying on our backs looking up at the stars, and we didn't ever feel like talking loud, and it warn't often that we laughed, only a little kind of a low chuckle" (Twain, 1996 [1884]: 84).

Huck's curiosity brings him into contact with the men who inhabit the river at night—gangsters on a wrecked boat, a sleeping watchman, thirty men drinking and fighting on a raft. When they discover him, they are deluded by his false identity and disarming tales and comically turn into protective hosts: "Overboard with you, and don't you make a fool of yourself another time this way.—Blast it, some raftsmen would rawhide you till you was black and blue!" (Twain, 1996 [1884]: 128).

Comedy is followed by an uneasy scene. As they near the fork in the river that is supposed to bring them to Cairo, Illinois, the atmosphere on the raft is tense. Jim is feeling "all trembly and feverish to be so close to freedom" (Twain, 1996 [1884]: 129). Huck catches Jim's mood and is aware of a nagging thought. The words he uses to describe this sensation reflect how Huck feels an almost physical presence visiting him: his conscience. It is a disturbing guest that refuses to leave him alone:

> It hadn't ever come home to me before what this thing was I was doing. But now it did; and it staid with me, and scorched me more and more. I tried to make out to myself that I warn't to blame, because I didn't run Jim off from his rightful owner; but it warn't no use, conscience up and says, every time, 'but you knowed he was running for his freedom, and you could a paddled ashore and told somebody'.
>
> *(Twain, 1996 [1884]: 129)*

At this stage, Huck's conscience appears to speak to him with the voice of local law; the legislation of this society regards the act of freeing a slave from his owner as a crime.

Huck's interior dialogue will repeat itself later after he has managed to divert two men with guns from getting to Jim, assuring them he would never let any runaway slave pass. Now Huck's nagging visitor returns, but Huck's empathy with Jim is gaining the upper hand against the voice of law.

> Then I thought a minute, and says to myself, hold on—s'pose you'd a done right and give Jim up; would you felt better than what you do now? No, says I, I'd feel bad—I'd feel just the same way I do now.
>
> *(Twain, 1996 [1884]: 133)*

These two scenes foreshadow Huck's third, crucial introspection later in the journey, which will be discussed as we get there.

With the Stephensons

Huck and Jim fail to find Cairo because of a dense fog. New events demand their response. The raft gets run over by a steamboat and they lose each other trying to get ashore. Huck runs across to a big log house, guarded by lots of howling dogs. The residents call out from a window and ask Huck suspiciously for his name, three times: "What did you say your name was?" (Twain, 1996 [1884]: 139). As the stranger presents himself as "George Jackson, sir. I'm only a boy" (Twain, 1996 [1884]: 139), they give him a hearty reception. Their son simply tells Huck that he should stay forever. Thirteen-year old Buck—his name so close to Huck—drags a gun along, because his family are caught up in a long-standing feud with another family. Huck is perfectly happy at this "mighty nice family home", where the cooking is good and "just bushels of it too!" (Twain, 1996 [1884]: 148). In this curiously lengthy episode, where Jim seems forgotten, Huck just absorbs the kindness of Buck and his extended family, who lavish on him the legendary Southern hospitality. But sadly, this idyll proves to be a lie—it is brutally ended by one of the most violent scenes in the book. From a cottonwood tree, Huck witnesses how Buck and his cousin get shot by their feudal enemies—a horrid scene, which will revisit Huck in his dreams forever. "I ain't ever going to get shut of them" (Twain, 1996 [1884]: 160).

The feud, the perpetual exchange of revenge, is here revealed as the poison destroying Southern hospitality. The neighboring clan, who is supposed to receive a hospitable welcome, has turned into a permanent enemy, leading to a brutal, uncompromising war. Shaken,

Huck swims back to the raft and is welcomed home by Jim. "Jim got out some corn-dodgers and buttermilk, and pork and cabbage and green" (Twain, 1996 [1884]: 161). This reunion is liberating for both of them: "We said there warn't no home like a raft, after all. Other places do seem so cramped up and smothery, but a raft don't. You feel mighty free and easy and comfortable on a raft" (Twain, 1996 [1884]: 161).

In the middle of the Mississippi

And here we are, out in the middle of the Mississippi, at the heart of the narrative. This is where the book might have ended if we had all been capable of the ultimate suspension of disbelief. We might have been able to believe in this Promised Land, this world beyond death, a starry night life, a dreamy paradise. We would have witnessed the new America, where Huck and Jim, the white boy and his black father, would be free to wonder about creation, their spirits lifted by the hospitable stream.

> Sometimes we'd have that whole river all to ourselves for the longest time. Yonder was the banks and the islands, across the water; and maybe a spark—which was a candle in a cabin window—and sometimes on the water you could see a spark or two—on a raft or a scow, you know; and maybe you could hear a fiddle or a song coming over from one of them crafts. It's lovely to live on a raft.
>
> *(Twain, 1996 [1884]: 164)*

Huck and Jim, Americans, not separated by their color, would have been free to exchange their observations of the universe, a mysterious but knowable force:

> We had the sky, up there, all speckled with stars, and we used to lay on our backs and look up at them, and discuss about whether they was made, or only just happened—Jim allowed they was made, but I allowed they happened; I judged it would have took too long to *make* so many. Jim said the moon could a laid them; well, that looked kind of reasonable, so I didn't say nothing against it, because I've seen a frog lay most as many, so of course it could be done.
>
> *(Twain, 1996 [1884]: 164)*

Unfortunately, this utopian scene is as fluid as it is ephemeral; the raft is a loose and floating place, isolated and due to be abandoned. And the completion of this "raft odyssey" is a great deal less heroic than that of one of Huck's ancient predecessors, the long-awaited Ulysses. This travelling hero, after completing his tour around the world, reclaims his wife and rightful home by killing his former guests, now hostile usurpers. Instead, one day Huck finds his beloved Jim gone: he has been captured and Huck hears he is held hostage on a nearby farm.

In the wigwam

Again Huck seeks out the wigwam on the raft—a symbolic dwelling inherited from Native Americans—to think, making room for the conflicting voices inside his head. This is an anguished scene in which Huck weighs his options, whether to betray Jim's hiding place and give him up by writing a letter to his prosecutors—or not. In this difficult dialogue between his two interior selves, one self strains to accord with society's morale, which says stealing a slave is a sin: "I was letting *on* to give up sin, but away inside I was holding on to the biggest one of all" (Twain, 1996 [1884]: 272). The other self, foreign to this society, remembers his deep companionship with Jim: "I see Jim before me, all the time, in the day, and in the night-time, sometimes moonlight, sometimes stars, and we a floating along, talking, and singing, and laughing" (Twain, 1996 [1884]: 273). Huck's conclusion, after his third introspection, confirms that he embraces the self who is a foreigner and will be cast out:

> I was a trembling, because I got to decide, forever, betwixt two things, and I knowed it. I studied a minute, sort of holding my breath, and then says to myself: "All right, then, I'll *go* to hell"—and tore it up.
>
> *(Twain, 1996 [1884]: 273)*

In remembering their shared existence, Huck accepts that his relationship with Jim now *belongs* to him. The realization seems to provoke in him that "uncanny strangeness" which the philosopher Julia Kristeva (1991) points out in relation to the concept of the foreigner. It is the unease that will be experienced by anyone who confronts the foreigner within himself, "situating myself with respect to the other" (Kristeva, 1991: 187). It seems that for Huck, this act of hospitality, which is the openness to welcome this uncanniness and to allow the resulting insights to enter his consciousness, sustains the "process of identification-projection that lies at the foundation of ... reaching autonomy" (Kristeva, 1991: 187).

At the Phelps farm

After this decision, Huck goes to find Jim. He finds out the black man is held hostage at a nearby place, the Phelps farm. When Huck goes there the farmer and his wife, Aunt Sally, mistake him for their nephew Tom Sawyer. The real Tom arrives a little later. He promises Huck to help him liberate Jim from the cabin where he was held captive. With his characteristic love of books, Tom resumes control and devises a plot in which they are the heroic liberators of the prisoner. Oddly, Huck falls again under the spell of Tom, who, unlike Huck, has not grown up. Huck is persuaded by Tom to treat Jim as a character in his play, staying inside his prison for a long time before he is let free. Jim, depressingly, does not resist the bullying. As he is captured by the townspeople, Jim does not look at Huck as he passes him. By pretending not to know Huck, he severs their relation.

Cruelty masked as playfulness is back. The plot reels into the much-debated absurd final episodes. Everything is chaos, everyone is mistaken for someone else, and all rationality has gone. As it turns out, the children's intricate attempt to free Jim was deluded, as Miss Watson had passed away some time before, and had already set Jim free in her will. Tom tells Huck he had planned it all differently:

> And [Tom] said, what he had planned in his head, from the start, if we got Jim out all safe, was for us to run him down the river, on the raft, and have adventures plumb to the mouth of the river, and then tell him about his being free, and take him back up home on a steamboat, in style, and pay him for lost time, and write word ahead and get out all slaves around, and have them waltz him into town with a torchlight procession and a brass band, and then he would be a hero, and so would we. But I reckoned it was about as well the way it was.
>
> *(Twain, 1996 [1884]: 360)*

The final scenes are inconsistent with the epic journey of Huck and Jim. Instead of allowing Huck and Jim to remain at the centre, Twain suddenly gives Tom Sawyer full rein; Tom is the director of the impulsive and egocentric scheme—a *childish* scheme—in which Jim is subjected to prolonged cruelty, and Huck is given the role of mindless assistant. Could this be Twain's way of shocking his readers into understanding what happens when society is run by children—a society governed by immature ethics? Its laws are incompatible with the law of hospitality—it cannot acknowledge others as they are and will do all it can to render them powerless.

Conclusions

In the world of the *Adventures of Huckleberry Finn*, hospitality appears as a fluid phenomenon in an infant society, lacking a mature moral system. Hospitality has been offered to Huck in various degrees of conditionality. We have seen that Huck has taken on so many identities, male and female, that he has practically turned into every one of us. We conclude that he has only been granted hospitality when he was *not himself*. And if we accept this, we realize the almost complete absence of the law of hospitality: Huck, who was everyone, has never been acknowledged *as himself*. Except by Jim, who was a temporary friend and created a fleeting home where they could be themselves. And what about Jim? We have seen how he spent much of the time waiting, sleeping in the shadows, imprisoned, consistently de-humanized into a prized object—coming alive and speaking in his magic jazzy speech only in the shared moments with Huck.

The book reveals a cynical reality, still relevant to our own society where so many seek a human welcome. Huck and Jim, crafting a barely human existence, are condemned to live like spirits in a fog—immaterial, untouched, and ignored by society. Life to them, whether it is directed by Providence or Fate, local law, or someone's wicked imagination, is a constant joke, a fraudulent reality as it is for any modern refugee. This elusiveness, the opposite of the desired welcome, has been captured by Julia Kristeva in her treatise on Derrida's concept of the foreigner:

> Riveted to an elsewhere as certain as it is inaccessible, the foreigner is ready to flee. No obstacle stops him, and all suffering, all insults, all rejections are indifferent to him as he seeks that invisible and promised territory, that country that does not exist but that he bears in his dreams, and that must indeed be called a beyond.
>
> *(1991: 5)*

Jim and Huck have been united briefly in their home on the river, but now separately seek that invisible beyond, a world where they will at last be allowed to be free. Huck regrets his creative act of writing his biography and opts for escape:

> If I'd a knowed what a trouble it was to make a book I wouldn't a tackled it and ain't ago-ing to no more. But I reckon I got to light out for the Territory ahead of the rest, because Aunt Sally she's going to adopt me and sivilize me and I can't stand it. I been there before.
>
> *(Twain, 1996 [1884]: 363)*

We close the book. Huck and Jim are part of us now. We have shared their fictive universe and return to the world as realists. Twain was right. Morals are not to be found inside this book. With Huck lighting out for the territory, it is up to us to decide if we follow him out there.

References

Benveniste, E. (1969) *Vocabulaire des institutions indo-européennes. 1. Economie, Parenté, Société*, Paris: Editions de Minuit.

Defoe, D. (1919 [1719]) *The Life and Adventures of Robinson Crusoe*, London: Seeley, Service & Co. Available as e-book at http://gutenberg.net.au/ebooks/z00018.html.

Derrida, J. and Dufourmantelle, A. (2000) *Of Hospitality: Anne Dufourmantelle Invites Jacques Derrida to Respond*, Stanford: Stanford University Press.

Hattink, H. M. and Lub, X. D (2015) Back to basics: how etymology could help us enhance a conceptual framework of hospitality, *Proceedings of EuroCHRIE Conference*, Manchester: MMU, pp. 1–7.

Kristeva, J. (1991) *Strangers to Ourselves*, New York: Columbia University Press.

Machinist, P. (2000) The man Moses, *Bible Review* 16, 2: 18–19. Available at http://www.biblicalarchaeol ogy.org/daily/biblical-topics/exodus/who-was-moses-was-he-more-than-an-exodus-hero. Accessed November 30, 2015.

Ricoeur, Paul (1991) Life in quest of narrative. In Wood, D. (ed.) *Paul Ricoeur: Narrative and Interpretation*, London: Routledge, pp. 20–33.

Still, J. (2010) *Derrida and Hospitality*, Edinburgh: Edinburgh University Press.

Twain, M. (1996 [1884]) *Adventures of Huckleberry Finn*, London: Bloomsbury.

Part III

Hospitality through time and space

23

Hunter and gatherer hospitality in Africa

Victoria N. Ruiter

Key themes

Hospitableness

Hunters and gatherers

African hospitality

Domains of hospitality

Visitor's footfalls are like medicine; they heal the sick.

(Proverb)

Hospitality is seen as an organic aspect of human life, an essential part of human existence and development, revealing much about societal and cultural values that bind a society. The hospitality norm and moral obligation of societies in Africa is incorporated in their daily way of living, where a good hunt is a communal pride, children belong to the community and the joy or fear of one person is deemed as everyone's concern. However, with globalisation and intercultural integration generating further interdependence of economic and cultural activities, these cultural values and norms seem to be disappearing. Nevertheless, for the majority of African foraging cultures, hospitality and hospitableness is still an honorably perceived act with many bound by *shereheka na mgeni wako kama vile ambavyo ungependa ushereheshwe ugenini*, meaning celebrate with your visitor as much as you would like to be celebrated as a visitor. Hence, hunter-gatherer hospitality in Africa can be summed up as an unconditional readiness to share freely without strings attached. It is, thus, the genuine inclination to give, to assist, to care, and to carry each other's burden and joy with no profit or reward motives as the driving force. Therefore, hunter-gatherer hospitality in Africa is simply African cultural and moral values, which are not theoretical, but a way of life.

All societies have had a degree of culturally defined obligations that are optimal for humans' well-being. Africa as a continent maintains a special niche of 90 percent of human

DOI: 10.4324/9781315679938-26

history origins entwined with hunter-gatherers as humans' earliest existence. Humans began the path to the present on the ancient savannahs, fighting for survival with other predators and perfected skills of hunting and gathering. Hunting and gathering was the subsistence strategy undertaken, and remained as the mode of survival for the human societies; 1.8 million years ago by Homo erectus and around 0.2 million years ago by Homo sapiens (Binford, 1986). This mode of human survival continued up till the end of the Mesolithic period and gradually transitioned with the spread of the Neolithic revolution some 10,000 years ago (Jean-Pierre, 2011). For the basis of this chapter, hunter-gatherers are people who are 'bonded' by their foraging culture of sustaining themselves by foraging, hunting and fishing (Shepard, 1998).

Over the years, as humans evolved, so did hospitality, transitioning between the social traditional forms and the commercial forms of hospitality. However, in order to review hunter-gatherer hospitality in Africa as a human activity with widespread antecedents, hospitality evolvement needs to be scrutinised through a multitude of hospitality lenses within the private, social and commercial domains. It appears that describing hospitality in Africa as a 'no roots' act does some injustice to the hunter-gatherer role in society in shaping today's hospitality behaviour from an anthropological perspective.

A number of modern anthropologists such as Richard Borshay Lee, Irven DeVore and Marshall Sahlins acquiesce that hunting and gathering, whether communal or individually, has been synonymous with humans' existence, since early human society's survival through obtaining food from wild plants and animals was humanity's first and most successful adaptation dating back 10,000 years (Marlowe, 2005). This chapter seeks to revisit this African hospitality albeit in a summarised form from a hunter-gatherer perspective, with content drawn from both existing literature and my personal experiences. I shall explore hospitality's existence and practices within the hunter-gatherer communities in the 'social', 'private' and 'commercial' domains in African hospitality by reflecting on Figure 1.1 'The domains of hospitality' (Lashley, 2000; see p. 2 this volume) which provides the context for this chapter.

Hunting and gathering played a big part in man's evolvement from Homo erectus to Homo sapiens, spreading throughout Africa and then Europe and eventually worldwide. Until about 12,000 to 11,000 years ago, when agriculture and animal domestication emerged in south-west Asia and in Mesoamerica, all humans were hunters and gatherers (Binford, 1986; Erdal and Whiten, 1996; Selwyn, 2000; Graeme, 2009; Wolff, 2014). The transition paved the way for a culture of agriculture and settlement. During human pre-historic period evolution, there was an adaptation of the mobile hunter-gatherer into non-nomadic society (Jared, 1998), as well as forest gardens. However, in understanding the hunter-gatherer (foraging) people, their hunting and gathering subsistence is a distinctive social characteristic, which worldwide sets foragers apart from farmers and herders. The band is the basic unit of social organisation of most, but not all, hunting and gathering peoples, a small-scale nomadic group of fifteen to fifty people related by kinship (Barnard and Woodburn, 1988).

Hunting and gathering practices brought the development of caring, sharing and cooperation with the need to carry things to a central sharing camp being a norm, for it is assumed that one's good harvests are worth more if shared and a good hunt is a communal pride. During hunting and gathering activities, a great deal of excitement occurs when the hunter-gatherer returns with the proceeds of hunts and gathering, accentuating relationships and a continuing shared societal benefit. These practices present hospitableness cues on the quality or disposition of receiving and treating kinsmen, guests and strangers in a warm, friendly and generous way (Lashley, 2008). In general, hunter-gatherer societies have maintained their cultures of hospitality and hospitableness in areas termed by the rest of humanity as 'inhospitable' – places of little water, thick jungles, impassable mountains and frozen Arctic regions – providing a setting in which both private and commercial activities take place, thus conforming to Derrida's description: 'Not only is there a culture of hospitality, but there is no culture that is not also a culture of hospitality' (2002: 361). Nevertheless, Derrida further elaborates that all cultures compete in this regard and present themselves as more hospitable than the others: 'Hospitality – this is culture itself' (2002: 361).

Conforming to the cultural and social lens of hospitality where each other's actions matter (Lashley, 2000), hospitableness is obviously rooted in hunter-gatherer society, with hunting-gathering undertakings such as scavenging for food, cultural sacrifices, rituals and symbols (as practices aimed at paying homage to the gods) seldom undertaken individually but as a band society where sharing is central. A typical hunter-gatherer society comprises bands of around thirty individuals. Bands are independent in their daily activities but connected to a larger tribe with clearly set values, interactions and practices. Reflecting on Lashley's hospitality domains, I position hunter-gatherer relationships in the social, private and commercial domains based on an analysis of personal experiences.

Hunter-gatherer hospitality domains in Africa

Hunting-gathering hospitality in Africa encompasses social and cultural obligations regarding the host's and the guest's behaviour towards each other. In as much as hunting and gathering activities are never undertaken individually, the hosting of kinsmen and strangers takes place in private domestic settings. Band societies live in smaller mobile groups of around twenty persons. However, each immediate family has a share of a private hut where hosting takes place as a private independent entity. Within the African band societies, there are rituals associated with hosting or being hosted. For example, it is a duty of the host to greet a visitor who does not belong to the direct kinship by shouting certain words before they enter the compound. Once the stranger enters the compound, it is the women's duty immediately to hand him a piece of the best-preserved hunt in their possession. The head of the band, normally the man, will in turn present to the stranger the traditional wine made from gathered plants. The duty of the guest is to accept all that is offered in a polite manner, such as kneeling when the lady of the house offers him the piece of meat. Once these two rituals have been completed, a special whistle is blown to alert the rest of the band members that there is a visitor within their compound. From this moment on, entertaining and protecting the guest becomes a social duty for the band community, where hospitality obligations are largely shared through the cultural and social norms of what is appropriate (Lashley et al., 2007). Entertaining guests in private settings allows for social performances and hospitality experiences with the desire to meet another's need, as shown within the domains of hospitality in Figure 23.1.

Lashley's three-domain model, presented as Figure 23.1, sets the context of hospitality and distinguishes between cultural and or social, private and or domestic, and commercial domains, as well as highlighting how the domains potentially overlap and influence each other. While exploring hunter-gatherer hospitality in Africa, throughout both Old and New Worlds, through a variety of lenses, the social and private lenses are revealed to be deeply rooted in African culture despite the destabilisation of traditional life by colonialism, foreign world-views, technology and modern living. Hunter-gatherer African hospitality has been upheld and instilled in all in the continent to the extent that it could be described as the way of the true African hospitality warrior. Hospitality practices are a vital aspect of existence in forager culture, which is still intact and strongly practised, in spite of the forces of recent external influences and internal pressure.

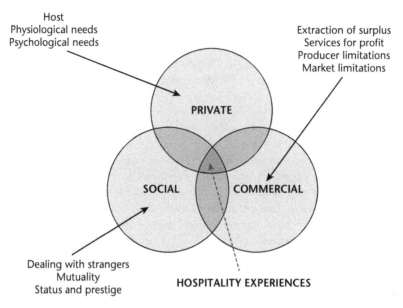

Host
Physiological needs
Psychological needs

Extraction of surplus
Services for profit
Producer limitations
Market limitations

PRIVATE

SOCIAL

COMMERCIAL

Dealing with strangers
Mutuality
Status and prestige

HOSPITALITY EXPERIENCES

Figure 23.1   Hospitality experiences model
Source: Lashley (2015: 4).

Based on the my personal experiences and observations while growing up in Africa's infinite beauty and abundance of flora and fauna, wild animals are a part of daily life and have shaped African hospitality and hospitable traditions, especially within the hunter and gatherer cultures. Culturally, African hospitality demands that it is everyone's moral duty to be hospitable to all and to protect each other.

In highlighting the hospitality domains, I have chosen to explore the 'hunting psychology' of animals with a focus on the big cats, with the lion species as a metaphor, and link it to hunter and gatherer hospitality in Africa. Hunting and gathering by humans is synonymous to hunting by wild animals within the food chain, since it is evident that there is a form of distinct 'social' value of decency forming hospitality relationships between the animals. The lion seldom moves or hunts without its pride's (clan's) presence. Interestingly to many of us, lions do have a hunting strategy, especially within their natural habitat. Hunting roles are 'divided' within the pride. The lioness has the predominant role of hunting, while the lion plays the role of the obstructer of the prey and protects the pride from any danger. During the hunt, there is a degree of hospitality and hospitableness, for once a prey has been hunted, it somehow becomes a social engagement where different animals play different roles at different times within the process. For example, after undertaking the responsibility of providing food and survival safety to its pride, the lion pride mostly only devours the blood and the softest parts of the meat, leaving the rest to the other members of the wild. Systematically, hyenas being the opportunists, but lacking speed, follow and only consume the lower part of the prey, leaving the rest to the fox who never hunts but only consumes the middle part of the leftover prey, and finally the vultures work on the clearance. Even for the wild animals, hunting and sharing of food is a communal engagement where there is a mutuality and exchange, and thus acts of beneficence.

However, it is quite evident that, with the modernisation of societies, cultural obligations do not have the same significance as they once did; even the wild animals hunting have had to take their share of the changes with foragers such as the Maasai people of Kenya inhibiting the process by seizing prey from the lion. Furthermore, the natural habitats of the animals have been turned into a commercial entity where hunting for the lions has had a price tag attached. It is known that huge financial deals are exchanged between the locals and the 'stranger' in return for consuming these supposed natural resources.

In comparison, human hunters and gatherers seldom hunt individually; it is a communal engagement where dancing and singing in privately owned locations is a norm to celebrate and devour a good hunt as a social tryst. Each hunter has their private huts where they never tire but thrive in welcoming both the kinsman and the stranger to share their exquisite hunt and gatherings. However, as within animal hunting, globalisation has paved the way for staged authenticity of the whole hunter and gatherer hospitality experience and acts commercialising hunting and gathering African hospitality. It is nowadays normal to see a typical hunter-gatherer society staging hunting and gathering hospitality experiences within their private territories with a price tag attached.

Nonetheless, it is my view that hunter-gatherer hospitality has been a primary feature and an essential part of human existence, dealing with basic human needs such as humans' well-being, food and shelter, whatever the form.

Hunter-gatherer hospitality governance

Hunter-gatherer societies are relatively egalitarian; there is no hierarchical leadership. Leadership is less formal and subject to constraints of popular opinion than in village societies governed by headmen and chiefs (Gowdy, 1998). Social norms and values of hunter-gatherer hospitality are instilled from generation to generation, for there is only a nominal leader who speaks for the band with the ability to persuade and find compromises regarding issues such as mobility. Mobility is another distinctive characteristic of the forager and the remarkable exhibition of concentration and dispersion. Hunter-gatherers tend to settle for either temporary and/or permanent settlements depending upon the community's mobility (Hall and Coles, 1994). Rather than live in uniformly sized groupings, they tend to be mobile, capitulating into smaller units and later aggregating into much larger units (Bellwood, 2004). In Germann Molz and Gibson's research (2007), the ethics of social relations in a mobile world pursued almost exclusively the use of hospitality as a means of better understanding the relations between communities and entrants from outside the community, which also reflects the full diversity of the human experience. According to Selwyn (2000), hospitality is used to establish a relationship or to promote an already established relationship.

Foraging culture is rich with numerous practical applications, including but not limited to increasing focus on personal relations. Socially, hunter-gatherer hospitality in Africa converts strangers into familiars, enemies into friends, friends into better friends, outsiders into insiders, non-kin into kin (Selwyn, 2000). Foraging culture does not condone violence, is egalitarian in social organisation, makes decisions by consensus, owns little property, readily shares what is owned and has little occupational specialisation except that based on gender (Kelly, 2007). Lashley's work in *Hospitality: A Social Lens* (Lashley *et al.*, 2007) continues the creation of a picture of hospitality that recognises the powerful origins of hospitality in human societies. Indeed, hospitality and the need to be hospitable is a central feature of human existence and experience. How and why humans evolved during the years is a fascinating and controversial topic, argued continuously by anthropologists, highlighting many facts and ideas about hunter-gatherers that are surprising and interesting, such as hunter-gatherers being a near distinct human species. In contrast, the usage of tools made of stone and bone that seem to be associated with hunting and gathering form a part of the intellectual mix of modern anthropology, presenting humans as a species based on the biological legacy inherited from our ancestors, hunter-gatherers also called foragers (Shepard, 1998). Even with the dawn of European expansion, hunter-gatherers still occupied almost one-third of the world's landmass, including all of Australia, the north-western half of North America and the southern part of South America, including parts of sub-Saharan Africa and parts of Asia.

Intriguingly, nearly all research about hunter-gatherer bands emphasises the extraordinarily high value they place on individual autonomy. Hunter-gatherers' sense of autonomy is different from the individualism of modern Western capitalist cultures. Western individualism tends to pit each person against others in competition for resources and rewards. It includes the right to accumulate property and to use wealth to control the behaviour of others. In contrast, as Tim Ingold (1999) has most explicitly emphasised, hunter-gatherers' sense of autonomy connects each person to others, in a way that does not create dependencies. The hunter-gatherer primary economic purpose is sharing, a concept different from the Western concept of sharing. For Western/modern societies, sharing is a praiseworthy act of generosity, for which a 'thank you' is due and some form of repayment may be expected in the future. For hunter-gatherers, sharing is not a generous act, nor an implicit bargain, but a duty. People are not thanked or praised for sharing, but would be ridiculed and scorned if they failed to share (Wiessner, 1996; Ingold, 1999).

Having explored the world of hunter-gatherer practices across societies and different geographical locations, calling for a bridge to link differences between societies and highlighting the uniqueness of each, I now attempt to map hunter-gatherer antecedents stretching back to the origins of human society from an African context.

The African social game of life

Africa, being the cradle of humankind, claims the majority of human hunting and gathering history. Hilary Deacon at the Klasies River Mouth site in the Eastern Cape reported fully human remains dating from 90,000 to 120,000 BP (Bankston, 2013), proving that the archaeology of Africa's hunter-gatherer people presents some of the earliest traces of human existence. The aim here is to further acquaint ourselves with hunter and gatherers' hospitality in Africa. Hunter-gatherer hospitality in Africa is a moral obligation defining the social and cultural expectations about spontaneous hospitable behaviour as a host both to the kinsman and the stranger, subsequently promoting inter-tribal hospitality and reciprocity.

The pre-colonial achievements of Africa, a continent with diverse culture, many languages and immense natural resources, have been well documented but rarely is there a focus on the hunter-gatherer's hospitality presence as flaunted on the magnificent rock art of the Sahara and the southern part of the continent. Yet it was the hunter-gatherers who had sole dominion over the continent for millennia before the advent of agriculture, the Bantu expansion and the rise of the great kingdoms of the savannah and Sudan.

Hunter-gatherer presence is traceable back to the widespread remains of ancient sites, even more subtly inscribed in the language clicks and sounds found, for example, in the Zulu and Xhosa languages (Anderson and Grove, 1987). Furthermore, in the last few millennia the encounter between resident hunter-gatherers and incoming farmers and herders has formed one of the key themes in African history and oral traditions (Kopytoff, 1987; Smith, 1992). The nature of this interface between foragers and others has become an area of lively debate in anthropology and archaeology (Clark and Brandt, 1984; Schrire, 1984; Wilmsen and Denbow, 1990). However, in as much as the hunter-gatherer of Africa represents a diverse origin, African hunters display the characteristics common to other societies in their regions, speaking local languages and adopting local customs; they have maintained distinct identities (Oliver, 1991; Lee and Daly, 2002).

Nonetheless, it is difficult to generalise across the continent. In fact, hunter-gatherer hospitality in Africa today is strikingly diverse socially, ethnically and economically, with some analysts presenting earlier dates as evidence that hunters everywhere were dominated for centuries by powerful Iron Age overlords (Wilmsen and Denbow, 1990). In contrast, others have argued of the persistence of relative independence of at least some foragers up to the present (Solway and Lee, 1990; Lee and Guenther, 1991, 1993, 1995).

It is an abomination for a hunter to gather his hunting equipment and walk out of the village to the wilderness to hunt alone. It is even worse for a hunter-gatherer to sit and enjoy his prey on his own. For hunter-gatherer hospitality in Africa, every undertaking for human cohesion is experienced as societal task or there is a danger of dire consequences; individualism would lead to sanctions and costly sacrificial cleansing. Thus, sharing and showing kindness to all, including strangers in need of any sort of hospitality, is a sense of duty, with the concern to please the other as the predominant motive (Telfer, 2000).

I recently revisited an African story highlighting the idea of reciprocity and communal closeness where a Western anthropologist, trying to understand the social behaviour of indigenous people, proposed a game to children of the San tribe. He put a basket full of fruit near a tree and told the children that whoever got there first would win the sweet fruits. When he gave them the signal to run for the basket, they all took each other's hands and ran together, then sat in a circle enjoying their treats. He asked them why they chose to run as a group when they could have had more fruit individually. One child spoke up and said: Ubuntu, 'how can one of us be happy if all the others are sad?' meaning 'I am sad because they are sad'. Strangely then, to the anthropologist, hospitality and experiences and acts of hospitableness in African culture are intertwined in the hunter and gatherers' daily life, as elaborated by Lumumba (2011).

Hunting and gathering has been and continues to be an important aspect of life in many African societies, especially rural African ones. The culture of hunting and gathering in Africa encompasses and includes the continent as a whole. The main split is between Northern Africa and sub-Saharan Africa. In Africa, modern humans and their hominid precursors have been using tools to acquire food for at least 2.4 million years (Lee and Daly, 2002). An area where African hospitality is manifested is in the communal willingness to assist each other, trusting that the host brings out his best things, not normally used. Since ancient times, Africans have displayed Good-Samaritan hospitality by showing care to each other in visiting, receiving, hosting and welcoming each other generously without expecting any returns other than the mutual well-being of the guest (Telfer, 1996).

Hunter-gatherers' role in shaping today's hospitality has received unjust recognition and societal perceptions, as in the work of Hobbes in the mid-1600s, who wrote that 'man without civilization lived lives that were "solitary, poor, nasty, brutish, and short"'. Hobbes' view has dominated and still prevails among modern societies where the majority of the general population still view hunter-gatherers as starving and sorry beings on the verge of extinction expressly as a result of growing modern agricultural and pastoral engagements, resulting in a continual decline of hunter-gatherer numbers, with only a few contemporary societies classified as purely hunter-gatherers. On the contrary, it is still common for African hunter-gatherers to show their care and hospitality by cooperating in achieving individual goals in a communal manner such as land cultivation, hunting and gathering, fishing and even building houses. In most, if not all, African societies your business is not your business, as portrayed by the Ubuntu culture where a person is a person through other people, meaning 'I am because we are' (Chuwa, 2014).

Born in a foraging culture in east Africa, I do have fond memories that translate to the true hospitality of hunter-gatherers in Africa. During my upbringing, it was common for children to engage in learning games of hunting small prey and gathering together with adults from an early age. The hunter-gatherer presence in Africa is woven into the fabric of daily life as myths, stories, proverbs and place names, and in the cultural imagination of the continent's peoples, both black and white (Lee and Hitchcock, 2001). As we progressed in age we graduated to hunting big game such as giraffes and warthogs. I explicitly remember when I got my first pair of shoes 'akala'. My shoes were hard-weather shoes made from old vehicle tyres that I treasured enormously and guarded with my whole being. This meant when we engaged in hunting and gathering activities, I had the privilege of not getting thorns in my feet. Naturally to me, these (my tyre shoes) were a commodity the clan kids were all proud of and we would take consensus turns as to who would enjoy the akala-wearing privilege. The akala was such a communal pride that whoever's turn it was to wear the shoes had the special responsibility of running after the prey once we had speared it. This was normally a task reserved for the more experienced in our team. My akala shoes became an all season and all requirement tool, for we used them to flatten weeds that were later to be gathered as our meal, as our toy in games, as our hunting weapon for small prey, as well as a relaxation pillow when we needed to catch our breath from the day's activities.

It is common in Kenya to hear the use of the term *tunakaa pamoja*, which means both 'we stay together' and 'we stay as one'. Furthermore, the private domain concerns of hospitality related to provision of food and accommodation (Lashley, 2008) are deeply reflected in hunter-gatherer hospitality in Africa, where it is common for a host to have their doors open for guests. Being kind and welcoming to a guest is a moral obligation expected of all and instilled in all as a cultural and moral value through daily activities and learning moments. During hunting-gathering sessions, the host (hunter-gatherer) expects that whatever is hunted and gathered must be more than sufficient for the needs of the immediate members of the band and will provide a reserve for both the expected and the unexpected guest.

While hunting and gathering tasks were, and still are, a means of survival aimed at bonding societies through socially described values of courtesy and obligations clearly extending back through human history, hunter-gatherer hospitality requires one to provide food and drink to all, irrespective of status or origin (Lashley, 2014), with moral sanctions for those who behave otherwise. However, in recent years, gathering and hunting areas in Africa have been encroached upon by the settlements of agriculturalists, forcing the majority of hunter-gatherer societies to supplement and/or adapt their original foraging livelihood to horticulture and/or herding. All in all, Africa today is a continent of city folk, traders, wage workers, farmers and herders, even though as recently as the 1990s, over 400,000 of Africa's population still identified themselves as foragers or former foragers (Lee and Hitchcock, 2001). Notably, two African hunter-gatherer groups, the Bushmen and the Pygmies, represent classic cases in the ethnographic canon (Murdock, 1959). Nevertheless, there are a number of other groups like the Hadza, Okiek, Maasai, Boni, Mikea, Dorobo, Capsian, Kwisi, Kung, Khoe-San, Nayaka, Innu and Ju'/Hoansi that are less well known but of equal interest.

I acknowledge that some tribes or groups will contradict these generalisations about hunter-gatherers. Nevertheless, the aim here is to emphasise that it is indeed possible to peruse the progression and onuses pertaining to host and guest behaviour across societies over different periods and hospitality domains, reinforcing Derrida's observation and Lashley's argument that hospitality and the need to welcome the stranger are at the heart of all human societies. This encouraged me to vow to maintain and contribute in preserving the true hunter-gatherer African hospitality, where we can all exhibit this same kind of reciprocity. In conclusion, hunter-gatherer hospitality in Africa was and is commonly practised in private domestic, social and cultural settings. The overlap between these domains within hunter-gatherer hospitality in Africa provides valuable insights as a learning source for modern hospitality societies. Hunter-gatherer African hospitality and hospitable acts are indeed real hospitality treasures, different from other versions of hospitality practised in other parts of the world, especially in Europe. Hunter-gatherer hospitality purely intends to enhance the mutual well-being of the parties concerned, making hospitality more than just food, drink and shelter (Telfer, 2000). It is a norm that each foraging band member is bound to offer a welcoming feeling, food and shelter to a band member or a stranger. Hunter-gatherer hospitality in Africa is perceived and practised as open-handed, instinctive and the most natural thing, and should be the adopted image of African hospitality globally. In summary, African hunter-gatherers eat, drink and socialise hospitality, provoking me to see hospitality as inherently African.

Conclusions

This chapter has sought to explore the concept of hunter-gatherer hospitality in Africa. In doing so, it has attempted to show that the manifestation of human evolution as a species is based on cultural influences inherited from our descendants, the hunter-gatherers. Our humanity evolved increasingly as we reflected in nature and kinship where we honed our obligation of survival through hunting and gathering for social bonding. Hunter-gatherers have played and still play a major role in maintaining African hospitality as found within their practices, norms and values, regardless of globalisation, and they are not on the verge of extinction. Therefore, this chapter has sought to expound how hospitality manifests itself in the two domains and its connections to lineage. Hunter-gatherer hospitality in Africa's social domain is portrayed as a cultural and moral obligation to display generosity and hospitality to the kinsmen and the stranger, as well as undertake hunting-gathering activities for the social well-being of the host and the guest regardless of private or commercial setting.

The chapter has also expounded on the general anthropological view of humans' roots in Africa. The main focus was on the contemporary hunter-gatherers of Africa and their attempts to preserve their hospitable cultural identities over different time periods. The chapter presented the practicality of hunter-gatherer African hospitality as experienced during my own upbringing and, in so doing, I have painted a general picture of what hunter-gatherer African hospitality is all about and how it is lived and practised right from the roots. The legacy of Africa's hunter-gatherers' entwinement with hospitality is further found in the daily way of life of both the young and the old. Of course, every band culture has its own norms and values to receive and host a guest. Within the general African foraging culture, hospitality manifests itself in social life through activities with hospitable motives, such as welcome dances, singing and rituals undertaken after a good hunt and gathering as a sense of duty to express solidarity and bind the community together. Regardless of which part of Africa they occur in, hunter-gatherer practices all maintain a similar trope of hospitality being inherently African. Loyalty and success and/or failure as a group are more important than the goals and possibilities of any one individual; being part of a global minority focusing beyond only themselves where there is no me, but always we, doing good for the sake of it without expecting rewards. In order to understand the true essence of hospitality, it was inevitable that I explore the roots with the intention of presenting the influence of hunter-gatherer hospitality in Africa on modern societies' adaptation of the hunter-gatherer attitude of Ubuntu or *tunakaa pamoja*. By incorporating the continuum of hospitality's different motives, I have questioned whether Western societies can tap into and learn from the authenticity of African hunter-gatherer practices of hospitableness.

References

Anderson, D. and Grove, R. (1987) *Conservation in Africa: People, Policies and Practice*, Cambridge and New York: Cambridge University Press.

Bankston, J. (2013) *Your Land and my Land Africa: We visit Kenya*, Hockessin, DE: Mitchell Lane.

Barnard, A. and Woodburn, J. (1988) *Property, Power and Ideology in Hunter-Gathering Societies*, Oxford: Oxford University Press.

Bellwood, P. (2004) *First Farmers: The Origins of Agricultural Societies*, Oxford: Blackwell.

Binford, L. (1986) Human ancestors: changing views of their behavior, *Journal of Anthropological Archaeology* 3: 235–257.

Chuwa, L. T. (2014) African indigenous ethics in global bioethics. In *Interpreting Ubuntu*, New York: Springer.

Clark, J. D. and Brandt, S. A. (1984) *From Hunters to Farmers: The Causes and Consequences of Food Production in Africa*, Berkeley: University of California Press.

Derrida, J. (2002) *Acts of Religion*, New York: Routledge.

Erdal, D. and Whiten, A. (1996) Egalitarianism and Machiavellian intelligence in human evolution. In Mellars, P. and Gibson, K. (eds) *Modelling the Early Human Mind*, Cambridge: MacDonald Monograph Series, pp. 139–150.

Germann Molz, J. and Gibson, S. (2007) *Mobilizing Hospitality: The Ethics of Social Relations in a Mobile World*, Aldershot: Ashgate.

Golub, A. (2013) *Theory in Social and Cultural Anthropology: An Encyclopedia*, Sage.

Gowdy, J. (1998) *Limited Wants, Unlimited Means: A Reader on Hunter-Gatherer Economics and the Environment*, Washington DC: Island Press.

Graeme, B. (2009) *The Agricultural Revolution in Prehistory: Why did Foragers become Farmers?*, Oxford: Oxford University Press.

Hall, D. and Coles, J. (1994) *Fenland Survey: An Essay in Landscape and Persistence*, Archaeological Report 1, London: English Heritage.

Ingold, T. (1999) On the social relations of the hunter-gatherer band. In Lee, R. B. and Daly, R. H. (eds) *The Cambridge Encyclopedia of Hunters and Gatherers*, Cambridge: Cambridge University Press, pp. 399–410.

Jared, D. (1998) *Guns, Gems, and Steel*, New York: Norton Press.

Jean-Pierre, B. A. (2011) When the world's population took off: the springboard of the Neolithic demographic transition, *Science* 333 (6042): 560–561.

Kelly, R. L. (2007) *The Foraging Spectrum: Diversity in Hunter-Gatherer Lifeways*, Clinton Corners, NY: Percheron Press.

Kopytoff, I. (1987) *The African Frontier: The Reproduction of Traditional African Societies*, Bloomington: Indiana University Press.

Lashley, C. (2000) Towards a theoretical understanding. In Lashley, C. and Morrison, A. (eds) *In Search of Hospitality*, Oxford: Butterworth-Heinemann, pp. 1–17.

Lashley, C. (2008). Studying hospitality: insights from social sciences, *Scandinavian Journal of Hospitality and Tourism* 8, 1: 69–84.

Lashley, C. (2014) Studying hospitality: an agenda, *Research in Hospitality Management* 3, 1: ii–iv.

Lashley, C. (2015) Hospitality and hospitableness, *Research in Hospitality Management* 5, 1: 1–7.

Lashley, C., Lynch, P. and Morrison, A. (eds) (2007) *Hospitality: A Social Lens*, Oxford: Elsevier.

Lee, R. and Daly, H. R. (2002) *The Cambridge Encyclopedia of Hunters and Gatherers*, Cambridge: Cambridge University Press.

Lee, R. and Guenther, M. (1991) Oxen or onions: the search for trade (and truth) in the Kalahari, *Current Anthropology*, 32, 5: 592–601.

Lee, R. and Guenther, M. (1993) Problems in Kalahari historical ethnography and the tolerance of error, *History in Africa* 20: 185–235.

Lee, R. and Guenther, M. (1995) Errors corrected or compounded? A reply to Wilmsen, *Current Anthropology* 36: 298–305.

Lee, R. and Hitchcock, R. K. (2001) African hunter-gatherers: survival, history, and the politics of identity, *African Study Monographs*, Suppl. 26: 257–280.

Marlowe, F. W. (2005) Hunter-gatherers and human evolution, *Evolutionary Anthropology: Issues, News, and Reviews* 14, 2: 54–67.

Murdock, G. P. (1959) Part Two: African hunters. In *Africa: Its Peoples and Their Culture History*, New York: McGraw-Hill, pp. 48–63.

Oliver, R. (1991) *The African Experience: Major Themes in African History from Earliest Times To The Present*, London: HarperCollins.

Schrire, C. (1984) *Past and Present in Hunter-Gatherer Studies*, Orlando: Academic Press.

Selwyn, T. (2000) An anthropology of hospitality. In Lashley, C. and Morrison, A. (eds) *In Search of Hospitality*, Oxford: Butterworth-Heinemann, pp. 18–37.

Shepard, P. (1998) *Coming Home to the Pleistocene*, Washington DC: Island Press.

Smith, A. (1992) *Pastoralism in Africa: Origins and Development Ecology*, London: C. Hurst.

Solway, J. and Lee, R. (1990) Foragers, genuine or spurious: situating the Kalahari San in history, *Current Anthropology*, 31: 109–146.

Telfer, E. (1996) *Food for Thought: Philosophy of Food*, London: Routledge.

Telfer, E. (2000) The philosophy of hospitableness. In Lashley, C. and Morrison, A. (eds) *In Search of Hospitality*, Oxford: Butterworth-Heinemann, pp. 38–55.

Wiessner, P. (1996) Levelling the hunter: constraints on the status quest in foraging societies. In Wiessner, P. and Schiefenhövel, W. (eds) *Food and the Status Quest: An Interdisciplinary Perspective*, Oxford: Berghahn, pp. 171–192.

Wilmsen, E. N. and Denbow, J. R. (1990) Paradigmatic history of San-speaking peoples and current attempts at revision, *Current Anthropology* 31, 5: 489–524.

Wolff, A. (ed.) (2014) *Political and Economic Systems: Bands, Tribes, First Peoples and Nations*, New York: Britannica.

24

The gift theory of Marcel Mauss and the potlatch ritual

A triad of hospitality

Leandro Benedini Brusadin

Key themes

Gift theory

Potlatch ritual

Mandatory and voluntary exchanges

Hospitality triad

Nobody can be as agreeable as an uninvited guest.

(Kim Hubbard)

'The Gift' (Mauss, 2008 [1925]) presents a notion on the theory of gift giving as a common denominator of human exercise involving three obligations: to give, to receive and to reciprocate. In symbolic articulation, the author reveals that 'in Scandinavian and many other civilizations, the exchange of goods and contracts is performed in the form of gifts, which are voluntary in theory, but in reality are mandatorily given and reciprocated' (Mauss, 2008 [1925]: 55). By describing the phenomena of the exchange of goods and contracts in primitive societies, in their forms of prestations and reciprocities, a system of total prestations is created. The triad obligation theory provides Mauss with a satisfactory fundamental explanation for the contract forms between primitive Polynesian tribes. These institutions 'uniquely express a *fact*, a social regime, mentality defined as: everything – food, women, children, land, labour, services, priestly positions and classes – it is the material used for transfer and delivery' (Mauss, 2008 [1925]: 71).

Indeed, the influence of exchanging does nothing more than translate the way social groups are constantly overlapping each other. In this chapter, we presume that the theory of gift giving represents hospitality, in the sense of being an act of human welcoming, and as such is a theoretical-methodological support for the epistemological understanding of this field of knowledge, while also contributing to the interdisciplinary construction of current scientific data which a priori appears to be opposite or distinct.

DOI: 10.4324/9781315679938-27

The word 'gift' comes from the Latin word *dativa* and etymologically is incomplete and should be combined with the word 'debt', which describes the condition where one depends on the other. 'However, no gift can eliminate the debt with the other, since it increases every time I give more. The gift, the debt, do not therefore expire' (cited in Noguero, 2013: 171).

Meanwhile, in his introduction to Mauss' *Essay on the Gift*, Lévi-Strauss states that 'the exchange is the common denominator for a great number of social activities, apparently heterogeneous among themselves' (Mauss, 2008 [1925]: 34). He also comments that Mauss' total social factor presents itself as a tri-dimensional character and needs to be matched with the proper sociological dimension of multiple synchronous aspects: the historical or diachronic dimension, and finally, the physio-psychological dimension.

Upon analysing the work of Mauss, Lévi-Strauss considers its importance for anthropological research:

> But such is that for the first time in the history of ethnological thought, there was made an effort to transcend empirical observation and attain deeper realities. For the first time, the social aspect ceases to depend on the domain of pure quality: episode, curiosity, material for moralizing description or scholarly comparison, and transforms itself into a system whose parts we can therefore use to discover connections, equivalence and solidarity.
>
> *(Mauss, 2008 [1925]: 30)*

Nevertheless, it is important to remember that the structuralism of Lévi-Strauss sought to overcome Marxism and functionalism, and therefore criticised the Mauss method by saying that that the author had allowed himself to be mystified by the indigenous theory, forgetting the scientific spirit. For Lévi-Strauss, the symbol was more real than what reality signified and Mauss failed because he was too empiricist and became a victim of the same beliefs he intended to theorise. From this perspective, the indigenous representations and practices of the gift would be fundamental for unconscious mental structure and collective thinking (Godelier, 2001).

However, the *total social phenomena*, as Mauss (2008 [1925]: 70) proposes to call them, include all types of institutions – religious, legal and moral – and these are political, economic and family at the same time. 'The total provision does not only imply the obligation of reciprocating the presents received, it presupposes two others that are equally important: the obligation to give gifts, on one side, and the obligation to receive them, on the other' (Mauss, 2008 [1925]: 70). Therefore, on an analytical basis, the gift does not presuppose a counter-position between the social and economic characters that we sometimes find in other epistemological lines of human thinking and the social dichotomous mode.

This system that Mauss (2008 [1925]) also terms the *total prestation system* from tribe to tribe is a system by which individuals and groups execute their exchanges – in such a manner that this constitutes the oldest system for economics and law that it has been possible to observe and design. In this manner, the giver establishes the morality of the gift – exchange, and this is then seen as a social obligation within the society. Upon studying the dark side of social life, Mauss (2008 [1925]) wished to illuminate the path to be taken by nations, morally as well as economically.

The potlatch ritual as per Marcel Mauss: a gift exchanging system

The methodology employed by Marcel Mauss (2008 [1925]) was one of comparison, and the areas he chose to study were Polynesia, Melanesia and north-western America. His study focused on their systems, which were described one after another in their entirety in a collective sense, demonstrating that there was a mutual obligation of exchange and contract. What these peoples exchanged were not exclusively goods and riches, but amiabilities, rituals and ceremonials. These acts are designated by Mauss as gifts and reciprocity, preferably voluntary, but understood to be mandatory as a social obligation. The name *potlatch* is indicated for such total prestations in the sense that the tribe utilises this system of rules and ideas to ensure a type of hierarchy among themselves when executing real contracts. The '*potlatch* itself, so typical as *fact* and at the same time so characteristic of these tribes, is nothing more than a system of gift exchanging' (Mauss, 2008 [1925]: 108).

Mauss (2008 [1925]) termed his system of study ethnographic, by which he used comparison to measure how much societies diverged in their approaches from the societies designated as primitive. In this way, Mauss identified his research as follows: 'what rule of the law and of interest in backward or primitive societies, determines that the gift received must be mandatorily reciprocated? What force exists in the thing that is given that causes the receiver to reciprocate?' (2008 [1925]: 56).

Thus, Mauss visualises how it would be possible to study total human behaviour with all its social life, and even more, understands that not only could this type of concrete study be conducted for the science of customs, a partial social science, but it could even provide conclusions on morals. Mauss (2008 [1925]) believed that studies of this kind could also effectively perceive, measure and weigh the various aesthetic, moral, religious, economic and material factors, as well as demographic reasons, that together create a society and constitute a life in common.

In the regions researched by Mauss (2008 [1925]: 195), potlatch is therefore a system of observed exchanges that was divided into essential elements: honour, prestige, the *mana* that gives wealth, and the obligation to reciprocate these gifts on pain of losing this *mana*, this authority, this talisman, this source of wealth that is its own authority. 'The unreciprocated gift makes the one who accepted it without the spirit of reciprocity, inferior', observed Mauss (2008 [1925]: 42).

It is important to state that potlatch is an English word originating from Native Americans and refers to a gift of sacred nature, constituting for the one who receives it a challenge to give an equivalent gift. In this chapter, we analyse this ritual in primitive societies with regard to their epistemological character through social significance, as did Marcel Mauss via his spatial and temporal limitations. However, we understand that this theoretical and methodological debate could also be performed using other social groups during their respective epochs in regard to their relationships with exchange, such as occurs in their welcoming practices and the exchange of primitive and modern hospitalities.

In the ancient societies described by Mauss (2008 [1925]), there exist four forms of potlatch that are synonymous of the gift: the obligation to give, the obligation to invite, the obligation to receive and, finally, the obligation to reciprocate. The individual that does not reciprocate his loan or his potlatch loses his social status or even his liberty. Taxes, talismans, copper and spirits of the chiefs are of the same nature and of the same function as the circulation of goods, of men, women, children, rituals, ceremonies and dances, these being the only other forms of currency that preceded our market societies.

Other symbolic instruments of these primitive societies are the *oloa*, which in brief refers to objects and movable instruments belonging to the husband, and the *tonga*, where the goods are feminine. Such gifts can be mandatory and are hoarded like treasures, talismans, cults and magic rituals. The *hau* involves the spirit of things and, above all, the form of power that animates or pursues whoever is the owner. This reveals that the gift received and exchanged is not inert, since through this we have the domain of the beneficiary. This seems to be the master idea that Mauss said presides in Samoa and New Zealand; in other words, the mandatory circulation of wealth, tributes and gifts. 'Actually, there are mixtures. Souls are mixed with things and things are mixed with souls. Lives are mixed with each other and just as people and the mixed things leave each of their domains, they mix: that is precisely the contract and exchange' (Mauss, 2008 [1925]: 90).

In this way, to accept anything from someone is to accept it from someone's essential spirit, contributing, as such, to the general theory that this mandatory exchange turns into something beyond the material object – that is, it is a spiritual tribute (*hau*). There is a series of rights and obligations for the consumer and the giver, corresponding to the rights and obligations of the givers and receivers. The complete theory of these three obligations supplied Mauss (2008 [1925]) with a fundamental explanation of the forms of contract between the primitive Polynesian tribes. All this passes as if there had been a constant exchange of matter involving spiritual things and men, between tribes and individuals, shared among classes, sexes and generations. Mauss saw this as proof that this interpretation is valid for other groups of societies, even though he limited his research to primitive societies.

As such, and from an epistemological point of view, material life, morality and exchange function in a form that is voluntary and mandatory at the same time. For Mauss, this obligation is expressed in a mythical way, imaginary or, if you like, symbolic and collective, assuming an aspect of interest connected to exchanged things: 'these are never completely disconnected from their exchange agents; the communion and alliance that they establish are relatively indissoluble' (2008 [1925]: 106). He also distinguishes two categories of objects: 1) those which are due and can be given or exchanged, the alienable; and 2) those which should not be given or exchanged, inalienable.

> If we give things and are reciprocated, it is because respect is being given and reciprocated – which we consider even more delicate. But we also give of ourselves when we give to others, and if we give of ourselves, it is because we owe something of ourselves – ourselves and our well-being – to others.
>
> *(Mauss, 2008 [1925]: 121)*

In our view, the triple obligation of giving, receiving and reciprocating is a socio-anthropological reality upon which primitive societies were built, of which some facets are also found in modern society, such as given relationships between parents and children, among men and animals, and gift giving to strangers (blood donation, for example). The aspect of this obligation, which is at the same time free and mandatory, builds the epistemological foundation of what may be called the gift or donation.

> The gift can be sociologically defined as: all services or goods effected without assurance of reciprocity, with the intent of creating, maintaining or reconstructing a social bond. In this instance, the gift of a relationship is more important than the goods. In a general definition, the gift is all service or goods effected without obligation, guarantee or assurance of reciprocity. The gift paradigm emphasizes the importance of the positive, normative, sociological, economic, political and philosophical ethics of this type of prestation.
>
> *(Caillé, 2002:142)*

As for Marcel Mauss himself, in the absence of an official biography, it is known that the author was born in 1872, in Épinal, France, almost 400 km from Paris, the same city in which fourteen years earlier his uncle Émile Durkheim had been born. Émile had a great influence on the management of Marcel's carrier. Mauss had a teaching degree in philosophy and dedicated his studies principally to the History of the Religions of Uncivilised Peoples, the title of his thesis, although he himself did not believe that there was such a thing as uncivilised people, but only people with different civilisations. Mauss defended the idea of a free market, lamented the imposition of a desire for violence and criticised Bolshevism because it did not support basic morals. Although a socialistic base opposes the class war, Mauss dreamt that power would be exercised by the workers provided they had sufficient political maturity. In 1925, Mauss founded the Institut d'Ethnologie de l'université de Paris and after the death of his uncle edited the journal *L'Année Sociologique*. Being of Jewish descent, he feared detention during the Second World War, and his health declined, together with his intellectual capacity, until his death in 1950 in Paris. Although *Essay on the Gift* was the highlight of Mauss' own work, in partnership with Henri Hubert he produced works of greater importance (Oliveira, 1979).

Mauss' uncle Émile Durkheim is considered to be the founder of modern sociology through his study of religion with Mauss and a group of colleagues. However, this group was separated during the First World War and many of the members were lost in the trenches or died a few years later. Only Mauss was left to continue the work they had begun, but he was never taken seriously in this presumptive role of heir. However, almost single-handedly, he founded French anthropology and gave it a complete ramification for sociological theory. Even though Mauss is considered to be a revolutionary socialist, he was not really a Marxist, since he rejected the communistic belief that society should be transformed by the actions of the state. In his opinion, the role of the state preferably consisted in providing a legal framework for socialism that should, above all, emerge from the base through the creation of alternative institutions (Caillé and Graeber, 2002).

Godelier (2001) reveals to us that Marcel Mauss was a socialist who ended up losing half of his friends in the First World War. He went against Bolshevism when he affirmed that it is necessary to preserve the market, and also against liberal capitalism when he claimed that the state should intervene, wanting the rich to re-encounter the ancient generosity of the Celtic or German chiefs in a social-democratic programme that combines a market economy with a socialistic state. In my view, Mauss did not worry about the relationships that men established in the production of things, but only that which they maintained among themselves, the virtue of their circulation.

Mauss (2008 [1925]) produced descriptive social studies with the use of ethnography, in which the Melanesian populations had, more so than the Polynesians, conserved or developed the potlatch, by means of the *kula*, which consisted in giving on the part of some, and receiving on the part of others, people being the receivers one day, and the givers the next, in a regular circular movement that seemed to encompass the totality of the economic and civil life of the Trobriand Islands. This system was observed and described directly by Malinowski (1978 [1922]), an author who influenced Mauss in his analyses of the role of the gift in primitive tribes.

The gift, its rites and legends: the soul of things

Once the facts have been defined, it is necessary to enter into contact with them – that is, to observe them, as Mauss put it, who even questioned: 'How to link a fact to a means, if not by demonstrating how the means reacted to this fact?' (1909: 128). The word 'ethnography' serves to describe the empirical and descriptive results of the science of mankind; the word 'ethnology' serves to refer one to the speculative and comparative theories such that anthropology should not escape from the study of that most intimate part of a human being, one's instinctive and emotional life. This line of thinking was also utilised by Malinowski who described his field work in the Trobriand Islands as follows:

> Living in a village without any responsibilities except to observe the native life, the ethnographer sees the customs, ceremonies, transactions, etc. … There is a series of important phenomena that in no way can be registered except with the assistance of questionnaires or

statistical documents, but should be observed in their complete reality. These phenomena can be given the name of the imponderables of real life.

(1978 [1922]: 29)

The tribes that live in the commercial and social environment of the *kula*, in the far east of the New Guinea mainland within the Trobriand Islands, are matrilineally related; in other words, as regards descent and inheritance issues, the maternal line is followed, whereby the women exercise functions of great influence with a friendly familiarity in the village. The *kula*, however, is essentially a masculine activity. Malinowski states that 'the native man works for reasons of social nature and highly complex traditions; his objectives certainly do not refer to the simple provision of the basic needs or utilitarian purposes' (1978 [1922]: 56).

When comparing the studies of Mauss and Malinowski, Weiner stated that the first was strongly influenced by the second in his theory about social exchanges, although he committed an error in his overall conception of reciprocity:

Marcel Mauss, drawing heavily on Malinowski's Trobriand ethnography, introduced the concept of exchange as 'total social phenomenon' containing elements at once social, economic, legal, moral, aesthetic, and so on. Mauss analyzed exchange by separating it into the acts of giving, receiving, and reciprocating. In order to expose the structure of exchange, reciprocity as a total concept was fragmented into discrete categories. Mauss's reciprocity was a major step toward a general theory of exchange, but the segmentation of reciprocity was a major conceptual error.

(1989: 219)

In spite of this, in the studies of Malinowski (1978 [1922]), the *kula* is a form of exchange and has an ample inter-tribal character, being practised by communities localised in an extensive closed cycle of islands. Each of the *kula* participants periodically (but not regularly) receives one or several *mwali* (seashell bracelets) or a *soulava* (a neckless of red seashell discs) that should be given to one of their partners, who reciprocates by exchanging another gift. As such, nobody keeps an article to himself for very long. This fact differentiates this type of primitive society from a modern one that is linked to the idea of permanent possession. However, a *kula* native, as any other human being, develops a passion for what is owned, but the social code of laws that regulate the giving and receiving overcome his natural acquisitive tendency.

Malinowski utilised the gift logic, although without conceptualising it as Mauss did, to study the sociological issues of the Trobriand Islands, when he wrote the following passage: 'for the ceremonial aspect of tribal life, we constantly came across this "give and receive", a permutation of gifts and payments ... the love to "give and receive" within themselves; the pleasure of possessing wealth expressed through their donations' (1978 [1922]: 136). I conclude that in the primitive societies studied by Mauss (2008 [1925]) and Malinowski (1978 [1922]), the relationships based purely on the exchange of material do not explain the actual society. The symbolism attached to magic, by means of rituals and enchantments, played an influential role in providing explanations of events and of the social structure and the key roles within it.

As for magic powers, Mauss questions:

do dreams really exist or is the individual in a state of ecstasy? What is there that is real, what is there that is fiction, the mythical tradition and the individual conscience? Is the individual really a victim of an illusion of his sentiments, and are his illusions imposed by tradition?

(1909: 76)

Mauss says that everything passes over a malleable territory in which the myth and the ritual, as feelings and acts, the inspirations, the illusions and the hallucinations mix to form a traditional image of magic, which is increased among tribe members, linking to their spirit a firm belief and a relatively little-simulated semi-sincerity. 'But these spirits, these powers, only exist because of social consensus, the public opinion of the tribe. It is this that the magic follows, and it is at the same time, explorer and slave' (Mauss, 1909: 101). Such analysis demonstrates that in Mauss' theory, there is no dichotomous relationship between the protagonist social agents, since they attain, in a dynamic sense, the dominating character and the dominated character at the same time. Would this not be a complex form of being, representing members of society acting as a shared culture?

Along these lines, the concept of *mana*, discovered in a small primitive Melanesian community by Mauss and Hubert (2005 [1898]), also figures widely in the beliefs and magic practices of the lives of all the natives. It was this principal that was criticised by Lévi-Strauss, in his Introduction to the work of Mauss, when he stated that the author became contaminated by the tribe's logic of magic and spirituality. However, the gift theory presupposes that spirituality is connected to things and vice versa.

The basic principal upon which the rules of transactions in these communities is based is the fact that the *kula* consists of a donation of a ceremonial gift in exchange for which, after a certain space of time, an equivalent present should be received. The exchange, however, can never be discussed, evaluated or bargained. Malinowski highlights:

> important, however, is that for the natives of the *kula*, to have is to give – and in this aspect, they are notably different from us ... The wealth is, then the principal indicator of power – and generosity, the sign of wealth. Indeed, avarice is the most despised addiction.
>
> *(1978 [1922]: 81)*

Furthermore, Malinowski (1978 [1922]) states that the *kula* is a gift that is reciprocated, after a certain period of time, by means of a counter gift and not a barter, and it is up to the donor to establish the equivalence of the reciprocated gift, that cannot be imposed, haggled or returned – the fundament of all transactions. For Malinowski, this moral injunction and the subsequent act of generosity, superficially observed and poorly interpreted, are responsible for the primitive idea of communism of the islanders.

It must be taken into consideration that although Malinowski (1978 [1922]) has described the *kula* in the Trobriand Islands in great detail, he did not understand, or poorly understood, the institutions which he analysed, an area in which Mauss became a specialist. Even though Lévi-Strauss has criticised Mauss for not positioning his discovery within the scope of modern structural analysis, it was the thinking of Mauss that gave to ethnology the sociological explanation of what people believe and think, that could reveal the common strands in all societies including the simplest hunter-gatherer groupings. Mauss, in contrast to a structuralist theory that deflates the reality lived by the agents, elaborates a very rich interpretation, going beyond the native interpretation, but without suppressing it (Oliveira, 1979).

It can be verified that almost all categories of gifts, including those in the modern world, have as a base some type of sociological relationship, but not necessarily all in the perspective of the gift. Annette Weiner (1989), in her studies on the Trobriand Islands, subsequent to Malinowski, suggested that care should be taken when generalising the gift concept in primitive societies. For Weiner, many of the things exchanged have an objective that goes beyond the gift, since the maintenance of the family's economic cycle between life and death represents much more, in apparent irrational contradiction of a vision of a world of those that are outside of the native system. In this specific case, Weiner (1989) tells us that there are women who have predominance in the social organisation of the tribe and in the articulation of cosmic and transcendent phenomena; they thus maintain a type of power different to that of the men.

In this sense, Weiner disagrees with Mauss on the logic of interest in the exchanges in which the anthropologist transformed the idea of the gift into a myth:

> The Trobriand informants who say they exchange for 'love' or 'generosity' are following a myth that serves in their society to hide a reality of self-interest. The anthropologist who then insists on labelling this act as a 'gift' seems to be perpetuating the Trobriand natives' myth. But this is probably only incidental to what she or he is doing. In weaving the 'gift' myth, is not the anthropologist hiding a reality that concerns his or her role in his or her society? Is he or she not perpetuating and creating an image of 'the primitive' as a person, or 'primitive society' as a way of life, that has survived on some fundamental principle other than self-interest?
>
> *(1989: 221)*

Therefore, still in the Introduction of his unfinished thesis, Mauss emphasises that 'on one side, the myth has little reality when not connected to a determined usage in a cult; and, on the other side, a ritual has little value if not it does not represent the employment of certain beliefs' (1909: 103). It is said that rituals become collective activities of the soul, more than attitudes of the body and enrichment of mental elements, of sentiments and ideas, differently from the thinking of Weiner (1989).

The use of courtesy and those courtesies of moral life possess forms as fixed as the more characteristic religious rituals. As such, a simple 'good day' is a true wish, clearly formulated but with only a conventional significance. In this manner, the rituals are 'effective traditional acts that relate with things considered sacred. For example, if I do not greet you, I offend someone, I expose myself to a censure of opinion; and if I greet you, I avoid all of this annoyance ... The rituals have, for sure, truly effective material', affirms Mauss (1909: 138). These make a link between material and the spirit of social logic.

In my opinion, the only problem with Mauss' theory is how to make it penetrate the historical method and the logic of time – in other words, how to interpret the rituals of a primitive society in the face of modern society in a dialogic sense? Sahlins (1990) helps us to understand this culture with different historicity, and also based on the action of the symbolic system that consists in the empiricism of a cyclical structure with a diachronic temporal character. With this reasoning, Sahlins points out that the difficulty is to explode the concept of history with the anthropologic experience of culture. In addition, he utilises the concept of the historicity of performative structures to admit varying cultural practices, known as 'Historical Structural Anthropology'.

While relating anthropology to history, Sahlins (1990: 63) congratulates the 'new history that finally learned the anthropologic lessons' and understands that society is constructed as an individual sum of its individual practices. The dialogue between these fields is also true for the way the author studies the mystical activity, sometimes as a practical activity, sometimes as a truly mystical one. In this case, the myth transforms into an event and vice versa, such as in his analysis of *Capitan Cook*. Thus, historians cannot ignore the exotic past simply for not being remotely cultural and for not having in-depth registers, since it is exactly because of this that the history of the islands of the South Seas and other civilisations merits special attention. Cultural and anthropological studies provide concepts that enable the understanding of a society's social and economic events through time.

Therefore, given the above, Mauss' theory raises questions of human social order that overlap the economic order or link to the same with interference from its logic of power. It is my understanding that primitive society held its exchanges through symbolic rituals that served as much for maintenance and power interests as for disinterested practices linked to the emotional aspects of honour and generosity. Nevertheless, there have been other studies that can be related to this perspective, although sometimes the economic analysis tends to prevail at the expense of the complexity of society.

Godelier (2001), for example, studied the Baruya, a tribe living in a provincial village in two mountain valleys of New Guinea. It is a society supposedly without potlatch, but where sacred objects exist the tribe must save and share their benefits with others, alienating themselves from their beneficial powers by putting them at the service of society. In this tribe, besides being signs and symbols, these objects possess a spirit and therefore powers of imaginary social origin. In the Hagen region, at the heart of the highlands of New Guinea, Godelier also found the *moka*: a vast system of ceremonial exchanges practised by a large number of tribes in which the domain of the donation largely exceeds the material, and is constituted by all that it is possible to share, creating other obligations and debts.

The studies of Godelier (2001: 255) indicate that the precious objects circulating in the exchange of gifts are symbolic 'double substitutes'; substitutes of sacred objects and substitutes of human beings. Godlier suggests three features are required to consider an object precious: uselessness of a routine function, abstractness incorporated into its material form, and beauty as defined by the cultural and symbolic universe as perceived by the society concerned. However, 'it is not the objects that sacralise all or part of the relationships between them and with the universe that surrounds them, it is the inverse' (Godelier, 2002: 74). This reminds us of Mauss when he identifies that 'it is the nature of society to symbolically express its customs and their institutions' (2008 [1925]: 14).

Mauss has said that rituals are 'effective traditional acts that relate to things held sacred' and that 'an ancient practice is only understood thanks to a new dogma' (1909: 142). In another study, Mauss (1926) stated that the family relationships within the Polynesian tribes are sacred, on the one hand, and on the other, profane. The reason for these opposite and entirely different behaviours can be found in each degree of the relationship and its function. Some relatives are protected by social etiquette; others are objects of shame and injustices.

Therefore, examples of primitive gifts can be seen in the following rituals: the potlatch, practised by indigenous tribes in north-west America, and referring to a notion of credit and honour; the *kula*, practised by the Trobriand Islanders, in which precious goods are defined and circulated by gender and according to their symbolic and utilitarian value. 'In a phenomenological perspective, it could be said that primary sociability constitutes a concrete intersubjective space and as such, that the gift is this concrete and specific mobility' (Godbout, 1992: 198). In lieu of this, it is a fact that the primitive society worried infinitely more about its reproduction than the production of things. However, a distinct magnetism between the object and the subject puts an end to archaic interchangeability.

The gift theory and its scientific and modern (counter) positions

We have in mind that primitive gift societies have something more to offer us, as if Mauss wished that something of the *kula* would come to irrigate modernity. However, the economy of modern society is constructed on what supposedly is the opposite of the gift: the individual, the merchandise, the currency and the market. Still, Christianity approaches such precepts of the gift, and aims to be an economy of grace. The example of Jesus eminently illustrates the aspect emphasised by Mauss: in the logic of the gift, to give is to give of yourself (Tarot, 2002). Therefore, many of the elements of primitive societies are present in other forms in our modern society.

In epistemological discussion about the gift, Godbout (1992) questions why sociologists and economists debate the interests of power or culture, or inherited traditions, but yet not in terms of gifts? This is due to a unilateral explanation of the gift; if there is an exchange it is not a gift from a utilitarian perspective. The idea that I defend and incorporate in this chapter is that the cycle of gift giving, receiving and reciprocating is important for understanding the human species not only in the giving, transmitting and reciprocating acts in which compassion and generosity can act, but also in a conception of self-appropriation or self-conservation, such as jealousy and egotism. According to our point of view, the gift constitutes a system of proper social relationships regarding intricate practices and relationships of economic interest or power.

We assume that research has only one objective: reflecting the social logic of human thought. Metaphysical freedom can be the privileged prerogative of man and is everywhere in statistical numbers to determine whether or not to exist. As Mauss said: 'I will say willingly that in sociology there is a need for more Anthropology and History. I would even say that a complete Anthropology could replace Philosophy, because it would include within it the very history of the human spirit that Philosophy assumes' (1923: 161).

Although the understanding of Mauss has set the boundaries of research in given primitive societies, we part from the presumption that the gift is as modern and contemporary as that characterised in primitive societies, since it refers not only to isolated and discontinuous moments of social existence, but to its totality. Jacques Godbout (1992) states that if modernity refuses to believe in the existence of the gift, it is because it represents an opposite image of a material egotistical interest. In his view, the 'true' gift could only be free and without any expectation of reciprocity. However, above all, the gift serves to establish relationships and a relationship without hope of reciprocation in the same manner, free and without motive, would not be a social relationship. The gift, as such, constitutes a system of proper social relationships, as irreducible forms are relationships of economic interest or power. For Godbout, the only hypothesis is that there exists in modern society, as well as in primitive society, a mode for circulation of goods that intrinsically differs from the mode analysed by economists, such as that found in Marcel Mauss.

The temporal issue of the gift was the first sign of hesitance shown by Marcel Mauss because he formulated the hypothesis that a modern gift does not correspond directly with that of primitive societies – thus avoiding extending his results beyond those cultures he had studied. However, the gift goes beyond the ideology of the imaginary and the opposition between the individual and the collective, considering people as members of a more ample concrete group in which goods circulate at the service of the social ties created, sustaining and re-establishing by means of services rendered without assurance of reciprocation (Godbout, 1992). It is my understanding that in an epistemic and methodological manner, the gift serves various fields of knowledge, supplying us with an understanding of the many facets of our society with its dynamic character.

In addition to this delimitation of the gift within primitive societies, there are a number of reasons why Marcel Mauss was a seriously underrated author. Mauss did not think to give up the pleasures of life, friendship and sport, and wrote only under compulsion, for passion and for pleasure, without taking into account that he had always wanted to be the militant of a civic cause and a socialist at the same time. Finally, his disciples became more famous than him, either by dissecting the complexity of his thinking or giving it unilateral emphasis.

Caillé (2002) works with the modern concept of the *gift paradigm*: the term paradigm to designate the gift, no matter how anti-systematic it seems to be, is necessary to fix it within some systematic modalities of concrete thinking, even concatenating them in an anti-paradigmatic manner. For Caillé, the first paradigm is the individual action known for a utilitarian approach to which Maussian sociology is opposed because it does not seek to impute in the action anything but its own positive and normative inherent determinants. The second paradigm refers to the holistic character of functionalism or structuralism, within which its members, Durkheim and Lévi-Strauss, explain all actions, individual or collective, analysing them as so many mani-festations of domination exercised by social totality over individuals and the need to reproduce them. The third paradigm defined by Caillé represents something beyond the 'holism as quickly self-assured and satisfied to play with its individualistic rival a game of simple and misleading mirrors. The gift paradigm overcomes the equally limited viewpoints of individuals and holism' (2002: 18). Therefore, is it possible to think of the gift as a paradoxical logic of the market?

Individualists aim to abandon the free market game for the organisation of a greater propor-tion of social existence, while holistics, on the contrary, demonstrate a preference for a state that has an important role in the social game. Such an established opposition between liberals and socialists is reinserted in the Maussian proposal in a social and political order that synthesises with common sense in opposition to reductionism and unilateral theorising. And this derives from the fact that before having economic interests, it is necessary that people, individually or collectively, exist and are constituted as such (Caillé, 2002).

In the Maussian gift system, there are a large number of authors who write about the gift and its rejection of gratuity, since the relationship of the gift is primarily one of reciprocity. Godbout stresses that there are several reciprocities for the gift: gratitude, recognition and even the imme-diate reciprocation of energy to the giver: 'He who calculates tends to be excluded from the gift system' (1992: 137). A clear example of this is when a couple enters the realm of telling of their donations to the system; it is a sign of a deterioration of the relationship, not a sign that a gift system has floundered, since the gift abhors equality and seeks alternate inequality.

In the study by Mauss (2008 [1925]), the 'thing given' is not an inert thing: the total presta-tion not only requires reciprocation of the gifts received, but also assumes the obligations of giving, on the one hand, and receiving, on the other. Hence, there arises the importance that human beings give to their relationships with others by the representation of being generous, helpful and important. Thus, feelings of gratitude emerge even if unconsciously. Therefore, the gift exchanging in the studied civilisations results in a definition of wealth as the abundance of voluntary and mandatory exchanges of gifts.

The act of exchange for these civilisations has much more importance than the object that was being replaced. In the case of potlatch, there was a reciprocity of gifts under the penalty of losing the *mana*, such as the authority and the talisman, which consisted in the power of its own authority and source of wealth. Another symbolic act analysed by Mauss in the primitive societies was the donation, since, it could be seen, on the one hand, as the fruit of the social moral of gift giving while, on the other hand, as a notion of sacrifice: 'The donation is the fruit of the social moral of gift giving and fortune on one hand, and the notion of sacrifice on the other' (2008 [1925]: 76). Therefore, we can conclude that there is no gift without some type of sacrifice.

The 'obligation to invite' is completely evident in the potlatch tribes and clans, since it demonstrates authority and fortune. The 'obligation to receive' is no less awkward: not to have the right to refuse a gift, since, in that primitive society, to react as such is to manifest that one is afraid to reciprocate and indicates humiliation. The 'obligation to reciprocate' in essence is, many times, one of destruction, sacrificial and of benefit to the spirits. This ritual implies that the sanction for mandatory reciprocation is slavery, since the virtues permuted by potlatch oblige the gifts to circulate, to be given and to be reciprocated. As seen from that society, a considerable part of our morals and of our own life remains always in the gift environment, mandatory and at the same time free. Therefore, it is possible to employ this order to economics, since the notion of value is impregnated in these same symbolic elements. All of the phenomena of gift giving are simultaneously economic, religious, judicial, aesthetical, morphological and so on. This is also evident in more advanced societies with the law of hospitality, stated Mauss (2008 [1925]) when referring specifically to the field of hospitality.

Furthermore, states Godelier 'for an Eastern observer, this giving and receiving of the same thing seems to be devoid of sense, since, if the thing is returned as soon as it is given, it seems to have been exchanged for nothing. And then the gift transforms into an "enigma"' (2001: 69). It is important to emphasise that, for Godelier, the processes of exchange in potlatch are nothing exceptional, since this occurs in our capitalistic and mercantile societies with production being followed by the sale and purchase of all types of merchandise. Be these items material or immaterial, of consumption or destruction, they only have importance when their use is supported by an exchange value and this value transforms into capital. For Godelier, the fetishism of the objects used for gifts corresponds to fetishism of the merchandise or sacred objects. What marked, and continues to mark, the exchange of gifts between those that are close to us is not the lack of obligation, but the lack of calculation regarding its sacrifice.

Mauss (1926) concludes that the facts known as potlatch assign an agonistic factor by rival generosity, the force and nobility of combat, by challenges in the case of injustices and by sentiments of hospitality. Along these lines, the primitive and contemporaneous practices of hospitality are situated in the centre of social and anthropological observations. The current problematic in debate is, whether some type of sacrifice exists in the practice of hospitality in societies of the market type?

Jacques Godbout explains the prerogatives of philosophical and sociological studies of the gift in the following manner: 'as soon as the issue appears, strange in principal, one needs to know if there exists a relationship between the gift of life, the art of conservation, loyal or patriotic love, the quest for a work well-done, the team spirit, the donation of blood, and business lunches' (1992: 22). It is necessary to conceive the gift forming of a system as reflecting the social context in which it takes place. Godbout reflects this approach when he relates that the only impediment to this type of study is the tradition of utilitarianism when he posted that the gift does not exist because the only disinterested gift would be the authentic gift, where being disinterested is impossible. According to Godbout, this unilateral vision of the gift does not express it as a system of social exchange or as an integrating formula for modern and primitive societies.

The triple acts of giving, receiving and reciprocating constitute a universal anthropology upon which primitive and traditional societies were constructed (Caillé, 2002). Mauss himself said that

> studies of this genre permit us, with effect, to see, measure, and ponder the various aesthetic, moral, religious, economic motives, as well as the various material *factors* and demography, which together found a society and constitute a life in common.
>
> *(2008 [1925]: 217)*

Therefore, even without all of the responses to the scientific problematics about the paradoxical issues of modern man, the gift theory brings to light the possibility of reaching beyond the postulated dichotomies between material and immaterial, the economic and social, the oppressed and the oppressor, the market and the human being which generate apologies and ideologies that many times aim to attend to their own interest of intellectual representation.

Conclusions

Why then has a term so marked throughout history by the stigma of nostalgia and ingenuity been transformed today into a relevant scientific and philosophical discussion? Such questioning by Camargo (2004) implies that it places us face to face with inherent social problems such as the ills of globalisation, since human migration (including that which emerges from tourism) continues to exist and furthermore, there is a preoccupation with the progressive homogenisation of habits and customs. Because of this, the gift system involving the triple act of giving, receiving and reciprocation should permit a better understanding of the correlated phenomena, such as human association, leadership and solidarity, and their exchange regimes. I conclude that the triad, *give-receive-reciprocate*, postulated by Mauss, consists of an epistemological and methodological base for hospitality.

The phenomenon of the gift is giving rise to increased academic interest to the extent of its concern to explain the constitution of the social link, without succumbing to the perplexities of the traditional methodologies – individualistic and holistic. In my view, due to its complexity and fragility, the gift allows us to once again encounter the idea of the inter-subjectivity of the social link in its classifying, identifying and circulatory functions. The gift appears to be a necessary step in establishing the identity of people and stakeholders in the hospitality field and can contribute to ways of thinking within various schools.

Therefore, we are not able to think of a society with utopian sentiments that are pure and absent of interest, much less one with deterministic opposition between dominants and oppressed, because in the paradoxes of exchange relationships there coexists both: interest and disinterest. The sociological and anthropologic character of the gift has provided us with the intellectual ability to rethink the human being (and the market) with a complexity whereby it acts in all institutions, be they family, work or public related.

References

Caillé, A. (2002) *Antropologia do dom: terceiro paradigma*, Tradução de Ephraim Ferreira Alves, Petrópolis, RJ: Vozes.

Caillé, A. and Graeber, D. (2002) Introdução. In Martins, P. H. (ed.) *A dádiva entre os modernos. Discussão sobre fundamentos*, Rio de Janeiro: Vozes.

Camargo, L. O. (2004) Os Domínios da Hospitalidade. In Dencker, Ada de F. M. and Bueno, M. S. (eds) *Hospitalidade: cenários e oportunidades*, São Paulo: Pioneira Thomson Learning.

Godbout, J. T. (1992) *O espírito da dádiva*, Colaboração de Alain Caillé, Paris: Edittions La Découverte.

Godelier, M. (2001) *O enigma do dom*, Rio de Janeiro: Civilização Brasileira.

Malinowski, B. K. (1978 [1922]) *Argonautas do Pacífico ocidental: um relato do empreendimento e da aventura dos nativos nos arquipélagos da Nova Guiné Melanésia*, São Paulo: Abril Cultural.

Mauss, M. (1909) L'origine des pouvoirs magiques dan les sociétes austaliennes: étude analytique et critique de documens ethnographiques. Ouvres, Ed. Cit. In Oliveira, R. C. (ed.) (1979) *Marcel Mauss: antropologia*, São Paulo: Atica.

Mauss, M. (1923) Mentalité primitive et participation. Oeuvres, Ed. Cit . In Oliveira, R. C. (ed.) (1979) *Marcel Mauss: antropologia*, São Paulo: Atica.

Mauss, M. (1926) Parentés à plaisanterie. Oeuvres, Ed. Cit. In Oliveira, R. C. (ed.) (1979) *Marcel Mauss: antropologia*, São Paulo: Atica.

Mauss, M. (2008 [1925]). *Ensaio sobre a dádiva*, trans. António Filipe Marques, Lisboa: Edições 70.

Mauss, M. and Hubert, H. (2005 [1898]) *Sobre o sacrifício*, São Paulo: Coisac Naify.

Noguero, F. T. (2013) La hospitalidad como condición necesaria para el desarrollo local, *Revista Hospitalidade* X, 2.

Oliveira, R. C. (ed.) (1979). *Marcel Mauss: antropologia*, São Paulo: Atica.

Sahlins, M. (1990) *Ilhas de história*, Rio de Janeiro: Jorge Zahar Editor.

Tarot, C. (2002) Pistas para uma história do nascimento da graça. In Martins, P. H. (ed.) *A dádiva entre os modernos*, Discussão sobre fundamentos, Rio de Janeiro: Vozes.

Weiner, A. B. (1989) *Women of Value, Men of Renown: News Perspectives in Trobriand Exchange*, Austin: University of Texas Press.

25

Hospitality, sanitation services and immigration

Leprosaria and hostels for immigrants in Brazil

Ana Paula Garcia Spolon

Key themes

Hospitality for immigrants

Hospitality and sanitation services

Leprosaria and hostels for immigrants

Hospitality and immigration to Brazil

> Guests bring good luck with them.
>
> *(Turkish proverb)*

The phenomenon of human displacement is ancient and closely associated with the idea of an ethics that envisages the practice of a cosmopolitan justice focused on the interests of the global citizen and a universal hospitality associated with 'the right of the foreigner not to be treated with hostility when he gets to the territory of the other' (Kant, 1970 [1795]: 105).

Rossello (2004) presents immigration as a phenomenon of utopic nature, always interspersed with negotiations, discourses and contradictions. For Rossello, migratory flow is a rite of passage, the moment when the individual abandons a previous *status* in order to acquire a new one, often unknown. Whatever the case, the one who emigrates hopes for a better future. From the one who receives, there is the perspective that this new interaction is positive or not. Historically, immigration has been a permanent phenomenon, caused by tragic events such as wars, terrorist attacks and plagues.

Gozálvez Pérez (2006) exemplifies the contemporary global situation in which one sees immigration as a social issue that somehow affects everyone. For Gozálvez Pérez, 'migrations have always existed', emigrate-migrate is 'a permanent feature of human history' (2006: 208). Likewise, the immigrant is an individual with rights and immigration is a 'structural phenomenon: it is not the person who decides, but social organisation and structures which determine, press forward and develop migratory flows' (Gozálvez Pérez, 2006: 209–210).

DOI: 10.4324/9781315679938-28

In the historical context of global-scale human displacements, challenges and opportunities are posed not only to people displaced but also to receiving societies; minor conflicts exist in situations where migratory flow is desired and stimulated by all players involved in the process. On these occasions, a proposal of immigrations is carried out, grounded on the idea that in order to receive the other, the receiving society itself needs to be transformed, based on the principle that any encounter 'with anyone different affects us and requires that we redefine the place and identity of both' (Gozálvez Pérez, 2006: 222). In this case, there is opportunity for change in the receiving society.

Whatever the context in which immigration takes place, there are oppositions between expectations and rights, the idea of justice and law, the welcoming of the other as a categorical imperative and the status of a state's sovereignty (Leung and Stone, 2009). Cavallar explains these oppositions from the point of view of the history of societies and argues that 'one-hundred years between 1750 and 1850 were a kind of "transition zone", with the right to hospitality being replaced by laws of immigration' (2013: 69). According to Cavallar, this was a time when, due to migratory flows recorded on a scale never seen before, requirements such as passports or entry bans on certain groups were introduced, as well as policies of isolation.

This chapter is about what is assumed to be *classical* or *traditional immigration*, the migratory flow towards colonial possessions in America, in a context marked by factors that, together, stimulated 'the most drastic change suffered by world population: the increase of inhabitants in the Americas from 30 to almost 160 million between 1800 and 1900' (Hobsbawn, 1998: 31).

In fact, in the second half of the nineteenth century and early twentieth century, there was the greatest migratory flow ever recorded worldwide. Segawa (1989) notes that between 1820 and 1930 the United States alone received 37 million of the nearly 50 million immigrants who headed towards the Americas. In Latin America, Argentina and Brazil were the primary destinations for immigrants, followed by Uruguay and Chile. According to Hobsbawn (1998), 6.15 million immigrants headed towards Argentina and Brazil between 1871 and 1911.

Encouraged human displacements – as is the case with so-called *classical immigration* – such as the coming of this enormous contingent of Europeans and Asians to the Americas, are movements that, by themselves, create a scenario of opportunities both for the receiving community and for those who arrive. It is an event in which the foreigner, in search of a better future, is duly 'authorised' or even invited to enter the host territory, recognising in it, at least temporarily, qualities that enable him to join the destination community. From both sides, encouraged immigration, mostly subsidised by states, is seen as a positive phenomenon.

Manzi and Toudoire-Surlapierre, speaking about the condition of the foreigner, discuss this issue of belonging:

> it is not enough ... for the foreigner to join a group or enter a certain place, but [it is necessary] that he is part of it, that is, he has the same recognised rights (even though they are limited or lower than those of the community). Thus he [the foreigner] complies to the codes and rules of the group which he joins.
>
> *(2004: 800–801)*

For Manzi and Toudoire-Surlapierre, in cases such as those of workforce encouraged immigration or even in the case of refugees in search of asylum when directed to countries willing to receive them, the condition under which the displacement takes place creates a context where the foreigner is 'authorised' to arrive, settle in and become a citizen. Rossello (2001: 7) highlights the difference between 'proposed' and 'imposed' hospitality (the same adjective might be applied to the concepts of mobility and immigration). It is in this sense that the flow of Europeans and Asians to America, from the second half of the nineteenth century until the mid-twentieth century, is characterised as a proposed immigration, considering that, on the part of immigrants, there was an urgent need to fight and search for a better life.

What has to be primarily considered is whether these immigrants had access – if not unrestricted, at least with few or only temporary restrictions. They were given the roles and condition of citizens. In them, competencies, abilities and capacities were recognised, providing them with the opportunity of 'merging with the receiving society and adopting its mentality, behaviour, rules and ways of life' (Duroux, 2004: 1057), while influencing its habits, language, traditions and beliefs. Indeed, as Duroux notes, 'the roles are the open sesame of hospitality' (2004: 1052).

The experience of recognising the characteristics of so-called *classical immigration* leads us to think about Binet-Montandon speaking on the paradoxical nature of welcoming, which is given through 'the emergence of different characters' *status* and conditions of their transformations under the angle of temporality' (2004: 1171). In the case of Brazil, at the end of the nineteenth century immigrants were desired, invited and attracted. For Europeans and Asians who opted to cross land and sea and head towards Brazil, an opportunity for a better future came true. As Binet-Montandon explains:

> the conception of welcoming depends on the institutional and cultural context within which it takes shape, of respective statuses and relations that were established between the one who receives and the one who is received, of the final horizon in which it is inserted.
> … thus, welcoming raises an identity question, both for the welcomed one and the one who welcomes, because the process through which welcoming is practised leaves identifying marks that structure their future relations.
>
> *(2004: 1177)*

In Brazil, between the years 1820 and 1914 the entry of approximately 3.4 million immigrants was recorded. Main nationalities were, from Europe, Italian, Portuguese, Spanish and German, and among the Asians, Japanese, Syrian and Lebanese. All these peoples left deep marks in Brazilian society, in both economic and cultural terms. Although spread all over Brazilian territory, their presence was strongly felt in the southern states and large urban centres (Rio de Janeiro, São Paulo and Salvador), but in a more concentrated way in the rural areas of São Paulo state, where coffee farms were located.

Historically, Brazil has always been a welcoming country for immigrants, but between 1960 and 1980, a large flow of immigrants from Europe, Japan and the United States was recorded. Nowadays, the country is again in demand for Bolivian, Haitian, Portuguese and, more recently, Syrian citizens. In the sixteenth and seventeenth centuries, Brazil experienced colonisation and settlement immigration – the country received mostly Portuguese and African citizens, promoting a movement of persecution and exploitation of Amerindians who would run to the backwoods, or be acculturated through mixing between peoples, giving birth to a population of *mamelucos* and *mestizos*. According to IBGE (2000), between 1500 and 1855 approximately 2.8 million Africans entered Brazil, characterising a forced migratory flow, an extremely profitable activity that had legal support until the mid-nineteenth century. Since then, Brazil has recorded the largest Portuguese population outside Portugal and the largest African population outside Africa. The profile of immigration that took place from the second half of the nineteenth century was different. Jürgens refers to the huge flow of people recorded between the years 1870 and 1920 as the 'great immigration', which ranked Brazil as 'the 4th most popular destination sought by immigrants from all over the world' (2012: 46) (Figure 25.1).

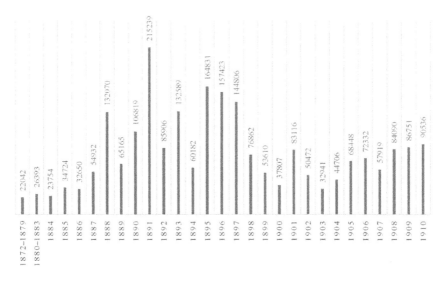

Figure 25.1 Arrival of immigrants to Brazil, per year, 1872–1910

Source: Elaborated by the author from data available in Skidmore (1998: 129).

Although there have been regional specificities, some general factors were decisive for this migratory flow towards Brazil. From a point of view of the issuing countries, it is worth noting (a) the crisis Europe was going through in the last quarter of the nineteenth century with unemployment, starvation and diseases, (b) population surplus both in the fields and in the cities, arising from the Industrial Revolution and the mechanisation of productive processes, and (c) the increasing urbanisation and the resulting degree of insalubrity in the cities, among other factors (Gerstner, 2008).

In the case of Brazil, several elements contributed to a context characterised by an intense migratory flow of people coming from Europe:

1 Movements in favour of the suspension of slave traffic from Africa and the replacement of slave labour by the labour of free men: the Queiroz Law (of 1850, that prohibited slave traffic from Africa to Brazil), the Free Belly Law (of 1871, that would free children born of slave parents), the Saraiva-Cotegipe Law (of 1875, that proposed the progressive extinction of slave labour) and, finally, the Golden Law (that formally abolished slavery in 1888).

2 Coffee culture expansion, that not only established a new economic system of mass production focused on export, but had an impact on cities' growth and the structuring of new urban services.

3 Progressive shortage of labour due to suspension of slave labour and the interest of farmers in coffee areas in promoting immigration and replacing slaves with employed immigrants.[1]

4 The end of the empire and proclamation of the Brazilian Republic in 1889, which gave the country a different political *status* in the world context, inaugurating a phase of new investments, including mobility, railways construction and port improvement.

5 The creation of the Immigration Official Agency in 1863 and of the Immigration Promotion Society in 1886.

6 The establishment of a federal subsidy for immigration until 1902 (which was subsequently resumed in 1907).

7   The provision of a coffee subvention by the São Paulo government, which guaranteed that 67–84 per cent of the total immigrants to Brazil between 1897 and 1901 were directed to São Paulo State.

Migratory flow to Brazil between the second half of the nineteenth century and the first decades of the twentieth century raised questions not only of a demographic nature, but also of public health, particularly in a country that in the mid-eighteenth century had begun to face cholera outbreaks and epidemics and where 'public health was virtually non-existent in colonial times' (Trindade, 2013: 41). In this context, Ignatian wards emerged and Brotherhoods of Mercy were formed – Holy Houses, in charge of treating travellers who, after a long ocean crossing that resulted in organic disorders, such as worm infections and scurvy, were sheltered and treated (Trindade, 2013: 33).

The theme of this chapter leads to the natural process of mapping and characterisation of leprosaria and hostels that, in Brazil, were dedicated to the care and/or accommodation of immigrants between the mid-nineteenth century and the first decades of the twentieth century. This mapping and characterisation has made it possible to understand how the creation and distribution of these institutions took place, as well as how cultural-historical heritage has been partially preserved today and established in memory spaces and museum institutions.

Human mobility and public health in Brazil: the emergence of places dedicated to immigrant lodging and medical care

As already said, between the second half of the nineteenth century and the mid-twentieth century a migratory flow was recorded, particularly from Europe towards the Americas. As Caponi relates, 'between 1880 and 1914, the world saw the formation of large colonial empires' and 'in this context of world economic expansion, followed by demographic growth in Europe and by an intense emigration in search of better opportunities in colonial areas' (2003: 50–51) a serious problem of infectious diseases took hold in the colonies.

Proliferation of diseases was a characteristic phenomenon of industrialisation, which promoted urbanisation and the growth of cities. Likewise, overseas expansion (that started in the early fourteenth century and widened from the seventeenth to the nineteenth century) bore close relation with questions connected to sanitary and epidemiological practices. Trindade (2013) discusses interfaces between public health and immigration issues, highlighting the problem of sanitary control policies and the construction of spaces designed to isolate international patients. The isolation of patients is a very ancient practice and the first leprosaria (places destined to receive patients with leprosy) were built in Europe during the eleventh century, reaching almost 19,000 units in the Middle Ages (Trindade, 2013). According to Trindade (2013), between 1750 and 1830 the foundations of a sanitary movement were laid based on the preservation of public health through structural reforms. All over the world countries adopted different solutions, with the common aim being the fight against endemic diseases and the promotion of community health and urban hygiene (Bynum, 2011). However, two international models were commonly pursued, based on the experiences of Norway and the United States (in Hawaii) concerning disease control and involving the construction of a legal framework of high social impact.

In the seventeenth century,

> Successive plague epidemics … increased awareness of communal health issues and resulted in a series of measures such as the routine quarantine of ships arriving from affected areas, the control of the movement of people and goods, and medical inspection.
>
> *(Bynum, 2011: 81)*

The practice of isolation would lead to the creation of the so-called cordons sanitaires, borders that would keep patients away from healthy people. Isolation was generally recommended in the form of quarantine and in many places in the world in the seventeenth century hospitals were built as temporary accommodation for patients, particularly those affected by bubonic plague and leprosy. They were called *lazaretos*, 'from Lazarus, the poor man whose wounds were licked by dogs, according to Jesus' parable in the Gospel of Luke – these isolation hospitals were adapted for plague, after the Black Plague, from their earlier use for people diagnosed as lepers' (Bynum, 2013: 34).

In Europe, with the disappearance of the plague in the second half of the seventeenth century, these hospitals were destined for other uses, while, according to Bynum, 'in the Middle East, where plague continued, they were kept as places to leave travellers and other people in transit under quarantine when the plague was close' (2013: 36). Isolation hospitals, along with medical police created in Europe in the late seventeenth century, fought against the plague, proliferation of malaria, yellow fever or sleeping sickness, typhoid fever and smallpox, as well as other illnesses.

During the eighteenth and nineteenth centuries, facilities dedicated to host immigrants proliferated in the world mainly because of the high migratory flow between European countries and from Europe to other continents, particularly the Americas. Many buildings dedicated to treat diseases were built in Brazil, most of them to receive people with leprosy. The generic name used to describe isolated colonies dedicated to treat Hansen's disease (also called leprosy, a disease transmitted by mycobacteria leprae) – one of the most lethal diseases in history, characterised by ulcerative wounds – was leprosarium or *lazaretos* (from the Italian *lazzareto*). Some leprosaria were world-famous such as those in Kalaupapa (Hawaii, United States) and Spinalonga (in Crete, Greece). Usually located on islands in order to facilitate separation of patients from population, leprosaria were very old institutions and had very specific characteristics.

Technically, Goffman (1974 [1961]) classifies them in the category of 'total institutions' dedicated to 'people incapable of taking care of themselves and who are a threat to society, although unintentionally (sanatoriums for those with tuberculosis, hospitals for those mentally ill, leprosaria)' (Ducatti, 2009: 146). Leprosaria are centuries-old institutions that historically 'fulfilled the function of separating the leper so that he would not contaminate any social environment' (Ducatti, 2009: 151).

Leprosy is a disease that has existed since the Roman Empire and arrived in Europe during the sixth and seventh centuries. The leprosy bacillus was detected in Norway, where one of the most important leprosaria in all Europe was located. Leprosaria multiplied in Europe during the sixth and seventh centuries, probably because of the urbanisation process and the expansion of overseas commerce. In their origin, they emerged 'in the spontaneous grouping of patients, institutionalised little by little', so that, during the Middle Ages, the church took the 'initiative of creating leprosaria that were small groups of miserable houses situated in the farthest areas of the city to confine patients' (Ducatti, 2009: 151).

It is estimated that by 1200 there were two dozen leprosaria in France, reaching 1,900 in other European countries. Although the institution had a purpose in itself – the isolation of patients affected by leprosy – it is important to distinguish that, at that time, diseases lacked precise diagnoses. However, the broader role of these places was care. The Catholic Church, during the Middle Ages until the early twentieth century, tried to offer this care, particularly to the poor. With this, religious institutions welcomed many patients in shelters, hostels, leprosaria and monasteries, and even in churches. Many of the leprosaria later became hospitals and gave origin to Holy Houses.

The physical form of the receiving institution would vary according to local environmental characteristics, recorded public health problems and also the kind of people who would arrive at these places. Thus, isolation hospitals, immigrant internment hostels and leprosaria many times would serve the same traveller, arriving in a country whose sanitary conditions were not the best.

In the late nineteenth century, as Trindade notes,

> the concept of health in Brazil had a bad reputation. The terrible plagues devastating the population would terrorise travellers. Immigrants would call Rio de Janeiro a *grave for foreigners*. Whenever they could, shipping companies would avoid docking their ships in Brazilian ports.
>
> *(2013: 116)*

The country was stricken by the bubonic plague (also called Black Plague) through the Port of Santos, where ships would arrive from Europe. Xavier *et al.* describe Brazil at the time as 'a country with many epidemiologies' and 'in each one of the phases – arrival, procedures of reception at hostels and integration to the marketplace – immigrants were always under the threat of yellow fever' (2004: 15).

Originally, leprosaria establishments, to which lepers were sent in order to be isolated from the rest of population, were unprotected, lawless and cruel colonies. In Brazil, several of them were built, and the most important ones were those in Pirapitingui (rural São Paulo State), Ilha Grande or Praia Preta (Rio de Janeiro coast), São Francisco do Sul (Santa Catarina coast), Ilha da Restinga (Paraíba coast) and Paricatuba, in Manaus, next to the Amazon rainforest.

Ilha Grande (or Praia Preta) leprosarium was the first one in the country (Figure 25.2). Built in 1884, it operated as a sorting centre and a place of quarantine for sick passengers. It operated for 28 years, received 4,000 vessels and afterwards was turned into a political jail. The building was decommissioned in 1903. Later, in 1942, it was re-established and became Cândido Mendes Penal Colony.

Figure 25.2   Ruins of Ilha Grande or Praia Preta Lazareto

Source: Image by Marcelo César Augusto Romeo (licensed by Creative Commons) and available at https://goo.gl/2e4nnO.

In Brazil, the roles of institutions dedicated to isolating patients and receiving immigrants are confused. Ducatti (2009) states that, although in Brazil compulsory isolation of patients only became a reality during the 1930s, already in the eighteenth century there were facilities that practised patient isolation and in the nineteenth century isolation was practised at hostels that received both immigrants and internal migrants. Segawa (1989) records that already in 1867 a report from the Brazilian Official Agency had recommended 'the foundation of hospices of immigrants modelled by American and German states' to be installed next to ports and railway stations that would dedicate themselves to isolating immigrants affected by diseases. Until this point, this isolation had taken place in small private hostels which often lacked hygienic conditions. The rental of private accommodation by the government for immigrants' temporary placement was, little by little, replaced by accommodation in more adequate establishments set up to receive people. According to Reznik, 'immigration hostels were one of the links in the extensive and complex migration chain stretching from the homeland village to arrival at the final destination' (2014: 248).

The characterisation of leprosaria and hostels for patients and/or immigrants in Brazil

There are four categories of establishments in Brazil in which policies relating to public health and immigration were applied and in which care for patients and the welcoming of immigrants were carried out. The first category comprises isolation institutions, generically called leprosaria or *lazaretos*, usually buildings with three distinct areas: the *leprosarium*, where patients would stay, the *preventorium*, where patients' companions who were not infected by the disease were assigned, and the *dispensary*, through which people who had been in contact with patients would pass. This category also includes Ignatian wards, later turned into Holy Houses of Mercy, which were already being built in the sixteenth century, but multiplied under the name of *lazaretos* and leprosaria during the eighteenth and nineteenth centuries, and some important leprosaria were built in the twentieth century.

In the second category are the internment hostels, dedicated to temporary internment of travellers affected by diseases who would complete an isolation period – called quarantine – before being able to effectively enter the territory. In Brazil there were three internment hostels: Morro da Saúde in Rio de Janeiro (1867–1881), and two in São Paulo, Homem de Mello (1880–1881) and Pari (1881–1882). In colonisation enclaves located particularly in the southern area of the country there were colonial enclave hostels exclusively serving settlers – national or foreign – who arrived in the area. These comprise the third category. Three colonial enclave hostels are recorded: one in São Paulo (Santana, 1877–1878) and the other two in its surroundings (São Caetano and São Bernardo Novo; both were operating in 1878, but there is no information on their closing dates).

Finally, governments established contracts with public and private hostels created to receive foreigners, and often subsidised accommodation and food expenses. These first hostels, installed in the mid-nineteenth century (Ilha de Bom Jesus Hostel in Rio de Janeiro was the first one, operating between 1850 and 1860), were very simple establishments, installed in adapted buildings and only received migrants who were healthy. Once their lack of adequacy was recognised, they were replaced by others, and new contracts were signed.

The picture started to change in 1882, when São Paulo State government recognised the importance of providing larger spaces for immigrants' accommodation, and rented a pottery in Bom Retiro district. Bom Retiro Immigrants Hostel was established, with a capacity to host 400 people. By 1885, it was already considered to be inadequate and the construction of a new hostel for immigrants was established through a Provincial Law (56 of 21st/03/1885).

In 1887 the new building received its first immigrants and its construction was concluded in 1888 in the district of Brás. It has operated as a shelter for immigrants and people displaced by flood, as a prison, as an aviation school and as a museum. In its 91 years of existence, Brás Immigrants Hostel received over 2.4 million people from 70 nationalities (Museu da Imigração, 2015), becoming the most important hostel for immigrants in the country. In 1982 the building was acknowledged to form part of the national heritage and in 1986 the Historical Centre of the Immigrant was created. Today, the complex includes the São Paulo State Immigration Museum (Figure 25.3) and also the Arsenal of Hope, an organisation supported by an Italian NGO that shelters 1,200 homeless men daily, offering them beds, and hygiene and food services, as well as support services such as a library, a laundry, leisure facilities and psychological support groups.

However, prior to Brás Immigrants Hostel there was Ilha das Flores Immigrants Hostel, located at Baía da Guanabara, in Rio de Janeiro. The first one in the country built specifically to host immigrants, it was opened in 1879, but the first guests had already arrived in 1877. Far away from everything for health care reasons, it received immigrants, refugees, migrants and prisoners and was also a torture area during the military dictatorship in Brazil. It operated as a hostel until 1966, having received approximately 300,000 immigrants. At that time, the building was transferred to the Navy and operated as a political jail from 1966 to 1971. Today it is an active military base, with a daily flow of over 1,000 service personnel from the Brazilian Marine Corps. Since 2012 the building has also hosted the Ilha das Flores Immigrant Memory Centre, supported by a partnership between the Brazilian Navy and Universidade Estadual do Rio de Janeiro (Figure 25.4). Recently, the Centre joined the world circuit of centres dedicated to immigration.

Table 25.1 lists leprosaria and hostels built in Brazil between 1713 and 1937, highlighting their typology and period of operation. The symbol (~) designates uncertainty related to the year of opening (when it comes immediately before the date) or closing (when it comes after the date). Figure 25.5 shows the distribution of leprosaria and hostels across the whole of Brazil.

Figure 25.3 Museu da Imigração do Estado de São Paulo/São Paulo State Immigration Museum
Source: Ana Paula Garcia Spolon, 2016.

Figure 25.4   Hostel for immigrants, Centro de Memória e Imigração Ilha das Flores, Rio de Janeiro/RJ

Source: Available at www.hospedariailhadasflores.com.br/galeria_02.asp, Coleção Leopoldino Brasil.

Figure 25.5   Geographical distribution of leprosaria and hostels in Brazil

Source: Elaborated by the author.

Table 25.1 Leprosaria, internment hostels, colonial enclave hostels and immigrants' hostels in Brazil

	Name of establishment	Region	Operation
1	Leprosário de Recife	NE	1713
2	Leprosário de São Luís	N	1718
3	Leprosário do Rio de Janeiro	SE	1756
4	Leprosário de São Paulo	SE	1779
5	Leprosário de Salvador	NE	1787
6	Leprosário de Belém	N	1838
7	Leprosário de São Francisco do Sul	S	1850~
8	Hospedaria da Ilha do Bom Jesus, Rio de Janeiro	SE	1850–1860
9	Leprosário da Ilha da Restinga	NE	1859
10	Hospedaria de Internação do Morro da Saúde	SE	1867–1881
11	Hospedaria Maçan d'Oro	SE	~1875
12	Depósito de Imigrantes e Hospedaria do Areal	SE	1875–1877
13	Hospedaria de Imigrantes da Vargem do Carmo	SE	1877
14	Hospedaria do Núcleo Colonial de Santana	SE	1877–1878
15	Hospedaria de Imigrantes do Campo da Luz	SE	1877-1878
16	Hospedaria do Núcleo Colonial de São Caetano	SE	1878~
17	Hospedaria do Núcleo Colonial de São Bernardo Novo	SE	1878~
18	Hospedaria de Imigrantes de Santana	SE	1879–1881
19	Hospedaria de Internação Homem de Mello	SE	1880–1881
20	Hospedaria de Internação do Pari	SE	1881–1882
21	Hospedaria de Imigrantes de São Paulo – Bom Retiro	SE	1882–1887
22	Leprosário de Sabará	SE	1883
23	**Hospedaria de Imigrantes da Ilha das Flores, Rio de Janeiro**	**SE**	**1883–1966**
24	Leprosário de Ilha Grande	SE	1886–1891(1903)
25	**Hospedaria de Imigrantes de São Paulo – Brás**	**SE**	**1886–1978**
26	Hospedaria de Imigrantes de Macaé	SE	?
27	Hospedaria de Imigrantes de Paraíba do Sul	SE	?
28	Hospedaria de Imigrantes de Paranaguá	S	?
29	Casa do Imigrante de Caxias do Sul	S	?
30	Hospedaria de Imigrantes do Pinheiro, Rio de Janeiro	SE	?
31	Hospedaria de Imigrantes Pensador, Manaus	N	?
32	Hospedaria de Imigrantes do Bairro do Calafate, Belo Horizonte	SE	?
33	Hospedaria de Imigrantes da Estrada de Vista Alegre	SE	?
34	Hospedaria de Imigrantes da Estrada da Soledade, Belo Horizonte	SE	?
35	Hospedaria de Imigrantes Horta Barbosa, Juiz de Fora	SE	1888~(1920)
36	Hospedaria de Imigrantes Mar da Esperança, Belo Horizonte	SE	1888~
37	Hospedaria São João del Rei	SE	1888~
38	Hospedaria de Imigrantes de São João Nepomuceno	SE	1889~
39	Hospedaria de Imigrantes de Rio Grande	S	1889–1894
40	Hospedaria de Imigrantes de Alfredo Chaves ou Pedra d'Água – Vitória	SE	1889–1924
41	Hospedaria de Imigrantes do Saco de Padre Inácio, Florianópolis	S	1890–1904
42	Hospedaria de Imigrantes de Campinas	SE	1891/1894
43	Hospedaria de Imigrantes Crystal, Porto Alegre	S	1891–1897
44	Hospedaria de Imigrantes do Itapema, Guarujá	SE	1892~(1910)
45	Hospedaria Provisória de São Bernardo	SE	1893–1895
46	Hospedaria de Imigrantes da Ilha de Outeiro, Belém do Pará	N	1893–1972
47	Hospedaria de Imigrantes de Paricatuba	N	1898~
48	Hospedaria de Imigrantes de Santos	SE	1912~
49	Leprosário de Paricatuba	N	1924~
50	Leprosário de Bauru – Asilo Colônia de Aimorés	SE	1933~
51	Leprosário de Pirapitingui, Itu	SE	1937~

Source: Adapted from Udaeta (2011, 2013), Reznik and Fernandes (2014) and Segawa (1989).

Of the 51 establishments listed in Table 25.1, 13 are leprosaria, most of them (six) located in the south-east, with three establishments in the north (São Luís, Belém and Paricatuba/Manaus), one in the south (São Francisco do Sul) and three in the north-east (Recife, Salvador and Ilha da Restinga/João Pessoa). In the north, three immigrants' hostels still operate (Pensador/Manaus, Ilha do Outeiro/Belém and Paricatuba/Manaus). In the south, besides the leprosarium mentioned, there were five hostels (Paranaguá, Caxias do Sul, Rio Grande, Porto Alegre and Florianópolis). The distribution of establishments in the south-east is wider and also more heterogeneous. Besides the six leprosaria mentioned, during the period between 1713 and 1937 three other internment hostels (Morro da Saúde, in Rio de Janeiro and Homem de Mello and Pari, both in São Paulo), three colonial enclave hostels (Santana, São Caetano and São Bernardo Novo, all of them in São Paulo) and 24 hostels for immigrants were recorded. Among them, those considered the most important are Ilha das Flores Immigrants Hostel in Rio de Janeiro and Brás Immigrants Hostel in São Paulo.

From the 24 hostels located in the south-east region of Brazil, 11 were in São Paulo State, seven in Minas Gerais, five in Rio de Janeiro and one in Espírito Santo. An analysis of the location of the 11 hostels for immigrants in São Paulo confirms the economic primacy of this area of the federation at the time of the so-called classical immigration. Of the 11 establishments identified, one stood in Campinas (in the rural area, close to the rail network), two on the coast, next to the port (Santos and Guarujá) and eight in Greater São Paulo, in locations always close to passenger transport stations.

Conclusions

Migratory flows have taken place for centuries and are often the result of people escaping conflict and insecurity. Historically, it would appear that many immigrants came from deprived backgrounds and arrived in an unhealthy state. The relation between migratory flows and the reception of foreigners in receiving societies and communal health led to the creation, during the eighteenth and the nineteenth centuries, of establishments that mixed functions of health care with hosting travellers.

In this context, leprosaria (or *lazaretos*) and hostels have emerged in Brazil as well as in many other places in the world – from colonial enclaves, internment camps and migrant camps. These institutions operated in buildings that would receive these displaced people as they arrived at the place of destination. Many of these buildings, besides providing space for lodging and meals to newcomers, would offer a space dedicated to the evaluation of their health and, if they were affected by some disease, adequate rooms for their isolation and treatment, until they were able to integrate themselves in the receiving society.

Leprosaria and hostels are places of waiting in which people cluster, spaces that mix feelings of fear, anxiety and hope. This chapter has been dedicated to mapping and characterising these spaces in Brazil, in the period between the second half of the nineteenth century and the early twentieth century, aiming to understand how the process of creation came about, how the logic of their geographical location was established, and how both the sites in which they were installed and their own edifications as historical-cultural heritage became important. Among the types of institutions created in this period for the care of those affected by disease or displaced (migrants, immigrants, refugees, etc.), leprosaria and immigrants' hostels are the most important ones.

Leprosaria are institutions dedicated primarily to the care of lepers, but they were adapted to receive people affected by several diseases. In many cases, they become general hospitals, asylums, field hospitals, jails and other kinds of establishments. Leprosaria, in turn, were the establishments destined to accommodate immigrants. Notwithstanding they have a specific function, quite often this function was confused with another, constituting in the country three kinds of hostels: internment, colonial enclave and immigrant.

Immigrants' hostels are the kind of facilities that interest us the most, precisely because they integrate in a very rooted manner the feeling of welcome (in spaces dedicated to immigrants' accommodation) with care (in spaces for health recovery and maintenance of these people). Brazilian immigrants' hostels are typical of the response to the large migratory flow from Europe and Asia towards the Americas in the late nineteenth and early twentieth centuries.

> [They] were buildings organically integrated to the structure of migration movements initially sponsored by the Empire and afterwards conducted by the Republic, linked to the present economic context and which respond to this correlation not only as lodges of individuals in transit, but as true architectural facilities specifically organised as infrastructure for medical and social care, providing them a status similar to those of hospitals in their daily performance.
>
> *(Segawa, 1989: 24)*

The support of health services in facilities destined to receive immigrants become necessary because of the conditions imposed by deadly epidemics, not only in their places of origin, but also in the locations they arrived at. Added to this is the problem of what Segawa refers to as the 'rudimentary medical-sanitary knowledge' (1989: 24) of that time.

As a solution to the problem of sanitary control, immigrants' hostels (and also other forms of accommodation recorded in this research such as *lazaretos* and leprosaria, colonial enclave and internment hostels) proved efficient, in a time when the migration process was characterised by a very fragile order in which there was lack of deep knowledge related to epidemiology and prophylaxis.

For Segawa:

> the first immigrants' hostels continued to be a variation of *lazaretos*, maritime hospitals specifically intended to receive passengers and cargos with contagious diseases, and to impose quarantine where such diseases were suspected.
>
> *(1989: 25)*

Segawa's analysis corresponds to Bois and colleagues' findings concerning world movements of immigration and social protection of patients: 'the history of social protection is articulated around the creation of institutions with longstanding imprecise borders and longstanding confused functions, at the same time social and moral' (2004: 541).

Much of the time institutions were indistinctly named and the term 'hostel' is only one amid a huge semantic confusion. The same confusion took place historically in relation to the role institutionally played by these institutions. For Bois *et al.*, 'two of the main functions of them – social, of the asylum and medical, of the hospital – blend in an older common concept, hospitality' (2004: 541). To receive with hospitality would mean, in this sense, not only welcoming, through the concession of a lodging and meal space, but also caring, providing for those who arrive conditions of survival for further integration in society.

From a patrimonial point of view these buildings and/or the places where they were installed constitute an important historical and cultural heritage to be preserved. In addition, they are the material representation of the architectural school of an epoch and the expression of hospitality of a people and an integral part of the development process of first colonial relations, in the terms proposed by Lee (2013). For Lee, 'the relation of hospitality with the nation building implicitly relates home and familiarity to outlining territory, creating thresholds and manufacturing a sense of entitlement, community and national identity' (2013: 48).

Located all over the national territory, not only on the coastline but also in important rural destinations, leprosaria and hostels (of internment, colonial enclaves, and immigrants) were symbols of both an important period and a social movement, and marked the immigrants' welcoming process in Brazil during the period of its utmost importance. Furthermore, the so-called classical immigration has left as a legacy a collection of material and immaterial culture that today is at least partially preserved and exposed in museums and in spaces dedicated to immigration memory and preservation of history in Brazil.

Note

1   Although there is a historiographical current that defends Brazilian labour shortages in coffee plantations due to the end of slavery and therefore the need for incentives to encourage European immigrants, there are other lines of thought suggesting that there was not a labour shortage and that the entry of immigrants was intended to promote the 'whitening' of the Brazilian population, particularly in São Paulo State, with the argument that Europeans were superior to Brazilians in cultural terms, which was not true, since immigrants to coffee plantations were ordinary people, natives from farming communities with very difficult socio-cultural and economic conditions.

References

Binet-Montandon, C. (2004) Acolhida: uma construção do vínculo social. In Montandon, A. *O livro da hospitalidade: acolhida do estrangeiro na história e nas culturas*, São Paulo: SENAC, pp. 1171–1183.

Bois, J., Puijalon, B. and Trincaz, J. (2004) Hospícios: modelos institucionais de proteção social. In Montandon, A. *O livro da hospitalidade: acolhida do estrangeiro na história e nas culturas*, São Paulo: SENAC, pp. 541–556.

Bynum, W. (2011) *História da medicina*, Coleção L&PM Pocket 957, Porto Alegre: L&PM Pocket.

Caponi, S. (2003) A saúde como objeto de reflexão filosófica. In Bagrichevsky, M. *et al.* (eds) *A saúde em debate na Educação Física*, Edibes: Blumenau/SC, pp. 43–59.

Cavallar, G. (2013) From hospitality to the right of immigration in the law of the nations: 1750–1850. In Baker, G. (ed.) *Hospitality and World Politics*, London: Palgrave Macmillan, pp. 69–95.

Ducatti, I. (2009) Aparelho ideológico de Estado e violência: o caso particular dos antigos leprosários, *Projeto História* 38: 141–163.

Duroux, R. (2004) Imigração: França/Europa. In Montandon, A. *O livro da hospitalidade: acolhida do estrangeiro na história e nas culturas*, São Paulo: SENAC, pp. 1051–1078.

Gerstner, L. O. (2008) El alojamiento de inmigrantes en el Río de la Plata, siglos XIX y XX: planificación estatal y redes sociales, *Biblio 3W – Revista Bibliográfica de Geografía y Ciencias Sociales* XIII, 779. Available at http://www.ub.edu/geocrit/b3w-779.htm. Accessed 12 November 2015.

Goffman, E. (1974 [1961]) *Manicômicos, prisões e conventos*, Coleção Debates, São Paulo: Perspectiva.

Gozálvez Pérez, V. (ed.) (2006) *La inmigración extranjera como desafío y esperanza*, Alicante: Universidad de Alicante.

Hobsbawn, E. J. (1998) *A era dos impérios (1875–1914)*, 12th edn, Rio de Janeiro: Paz e Terra.

IBGE (2000) *Brasil: 500 anos de povoamento*, Rio de Janeiro: IBGE. Apêndice: Estatisticas de 500 anos de povoamento, p. 223.

Jürgens, P. (ed.) (2012) Uma ilha de muitas nacionalidades, *Rio Pesquisa* (História), Fundação de Amparo à Pesquisa do Rio de Janeiro (FAPERJ) VI, 21: 44–46.

Kant, I. (1970 [1795]) Perpetual peace. In *Kant's Political Writings*, ed. Hans Reiss, Cambridge: Cambridge University Press, pp. 93–130.

Lee, M. K. (2013) Captivity and hospitality in the New Americas, *Hospitality & Society* 3, 1: 43–55.

Leung, G. and Stone, M. (2009) Otherwise than hospitality: a disputation on the relation of ethics to law and politics, *Law Critique* 20: 193–206.

Manzi, J. and Toudoire-Surlapierre, F. (2004) O estrangeiro: o desconhecido que bate à minha porta. In Montandon, A. *O livro da hospitalidade: acolhida do estrangeiro na história e nas culturas*, São Paulo: SENAC, pp. 795–817.

Museu da Imigração do Estado de São Paulo, at http://www.museudaimigracao.org.br. Accessed 20 December 2015.

Reznik, L. and Fernandes, R. A. N. (2014) Hospedarias de imigrantes nas Américas: a criação da Hospedaria de Imigrantes da Ilha das Flores, *História* 33: 234–253.

Rossello, M. (2001) *Postcolonial Hospitality: The Immigrant as a Guest*, Stanford: Stanford University Press.

Rossello, M. (2004) Imigração: discursos e contradições. In Montandon, A. *O livro da hospitalidade: acolhida do estrangeiro na história e nas culturas*, São Paulo: SENAC, pp. 1079–1087.

Segawa, H. (1989) Arquiteturas de imigrantes, *Revista do Instituto de Estudos Brasileiros* 30: 23–42.

Skidmore, T. E. (1998) *Uma história do Brasil*, Rio de Janeiro: Paz e Terra.

Trindade, D. F. (2013) *Médicos e heróis: os caminhos da medicina brasileira desde a chegada da Família Real até as primeiras décadas da República*, São Paulo: Ícone.

Udaeta, R. G. S. (2011) Hospedarias de Núcleos Coloniais: os casos de Santana, São Caetano e São Bernardo (1877–1979), *Anais do XXVI Simpósio Nacional de História* (ANPUH), July: 1–12.

Udaeta, R. G. S. (2013) *Nem Brás, nem Flores: hospedaria de imigrantes da cidade de São Paulo (1875–1886)*. 228 f., il. Dissertação (Mestrado). São Paulo: Faculdade de Filosofia, Letras e Ciências Humanas da Universidade de São Paulo (FFLCH-USP).

Xavier, J. *et al.* (2004) Relato do 6° Congresso Brasileiro de Epidemiologia. 'Cidade mais justa e saudável'. *Radis – Comunicação em Saúde* 24: 8–28.

26

Experiencing hospitality and hospitableness in different cultures

Javed Suleri

Key themes

Hospitality

Hospitableness

Hospitality as experience

Genuine hospitality

The experience of working collaboratively in culturally different environments can be rewarding and challenging (Jordan, 2008). A new set of transformations have made daily life more global, uncertain, and dynamic (Tribe, 2010). Internationalization has encouraged the study of cultures, traditions, and societies (Stier, 2003). Factors such as globalization of hospitality, global migration, altruistic hospitality, and vigorously emerging economies such as those of Brazil, China, and India have added to the intensifying interest in internationalizing (Enders, 2004; Yang, 2004; Munar, 2007). I started to explore the world myself because I wanted to become acquainted with people from different parts of the world and to discover global hospitality, and, therefore, that is the focus of this chapter. There are a number of possible motives for hosts offering hospitality to guests, as suggested by Figure 26.1. This chapter is based on a review of the relevant literature and my personal observations, interviews, and experiences in different cultures and countries.

Ulterior motives hospitality	Containing hospitality	Commercial hospitality	Reciprocal hospitality	Redistributive hospitality	Altruistic hospitality

Figure 26.1 A continuum of hospitality

Source: Lashley (2015).

DOI: 10.4324/9781315679938-29

First, what is the concept of hospitality and hospitableness? It is the relationship between host and guest; that of inviting, welcoming, and giving the guest one's home and generosity without asking for any reimbursement, or the accomplishment of even the smallest condition (Derrida, 2000; Derrida and Dufourmantelle, 2000). However, the *Oxford English Dictionary* defines hospitality as "the friendly and generous reception of guests or strangers" (*Oxford English Dictionary*, 2015). Hospitality is a feeling of generosity, a desire to please, and a genuine regard for the guest. Lashley and Morrison (2000) define it as the willingness to be hospitable for its own sake without any expectation of reward. Furthermore, hospitality and hospitableness are designed to enhance the mutual wellbeing of the parties concerned; nevertheless, it is more than food, drink, and shelter (Brotherton, 1999; Telfer, 2000).

I was born in Lahore (Pakistan) in the province of Punjab, and that is where my itinerary will start. One of the ancient civilizations dating back to 2500 BC and stemming from numerous empires—Afghan, Arab, Aryan, British, Ghaznavid, Greek, Indus valley civilization, Kushan, Mughal, Persian, Sikh, Scythian, Turkish, and Timurid—"Punjab" is a blend of two Persian words, *Punj* meaning five and *ab* meaning water. Punjab, mainly Lahore, is famous for its hospitality in Pakistan and there is a common saying: *Jinnay Lahore ni vikhya o jamiya e ni*, which means those who have not seen Lahore are not born yet. Another renowned term *Zinda dilan-e-Lahore*—or the lively Lahorian—reveals the pleasant and hospitable character of the inhabitants and their hospitality. It was in 1989 that I decided to leave Pakistan to explore the world and I have since visited forty countries. Hence, in this chapter, the focus is on sensitivity to the guest. Some personal experiences around the world with different cultures will be shared as they are unforgettable and add value to life. Indeed, this chapter is not about goods or materials but about admiring rich experiences, memories, and occasions far away from home (Gilmore and Pine, 1997; Hemmington, 2004).

Due to the increase of the global workforce, it is hard to find a place on the globe where original cultures are comprehensively protected. They are all, more or less, engineered through various factors, such as the Zwarte Piet (Black Pete) discussion in Holland. Zwarte Piet is a character who first appeared in his current form in an 1850 book by Jan Schenkman and he is commonly depicted as a blackamoor. Traditionally he is said to be black because he is a Moor from Spain. In recent years, the character has become the subject of controversy, especially in the Netherlands (Zwarte piet, 2015). Hence, in Amsterdam and other major cities, Black Pete has been introduced with different colors. A man shaking hands with a Muslim woman anywhere in an Islamic country provides another apt example. Muslims should refrain from acts disliked by their Prophet, and shaking hands with a woman is something that was personally disliked by the Prophet. Hence, it is a moral standard that it is highly desirable to follow (Ghamadi, 1999), though in my experience there are very few women at work who would avoid shaking hands with men. Besides, we are not likely to forget that people are forever the movers and shakers of the world (O'Shaughnessy, 1873). Diverse mannerisms leading to unique ways of dealing with different people from different places are undoubtedly real, and genuine hospitality can positively transform an alien into an acquaintance and a foe into a friend. After presenting welcoming experiences along with diverse hospitality motives for hosts offering hospitality to guests, this chapter will also highlight some cultural or societal ambiguities in hospitality.

Welcoming experiences

The private (domestic) domain of hospitality reflects the range of concerns related to the provision of food, drink, and accommodation, along with the effect of host and guest obligations (Lashley, 2008). Every culture has its own norms to welcome guests. In Pakistan, wherein my roots lie, the host and guest shake hands with the right hand, firmly but gently, in greeting and departure. Once a relationship is developed, they may hug as well as shake hands and display intentions of reciprocal hospitality (Lashley, 2015). In brief, focusing on the relational, dyadic aspects of relationships has led to a much better understanding of both social cognition and interpersonal processes (Holmes, 2000). On the one hand, in the welcome phase, it is common to ask about guests' health, family, and business, which is a corresponding sign of valuing and developing the relationship. Establishing more open relationships can be seen as a strategy for re-forming steadiness and grooming value-creating occasions in new ways (Ballantyne, 2003). On the other hand, there is a clear segregation between men and women. Usually, women kiss each other once on the cheek, whereas men are not endorsed to kiss the opposite sex; though there are examples in certain regions where men kiss each other too as a sign of welcoming and showing genuine hospitality. Similarly, in most Western countries shaking hands is normal and hugging when knowing someone better, whereas a kiss on the cheek would show an added value of the relationship and be a sign of generous and benevolent motives of hospitality, which Lashley (2015) expresses as reciprocal hospitality. However, the Dutch kiss three times, unlike in other Western countries.

There are diverse ways to feel welcomed. For instance, I am privileged with Irish hospitality because I always ask *conas atá tú* in Irish, meaning 'how are you'. This small sentence opens a corridor of friendship and kindness towards each other. Likewise, there are different ways to express altruistic hospitality. For example, while in Singapore I was standing in front of thirty-odd stairs along with my luggage and was wondering how to enter the airport. All of a sudden, a young man appeared, took my luggage, and carried it upstairs, waved to me and wished me a good day. That was one of the most incredible signs of generosity and unconditional hospitality I have ever come across, as unconditional hospitality concludes that you don't ask the other to give anything back (Derrida, 1998).

Another altruistic hospitality experience occurred in Australia, with regard to my first encounter with a lady customs officer at Sydney airport. While examining my baggage she was inquisitive about me, predominantly for the purpose of my stay in Australia, which I believe to be a part of her duty as well as public relations. After my satisfactory question and answer session, she pleasantly told me how to find the way to a youth hostel. I must acknowledge she gave me a reason to reconsider my opinion of custom officers around the world. Despite their notoriety, I was pleasantly surprised by this officer's behavior. I experienced it as a sign of unconditional hospitality (Derrida, 1999). Hence, my first encounter with an Aussie gave me a very good impression of Australian hospitality. While I do not know whether I would recognize her again, her positive behavior shows that sometimes just one good experience can have a positive impact on a human being's life. People do not buy service delivery; they buy and desire experiences, memories, and occasions (Gilmore and Pine, 1997; Hemmington, 2004).

One more noteworthy experience of inimitable hospitality happened when I was in Rhodes (Greece), where I met a couple who were running a cafeteria at the beach. I was inquisitive to know about their specialty, mainly some local food after tasting tzatziki and moussaka as they were scrumptious! It was not only the food but a mixture of servicescape and their personal touch of treating me as guest that made me return to their cafeteria. In just a few days, to follow Lashley's terms (2015), commercial hospitality converted into real friendship – a unique experience without commercial motives. Even though commercial hospitality cannot deliver true hospitableness (Telfer, 2000; Ritzer, 2004, 2007), within a short period of time they had given me a homely feeling as if we had known each other much longer, and therefore I experienced commercial hospitality that eventually converted into altruistic hospitality. After I left, they sent me a video they had made with the intention of remembering me and being remembered.

In contrast, while in Istanbul (Turkey), due to a delayed flight, I had to stay in a hotel. The airline had arranged my visa and stay, as it was responsible for the inconvenience. The following evening I encountered an unusual experience of commercial cum ulterior motives hospitality at the time of checkout when I was asked to pay for the food. I declined and called for the manager for explanation. After a short conversation, he apologized for the trouble and wished me a nice journey, although I had observed that the other passengers who had been affected by the delay were asked by the hotel to pay and most of them did. I found this action to be ill-mannered and creating negative word of mouth. It was more an experience of hostility than hospitality, or even discriminative, as most of the passengers were having communication problems, which the hotel management was using to its advantage. As Visser (1991) notes, hospitality and hostility have a similar root.

Another encounter involving ulterior motives hospitality occurred while I was at Minneapolis airport in Minnesota. After a long journey, I encountered the rudest ever behavior from an immigration officer, which I have no hesitation in calling discriminative, given the exceptionally hard-nosed way he enquired about me, my spouse and my children. The only difference I can feel, compared to my earlier travels, especially in Australia, was that the former was before 9/11 and the latter—my arrival in America—was post-9/11. That was indeed the largest catastrophe ever in airline industry and one of the worst in recent history. But that does not mean innocent people should suffer because of others' criminal and barbaric acts. The officer went so far as to ask my wife how she had met me and how long we had been together and other disconcerting questions in the presence of my 14- and 12-year-old children. In my thirty years of traveling, I have never came across such an officer in any country, and therefore it's difficult to make a statement about American concepts of hospitality or immigration, but one thing is sure—one bad fish can destroy the whole pond and replicate negative motives of reciprocal hospitality. Quite interestingly, in America, if you are in a shop or restaurant, you will be addressed with 'how are you doing today' and 'how can I help you', portraying the American standards for hospitality, yet it can have no meaning, and if it is not reflected in daily life, then such a welcome does not relate to the authenticity of the hospitality provided (Lashley, 2015). Nonetheless, Native American hospitality is more meaningful, as a member of the Ojibwe tribe has elucidated (Ojibwe, 2015), and reflects motives of redistributive hospitality. To sum up, genuine hospitality is not a concept but a feeling that makes a stranger think he or she is included (Lashley, 2000).

Sensitivity to the guest

Unconditional hospitality entails the host to permit the guest to behave as they wish; there must be no stress or compulsion to behave in any particular fashion (Derrida, 1999). Offering hospitality to strangers is a vital characteristic of a Pakistani and the guest is seen as *Rahmat*, which means sympathy, mercy, compassion, and kindness, whether he or she is expected or not. Although India and Pakistan have had many tensions and grievances regarding their bilateral relations, Bollywood actress Swara Bhaskar, upon visiting Pakistan, described her feeling about its hospitality with the words, "if enemies treats you like this then why do I need friends" (Mazaqraat, 2015). In addition, it is very common to receive guests warmly and provide them with a pleasurable experience. However, the guest has a social responsibility to contribute to the relationship by being good company (King, 1995). In other words, the host–guest relationship is the key distinguishing characteristic of hospitality from which several other dimensions emerge (Pritchard, 1981).

For instance, during a flight to Hong Kong I noticed the gentleman sitting next to me placing his seat cushion on his knee with the consequence that the stewardess's quick glance missed him. I knew he had not fastened his seatbelt and his body language showed he had no clue how to fasten it. I felt his awkwardness and had compassion for him. Choosing not to add to his mortification, I started playing with my seat belt by opening and closing the buckle and, thus, provided an intangible and unconditional service to him (Derrida, 1998). I noted him observing me and he finally buckled his belt—this swift gesture of altruistic hospitality helped me accomplish my mission. In fact, I was a guest as well but it was my concern for others that persuaded me to help a fellow guest during takeoff. I was enjoying my flight as my physiological needs had been basically fulfilled, but I became increasingly interested in finding safe circumstances, stability, and protection (Norwood, 2014). Nevertheless, my actions represented generous giving without any motives for return or repayment (Lashley, 2015).

In another instance during my stay in Sydney, I met an admirable thought-provoking British migrant to Australia who had been living there for the past twenty-five years. He was not only an auto mechanic but a good artist too—specializing in painting sixteenth- and seventeenth-century history. Painting was his hobby and I have seen many of his paintings that were quite admirable. On one side, he was a solitary person but relatively positive, whereas, on the other, he was a man full of life and color. He would be thrilled to see me and would always show me his new paintings. Correspondingly, I would update him about my studies and work. I was doing it to show him how special he and his work was (and still is) for me, and the way he would nod and cherish my compliments was indescribable. Although we were two strangers from different countries, we had developed a bond through our companionship and exhibited feelings of generosity to each other (Lashley, 2000). Telfer (1996) nicely described that turning friends into family is the essence of hospitality because it allows each to feel at home with the other.

At the time of my graduation ceremony, my Australian friend brought a formal suit for me, which surprised me as I had never seen him in formal clothes—only in jeans. Upon inquiring about the outfit, he told me that he had bought it a while ago, yet had never worn it. Besides, he had seen me wearing suits and thought it would be a good gift for my graduation. This one meaningful gesture and his intentions touched me and left me exhilarated, and at the same time I wanted to salute him for his redistributive hospitality. His way of showing his genuine hospitableness is unarguably a part of his personality (Telfer, 1996; Lashley, 2015). On one hand, intentionality is hospitality—a gesture of welcoming (Derrida, 1999); on the other, metaphoric gestures can play a vital part in life, and friendship is meant to create a symbolic tie between people (Müller, 2004) that establishes bonds between those involved in sharing hospitality (Lashley, 2000).

In the same way, when I moved to a small town in Friesland in the Netherlands, most of my friends thought my decision was wrong; according to them, I would isolate myself, since, in Friesland, a specific dialect is spoken and the culture is quite distinctive. Nonetheless, I had a very congenial experience; the first thing I did after moving was to invite my neighbors for an introductory high tea. During these gatherings I came to know more about them and vice versa. Hence, by taking one good hospitable step, a healthy relationship was developed with my neighbors, as, by showing unconditional hospitableness, you welcome visitation and the invited guest (Derrida, 1998). Consequently, stimulated by my idea of inviting them, all of them invited me back and, in particular, one of them told me they had been living there for thirty years and they had never experienced such an invitation. This approach of reciprocal hospitality has provided not only lots of comfort to my family and me, but has taught me that just one good gesture can develop healthy relationships. Hence, taking the first step as a new entrant and maintaining contact with neighbors and surroundings will result in respect and love. In short, if a guest respects the host's customs, there is no need for the host to be heedless as cordiality is reciprocal (Lashley, 2015).

Hospitality concepts can be used to develop the relationship between host societies and their relationships with non-hosts, for instance immigrants, asylum seekers, and refugees (Hage, 2005; Molz, 2005). There is always a little hostility in all hosting and hospitality— establishing what Derrida termed a persuaded 'hostipitality' (Derrida, 2000: 13). On the contrary, it is the new entrants' responsibility to behave as if they are visiting their best friend's, where they always demonstrate their best behavior for benevolence and reputation, corresponding to my experience of Friesland. Besides, if immigration is experienced in this way, then it will not be too long before a migrant has more friends than enemies. Though Derrida (1999) advocated unconditional hospitality, at the same time it is the guest's obligation as well not to misbehave or endanger the host (O'Gorman, 2007). They will receive friendship from others and provide friendship in return, thereby generating reciprocal hospitality (Lashley, 2015). In a healthy society, every positive motive and action has consequences: "For every action there is equal and an opposite reaction" (Newton, 1686). In short, globalization is the real life and we must be prepared, or prepared to be prepared, for the unexpected arrival of any other (Derrida, 1998).

All welcome, but not you!

During my travels I met many people with diverse characters from different cultures – among them were Hindus, Muslims, Christians, Jews, Sikhs, atheists, and gays from all different areas of life. What fascinated me most were the common grounds of hospitality and their genuine hospitableness. People from all over the place are the same and there is only one race in this world—the human race (Suleri, 2008). It is due to social forces and beliefs that people form cultures and develop a specific conduct of hospitality and act accordingly (Telfer, 1996; Lashley et al., 2007).

As the saying goes, "charity begins at home," therefore, as I was the guest, I adhered to the norms of different societies and, as a result, developed a certain bond with the host(s). In my opinion, those who visit different countries or different cultures are the ambassadors of their birth countries. This is one of the best opportunities and ways to make an impact on others. A good impression can help in developing respectable relationships, as in my experience in Australia, whereas a negative impression can spoil their image as well, as in my encounter in Minnesota, although "hospitality does not always imply reciprocity" (Ben Jelloun, 1999: 3). Above all, word of mouth is a vital element—it mostly delivers what people spread, the power of which is evident and is seen as credible. It is perceived as having passed through the unbiased filter of "people like me" (Allsop et al., 2007: 398).

While walking through Ilford, a large town in London, England, I came across a very nice temple that my family and I decided to visit without knowing anything about the visitation norms of the temple. After enquiring about visitation possibilities, we received a positive reply and were invited to have a tour of the temple and were told any assistance required would be provided. We were all bare headed and were asked politely to cover our heads as well as take off our shoes. We complied, keeping in mind to do in Rome as Romans do, and enjoyed the temple tour along with very nice hospitality—free food was served and the kids were given special sweets. We had an astonishing experience of altruistic hospitality—we are not Sikhs and had no idea about their religion. Nevertheless, as we showed interest and respect for their faith and belief, in return we received respect and recognition. That little incident made me think—sometimes just one little action can bridge and fill the gap between people and societies, as well as develop reciprocal hospitality. It can also encourage the reform of a society, welcoming all, irrespective of religious affiliation, gender, and race, and generating harmonious living (Telfer, 2000).

Talking about diverse ways of living, the use of the traditional knife and fork is not customary in all Asian countries. While I was traveling from Hong Kong to Bangkok, the food was served with the airline's modish cutlery and a few people were uncomfortable with the fork and knife combination. As the saying goes, "practice makes a man perfect"—these people, having had no practice were thus eating with apparent discomfort. The flabbergasting fact was that none of them had even asked for spoons. Nevertheless, I heard someone whisper in their local language, which, coincidently, was familiar to me that "It is YUK to eat with a knife and fork" (Suleri, 2008: 3). However, no one thought of simply asking for spoons and enjoying their meal and utter hospitality (Derrida, 1999). I understood it as more of a language barrier than the act of asking for a spoon. They might not have been aware of how to assertively ask for spoons. However, their non-assertive behavior was discomforting not only them, but also those sitting around them. As Ben Jelloun (1999) states, if guest and host are from different cultural backgrounds and language, it leads to confusion between how to extend and accept requests. After a while, I asked for a spoon for myself and, as we were sitting adjacently, I enquired whether anyone else needed spoons as well, to which they replied affirmatively and finally enjoyed their meal, and I was delighted in my unconditional amenity (Derrida and Dufourmantelle, 2000). My ulterior motive was to comfort them and the people sitting around them; Lashley (2015) describes this as altruistic hospitality.

As a matter of fact, habitually we have different standards, mainly when we deal with someone who does not belong to our culture or who speaks a different language, which shows a lack of knowledge about diversity and inclusion, whereas globalization and the emerging global workforce is the reality, and the benefits of diversity in an international market are well recognized (Allen *et al.*, 2008). In the twenty-first century, we need to be equally vigilant about 'I' and 'We' (Cashman, 2008). Our approach should be more inclined towards "Care for you and me" than "Care for me" only, as advocated by Cavagnaro and Curiel (2012). It requires more effort to come out of one's comfort zone or think out of the box. For instance, as a guest in Hong Kong, I had to think out of my comfort zone when I encountered the same kind of experience in a bar where the majority of people were Chinese. I am not familiar at all with the Chinese language but while enjoying myself and having fun, a Chinese guy, whom I had never met or seen before, came up to me and started talking to me in full flow. I tried to interrupt to tell him I had no clue what he was talking about, but to no avail. He kept going on and I showed all my patience by quietly listening. On the one hand, I had the same feeling as put forward by Derrida, "the unexpected surprise ... If I could anticipate, if I had a horizon of anticipation, if I could see what is coming or who is coming, there would be no coming" (2001b: 67). On the other hand, my contentment was that he was comfortable communicating with me. After a while, when he had finished with his catharsis, he departed by bowing his head, which is a polite gesture—leaving me with a great feeling that I had provided some effective service to him, which Lashley (2015) terms as redistributive hospitality. He got his desired service from me; as similarly described by Zeithaml and colleagues (2009) customers assess service performance on the basis of two boundaries: what they desire and what they consider acceptable. I have learned how effective listening can be in fulfilling a valuable psychological need in a lonely person. Telfer (1996) terms this 'Good-Samaritan hospitality'.

Ambiguity in hospitality

Envision a woman with long hair from the Indian sub-continent or Middle East arriving in the Netherlands visiting a new place where people already presume such women to be unintelligent, for the reason that they have an expression—"long hair small brains" (Suleri, 2008).

Presumptions do not involve an explicit rule—killing is usually not done in self-defense—instead they are an example of an implicit exception. Some presumptions are backed as being defined in statutes (source-based presumptions), whereas other presumptions are declared as such in precedents. Furthermore, presumptions are empirically probable and to an extent can be treated as a logical phenomenon (Prakken and Sartor, n.d.). Hence, damaging assumptions about fellow human beings in any society are not a sign of hospitality and will not replicate welcome feelings. On the other hand, this reflects a little hostility in hosting (Derrida, 2000). By spreading such ideas through media or otherwise, what is being done is an attempt to ghettoize people and create a big gulf among cultures. New entrants feel they are not receiving welcome feelings, nor are they getting the benefit of radical hospitality (Derrida and Dufourmantelle, 2000). On one hand, we are prompting diversity and inclusion globally, yet on the other, media coverage of such topics can create a hurdle for assimilation. Healthy and genuine hospitality requires accepting each other in spite of our differences; in the twenty-first century, diversity is becoming a must, and we are beginning to benefit from real synergy (Gerstandt, 2007). In short, it is not possible to give any statement about a person's intelligence simply by looking at them superficially. The length of one's hair is totally a personal matter, and if having long hair adds to the beauty of a person, then so be it. The best way to show our altruistic hospitality to fellow human beings is to allow them to be—as Mahatma Gandhi said, "The only way to live is to let others live."

Even when it comes to adopting children there are dubious and ambiguous political criteria regarding color, creed, and culture, which Lashley (2015) delineates as ulterior motives hospitality. For instance, in Washington I personally met white families with black adopted children, and found them to be happy and content. Washington, DC has been a relatively hospitable place for decades since it has a high rate of interracial marriage (Frey, 2003). Yet there is an example of a white woman who shared her story of adopting a black child. She was not pleased with the approach of the community workers and their ulterior motives. They had counseled her not to adopt a black child since it could bring cultural problems. There could be questions of differences of skin color that could lead to an identity crisis. In spite of the fact that people place more weight on negative information in making decisions (Weinberger and Dillon, 1980), the woman ignored their advice. Her caring, worrying, and affection clearly exhibited how much she loved her child regardless of skin color. I felt very proud to see such an affection and bond between a mother and child with different origins. Telfer rightly said, "Liking and affection are inherent in friendship—the liking produces a wish for the friends' company, the affection a desire to please them" (1996: 93). I found it preposterous that official agencies were playing such a negative role in child adoption instead of encouraging people and trying to solve the adoption problem worldwide. On the one hand, governments are promoting and striving for human rights and equal rights for gay people – allowing them to get married and adopt children – and, on the other hand, we are discouraging interracial mingling. In short, this ambiguity and duplicity is harming global growth as well as genuine hospitality among different cultures.

Researchers have carried out many studies about children's nature and behavior. Moreover, they have speculated on how surroundings affect the child. As a result, the upbringing of every child is important, from the first five to ten years, and adults must provide clarity and organization (Thompson, 2001). Hence, parents with adopted children need to be fully aware of this fact and the adoption of a child ought to be based on equality with much love and care meted out to the child, irrespective of color, creed, and culture, which Lashley (2015) outlines as altruistic hospitality and Derrida (1999) expresses as unconditional hospitality. Interracial adoption can be a corridor for genuine hospitality and can "open windows in the house of silence, indifference and fear" (Ben Jalloun, 1999: 39). One of my close acquaintances in the Netherlands has adopted three children from three different countries, and I have experienced their way of hospitality and hospitableness with me as open and welcoming. Their children share their feelings with them and make them aware of how society thinks about them. Hence, the parents are experiencing and seeing the other side of the coin—society's ambiguity and ulterior hospitality motives. Their varied origins help these children to recognize other societies and ways of being and they are sensitive to altruistic hospitality – being hospitable for its own sake.

We talk about globalization, genuine hospitality, and hospitableness, but if our authorities are not facilitating people with their basic rights, countries and cultures will not be able to grow unconditionally and produce altruistic hospitality. In fact, laws tend to be always conditioned and conditional when it comes to family and civil society (Derrida and Dufourmantelle, 2000). On another note, universities and colleges are endorsing exchange student programs to familiarize students with the other parts of the world. For instance, The George Washington University mission, in order to help the community, brings about transformation by attracting, retaining, and leveraging the talents of diverse individuals to facilitate first-rate teaching, learning, scholarship, and service in a way that is welcoming and inclusive (Thomas and Creary, 2009). It reveals that every individual in society counts and has the right to feel included. In conclusion, I would reiterate my example regarding the Dutch family with adopted children, where I was made to feel not only welcome but part of the family as well due to the parents' unconditional and genuine hospitality (Derrida, 1999; Lashley, 2015). There is no doubt in my mind that interracial adoption, marriages, and relationships are the future of the world, and key to promoting genuine harmony, hospitality, and hospitableness in our societies.

Conclusions

This chapter has attempted to identify a number of motives of hospitality that hosts offer to guests, ranging from ulterior to altruistic hospitality. Due to the progression of globalization, countries and cultures are becoming enhanced, leading to the development of the hospitality industry and making the world a better place (Sorman, 2008). Our globe is becoming enriched by economic development, democracy, cultural enrichment, political and cultural norms, information, and internationalization of the rule of law (Sorman, 2008). Hospitality to foreigners can be revealed worldwide and throughout human history (Meyer, 2008). Nonetheless, the credit for how it is forming into shape in the service industry goes to internationalization as well as the global workforce. Frequent traveling, information facilities, migration, and novel and innovative ideas are becoming part of various cultures, thus comparatively modifying the remaining cultural deadlocks and increasing respect for other cultures (Sorman, 2008).

It is evident that we are living among diverse societies and cultures, no matter where we live, be it New York, Sydney, Amsterdam, or Lahore (Norris and Inglehart, 2009). There is an urge to form a universal culture that will entail not only less diversity among us, but more inclusion as well. In short, innovation in societies is not possible without inclusion (Forbes, 2015). Nevertheless, just as every society has the right to keep its customs and values intact, equally, the other society's standards and values have a right to be accepted. Hence, respecting others' hospitality and showing your genuine hospitableness is the key to success in the emerging world of the global workforce. For that reason, in the twenty-first century, we don't need experiences such as that pronounced by Deutscher: 'his successive experiences as a young student in Paris were isolated and unhappy' (2005: 10).

In conclusion, we need a society where the stranger who is not even a member of the host's family still receives hospitality with a conviction and enjoys the qualities of hospitableness—a desire to please and meet the other's needs and a desire to make friends and help them in trouble (Telfer, 2000). Moreover, we need a society where hospitality consists of responding to psychological needs such as loneliness and the desire to be valued, and promotes altruistic hospitality (Telfer, 1996). In short, altruistic hospitality can transform aliens into acquaintances, foes into friends, and strangers into family (Selwyn, 2000).

References

Allen, R. S., Dawson, G., Wheatley, K. and White, C. S. (2008) Perceived diversity and organizational performance, *Employee Relations* 30, 1: 20–33.

Allsop, D. T., Bassett, B. R. and Hoskins, J. A. (2007) Word-of-mouth research: principles and application, *Journal of Advertising Research*, December. DOI: 2501/S0021849907070419.

Ballantyne, D. (2003) Relationship marketing: looking back, looking forward, *Marketing Theory* 3, 1: 159–166.

Ben Jelloun, T. (1999) *French Hospitality: Racism and North African Immigrants*, New York: Columbia University Press.

Brotherton, B. (1999) Towards a definitive view of the nature of hospitality and hospitality management, *International Journal of Contemporary Hospitality Management* 11: 165–173.

Cashman, K. (2008) *Leadership from the Inside Out*, San Francisco: Berrett-Koehler.

Cavagnaro, E. and Curiel, G. H. (2012) *The Three Levels of Sustainability*, Sheffield: Greenleaf.

Derrida, J. (1998) Hospitality, justice and responsibility: a dialogue with Jacques Derrida. In R. Kearney and M. Dooley (eds.) *Questioning Ethics: Contemporary Debates in Philosophy*, London: Routledge.

Derrida, J. (1999) Responsabilité et hospitalité. In M. Seffahi (ed.) *Manifeste pour l'hospitalité*, Paris: Paroles l'Aube.

Derrida, J. (2000) Hostipitality, *Angelaki: Journal of the Theoretical Humanities* 5, 3: 3–18.

Derrida, J. (2001) *On Cosmopolitanism and Forgiveness*, trans. Mark Dooley and Michael Hughes, New York: Routledge.

Derrida, J. and Dufourmantelle, A. (2000) *Of Hospitality: Anne Dufourmantelle Invites Jacques Derrida to Respond*, trans. R. Bowlby, Stanford: Stanford University Press.

Deutscher, P. (2005) *How to Read Derrida*, London: Granta Books.

Enders, J. (2004) Higher education, internationalization, and the nation-state: education to developing and transitional economies, *Higher Education* 47: 361–382.

Forbes, I. (2015) *Global Diversity and Inclusion Fostering Innovation through a Diverse Workforce*. Available at: http://images.forbes.com/forbesinsights/StudyPDFs/Innovation_Through_Diversity.pdf. Accessed 14 August 2015.

Frey, W. H. (2003) Untitled, *Milken Institute Review*, 3: 7–10. Available at http://www.frey-demographer.org/reports/Rainbownation.pdf. Accessed 24 February, 2015.

Gerstandt, J. (2007) A perspective: Diversity 2.0 – what we must become, *Diversity Factor* 15, 4: 36–40.

Ghamadi, J. A. (1999) Shaking hands with a woman. Available at http://www.javedahmadghamidi.com/renaissance/view/your-questions-answered88. Accessed 3 April 2015.

Gilmore, J. H. and Pine, B. J. (1997) Beyond goods and services: staging experiences and guiding transformations, *Strategy & Leadership* 25, 5: 10–17.

Hage, G. (2005) Nomadic hospitality and the gift of rest, conference abstracts, *Mobilising Hospitality: The Ethics of Social Relations in a Mobile World*, Lancaster: Lancaster University.

Hemmington, N. (2004) Concepts of hospitality—from service to experience. Proceedings I- CHRIE Conference, Philadelphia, July.

Holmes, J. G. (2000) Social relationships: The nature and function of relational schemas, *European Journal of Social Psychology* 30: 447–495.

Jordan, F. (2008) Internationalization in hospitality, leisure, sport and tourism higher education: a call for further reflexivity in curriculum development, *Journal of Hospitality, Leisure, Sport and Tourism Education* 7, 1: 93–103.

King, C. A. (1995) What is hospitality?, *International Journal of Hospitality Management* 14, 3/4: 219–234.

Lashley, C. (2000) Towards a theoretical understanding. In Lashley, C. and Morrison, A. (eds.) *In Search of Hospitality*, Oxford: Butterworth-Heinemann, pp. 1–17.

Lashley, C. (2008) Studying hospitality: insights from social sciences, *Scandinavian Journal of Hospitality and Tourism* 8: 69–84.

Lashley, C. (2015) Hospitality and hospitableness, *Research in Hospitality Management* 5, 1: 1–7. Available at http://www.stendenaihr.com/media/77/NL/algemeen/original/RiHM5.1.April%202015.pdf.

Lashley, C. and Morrison, A. (eds.) (2000). *In Search of Hospitality: Theoretical Perspectives and Debates*, Oxford: Butterworth-Heinemann.

Lashley, C., Lynch, P. and Morrison, A. (eds.) (2007) *Hospitality: A Social Lens*, Amsterdam: Elsevier.

Mazaqraat (2015) available at http://video.dunyanews.tv/index.php/en/pv/Mazaq%20Raat/9684/ep-13034/All/2015-04-27#.VUSvR-L8LDc. Accessed 1 May 2015.

Meyer, D. (2008) *Setting the Table: The Transforming Power of Hospitality in Business*, London: HarperCollins.

Molz, J. G. (2005) Cosmopolitans on the couch: mobilizing hospitality and the internet, conference abstracts, *Mobilizing Hospitality: The Ethics of Social Relations in a Mobile World*, Lancaster: Lancaster University.

Müller, C. (2004) Metaphors, dead and alive, sleeping and waking: a cognitive approach to metaphors in language use, Habilitationsschrift, Free University, Berlin.

Munar, A. M. (2007) Is the bologna process globalizing tourism education?, *Journal of Hospitality, Leisure, Sport and Tourism Education* 6, 2: 68–82.

Newton, I. (1686) Newton's laws of motions, Glenn Research center. Available at http://www.grc.nasa.gov/www/k-12/airplane/newton.html. Accessed 9 March 2015.

Norris, P. and Inglehart, R. (2009) *Cosmopolitan Communications Cultural Diversity in a Globalized World*, Cambridge: Cambridge University Press.

Norwood, G. (2014) Maslow's hierarchy of needs. The truth vectors (Part I). Available at http://www.deepermind.com/20maslow.htm. Accessed 2 March 2015.

O'Gorman, K. D. (2007) The hospitality phenomenon: philosophical enlightenment?, *International Journal of Culture, Tourism and Hospitality Research* 1: 189–202.

Ojibwe (2015) at http://en.wikipedia.org/wiki/Ojibwe. Accessed 27 April 2015.

O'Shaughnessy, W. E. (1873) Ode. Available at http://www.ballinagree.freeservers.com/ode.html, (accessed 21 February 2015).

Oxford English Dictionary (2015) at http://www.oxforddictionaries.com/definition/english/hospitality. Accessed 23 February 2015.

Prakken, H. and Sartor, G. (n.d.). Presumptions and burdens of proof. Available at http://www.umiacs.umd.edu/~horty/courses/readings/prakken-sartor-2006-presumptions.pdf. Accessed 6 March 2015.

Pritchard, M. (1981) *Guests and Hosts*, Oxford: Oxford University Press.

Ritzer, G. (2004) *The McDonaldization of Society*, rev. New Century edn, London: Sage.

Ritzer, G. (2007) Inhospitable hospitality? In Lashley, C., Morrison, A. and Lynch, P. (eds.) *Hospitality: A Social Lens*, Oxford: Elsevier, pp. 129–140.

Selwyn, T. (2000) An anthropology of hospitality. In Lashley, C. and Morrison, A. (eds.) *In Search of Hospitality: Theoretical Perspectives and Debates*, Oxford: Butterworth-Heinemann, pp. 134–156.

Sorman, G. (2008) *Index of Economic Freedom*. Available at http://www.heritage.org/index/pdf/2008/index2008_chapter3.pdf. Accessed 10 August 2015.

Stier, J. (2003) Internationalization, ethnic diversity and the acquisition of intercultural competencies, *Intercultural Education* 14, 1: 77–91.

Suleri, J. I. (2008) *Cultural Differences or Discrimination?*, New York and Bloomington: iUniverse.

Telfer, E. (1996) *Food for Thought: Philosophy of Food*, London: Routledge.

Telfer, E. (2000) The philosophy of hospitableness. In Lashley, C. and Morrison, A. (eds.) *In Search of Hospitality*, Oxford: Butterworth-Heinemann, pp. 255–275.

Thomas, D. A. and Creary, S. J. (2009) Meeting the diversity challenge at Washington University, Office of Diversity & Inclusion. Available at http://diversity.gwu.edu/vision-and-mission. Accessed 7 February 2015.

Thompson, R. A. (2001) Development in the first years of life, *Caring for Infants and Toddlers* 11, 1: 20–33.

Tribe, J. (2010) *Strategy for Tourism*, Oxford: Goodfellow.

Visser, M. (1991) *The Rituals of Dinner: The Origin, Evolution, Eccentricities and Meaning of Table Manners*, London: HarperCollins.

Weinberger, M. G. and Dillon, W. R. (1980) The effects of unfavorable product rating information, *Advances in Consumer Research* 7: 528–532.

Yang, R. (2004) Openness and reform as dynamics for development: a case study of internationalization at South China University of Technology, *Higher Education* 47, 4: 473–500.

Zeithaml, V. A. and Bitner, M. J. (2009) *Service Marketing: Integrating Customer Focus Across Customer Focus Across the Firm*, New York: McGraw-Hill Higher Education.

Zwarte piet (2015) at http://en.wikipedia.org/wiki/Zwarte_Piet. Accessed 3 April 2015.

27

Transcending the limits of hospitality

The case of Mount Athos and the offering of philoxenia

Prokopis Christou

Key themes

The origins of philoxenia

Philoxenia in the Orthodox world

Philoxenia at Ayion Oros (Mount Athos)

Identifying philoxenia

> From all those who offer hospitality to him, the stranger always remembers him, who with distinct love welcomed him.
>
> *(Homer, Odyssey)*

Skandrani and Kamoun (2014) argue that perceptions of hospitality may foster behavioural and affective loyalty and that cultural sensitivity is a critical skill that may help hospitality providers cope with guests' cultural differences. They argue that the hospitality conception seems to have a pentagonal structure revolving around personalisation, comfort, relationship of guest/host, hospitableness and warm welcoming dimensions. Lashley (2015) makes reference to the contemporary use of the word hospitality to describe a variety of sectors initially motivated by a public relations need to cloud over the commercial nature of enterprises (i.e. hotels). Even so, he argues that the nature of 'genuine hospitality' and the array of motives for offering hospitality should be at the heart of an understanding of the hospitality experiences and human resource aspects (i.e. recruitment and rewarding) which are the foundation of any competitive advantage. The sector needs also to consider some of the small firm providers (i.e. B&Bs) where the domestic and commercial aspects of hospitality and hospitableness overlap.

A decade ago, the same researcher offered a simplistic, yet noteworthy, three-domain model as a means of comprehending the broad concept of hospitality (Lashley, 2000). The model places the relationship between hosts and guests in the centre. The three inter-related domains consist of the socio-cultural, private and commercial domains. The socio-cultural domain covers the

DOI: 10.4324/9781315679938-30

various degrees of obligations of different societies to be hospitable towards the guest. These obligations, however, alter over time due to the increased interaction with guests and modernity. Lashley (2008) mentions that many industrialised societies no longer have strong (i.e. cultural) obligations to offer hospitality to strangers. The other domain (private) covers those obligations to be hospitable which are learnt by individuals in their home settings. This private/domestic hospitality may be seen by some as more genuine and authentic. Finally, the commercial domain is concerned with the industrialisation of hospitality and is influenced by the other two levels/domains, the social and the private. Even so, Lashley stresses the importance of those guests' emotions which are stimulated by the hospitableness involved in the host–guest transaction: 'By recognizing the core importance of the host–guest transaction and the emotional dimensions of the guest's experiences, it is possible to build a loyal customer base' (2008: 27). He essentially suggests a 'culture of hospitality' (Lashley, 2008: 21) whereby among others the stranger is treated as a guest and potential friend. Individuals, by being members of this 'culture of hospitality', have to practise qualities of hospitableness (e.g. friendliness, benevolence, compassion, the desire to please, entertain and help those in need).

Even so, Severt *et al.* (2008) make reference to a 'Hospitality Centric Philosophy' (HCP) which may be put into place by hospitality provision organisations. The researchers believe that an effectively managed HCP can be modified by culture to enhance the service excellence of the patient/guest experience in hospitals and the hospitality industry. The extreme context of a hospital where the importance of hospitality is magnified due to treating and caring for sick guests offers a different frame of reference which may lead to more cutting edge ideas for refining and customising the service design and delivery, for both hospitals and hospitality businesses.

Researchers have examined thoroughly the notion of 'hospitableness' and the extent to which this is an innate characteristic or something that can be nurtured and developed. O'Connor (2005) argues that only once an understanding of hospitality's origins and its place in human nature is achieved can one expect to discover what hospitality means today, and more importantly what it will mean to those entering the industry in the future. O'Gorman (2007) makes reference to a coherent philosophy of hospitality which seems to be an enigma; possibly because hospitality is not a matter of objective knowledge.In order to inform the emergent paradigm of hospitality studies there needs to be a continuing multidisciplinary study of hospitality; further inter- and intra-disciplinary research and investigation is required.

Lashley (2007a) agrees that the study of host and guest transactions extends beyond commercial hospitality management activities. A large number of human interactions, employee relations and the development of customer loyalty can be better understood through host and guest transactions. He suggests (Lashley, 2007b) that too much academic research appears managerial in focus and is weakened by the lack of critical ways of thinking about hospitality. The outcome of his research implies that commercial and educational hospitality practice would be better informed by both critical perspectives and reference to a number of social science and arts perspectives on hospitality.

'Philoxenia'– origins and its offering in the Orthodox world

> Philoxenia is a soul mood, it is the affectionate behavior for others. It is not taught with words; it is experienced instead.
>
> *F. Ramantanakis (2011)*

'Philoxenia', like other compound words that commence with *philos* (friend) such as philoptochos (friends of the poor), philadelphia (brotherly love) and philanthropy (friends of humans), is a Greek word composed of *philos* (friend) and *xenos*. The Greek noun *xenos* initially meant 'guest', acquiring the meaning of 'foreigner' at a later stage. The word apparently derives from *Xenos* (Greek: Ξένος), *Ksenos-Skenos* (Skini: Tent); the guest during his stay used to put up his tent in the fresco of the hosting house. *Xenia* in ancient Greece was divided into three stages:

1   The *xenos* entered the house of the host and in the name of Xenios Zeus, requested protection.
2   The owner offered presents (*xeniia*) to the *xeno*, food and a place to rest/sleep.
3   The *xenos* departed with exchange of gifts (i.e. linen and jewellery).

After the *xenia*, families were connected with 'xenian links' which were inherited by their descendants. In fact, they wrote their names, along with a passage, on piece of gold or silver and broke this into two. Each took a piece. This confirmed and renewed the friendship among the descendants. The power of 'xenian links' is evident in Homer's *Iliad*, when Deomidis and Glavkos were getting ready for a duel. Once they announced their family names it was revealed that they were related with 'xenian links'. They embraced each other, renewed their relations and exchanged their panoplies (Knossopolis, 2012).

Chronologically speaking, the concept and offering of philoxenia is evident from biblical times. The Old Testament makes reference to the proverbial story of Abraham and Sarah's generous 'Philoxenia of Abraham'. It is also apparent in the story of Lot, who was unaware that his two guests were angels and sheltered them from the Sodomites. He placed himself and his family at a risk, but he was rewarded with the exhortation to depart from the city which was about to be destroyed. In the New Testament, Christ calls:

> Come, you who are blessed by my Father, inherit the kingdom prepared for you from the foundation of the world. For I was hungry and you gave me food, I was thirsty and you gave me drink, I was a stranger and you welcomed me, I was naked and you clothed me, I was sick and you visited me, I was in prison and you came to me.
>
> *(Matthew 5:1–19)*

Likewise, the apostle Paul urged people not to neglect to show philoxenia to strangers (Hebrews 13:1). St Samson, a Roman descendant from a wealthy family who studied medicine, while he was living in Constantinople, cured the Emperor Justinian. In return, as a gesture of gratitude, the Emperor built for him a hospital which also acted as a hotel. There he hosted free of charge the poor and paupers. For this reason he was called *xenodoxos* (accepting/treating strangers) and he is still today regarded as the Patron Saint of those who work in the hospitality industry. He offered generously without expecting anything in return while people of his era used to say that 'his pockets had holes'. He welcomed everyone because he well knew that love knows no boundaries. He valued the bother and the drudgery for the love of people; a kind of love that is offered wholeheartedly without placing logic first. This approach challenges as well as seems to contradict Sigmund Freud's insistence that

> if I love someone, he must deserve it in some way … He deserves it if he is so like me in important ways that I can love myself in him; and he deserves it if he is so much more perfect than myself that I can love my ideal of my own self in him.
>
> *(1962: 56)*

Yet, his view was criticised as highly problematic 'since the human beings that disability studies is concerned with often cannot aspire to represent our culture's narcissistic ideals' (Brock and

Swinton, 2012: 297). In another case, a bishop visited an Orthodox monk who with great love offered philoxenia to him; the virtuous monk eventually apologised for having only bread and salt to offer, but the bishop being overwhelmed by his kindness, said: 'I wish when I return, to find not even salt'. St Makarios the Egyptian, equipped with love and sympathy, travelled 50 miles to Alexandria to find flour in order to prepare a soup for a sick monk (Ahdoni, 2013; Orthodox Synaxaristis, 2015). Great Basilios, known for his philanthropic actions, founded in the outskirts of Kaisareia town in Cappadocia a new city for the care of the poor and the orphans, the sick and the elders. The city was named Basiliada. Through not only his words, but also his actions, he stressed *philallilia*, love for others, over *philaftia*, love for one's self (Gregory the Theologist, 577CD; Mantzarides, 2005a).

However, philoxenia in the Orthodox world is not offered only by monks, Elders or Anchorites. For instance, St Xenophon and St Maria, a married couple who lived in Constantinople during the sixth century, offered philoxenia to all those in need or in difficult positions. In fact they used to actively seek out the deserted, sick and orphans. Prior to that, another couple, St Timothy and St Mavra, who actively practised philanthropy, were accused of attempting to proselytise Pagans. They were crucified and gave courage to each other while on their crosses for as long as nine days, until they died (Lekkou, 1992). In the twentieth century, touching is the word used to describe the actions and overwhelming emotions that Elder Gabriel exhibited towards his guests:

> Sometimes he stared [at] a (person's) face with *eyes which shined from love,* suddenly uplifting himself and exclaiming ... 'my dear, can I embrace you?' ... He counted all adults as children and treated them as if he was their mother. When he served tea or food he added more sugar, or over-floated the cup with cream, saying 'Ooop!' And continued: 'Eat for the love of God, my child'. With the same care Ft Gabriel behaved towards his visitors in all aspects. If they were cold in the hosting area, he sent blankets and bed covers, even his personal winter coats ... Such love is true that only from his own mother someone could receive ... Once he wanted to comfort one of his spiritual children who had recently lost his mother. He sent a letter which concluded: 'If it is hard for you to bear it, and if you can, come to me. I hope that here, you will feel motherly love ... Please forgive me for what I'm saying to you, but I'm not exaggerating. I think that's how it is, I am writing to you what I feel'.
>
> *(Kolmogkorof, 1998: 198–199)*

The offering of philoxenia is not necessarily associated with the provision of a bed to sleep in or food to consume. Neither is it restricted to the offering of shelter and other physical items; it also involves the offering of support, psychological comfort and spiritual advice, or guidance. Based on St John of Climacus and St Symeon the New Theologian, there are three qualities of a spiritual father/mother that are above all emphasised: counsellor, intercessor and burden-bearer. A charismatic Elder is in the first place a counsellor (*symvoulos*); he may give help through his silence, through being a good listener. But in most cases he will provide spiritual healing through his words, through his counsel or advice (Speake, 1990; Ware, 2000). St Antony of Egypt withdrew into the desert and enclosed himself in a ruined fort, with no idea at all of acting as a director and teacher of others. If he eventually became 'a physician given by God to Egypt' (Athanasius of Alexandria), it was because others took the path into the remote desert and implored him to act as their guide. The same is true of St Seraphim of Sarov (nineteenth century), known largely for his unique relationship with animals and palpable love for all people: 'Deep discussions of spiritual practices ... we feel his presence and receive a taste of that extraordinary peace, sweetness and joy for which he is known and loved by so many' (Moore, 2009: 38).

Under constant pressure, he began to receive visitors, at first listening to them in silence and praying for them. It was only towards the end of his life that he embarked fully on the apostolic ministry of the *Starets* (in Russian: старец) (Speake and Ware, 2015).

Today, a plethora of pilgrims and other visitors who travel to Mount Athos, or Ayion Oros, the spiritual heartland of the Orthodox world (Mantzarides, 2005b; Speake and Ware, 2015), are offered philoxenia (Cherouveim, 1996; Isaak 2004; Farasiotis, 2005).

Mount Athos (Ayion Oros)

Mount Athos is located in the third eastern peninsula of Halkidiki (northern Greece). It is the only place in Greece that is completely dedicated to prayer and the worship of God and for this reason it is called the 'Holy Mount' or in Greek, 'Ayion Oros'. The Holy Mount is about 50 km in length, around 10 km in width and it covers an area of about 350 km². The highest point of Mount Athos is like a huge cone, reaching 2,033 metres in height. The Holy Mount is a self-governed part of the Greek state, subject to the Ministry of Foreign Affairs in its political aspect and to the Ecumenical Patriarch of Constantinople in regard to its religious aspect. An Orthodox spiritual centre since 1054, Mount Athos has enjoyed an autonomous status since Byzantine times. The Holy Mount, which is forbidden to women and children, is also a recognised artistic site. The layout of the monasteries had an influence as far afield as Russia and its school of painting has influenced Orthodox art. Cloaked by chestnut and other types of Mediterranean forest, the steep slopes of Mount Athos are punctuated by twenty imposing monasteries and their subsidiary establishments. The subsidiary establishments include *sketae* (daughter houses of the monasteries), *kellia* and *kathismata* (living units operated by the monks), where farming constitutes part of the monks' everyday life. Certain criteria highlight the uniqueness of Mount Athos:

1   The transformation of a mountain into a sacred place made Mount Athos a unique artistic creation combining the natural beauty of the site with the expanded forms of architectural creation.
2   Mount Athos exerted lasting influence in the Orthodox world, of which it is the spiritual centre, on the development of religious architecture and monumental painting.
3   The monasteries of Athos present the typical layout of Orthodox monastic establishments (i.e. a fortification flanked by towers, which constitutes the *peribolos* of a consecrated place, in the centre of which the community's church stands alone).
4   The monastic ideal at Mount Athos has preserved traditional human habitations, which are representative of the agrarian cultures of the Mediterranean and have become vulnerable through the impact of change within contemporary society.
5   An Orthodox spiritual centre since the tenth century, the sacred mountain of Athos became the principal spiritual home of the Orthodox Church in 1054. It retained this prominent role even after the fall of Constantinople in 1453.
6   The harmonious interaction of traditional farming practices and forestry is linked to the stringent observance of monastic rules over the course of centuries, which has led to the excellent preservation of its Mediterranean flora.

Ayion Oros for Christians is regarded as the Garden of the Virgin, the priceless gift that Christ *gave* to his mother. The precise date of the first Christian establishments on Mount Athos is unknown. However, the monastic movement began to intensify in 963, when St Athanasius the Athonite founded the monastery of Great Lavra. Soon after, the first *Typikon* (agreement) was concluded at Karyes (capital) between the Emperor and the monks there. A self-governing region enjoying a special status, Ayion Oros includes twenty monasteries, twelve *sketae*, and about 700 houses, cells or hermitages. Over 1,000 monks live there in communities or alone, as well as in the desert of Karoulia where cells cling to the cliff face rising steeply above the sea.

Ayion Oros is the spiritual capital of the Orthodox world. All its permanent residents are monks. Even though it is located in Greece, it's not Greek, but pan-Orthodox. The majority of the monasteries are Greek speaking. There is a monastery for Russians, one for Serbians and one for Bulgarians. Besides monks from traditional Orthodox countries, others come from all over the world, such as from Western Europe, the USA, Australia and South America (i.e. Peru). In 1963, Ayion Oros celebrated its millennium, although there is evidence of monk communities being established there many years prior to that (Speake, 2005; Speake and Ware, 2014). According to Gothoni and Speake (2008), monks have been drawn to Mount Atho's forests, cliffs and caves in search of tranquillity and the inspiring teaching of charismatic elders since the ninth century. Today, the magnetism (for monks, pilgrims and visitors) has lost none of its force and despite threats to its environment and its unique way of life, Athos continues to operate as a spiritual powerhouse offering refreshment to all who turn to it. According to Ft Nikolaos:

> the naturalness of life, the authenticity of faith, the source of feelings, the transcendency of logic, the otherness of its expressions, make you feel close to it, different but relative, human but with divine prospects, small but comforted, with awe but acquainted. Next to it, you forgive, you believe, you hope. You live the divine experience, the eternity, the miracle, God's grace. Next to it you crave eternity … Next to it you live. At Ayion Oros you live the Holy Spirit. Even today.
>
> *(2000, synopsis)*

Mount Athos has been exercising its magnetic attraction on monks, pilgrims and other visitors for over 1,000 years while the Athonite pilgrim is not necessarily looking for a priest but rather a Sprit-bearer or Elder who can guide him to Christ. Even so, 'most pilgrims do not go to Athos to find the intellectual solution to theological problems but to participate, if only for a few days, in the liturgical life of the monastery' (Speake and Ware, 2015: 74).

Philoxenia at Ayion Oros

To enter Ayion Oros one must obtain a *diamonitirion* which is the official permit, or visa, that permits a pilgrim/visitor to enter Athos and to enjoy hospitality at the monasteries. Providing hospitality without a fee is one of the principal *raisons d'être* of the monastery (Speake, 2005) and visitors may even stay in Ayion Oros for months. 'I visited the Holy Mount and I was staying as a guest in a hut of a "Quieter", for several months' (Farasiotis, 2005: 303). However, it should be stressed that Ayion Oros cares for women as well as men. For instance, the Holy Convent of the Annunciation at Ormylia (outside Ayion Oros), which is a daughter house of the monastery of Simonopetra (in Ayion Oros), provides countless benefits to its visitors. Its community centre cares for both the physical and the spiritual needs of the local population and specialises in the early diagnosis of cancer in women while it too provides hospitality for numerous pilgrims (Speake, 2005).

Reaching a specific monastery, or a *skete*, at Ayion Oros may be a challenging task, yet visitors are willing to go through (in some cases) a lengthy or tiring journey, especially if they wish to visit a particular Elder. Farasiotis states: 'It took us three hours to get from Thessaloniki (town) to Ouranoupoli with public transportation. Upon our arrival we boarded the boat to proceed towards the Mount. We were sailing for one and a half hours' (2005: 46). In another case:

> Father Porfirios was staying in the Skete (organized community established by several monastic huts) Kafsokalivion. This Skete is one of the most remote of the Mount. It's located in a steep slope of Athos ... Around 30 little houses ... Life there is harsh. People there live with constraints. One can't have too many things ... A couple of days on the Mount were needed to get there ... My desire to see Elder Porfirios was so great ... that I decided to pay him a visit.
>
> *(Farasiotis, 2005: 305–306)*

Speake (2005), who experienced philoxenia in Ayion Oros, makes reference to his first spiritual Orthodox journey which was facilitated by the fathers of Vatopedi Monastery to whom (as he claims) he owes a 'great debt'. According to an article published in *Eleftherotypia*, the coenobitic (a monastic tradition that stresses community life) of Ayion Oros continues the tradition of the first Christian coenobitic life: 'What's important is that all visitors will feel immediately that they belong to the team, who is ready to serve them in whatever they want discreetly; and with love' (I epananstasi twn koinoviwn, 1993). Elder Isosif (Joseph) o Isihastis ('The Quieter') of Ayion Oros was characterised by his love towards God, with all his soul and heart, and towards his fellow-people. When others (monks) described to him a tragedy or someone's agony, he would cry (Iosif, 1983). His behaviour puts in action what one of the greatest ascetic writers of Orthodoxy, Abba (Desert Father) Isaak the Syrian accentuated in his maxim: 'rejoice with those that rejoice and weep with those that weep, because this is a feature of purity' (NH', 239 in Maxim of Abba Isaak, 2011: 99). Germane in this case are also the contradictory concepts of *philaftia* (love for one's self) and *philallilia* (love for others).

> *Philaftia* entraps a person to his Ego, whereas a *philallilos* is a person of love. Each person regards [it as] a normal thing to love himself. But the egocentric love of a person towards himself which *philaftia* is identified with, leads to antithesis towards the neighbor. So it clashes with *philallilia*. Likewise, from the other side, *philallilia* puts aside the individual interest and clashes with *philaftia*. And because a person finds it hard to put aside his individual interest, usually he sacrifices *philallilia* on the altar of *philaftia*.
>
> *(Mantzarides 2005a: 92)*

Great Basilios emphasises that a coenobitic (i.e. monastery) is not built with *philaftia*, but with *philallilia*. He adds that 'whoever loves his fellowman does not possess anything more than him. Cause if he does that, it means that he prefers his own wellbeing than the needs of others' (G. Basilios, quoted in Mantzarides, 2005a).

> I was impressed by the coenobitic organization of their lives. There was not at the monastery such thing as private ownership. Everything belonged to everyone – common ownership. Everyone was dining together with their Philoxenoumenous (guests who were offered philoxenia), the same food, on the same table.
>
> *(Farasiotis, 2005: 46–47)*

When Elder Paisios (who lived in Ayion Oros) used to go in the countryside to pray he 'always left the dining door open. If someone was passing from there, to find something to eat. There was bread, tins, tomatoes etc.' (Isaak, 2004: 133). In one of his letters, sent in

December 1971, he wrote:

> I have all the good intention to *philoxenw* (provide philoxenia to) you with all my gypsy philoxenia, in my hut, and to be yours not semi Paisios but complete. Whenever you want do not hesitate, (cause if I realize that you hesitate I will be sad). Only now in Winter, only one person can my hut host. Unfortunately my hut does not agree with my heart.
>
> *(Isaak, 2004: 208)*

Elder Paisios used to treat his guests with dry figs, hazelnuts, simple cuisine such as spaghetti or lentils and with sweet delights (Isaak, 2004). Poet and professor of literature Professor Cairns, in his spiritual journey to Mount Athos, stresses the philoxenia which he received. Among others he mentions: 'After the Divine Liturgy, I said my good-byes to *Ft* Zosimas, thanking him for his hospitality' (2007: 182). Speake (2005) also makes reference to a youngish monk who brought guests the traditional hospitality tray. Moreover, he mentions 'Upon our arrival we were received with traditional hospitality and shown to a room that contained 8 beds' (Speake, 2005: 66). Even so, philoxenia is not restricted to physical offerings (i.e. shelter, bed, food) and a tray of hospitality. It extends beyond a 'warm welcome', to the offering of unconditional and unrestricted love. This puts in action the words of the apostle Paul about love:

> Love is patient, love is kind. It does not envy, it does not boast, it is not proud. It does not dishonour others, it is not self-seeking, it is not easily angered, it keeps no record of wrongs. Love does not delight in evil but rejoices with the truth. It always protects, always trusts, always hopes, always perseveres.
>
> *(1 Corinthians 13: 4–8)*

Visitors were impressed by the 'rare kindheartedness' (Cherouveim, 1996: 65) which Elder Kallinikos o Isihastis ('The Quieter') showed towards people. Likewise, others highlight the love they experienced in more recent years:

> Father Paisios received me, he opened once more his arms for me and that was enough. He truly loved me, regardless of how I was ... healthy or sick, handsome or appalling, strong or weak, clever or irrational ... He always loved me ... under all circumstances ... What a relief!!! ... How comforting! ... What a joy!!! ... What else did I want?
>
> *(Farasiotis, 2005: 246)*

Philoxenia, in several cases, appears also to be accompanied by words of comfort, a burden-relief stance and spiritual advice or guidance when needed and asked for by guests. This thrusts philoxenia up to a spiritual height, while this rather mysterious element makes it hard to fully comprehend, measure and explicate: 'The hospitality, the prayers, all of these express something of this Mystery' (Speake, 2005: 79). Visitors may be led to a Father, or Elder, at certain monasteries, or *sketae*, to have spiritual conversations, or to seek guidance or search for a spiritual father. As Speake and Ware mention:

> few people are good judges of themselves. It is through our spiritual father that we learn to see our true self ... The (spiritual father) ... offers advice in the form of an open dialogue, and so he is to be regarded as a fellow-traveller or 'soul-friend' on the road to perfection.
>
> *(2015: 23)*

Elder Kallinikos o Isihastis ('the Quieter') received visitors and well-known people (i.e. doctors and professors) who turned to him for advice. Elder Isaak also received people at Ayion Oros who turned to him in times of sorrow and in need (Cherouveim, 1992). Abba Isaak states in this regard that 'If you want to sermonize someone towards good, firstly relieve him physically and honor him with a word full of love' (ΟΓ', 291, in Maxim of Abba Isaak, 2011: 116). Author Metropolitan Hierotheos, a frequent pilgrim to Mount Athos, stresses his 'particularly fruitful visit' with a hermit monk and gives a strong emphasis on the spiritual discussions he had with him (Vlachos, 2003). In 1988, a law student stated: 'I went (to Ayion Oros) more like for spiritual tourism, and also because I wanted to prove to Elder (Paisios) that there is no God and that he wrongfully wasted so many years as a monk'. He was impressed and touched by his 'sweet smile', delightful offerings and the spiritual conversations he had with him (Isaak 2004: 330). Ironically the atheist young man, six years after this 'spiritual meeting', became a monk. Obviously this does not imply that the motive of such charismatic Elders is to lead people to the monastic life. In fact, Fr Andreas (a priest serving a parish in the UK and Reader in Orthodox Christianity at the University of Winchester) makes reference to the monasteries in Athos which operate like a network of 'spiritual hospitals' (Speake and Ware, 2015):

> In a while, they (monks) appeared to carry a little old man (Elder Porfirios) who couldn't stand on his feet and seemed to be in great discomfort in each move ... I felt great joy being next to him ... He watered and fed me spiritually, and I was receiving with gratitude and joy ... Words were needless. The oxymoron was happening. The close to death old man, to donate life, biological and spiritual, to the 25 year old ... We exchanged a few sentences, yet had so much depth! 'I shall be praying for you and come and see me again', he said.
>
> *(Farasiotis, 2005: 305–306)*

Elder Sofronios (founder of St John the Baptist Monastery in Essex, UK), who also lived as a monk in Ayion Oros, was viewed as a spiritual father (by pilgrims and visitors) who did not wish to lead, but to fellow-travel:

> Open-minded and hearty towards everyone ... He respected his interlocutor whatever his position or age ... His respect towards human freedom was unlimited ... With great sympathy he viewed the fatiguing struggles and sacrifices of a person in his different levels of his life. He lived his (others') pains. He participated in his agonies. He suffered for his fails and dead-ends. He looked after with every means to relief the unfortunateness he saw around him.
>
> *(Mantzarides 2005b: 194)*

As a final note, it should be stressed that among other factors, visitors who enjoy philoxenia may pose a threat to the tranquillity of Ayion Oros. The words of Mantzarides acknowledge this: 'Besides, the number of pilgrims and visitors ... the many modes of transportation, communication, conservation and service provision of the particularly increased needs of the monasteries imply intense human presence, noise and distraction' (2005b: 187). Elder Paisios was against the construction of a large road passing through the whole peninsula on the basis that this would negatively affect the peacefulness of Mount Athos and alter its spiritual physiognomy. 'Don't they understand this? It's like, let's assume, in a way, to beat with an axe the backbone of Athonas. If this situation continues, then what will happen? Many will thresh with their cars the whole mountain for tourist reasons and some will be selling and soft drinks' (Isaak, 2004: 245).

Conclusions

Philoxenia can be traced back to biblical times, yet its significance is highlighted and offered up to today, such as in Ayion Oros – the spiritual heartland of the Orthodox world. Its features include, yet are not limited to, that it is offered without charge, with a kind of love that takes sincere forms (i.e. motherly, palpable) by people who offer it wholeheartedly without placing logic first. At times of philoxenia offering, rare kindheartedness is shown by people whose genuine emotions, behaviour, actions, physiognomy and physical stance betray honest intentions, sympathy and love in all circumstances. People who offer philoxenia may even do so by actively seeking to comfort others for the love of God and others – *philallilia* – by neglecting completely their personal interest, any *philaftia* motives and if deemed necessary, even in exchange for their own lives. Although offerings for physiological comfort are often provided in different forms (i.e. shelter and food), these may be kept to the bare minimum, while watering and feeding may also take a spiritual form (i.e. provided by a charismatic Elder), if the guest wishes to, in an open-dialogue and above all in a manner that respects human free speech.

Despite this, drawing graphical presentations and reaching conclusions as to what precisely philoxenia is can be a very challenging task, especially if it is accompanied by a spiritual element and a burden-relief host stance. This moves philoxenia up to a higher level beyond the basic features of hospitality, or even hospitableness. The unpretentiousness and humbleness of people who offer philoxenia and wish their actions to remain undisclosed, the fact that logic is jostled away by wholehearted love and the mystery element which it may carry, may partially explain the limited existing bibliography, the perplexed task of identifying possible links with other terms, and reaching conclusions in regards to its definition. Despite that, further investigations, such as examining the applicability of philoxenia in the tourism and hospitality field, may be thought-provoking and conceivably valuable, yet such research must not be taken lightly. Such investigations must be undertaken in an ethical, thoughtful, discreet and careful manner so that the researcher does not violate the humble yet noble, sincere, self-sacrificing and cherished to the extent of sacred notion of philoxenia.

References

Ahdoni (2013) *Ayios Sapson*. Available at http://ahdoni.blogspot.com/2013/06/blog-post_7450.html. Accessed June 2015.

Athanasius of Alexandria (1998) *Life of Antony*, trans. Caroline White, London: Penguin.

Brock, B. and Swinton, J. (2012) *Disability in the Christian Tradition: A Reader*, Grand Rapids, MI: Eerdmans.

Cairns, S. (2007) *Short Trip to the Edge: Where Earth meets Heaven – A Pilgrimage*, New York: HarperOne.

Cherouveim Archimandritou. (1992) *Isaak Dionysiatis*, 6th edn, Holy Moni of Paraklitou.

Cherouveim Archimandritou. (1996) *Kallinikos o Isihastis*, 7th edn, Oropos, Attica: Holy Moni of Paraklitou.

Farasiotis, D. (2005) *The Gurus, the Young and Elder Paisios*, 7th edn, Thessaloniki.

Freud, S. (1962) *Civilization and Its Discontents*, trans. James Strachey, New York: W. W. Norton.

Gothoni, R. and Speake, G. (2008) *The Monastic Magnet: Roads to and from Mount Athos*, Oxford: Peter Lang.

Great Basilios, *Pros Ploutountas* 1, p. 31, 281B.

I epanastasi twn koinoviwn (1993) *Eleftherotypia*, August.

Iosif (Monaxou) (1983) *Elder Iosif o Isihastis, Ayion Oros*, Thessaloniki: Panayias.

Isaak (2004) *Life of Elder Paisiou the Ayioritou*, Ayion Oros.

Knossopolis (2012) Xenos-Xenia. Available at http://knossopolis.com. Accessed June 2015.

Kolmogkorof, St Symeon (1998) *Elder Gabriel the Anchorite*, Attica, Athens: Botsis.

Lashley, C. (2000) Towards a theoretical understanding. In Lashley, C. and Morrison, A. (eds), *In Search of Hospitality: Theoretical Perspectives and Debates*, Oxford: Butterworth-Heinemann, pp. 1–17.

Lashley, C. (2007a) Studying hospitality: beyond the envelope, *International Journal of Culture, Tourism and Hospitality Research* 1, 3: 185–188.

Lashley, C. (2007b) Discovering hospitality: observations from recent research, *International Journal of Culture, Tourism and Hospitality Research* 1, 3: 214–226.

Lashley, C. (2008) Marketing hospitality and tourism experiences. In Oh, H. (ed.) *Handbook of Hospitality Marketing Management*, Oxford: Butterworth-Heinemann, pp. 3–31.

Lashley, C. (2015) Hospitality experience: an introduction to hospitality management, *Journal of Tourism Futures* 1, 2: 160–161.

Lekkou, E. (1992) *Holy Married Couples in the Church's Life*, Thessalonika: Saitis.

Mantzarides, G. I. (2005a) Social theory and act according to Great Basilios. In *Odoiporiko of Theological Anthropology*, Holy Great Monastery of Vatopedi, Ayion Oros.

Mantzarides, G. I. (2005b) *Odoiporiko of Theological Anthropology*, Holy Great Monastery of Vatopedi, Ayion Oros.

Maxim of Abba Isaak the Syrian (2011) *Enomeni Romiosini*, Thessaloniki.

Moore, L., Archimandrite (2009) *An Extraordinary Peace: St Seraphim, Flame of Sarov*, Port Townsend, WA: Anaphora Press.

Nikolaos Metropolitan Mesogaias and Lavreotikis (2000) *Ayion Oros – The Highest Point on Earth*, Athens: Kastanioti.

O'Connor, D. (2005) Towards a new interpretation of 'hospitality', *International Journal of Contemporary Hospitality Management* 17, 3: 267–271.

O'Gorman, K. D. (2007) The hospitality phenomenon: philosophical enlightenment?, *International Journal of Culture, Tourism and Hospitality Research* 1, 3: 189–202.

Orthodox Synaxaristis (2015) available at www.saint.gr. Accessed June 2015.

Ramantanakis, C. (2011) *Philoxenia*. Available at www.paravouniotissa.gr. Accessed May 2015.

Severt, D., Aiello, T., Elswick, S. and Cyr, C. (2008) Hospitality in hospitals?, *International Journal of Contemporary Hospitality Management* 20, 6: 664–678.

Skandrani, H. and Kamoun, M. (2014) Hospitality meanings and consequences among hotels employees and guests. In Woodside, Arch and Kozak, Metin (eds) *Tourists' Perceptions and Assessments*, Advances in Culture, Tourism and Hospitality Research 8, Bingley: Emerald, pp. 147–156.

Speake, G. (1990) The Spiritual Father in Saint John Climacus and Saint Symeon the New Theologian. In Hausherr, Irenee, *Spiritual Direction in the Early Christian East*, Cistercian Studies Series 116, Kalamazoo, MI: Cistercian Publications.

Speake, G. (2005) *Mount Athos, Renewal in Paradise*, New Haven: Yale University Press.

Speake, G. and Ware, K. (2014) *Mount Athos: Microcosm of the Christian East*, Oxford: Peter Lang.

Speake, G. and Ware, K. (2015) *Spiritual Direction on Mount Athos*, Oxford and Bern: Peter Lang.

Vlachos, H. Metropolitan of Nafpaktos (2003) *A Night in the Desert of the Holy Mountain: Discussion with a Hermit on the Jesus Prayer*, Greece.

Ware, K. (2000) *The Spiritual Guide in Orthodox Christianity, The Inner Kingdom*, Crestwood, NY: St Vladimir's Seminary Press.

28

Fifty shades of hospitality

Exploring intimacies in Korean love motels

Desmond Wee and Ko Koens

> **Key themes**
>
> Sex and South Korea
> The city and sex
> Mapping public space
> Intimate spaces

People are born hosts or born guests.

(Max Beerbohm)

The relationship between the hospitality industry and intimate encounters is highly complex, comprising many shades of hospitality formed across dynamic intersections of space, time, and culture. Within the social imagination of the West, the two are often placed in a context brimming with clandestine encounters in seedy environs. Indeed, hotels have been described as ideally suited for "transgressive behaviours and illicit sex," while references to brothels and disreputable parts of the city seem to accompany the writing on the subject (Pritchard and Morgan, 2006: 763). Pritchard and Morgan (2006) explore the notion of the hotel as a liminal, complex, and culturally contested place where dominant discourses of space are resisted, contested, and affirmed. But what would this mean in the East? How does this relate to the neo-liberal economies of the West in South Korea and particularly Seoul? Or has the capital(ist) city overshadowed normative ideas of what it means to be "Western"?

Research done on Asian hospitalities has revealed how, in these areas, the connotation between intimacy and hospitality needs to be considered using different approaches. For example, research across "love motels" in Japan and Taiwan has revealed how these are used predominantly by couples for personal consumption and that the sexual association is almost coincidental (Chaplin, 2007; Alexander *et al.*, 2010; Chang *et al.*, 2012). This seems to defy Western delimitations of the relationships between public, private, and commercial urban spaces alongside hospitality and

DOI: 10.4324/9781315679938-31

intimate sexual encounters. In other words, what are known as the "love motels" of South Korea in Western discourse are really "motels" (모텔, pronounced literally mo-tel) for South Koreans without the need for explication and the negative connotations that may exist in Western discourse. However, there still appears to be some trepidation towards initiating further academic dialogue in this field with the number of publications on the subject remaining limited.

In this chapter, we further the conceptualization of love motels by focusing on the Korean motel (모텔). We consider questions of the intimate practices of young people and the discursive role of the motel within public, private, and commercial spaces in a wider city hospitality context within the city of Seoul. The chapter does not claim to be a substantive, all-encompassing research of informal encounters in Korean motels. Instead, it provides an exploration of the liminal edges of hospitality in South Korea, which are really not so shady, but replete with shades of everyday life. We hope this research will spur on other researchers to undertake a more global perspective when conceptualizing hospitality and that it will help address the critique that tourism and hospitality research remains too focused on Western discourses (Rogerson and Visser, 2012). To achieve this, we will provide exploratory research based on secondary sources comprising Internet discourses and literature research, and primary interviews involving spatial mapping to further the conceptualization of how discursive ideas of Korean motel spaces are constructed in the light of everyday intimacies. In order to gain a better perspective, we start with the highly useful notion of the three conflating domains of hospitality as postulated by Lashley:

> The *social domain* of hospitality considers the social settings in which hospitality and acts of hospitableness take place together with the impacts of social forces on the production and consumption of food/drink/and accommodation. The *private domain* considers the range of issues associated with both the provision of the "trinity" in the home as well as considering the impact of host and guest relationships. The *commercial domain* concerns the provision of hospitality as an economic activity and includes both private and public sector activities.
>
> *(2011: 5)*

To explore how we can further extrapolate this notion to increase understanding of motel spaces in South Korea, we pose a critical framework as follows (in the same order as above):

1 *Where (in the city) does hospitality take place?* Can hospitality happen in the bedroom?
2 If we consider hospitality as an instrumentation of the host–guest relationship, we need to ask: *Who is the host?*
3. How are spaces (public, private and liminal) conceived and reproduced in terms of discursive flows?

How are spaces (public, private and liminal) conceived and reproduced in terms of the discursive flows of consumption? City and the sex in a changing South Korea

The exploration of the modern city as part of an emergent socio-spatial process has been the focus of critical enquiry in the last decades (Gottdiener, 1985; Lefebvre, 1991; Zukin, 1995; Soja, 1996). At the same time, the subject has developed in social theory and society at large (Turner, 1984; Featherstone *et al.*, 1991; Shilling, 1993; Rodaway, 1994). This chapter strives to link these two foundational aspects and to follow on from the comprehensive work of Phil Hubbard (2012) to understand how the city creates intimate spaces for sexual practice and provides a stage for performances that shape our sexual lives. Mort and Nead (1999: 7) emphasize the need to explore urban spaces within the city and its connection to the distribution, regulation, habitation, and negotiation of the sexual subject. It becomes evident that "[s]pace and place work together in the formation of sexual space, inspiring and circumscribing the range of possible erotic forms and practices within a given setting" (Green *et al.*, 2008: 15). It is within these dynamic spaces that material features of the city thrive in ways that stimulate the desire for intimate encounters (Brown, 2008; Hubbard, 2012; Johnston, 2012). Hence the manner in which we see, feel, taste, smell, and hear all contribute to how the city is sensualized.

Latham's conception of urban space as part of a greater "socio-cultural project" (2003) is particularly useful here to understand the commingling of particular spaces of hospitality and the types of social practices that are enabled in the urban landscape. Hospitality can be understood then as a development of human relations in the city and the intersections between what public, private, and commercial spaces entail. The "hospitable city" (Lashley *et al.*, 2007; O'Gorman, 2010; Lashley and Morrison, 2011) latches on to a dynamic understanding of hospitality that

> accommodates the complex fabric of relationships which constitute the modern urban environment, with its variety of groups, work activities and laws, among many other aspects of modern life, like the anonymity, the individualism and the fluidity of transactions and categorizations fostered by the industrial society.
>
> *(van den Broek Chávez* et al., *2012: 1)*

Hence, hospitality exists as a social phenomenon that incorporates the everyday expectations of host–guest relations and their multimodal networks across various stakeholders across the city. In similar fashion, the hospitality of a city towards certain behaviors is created in an iterative process between its different users and city planners. As argued by Bell, cities provide space for transactions across both day and night, meaning that city planners need to "create opportunities for these variegated transactions to take place" (2007: 18).

The reign and dictatorship of Park Chung-Hee as President of South Korea marked the period of late-industrialization characterized by the need for sacrifice and hard work under an iron grip from the 1960s to the 1980s. Despite his death in 1979, the "Miracle of the Han River" continued with unprecedented economic growth (Amsden, 1992). It is not surprising that with this boom the nation also witnessed an increase in the leisure, entertainment, and hospitality industry. "Indeed, south Korea was judged a miracle of rapid economic development, marked in the 1980s by the nation's entry into the ranks of the Newly Developed Nations and celebrated in its hosting of the 1988 Olympics" (Kendall, 2002: 3). To highlight the development of the hospitality industry in Seoul in the 1980s, "[w]hile there were 713 pleasure resorts in 1983, there were 1,211 by 1986. In the same period the number of hotels increased from 658 to 853, and massage parlours from 57 to 122" (Cotton and van Leest, 1996: 191). During this period, sexual promiscuity on film was first evidenced, and 애마부인 (*Aema Puin*), released in 1982, became the first Korean X-rated film. It comes as no surprise that the 1990s epitomized "a loosening of censorship and social control, and with global economic success, the emergence of a full-blown consumer culture" (Kendall, 2002: 3). These societal trends impacted on city spatial culture and led to a strong rise of the "motel":

> The notion of escape (from the city and from the responsibilities associated with work and family) came to be a motivating force behind the emergence of love motels in South Korea throughout the 1980s and 1990s. That period of increased commerce, consumption, and democratic freedoms – following decades of political turmoil and authoritarian rule … has

been characterized as a "golf boom" by economic analysts who see the nation's burgeoning middle-class aspirations as a kind of consumer-driven corrective to preexisting social problems.

(Diffrient 2009: 302)

Diffrient defines the love motel as

a polymorphous space signifying the physical entanglements and spiritual bankruptcies behind South Korea's modernization drive. Reserved for liaison between the sexes, the ubiquitous love motel is where upwardly mobile men and downhearted women enact gender-coded rituals in a space that is marginal yet central to the understanding of sexual mores in a patriarchal society.

(2009: 299)

The motel is not known as a brothel or as part of the sex industry where prostitutes are provided. Rather, sex itself as an activity is generally not commercialized and a part of the process of courtship and desires. Like their counterparts in Taiwan and Japan, motels in South Korea are more about non-commercial intimacies in commercial contexts. What became apparent while investigating motels in South Korea was, on one hand, the thriving embodied economies of what we understand by the so-called Western imagination and, on the other, the ubiquity of such places evident though a vibrant materiality. Equally, and more importantly, the symbolic status of motels appears to be an inherent part of the everyday, hence the lack of the redundant adjective "love" in the Korean understanding of the motel.

An Internet search for "Korea" and "Motel" reveals not only sexually explicit films and video reviews of motels, but also, more interesting for this chapter, self-made videos documenting traveller stay in Korean "love" motels. The videos describe the conditions of stay and most of them feature the Western traveller's perspectives of a stay in a Korean motel. They present a rough idea of what the motel room looks like, as well as the amenities the room comes with, including a flat-screen TV, computer, fridge containing beverages, toiletries including toothpaste and condoms, and food menus with various delivery options (see Good Morrows, 2012; ROK On!, 2012; Miller, 2013; Whyte, 2015). There are also renowned, fancy motels in Seoul that "feature swimming pools, karaoke machines, barbecue grills and decor so garish it's awesome" (Kim, 2011).

One particularly relevant video on YouTube, *Korean Love Motels and Dating* (UUtvProductions, 2015), promotes itself through the caption that it

takes a closer look at the Love Motels in South Korea. Young couples in South Korea have a unique outlet to spend time at while on a date. Because of the current social and economic culture, it is hard for young couples to find private time.

One of the most interesting things about this caption is the fact that the authors at UUtv chose to prioritize "time" as opposed to "space," although one is technically buying time in a space. Clarification of this perspective is provided in the first lines of the clip, as the presenter introduces the concept of Korean motels to an audience unfamiliar with their existence:

One of the things I am going to focus on here is the motel. It's not like any motel, they're a love motel. In America, that kind of brings ideas of nasty, dirty, dingy motels where you get a hooker for an hour and you go inside. It's really not like that, it's kind of out in the open where, couples kind of get the place for a couple of hours and they do what they do, because they can't do it where they want to do it.

What the presenter is alluding to is the commercialization of the motel as a space for intimacy, juxtaposed with the stigmatization of an outward demonstration of affection and the lack of access to privacy. The economic success of South Korea as evidenced earlier and the rapid commercialization of the city seem to have displaced the personal space of individuals. As such, it can be argued that for young Korean couples, time and space are variants of the same thing. Having private time largely depends on finding a private space, which cannot be taken for granted in a country where young adults tend to live either with their parents or in shared housing. Yet in contemporary Korea, especially in the pulsating capital Seoul, the motel becomes a place where privacies are guaranteed (Lee, 2012). This reconceptualization of the way public/private space is set against public/private time may help to provide an understanding of different perceptions of commercial hospitality outlets as places of intimacy against dominant Western discourse. It would seem that this intimate *space* (or personal space with another) and *time* within the enclosure of the place needs to be purchased, albeit at an affordable price. Hence these motels begin to encapsulate patterns of urban living and form an intricate part of the city hospitality of Seoul, especially in a context of urban regeneration, not too dissimilar from those described in a Western context (Bell, 2007).

Unlike the other videos of self-styled Western travellers, the host of UUtv, probably of Korean origin and with adept Korean and English language skills, interviews the owner of one of the motels about the price of the rooms. The operator signifies that there are two different price brackets: $20 for three hours or $50 for the day. When asked what type of customer gets a room for three hours, the operator answers:

> Customers on a date. When on a date, motel rooms provide a total experience. They are economical and private. You get free movies and drinks. We provide computers too. We provide everything.

The provision of "everything" suggests an all-encompassing hospitality experience. Indeed, the motel provides a broth of private space, negotiated time, and total experience. The host here is not so much just a person simply running the motel, but the personification of a silent provider who takes care of whatever is required for a home-like hospitality. The notion of privacy must also assume that the host should be as invisible as possible. A different motel operator in another interview with UUtv (2015) said, "Motel rooms provide privacy. ["NO ID REQUIRED" and "TOTAL PRIVACY" were imprinted onto the screen as part of the backdrop]. We can't see you and you don't see us." This very strong statement alluding to the gaze, its blockage and sense of empowerment at the same time needs to be reconsidered especially in terms of how (in)visibilities actually constitute a transformation of the traditional host, towards one that excludes herself from the hospitality experience. Instead, hospitality is personified within and through dynamic and embodied spaces where the host is no longer visible as a person.

In the film *Fifty Shades of Grey*, directed by Sam Taylor-Johnson (2015) based on E. L. James's book of the same name (2012), Christian Grey invites Anastasia Steele to his "Playroom":

> Christian Grey: "Come, it's just behind this door"
>
> Anastasia Steele: "What is?"
>
> Christian Grey "My Playroom"
>
> Anastasia Steele: "Like your Xbox and stuff?"

Christian's "Playroom" provoked an "Oh my God" response from Anastasia upon the shock of seeing its contents. She realized it was not Nintendo she was about to be playing with. The motel, in contrast, does just the opposite: it claims to provide the "Xbox and stuff" lock, stock, and barrel, stuff that one would be comfortable seeing, to the point of being familiar with. Somewhere in the room are the usual household objects right down to toothpaste and tooth-brushes that will resolve any oral fixation.

On opening the door and entering the motel room, one is confronted with a secret place, yet this place is built around a familiarity that appears to cultivate a sense of homeliness. In Whyte's video clip (2015), he showcased a menu in his room in which one could order take-out. Note that the suppliers of this food are not the people who run the motel, but a collection of hole-in-the-wall restaurants operating within the vicinity of the motel. Again, a very homely hospitality experience is interspersed with references to privacy and anonymity. The menus are usually exhaustive and, upon a phone call, a full meal with separate dishes, soups or even steaks will be delivered to the door in minutes. In this way, the motel provides a very comprehensive, individualized, and anonymous hospitality experience, without obligations towards the host. There is a shared understanding between owner and host that the hospitability in these encoun-ters stems from interaction between guests themselves, with the host merely facilitating this by providing hospitality and taking away all barriers that may inhibit interaction (see Lugosi, 2008).

Lee (2012) considers the motel as a place where one can freely express three basic human desires, which are accommodation (宿), food (食), and sex (性). So for three hours (or the more expensive overnight option), what potentially takes place are the elemental needs of Maslow's triangle, the complete household or the everyday routine comprising sleep, sex, food, drink, excretion, all sorted in the space of a "homely" motel room. In a way, these motels act as "liminoid" spaces where participants temporarily become detached from social structures or institutions and enjoy moments of "blissful togetherness" (Lugosi, 2007: 167).

Mapping public spaces around motels

To better appreciate the intricacies of the Korean motel, the relations between public openness regarding motels in society, and the personal emphasis on privacy in these motels, we inter-viewed six Korean university students (five females and one male) on exchange semesters. More specifically, we collated hand drawn mental maps, given that these are useful to tell a story and create mental images of space, and how spaces are consumed in the larger scheme of things, as demonstrated by Lynch:

> In the process of way-finding, the strategic link is the environmental image, the generalized mental picture of the exterior physical world that is held by an individual. The image is the product both of immediate sensation and of the memory of past experience, and it is used to interpret information and to guide action. The need to recognize and pattern our sur-roundings is so crucial, and has such long roots in the past, that this image has wide practical and emotional importance to the individual.
>
> *(1960: 4)*

We were careful to approach the subject of "motels" in an indirect way, without the risk of embarrassing or offending the interviewee. This led us to ask for their mental maps based on familiar habitation rather than how they would get from point A to point B. We asked them to map out an area in which they recalled being at where they have walked past motels.

"On the way" to actually drawing the map, we conducted an unstructured interview asking what they thought about the idea of "motels" and their wider perception of the motel phenomena in Korea.

To start with, it is important to signify the abundance of motels, at least in certain parts of the city of Seoul. To give an example, Figure 28.1 illustrates a relatively small area near Seoul National University, Sillim-Dong, which is a 대학로 (Daehak-ro) or "university street" renowned as a motel hot-spot. The motels are situated in an area together with food and convenience stores, providing an overarching hospitality experience.

Even while there are many motels around Sillim-Dong, one thing that surfaced repeatedly was how motels are a part of the "back stage" of the city. This was exemplified in the map arising from interview Y3 (Figure 28.2) that consisted of another "Daehak-ro." In essence, this drawing represents the perimeter of a generic "city," located beside a large university, with outlets providing food, accommodation, and entertainment.

What is obvious from Figure 28.2 is the location of motels in the "narrow" backstreets and surrounded in the peripheral by restaurants, cafés, and pubs. The next tier, comprising restaurants and cinemas, mostly retail, follows the shops closest to the main street. The first parallel street is marked by drink havens (pubs such as Hofs), DVD-Bangs (where one watches videos with cheap make-out possibilities), and Norebangs (Karaoke bars). Motels usually appear on the second parallel street. They are thus "out of sight" yet in close proximity to other facilities and

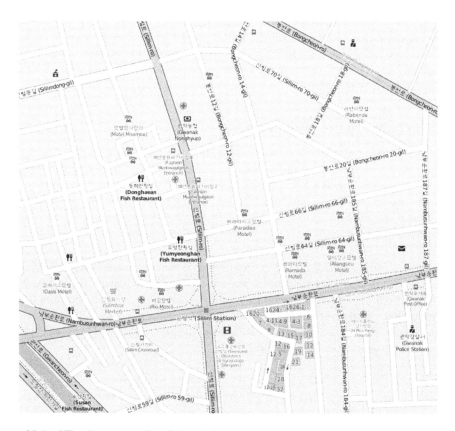

Figure 28.1   Sillim-Dong area, Seoul, South Korea

Source: OpenStreetMap.org.

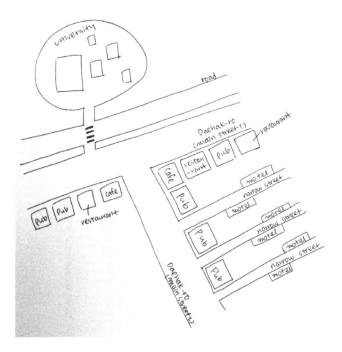

Figure 28.2 Motels in the city as drawn by interviewee Y3

transport options. Interviewee Y5, who drew a similar map, first charted the subway stations ("S") on the main street before she penned in the other establishments. This points towards the importance of easy access to the motels. Similarly, interviewee Y6 emphasized the importance of specific motel parking lots. In keeping with the private nature of motels, their parking facilities are always built underground and away from public view.

The map provided by interviewee Y4 (Figure 28.3) focused on yet another "University Street" and places the motels in relation to its wider neighborhood, including supporting pubs (Hof), restaurants (Chicken, Galbi), cafés (Angel in Us), and Sulzip (literally "drinking place"), which is also a kind of pub.

Interview Y4 noted down "hunting" (헌팅) at the "Sulzip" (술집) in her schema, which represents a kind of courtship in which all-male/all-female groups enter a premises and hopefully move on as one group of friends to the next destination. Before entry into the Hunting Sulzip, the bouncer will ask the "female" group if they would like to "participate" (or not). The concept of "hunting" (referring to the pick-up along the beach or the street) has always been around discursively, but what was most interesting was the reiteration and facilitation of this "new" phenomenon of hunting in drinking holes (within the last four years) as an organized process. This again points to the complex relationship between the widespread acceptance and public knowledge regarding sexual relations and the need for privacy within these Korean sub-cultures. The public practices that take place in the "hunting" process require the close proximity of motels and the privacy they bring to enable young men and women to further their amorous practices.

Motels were also described using the concept of 대실 (Dae-shil) meaning "Borrow-room" by interviewee Y8, implying a short-term hourly lease (usually three hours). An interesting underlying implication in this interview is that visitation primarily happens during the daytime.

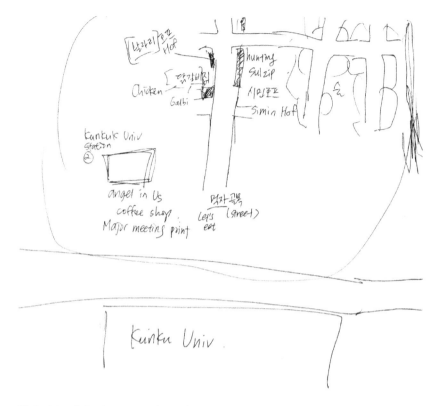

Figure 28.3   Motels in the city as drawn by interviewee Y4

One of the ways to invite someone to a motel is "Is it cold/hot outside?" or "Would you like to 'borrow-a-room' and stay in?" Interviewee Y5 also discussed the "resting" idea (Dae-shil) versus spending the full night at the motel. In her opinion, most people take the "resting" option as it is a lot cheaper. In terms of payment for the motel, she said that it is usually the male who pays, and when asked if the male usually pays for everything else, she provided the following typology, "he gets movie, she gets popcorn and cola, he gets dinner, she gets coffee."

In talking about the motel as a naturalized experience, interviewee Y4 discussed the kinds of relationships that are in place to consume the motel:

1   Boyfriend–girlfriend
2   One-night stand (which might or might not culminate into 1)
3   Affairs (understandably for "older" people around 40 years of age)

Whereas previous generations had predominantly sexual connotations of motels in general, university students see the existence of the motel in Korean society as a diverse and complex place rather than one with sexual, immoral, and pleasure-seeking connotations. In a way, the motels provide a very transparent hospitality experience, in that it is clear what the host offers (privacy and homeliness) and requires (financial remuneration). However, the way the guests make use of this space differs. Hence, the motel could be a "private place for couples and at the same time it can be a public space where group of students go to motel to study" (Y4). The motel could also be "a cultural place where people throw a party and practical place to spend the day with cheap prices" (Y4). She added that "The meaning and value of motel is not settled or defined yet among these generations. It is depending on what they do in the space and the boundary of it is very vague" (Y4).

Indeed, interviewee Y8 emphasizes the visitation of motels as a common activity among students. She estimated that more than 60 percent of her friends had been to a motel, the reason being that there was "no way to home" since most of her friends lived with their parents. Those who did not were usually housed in dormitory-style apartments near the university with a security guard at the front gates and a warden located within each building. The exclusive few who did actually have their own apartments might still end up at a motel because "Facilities good, mood different, atmosphere, facilities neat, better than what people think" (Y8). Interviewee Y5 was quite vocal about how motels have the "perks to make boy and girl together … designing that makes them come out of the idea." This suggests that motels are spaces that "do more than reduce hospitality to monetary exchange. They produce forms of hospitality and hospitableness between hosts and guests, and between guests and guests, that are not confined solely to the economic" (Bell, 2007: 19). Instead they provide students with liminal spaces to share a host–guest experience in a semi-homely setting.

Similarly to their physical spatial presence especially in a social context, motels are an important aspect within everyday life, albeit always existing within the emotional backstage. Details are to be shared only with an intimate few, while, in daily social life, experiences with motels are hidden behind a façade of normality. This was particularly discussed by interviewee Y3, who highlighted how motels were not talked about explicitly, but were always there for a purpose. Such was the discretion of this place that, "if you talk about this, it is usually with close friends." Consequently, the more the topic is talked about between friends, the closer friends they become, given that sharing knowledge regarding motels requires trust. The role of "hunting" as courtship and consummation in motels seems to rest on a private backstage, yet this experience needs to be shared in order to foster a different social order and cultivate a kind of collective privacy. Interviewee Y5 spoke of someone whom she knew who dated for two years without having been to a motel. She emphasized that the stereotype among students is such that the fact that they have not been to a motel means that "nothing ever happened between them." This seems rather contradictory, the "bad impression" of those being seen visiting motels, especially since some people "cannot have relationship before marriage" put against the stigmatization of not consummating a relationship.

Love motels are an integral part of Korean student life, albeit often out of direct physical and social view. The way in which motels operate in South Korea provides useful insights into a different way of experiencing hospitableness and hospitality. Instead of an interpersonal reciprocity when we think about hosts and guests, it would seem more like an *intrapersonal* reciprocity that is negotiated through an established cultural practice. Private time and space needs to "accommodate" both the guests and the disappearing hosts to maintain the notion of total experience and total privacy at once. The point about what constitutes the commercial domain needs to be clarified in that, unlike the way it was discussed in Telfer (2000) and van den Broek Chávez *et al.* (2012), in which the hospitableness of the industry is controversial due to the profit motive, the commercial domain here does not compromise the notion of hospitality, but almost enhances it or at least the comfort of the guest. The level of discretion, the lack of need for conversations, and the quick entrances and exits allow the guests to pay for a familiar level of comfort in an anonymous space which they cannot find within their homes.

One of the things Wood (1994: 78–79) alludes to is the link between domestic and touristic experiences, and, particularly, the need to explore the meanings of home alongside hotels, a kind of "pseudo-domestication" of the hotel. It is in relation to this that the notion of a modern development of Korea can be seen, one that displaces and replaces "home"; commercial hospitality is being domesticated, and provides a new kind of home. From the maps of motel spaces, what is evident is not merely the intimate liaisons that occur within the confines of the motel, but a dynamic intermesh with cafés, restaurants, and convenience stores, culminating in a new order of habitability, a new order of home in Korea.

The ubiquity of the motel (as demonstrated by the interviewees) enables intimacy to be practiced within the cityscape. The historical imprint and constant discursive reiteration make it difficult to escape "the altered perceptions of sexuality and gender among the latest generation of South Koreans, who seem just as eager to cast off the shackles of Confucian ideology as they are in putting the country's poverty-stricken past behind them" (Diffrient, 2009: 302). Once again, this remains in stark contrast to the fifty shades of shackles Christian Grey puts onto Anastasia. Unlike a more mainstream approach where couples might approach hotels based on values and conditions related to lifestyle, affluence, comfort, and quality, the motel as discursive practice seems to be the very category of hospitality, existential and omnipresent within the fabric of South Korean culture.

Latham emphasizes that it is "new solidarities and new collectivities" (2003: 1719) that add to the sense of belonging and the acquisition of identity. When asked about whether the motel was a part of Korean identity (in the sense that it was an inherent part of the Korean landscape), all respondents were rather enthusiastic in pointing out that this was the case, although some were careful to point out that these places were the "negative" aspect to what contributed to Korean culture. Perhaps the imbued sense of justification needs to be explicit in order to protect the mainstay of what it means to be Korean. This elucidates the creation of "new, equally confining (and life-defining) codes of normative behavior for the supposedly upwardly mobile man and (especially) woman" (Diffrient, 2009: 302) evidenced in the formulation of a

> new sexual subjectivity and morality within the spatial confines of love motels/hotel rooms, [where] contemporary cultural producers are not only challenging hidebound notions of chastity and fidelity that have dictated the social realities of Korean women for centuries; but also revealing a paradox at the heart of paradigm-altering attempts at social change.
>
> *(Diffrient, 2009: 302)*

What is "new" are not the motels or the associated idea of love motels, but how they have been assimilated into the everyday discourses of sociality and performed as a part of culture and identity.

What we are seeing is an emergence of a "polymorphous public culture" (Latham, 2003: 1707) in which cafés, restaurants, convenience stores, and motels have been organized around a new kind of sociability in the city. This means that consumption is productive or co-productive in the making of social realities. The question asked by Latham becomes ever more crucial, "what is to be made of the companies and entrepreneurs that own and run the hospitality establishments on the Roads?" (2003: 1714). Latham was referring to the Ponsonby and Jervois Roads and the kinds of commercial relations to which the places were bound. In a similar way, 대학로 (Daehak-ro) or university streets, entire precincts close to big universities within the cityscape that provide food, accommodation, and entertainment, are full of the bustle of young people in city spaces (see Figures 28.2 and 28.3). To answer the question posed by Latham above, perhaps the companies and entrepreneurs that run the hospitality establishments around University Road are the invisible ones who become the visible, deputy hosts to the guests at the motel. These pseudo-hosts define the atmosphere of the region which the Korean student frequents, especially in the partaking of informal encounters through formalized conviviality and hospitableness in commercial venues.

Conclusions

Berman defines modernism as "any attempt by modern men and women to become subjects as well as objects of modernity, to get a grip on the modern world and make themselves a home in it" (1988: 5). Young Koreans in the ever-evolving Korean modernity of the last 30 years are *doing* just this, *making* themselves a home, or as one of our respondents clearly reiterates about motel activities, "*making* babies." Since the outcome of babies and the resultant stigmatization is not an option for unmarried couples in Korean society, the *making* is what matters. This kind of *making* is reminiscent of Dostoyevsky's *Notes from the Underground* (1864) in which "Man likes to make roads and to create, that is a fact beyond dispute", and yet *he* seems to be afraid of attaining his goal, "Who knows, perhaps he only loves that edifice from a distance, and is by no means in love with it at close quarters; *perhaps he only loves building it, and does not want to live in it*" (Dostoyevsky, 2016 [1864]: 361). There was something that all the interviewees mentioned consistently without fail, that the commercial motivation was what motivates the patronization of the motel as opposed to the hotel. It was a lot cheaper. While it seems rather obvious, what is more intriguing is how this has found its way into common discourse, that the way to the motel is by virtue of price. We would argue that it also probably has something to do with feeling at home, exploring illicit spaces and intimate encounters that legitimize everyday behavior. In other words, the motel becomes a commercial extension of home.

We need to consider once again: how should the relationship between public spaces and commercial hospitality be framed? As opposed to looking at profit orientation, it is as important to understand the narratives of the city and its spaces as sites of accumulation. Through this exploration of Internet discourses, secondary literature research and primary interviews involving spatial mapping, we have seen the emergence of particular kinds of spaces and the embodied cityscape of socio-cultural practices in the hospitality industry. What becomes clear is that hospitality spaces and their complexities do transform public culture and patterns of living around the neighborhood.

Coming back to the main questions of this chapter, motels in Korea provide hospitality and even hospitableness to their users, albeit in a way in which the host–guest relationship is such that it is the guests themselves who create a joint liminal space in the bedrooms of these motels. While the traditional host may be present to offer hospitality, they aim to make themselves invisible in the eye of privacy. Korean students conceive and reproduce motels in ways similar to the physical presence of the motels; publicly present, yet always backstage. The fact that motels for younger users do not exclusively signify sexual encounters highlights how they represent the increasingly complex and nuanced perspective among Korean students towards the hospitality of these places.

There are three main findings that surface from this research in response to the three questions that were posed in the beginning. First, it is imperative to think about time existing alongside space and to measure our construction of public/private spaces against public/private time. Hospitality "takes place" in the motel, in the confines of the room, yet this hospitality also "takes time" in the room. The three hours of "Dae-shil" (borrow-room) or a kind of "Nightlight saving" (if the term exists at all) legitimize an intimate time of consumption. With the recent proliferation of daytime hotel accommodation such as dayuse.com and hotelsbyday.com, further research needs to be explored in this area, if private time can be offset with "public time," and the implications of this in hospitality studies. Second, the answer to "who is the host" needs to be considered in terms of hospitality spaces. The city, or the spaces of the city, is not only just host to the supply side of the hospitality industry, but also an agent to the consumers of hospitality. The materiality of the host needs to be reflected on in terms of an accumulated plethora of hospitality services and entertainment, and not as sole proprietor. Third, the way space is consumed seems to be intimate and private based on practice, but explicit in discourse. This play between intercourse and discourse is the same mesh that collapses the notion of public and private space, commercial and domestic space, exotic and familiar space. In fact, we need to reposition the Korean motel as an extension of a home-like space of everyday habituation and the fulfillment of basic desires such as food, sleep, and sex.

Korean motels do not exist in a vacuum. They thrive within and alongside an agglomeration of commercial and hospitable enterprises. What is more important is the practice of how these spaces are being condoned, discoursed, and practiced relating to "new" typologies of usage, especially the ways in which they are constantly being labeled and formulated into a cultural practice for young people. It is about applying insights of hospitality in order to enhance our knowledge of hospitalities, making explicit the realities of shades and visibilities of the phenomenon. This chapter calls for further in-depth exploration of the kinds of social hospitalities and intimate encounters (be it the facilitation of food, drink, sleep, or sex) and how these modalities constantly intermesh and evolve into new forms of reflexive everyday encounters which young people in Korea embrace outwardly. Such a study would spur future researches, especially those coming out of South Korea and other Asian contexts, to further engage with hospitality in the city and explore its implications for the future.

References

Alexander, M., Chen, C. C., MacLaren, A. and O'Gorman, K. D. (2010) Love motels: oriental phenomenon or emergent sector?, *International Journal of Contemporary Hospitality Management* 22, 2: 194–208.

Amsden, A. H. (1992) *Asia's Next Giant: South Korea and Late Industrialization*, New York: Oxford University Press.

Bell, D. (2007) The hospitable city: social relations in commercial spaces, *Progress in Human Geography* 31, 1: 7–22.

Berman, M. (1988) *All that is Solid Melts into Air: The Experience of Modernity*, New York: Penguin Books.

Brown, G. (2008) Urban (homo)sexualities: ordinary cities and ordinary sexualities, *Geography Compass* 2, 4: 1215–1231.

Chang, J., Ryan, C., Tsai, C.-T. (Simon) and Wen, H.-Y. (Sally) (2012) The Taiwanese love motel – an escape from leisure constraints?, *International Journal of Hospitality Management* 31, 1: 169–179.

Chaplin, S. (2007) *Japanese Love Hotels: A Cultural History*, London: Routledge.

Cotton, J. and van Leest, K. (1996) The new rich and the new middle class in South Korea: the rise and fall of the "golf republic". In Robison, R. and Goodman, D. (eds.) *The Rich in Asia: Mobile Phones, McDonalds and Middle-Class Revolution*, London: Routledge, pp. 185–203.

Diffrient, D. S. (2009) No quarter(s), no camel(s), no exit(s): *Motel Cactus* and the low heterotopias of Seoul. In Clarke, D. B., Pfannhauser, V. C. and Doel. M. A. (eds.) *Moving Pictures/Stopping Places: Hotels and Motels on Film*, Lanham, MD: Lexington Books, pp. 297–324.

Dostoyevsky, F. (2016 [1864]) *Fyodor Dostoyevsky*, Dover, NY: Courier Dover.

Featherstone, M., Hepworth, M. and Turner, B. S. (1991) (eds.) *The Body: Social Process and Cultural Theory* (Vol. 7), London: Sage.

Good Morrows (2012) *Hotels/Love Motels in South Korea*. Available at https://www.youtube.com/watch?v=a_-EQcXx8DI. Published 15 August.

Gottdiener, M. (1985) *The Social Production of Urban Space*, Austin: University of Texas Press.

Green, A., Follert, M. Osterland, K. and Paquuin, J. (2008) Space, place and sexual sociality: towards an "atmospheric analysis", *Gender, Work, Organization* 17: 7–27.

Hubbard, P. (2012) *Cities and Sexualities*, Abingdon: Routledge.James, E. L. (2012) *Fifty Shades of Grey*, London: Arrow Books.

Johnston, L. (2012) Sites of excess: the spatial politics of touch for drag queens in Aotearoa New Zealand, *Emotion, Space and Society* 5, 1: 1–9.

Kendall, L. (2002) Introduction. In Kendall, L. (ed.) *Under Construction: The Gendering of Modernity, Class, and Consumption in the Republic of Korea*, Honolulu: University of Hawai'i Press, pp. 1–24.

Kim, V. (2011) The crazy wonderland of Seoul's party motels, *CNN Travel*, 15 November. Available at http://travel.cnn.com/seoul/play/why-you-should-love-motels-659935/.

Lashley, C. (2011) Towards a theoretical understanding. In Lashley, C. and Morrison. A. (eds.) *In Search of Hospitality: Theoretical Perspectives and Debates*. Oxford: Butterworth-Heinemann, pp. 1–17.

Lashley, C. and Morrison, A. (2011) (eds.) *In Search of Hospitality: Theoretical Perspectives and Debates*, Oxford: Butterworth-Heinemann.

Lashley, C., Lynch, P. and Morrison, A. J. (2007) *Hospitality: A Social Lens*, Oxford: Elsevier.

Latham, A. (2003) Urbanity, lifestyle and making sense of the new urban cultural economy: notes from Auckland, New Zealand, *Urban Studies* 40, 9: 1699–1724.

Lee, N.Y. (2012) 욕망의사회사, "러브모텔" Socio-histori[c]al deployment of sexuality, "Love Hotel" in South Korea, *Society and History* 96, 12: 183–224.

Lefebvre, H. (1991) *The Production of Space*, Oxford: Blackwell.

Lugosi, P. (2007) Queer consumption and commercial hospitality: communitas, myths and the production of liminoid space, *International Journal of Sociology and Social Policy* 27, 3/4: 163–174.

Lugosi, P. (2008) Hospitality spaces, hospitable moments: consumer encounters and affective experiences in commercial settings, *Journal of Foodservice* 19, 2: 139–149.

Lynch, K. (1960) *The Image of the City*, Cambridge, MA: MIT Press and Harvard University Press.

Miller, S. (2013) *Inside a Sexy Korean Love Motel* [GoPro Hero2], 22 August. Available at https://www.youtube.com/watch?v=9pOhJaQj4MY.

Mort, F. and Nead, L. (1999) Introduction – sexual geographies, *Sexualities* 37: 5–10.

O'Gorman, K. D. (2010) Introduction to the origins of hospitality and tourism. In *The Origins of Hospitality and Tourism*, Oxford: Goodfellow.

Pritchard, A. and Morgan, N. (2006) Hotel Babylon? Exploring hotels as liminal sites of transition and transgression, *Tourism Management* 27, 5: 762–772.

Rodaway, P. (1994) *Sensuous Geographies: Body, Sense and Place*, London: Routledge.

Rogerson, C. M. and Visser, G. (2012) Rethinking South African urban tourism research, *Tourism Review International* 15, 1–2: 77–90.

ROK On! (2012) *Love Motels in Korea* [Banchan #24], 30 April. Available at https://www.youtube.com/watch?v=BBCqdziy8cM.

Shilling, C. (1993) *The Body and Social Theory*, London: Sage.

Soja, E. W. (1996) *Thirdspace: Journeys to Los Angeles and Other Real-and-Imagined Places*, Oxford: Blackwell.

Taylor-Johnson, S. (dir.) (2015) *Fifty Shades of Grey*, Universal Pictures, USA.

Telfer, E. (2000) The philosophy of hospitality. In Lashley, C. and Morrison, A. (eds.) *In Search of Hospitality: Theoretical Perspectives and Debates*, Oxford: Butterworth-Heinemann, pp. 38–55.

Turner, B. S. (1984) *The Body and Society: Explorations in Social Theory*, Oxford: Basil Blackwell.

UUtvProductions (2015) *Korean Love Motels and Dating*, 12 April. Available at https://www.youtube.com/watch?v=Nb23VVtshzM.

van den Broek Chávez, F., Wiegerink, K. and van der Rest, J. P. (2012) City hospitality: in search of host-guest relations. In *2nd Advances in Hospitality and Tourism Marketing and Management Conference*, Corfu.

Whyte, J. (2015) *My $40 A Night Love Motel in Insadong, Seoul, South Korea*, 6 February. Available at https://www.youtube.com/watch?v=pnpsr5IcyCI.

Wood, R. C. (1994) Hotel culture and social control, *Annals of Tourism Research* 21, 1: 65–80.

Zukin, S. (1995) *The Cultures of Cities*, Oxford: Blackwell.

29

Hospitality between the sheets

Leisure and sexual entertainment for tourists in large urban centres in Brazil

Ricardo Lanzarini and Luiz Gonzaga Godoi Trigo

Key themes

Leisure and sexual entertainment

Sex market

Tourism and hospitality

Sex tourism

> Remember, remember always, that all of us, and you and I especially, are descended from immigrants and revolutionists.
>
> *(Franklin D. Roosevelt)*

Sexual intercourse is part of human nature, as well as that of many other species that need it in order to reproduce and/or feel pleasure as the utmost expression of well-being and contentment. Since ancient times, human beings have had sex for pleasure, as a momentary enjoyment, a satisfaction often sought and repeated. Today, specialisation of pleasure by sex gains sumptuous markets and supporters from all social tribes, with their fetishes and fantasies, transcending the sphere of private lives for the leisure and entertainment sector. For each new tourist destination there is a sexual market fostered by tourists who search for pleasure with new flavours in moments of leisure during a trip, overcoming barriers that society and their social group impose on them through hetero-normativity and monogamy.

Entertainment offers great possibilities in contemporary societies and sex is one of the most developed sectors, encompassing many desires, both possible and fantasised. In the broad and wide imaginary of sexual preferences, attraction for beauty is quite significant. The celebration of this beauty in the West has occurred since the Greco-Roman world and has deepened in modern societies where aesthetic standards influence both the media and peoples' imagination while influenced by the media.

DOI: 10.4324/9781315679938-32

Youth, beauty, health, desire and sexual arousal are amalgamated in standards more or less universal and systematically reproduced by the media. Fashion, cinema, sexual services and advertising, services that specialise in well-being (massage, hair style, make up, perfumes, fitness gyms, diets, etc.) – all praise glamour and human being's pre-dawn freshness with endless offers of satisfaction constantly renewed.

Sex as leisure and entertainment has become an increasingly professionalised and profitable business, offered through several products and services. Films, photos, websites on the Internet, 'massage' houses, saunas, bars, nightclubs, conventional brothels, advertising in newspapers, trips, sex-shops, hotels and motels are some of the legal businesses involved in the sexual market. These challenge social morality and encourage the rejection of taboos that still persist in contemporary society.

The construction of the sex market

People have an ideal sexual partner. This idealisation varies and depends on each individual's taste and personal story according to his/her preferences, experiences and sexual opportunities. However, especially in today's societies, youth, health and aesthetics exert strong attraction on a significant number of people. Analysing the icons and standards consecrated in the early twentieth century, one notes that they have altered through the centuries. Certainly literature and cinema, press and electronic media have been vital in the elaboration of what might be called 'sexual aesthetical standards' that attract peoples' attention and desire.

Western civilisation (including Asian developed countries) highlights its contradictions and paradoxes in many ways. One of them, in the aesthetic field, is inserting extraordinary advertising photos in sophisticated stores. In temples of consumption there is a careful exhibition of perfumes, clothes, watches and crystals surrounded by photos of the most beautiful human specimens from both sexes, usually at the sexual height of their youth, right in the middle of their biological procreation stage. There is a twofold objective in this aesthetical organisation: to call attention to the products and to make people melancholic when they think on the beauty of these creatures and the impeccable technical reproduction of this beauty through well-edited pictures. Biology and technology join to cause astonishment before beauty. Full aesthetics: the models, the photographer, lighting, graphic computing and experts explore beauty and desire at their full extent. They try, through a 'perfect' image, to seduce the consumer and encourage them to buy something that gives them a pale idea of sharing the archetype perceived.

These airport and shopping centre icons that sanctify youthful sensuality ally with the architecture of immensities outlined by translucent glass and lights, mirrors and decorations, in order to involve us in a monad of consumption, a capsule of desire. Consumption and desire: consumption of desire, desire of consumption. The fetish of beauty is a commodity desired and feared, both transient and essential to the imaginary and allied to the mythic imaginary of trips, it enhances its delusions in search of adventures and sensual experiences in shifts.

Market appropriation has taken place in two main ways. The first advancement was held through the general insertion of revolutionary segments in the market during the 1960s, including products designed for women, afro-descendants, youth, adolescents and children, cultural minorities in general (vegetarians, environmentalists, macrobiotics, alternative) and, obviously, homosexuals. Capitalist appropriation of rebellion and contestation became a promising market and would become, in the future, 'politically correct'.

Another aspect is the market evolution itself, led by experts who analysed these political, social and cultural changes and defined new parameters and methods for products and services for more democratic and pluralist societies in terms of options, and qualitatively more diversified.

One of the founding texts of this new marketing management was *The Long Tail* (2006), published by Chris Anderson at the magazine *Wired*. The term is used in statistics to identify contributions of Pareto's curve data, where the volume of data is structured in decreasing order. In a conventional market, these curves show what consumers search for. Usually, there is a high demand for a small set of products or services and a decreased demand for a large number of other options. In the classic market, it is hard to calculate the demand for small niches, but in more computerised economies it is possible to attend to a larger number of consumers in an individualised and targeted manner. In this dynamic and highly differentiated market, products and services offered to people are highly diversified and elaborated. With two aspects so stimulating such as sex and travel, the promise of an unforgettable experience becomes the hedonist-hyper-modern Holy Grail.

In 1999, B. Joseph Pine II and James H. Gilmore popularised the concepts of 'experience' 'spectacle' and 'sensations' in their book *The Experience Economy*. After economic phases involving commodities (farming societies), goods (industrial society) and services (services society), the sensations phase (sensations or experience societies) would be something involving the 'domains' of education, escapism, aesthetics and entertainment. The sexual market is just a market concerned with aesthetics and entertainment, pleasure and even sophistication, whether 'authentic' or even farcical.

An innovative and important factor in the creation of niches and new market options has been the union of telecommunications with computing and digitalisation, creating the vast virtual space where desires and sensations can be created and recreated according to the will of an audience looking forward to novelties, communication and stimulating possibilities. In this 'flat' world, dominated by information and social networking (Friedman, 2005: 176), viewers interested in sexual pleasures find websites and networking opportunities to express themselves and sell and provide ideas, attitudes, products and services.

Tourism and the sex market: the emerging segment

The search for sexual pleasure in places far from home is not a new concept. There is a famous nineteenth-century Portuguese motto (mentioned in a song by Chico Buarque) that says: 'there is no sin south of the equator'. The possibility of going to another region and being able to do something forbidden in your place of origin has always attracted defenders and admirers, particularly towards warm and poor countries in the Americas, Africa or Asia.

Travel literature is full of sensual and paradisiac destinations where settlers, without fear, shame or guilt, may enjoy local delicacies, including those of the natives. André Gide and Paul Bowles went to Africa; naturalists came to Brazil in order to register its beauties; hordes of tourists go to Thailand, the Caribbean and Brazil in search of sexual tourism.

Aspects of art and literature initially designated as pornographic have unfolded and gradually advanced over Western culture. With the development of cinema, television, cheap and high quality graphic methods and then super-8 and VCR, possibilities of production and advertising without censorship have simply multiplied. Entertainment appropriates cultural production, including one more segmented and targeted to specific audiences. Human beings are no longer satisfied to look at beauty from afar, lost between the sun and the sea. Tourism, leisure and entertainment, allied to new technologies of transportation and communication, allow beauty to be reproduced and consumed on a global scale, forming new cultural facets related to sexuality.

With the development of new communication technologies (interconnected systems, digitalisation, graphic computing), the increase of freedom all over the world and civil actions for human – including sexual – rights, distribution of eroticism grew exponentially. Art and entertainment became segmented. The production of centuries, restricted to libraries and specialised bookstores, became accessible to millions of people at low cost. Where once only insiders knew about the artist Paul Cadmus, nowadays there are several websites on the Internet showing his works and providing discussion groups. All this material is connected through links and search providers that access thousands of text pages and illustrations. Once the classical work of Professor Gregory Woods (1998) was hard to find, but today it is available at virtual bookstores, as is information on his field of research (gay and lesbian studies).

There is an expanding sexual market (sex market) worldwide and there are many discussions on issues such as prostitution, pornography or alternative sexual options. For instance, the feminist Andrea Dworkin led a crusade against pornography in the United States during the 1970s, in a movement that tried to prove, according to the theory of another radical feminist, Robin Morgan, that 'pornography is the theory, and rape is the practice' (Friedman, 2005: 195). Despite constant pressure from Evangelical churches and American conservative groups against pornography, the movement was a failure, for this more liberal time was not consistent with repression. The 'spirit' of the 1970s, following the influence of the beats and hippies since the 1950s and 1960s, questioned the conservative status quo. Morgan's phrase did not resonate with the research on rape either. For example, as Friedman states, 'in Japan, where violent pornography is easily found, rape is practically nonexistent' (2005: 195). On the other hand, economic interests in a sex market appeared and soon an icon of pornographic movies would emerge. In 1972, actress Linda Lovelace starred in a movie called *Deep Throat*, a breakthrough in conventional pornography as it showed fellatio explicitly to a wide audience. The movie made over US$25 million. Afterwards, male pornography emerged, viewed mainly by a gay audience. One of its greatest stars was Jeff Stryker, an actor who made over 40 homosexual movies and later 'traded a 25-centimetre artificial penis supposedly modelled on his own member' (Friedman, 2005: 196).

Liberalised culture enabled pornography to emerge as a legitimate form of entertainment and it could count on the support of profitable sectors, such as those in the field of medicine. To give an example, Viagra produces revenues of one billion dollars yearly. It is hard to evaluate the amount of profit generated by sex. The growth of the sexual market has encompassed heterosexual, homosexual and bisexual segments. The segmented and mass-oriented web of domestic and travelling pleasures has only just been formed.

Lanzarini and Trigo (2014) argue that with the increase of travel in the twentieth century, the expansion of civil liberties and the exchange of culture provided by tourism, borders of pleasure have also expanded. By breaking out of routine, the tourist may allow himself to have new experiences and emotions where sex plays a vital role in the endless search for pleasure.

Tourism as a growing market articulates sexual consumption as one of its segments; perhaps one of the most consumed, as it is present (or sub-present) in almost all other forms of tourism, a fact that complements sexual tourism, but does not correspond to it. Not everybody travels to have sex, but everybody can have sex while travelling, besides consuming pornography and spaces of sexual entertainment such as movie theatres and brothels.

Leisure and sexual entertainment in São Paulo and Rio de Janeiro

The cities of São Paulo/SP and Rio de Janeiro/RJ, located in the south-east of Brazil and the two largest urban centres of the country with the largest national tourist demand according to the Ministry of Tourism (2012), were chosen as case studies for the sexual market of leisure and entertainment for tourists. Among all these tourists, over half are men who travel by themselves, especially for business.

Research focused on the provision for heterosexual, bisexual and homosexual male travellers found in the main leisure and entertainment sights displayed by city tours and virtual sex guides in these cities. This was to better understand the motivation and consumption of tourism shaped by the traveller's sexuality.

Leisure, even for short periods of time, is part of the trip, whether motivated by holidays or business. New social relationships are established from carefree and ephemeral encounters, a fact that gives to the trip a sense of freedom in the face of society's regulation of public and private behaviours such as sex. Therefore, leisure and entertainment attractions of urban tourist centres, such as historic centres, constitute the main means of sociability to tourists, as well as attractions for specific audiences such as saunas and sex houses. This scenario, typical of large urban centres, consecrates a sexual market open to all possibilities of individual consumption, affirming the notion of urban sexual hospitality addressed by Lanzarini (2013a).

Two distinct groups of contexts have been observed in the environment of a search for partners: the first, related to the use of bars and nightclubs, where social behaviour is limited by the rules and norms set by the establishment; the second, whose interactions are focused on sexual practice such as saunas and sex clubs, both selected from adverts aimed at tourists in general and found in press guides, travel agencies and the virtual environment.

The research took six months, and was undertaken in 2013. The method used was ethnographic and based on personal experience and approaches between researchers and researched, of an essentially qualitative character, given the impossibility of measuring sexual consumption. Debray (1992) highlights that ethnography examines practices and individual and social knowledge using techniques such as observation and dialogue. The main analysis tools adopted were participant observation and interviews, as well as informal dialogues carried out in virtual space, the main means used by the research participants to meet each other. For Lapassade (2001), participant observation designates all fieldwork and participation as part of the analysed field. This starts with the investigator's arrival and the beginning of negotiations to access the research field up to the moment he ends his participation. The relationships established between the researcher and the participants are also a feature of the research.

Research participants were identified from two distinct contexts. First, by a straight search on Universo on-line via chats of UOL (Universo On-Line), a provider that, according to Lanzarini's research (2013b), is the most famous provider in Brazil for sex searches and social relationships developed in chat room settings. As users, the researchers had the opportunity to talk with men who identified themselves as travellers or as not belonging to the local social group. They were chatting in search of casual and immediate sex. Furthermore, respondents were identified through their use of sex apps via Android and iPhone systems. These apps work as trackers that filter users' preferences and make suggestions for contact, as well as identifying people close by who are looking for sex with the same preferences or fetishes. Basically, they are segmented by sexual orientation, with Grindr, Growlr, Scruff and Hornet for homosexuals, and Blendr and Tinder for heterosexuals, with large concentrations of bisexual women in the case of the two cities researched.

The second step of the research involved participant observation in places of sexual sociability such as sex houses, bars and saunas located in regions with the highest concentration of hotels and tourism attractions in São Paulo/SP and Rio de Janeiro/RJ. During these visits, interviews were carried out to observe the sexuality and gender social dynamics that each place offers to the tourist.

In virtual space there is always opportunity to meet men who identify themselves as 'tourists', 'businessmen', 'travellers' or 'gringos' (a native category related to foreigners) among others, searching for sex with men and women anonymously, without any identification as to origin or social identity. To that end, virtual characters are created to meet all tastes and sexual preferences. Ephemeral and merely sexual relations are established, very often in just one encounter.

These sexual partners present several motivations that vary from a prostitution trade relation, where someone pays for a service offered and the one who offers usually has payment as their selection criterion, to cases in which these dates are promoted by the desire to feel pleasure from both parties, without any financial exchange. However, dates promoted by pleasure feed the sexual leisure and entertainment market anyway, as there is consumption of images and objects, use of spaces intended for sex and the comfort of the trip in the promotion of anonymity that allows the tourist to feel new pleasures, far from social sanctions.

During the research, 500 male tourists were found looking for a sexual partner/s in virtual space. It is important to highlight that this number does not refer to any real sampling, as chat rooms work 24 hours a day and there are many rooms and providers. Therefore, this number is just a statement of approximation of the universe researched, without any statistical claim. From the total, 34 per cent were searching for heterosexual relations, 24 per cent for bisexual and 42 per cent for homosexual. Regarding the cities, 58 per cent were in São Paulo and 42 per cent in Rio de Janeiro, with ages ranging from 20 to 65.

All of them searched for sex for the exchange of pleasure, and did not involve prostitution agencies. They found themselves in the position of tourists, mostly travelling for work but also for shopping or on holiday. Among men who travel for business, there is a more contained profile of sexual behaviour based on morality. They are men older than 30 and usually married to women, who preserve their heterosexual self-image, even when they search for sex with other men. On holiday it is possible to find younger and single men (and for this reason travelling alone), notably from cities close by, who visit the large urban centres in search of differentiated (and sexual) opportunities for leisure and entertainment.

In general, these men present several motivations and occupations during the trip, with free time that can be filled by pleasurable and relaxing activities, with carefree sexual practice, corresponding to leisure or entertaining activity on the trip. Chat rooms and apps usually get straight to the point. Physical characteristics and sexual preferences are privileged, such as desires and fetishes, leading straight to the blind date for sex. The hours when searches and dates take place vary as follows:

(SP-15h) 'Macho-tourist': engineer, 40, alone at the hotel. I'll pay women up to 30 for sex tonight.

(RJ-18h) 'Hde-fora_Bi': 37, versatile, in shape, 190 cm, 80 kg. Feel like having sex now. With a car in Ipanema. I like couple or macho.

(SP-21h) 'Hinterior x H': 53, active, 20 cm dick, 165 cm, 90 kg, in SP for the week. Is anyone passive in the surroundings of Rua Frei Caneca?

(RJ-20h) 'EmpresárioSP wants active': 40, passive bear. Is anyone active in Zona Sul between 30 and 50?

The accounts above exemplify the diversity of cases easily found in virtual space, where the tourist has the opportunity to search for local sex, but is protected by the anonymity of the trip, safeguarding himself from any moral judgement from his group of origin. Initially, there is a physical description of each participant so that a prior selection of the candidate is possible. Then sexualities (an act of partner selection and not of social repression) and the search for men, women or both are defined, with a focus on sexual practice preferences like 'active' (the one who wants to penetrate), 'passive' (the one who wants to be penetrated) or 'versatile' (the one who acts freely as active or passive). The act of penetrating or being penetrated, in the case of men, intertwines relations of power and organisation of males in society, creating stereotypes of groups marginalised or oppressed by standard heterosexuality. In this view, the greatest expressivity of male sexual searches in virtual space researched here appear in the desire to be penetrated, whether as a relief from social tensions that regulate daily sexual behaviour or as a resistance to the sublimation of desires by morality.

With regard to apps, users search for sex in the surroundings of their locality in a quick and anonymous manner, and may freely expose their fantasies and sexual desires within a group of people with common interests, already segmented by the app. Some of them, such as Tinder and Bang With Friends, can be downloaded for free through social networks such as Facebook. Other paid apps that also have simpler (and free) versions for users, such as Grindr and Blendr, claim to have over 180 million users worldwide and their main function is to identify the distance between people interested in casual sex. In this case, the app works as a radar that tracks other users in the vicinity, as long as they are connected to the Internet. It also allows chat and file exchanges with users' images without any censorship of the picture content.

The two possibilities for interaction offered in virtual space attract more and more supporters every day, particularly in large urban centres where there is further technological development. Among the users of these apps, foreigners appear with more frequency, especially because they have versions in several languages, unlike national chat rooms such as UOL. Like chat rooms, the apps gather people who just want to break the social barrier of the blind date, but with focus on casual and immediate sex, in the case of the tourist who has little time available to flirt. A characteristic of this condition is that in the apps, particularly those using GPS, the dialogue between interested parties is even more objective, with exchange of information on possible sexual practices as well as pictures, which reinforces the discussion that sex is strictly linked to the notion of beauty and aesthetics, in a game of attraction using images of nude – preferably young and healthy – bodies.

All attempts to meet with people for interviews generated by apps were unsuccessful, given the mere interest in quick sex, both in hetero and homosexual groups. As for the profile of this resource, searches for homosexual and bisexual interactions predominate, including in apps designed for use by heterosexuals, as there is an expressive number of male users in Brazil and a timid participation of female heterosexuals, except for sex professionals. Both in Rio de Janeiro and São Paulo, homosexual searchers prevail.

In the case of bisexuality, there is a greater predisposition for homosexuality than for heterosexuality – that is, in cases where there is no hetero couple, finding a man is always a viable second option, considering the offer is predominantly masculine. In general, men who search for heterosexual pleasure seem to be bound to a macho prostitution consumption culture, which provides sex spaces designed for heterosexuals that, historically, have a commercial connotation, not only in tourism activity but also in daily life.

During the second phase of this research, twelve field visits were made in each city, twice to each leisure and entertainment spot, including nightclubs, saunas and sex houses. Considering that the time available for leisure – except for tourists on holiday – is relatively short, sexual searches are always very quick and similar in all sexual practices, as in virtual space. In this context, spaces designed for sexual practice are always strengthened to the detriment of spaces of more social order, such as nightclubs and bars, where there is need for more social interaction between interested parties.

In pub-style nightclubs and bars there is a clear search for sex among clients, in a dynamic they call 'hunting'. This search is established from an exchange of glances that provoke approach behaviour. In these places, many sex professionals can be found, looking mainly for male foreigners. In interviews, four managers of nightclubs attest:

(SP) Manager-1: Many tourists come here in search of fun and sex. There are many call girls, but they don't belong to the nightclub. They get in as clients, do their work without disturbing anybody and are hardly noticed. Usually they hang around with foreigners. But many people stand here searching for a sexual partner, so it is difficult to pinpoint who charges and who doesn't.

(SP) Manager-2: Here we choose to serve the LGBT (Lesbian, Gays, Bisexuals and Transgenders) community so it is common to see men arriving alone or with a few friends and the 'hunting' atmosphere is constant. Once a week we throw a party here: the bar turns into a nightclub, the environment gets darker, the music gets louder and sexual desires are more evident. It's hard to see someone getting out of here unaccompanied! We also have a page on Facebook as a closed group, where participants can make comments on the parties and get to know each other: a friend of mine even got married to another guy he met this way! We have much acceptance on the Internet, always with new requests from users. There they confirm their presence and even say whether they are available for dates. Many tourists show up – particularly from cities close by – coming to enjoy the weekend in the capital.

(RJ) Manager-3: Almost everybody here arrives in groups or alone, but you rarely see couples on the entrance line. When leaving, most of them are accompanied and seem ready for another party. Many are male tourists and many women are from here. I wouldn't say everybody here just wants sex, but even those who don't want it end up falling into temptation [laughs].

(RJ) Manager-4: The climate of sun and beach, beautiful people, tourists … everything favours the person in search of an adventure, a night of pleasure, a summer love, and especially considering that here we have summer all year round! My bar is not intended for sex, and we don't see explicit things here, but of course there are searches and happy encounters both between people who want to 'enjoy' themselves and those who pay for sex. I just exercise discretion and don't let the thing get out of control. Every day I see some 'sexual affair' happening between clients, mainly with tourists.

In saunas and sex houses, approach behaviours are direct and sexual activities usually take place on the spot, unlike nightclubs, bars and virtual spaces, which serve only as a first contact. In this atmosphere, people circulate in bathing suits or nude, searching for sexual partners through visual attraction, many times without exchanging basic information such as their name or age. For them, what really matters is sexual pleasure and not the partner. In all these environments there are private rooms for sex and other collective spaces for group sex and/or mere voyeurism, as well as darkrooms: rooms and aisles where people can have sex without fear of the possibility of seeing each other, avoiding any kind of rejection, as everything is controlled by touch.

Two saunas were visited in both cities, two sex houses exclusively for men and two for couples. In these environments, people search for sex among visitors, and ask staff to point to individuals who might also be of interest to them, possibly 'from outside'. There are always accounts of increased numbers of travellers in these environments during holiday times. In addition to visits from foreigners, men living in areas outside the cities and executives travelling on business increase the use of saunas and sex houses not meant for couples.

In addition to informal remarks and personal observations, some interviews were possible, notably with men who were in these spaces momentarily, as viewers or onlookers. According to Broeck and López (2015: 793), 'this kind of sexual date' has not always been associated with sexual intercourse or may take several forms such as masturbation or voyeurism, as in the observation of nude bodies through windows in Amsterdam or in gay parades or in stripper shows such as live sex in dark rooms or in sex museums among many other examples.

It is worth considering that in this environment of hunting for sexual partners, interviews are rare. Once we had identified that we were undertaking research, as required by scientific ethics, both clients and managers began to offer denials in their testimonies. For managers, there was a concern that clients would feel threatened or disturbed, which demanded from us the utmost discretion and sensitiveness during our approaches. For clients, besides the fear of being identified, there was also disinterest; they enter that environment only to have sex and not to formally interact. Therefore, the main learning resource for our research was direct observation and very informal data about the audience in each premises.

Without fear of social compromise, even in person, the detached condition of public relationships grants to visitors the opportunity to create characters, as in virtual space (except for physical features), making up names or professions in the absence of any identification: what really matters is the exchange of sexual pleasures, not the social identification of participants, a fact that hinders data collection on origin, profession, marital status and so on for researchers.

During the research visits, fifty male tourists were found: 46 per cent at sex houses in São Paulo and 54 per cent at houses in Rio de Janeiro, with ages ranging from 20 to 65. Of the sexual searches, 78 per cent were for other men, 12 per cent for women and 10 per cent classed themselves as bisexual and prone to sex between men, as long as women took part, unlike in virtual space where the absence of women does prove an obstacle to the date. All tourists who claimed they were searching for women (22 per cent) were found in sex houses for couples. While in virtual space the largest number of results was for São Paulo, Rio de Janeiro is highlighted in the on-site research. The climate of beach and leisure created in the city is the main reason for travelling rather than business, as in the case of São Paulo. At any rate, homosexual interactions still prevail.

On reasons for travelling, a striking factor is that 56 per cent are men on business trips, using a brief moment of leisure for sex far from family and friends. Most of them are married to women and have children. They did not search for prostitution as a sexual resource, nor did they often use sex apps. They preferred the informality and impersonality of sex spaces, where it is possible to make their wishes come true freely and momentarily, without having to make commitments or engaging emotions.

In general, the fifty respondents claimed to be entrepreneurs, civil servants or professionals, ranging from middle to upper class. As far as their marital status was concerned, 6 per cent were single and searching for men and/or women, 16 per cent were married to women and searching for other women, 52 per cent were married to women and searching for other men, and 26 per cent were married to men and searching for other men. It is worth highlighting that of the socially heterosexual tourists who were married to women, 75 per cent were found in exclusively homosexual sex houses.

As some respondents commented:

(SP) Interviewee-1/39 (sex house for couples): I'm married but always travel on business and use my time off to relax and have different sex. I don't like prostitutes. I prefer coming here to this swing house and having sex with someone who also wants to have sex with me as many times as I want. It is more expensive to enter unaccompanied, but my wife would come and I don't know if I'd like her to come [laughs].

(RJ) M-2/31 (sex house for couples): I'm bisexual and like to have sex with couples. That's why I come to swing houses, where there is a varied offer and I can choose carefully who I will have sex with, more than on the Internet. Here I can do everything I like, without social rules and without having to pay for sex. In my city it is impossible because it is small. So I use my holidays to realise my fantasies.

(SP) M-3/48 (gay sauna): I have a wife and children, but use my business trips to do what I like the most: come to a gay sauna and realise my homosexual fantasies with somebody else or in a group. I like being passive, but have few opportunities to doi this; only when I travel without family, on business, for a few days and hours off, usually at the end of the day.

(RJ) M-4/44 (sadomasochism house): I'm passive/submissive. I visit sadomasochism houses because they are the place where I can realise my fantasies the most. And here there are items I use in sex and cannot have at home because of my family, for I live with my parents.

(SP) M-5/60 (gay sex house): I always come to São Paulo on business and, whenever I can, I try to have sex and do crazy things I don't do with my wife. I enjoy everything and depending on my desire I come to a gay or mixed sex club. ... I don't know if I'm bisexual, but I prefer to think that pleasure has no rules or limits! But with men it is easier than with women: they usually want money, while guys have sex for pleasure.

(RJ) M-6/29 (gay sauna): A sauna is very practical because everybody here has the same intention and through signs and approach behaviour you know who likes you or not; and sex happens right here. In my case, I don't have time during the week because of my work and on the weekend because of my friends and boyfriend. Then when I travel on business I come here to relax a bit. I like sex so much and here I can exchange partners as many times as I wish. It is guaranteed sex: you never get out of a sauna without feeling totally relaxed [laughs]!

(SP) M-7/28 (pub close to several sex houses): I usually come here when I want to find someone to have sex with. I'm bi, but confess that on the street and in the bars women I often meet for sex are prostitutes. Not the men. Many just want to have sex. So it is easier and cheaper! In this area of Rua Augusta and Frei Caneca you find everything: tourists wanting sex at any time of the day. I'm from Minas, but often come here on business and always take a tourist to an Inn where I stay near here. The manager doesn't even say a word when he sees I have company. I think they are used to it. And my companions are almost always men. Many don't like saunas and prefer to stay in bars. But tourists very often want quick contacts: a half-hour of conversation and two hours of sex [laughs].

(RJ) M-8/25 (pub close to the beach and sex houses): I live in a city in the metropolitan zone and always come here. I like this beach because it is one of the favourites for tourists. It is always crowded with beautiful people, foreigners, and people from other states. This region is full of sex houses for all tastes; and also cheap hotels (2 hrs cost R$30 on average). We get to know each other here at the beach or in the bar and go straight to the hotel to have sex. It is fast, safe, practical and you can go on foot.

The transcriptions describe the association that men from the most varied ages made concerning the idea of leisure and travel, associating sexual activities repressed by daily life because of family and social groups to an activity that gives them pleasure and personal satisfaction, despite the rules of conduct of their social groups of origin, once they are far from home.

Lanzarini argues:

> sexual dates are the main focal point between daily life and the new socialisation that foments trips, which characterises itself in the disruptions arising from social invisibility and the contact between men with the same sexual impulses. When the individual travels on business to a large urban centre he has the opportunity to converse with other men far from home in a universe of safer relations that, with the help of the Internet, enables him to exchange sexual pleasures under conditions of similarity and friendship.
>
> *(2015: 946)*

This brief sampling shows the diversity of cases and situations that form the universe of interactions between sex and tourism that are silenced by social morality. Among the possibilities for male sexual practices, the issue of women is still a dilemma: M-5 and M-7 report that the interests are different between the genders, possibly because of different historical conditions of pleasure and commercial use of sex, a fact that is also present in tourist destinations all over the world, where the female presence is more associated with prostitution than exchange of pleasures.

Thus, leisure and entertainment work as a kind of escapism for social tensions that involve moralisation of sex, breaking rules and conventions such as monogamy or standard heterosexuality. Its movement is subtle in large urban centres, taking place without changing the routine of the place or in places where searching for sex is routine, a part of people's daily life.

Final considerations: sexual hospitality for tourists

Leisure and entertainment, desire and pleasure, travelling and social freedom are mixes that are present in the post-industrial culture of consumption. Every day, the search for moral freedom and satisfaction of personal pleasures is valued and optimised by the tourism market, which enables temporary and safe sexual experiences far from home.

This market, particularly in large urban centres, gives new significance to spaces of leisure and entertainment as well as all city structures and creates its own spaces and structures for sexual consumption. Similarly, the Internet has shown its power to unite and socialise: people who have never met before and probably will never meet again are able to, for a brief time, relate socially and sexually, without affective bonds and, in many cases, without trade relations. Dates according to affinity and interest are established and linked to desire and sexual pleasure, based on the aesthetics of the body and on the convenience/ease of a personal encounter.

Sexuality, in travel, manifests itself purely and simply as an expression of intimate desire, of fetish, and through the social condition that imposes classes of sexual behaviour such as hetero-, bi- or homosexual. These classes publicly dictate a behaviour that may not correspond to reality, but is supported discursively (particularly during trips and sexual practices contrary to this discourse). It is not rare to find socially heterosexual men in sex houses for homosexuals. For them, the exchange of pleasure between 'machos' does not diminish their maleness or even characterise them as homosexuals because they do not assume this behaviour publicly. Therefore, they are heterosexuals having sex with other men and only this.

Sexual identity, in this case, merges with social identity, referring to public behaviour and not really to sexual behaviour, which is secret. Thus, for these tourists, to be homosexual goes far beyond enjoying sexual practices with other men; it requires assuming publicly a homosexual attitude before society. Therefore, in the conception of the respondents, to maintain marriages with women guarantees their social heterosexuality, and having sex with other men, as long as they are far from home, does not interfere with their daily life.

Prejudice and marginalisation of sexual pleasure appear in a very present form in the social life of these men who do not publicly assume their desires for homoerotic pleasure. Thus, they end up disseminating distorted ideas on sexuality as they uphold to their children and closest associates monogamous heterosexuality as a standard of social conduct. Any act out of this context is kept underground, silencing their sexual practices in ghettos and sporadic refuges such as business/holiday trips. In turn, such trips have gained more value in the imagination of these men who find in them their particular universe, safe and anonymous, in which they can briefly break away from their own prejudices and taboos.

Both for studies of tourist phenomena and leisure, sexuality treated as a decisive element in social behaviour is still a marginal issue that involves not only social confrontation, but also the breaking of morality taboos that oppress people. These taboos are usually left out in the moment of the tourist trip. Family and friends are very often kept out of reach from our individual sexual desires. In this way travelling configures itself as the right moment to break with fixed structures of social living.

Sexual hospitality refers to the cultural and infrastructure opening that predisposes people to a sexual encounter, offering physical and emotional safety. Large urban and tourist centres are the greatest promoters of sexual freedom during trips, since they offer leisure and entertainment tools suitable for sex, and there is also an interested audience, considering the high circulation and turnover of people. This factor acts as a facilitator of encounters: in tourist destinations there are different people every day, with differentiated needs and tastes from all over the world. So leisure and entertainment tools that serve tourists in their sexual practices complement the offer of destinations. Flavours and aromas mix with desire.

Mysticism, consumption, aesthetics and desire involve all privileged places of a post-industrial market. Desire is offered as 'customised' (or in segmentations of market), to be consumed, whether in the city of origin (many times in a way limited by the social group) or through trips around the world. Every day tourist destinations become more expert in sexual hospitality. They meet a latent and diverse demand, increasing the profits of the sex market and increasing the satisfaction of guests who find pleasure and hospitality between the sheets.

References

Anderson, C. (2006) *The Long Tail: Why the Future of Business is Selling Less of More*, New York: Hyperion.

Broeck, A. M and López, Á. L. (2015) Turismo y sexo: Una reflexión teórica desde el homoerotismo y el espacio, *Estudios y Perspectivas en Turismo* 24: 787–808.

Debray, R. (1992) *Vie et mort de l'image*, Paris: Gallimard.

Friedman, T. L. (2005) *The World is Flat*, New York: Farrar, Strauss and Giroux.

Lanzarini, R. (2013a) A hospitalidade sexual urbana na relação viajante-residente, *Revista Hospitalidade* X, 1: 3–27.

Lanzarini, R. (2013b) Jorge: empresário de fora, casado e versátil – homoerotismo no anonimato das viagens, Doctoral thesis, UFSC, Florianópolis.

Lanzarini, R. (2015) Homoerotismo durante los viajes: el placer sexual entre hombres en espacios anónimos en Brasil y Portugal, *Estudios y Perspectivas en Turismo* 24: 943–962.

Lanzarini, R. and Trigo, L. G. G. (2014) Lazer sexual masculino no Brasil, *Journal of Tourism and Development* 2, 21/22: 59–67.

Lapassade, G. (2001) L'observation participante, *Revista Europeia de Etnografia da Educação* 1: 9–26.

Ministry of Tourism, Brazil (2012) *Anuário estatístico 2012*, Brasília: Mtur.

Pine, B. J. II and Gilmore, J. H. (1999) *The Experience Economy*, Boston, MA: Harvard Business School Press.

Trigo, L. G. G. (2003) *Entretenimento: uma crítica aberta*, São Paulo: Senac.

Woods, G. (1998) *A History of Gay Literature: The Male Tradition*, New Haven: Yale University Press.

Part IV
Sustainable hospitality

30

Creating value for all

Sustainability in hospitality

Elena Cavagnaro*

> **Key themes**
>
> Hotel sustainability
>
> Social inclusivity
>
> Disability and hospitality
>
> Multiple usage hotels

Over a decade ago Bader (2005) noted that sustainability was becoming one of the most relevant issues to hoteliers. The main reason given by Bader (2005) is that hoteliers recognise that they are in an interdependent relationship with the surrounding environment. Considering that the focus of the hospitality industry is on guest satisfaction and long-term relationships, one would expect the industry to favour the social dimension of sustainability (Milhalic *et al.*, 2012). Yet, sustainable business practices in the sector are more often than not based on a desire for cost reduction, so that environmental issues and eco-efficiency are prioritised above social ones (Xu *et al.*, 2011; Milhalic *et al.*, 2012). External pressure from legislative bodies reinforces the hoteliers' focus on energy savings and cost reduction. At the European level a clear example is offered by the European Directive on Energy Performance of Buildings (EC 2002). Yet member states have also passed laws concerned with buildings' eco-efficiency such as in the case of Portugal discussed by Galvão and colleagues (2011). Voluntary certification initiatives, such as the Dutch GreenKey, have also predominantly had an environmental focus.

The appeal of eco-efficiency to the commercial hospitality sector is understandable, but deceptive from a sustainability viewpoint. It is understandable both because of the role that the environmental movement has played in framing the concept of sustainability (Cavagnaro and Curiel, 2012) and also because eco-efficiency has an immediate economic return. It is deceptive because, from its start, the concept of sustainability has included a social dimension

DOI: 10.4324/9781315679938-34

(see, e.g., WCED, 1987). In addition, it could be argued that eco-efficiency is a product-related sustainability measure and therefore does not touch on the specific core of hospitality, the host–guest relationship. In other words, hospitality is a people-related business and is thus in a perfect position to favour the social and ethical dimension of sustainability (Milhalic *et al.*, 2012; Lashley, 2016).

In this context it is not surprising that when the social dimension is considered by the hospitality industry philanthropy is the predominant paradigm (Holcomb *et al.*, 2007). Philanthropy, though, by its nature does not require a change in the strategy and the processes of organisations. In other words, organisations may engage in charitable giving even when they act unethically (Cavagnaro and Curiel, 2012; Lashley, 2016). As Carroll (1991) has observed, philanthropy is the icing on the cake, and cannot be seen as a substitute for the ethical and social responsibilities facing an enterprise.

Therefore, it may sadly be concluded that more than ten years after Bader's observation that sustainability was becoming a salient issues to hoteliers, the hospitality industry has still not delivered on its potential to create value not only on an economic but also on a social and environmental bottom line. To overcome this unsatisfactory situation it has been argued that it is 'especially relevant to assess whether (at least) sustainability leaders/champions are present in this industry to instigate the necessary changes' (Melissen *et al.*, 2015: 6). Highlighting the work of sustainability leaders through presenting best practices may encourage the necessary change by offering a perspective for action. Following this appeal, this chapter presents two best cases of hotels that with a different cultural background and ownership structure have engaged with sustainability by tackling a social challenge. The first case describes a project by Meliá Roma Aurelia Antica where people with a disability were offered the opportunity to develop their talents as trainees. The second case highlights the power of new, sustainable business models by referring to a hotel in Amsterdam, Casa 400, which back in the 1960s developed a business solution to the social problem of student housing. An overall conclusion briefly ties the discussion together and looks forward to the future of sustainability in hospitality.

Creating value for everyone: inclusivity and hospitality at Meliá Roma Aurelia Antica, Rome

This section reports on a project developed by Meliá Roma Aurelia Antica in cooperation with the Italian Association of People with Down Syndrome (AIPD) in which six youngsters with Down syndrome were trained as hotel employees. The section is divided into three subsections: the first frames the social issue of inclusivity as a sustainability challenge; the second introduces the company, Meliá Hotels International; the third and last subsection showcases the project 'Hotel with 6 Stars' that was designed and implemented at Meliá Roma Aurelia Antica. A brief conclusion closes the section.

The disabled guest

The integration of specific groups, such as disabled people, is one of the most pregnant social issues of the modern-day economy. Accessibility and inclusiveness have therefore become a heavily discussed theme in general, and in the tourism and hospitality industry in particular. From a business perspective, accessibility is often addressed as an opportunity to enlarge the market base (see, e.g., O'Neill and Knight, 2000) by suiting the special needs of differently able guests (e.g. Eichorn *et al.*, 2008; Darcy and Pegg, 2011). Accessibility, though, implies the inclusion of persons with disability not only as guests but also as hosts.

The UN World Programme for Action Concerning Disabled Persons, issued in 1982, aimed at full participation and equalisation of opportunities for persons with disabilities in order to strengthen their role as agents and not only as beneficiaries of development (UN, 1982). This double focus is present in all UN documents related to the theme, and has been reinforced in the UN report on a disability inclusive agenda issued in 2013 (UN, 2013). In this report, moreover, inclusiveness is framed as a necessary prerequisite for sustainable development. The inter-linkage between sustainable development on the one hand and the full participation of persons with disability in economic life on the other had already been stressed in 2012 by the UN Conference on Sustainable Development (UN, 2012). It can therefore be stated that accessibility and inclusiveness are becoming major themes in the debate around the socio-economic dimension of sustainable development. Commercial and non-commercial organisations are in the front line in fighting this challenge, because they own the means to include (or exclude) disabled people as employees and as clients. In this context it should be remembered that the hospitality and tourism industry is one of the leading employers worldwide: 1 in 11 jobs are in this sector (UNWTO, 2013). Accessibility for and inclusiveness of disabled people in terms of their opportunity to participate as actors in economic activities are therefore of particular relevance to the tourism and hospitality industry.

One of the difficulties of addressing the needs of differently able people, both as hosts and as guests, is the lack of consensus on a definition of 'ability' and 'disability'. Generally speaking, two approaches can be distinguished in the literature. One approach propagates a strict definition based on medical conditions. From this perspective disability is a deficiency to be measured on the basis of its deviance from the norm. The other approach sees disability as a social phenomenon and tends to examine it in the context of exclusion and discrimination (Buhalis and Micopoulou, 2011). This is not the place to enter into the details of this debate. However, it can be noted that while the physical dimension of disability should not be overlooked, it cannot be denied that what is considered a 'disability' depends also on individual attitudes and on the social context. Both approaches should therefore be integrated when looking at the accessibility of the labour market for disabled people.

Considering a wide definition of disability, it has been estimated that worldwide one billion people have some level of disability (WHO, 2011). In Italy 6.5 million people between the ages of 15 and 64 years (i.e. 16.5 per cent of the population) are confronted with (chronic) illness or a form of disability (Istat, 2013). Notwithstanding several mechanisms aimed at enhancing the opportunities of disabled people in the Italian job market, the percentage of unemployed in this group is higher than in all other groups. In this context, Italian employers have been accused of being unresponsive. Unfortunately, this situation is not limited to Italy. As has already been noted above, the lack of inclusivity worldwide is considered to be one of the major impediments to sustainable development (UN, 2013). Sharing examples of best practices, such us the training programme for people with Down syndrome at Meliá Aurelia Antica in Rome, may help to showcase that it is indeed possible to create value for everyone.

Meliá Hotels International

Meliá Aurelia Antica in Rome is part of Meliá Hotels International, a leading hotel company in Spain and one of the most important hotels and resorts enterprises worldwide. It owns a portfolio of more than 350 hotels distributed in 41 countries on four continents and employs more than 35,000 people. Sustainability is regarded by Meliá Hotels Internationals (MHI) as one of the backbones of the business model, since it ensures the long-term creation of economic value. From the start of the company, the commitment to protecting the environment, sharing the local culture and contributing to cultural integration has been included in MHI's fundamental values. The level of integration of these values in MHI's strategy, processes and procedures has increased over the years (see Figure 30.1), following a pattern that is described in several models on the development of corporate social responsibility (CSR): from a self-protecting stage where CSR is considered as a value protector and reveals itself in activities that are not directly linked with the business processes (such as philanthropy) to an embedded phase where CSR is understood as value creation and is intertwined with the principles, strategy and processes of the organisation (Maon *et al.*, 2010).

Interestingly, in its sustainability policy MHI gives equal attention to the environmental and the social dimension of sustainability (MHI, n.d.). MHI claims that the backbone of its social involvement is the conviction that MHI's activity will only be sustainable in the long term if it is able to contribute to the reduction of social differences and poverty. This includes looking for inclusion of the most disadvantaged groups such as the elderly or the disabled. In addition, MHI does not see inclusivity of these groups only as an opportunity to enlarge its marked base (see, e.g., O'Neill and Knight, 2000) but also as an opportunity to enlarge its pool of human resources. In this way MHI seeks to simultaneously address a major social issue (labour opportunity for the disabled) and a major business issue (shortage of employees). Finally, MHI's commitment to inclusiveness has been framed as a policy for its international operations. To this aim in 2013 MHI created the Global Model of Disability Integration in co-operation with the ONCE Foundation, an organisation with a long-standing commitment to less fortunate people. Basically, the MHI Global Model of Disability Integration looks at opportunities for inclusiveness in MHI relations with each of its main stakeholders: suppliers, guests, owners and employees. For example, in its relationship with suppliers MHI strives for an inclusive value chain where special attention is given to local suppliers and suppliers from

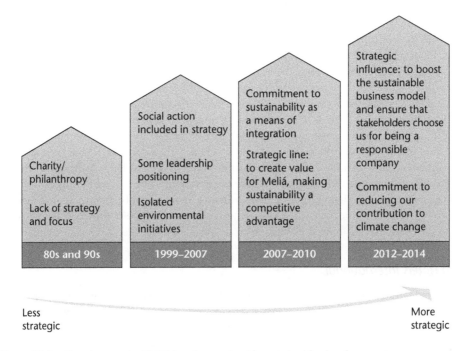

Figure 30.1 Development of MHI involvement with sustainable development

Source: CSR Department, Meliá Hotels International (P. Noschese, Rome, 2014, personal communication)

less advantaged groups such as (in specific countries) women. The design of the hotel premises, where barriers are removed as far as possible, shows MHI commitment to inclusiveness towards guests. Employment of disadvantaged groups forms part and parcel of this policy (P. Noschese, Managing Director Italy – Meliá Hotels International, Rome, 2014, personal communication).

Against this backdrop it can safely be stated that the offer of a traineeship to six youngsters with Down syndrome at Meliá Hotel Aurelia Antica in Rome is not a standalone activity, but finds its roots in a longstanding commitment to environmental and social sustainability by MHI. This project, known by the name 'Hotel 6 Stelle' (Hotel with 6 stars), will be illustrated in the remainder of this section.

Hotel with 6 Stars[1]

The aim of the project 'Hotel with 6 Stars' was the integration of six young people with Down syndrome into a real work environment while its objective was to create for them a professional and complete experience by focusing not on their disability but on their ability to contribute to the daily work. To reach this aim it was essential that a professional and complete work experience would be offered to the trainees, six young people with Down syndrome – the six stars in the project title. This meant that they should fully contribute to the daily work according to their abilities and be able to join as a trainee all departments of the hotel. The setting, Meliá Roma Aurelia Antica, is a 4-star hotel: work standards are therefore high and could be considered quite challenging for the trainees.

The project's planning phase started in October 2013. While approval of the project by the competent authorities was sought, the trainees' selection was carried out by AIPD (Italian Association of People with Down Syndrome) in close consultation with the hotel management. After the selection of the six trainees, a second assessment individuated their attitudes and abilities and matched them to the six hotel departments with six different roles: receptionist, chambermaid, waitress during breakfast, waitress at the bar and restaurant, cook and maintenance. Thus, in line with the aim and objectives of the project, the trainees were integrated in all hotel departments, including those departments such as front desk and room division where direct contact with guests is expected. This is remarkable because when jobs are offered in the hospitality industry to people with Down syndrome these are mostly in the back office, far from contact with guests (P. Noschese, Rome, 2014, personal communication).

A staff member of Meliá Roma Aurelia Antica tutored each trainee. Tutors were selected considering their character traits, their empathic attitude and their capability to create an interpersonal relationship to facilitate learning. The human factor was of paramount importance for the success of the project because the trainees would be confronted with several new and challenging activities, such as travelling alone and working in a professional organisation. Tutors were challenged, too: most of them had never worked with people with Down syndrome. By establishing a warm contact between the tutor and the trainee almost from the beginning the fear connected with the novelty of the work environment and the tasks could be softened and the threshold for asking help lowered.

The tutors were well aware of the challenges faced by their trainees, as the following quote from one of the tutor shows:

> Since my trainee's arrival, it was clear that he was the right person for the role of cook because he had already practised in a kitchen and also studied at a hotel school. His big challenge was learning and working in a different environment, with a new team and cooking with new installations and equipment that can only be found in large restaurants.
>
> *(Chef at Meliá Roma Aurelia Antica,*
> *Rome, 2014, personal communication)*

The traineeship lasted three months, from 18 November 2013 to 7 March 2014 with a Christmas break. It was organised as a part-time job, with four working hours a day. Three trainees worked in the morning, from 9 a.m. till 1 p.m., and the other three in the afternoon, from 2 p.m. till 6 p.m. When scheduling tasks each trainee's ability was taken into account, and allowance was made for the possibility that they would get tired sooner than other staff members. Instructions were also carefully doled out considering the limited amount of information that each trainee could daily acquire. On the other hand, no concessions were made to quality, and trainees were constantly challenged to reach the next level.

A clear example of the tension between the quality standards of the hotel and the trainees' capacity to cope with them can be seen in the difficulties that the trainee assigned to the role of chambermaid faced in cleaning rooms. She could not properly manage her time, and was constantly lagging behind schedule. This issue was solved by dividing operations into small chunks of activities and by constantly practising those so that memory and speed could both be improved. The personal growth of this trainee is well expressed in the following quote: 'I wasn't able to do anything at first … I could not match the required timings, the bathroom was not perfect … Yet in the end I managed it!' (Martina, Rome, 2014, TV series *Hotel a 6 stelle*).

A very important point to be highlighted is that during this experience the trainees learned a job, earned their first salaries and gained the knowledge needed to work for an enterprise. The sentiments of the trainees are well depicted in the following quote: 'The joyous reaction of the trainees in the dressing room: for the first time they were wearing a real job outfit and were seeing each other as real professionals' (A. Previde Massara, Rome, 2014, personal communication).

In addition, the trainees also 'infected' the hotel staff with their pure enthusiasm, by bringing their positive energy and unfiltered approach to their work challenges. This is something that would be impossible to forget, as Francesco, one of the tutors, remembers: 'my trainee's passion, proactive attitude and uncomplicated approach to life are a constant inspiration for me and the Front Office Team today. His presence here represented an undisputed enrichment for us, from both a professional and a human point of view' (personal communication, 30 May 2014).

At the end of the experience a debriefing of the activities was organised by AIPD, the NGO that followed the whole project. During the debriefing, the hotel tutors and management shared information and evaluated the experience together. In short, the lesson learned is that to successfully integrate people with a disability into a working environment three major ingredients are needed: first, careful preparation with the support of a specialised organisation; second, a thorough choice both of trainees and tutors; and, last but not least, an unrelenting commitment to make a difference by creating value for all. To quote one of the employees involved: 'It's not a matter of costs, it's a matter of culture, we must contribute to change' (P. Noschese, Rome, 2014, personal communication).

Concluding remarks

Accessibility is often addressed as an opportunity to enlarge the market base by suiting the special needs of differently able guests (O'Neill and Knight, 2000; Eichorn *et al.*, 2008; Darcy and Pegg, 2011). Accessibility, though, implies the inclusion of persons with disability not only as guests but also as hosts. The hospitality and tourism industry is one of the leading employers worldwide. It can therefore not escape the responsibility to offer real work opportunities for people with a handicap. In doing so it creates value not only for these people and society, but for the company itself as the experience at Meliá Roma Aurelia Antica shows. This experience illustrates that inclusion is feasible and that, under the proper conditions, does not form a liability but rather an asset enhancing the 4-star service offered by the hotel.

The next section goes a step further: it showcases a hotel where creating value for society is not only a special project but constitutes the reason why the hotel was developed in the first place.

Solving social problems with a business solution: Hotel Casa 400, Amsterdam

This section reports on an example of social entrepreneurship – that is, a business founded to solve a social problem. In the case illustrated here the business is a hotel and the social issue addressed is student housing in Amsterdam in the 1960s. The section is divided in three subsections: the first introduces the case by briefly addressing the concept of 'social enterprise' and then describing the situation in Amsterdam in the early 1960s, focusing on the student housing problem. In the second subsection the foundation Casa Academica is introduced and it is shown how the company that Casa Academica started, Hotel Casa 400, represents an example of a social enterprise in the hotel industry. The third section looks forward, at further developments at Hotel Casa 400, and offers a brief conclusion to this section.

A flexible provision

The major challenge of linking sustainable development to business activity is to create a business model that 'capture[s] economic value for itself through delivering social and environmental benefits' (Bocken *et al.*, 2014: 44). Already in the first pages of this chapter it has been noted that the hospitality industry seldom addresses sustainability integrally by creating social and environmental value alongside economic value. In the majority of cases, for hoteliers sustainability equals reducing energy and water use. Reduction, though, addresses only a specific aspect, eco-efficiency, of the environmental dimension of sustainability and leaves untouched its socio-cultural dimension. With the project 'Hotel with 6 Stars' presented above, Meliá Roma Aurelia Antica championed an approach to sustainability that goes beyond eco-efficiency because it directly engages with inclusivity and inclusivity is a major socio-economic issue. As observed above this engagement had deep roots in the mission and vision of the Meliá International Hotel chain and – as far as it can be foreseen now – Meliá Roma Aurelia Antica will continue in its efforts to be inclusive, even though 'Hotel with 6 Stars' is a project and may not be continued. In other words, to foster inclusivity is not the reason why Meliá Roma Aurelia Antica was set up as a business: its business model was not based on the need to solve the social problem of inclusivity. In this sense, Meliá Roma Aurelia Antica cannot be characterised as a social enterprise. However, Hotel Casa 400 can: it has been developed with the specific purpose of solving a social problem by offering comfortable and affordable housing to the student population of Amsterdam, a city that in the 1960s and today is struggling with the increasing number of young people willing to pursue their studies in this enchanting and vibrant Dutch city.

To better understand the difference between the Meliá Roma Aurelia Antica and Hotel Casa 400 approaches, it is useful to refer to the business typology proposed by Short and colleagues (2012). These authors distinguish nine sustainable business models ranging from more conservative to more visionary. These nine approaches are (1) maximise material and energy efficiency, (2) create value from waste, (3) deliver functionality, rather than ownership, (4) encourage sufficiency, (5) adopt a stewardship role, (6) re-purpose the business for society/environment, (7) integrate business in the community, (8) develop scale-up solutions, and (9) radical innovation.

As argued by Melissen *et al.* (2015), whereas focusing on material and energy efficiency and creating value from waste can definitely contribute to the environmental component of sustainable development, actually aligning a business activity with environmental and societal needs requires more advanced approaches, such as represented by models (6), (7), (8) and (9). Meliá Roma Aurelia Antica's 'Hotel with 6 Stars' project may be framed between models five (adopting a stewardship role by engaging with stakeholders to ensure their long-term well-being) and seven (integrated business in the community through its collaborative approach with the Italian Association of People with Down Syndrome). As the next subsection illustrates, from its start Hotel Casa 400 constituted a radical innovation in the way student housing was approached and is therefore better understood as an instance of the ninth business model.

Before describing Hotel Casa 400's business solution to student housing, it is necessary to look briefly at the situation of Amsterdam in the late 1950s and early 1960s. At the end of the 1950s, as in most European countries, the Dutch economy and society had started to recover from the tragic scars left by the Second World War. While the older people in Dutch society wished to go back to the pre-war situation, young people were looking westwards, to the USA, and forwards, to a new and more equal society. Young people wished for a life different to that of their parents, and young women certainly also wished to develop their talents outside the family. It is useful to remember here that in the 1960s in the Netherlands it was perfectly lawful and socially acceptable for an employer to fire a woman when she was expecting her first child. An increasing number of men and women, who longed for emancipation, chose to enrol for higher education, preferably in major cities such as Amsterdam. As a consequence, student housing in Amsterdam became a significant problem. In 1957 the General Students' Association of Amsterdam (ASVA) reckoned that for every 100 students only 35 rooms were available. Often these were uncomfortable, small and very expensive accommodation offered for rent by private owners. For many students there seemed to be no alternative but to keep living with their parents. Protesting and occupying empty houses constituted a more radical alternative, and one that often led to tense situations in the Amsterdam of the early 1960s. Clearly student housing was a social problem that the Municipality of Amsterdam was not able to address alone.

Casa Academica and Hotel Casa 400[2]

Hotel Casa 400 was designed with the specific purpose of offering a long-term solution to the social problem of student housing in Amsterdam. Four young men found the archetype for this solution during a trip to Copenhagen in the late 1950s. In Copenhagen they discovered a property that was operating as a traditional hotel in the summer and as student housing in the winter. This idea struck them and they immediately thought of the possibility of replicating it in the Netherlands. Even though they had no specific experience in the hotel business, in 1957 they started a foundation, Casa Academia (Academic House), by donating 25 guilders (around 12 euros) each with the aim of opening a similar hotel in Amsterdam. Their plan caught the interest of some major Dutch companies, such as KLM, and the Municipality of Amsterdam. By what in our time would be called a process of crowdsourcing, the four managed to fulfil the funding requirements of the Dutch government. Finally Hotel Casa 400 could be built.

The building, with 400 rooms, was officially opened on 31 October 1962. At its opening Hotel Casa 400 represented a radical innovation not only in student housing but also in the hospitality business. It offered a business solution to a social problem because it financed student housing in the winter via the profits earned by exploiting the building as a commercial hotel in the summer. In this way it could offer affordable and comfortable student housing.

Notwithstanding some changes, providing inexpensive but comfortable housing to students through profitably exploiting hotel accommodation is still today at the centre of the mission of Hotel Casa 400. As Bernadine Egbring, Executive Assistant Manager at Casa 400, puts it: 'though we do not always advertise ourselves as a social enterprise, our end goal is not to earn money; money from the commercial exploitation of hotel rooms is a means to serve our end goal: to offer students affordable accommodation' (Amsterdam, 2015, personal communication).

'Social enterprise' is a rather new concept, not known in the 1960s, and still today it is not widely used. This at least partially explains why Hotel Casa 400 does not advertise itself as such. Moreover, Hotel Casa 400 management feared that hotel guests might feel uncomfortable at the idea of sleeping in a structure that for part of the year was also functioning as student accommodation. This fear increased when Casa 400 decided to accommodate guests not only in the summer, but also during winter by building a new structure with more rooms. As a consequence, a part of the hotel was dedicated to paying guests the whole year round, while a part saw a mixed occupancy: guests in the summer and students in the winter. Interestingly, thanks to conversations with other stakeholders such as suppliers and academia, this attitude has changed and Hotel Casa 400 is more and more seeing that the uniqueness of its concept has a marketing value, as the following quote shows:

> We are developing a new website where our unique nature will be openly communicated to all our guests. This new website will integrate the functions that are now served by four, distinct websites dedicated to our two major target groups: hotel guests and students. It is a step in the attempt to let these two worlds, which thus previously we were very carefully to keep separate from each other, meet.
>
> *(Anne-Mieke Mulder, Amsterdam, 2015, personal communication)*

The original ownership structure was a foundation precisely to underline the special aim of Hotel Casa 400 where, as stated above, making a profit is a means to offer to students affordable accommodation. Now Hotel Casa 400 is a privately owned company, even though all shares are owned by the foundation 'Casa Academica' and all profit is still reinvested in the company. The change in the ownership structure is linked to other major changes in the way Hotel Casa 400 is operated. In 2010 Hotel Casa 400 took over a new building, which in contrast to the first one is not owned but rented. The new structure features 520 rooms, 12 conference rooms, a restaurant and a bar. Since 2010, 150 out of the 520 rooms have been exploited as hotel rooms for the whole year round. These 150 rooms generate the revenues needed to cover the increased costs of the building, and to compensate for the withdrawal of the Municipality as an investor. The management structure has also been strengthened and professionalised due to the need to operate a major hotel not for four but for twelve months a year.

Though successful, the concept has never been upscaled. This is interesting, considering the mission of the foundation 'Casa Academica' and the fact that in Amsterdam and other major Dutch cities it is still rather difficult for students to find affordable housing. Moreover, it could be argued that also from a sustainability perspective a successful concept should be delivered on a larger scale to maximise the benefits for society and the environment (Short *et al.*, 2012). There are reasons, though, why this has not happened. To quote Anne-Mieke Mulder:

> From the opening of the first Hotel Casa 400 onwards the focus has been on delivering affordable housing for students more than on the commercial side of the operation. This internally directed focus explains why no resources have been developed to up-scale our solution. Moreover the market served by Hotel Casa 400 is very specific: we need to find places where there is a strong demand both from students and from hotel guests. In the Netherlands this limits us to Amsterdam, because other major academic cities such as Rotterdam and Utrecht do not attract the same amount of tourists as Amsterdam. As a

foundation we are bound to a low risk strategy: the whole mix should be perfect before we make a move. That is the reason why, even though in the last few years the Foundation has regularly been approached with requests to expand, no other Hotel Casa 400 has been developed yet.

(Amsterdam, 2015, personal communication)

Bernadine Egbring adds: 'Moreover the hotel premises should not be too expensive, and this means that we cannot build on too expensive ground – which unfortunately has become the case in Amsterdam' (Amsterdam, 2015, personal communication).

Further developments

Hotel Casa 400 now has several competitors. A similar formula (students in the winter and tourists in the summer) is operated by The Student Hotel in Amsterdam, Rotterdam and The Hague. The average price of a room in The Student Hotel, though, lies more than 200 euros above the price of a room at Hotel Casa 400. Here, once again, the social mission of Hotel Casa 400 has led to a different outcome than its commercially minded competitors. Since the economic crisis in 2008 more competitors have entered the market for student housing in Amsterdam as office-building owners have discovered that providing student housing in their buildings can be a profitable option. These developments, combined with an expected decline in the student population due to demographic reasons, may lead to a new situation where the student housing problem in major Dutch cities is solved, although new and even more challenging housing problems are emerging, such us housing for elderly people and for war refugees. This is probably the area where Casa Academica and Hotel Casa 400 can still make a difference in the future.

Many people may think that student housing is a less pressing social problem than the exclusion of people with disability from work, even though both are problems society is struggling with. Clearly governments alone seem unable to offer a suitable and feasible solution to both, and therefore they represent an opportunity for businesses to step in and create economic value through delivering social and environmental benefits (Bocken *et al.*, 2014). Moreover, Hotel Casa 400 showcases that engaging with a social problem can become the reason why a business is developed. In this sense, Hotel Casa 400 offers to the hotel industry a clear example of social entrepreneurship.

Conclusions

The two case studies described in this chapter illustrate that at least some hoteliers recognise the truth of Bader's statement (2005) that sustainability is one of the most relevant issues to the hospitality sector. Both examples moreover testify to the fact that implementing sustainability in hospitality does not need to remain limited to cost-driven measures (Xu *et al.*, 2011; Milhalic *et al.*, 2012), and that a more integral approach to sustainability is not only wishful thinking but also possible. When managers look at sustainability from a cost perspective, they are led to focus on its environmental dimension and on eco-efficiency measures such as reducing the amount of the water and energy used. Eco-efficiency measures may result in a smaller environmental footprint, and should therefore be encouraged. However, as pointed out above, eco-efficiency falls short of sustainability for at least two reasons: first, because it does not directly address the social (or people) dimension of sustainability and, second, because, being product related, it does not touch the ethical component subtending genuine hospitality (Lashley, 2016).

The examples of Meliá Roma Aurelia Antica and Hotel Casa 400 show that while the hospitality industry in general seems not yet ready to fully and integrally engage with sustainability (Melissen *et al.*, 2015) in cases where this happens the potential of hotels to generate economic benefits while creating social value is tremendous. Even more interestingly, both examples showcase that the hospitality industry is in a perfect position for favouring the social and ethical dimension of sustainability without resorting to philanthropy. Philanthropy is still the predominant paradigm from which most industries, including hospitality, address social issues such as creating job opportunities for disadvantaged people or catering for guests with a small purse. Similarly to eco-efficiency, philanthropy is praiseworthy but not sufficient to fulfil the requirements of sustainability. For one thing, supporting a good cause with money does not reveal whether this money is gained ethically. Meliá Roma Aurelia Antica and Hotel Casa 400 have chosen, respectively, to address the issues of job opportunity for disabled people and of affordable student housing not through philanthropy but by developing new and more sustainable business models (Short *et al.*, 2012). In doing this they have demonstrated that hospitality is not only willing but also able to integrate sustainability in its processes and operations, and thus contribute to a solution to tough social problems (Cavagnaro and Curiel, 2012). In a society characterised by increasing socio-political and ecological instability, the hospitality industry has a choice: to engage in these challenges or to escape to the fairy-tale land where the only business of business is making money. It does not require 20/20 vision to see that only one strategy may lead to success, and that engaged hotels such as Meliá Roma Aurelia Antica and Hotel Casa 400 are leading the way in creating innovative and sustainable business models and thus securing the future of the hospitality industry.

Notes

* This article would not have been possible without the collaboration of Palmiro Noschese (Managing Director Italy – Meliá Hotels International), Alessio Previde Massara (Resident Manager at Meliá Rome Aurelia Antica) and Bernadine Egbring (Executive Assistant Manager at Casa 400) and Anne-Mieke Mulder (Project and Development Manager at Casa 400).

1 Information for the writing of this subsection has been gathered through interviews with management and employees of Meliá Roma Aurelia Antica in Rome and study of different materials such as MHI reports and a short TV series on the project filmed by Italian television (RAI3 and Magnolia). To respect the privacy of the people involved their names have not been revealed unless permission to do so was given. One quote was taken from the broadcasted TV series, and therefore the name of the trainee is given. Information on the TV programme, in Italian, and some photo material is available from http://www.rai.tv/dl/RaiTV/programmi/media/ContentItem-e7ac2021-362c-457d-9497-12696849ea91.html (accessed 1 December 2015).
2 This chapter is based on interviews with management and employees at Hotel Casa 400.

References

Bader, E. E. (2005) Sustainable hotel business practices, *Journal of Retail and Leisure Property* 5, 1: 70–77.
Bocken, N. M. P, Short, S. W., Rana, P. and Evans, S. (2014) A literature and practice review to develop sustainable business model archetypes, *Journal of Cleaner Production* 65: 42–56.
Buhalis, D. and Michopoulou, E. (2011) Information enabled tourism destination marketing: addressing the accessibility market, *Current Issues in Tourism* 14, 2: 145–168.
Carroll, A. B. (1991) The pyramid of corporate social responsibility: toward the moral management of organizational stakeholders, *Business Horizons* 34, 4: 39–48.
Cavagnaro, E. and Curiel, G. H. (2012) *The Three Levels of Sustainability*, Sheffield: Greenleaf.
Darcy, S. and Pegg, S. (2011) Towards strategic intent: perceptions of disability service provision amongst hotel accommodation managers, *International Journal of Hospitality Management* 30: 468–476.
EC (2002) Directive 2002/91/EC, On the energy performance of buildings. Available at http://ec.europa.eu/energy/demand/legislation/buildings_en.htm.

Eichorn, V., Miller, G., Michopoulou, E. and Buhalis, D. (2008) Enabling access to tourism through information schemes?, *Annals of Tourism Research* 55, 1: 189–210.

Galvão, J. R., Leitão, S. A., Silva, S. M. and Gaio, T. M. (2011) Cogeneration supply by bio-energy for a sustainable hotel building management system, *Fuel Processing Technology* 92, 2: 284–289.

Holcomb, J. L., Upchurch, R. S. and Okumus, F. (2007) Corporate social responsibility: what are top hotel companies reporting?, *International Journal of Contemporary Hospitality Management* 19, 6: 461–475.

Istat (2013) *Limitazioni nello svolgimento dell'attività lavorativa delle persone con problemi di salute*, Anno 2011, Statistiche Report, Roma.

Lashley, C. (2016) Business ethics and sustainability, *Research in Hospitality Management* 6, 1: 1–7.

Maon, F., Lindgreen, A. and Swaen, V. (2010) Organizational stages and cultural phases: a critical review and a consolidative model of corporate social responsibility development, *International Journal of Management Reviews* 12, 1 20–35.

Melissen, F., Cavagnaro, E., Damen, M. and Düweke, A. (2015) Is the hotel industry prepared to face the challenge of sustainable development?, *Journal of Vacation Marketing* 22, 3: 227–238.

MHI (Meliá Hotels International) (n.d.) *Sustainability at Meliá Hotels International*. Available at http://www.meliahotelsinternational.com/en/corporate-responsibility. Accessed 12 January 2015.

Mihalic, T., Zabkar, V. and Knežević Cvelbar, L. (2012) A hotel sustainability business model: evidence from Slovenia, *Journal of Sustainable Tourism* 20, 5: 701–719.

O'Neil, M. and Knight, J. (2000) Disability tourism dollars in Western Australia hotels, *Hospitality Review* 18, 2: 72–88.

Short, S. W., Bocken, N. M. P., Rana, P. and Evans, S. (2012) Business model innovation for embedding sustainability: a practice-based approach introducing business model archetypes. In *Proceedings of the 10th Global Conference on Sustainable Manufacturing (GCSM): Towards Implementing Sustainable Manufacturing*, 31 October–2 November, Istanbul, Turkey.

UN (1982) *World Programme for Action Concerning Disabled Persons*, UN General Assembly Resolution 37.52.1/. Available at http://www.independentliving.org/files/WPACDP.pdf. Accessed 12 March 2014.

UN (2012) *Future We Want*, Outcome document of the Rio+20 Conference. Available at http://sustainabledevelopment.un.org/futurewewant.html. Accessed 12 March 2014.

UN (2013) *The Way Forward: A Disability Inclusive Development Agenda Towards 2015 and Beyond*, Report to the Secretary-General, A/68/95. Available at http://www.un.org/disabilities/default.asp?id=1590. Accessed 12 March 2014.

UNWTO (United Nations World Tourism Organization) (2013) *Tourism Highlights, 2013 edition*, Madrid: UNWTO.

WCED (World Commission on Environment and Development) (1987) *Our Common Future*, Oxford: Oxford University Press.

WHO (2011) *World Report on Disability*. Available at http://www.who.int/disabilities/world_report/2011/en/. Accessed 12 March 2014.

Xu, P., Chan, E. H. and Qian, Q. K. (2011) Success factors of energy performance contracting (EPC) for sustainable building energy efficiency retrofit (BEER) of hotel buildings in China, *Energy Policy* 39, 11: 7389–7398.

31

Liberating wage slaves

Towards sustainable employment practices

Conrad Lashley

Key themes

Slavery today

Autocratic management practices

Participatory involvement

Workers control

> When we acknowledge the kingdom of the self, we will no longer accept slavery either for ourselves or for others, no matter how it is disguised.
>
> *(Spence)*

As a proportion of the total employee population, those who are slaves are a relatively small number, but there are millions of people who are in effect slaves, forced to undertake work at inadequate pay rates that are imposed upon them. For others in the workforce there may be freedom of movement and employment, but the rates of reward for their efforts are derisory. In principle, the national minimum wage protects employees from the power of employers to pay wages below the level to sustain the cost of living. In practice, however, the UK minimum wage rate is below the 'living wage', and many low-paid employees are forced to work longer hours, or take on another job to cover the cost of survival.

This chapter explores the employment relationship in the hospitality sector, and suggests that, for all sorts of structural reasons, the ability of individual employees to protect their rights via collective bargaining is limited. In these circumstances, forms of employee resistance take individualised forms – high levels of staff turnover are one manifestation of this situation. The chapter goes on to suggest that it is in the long-term interest of employers to see employees as the key asset capable of delivering customer loyalty and competitive advantage. There is a need to adopt management practices that engage the wisdom of front-line personnel, and prioritise employee retention.

DOI: 10.4324/9781315679938-35

Slavery today

According to the International Labour Organization (ILO, 2015), approximately 21 million men, women and children live in slavery across the world. While it is assumed that slavery ended in the early nineteenth century, there are an estimated 13,000 people currently living as slaves in the UK. In 2013, some 1,746 referrals were made to the official National Referral Mechanism. Of these, 1,122 were women and girls, and 624 were men and boys. The Anti-Slavery Society states;

> There are many different characteristics that distinguish slavery from other human rights violations, however only one needs to be present for slavery to exist. Someone is in slavery if they are: forced to work – through mental or physical threat; owned or controlled by an 'employer', usually through mental or physical abuse or the threat of abuse; dehumanized, treated as a commodity or bought and sold as 'property'; physically constrained or has restrictions placed on his/her freedom of movement.
>
> *(2015)*

The society then describes a number of forms that slavery takes in the contemporary world. *Bonded labour* is when the person is forced to work in repayment of a loan. *Child labour* involves the exploitation of children by forcing them to work for another person's gain. The ILO estimates that there are 5.5 million children in slavery or in situations like slavery around the globe (Anti-Slavery Society, 2015). *Child and forced marriage* occurs where young people under the age of 18 are forced into marriage. While both girls and boys experience this, most victims of forced marriage are females. The Society quotes a UNICEF estimate that 11 per cent of women worldwide were married under the age of 15. *Forced labour* involves punishment or threats of punishment to make individuals undertake work against their choice. *Descent-based slavery* results from children of slaves or a slave class being born into a society, where the children are regarded as the property of the slave owners. 'They are treated as property by their "masters". They can be inherited, sold or given away as gifts or wedding presents' (Anti-Slavery Society, 2015). *Human trafficking* takes place when men, women and children are exploited to work against their will in prostitution, forced marriage, domestic servitude, farming or other industries. In some cases, human trafficking results in forced organ removal for the benefit of the owner, for trade or personal use. And this in the twenty-first century?

Modern slavery, therefore, takes a number of forms and encompasses a range of motives. However, bonded labour and child labour are the forms that are most likely to involve work within hotels, restaurants and other hospitality organisations. In some cases, bonded labour is used directly in hospitality businesses, typically in low-skilled jobs in cleaning and housekeeping services. In other settings, women are forced to work in the sex industry in brothels or in other 'love hotel' settings. The initial debt incurred is used as a device to force individuals to work for low wages with little opportunity to escape or repay the debt. This involves the poorest or most stigmatised individuals in the society. Loans taken out so as to be able to survive can result in a bonded relationship. 'Widespread discrimination against some social groups means they have limited access to justice, education, and ways to get themselves out of poverty, which is one of the main reasons the debt is taken in the first place' (Anti-Slavery Society, 2015). In other cases, the bonded labour involvement in the hospitality is indirect, because it occurs further down the supply chain in agricultural supply of food and drink, and cotton-based uniforms for example.

It is estimated by the ILO (2012) that there are 168 million children, aged between 5 and 17 years of age, working across the globe. Of these, it estimates, 5 per cent are employed in the most dangerous and unhealthy conditions. 'Worldwide, 5.5 million children are in slavery, trafficking, debt bondage and other forms of forced labour, forced recruitment for armed conflict, prostitution, pornography and other illicit activities' (ILO 2012). The main activities are in prostitution or pornography, illicit activities such as forced begging and petty theft, and the drug trade. The main industries cited by the United Nations Supplementary Slavery Convention (1956) include agriculture, factories, construction, brick-kilns, mines, bars, restaurants and the tourist environment.

Enslaving non-slaves

The previous section has shown that slavery in its various forms has an involvement in hospitality service provision across the globe. This section employs slavery as a metaphor to describe the employment experiences for workers in the sector where employee remuneration, even on the minimum wage, is below a level to sustain a decent standard of living. They may not be slaves technically, but their position in the labour market is such that they are forced to work in jobs where their power and choices are limited. This situation is particularly difficult in the hospitality industry where union membership is low, and opportunities for collective resistance are limited.

Before looking at the employment relationships in the sector, it is important to establish the dominant frames of reference used when examining the organisational relationships and the power of the various stakeholders. Fox (1974) and Cradden (2011) identify three frames of reference when discussing employment relationships. These frames of reference suggest that there are different views of employment and these determine the actions of various parties in the organisation such as between owners, managers and front-line employees, but also among commentators, academics, researchers, politicians, governments and legislators. Indeed, the 1970s and 1980s involved a high level of public debate about the 'industrial relations problem' in the UK.

The *unitary perspective* views the employment relationship in organisations as being one of mutual interest in the aims and activities of the organisation. All parties have a common interest in organisational purpose and outcomes. According to this view, organisations are one social entity with 'a general will', as Rousseau might have said. Cooperation and working collaboratively towards common goals is thereby deemed to be the natural order of things. Conflict is judged to be irrational and malign, and a failure to grasp 'the way things are'. This view has informed the dominant view about employment and the direction of much employment legislation in the UK over recent decades. The unitary perspective has informed legislation restricting the ability of trade unions to organise workforce resistance to owner/management policies. It has also informed a whole tranche of employment polices – the level of the minimum wage being set below the living wage rate, the rate needed to exist within the social and cultural setting.

The *pluralist perspective* asserts that organisations are made up of groups with different needs and interests. Owners, managers and employees are three major groups with different interests, and these need to be reflected in the organisation's control and accountability structures. Unlike those holding a unitary perspective, the pluralist view recognises that these different interest groups may indeed have conflicting needs and priorities, and the power of ownership should be tempered so as to reflect the needs of other stakeholders. Membership of the organisation is predicated on recognition of these mutually dependent relationships. Policies need to be developed in contexts where the various sectional interests participate so that policies, priorities and practices of the organisation reflect the needs and ambitions of the various stakeholder groups. This perspective has been dominant in mainland Europe, leading to formal negotiation structures where the needs of employees are reflected. Works Councils are one widespread structure whereby employee representatives are consulted on issues related to organisational aims, objectives and policies. In some countries, Worker Directors take seats on the Board of Directors, and, although outnumbered by shareholder appointees, they do at least enable the employee perspective to be heard and considered. In Germany, all public companies are required to have two boards of directors. The Management Board is appointed by the owners, although it includes at least one Worker Director, and is responsible for the day-to day running of the organisation. The Supervisory Board is, in the largest organisations, composed of equal numbers of owner and employee appointed directors, and this oversees the long-term conduct and direction of the firm.

The *radical pluralist perspective* suggests that, in capitalist organisations, there is a systematic conflict of interests. Owners and managers prioritise financial outcomes, profitability, return on capital and increasing share value for the owners. In most capitalist organisations, these financial measures define organisation success, and thereby the accountabilities of manager performance. By definition, the value created by employees is partly extracted so as to create owner benefits. The extraction of this surplus value inevitably leads to conflict between those who own and those who produce the goods and services concerned. Given any level of productivity, the labour cost for owners is the source of increasing profitability – the labour cost to owners is a cost to be kept to a minimum. Reducing wage rates, or at least pay wage rates that are as low as the acquisition of labour will allow, are clear drivers in many decisions. In other cases, the redesign of jobs by deskilling work, so as to make it available for a more plentiful, low-skilled workforce, is also an example of these conflicts of interest. Fundamentally, the wage represents an income to the employee upon which he/she survives, while it is an important cost stream to the employer whereby extra profits will flow from reduced labour costs.

The relocation of production around the globe so as to exploit low cost labour is also an example where the power of ownership results, in one way or another, in the exploitation of labour. Fox states:

> Negotiation of order within the enterprise takes place only at the margins. Management and the employee interests do not jointly build up their collaborative structure from the ground floor up. Power and social conditioning cause the employee interests to accept management's shaping of the main structure long before they reach the negotiating table.
>
> *(1974: 286)*

The radical frame of reference shares much with the pluralist perspective, but recognises that these inequalities of power are implicit in the capitalist mode of production, and ultimately these inequalities are central to organisational priorities and management. Ultimately, this implies workers' control, via such mechanisms as co-operatives, is one way of organising production so that the workers creating goods and services have a full share of what they produce.

This chapter takes a radical pluralist perspective because, in my opinion, it best describes the essential relationship between owners and employees. The uneven power that the employment relationship involves always has individual employees in a weaker position than employers. The employer decides on the level of demand for labour, pay, the tenure of the post, the terms and conditions of employment, training and development of the workforce and so on. While collectively organised labour can offer some resistance to employer power, individual workers are generally in a subservient role. For this reason, collective organisation of labour through trade union membership has been a major means of strengthening the employee negotiating position.

The hospitality industry in the UK, however, does not have a high level of union membership, and most employees are not able to take advantage of collective bargaining.

As a result of the lack of organised worker opposition to employer power, pay rates have historically been low in the hospitality industry. In 1909, the Trade Boards were introduced, and these set minimum wages across a cluster of what were described as the 'sweated' industries, including work in the hotel and catering sector. Small firms have traditionally dominated the sector, with few employees per employer and high levels of labour turnover. Even larger chain hotel and restaurant organisations may employ large numbers at company level but with relatively small numbers in any one site. This situation made trade union organisation difficult, and the Boards set minimums that protected employees against labour market conditions that worked excessively in employers' interests. Subsequently, the Boards were replaced by Wages Councils and ultimately by introduction of the National Minimum Wage (1999).

The Low Pay Commission advises government on the appropriate national minimum pay rate. The Commission comprises three employers, three trade union members and three independent labour market experts. As of October 2015, the UK national minimum wage (NMW) for adults (21 years and above) is £6.70 per hour, for employees between 18 and 20 years of age the rate is £5.30 per hour, and for workers under 18 the rate is £3.70 per hour. All these are minimum rates for outside of London – the capital city attracts added pay rates because of higher living costs. These rates may be reduced where the employer provides accommodation. Many hotel sector employers make living accommodation available for full-time employees. There is a National Minimum Wage compliance team associated with HM Revenue and Customs, and the team investigates complaints made by workers who believe they are under paid. This system sets a legal minimum wage rate, but enforcement is not monitored by an on-going independent team; complaints have to be made first. In a setting where overseas workers may not know their rights or how to complain, or where employees may fear dismissal, or they are persuaded that their employer cannot afford to pay the rate, the system of ensuring the workers get a living wage is flawed.

The National Living Wage Foundation is a pressure group that sets and updates annually the pay rate required to 'meet the basic cost of living in the UK'. This was set at £8.25 per hour compared to the NMW rate quoted above. The National Living Wage is not legally enforceable, though is used by many employers as the pay rate. Research conducted for the 'foundation' suggests that paying the living wage, rather than the legal minimum, is good for business. It reduces employee turnover and absenteeism, increases work quality and improves the employer's profile as an ethical business. On a personal level, the living wage helps people live within the first job income and reduces the need for some employees to have second or even third jobs (Toynbee, 2015). At a society level, it increases collective economic activity and increases both GDP and employment. Furthermore, added spending by the lowest paid generates higher economic activity and more jobs, because the poorest spend on immediate living expenses, rather than 'squirreling' it away in savings (Piketty, 2014).

Those holding the unitary perspective have sought to excuse low pay rates in the hospitality sector through the added income gained from tips, gratuities or service charges paid by guests. There is a need to define the differences between tips and gratuities, and service charges. Tips and gratuities are voluntary payments made by guests supposedly in recognition of the quality of the goods and services received. A service charge is a fixed amount added to the guest bill. As from 2009, it was made illegal for employers to pay wages from tips, hence the employer pays the wage and the tip/service charge provides added income (Department for Business Administration, 2009). The Code of Practice developed at the time did allow for some potential deductions for administrative costs on service charges on credit card transactions.

While these may add considerably to the incomes of workers in the hospitality sector, they are not generalised across all employees. Hence it is necessary to explore two basic questions about the value of gratuities for hospitality sector employees. First, which jobs do/do not attract tips from customers, second, what is the typical amount paid by customers and, finally, how are these distributed among the workforce?

While the payment of tips and gratuities and service charges is widespread across the hospitality sector, the job roles entitled to share in them vary between roles and establishments. In some operations, the tip is collected directly by individuals and not shared with others. In other cases, tips are pooled and shared out among others in the service setting. In other situations, tips are pooled in the 'tronc' and management may receive a share. In restaurant settings, kitchen staff may, or may not, be included in the distribution of tips. In hotel settings, it is highly unlikely that housekeeping, cleaning and other 'backstage' personnel share in the tips. The service charge is a fixed fee typically added to restaurant bills, though there is no formal legislation as to how these are distributed, and in some cases they may be subject to some management deductions. In fact, it was recently reported that a London hotel was using tips intended for service staff to top up managers' salaries. A spokesperson for trade union Unite suggested that the company was exploiting a legislation which forbids workers' salaries to be paid from tips by using it as managerial pay top-up (Butler, 2016).

In the UK, there is a cultural expectation that the tip will represent 10 per cent of the customer bill, while in the USA the expectation of the tip size ranges between 15 and 25 per cent. In the UK, the payment of tips in the restaurant sector represents a cultural expectation, but is a much looser expectation than in other countries, such as the USA. In some countries, tipping is discouraged; Iceland, Slovenia and Germany are examples of countries where tipping in restaurants is unlikely. In the Netherlands, pay rates are set by government at levels where there is no need for restaurant staff to supplement their income with tips, though there may be some 'rounding up' by a few euros to the appropriate figure. In the UK, service charges are added to the bill by many restaurant and bar organisations, and this is typically 12.5 per cent, though the distribution may, or may not, include all staff. While the service charge is automatically added to bills in participating restaurants, there is no legal obligation to pay it, and customers may decide to opt out, though this is highly unusual. Where a service is to be added to the bill, the restaurant operator has to make this clear to the customer.

Liberating the enslaved

Arrangements for giving employees more power in the workplace involve several approaches. At its most fundamental, the employee response to owner power has been collective and unified resistance, whereby employees go on strike or on go-slows that stop production or increase employer costs in one way or another. As industrialisation grew in the eighteenth and nineteenth centuries, workers increasingly organised themselves collectively in the form of trade unions. Collective bargaining at plant, firm, industry or even national governmental level enables employees to counter the power that employers have over individual workers.

The role of trade unions has been the subject of different perceptions. Those holding the *unitary view* see trade unions as malevolent, interfering with the national order of business systems. Hence, they are to be resisted with all that power and wealth can muster. The Anglophone countries, dominated by a pro-business culture and neo-liberalist economics, have been particularly good examples of this approach over the last three or four decades. Trade union restriction and open conflict with organised labour is used to delegitimise and limit the power of trade unions to protect individuals from employers. The *pluralist view* of trade unions dominant in many mainland European countries has been to value their role as representatives of employee experiences, perceptions and concerns. Legislation accepts trade unions as a means of reflecting employee interests, and there are a number of different approaches explored later in the chapter. For *radical pluralists*, trade unions are the means by which employees are able to resist employer power and promote worker interests. To be effective, however, the collective has to be able to exert economic and public relations pressure on employers.

If trade unions are to be able to act as the defender of employee rights, they require large numbers, solidarity and the ability to exert pressure. It has been easier to organise effective opposition where employees were organised in high numbers on a few sites. The large car plants, as well as general manufacturing and mining sectors, are all examples with a highly unionised workforce. As the service sector has grown, local government, education and the health service have grown typically to include a more unionised workforce, though not as heavily unionised as in the 'industrial sector'. Currently, 26 per cent of the UK workforce is a member of a trade union. Over 56 per cent of employees in the public sector are union members, though membership density in the private sector is a mere 14 per cent.

Trade union membership in the commercial hospitality sector in the UK has been traditionally low. Large numbers of small employers with few workers on any one site, high levels of staff turnover, heavy reliance on part-time, casual or seasonal staff, together with the ability to tap into plentiful low skilled sectors of the labour market, all militate against collective organisation and high levels of trade union membership in hotels, restaurants and bar operations. Union membership is less than 10 per cent across the private sector, though individual firms may have more union members. There are also regional variations, with northern regions of the UK having larger numbers of union members. The sectors where hospitality services operate in a supporting role do tend be more unionised – school meals services, hospitality workplace catering, as well as contract catering, all tend to be more unionised, often as a by-product of unionisation within the wider business organisation.

Given the difficulties of organising collective opposition in the private sector, employee resistance has taken more individualised forms. High levels of employee turnover and absenteeism, together with low quality working, are all examples of employee behaviour resisting the employer. Although this is rarely considered in these terms, the cost to an organisation of high levels of labour turnover can be enormous, though the cost of staff replacement is rarely measured and considered. The cost of losing, recruiting and replacing a member of staff is considerable. When labour turnover reaches levels commonly found in the commercial hospitality sector, it is downright reckless. As directors and mangers are not required to account for staff turnover in company annual accounts, it is not measured or costed. Failing to recognise this as a major impairment to business effectiveness does not mean that it does not have a negative impact on business costs.

Given the key role employees play in delivering hospitality services, together with the concern for the costs of employee dissatisfaction, some employers have adopted more consultative and participative management styles. An array of techniques that empower employees to become more involved in workplace decisions is one approach. The second includes initiatives that involve either employee consultation or employee participation in decision-making at senior levels. Co-determination is best defined as a number of arrangements that involve some form of joint decision-making with managers at establishment or organisational level. In Continental Europe, initiatives that include Works Councils and Employee Directors are rooted in a pluralistic view of organisations and are mechanisms for governing enterprise through co-determination. Workers' control is again an approach more prevalent in mainland Europe, but which involves employees controlling the ownership of the organisation through some form of workers' co-operative. Both approaches reflect a stakeholder view of capitalism (Keep and Rainbird, 2000).

Employees are empowered through their participation in decisions at a level beyond the task. In most cases, there is also a corresponding growth in a representative form, and employees are empowered as a collective interest set rather than as individuals. Although most individuals do not normally attend Works Council meetings or sit on Supervisory Boards, their interests as employees are represented at these meetings, and, no matter how limited, they do have opportunities to influence, or at least have a say in, decisions that affect employees.

Forms of employee participation that involve co-determination incorporate some processes whereby employees join with managers and/or owners to make decisions, or at least hold decision-makers to account for their decisions. These mechanisms are usually at the level of the enterprise, though in the German situation Works Councils can be established at unit level. Given this enterprise focus, it is not surprising that they become more representative in nature. The practical organisational difficulties are usually cited as reasons why selected representatives participate with management decision-making on behalf of the workforce as a whole. The range of issues discussed varies in different legislative contexts and forums. The degree of power that employees have to make decisions stick also varies, but power is constrained by the balance of interests in the decision-making process. Where managers/owners form the majority of the committee, council or board, it is less likely that employees will be able to make decisions stick. From an empowerment perspective, employees are empowered to participate in some decisions that in more traditional organisation structures would exclude them, and there may be some sense of personal efficacy felt by employees. The representative nature of the participation may well limit impacts for the workforce as a whole.

Works Councils

Although there are a few examples in the UK and the USA, Works Councils have a long established tradition on mainland Europe, and the European Union passed a Directive in 1994 requiring all companies operating in more than one European country to set up Union-wide Councils. Though the UK was not a signatory to the Social Charter, and opted out of the Social Chapter of the Maastricht agreement, many British companies with operations on the Continent have established Works Councils. In many cases, these include representatives from their British establishments.

The Works Councils set up under European provisions are consultative, requiring employers to inform employees about planned developments. The system in Germany extends the legal rights of Works Councils beyond consultation, and could be a model for an organisation wanting to take empowerment of its employees to another level. Works Councils play an important role in German industrial relations. All employees in establishments employing five or more workers have a legal right to establish Works Councils. The provisions relate to establishment, and thereby encompass most service sector organisations. Jacobi *et al.* (1992) estimate that some 33,000 councils exist involving 180,000 workers and include between 70 and 80 per cent of the eligible workforce.

The Works Constitution Act requires that the Works Council is elected from all employees. The Councils have several legal rights. Works Council members, as the formal representatives of the workforce, have the right to information covering the employer's manpower planning, and the general economic development of the organisation. They have the right to be consulted over issues such as training provision, job structures, alterations to working methods, plans for new technology and mass redundancies. Works Councils also have the right to jointly decide, through negotiation with the employer, a whole host of general employment issues, some of which relate to the implementation of national agreements, and others relating to training and recruitment, through to the transfer of operations and mass lay-offs. Many of these issues enable employees to be involved, via their representatives, in management decisions beyond the operational issues that include most task level forms of empowerment.

As stated above, Works Councils play an important role in German industrial relations, in that they perform many of the roles and responsibilities that might be fulfilled by a trade union in British organisations, and it is a mistake to think that individual arrangements can be plucked from one industrial relations environment and transplanted in another. Royle's research (1996) does show, however, that Works Councils could achieve some benefits for employees, particularly in developing a wider sense of employee empowerment in relation to the employer. He reports that Works Councils established in German McDonald's restaurants had stopped unfair dismissal, acted as a check on employment practice and 'created a better working environment where management no longer ruled by fear' (Royle, 1996: 92). It is an interesting commentary on the restricted nature of employer definitions of empowerment that the company in question actively worked against the establishment of Works Councils and ultimately paid out substantial sums in buying off employees who were actively involved in the Works Councils (Royle, 1996: 93).

Employee Directors

Employee Directors represent another initiative that has more of a history on mainland Europe than in the UK. Notably, two organisations – British Steel and the Post Office – did introduce Employee Directors in the 1970s, and both were public sector organisations at the time. In addition, the Bullock Committee (1977) on Industrial Democracy also featured proposals for employees to be represented at Board level. The Committee's proposals were greeted with a howl of opposition from UK employers, and the subsequent watered-down proposals, which were written in the Labour Government's White Paper, were dropped when the Conservative Government came to office in 1979.

The European Union has a draft directive on Employee Directors under way, but at the time of writing this has not yet produced a workable set of proposals through which to establish a Europe-wide approach. If the Vredeling proposals of the mid-1970s are anything to go by, there are considerable international and employer barriers to overcome. The Japanese employers in particular played a key role in political opposition to the European Commission's plan to require companies to institute some form of employee representation on the Board. As might be expected, the Conservative Government in Britain has been firmly opposed to such ideas and, given its opt-out of the social legislation, has attempted to prevent legislation introduced by the other member countries from having effect in the UK. However, as with European Works Councils, there may be companies who will introduce these arrangements to their British operations, just for organisational consistency. Cotton (1993: 113) notes that a significant number of EU member countries already have these arrangements in their company legislation, and it is likely that some form of directive on Employer Directors will eventually emerge.

Cotton (1993: 120) indicates that research on the impact of Employee Directors in terms of organisational performance is mixed. Opponents of the initiative generally point to the risk borne by owners as not being matched by Employee Directors, and state that employees should not be allowed to interfere with commercial decisions. Supporters, on the other hand, point to the benefits of winning support for strategic decision by involving employees, and argue that the involvement of employee representatives may improve the quality of decisions. Again, these views often reflect different concepts of the nature of capitalism, shareholder or stakeholder models, to use the Keep and Rainbird (2000) phrase.

From an empowerment perspective, employees individually have little involvement in the decisions, though the knowledge that their views have a voice at the most senior levels could be an important element in the creation of a culture of empowerment. Ultimately, the precise nature of the arrangements will determine whether Employee Directors have any real power to influence decisions. The experiences in German companies show that the balance of numbers on the Board can be crucial (Jacobi *et al.*, 1992: 227). The German system is based on two-tier boards. A small management board, including one employee director, is appointed by the owners and is responsible for the day-to-day running of the company. The Supervisory Board, including employee and owner directors, oversees the running of the company and makes all strategic decisions. There are different arrangements for the balance of numbers of employee and owner directors. In organisations employing fewer than 2,000 employees, the balance is one-third employees to two-thirds owner directors. In organisations employing more than 2,000 employees, the Co-determination Act (1976) creates an apparent equal balance between owner and employee representatives (Jacobi *et al.*, 1992: 228), though the composition of the 'employee' representation includes middle managers and, ultimately, this means the balance is stacked in favour of owners. The Montan industries (coal and steel) are equally balanced, though Jacobi *et al.* (1992: 228) estimated that this later type of arrangement covers approximately 30 establishments. Clearly, the ability to shape senior level decisions will be largely influenced by the balance of numbers. Where Employee Directors are in the minority, their role is likely to be more consultative than based on co-determination.

Considering the psychological aspect of empowerment, the representative nature of these arrangements, the potential remoteness of the bodies to shop-floor workers and the ultimate balance of power, owners are less likely themselves to create a sense of empowerment. But used as part of a wider strategy that genuinely recognises the importance of the employee contribution to organisation success, they could provide a valued device in establishing a trust culture and a sense of mutuality of interest among all organisation members.

The John Lewis Partnership is one of Britain's most successful retailers (Rawnsley, 1996). It is a long-established example of employee ownership in a service industry. It has been owned by employees (partners) for over seventy years. All profits of the enterprise, after payments of loans, dividends and so forth, are distributed among the employees. On average, this can be 15 per cent of the final pay packet. In addition, a system of committees involve, to varying degrees, representatives of employees who have rights to be involved in some decisions. One recent spokesperson for the company said that a recent decision to open stores half an hour early and close half an hour later 'took hours of meetings to get approval' (Rawnsley, 1996). It is a system avowedly democratic, yet it is a form in which democracy should not 'influence business decisions at the cost of efficient management' (Flanders *et al.*, 1968: 182). Furthermore, 'the effect of the system on management is paradoxically to reinforce its authority so it is stronger and commands greater power than is usual' (Flanders *et al.*, 1968: 183). The John Lewis Partnership confirms that ownership of shares in the enterprise, even where these represent a majority holding, do not automatically produce control over managerial decision-making.

For most employees, this form of participation is indirect because it is representatives who participate within the decision-making process. The level of participation is beyond the task, and employees have some valuable communication links to the most senior managers who can be held to account by the partners. That said, partners have no real sanctions against managers – they cannot dismiss a manager, and the house magazine does reveal controversy among partners about the levels of senior managers' pay (Tredre, 1996). The range of issues to be considered is constrained, and employees' power to make decisions that stick is limited. The extent that these arrangements develop a sense of personal efficacy is an issue that requires further study, though the study by Flanders and colleagues did show that there were generally high levels of job satisfaction, labour stability and general support for the system.

The Mondragon network of worker co-operatives in the Basque region of Spain is an example of a more worker-driven attempt at empowerment. Here, the arrangements were established as a device to provide a work and economic activity from within the community without reliance on traditional commercial and exploitative structures. In this case, it is argued that employees empowered themselves by avoiding situations that disempowered them. 'The Mondragon experiment has shown, above all, how workers can create and extend a system of self-management in an environment which is changing rapidly and becoming more and more competitive' (Thomas and Logan, 1982: 1). The network of co-operatives spans manufacturing as well as service industry contexts, including colleges, banks and retail outlets. Moreover, 'their growth record of sales, exports and employment, under favorable and adverse economic conditions, has been superior to that of capitalist enterprise' (Thomas and Logan, 1982: 127).

Almost 100,000 people are involved in the co-operatives, though most are not bigger than 500 members. Each person employed in the co-operative has the opportunity to take a financial stake in the shares of the enterprise – this cannot be sold on, and there is a maximum holding. Dividend payment is paid on the basis of share holding. Those who work in the enterprise elect individuals to represent their interests on various committees and boards. They have the power to both hold managers to account and appoint, as well as dismiss, managers. Employees are involved in directly and indirectly making long-term decisions, though day-to-day decision-making is in the hands of managers.

In this case, employees are in control of the enterprise, its direction and policy. They share in its profits and losses. Individuals are directly, indirectly and financially involved at the level of the enterprise, which is restricted in size. The range of issues is largely on a more strategic level, and they have the power to make decisions stick. That said, there are constitutional constraints on participants that limit complete freedom of action. Employees are empowered as owners of an enterprise in a location where there is a strong cultural acceptance of co-operation. The size of the venture seems to be an important factor, because early co-operatives were allowed to grow in size, and a long, bitter strike took place in one of the largest. This may show that the sense of involvement in the co-operative becomes diffused when enterprises grow too large. It is also confirmation of how fragile the state of empowerment can be and that immediate work experience, relations with managers and supervisors, communications and training have a powerful influence even when the employees are the owners.

Conclusions

The pay rates and other employment benefits in the hospitality sector are typically a product of labour market conditions. A plentiful supply of low skilled and low paid labour allows managers to manipulate labour market conditions for the short-term benefit of business owners. This chapter has argued that, while this is the reality of employment conditions, it is not the only way of operating hospitality businesses.

The recognition of employees as the key asset to hospitality service organisations requires a shift in the dominant managerial mindset. This would then result in a change in managerial priorities and practices so as to retain employees and build competitive advantage through the quality of the personal interactions between the employee host and the customer guest. Importantly, it needs managers to see that employees are potentially the key to building personal relationships with customers that build customer loyalty and competitive advantage.

References

Anti-Slavery Society (2015) What is Modern Slavery? Available at www.antislavery.org. Accessed 20 October 2015.

Bullock Committee of Inquiry (1977) *Report on Industrial Democracy*, London: HMSO.

Butler, S. (2016) Hotel accused of using staff tips to top up manager's pay, *Guardian*, 6 February, p. 16.

Cotton, J. L. (1993) *Employee Involvement*, London: Sage.

Cradden, C. (2011) Unitarism, pluralism, radicalism and the rest? Working paper No. 7, University of Geneva: Geneva.

Department for Business Administration (2009) *A Code of Practice for Department for Business Administration, 2009. Tips, Service Charges, Gratuities and Cover Charges*, HMSO: London.

Flanders, A., Pomeranz, R. and Woodward, J. (1968) *Experiment in Democracy: A Study of the John Lewis Partnership*, London: Faber and Faber.

Fox, A. (1974) *Beyond Contract: Work, Power and Trust Relations*, London: Faber and Faber.

ILO (2012) *Global Estimates of Forced Labor – 2012*, ILO: Geneva.

ILO (2015) *Global Estimates of Forced Labor – 2015*, ILO: Geneva.

Jacobi, O., Keller, B. and Müller-Jentsch, W. (1992) Germany: codetermining the future. In Ferner, A. and Hyman, R. (eds) *Industrial Relations in the New Europe*, Oxford: Blackwell, pp. 218–269.

Keep, E. and Rainbird, H. (2000) Towards the learning organisation. In Bach, S. and Sisson, K. (eds) *Personnel Management: A Comprehensive Guide to Theory and Practice*, Oxford: Blackwell, pp. 173–194.

Piketty, T. (2014) *Capital in the Twenty-First Century*, Cambridge, MA: Belknap Press.

Rawnsley, A. (1996) Stake and chips (hold the unions), *Guardian*, 21 January.

Royle, T. (1996) Avoiding the German system of codetermination: the McDonald's Corporation. Paper presented at the Fifth Annual CHME Research Conference, Nottingham: Nottingham Trent University.

Thomas, H. and Logan, C. (1982) *Mondragon: An Economic Analysis*, London: George Allen & Unwin.

Toynbee, P. (2015) Support the National Gallery strikes while they are still legal, *Guardian*, 1 August.

Tredre, R. (1996) A reader rants: store poison pens, *Guardian*, 25 February.

32

Hospitality studies

Developing philosophical practitioners?

Conrad Lashley

Key themes

Hospitality management

Education for hospitality

Hospitality studies

Reflective practitioner

> Ignorant people think they know everything, whilst knowledgeable people are aware of how little they know.
>
> *(Anon.)*

Higher education provision to meet the needs of management within the hospitality industry is now well established in most countries. In the UK, for example, degree programmes appeared in the late 1960s and burgeoned alongside the general expansion of higher education in the 1990s. This chapter draws on recent reports on higher education for the hospitality industry, and on recent academic research into the nature of hospitality to suggest that higher education programmes would better serve both students and industry if they reflected more social science underpinnings. Paradoxically, an overly managerial focus in content is not always consistent with the needs of manager education. Various studies suggest that reflective practitioners are needed for a turbulent and changing hospitality industry. This chapter argues that 'philosophical prac-titioners' are more appropriate because the development of analytical and critical thinking skills is essential for managers who are increasingly being asked to 'think outside the box'. I conclude that these skills are best developed in a framework of critical education which is as concerned with the study *of* hospitality management as it is with the study *for* hospitality management.

This chapter explores some of the issues arising from reports and from other work I have undertaken on the nature of management in hospitality businesses. It suggests that recent work exploring the nature of hospitality from an array of social science perspectives provides

DOI: 10.4324/9781315679938-36

opportunities to support the development of those being prepared *for* management in the hospitality industry by encouraging the study *of* hospitality and management through critical and theoretical perspectives. It advocates that the hospitality field of study needs to refocus to reflect these social science perspectives and suggests that Hospitality Studies as a title for the field provides an opportunity to encompass the study *of* and the study *for* hospitality. Indeed, the contents of the current book provide an example of the scope of the study and the richness of insights to be gained from academic fields in the social sciences and arts.

Hospitality management education

Although conducted some years ago, a review of hospitality management conducted in the late 1990s remains the only systematic analysis of hospitality management education provision in the UK. The *Review of Hospitality Management* defined hospitality management as 'having a core which addresses the management of food, and/or drink, and or accommodation in a service context' (HEFCE, 1998: 2). When all these activities are taken into account, hospitality activities employ approximately 2.4 million people in Britain, and Oxford Economics (2010) suggests it accounts for 8 per cent of total employment. When indirect employment and contribution impacts are accounted for, somewhere in the region of 3.6 million jobs are related directly or indirectly to the sector. The HEFCE report acknowledged that the industry is complex, covering different sectors including those where hospitality services are core business activities in hotels, restaurants, pubs and bars, and contract catering, as well as indirect provision in the welfare sector in schools and hospitals, and in health clubs, cinemas and theatres, where hospitality services are a subset of the operation. Small firms dominate commercial sectors of the industry. Some 99 per cent of hospitality firms in these sectors employ fewer than 50 people, yet these firms account for only 45 per cent of total sales and 50 per cent of employment (Thomas *et al.*, 2000). At the other end of the scale, in each of these commercial sectors a small number of branded businesses own and manage hundreds, or thousands, of units. These businesses offer management careers in multi-layered organisations at individual unit, multi-unit, middle and senior management positions.

The report confirmed that courses were designed to match these occupations incorporating a mixture of operational management subjects together with topics that supported the development of management competences in people management, marketing, finance, business strategy, small firms and entrepreneurship. It was recognised that programmes showed some variations between institutions but much of the provision had common content and objectives. Presentations at the CHME Research Conference and other hospitality research conferences confirm that this cluster of topics still reflects the majority of these courses.

The HEFCE report was undertaken at a time when the Higher Education Funding Council – England was considering the introduction of a revised mechanism for funding courses that potentially would have placed hospitality management programmes in the lowest funding band along with programmes like Business Studies, which are solely classroom based. In fact, the report showed that all courses included some element of 'laboratory' time in kitchens, bars, restaurants, reception and accommodation suites. Litteljohn and Morrison (1997) estimated that, on average, 23 per cent of students' contact hours at university or college were spent in laboratory situations and 64 per cent of these in food and beverage activities. In addition, most courses incorporate a one-year work placement as part of the programme.

Although there were estimated to be 2,000–3,000 graduates in the late 1990s, numbers on hospitality management programmes have reduced in the last few years, as new competing programmes in 'licensed retail management', 'event management' and 'leisure management', together with the impacts of the introduction of student fees and changes in university management structures, have reduced student enrolments even at a time of increased participation in university education. The number of graduates entering the labour market in 2002 was closer to 2,000 than the higher figure shown above. Given an estimated 250,000 managers employed in accommodation, bars and restaurant services alone (Hospitality Training Foundation, 2000), it is still true to say that, 'there is no question of graduates flooding the market' (HEFCE 1998: 15). Commenting on graduate entry into the industry, the same report stated that 'initially, 80 per cent went into work connected with the industry' (HEFCE 1998: 7). Most educators are also aware of the strong competition for hospitality graduates from traditional high street retailers who like the array of skills they possess.

The HEFCE report acknowledged a failure in communication with the industry at large that has sometimes resulted in comments from practitioners that educators produce too many graduates, and not enough graduates go into the industry. The somewhat contradictory nature of these comments is in part a reflection of these communication failures but also a reflection of the relatively low level of graduates working in the industry. This stands at just 5.5 per cent of all employees and employers, compared with 17.9 per cent across all industries (HtF, 2000). It is estimated that approximately 20–30 per cent of managers in the hospitality industry are graduates; hence some seven or eight out of ten practising managers are not graduates and have no higher education.

While acknowledging these communication difficulties with the industry at large, Airey and Tribe describe hospitality courses as being prominently influenced by industry: 'The emphasis on practical and industry-oriented content is clear from module titles, such as food preparation techniques' (2000: 183). The Council for National Academic Awards suggested that these programmes 'combined a range of business studies components' as well as more generic management studies and 'these are combined with specific hotel and catering studies which invariably include a science element' (Council for National Academic Awards, 1992: 7). Airey and Tribe note that over recent years course titles have shifted from hotel and catering management to include 'hospitality', and while they recognise the change in title opens up a wider conceptual framework, 'at the same time it is clear that the vocational orientation remains at the core of the curriculum' (2000: 282). In fact they go on to establish these programmes as located in the vocational action quadrant when higher education provision in general is mapped against two continua – stance as reflection/action, and ends as liberal/vocational (Figure 32.1). They suggest that while this meets the needs of industry and employers, these programmes can be criticised as being 'dominated by the tyranny of relevance' (Airey and Tribe, 2000: 290). The study of hospitality in its broadest sense provides opportunities to locate the subject in the wider social sciences, and provide a more reflective agenda for educators. Certainly the link with industry and the vocational aims of these programmes locates them within one of several potential positions in higher education provision.

Ends \ Stance	Reflection	Action
Liberal	Reflective liberal	Liberal action
Vocational	Reflective vocational	Vocational action

Figure 32.1 The use of curriculum space

Source: Airey and Tribe (2000).

These potential positions will be discussed in more detail, but the tyranny of relevance is further compounded by the learning style preferences of students entering hospitality management programmes. There is now a weight of research in the UK and internationally (Lashley, 1999; Barron and Arcodia, 2002; Lashley and Shaw, 2002; Charlesworth, 2003; Lashley and Barron, 2005) showing that hospitality management has a predominant preference for activist learning styles (Honey and Mumford, 1986).

Student learning styles

Several studies have been undertaken that attempt to identify the learning preferences of hospitality, tourism and travel management students in the UK, Asia and Australia. In a study of predominantly domestic students in the UK, Lashley (1999) found that the vast majority of students who were recruited to a particular hospitality management programme in the UK displayed preferred learning styles which indicated that they enjoyed practical activity, but were less comfortable with theorising and reflection. Students display preferences for activist learning styles (Lashley, 1999). Activist learners thrive on the challenges associated with new experiences and they were described as tending to 'act first and consider the consequences later' (Lashley, 1999: 181). In Australia, Barron and Arcodia (2002) also found that Australian hospitality and tourism students were also predominantly Activist learners. The dominance of the activist style of learning on hospitality and tourism programmes has been explained by the nature of the vocational and people centred nature of the programme (Lashley, 1999). In other words, people who like working with other people are likely to display extrovert personality characteristics and 'right-hand brain' preferences that ultimately underpin Kolb's model and thereby define the activist learning style. Armstrong points out that the split-brain formulation can be criticised as an over-simplification, but it does 'serve as a useful metaphor for describing these cognitive differences' (2002: 15).

Table 32.1 details the responses from students on different courses in the UK student programme. There are some variations across courses, though the general patterns across the intake as a whole are consistent. The majority of students register strong or very strong preferences for the activist learning style, though minorities register (18 per cent) strong or very strong preferences for the reflector style. The numbers registering strong preference for theorist and pragmatist styles are limited to a handful of individuals. Many of these students registered low or very low preferences for the theorist style (49.6 per cent) and for the pragmatist style (66.1 per cent). The reflector style was also a low preference for some 23 per cent of the respondents.

In contrast, students studying hospitality management, hotel and catering management, tourism management, and travel and tourism studies at Higher Diploma level and above in various colleges and universities in Hong Kong, Singapore and Taiwan displayed preferences for reflector learning styles (Wong et al., 2000). It was found that all but one of the student groups questioned displayed a strong preference for the reflector learning style. These students prefer to learn through observation and benefit from the opportunity to think before acting. They appreciate the opportunity to undertake research before an activity and think about what they have learned. Reflectors find it more difficult to learn from activities where they are forced into the limelight, for example through peer presentations or role-playing. Similarly, methods of learning such as case studies may prove problematic for these students as they are not keen on undertaking a task without prior notice or sufficient information (Honey and Mumford, 2000). Interestingly, Barron and Arcodia (2002) found that 'Confucian Heritage' students appeared to change their learning

Table 32.1 UK students Year One learning style preference, 2000/2001

Preference	Course and degree type	No. of students	Activist %	Reflector %	Theorist %	Pragmatist %
Strong and	BALRM	35	68.5	20.0	10.0	0
very strong	HND Hospitality	30	56.0	20.0	4.0	0
preference	BA HM	45	66.7	16.7	0	0
	HND Tourism	45	60.0	17.8	8.9	0
	BA Tourism	45	62.2	22.2	6.7	4.4
	BA International Tourism	35	71.4	11.4	11.4	2.9
Moderate	BALRM	35	31.5	51.4	57.1	40.0
preference	HND Hospitality	30	44.0	60.0	32.0	24.0
	BA HM	45	33.3	66.7	50.0	35.0
	HND Tourism	45	35.6	62.2	44.4	31.1
	BA Tourism	45	35.6	55.6	48.9	28.9
	BA International Tourism	35	28.6	57.1	28.6	37.1
Low and	BALRM	35	0	28.6	32.9	60.0
very low	HND Hospitality	30	0	20.0	64.0	76.0
preference	BA HM	45	0	16.7	50.0	65.0
	HND Tourism	45	4.4	20.0	46.4	68.9
	BA Tourism	45	2.2	22.2	44.4	66.7
	BA International Tourism	35	0	31.5	60	60

style preference as they studied in the Australian context. Students on the later stages of the degree were closer to Australian students and registered stronger preferences for activist learning styles.

Thus, there are two significant issues that might challenge current models of effective teaching in hospitality and tourism management programmes in universities. First, it is important to understand the learning style preferences of *all* students studying hospitality and tourism management and to attempt initiatives that encourage students to adopt a more reflective approach to their studies. Second, it is important to recognise the diversity that is currently common in university classrooms and acknowledge the preferred learning styles of students from different educational backgrounds. Equally, it is essential to nurture and encourage the use of more 'balanced' learning strategies so as to support more reflective approaches to information processing. Fundamentally balanced approaches discourage short-term surface learning as typified by the 'McDonaldisation' of higher education (Ritzer, 2004).

Figure 32.2 compares the learning style preferences of the key groups and some interesting patterns emerge. A substantial majority of UK students on hospitality and tourism programmes, Australian home students and 'other Australian' students register strong or very strong preferences for the activist style. Using Honey and Mumford's instrument (1986), activist learners will have agreed or strongly agreed with statements that suggest they prefer to learn through experience and experimentation rather than through reflection and conceptualisation. Table 32.2 lists the twenty statements that Honey and Mumford use to identify the learning style preferences. In their original study respondents register agreement with the majority of the statements so as to identify a strong or very strong preference for the style. In this instrument, respondents would score 4 or 5 against the majority of these statements. Those registering a low preference for a style score the item 0 or 1.

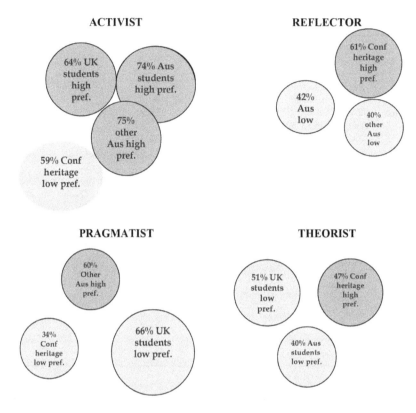

Figure 32.2 Patterns of high and low learning style preference among UK and Australian students

Table 32.2 Honey and Mumford's statements identifying learner preferences

Activist	Reflector
I often act without considering the possible consequences.	I like the sort of work where 1 have time for thorough preparation and implementation.
I believe that formal procedures and policies restrict people.	I take pride in doing a thorough job.
I often find that actions based on feelings are as sound as those based on careful thought and analysis.	I take care over the interpretation of data available to me and avoid jumping to conclusions.
I actively seek out new experiences.	I like to reach a decision carefully after weighing up many alternatives.
I'm attracted more to novel, unusual ideas than to practical ones.	I pay meticulous attention to detail before coming to a conclusion.
I thrive on the challenge of tackling something new and different.	I am careful not to jump to conclusions too quickly.
I enjoy fun-loving, spontaneous people.	I prefer to have as many sources of information as possible – the more data to think over the better.
I tend to be open about how I am feeling.	
I prefer to respond to events on a spontaneous flexible basis rather than plan things out in advance.	I listen to other people's points of view before putting my own forward.

Activist	Reflector
Quiet, thoughtful people tend to make me feel uneasy.	In discussions I enjoy watching the manoeuvrings of the other participants.
It is more important to enjoy the present moment than to think about the past or future.	It worries me if I have to rush out a piece of work to meet a tight deadline.
In discussions I usually produce lots of spontaneous ideas.	I often get irritated by people who want to rush things.
More often than not, rules are there to be broken.	I think that decisions based on a thorough analysis of all the information are sounder than those based on intuition.
On balance I talk more than I listen.	I prefer to stand back from a situation and consider all the perspectives.
I enjoy being the one that talks a lot.	I tend to discuss specific things with people rather than engaging in social discussion.
When things go wrong I am happy to shrug it off and 'put it down to experience'.	If I have a report to write I tend to produce lots of drafts before settling on the final version.
I find the formality of having specific objectives and plans stifling.	I like to ponder many alternatives before making up my mind.
I'm usually one of the people who puts life into a party.	In discussions I'm more likely to adopt a 'low profile' than to take the lead and do most of the talking.
I quickly get bored with methodical, detailed work.	It's best to think carefully before taking action.
I enjoy the drama and excitement of a crisis situation.	On balance I do the listening rather than the talking.
	I'm always interested to find out what people think.

Pragmatist	Theorist
I have a reputation for saying what I think simply and directly.	I have strong beliefs about what is right and wrong, good and bad.
What matters most is whether something works in practice.	I tend to solve problems using a step-by-step approach.
When I hear about a new idea or approach I immediately start working out how to apply it in practice.	I regularly question people about their basic assumptions.
I accept and stick to laid down procedures and policies so long as I regard them as an efficient way of getting the job done.	I get on best with logical, analytical people and less well with spontaneous 'irrational' people.
In discussions I like to get straight to the point.	I find it difficult to produce ideas on impulse.
I believe in coming to the point immediately.	I don't like disorganised things and prefer to fit things into a coherent pattern.
I tend to be attracted to techniques such as network analysis, flow charts, branching programmes, contingency planning, etc.	I like to relate my actions to a general principle.
I tend to judge people's ideas on their practical merits.	I tend to have distant, rather formal relationships with people at work.
In meetings I put forward practical realistic ideas.	Flippant people who don't take things seriously enough usually irritate me.
I can often see better, more practical ways to get things done.	I tend to be a perfectionist.
	I can often see inconsistencies and weaknesses in other people's arguments.
	I believe that rational, logical thinking should win the day.

(Continued)

Table 32.2 (Continued)

Pragmatist	Theorist
I think written reports should be short and to the point.	I am keen to reach answers via a logical approach.
I like people who approach things realistically rather than theoretically	In discussions with people I often find I am the most dispassionate and objective.
In discussions I get impatient with irrelevancies and digressions.	I like to be able to relate current actions to a 1onger term bigger picture.
I am keen to try things out to see if they work in practice.	I tend to be tough on people who find it difficult to adopt a logical approach.
In discussions I often find I am the realist, keeping people to point and avoiding wild speculations.	I am keen on exploring the basic assumptions, principles and theories underpinning things and events.
I tend to reject wild, spontaneous ideas as being impractical.	I like meetings to be run on methodical lines, sticking to a laid down agenda, etc.
Most times I believe the end justifies the means.	I steer clear of subjective or ambiguous topics.
I don't mind hurting people's feelings so long as the job gets done	
I do whatever is expedient to get the job done	
People often find me insensitive to their feelings.	

Source: Honey and Mumford (2000).

The activist style is consistent with Kolb's accommodator style derived from the interaction of two continua of learning preferences – learning through *concrete experience* or *abstract conceptualisation* and learning by *active experimentation* or by *reflective observation*. The accommodator prefers to learn through concrete experience and active experimentation. In fact, Kolb's model is founded on learning preferences that are shaped by personality type and preferences to learn using the left or right brain domains.

Large numbers of students on these programmes registering preference for activist/accommodator learning are likely to be extrovert personalities who prefer to learn with right-hand brain domains. That said, conceptual problems associated with Kolb's model question the robustness of this conclusion. The key point is that using the Learning Styles Questionnaire we know that respondents largely agree or disagree with statements listed in Table 32.2.

Honey and Mumford point out that activist learners are at an advantage when they are in contexts where they are working with other people, and through talking with other people as guests or as fellow workers. They enjoy contexts where there is a great deal of variety and situations are difficult to predict. Many aspects of the hospitality working environment could be said to match these requirements. Often, demand is difficult to predict precisely. Unusual customer requests, or customer complaints, require quick responses, and the work usually involves immediate contact with other employees and customers. Hospitality and tourism management university programmes have been described as 'vocation/action in orientation' (Airey and Tribe, 2000: 183) because they prepare graduates for specific occupations, and activist learning styles could be seen as compatible with this type of programme.

In these circumstances, university educators are faced with some difficult challenges. First, given the pragmatic vocation content of hospitality management programmes, their immediate focus on job roles, applied knowledge and skills, there is a tendency towards 'relevant content'.

Second, there is a general learning style preference among many students for a learning style that prioritises practice and action and is less comfortable with theory and reflection. Programmes may become dominated by a 'how to do' agenda where social science content and critical thinking are not encouraged. It is important, therefore, to undertake learning styles research with all students and share the results with them, including the implications for their successful performance in higher education.

The study *of* hospitality

Although the hospitality title may have initially been intended as something of a public relations device (Lashley, 2015) it did open up the study of hosts and guests, and hospitableness, which has resulted in the study of the hosting phenomenon from an array of social science perspectives that is the basis of the hospitality studies agenda. The study of hospitality, therefore, concerns the relationship between hosts and guests in all domains, domestic and commercial, as well as their cultural settings. From these perspectives, hospitality can be seen as a fundamental and ubiquitous feature of human life. Studied through anthropology, and other social sciences, hospitality and hospitableness present fascinating subjects in their own right, but they also develop critical tools through which to better inform the study of commercial hospitality and hospitality management (Blain and Lashley, 2014).

Bearing in mind these wider definitions of hospitality demands a breadth of academic study that allows the analysis of hospitality activities in 'cultural' and 'domestic', as well as 'commercial' domains (Lashley and Morrison, 2000). Put simply, each domain represents an aspect of hospitality activity that is both independent and overlapping. The cultural domain of hospitality considers the social settings in which hospitality and acts of hospitableness take place, together with the impacts of social forces and belief systems on the production and consumption of food and/or drink and/or accommodation. The domestic domain considers the range of issues associated with the provision of food, drink and accommodation in the home, as well as considering the impact of host and guest obligations in this context (Heal, 1990; Visser, 1991; Nouwen, 1998; O'Gorman, 2007). The commercial domain concerns the provision of hospitality as an economic activity providing food, drink and accommodation for money exchange. Clearly, this commercial domain has been the focus of academic study for the hospitality industry, but there has, until recently, been limited study of the cultural and domestic domains and their impact on the commercial. Fundamentally, the actual experiences of hospitality, in whatever setting, are likely to be an outcome of the influence of each of these domains.

The study of hospitality engages with research and academic enquiry informed by social science, and encouraging the development of critical thinking. This aids and informs research, academic thought and the development of reflective practice within future sector managers. Hospitality represents a robust field of study in its own right, but it also encourages critical thinking and a concern for host–guest relations that influence the practice and development of those entering managerial roles in the sector. Flowing from this is the study of the motives engaged by those offering hospitality. These motives can be perceived in a ranking system that ranges from hospitality offered for ulterior motives through to hospitality offered for the joy of giving.

Academics from hospitality management programmes have compiled two books, *In Search of Hospitality: Theoretical Perspectives and Debates* (Lashley and Morrison, 2000) and *Hospitality: A Social Lens* (Lashley, Lynch and Morrison, 2007), which extend the focus on hospitality beyond commercial activities. Around the same time, academics from social science backgrounds published *Mobilizing Hospitality: The Ethics of Social Relations in a Mobile World* (Germann Molz and Gibson, 2007) which looked at hospitality as a metaphor for understanding how in-group members respond to out-group members entering their space. This presented an interesting insight that suggested the host–guest relation might be applied in such places where aircrew and bus drivers hosted passengers or prison guards hosted prisoners as their guests. A new journal, *Hospitality & Society* (2010), has also emerged to engage these social science studies of hospitality and it is edited by academics from both hospitality and social science communities (Lynch *et al.*, 2011).

Hospitality education: a philosophical future?

The strands of research discussed above suggest some important directions for the future of higher education provision in hospitality. I have argued for some time that the programme field should adopt the 'hospitality studies' title (Lashley, 2003, 2007, 2009). This suggestion is not to diminish the link to industry or the university role in developing management talent for the sector. The 'studies' title allows educational provision to be more flexible and wider in scope. The 'hospitality management' title, while not constraining of itself, does reinforce the tendency towards programmes located in practicality and relevance. The 'management' title implies content shaped by the day-to-day practicalities of hospitality business operations and decision-making. The current programme content, in most universities, is packed with modules that provide practical skills and theoretical material associated with hospitality businesses. As a by-product, courses are frequently dominated by the dissemination of management knowledge and didactic teaching methods. Superficially, courses appear to be meeting the needs of industry for a pre-trained management workforce, and the needs of students for programmes that will make them attractive to employers, as well as easy transfer into the employing organisation. However, this practical content, accompanied by these didactic teaching methods, does result in a somewhat pragmatic 'how to do' agenda and uncritical thinking. Future managers need to be more analytical and critical, and programmes developing them must enable the development of these ways of thinking.

The widespread adoption of the 'studies' title would signal a move away from this culture of pragmatism, and the potential for a curriculum drawn from an array of academic perspectives. This, in turn, might allow the development of future managers who have the skills to be critical and analytical, but who also perceive commercial provision within the wider contexts in which hospitableness is practised. It is interesting that undergraduate programmes at generic business programmes have 'business studies' titles, even though courses are clearly intended to develop future managers in business organisations.

The *cultural domain* in particular allows for the study of hospitality as a human phenomenon experienced in all societies. The obligation for hosts to welcome and protect guests is ubiquitous. The obligation that cultures require of hosts and guests opens up interesting study areas, showing similarities and differences across the globe. At the centre of the revised curriculum, therefore, would be the study of hospitality and hospitableness. This might incorporate the study of insights from philosophers (Telfer, 2000; Derrida, 2002), historians (Heal, 1990; Walton, 2000), anthropologists (Selwyn, 2000; O'Gorman, 2007) and others to establish a more fundamental understanding of hospitableness. This would have the dual impact of aiding the development of more critical thinking among students and providing an underpinning rationale for building a competitive strategy based upon the delivery of hospitable experiences to guests.

The study of the *private domain* of hospitality also proves a potentially valuable arena. Students enter these programmes with personal experiences of being hosts and guests in their own private lives. These experiences should be explored, compared and analysed through the programme and theoretical observation (Lashley *et al.*, 2003; Morrison and O'Mahony, 2003). Working from students' own personal experiences towards theoretical principles is also consistent with the dominant 'activist' learning style of students in these programmes. Contrasting and comparing student experiences may also underpin the impact of cultural aspects on the expectations of both guests and hosts in these domestic settings, as well as inform potential hosts of the varied expectations of guests in commercial contexts. Flowing from this, the overlap of the private and commercial domains might help investigate the host and guest experiences in small hotels, guesthouses, bed and breakfast establishments and other contexts where commercial provision is located in the same establishment as the domestic/private dwelling.

This study of hospitality will also assist in critical analysis of the *commercial domain*. To what extent are guests treated as truly welcome, and made to feel that they are recognised as guests rather than as clients who are only welcome so long as they pay the bill? It is not inevitable that commercial provision will always be dominated by the economic transaction (Warde and Martens, 2000; Ritzer, 2007), the welcome extended by hosts even in commercial settings may be genuine and engender guest feelings of welcome (Sherringham and Daruwalla, 2007). Hospitableness and the quality of the guests' experience may be a source of competitive advantage that serves as a business strategy that extends beyond the generic service quality model. Guest loyalty founded on the quality of hospitableness is likely to be more robust in establishing long-term links with guests as fellow human beings.

Front-line staff act as immediate hosts to guests and therefore their performance is essential. The recruitment, training, reward and retention of these employee hosts are crucial. Firms adopting a competitive strategy founded on hospitableness and the quality of guests' experiences cannot get by with sloppy and ill-conceived recruitment practices, poorly trained staff, a demotivated workforce and the sky-high levels of labour turnover typical of many commercial business operations. Front-line employees are the corner stone for developing competitive advantage and need to be treated accordingly. Programme content has to reflect these business strategies in the way that competitive strategy and, most importantly, employment strategies are translated into practice.

The teaching and learning context in which these studies are set needs to be informed by, and based upon, a clear understanding of student learning style preferences, starting with learning styles research and planning the learning from the practical to the theoretical. The examples quoted earlier suggest that the students' own experiences as both hosts and guests are a potentially valuable starting point. Theoretical inputs can then be used as both analytical tools and an introduction to some of the wider themes suggested earlier in this chapter.

While an immediate objective is to ensure that programmes truly encourage these would-be practitioners to be reflective (Airey and Tribe, 2000), the ultimate aim should be to produce 'philosophical practitioners'. The conceptual model suggested in Figure 32.1 is helpful in steering programme designers' thinking. Graduates should be able to act and think, and be concerned for the pursuit of knowledge for its own sake, but also committed to apply, where applicable, the knowledge gained within practical contexts.

All this has implications for the more practical and 'laboratory' elements of these programmes. Many universities involve some form of laboratory experience in kitchen and restaurant provision used to develop insights into the operational aspects of hotel and catering operations. Often these facilities occupy large amounts of rigid space that cannot be adapted for generic education use. Restaurants and kitchens are also expensive to maintain at an industry-consistent quality. It is not surprising, therefore, that many universities have linked up with local further education provision, and removed their own on-site facilities. While this appears to be a sensible solution in cash-strapped times, it fails to address two fundamental issues. First, why simulate experience when programmes could be more formally involved in managing student part-time and holiday work? Content is often overly concerned with technical skills that are unlikely to be required in future graduate employment (Lashley, 2009, 2014). Student part-time and holiday work undertaken in real life hospitality business organisations would be more insightful. With a more structured management of this experience, students could be required to work in a variety of settings and roles, hence expanding their understanding of the operational experiences of hospitality businesses. Second, laboratory provision could be more truly set in laboratories, involving experiments with food and drink. This could allow the study of gastronomy, food science and microbiology, for example, relevant inputs rarely touched upon in most programmes, but requiring laboratory space that might be more readily used across the wider university.

Beyond these technical dimensions to the curriculum, it is possible to identify an array of arts subjects that might be included in a more philosophical agenda. The study of painting and sculpture might help to provide insights into visual presentation. This has high relevance for individuals where the visual appearance of dishes and decor are important aspects in the delivery of food, drink and accommodation. Similarly, theatre studies can help the development of a sense of drama and mood that impacts on the ambience created in hotel, restaurant and bar venues. Acting studies might also be a related aspect of the curriculum, assisting students to understand the performance needs associated with the delivery of guest experiences, as well as the management of the emotional labour demands of their work. Music studies and the moods influenced by sound is another potential input that might help with the development of a more rounded education for individuals as citizens and as managers. Fundamentally, programmes should be primarily concerned with encouraging learning for its own sake, rather than because it has relevance to future careers. Perhaps the truly liberating impact of education is not so much about providing students with new knowledge, but giving them insights into the boundaries of their own ignorance, and engendering a desire to learn?

Conclusions

This chapter has argued principally for a move away from a curriculum rigidly locked into a checklist of management content and skills. While most courses will continue to be concerned with developing management personnel for the sector, it is necessary to focus more on the development of graduates who are at least reflective, if not philosophical, practitioners. With this breadth of thinking and tools, graduates will be more readily able to respond to a fast changing and increasingly competitive environment. At the heart of this more open curriculum, this chapter has argued that the study of hospitableness both allows for the inclusion of more social science content, and thereby critical study, and provides the basis of competitive advantage through a concern for the quality of guest experiences. While a move away from 'management' in programme titles is not essential for this to take place, the use of 'studies' might more clearly signal this wider programme focus. In the long term, it may be that programmes will emerge that study hospitality and hospitableness as a human phenomenon, and are not immediately concerned with the preparation of management personnel.

References

Airey, D. and Tribe, J. (2000) Education for hospitality. In Lashley, C. and Morrison, A. (eds) *In Search of Hospitality: Theoretical Perspectives and Debates*, Oxford: Butterworth-Heinemann.

Barron, P. and Arcodia, C. (2002) Linking learning style preferences and ethnicity: international students studying hospitality and tourism management in Australia, *Journal of Hospitality, Leisure, Sport and Tourism Education* 1, 2: 1–13.

Blain, M. and Lashley, C. (2014) Hospitableness: the new service metaphor? Developing an instrument for measuring hosting, *Research in Hospitality Management* 4, 1/2: 1–8.

Charlesworth, Z. (2003) The influence of culture on learning styles, *Eighth Annual Conference Proceedings European Learning Styles Information Network*, Hull: University of Hull, pp. 103–113.

Council for National Academic Awards (1992) *Review of Hotel and Catering Degree Courses*, London: CNAA.

Derrida, J. (2002) *Acts of Religion*, London: Routledge.

Germann Molz, J. G. and Gibson, S. (eds) (2007) *Mobilizing Hospitality: The Ethics of Social Relations in a Mobile World*, Aldershot: Ashgate.

Heal, F. (1990) *Hospitality in Early Modern England*, Oxford: Clarendon Press.

HEFCE (Higher Education Funding Council for England) (1998) *Review of Hospitality Management*, London: HEFCE.

Honey, P. and Mumford, A. (1986) *The Manual of Learning Styles*, 2nd edn, Maidenhead: Peter Honey.

Honey, P. and Mumford, A. (2000) *The Learning Styles Questionnaire: 80 Item Version*, Maidenhead: Peter Honey.

Hospitality Training Foundation (2000) *Estimating the Benefits of Training*, Leeds: Leeds Metropolitan University.

Lashley, C. (1999) On making silk purses: developing reflective practitioners in hospitality management education, *International Journal of Contemporary Hospitality Management* 11, 4: 180–185.

Lashley, C. (2003) Studying hospitality: some reflections on hospitality management education, *International Journal of Hospitality Management* 21, 2: 233–261.

Lashley, C. (2007) Discovering hospitality: observations from recent research, *International Journal of Culture, Hospitality and Tourism Research* 1, 3: 214–226.

Lashley, C. (2009) The right answers to the wrong questions? Observations on skill development and training in the UK's hospitality sector, *Tourism and Hospitality Research* 9, 4: 340–352.

Lashley, C. (2014) Insights into the study of hospitality, *Research in Hospitality Management*, 4, 1/2: iii–v.

Lashley, C. (2015) Hospitality and hospitableness, *Research in Hospitality Management* 5, 1: 1–7.

Lashley, C. and Barron, P. (2005) The learning style preferences of hospitality management students: observations from an international and cross cultural study, *International Journal of Hospitality Management* 23, 2: 253–269. Lashley, C., Lynch, P. and Morrison, A. (eds) (2007) *Hospitality: A Social Lens*, Amsterdam: Elsevier.

Lashley, C. and Morrison, A. (eds) (2000) *In Search of Hospitality: Theoretical Perspectives and Debates*, Oxford: Butterworth-Heinemann.

Lashley, C. and Shaw, M. (2002) The effects of learning styles on student achievement in HE and the implications for curriculum design, development and delivery, *Seventh European Learning Styles Information Network Conference Proceedings*, Ghent: University of Ghent, pp. 386–399.

Lashley, C., Morrison, A. and Randall, S. (2003) My most memorable meal ever: some observations on the emotions of hospitality. In Sloan, D. (ed.) *Culinary Taste*, Oxford: Butterworth-Heinemann, pp. 165–184.

Litteljohn, D. and Morrison, J. (1997) *Hospitality Management Education Report*, Council for Hospitality Management Education

Lynch, P., Germann Molz, J., McIntosh, A., Lugosi, P. and Lashley, C. (2011) Theorising hospitality, *Hospitality & Society* 1, 1: 3–24.

Morrison, A. and O'Mahony, G. B. (2003) The liberation of hospitality management education, *International Journal of Contemporary Hospitality Management* 15, 1: 38–44.

Nouwen, H. (1998) *Reaching Out: A Special Edition of the Spiritual Classic including Beyond the Mirror*, London: Fount.

O'Gorman, K. D. (2007) The hospitality phenomenon: philosophical enlightenment?, *International Journal of Culture, Tourism and Hospitality Research* 1: 189–202.

Oxford Economics (2010) *Employment in the Hospitality Industry*, Oxford: Oxford University Press.

Ritzer, G. (2004) *The McDonaldization of Society*, rev. New Century edn, London: Sage.

Ritzer, G. (2007) Inhospitable hospitality? In Lashley, C., Lynch, P. and Morrison, A. (eds) *Hospitality: A Social Lens*, Amsterdam: Elsevier.

Selwyn, T. (2000) An anthropology of hospitality. In Lashley, C. and Morrison, A. (eds) *In Search of Hospitality: Theoretical Perspectives and Debates*, Oxford: Butterworth-Heinemann, pp. 18–37.

Sherringham, C. and Daruwalla, P. (2007) Transgressing hospitality: polarities and disordered relationships? In Lashley, C., Lynch, P. and Morrison, A. (eds) *Hospitality: A Social Lens*, Oxford: Elsevier, pp. 33–46.

Telfer, E. (2000) The philosophy of hospitableness. In Lashley, C. and Morrison, A. (eds) *In Search of Hospitality: Theoretical Perspectives and Debates*, Oxford: Butterworth-Heinemann, pp. 38–55.

Thomas, R., Lashley, C., Rowson, B., Guozhong, X., Jameson, S., Eaglen, A., Lincoln, G. and Parsons, D. (2000) *The National Survey of Small Tourism and Hospitality Firms: 2000 – Skills Demand and Training Practices*, Leeds: Leeds Metropolitan University.

Visser, M. (1991) *The Rituals of Dinner: The Origin, Evolution, Eccentricities and Meaning of Table Manners*, New York: HarperCollins.

Walton, J. (2000) *The British Seaside: Holidays and Resorts in the Twentieth Century*, Manchester: Manchester University Press.

Warde, A. and Martens, L. (2000) *Eating Out: Social Differentiation, Consumption, and Pleasure*, Cambridge: Cambridge University Press.

Wong, K. K. F., Pine, R. J. and Tsang, N. (2000) Learning style preferences and implications for training programs in the hospitality and tourism industry, *Journal of Hospitality and Tourism Education* 12, 2: 32–40.

33

Conclusion

Hospitality and beyond...

Conrad Lashley

Key themes

Investigating the domains

Exploring the continuum of hospitality

Researching hospitableness

The hospitality metaphor

This volume is dedicated to developing a wider understanding of hospitality and hospitableness. This chapter suggests some potential avenues for future research. The domains of hospitality assist in shaping broad themes that might shape research into hospitality beyond the scope of this book. Hospitality in the private or domestic domain in particular would benefits from more investigation.

The hospitality continuum suggests an array of motives for offering hospitality. Altruistic hospitality was the focus of Blain's development of an attitude survey that appears, on the basis of initial findings, to provide an instrument for identifying individuals who, as hosts, offer hospitality because they are 'hospitable' people. The questionnaire needs to be more widely used and developed so as to firmly establish its reliability and validity. The study of hospitableness can be applied in settings that are not primarily related to the service of food, drink and accommodation. Any setting where one individual enters the space of another can be said to be about the receiving of a guest by a host. So the metaphor could be applied in many 'non-hospitality' settings that involve hospitableness.

Understanding the domains of hospitality

It is perhaps not surprising that many of the contributions to this book comment on the social and cultural domain of hospitality. In part the aim of the study of hospitality is to explore the

DOI: 10.4324/9781315679938-37

universal nature of the duty to be hospitable to strangers. These chapters confirm this human obligation across different nations and continents, through time as well as across various social and cultural backgrounds.

The study of hospitality in its social and cultural contexts will continue to be an issue to research, as there is much to learn about cultural commitments to be hospitable in different social settings and at different economic levels. In Chapter 23 Victoria Ruiter highlights hospital practices in African hunter-gatherer communities, similarly Leandro Brusadin in Chapter 24 discusses potlatch traditions among North American indigenous tribes who were also hunter-gatherers. In Chapter 9 I explore religious obligations about hospitality and also mention hunter-gatherer communities in Australia. Future research is likely to continue these lines of enquiry, building an increasingly sophisticated understanding that hospitableness and the obligations to welcome the stranger are found even in the smallest of human communities living off natural resources before the emergence of farming.

The development of settled communities, based initially on simple forms of farming also involved moral and social codes about hospitality and this extended beyond the obligations to strangers and required communities to offer hospitality to other community members who for one reason or another found themselves in need of food and drink, or shelter. Martine Berenpas, in Chapter 13, explores these obligations in Confucian, Daoist and Buddhist contexts in what were essentially agricultural communities stretching back several thousand years, while in Chapter 15 Barry O'Mahony discusses the experiences of those transported to Australia – guests in an alien land. The hospitality experienced in these agricultural societies will also continue to be a key focus for some researchers, and a theme that enriches by comparing and contrasting community obligations across different societies and through time.

The study of these obligations and the delivery of hospitality experiences in contemporary societies is another theme that will continue to attract research. In Chapter 8 Szilvia Gyimóthy highlights some of the contemporary features of hospitality on offer through the advent of the sharing economy and new developments with platforms such as Airbnb that shape the nature of the choices available to guests in the modern world of tourism and the mass movement of people for both business and leisure activities. More important, perhaps, is the fact that contemporary societies seem to have lost the central obligation to be accepting of travellers. Indeed the mass movement of people away from war-torn regions has become a highly discussed feature of many nations in Europe, the USA and across the globe. The assumed culture of hospitality and welcome articulated by many is often contradicted by the selective nature of who is welcome, and who is not. The study of these limits to hospitableness and selectivity of the offer of welcome promises much in future research studies.

The study of hospitality needs to extend beyond these social and cultural features of hospitality. Indeed few of the chapters in this text deal with private or domestic dimensions of hospitality. Elizabeth Telfer, in Chapter 5, provides some linkages through the discussion of authenticity, which is the extent to which domestic hospitality offered in the private domain is more authentic than that experienced in commercial settings – 'hospitality at a price', being the key issue. If hospitality is being provided as a commercial activity then by definition it lacks authenticity because if the guest cannot pay for the hospitality provided then the host withdraws the offer. This is not as clear-cut as it first appears, because domestic hospitality is likely to be a by-product of the host's motives and performance. In some cases, the commercial offer allows more choice and is less dependent on the host's hosting skills. The authenticity theme is likely to be one that continues to stimulate questions and academic interest.

The private domain is also worthy of further enquiry because it allows the consideration of similarities and differences of both guest experiences and host practices. The way guests are treated and the expectation of the behaviour of guests are worthy of study particularly within and between communities. Also, hospitality offered in domestic settings provides a training ground for both would-be entrepreneurs and employees. For entrepreneurs the hospitality business based around the provision of food, drink and accommodation can create a simplistic assessment of the skills needed for effective performance, and lead ultimately to high turnover in business ownership. For employees the private sector provides opportunities for learning about how to act as both host and guest. For these reasons, employers will often target young men and women from affluent backgrounds to work in the sector. They are seen as a valuable source of recruits who understand the nature of hospitality and the performance required of hosts. The private/domestic sector is therefore an important context in which to study the nature of those who enter the commercial sector.

The overlap between the commercial and private domains is much under-researched yet offers fascinating insights. Many smaller hotels, restaurants and pubs include private domestic space in the commercial setting. The business owner and family frequently share the commercial property. Family quarters are included and the family has to varying degrees to share the hotel, pub or restaurant premises with commercial guests. The way that these spaces are managed is a topic worthy of a programme of research. In some hotels, for example, the property is principally domestic and involves a few paying guests. In other cases, the space is principally a commercial operation with private quarters included. Again the study of these arrangements offers many possibilities. The impact on family members and family relationships brought about by sharing the domestic space with commercial activities is one interesting theme. To what extent are individuals reared in these circumstances more or less likely to enter the commercial sector as an occupation?

The commercial domain and trends towards in-hospitality are interesting. The search for increased profits by reducing labour costs leads to trends towards practices that deskill work and practices that minimise the cost of the labour element of the services provide. The use of techniques that George Ritzer (Chapter 19) described as McDonaldisation involved service production that was heavily influenced by mass production, but has now moved on to 'pro-consumption'. In other words, services are now increasingly using techniques that involve customers producing, or part producing, the service that they consume. In hotels, self-check-in, and the use of vending machines to replace room service for drinks, are examples whereby guests undertake the commercial hospitality service. Ongoing research into customer reactions to this and the impact on competitive advantage is required as industrial practices and consumer trends and tastes develop. Commercial provision does not always match customer expectations. Recent reaction against mass-produced foods in commercial pub and restaurant menus in the UK has resulted in a drive towards more menus designed round onsite cooking. The role of hospitableness, or the absence of it, in commercial provision will provide interesting avenues for research in this evolving scene. Will there be negative customer reactions to the trend towards 'service-less service' in many hotel organisations?

Exploring the continuum

The continuum of hospitality arises initially from Telfer's (Chapter 5) notion that there are sometimes ulterior motives for offering hospitality as opposed to what she terms 'genuine hospitality', and what I have termed 'altruistic hospitality' (Chapter 1). The more elaborated continuum suggests that there are a variety of motives for offering hospitality, and these variations need to be explored more fully in the future. Ulterior motives hospitality in the form of business lunches, sales force weekends and so forth could all be subject to research. To what extent do guests feel more positively about their hosts, or do they see through these 'schmoozing manoeuvres'? Is it better than nothing, or an expectation of business transactions – that is, there are negative consequences for those who do not do it, but no positive shifts in feelings for the host when it is an expectation of the way things are done? Containing hospitality is founded on the antithesis of the notion of altruistic hospitality – the fear of strangers leads to the assumption that they are a threat and need to be put under surveillance. Research needs to explore the workings of this in detail – is the contained guest treated differently, and if so, how?

The commercial provision of hospitality is also potentially a distorted form of hospitality because the exchange of hospitality for money brings into question the genuineness of the hospitality on offer. Research needs to be undertaken to explore the way customers see hospitality on offer in commercial settings. Do guests merely suspend disbelief, and enter the hosting context with lower expectations than when entering a private dwelling? I have argued that the cash exchange makes it less genuine, motivated by the potential sale or the gratuity, though Telfer (Chapter 5) suggests that this is not inevitable. Perhaps hospitable people are drawn to work in the sector?

Reciprocal hospitality needs to be explored in a variety of social and cultural settings. How rigidly followed is the expectation that guests offer hospitality to their former hosts? Are there variations in this among different social groups in the same culture? Are there pressures to be an even more generous host? Does offering hospitality become another feature of the game of one-upmanship? Do some people withdraw from reciprocal hospitality because they fear they cannot compete with their former hosts?

Redistributive hospitality has its most obvious application in hunter-gathering communities, where the inconsistencies of hunting success mean that there is a need to share, and where generosity is highly valued. The community as whole benefits from sharing and social status is linked to giving not taking, and this needs more detailed research. The extent that the host gives to the guest in preference to their own consumption is a feature of the expectations in many cultures; we need to know more about these.

Altruistic hospitality offers up some interesting opportunities for research. The Matthew Blain instrument, to be discussed in more detail below, provides a potential devise for assessing individual levels of hospitableness and for measuring the distribution of hospitableness across and between populations. It can also be used to evaluate potential change through time. Are hospitable people always hospitable? Does exposure to more guests reduce the feeling of welcome or is it consistent? How do individuals vary in these respects?

Researching hospitableness

'Genuine hospitality' (Telfer, Chapter 5 this volume) 'radical hospitality' (Derrida, 2002) and 'altruistic hospitality' (Lashley, Chapter 1 this volume) are three terms used to denote hosts providing hospitality to guests without any ulterior motive, other than a motive that would ultimately benefit the host. Telfer provides a useful checklist of the features of hospitableness (Table 1.1 this volume), although there has been limited research, thus far, to measure individuals and communities in their propensity to be hospitable.

Matthew Blain, while studying for his DBA, went through an interesting research process involving several stages until he eventually produced a questionnaire that contained 13 statements embedded in a 30 question instrument (Figure 33.1). The instrument developed by Blain

Desire to put guests before yourself	• I put guests' enjoyment before my own • I do whatever is necessary to ensure that guests have a great time • I always try to live up to my idea of what makes a good host • The comfort of guests is most important to me
Desire to make guests happy	• I get a natural high when I make my guests feel special • I enjoy taking responsibility for the wellbeing of guests • It means the world to me when guests show their approval of my hospitality • It's important to do the things that people expect of a good host • I seek out opportunities to help others
Desire to make guests feel special	• When hosting I try to feel at one with the guests • I try to get on the same wavelength as my guests • Guests should feel that the evening revolves around them • I find it motivating to take accountability for other people's welfare

Figure 33.1   Blain's hospitableness question bank

contains three themes covering the 13 attitude statements employing a 7 point Likert scale. This established a tendency to respond positively among a significant minority of respondents. The research used a convenience sample from immediate personal and business colleagues, and was therefore formally stratified. The instrument at this stage is to be seen as an initial draft that needs to be subject to considerable testing to establish reliability and validity.

The complete questionnaire is included as an appendix to this chapter and readers are invited to test it out and share the results.

The hospitality metaphor

Earlier chapters have demonstrated that the study of hospitality and hospitableness has been driven by academics interested in the development of managers who will engage with the delivery of food, drink and accommodation services, together with academics interested in the acceptance of the stranger in societal and domestic contexts. The treatment of one individual (the guest) in the space of another (the host) can be used as a metaphor in a much wider array of contexts. Consequently, the sense of being welcome and safe can be applied in many settings where the host might be better prepared to receive the stranger if he/she were seen as a guest.

The induction processes in the recruitment of new employees, school children or university students in essence are about these guests entering the space of the hosts – employers, teachers, academics. Patients and their families being received into the doctor's surgery, or hospital, might have their anxieties eased if attention were paid to the welcome they receive as guests. Retail customers entering a shop or mall are in effect guests and could be greeted in a hospitable way.

These are just a few examples of how the hospitality metaphor might be applied in all settings where one person enters the space of another. If the guest is made to feel welcome on their own terms and for themselves, it is likely that they will not only feel comfortable, but will also want to return. Hospitableness has the potential to be the source of competitive advantage because it enables the development of bonds between individual hosts and guests that cannot be replicated. The guest has a personal relationship with the host. It is based on links between

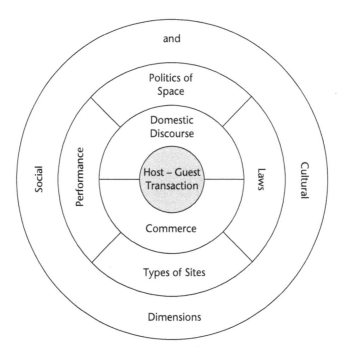

Figure 33.2 The host–guest transaction

specific individuals and this is the aspect that cannot be reproduced by a competitor. Front-line staff are the source of uniqueness that cannot be reproduced. In these circumstances the nature of hospitableness and its use outside of the immediate 'hospitality sector' should be the subject of research attention and focus.

Whether it be directly in the provision of hospitality services or in other service transactions the relationship between host and guest is at the centre of successful or unsuccessful transactions. Figure 33.2 provides a graphic representation of this and reflects the need to research these transactions in all service relationships.

Conclusions

This chapter has argued that the content of this volume contributes to a wider understanding of hospitality and hospitableness. However, it should be viewed as a single step on the voyage of discovery, not as an end in itself. There is so much more to learn about the domains of hospitality. A majority of the contributions focus on the cultural or social domain, yet this domain could yield so much more, with a more systematic study of culturally, historically and geographically diverse settings. The private or domestic domain of hospitality is still grossly under-researched. Apart from the immediate study of experiences and practices, this domain acts as an important training ground for learning rules of what to do, and what not to do, as hosts and guests.

This chapter has also briefly introduced the development of a research instrument that seems to identify individuals who are more naturally hospitable. The instrument itself requires further application to test out its reliability and validity. If necessary this may lead to further amendment and testing. Importantly, it leads to the potential investigation of who these hospitable individuals are. What are their personality profiles? Do they change over time? Particularly in commercial contexts, do they eventually suffer from 'hospitality fatigue' in their day-to-day experiences of offering hospitableness to guests who vary in their worthiness of welcome? Despite industry pronouncements, there may be limits to treating customers as though 'they are guests in your own home'. For some guests the service encounter suggests a relationship of superiority and inferiority between commercial guests and their hosts.

Appendix 33.1 Hospitality questionnaire

Dear Future manager,
Educational and research institutions are the heart of providing the service industry with a zealous skilled workforce that will drive the future economy. 'The future is now'.

This pilot study comprises a phase of a PhD research project at the University of Derby, UK, working with Mrs. Victoria Naisola Ruiter. The study targets to identify and understand the personality traits of people.

Please be so kind as to fill out all parts of the questionnaire which is very important for the research and for the development and validation of a research measurement instrument to be used on a wider scope within the service industry.

You will be presented a series of statements relating to your experiences as a host.

Think about a time you have entertained friends, family or colleagues. It may have been a dinner party, people staying over, a big celebration or simply a friend coming around for a few drinks and a takeaway.

Try to decide quickly (as your initial reaction is likely to be the most accurate) and then move on to the next question. Please don't try to second guess the questions as they are often not measuring what they appear to be.

By filling in this questionnaire means that you have read and understood the consent document attached. It will take approximately 20 minutes to complete this questionnaire.

For any questions regarding this research, feel free to contact me on: Victoria.naisola.ruiter@stenden.com

Thank you for influencing the future of the service industry by participating in this research!
Victoria Naisola Ruiter

For each statement please rate how much you disagree or agree with what is being stated on a scale of 1–7 (1 being disagreement and 7 being agreement).

Please rate how strongly you agree with the following statements on a scale of 1–7 (with 1 being 'totally disagree' and 7 being 'completely agree')

	Statement	totally disagree	strongly disagree	disagree	neutral	agree	strongly agree	completely agree
1	I know and enjoy being a genuinely hospitable person	1	2	3	4	5	6	7
2	Given a choice I much prefer to be a guest than a host!	1	2	3	4	5	6	7
3	I seek out opportunities to help others	1	2	3	4	5	6	7
4	I'm disappointed when people I host don't demonstrate gratitude (give me a return invite)	1	2	3	4	5	6	7

(Continued)

	Statement	totally disagree	strongly disagree	disagree	neutral	agree	strongly agree	completely agree
5	I'm the one who normally ends up cleaning after our guests in our house	1	2	3	4	5	6	7
6	I don't find it necessary to stop and think every few minutes about whether or not my guests are okay	1	2	3	4	5	6	7
7	The comfort of my guests is very important to me	1	2	3	4	5	6	7
8	If I think people have enjoyed themselves, I can't resist prompting them to tell me	1	2	3	4	5	6	7
9	Whatever the time I like it when I am of service to others	1	2	3	4	5	6	7
10	You've got to love being a host to be great at it	1	2	3	4	5	6	7
11	If I had to prioritise, the physical comfort is lower down my list than the quality of the service experience	1	2	3	4	5	6	7
12	I have concern for other people	1	2	3	4	5	6	7
13	Anyone can learn to be an outstanding host	1	2	3	4	5	6	7
14	It doesn't matter whether or not guests warm to my personality so long as they have a good time	1	2	3	4	5	6	7
15	I always try to live up to my idea of what makes a good host	1	2	3	4	5	6	7
16	So long as I know that I've done a good job I'm not overly concerned with what my guests think	1	2	3	4	5	6	7
17	You can still be a great host without going over the top to make guests feel special	1	2	3	4	5	6	7
18	I find it motivating to take accountability for other people's welfare	1	2	3	4	5	6	7
19	I enjoy taking responsibility for the wellbeing of my guests	1	2	3	4	5	6	7
20	It means the world to me when guests show their approval of my hospitality	1	2	3	4	5	6	7
21	Guests should feel that the moment revolves around them	1	2	3	4	5	6	7
22	I get a natural high when I make my guests feel special	1	2	3	4	5	6	7
23	It is important to always do the things that people expect of a good host	1	2	3	4	5	6	7
24	You can't be a good host if people don't naturally warm up to you	1	2	3	4	5	6	7
25	Hosting can sometimes be a bit of a chore	1	2	3	4	5	6	7
26	You must actually like your guests in order to be a good host	1	2	3	4	5	6	7
27	At school I am the class entertainer	1	2	3	4	5	6	7
28	I regularly play host for my friends and family	1	2	3	4	5	6	7
29	I try to get on the same wavelength as my guests	1	2	3	4	5	6	7
30	I try to feel at one with my guests	1	2	3	4	5	6	7
31	Guests have to take me as I am	1	2	3	4	5	6	7
32	I do whatever is necessary to ensure that my guests have a good time	1	2	3	4	5	6	7
33	I put my guest's enjoyment before my own	1	2	3	4	5	6	7

You will now be presented with twelve sets of questions focusing on basic dimensions of personality. This section is designed to be a quick fire so try to decide each answer in 3–4 seconds (as your initial reaction is likely to be the most accurate). Then move on with the next question.

For each trait please rate how you believe that other people see you on a scale of 1–7 (with 1 being 'not at all' and 7 being 'completely')

	Statement	not at all	mostly not	sometimes not	neutral	sometimes	mostly	completely
34	A high concern for others	1	2	3	4	5	6	7
35	Friendly	1	2	3	4	5	6	7
36	Affectionate	1	2	3	4	5	6	7
37	Entertainer	1	2	3	4	5	6	7
38	Warm	1	2	3	4	5	6	7
39	Self Confident	1	2	3	4	5	6	7
40	Compassionate	1	2	3	4	5	6	7
41	Happy	1	2	3	4	5	6	7
42	An affection for others	1	2	3	4	5	6	7
43	Pleasure Seeker	1	2	3	4	5	6	7
44	Charitable Sensitive	1	2	3	4	5	6	7
45	A need to share with others	1	2	3	4	5	6	7
46	Talented	1	2	3	4	5	6	7
47	Willing	1	2	3	4	5	6	7
48	Comforting	1	2	3	4	5	6	7
49	A need to help others	1	2	3	4	5	6	7
50	Enthusiastic	1	2	3	4	5	6	7
51	Caring	1	2	3	4	5	6	7
52	Selfless	1	2	3	4	5	6	7
53	Kind	1	2	3	4	5	6	7
54	Welcoming	1	2	3	4	5	6	7
55	Humble	1	2	3	4	5	6	7
56	Generous	1	2	3	4	5	6	7
57	Trusting	1	2	3	4	5	6	7
58	Public spirited	1	2	3	4	5	6	7
59	Sympathetic	1	2	3	4	5	6	7
60	Sociable	1	2	3	4	5	6	7
61	Amusing	1	2	3	4	5	6	7
62	Giving	1	2	3	4	5	6	7
63	Self Centred	1	2	3	4	5	6	7
64	Delightful	1	2	3	4	5	6	7
65	Loyal	1	2	3	4	5	6	7
66	Determined	1	2	3	4	5	6	7
67	Trusting	1	2	3	4	5	6	7
68	Ambitious	1	2	3	4	5	6	7
69	Observant	1	2	3	4	5	6	7
70	Respectful	1	2	3	4	5	6	7
71	Mature	1	2	3	4	5	6	7
72	Alert	1	2	3	4	5	6	7
73	Lucky	1	2	3	4	5	6	7
74	Imaginative	1	2	3	4	5	6	7

(Continued)

(Continued)

	Statement	not at all	mostly not	sometimes not	neutral	sometimes	mostly	completely
75	Leader	1	2	3	4	5	6	7
76	Organised	1	2	3	4	5	6	7
77	Risk-taker	1	2	3	4	5	6	7
78	Productive	1	2	3	4	5	6	7
79	Follower	1	2	3	4	5	6	7
80	Insightful	1	2	3	4	5	6	7

How many years of practical experience do you have in the service industry?

0–1 year

2–3 years

3–4 years

The reporting of these research findings will be anonymous. The results will be used as part of a research project by the University of Derby into personality types within the service industry.

Gender: Male/Female

Your Age: _____

Education (programme): _____

Your Names: _____

Nationality: _____

References

Derrida, J. (2002) *Acts of Religion*, London: Routledge.

Index